# TOWARD AN UNDERSTANDING OF CRIME IN AMERICA

Here in one volume are concrete, practical goals for reduction of high-fear crime (such as homicide, rape, and robbery); reform and improvement of criminal justice systems at State and local levels; increased efforts to involve all citizens in crime prevention; improvement in police services at the municipal level; major streamlining of court procedures and practices; fundamental changes in the American system of corrections; and nationwide action at the State level to confront the dangers posed by widespread possession of handguns.

Two of the Commission's recommendations in particular have received headline attention: the proposal for a ban on possession, sale, and manufacture of *all* handguns (except for military and police); and the recommendation for re-evaluation of "victimless crime" laws (those applying to various sex acts, pornography, marijuana, drunkenness, minor traffic offenses, and vagrancy).

But even more revolutionary is the Commission's belief, both explicit and implicit, that our present criminal justice systems perpetuate, if not actually create, crime.

Taken as a whole, the Commission's statement of priorities, goals, and standards comprises one of the most important and provocative documents of our time. It is an impressive and substantial contribution to the understanding of crime—and what can be done about it—in America today.

Report by the National Advisory
Commission on Criminal Justice
Standards and Goals

# A NATIONAL STRATEGY TO REDUCE CRIME

with extensive excerpts from the
Commission's Task Force Reports

With a critical introduction by
**ISIDORE SILVER**

AVON
PUBLISHERS OF BARD, CAMELOT, DISCUS, EQUINOX AND FLARE BOOKS

AVON BOOKS
A division of
The Hearst Corporation
959 Eighth Avenue
New York, New York 10019

First Avon Printing, January, 1975.

Printed in the U.S.A.

# Contents

v

This project was supported by the Law Enforcement Assistance Administration, U.S. Department of Justice, under the Omnibus Crime Control and Safe Streets Act of 1968, as amended. Points of view or opinions stated in this document are those of the National Advisory Commission on Criminal Justice Standards and Goals, and do not necessarily represent the official position of the U.S. Department of Justice.

# Chapter VIII
# Criminal Code Reform and Revision

# Chapter IX
# Handguns in American Society

# Chapter X
# A National Commitment to Change

# Introduction

Within the past decade, at least six national commissions[1] have reported upon either social disorder or crime in the United States and have reached the same general conclusions. As a nation, we have yet to face our festering and almost intractable social problems resolutely. We have over-relied upon and overused the criminal law and the criminal justice system to deal with those problems, and our national failures may well lead to social disorganization and social and racial polarization. The effect of these reports upon governmental officials, criminal-justice practitioners, and public opinion generally has been minimal; depending upon the "style" of the president who has received them (LBJ was effusive but ultimately uninterested: Richard Nixon was churlish and antagonistic), they have been either ignored, shelved or denounced. Each report seems only to have provided source material for each subsequent report, and they have followed each other like lemmings to the sea. Indeed, the only discernible change appears to be in the commissioners themselves; their endeavors have almost invariably tended to radicalize them.

What might be termed the "rule of radicalization" has been particularly apparent in the case of the National Advisory Commission on Criminal Justice Standards and Goals. Unlike most of its predecessors, this commission was composed of "lesser lights"—in the main, criminal-justice practitioners (although its chairman was the little-known gover-

---

[1] The National Advisory Commission on Civil Disorders ("The Kerner Commission") (1968); The President's Commission on Campus Unrest ("The Scranton Commission") (1970); The President's Commission on Law Enforcement and the Administration of Justice ("The Katzenbach Commission") (1967); The United States Commission on Marijuana and Drug Abuse ("The Shafer Commission") (1972); The National Commission on Obscenity and Pornography (1970); The National Commission on the Causes and Prevention of Violence (1969).

nor of Delaware, Russell W. Peterson). Of the twenty-two commissioners, perhaps a handful were even vaguely known to the public, and the range of views represented probably meandered no further left than "moderate" and no further right than "respectable conservative." The Commission was not graced by such eminences as Nicholas DeB. Katzenbach, William Scranton, or even Otto Kerner.[2]

The Nixon administration—which had found itself in the embarrassing or even ludicrous position of appointing some of the previous commissions only to disclaim their findings—could reasonably have believed that the new "crime commission" would render a safe law-and-order report. When that body formally tendered its main findings (in a 318-page document) on August 9, 1973, Attorney General Elliot Richardson was only slightly less flabbergasted than was the president himself (who neither admitted that he had received and read the report in advance nor summoned the chairman to the White House for the obligatory ceremonial presentation). Richardson could only note that "The federal government is neither endorsing nor opposing the . . . goals contained in this report"; with a sure instinct for finesse, he hastily added that the document was one "of uncommon importance." And so it is.

Only two aspects of the Report received major publicity at the time of its release. The Commission's blunt, unstartling, and hardly novel conclusion that all handguns should be banned for all citizens (except for the police and the military) by every state by 1983 and its recommendation of a thorough reevaluation of victimless-crime laws (those penalizing drunkenness, vagrancy, minor traffic offenses, various sex acts, and possession of marijuana and pornography) became the object of intense though short-lived debate. Earlier in 1973, the Commission had caused a minor flurry by advocating (in a preliminary report) abolition of plea bargaining by 1978; after August 9, 1973, other particulars of the Commission's wide-ranging proposals would become matters of public concern, and there would be a lively, though unsustained, controversy

[2] An interesting bit of Commissioniana is the question of what happens to chairmen after they report. Apparently, their commission experiences had decisive effects upon their careers: Katzenbach retreated to law school teaching; Scranton went back to banking and a vow never to serve Richard Nixon again and Kerner became a federal appellate judge in which position, until he was convicted of bribery, he compiled a distinguished, progressive record.

about prison reform (the Commission recommended a moratorium on building new prisons), abolishing grand juries, and tough proposals for safeguarding the burgeoning files of criminal-justice information and intelligence.

What was overlooked by both critics and defenders is the most startling proposition of all—the Commission's belief, both explicit and implicit, that crime will abate only when the role of the criminal-justice system in general is reduced. This fundamental belief underlies a spate of significant suggestions including (1) redrafting criminal codes to eliminate drunkenness, vagrancy, and minor traffic violations as criminal offenses and to prohibit incarceration as a penalty for other "victimless crimes"; (2) formulating alternatives, such as citation and summons, to arrest for many misdemeanors and even some felonies; (3) diverting many accused from the criminal-justice process; (4) creating non-criminal-justice institutions to deal with problems such as mental illness and drug abuse; (5) replacing juvenile courts by family courts; (6) increasing use of probation and community-treatment facilities for those convicted; (7) abolishing juvenile correctional institutions; and (8) the aforementioned moratorium on new prison construction. Thus, the Commission bluntly informed the public that our criminal-justice institutions and processes perpetuated (if they did not create) crime.

The Commission did not mince words—our criminal-justice institutions are not only ineffective; they are, to use contemporary jargon, both "counterproductive" and "criminogenic." Thus the Commission, by its own examination of the "system," reached back into the past to reiterate the old liberal notion (perpetuated by a great English reformer, Jeremy Bentham) that punishment is not a "service" but an evil, a necessary one to be sure, but justifiable only insofar as it *is* absolutely necessary to deter greater evil. That perspective must be kept in mind as we review the Commission's work in greater detail.

# 1: "Crime" and the Commission

Although the National Advisory Commission did not succumb to the (almost inevitable) temptation to rely heavily upon social scientists—both the main and the Task Force reports are refreshingly free of the often tendentious and arcane "expert" analyses that deformed the 1967 Crime Commission Report—it did reflect some of the newer academic concerns about crime. Despite the Report's lack of overt acknowledgment of academic influence (indeed, it exhibits a certain impatience with "basic research" that seems to have no immediate payoff), the Commission does recognize that criminality is not a simple social event.

To understand the Commission's position, a preliminary word about the new criminology is necessary. Today, many students of the phenomenon of crime have concluded that the focus of study must be not the criminal but the society in which he functions. They have abandoned the fruitless search for the "criminal type" simply because many people commit many acts condemned by society for many reasons or because of many impulses. Murderers are not particularly alike, nor do they resemble others who commit (either once or habitually) other kinds of criminal acts (indeed, there are no "murderers," only people who have committed a certain act legally defined as culpable homicide). Some forms of crime are intimately related to certain mental states, others to encouragement by cultural milieus, while others are simply matters of need and opportunity. Some forms of crime are perceived as morally wrong, even by their perpetrators, while others are not.

To the new criminologists, criminality is often a function not of an act, but of the way that society (or an influential part of that society) views that act, and they have concluded that labeling certain conduct as first "deviant" (i.e., disapproved) and then "dangerous" (i.e., criminal) is the most significant event in the creation of "criminality." A person's involvement in the criminal-justice system is *itself* conclusive proof, both to society and to himself, that he is a criminal; the fact that he has committed an act punishable by criminal penalties is not enough. The society adds the label and the offender accepts it—indeed much criminal-justice activity is designed specifically to induce the person to accept the label.

The Commission has adopted a common-sense version of that stance. It recognizes that incarceration for a crime produces more "recidivists" (repeaters) than does release on probation, that awaiting trial in jail rather than on bail increases the chances for conviction (i.e., the authoritative labeling of "criminal"), that parolees are questioned more often by police and parole officers than average citizens would be in similarly suspicious circumstances. Thus, the Commission obliquely accepts the new criminology's recognition that the system determines the definition of criminality. Indeed, the Commission's recommendations attempt to limit the occasions for imposing the label or, alternatively, to limit the implications and consequences of the label.

The Commission is more reluctant to acknowledge, either explicitly or implicitly, another theoretical perspective about crime—the belief that crime is endemic to all societies (though it may take different forms), and that condemnation of certain forms of conduct and the use of something resembling a criminal-justice system is necessary for social cohesion. Crime, in this perspective, becomes an inevitable and necessary concomitant of the deepest values of people. The Commission is discomfited, as we all are, by the possibility that crime may be, as one scholar has put it, "the queer ladder of social mobility" (recent findings that control of organized crime in some cities is passing from Italians to Blacks and Hispanics tend to substantiate this insight). If our deepest values—those relating to success, mobility, wealth, minorities and the poor, and corruption—give rise to "crime," then it follows that there is no "crime" problem—only the problem(s) of society. Clearly, neither the Commission nor the public wishes to hear this, for the implication (borne out by our history) is that crime is the price we pay for being what we are.[3]

For the discerning reader, hints are present—although by being couched in the neutral jargon of "community responsibility" for crime and the need for development of "community correctional facilities" to combat the crime rise, they are obfuscated. Whatever the rhetoric, the Commission recognizes that crime has roots. Thus, the report's emphasis is not upon the wrongdoer but upon community conditions that are criminogenic (crime-inducing), and one significant Task Force Report deals with unemployment, undereducation, substandard housing, and other "poverty" syndromes that correlate with crime. Although the Commission fails to answer the

---

[3] Ultimately, the public will listen. As this is being written, the June 10, 1974 issue of *U.S. News and World Report*—an influential "middle-American" journal—alarmingly notes (in a special report entitled "Crime Surge Defies All Efforts, Survey of Cities Shows") that crime, "after all the things we've tried is still rising." The three-page report, predictably devoted to police attempts to curb crime, acknowledges certain heresies such as "crime will never be checked until this nation begins to solve the underlying social problems which cause crime," and "There is too much instability in our cities. As long as we have unemployment, underemployment, broken homes, alcoholism, drugs and mental-health problems, we are going to have crime."

questions whether these conditions cause—rather than merely correlate with—crime and whether they are symptomatic of something else, it does not adopt the chimerical posture that crime is alien and can be eradicated by "crusades" and "wars" (the rhetoric of LBJ and the 1967 Crime Commission). Thus, the Commission took the vital first step in recognizing at least the symptoms; if crime is as multifaceted as I have indicated, perhaps, in part, the symptoms are also the causes. In any event, some of the right questions are being asked about crime and criminality.

## 2: Naïveté and the Commission

Much of the Report's language is chiliastic. Many have criticized the Commission's sanguine optimism that there can be a 50-percent reduction in major crimes (or, at least, those which most frighten the public) by 1983. The Commission's artless assumption that handguns can be banned by 1978 has disconcerted others. (Five months after the Report, Attorney General William Saxbe said of gun control, "I just don't think it is possible—it is an idealistic dream.") The apparently limitless faith in community treatment facilities (many of which do not exist) has confounded others. Skeptics have asked whether the Commission had any clear idea about what "community" means in this context—will affluent neighborhoods permit drug-rehabilitation centers or halfway houses in their midst? On the other hand, can reintegration with law-abiding society occur in a high-crime environment? The findings that prison has no rehabilitative value and that punishment is meaningless in a system which returns most offenders to society tests the indignation quotient of many. (Again, it was the irrepressible Saxbe who said, upon learning that serious crime had risen 5 percent in 1973, "We're on a kick where nobody believes in punishment.")

If the Commission can be faulted for a certain pervasive equanimity and political naïveté, its perspective must be clearly understood. The Commission is simply arguing that, given our national attitudes and perceptions, given our concern with rising crime, given our ambivalence about the purpose(s) of corrections, its proposals are indeed practical. Certainly they are more practical than today's irrational and confused "solutions." Perhaps, the Commission implies, it is too much to expect a wholesale reevaluation of our attitudes, but barring that, at least some retail change must occur. If our ambivalences (Is the purpose of corrections to punish or to rehabilitate? Is our demand for long prison terms consistent with social approval of plea bargaining? Does it make sense to incarcerate for theoretically lengthy periods of time and then to quickly release prisoners on parole?) defeat any reasonable attempts to make the criminal-justice system work, then we have the worst, not the best, of all possible worlds. Since 99 percent of those imprisoned will eventually be released and since more than 50 percent of those so released will, under present conditions, continue their criminal careers, the Commission reasonably assumes that new approaches are necessary. "Realists" who are content with no change or merely incremental change are what one prominent social critic has labeled "crackpot realists."

The true naïveté of the Report is not to be found so much in its reasonable and common-sense response to the "crime" problem, but in its steadfast optimism about the political realities of the criminal-justice system. If our national attitudes create the matrix for much confused thinking about crime and the criminal, then our political and law-enforcement leadership have consistently played upon and shaped those attitudes for their own purposes. The Commission only faintly recognizes that the agencies entrusted to contain crime have a vested interest in perpetuating present definitions of criminal conduct and present modes of dealing with the "problem." Ironically enough, the most controversial proposal—the abolition of private possession of handguns—is an exception to the above generalization, for public attitudes, at least as measured consistently in the polls, are overwhelmingly more enlightened than are those of the National Rifle Association and its political votaries. The Commission's recommendation was addressed to the states, evidently because of its belief that Congress would not act on a national level, and it is hard to say whether Commission sophistication (forgetting about Congress) was greater than its naïveté (assuming that NRA pressure on state legislatures would have less influence) or vice versa.

# 3: Perspectives on Crime

There are three fundamental perspectives about crime, although the range of most popular writing encompasses only two. The "conservative" law-and-order position assumes that offenders have free will and rationally choose to violate the law, so that prompt and effective law enforcement can deter the malefactor (at one extreme, severity of punishment as well as promptness is the deterrent). The "moderate liberal" middle-ground position acknowledges certain social and economic roots of crime, but vacillates between conservative notions of criminality and punishment, and usually hortatory and fruitless appeals for vague and unspecified changes to eradicate the causes of crime. Contradictions inevitably abound. Of late, the primary confusion revolves about the recognition of the community's role in fostering crime and the remedy of returning the offender to that community as rapidly as possible. The "radical" perspective, as I have previously mentioned, would concentrate not upon some mythical community, but upon the society at large to discover why it perceives and labels certain conduct as criminal, what needs (for social order, stability, collective indignation, or perhaps just reassurance) these perceptions and labels serve, and of more recent vintage, what groups politically benefit from these perceptions. Of course, since radicals live in the society, they also want the muggers and rapists to be apprehended, but argue that law-enforcement "survival tactics" are simply a temporary and inadequate solution—really a holding action—to only part of the problem. Clearly, the concerns of these different positions will differ, often startlingly, although the "moderate" perspective overlaps the other two and so stretches and dilutes its concerns. Much of this critique, as will become apparent, is written from a "radical" orientation. It should be observed that "radical" literally means "to the root" and, at times, is synonymous with "conservative" (see my comments on retention of the twelve-person petit-jury system, for instance).

Not all of this analysis is "radical," for it is inevitable that the Commission's choice of the middle ground (which it aggressively stakes out and occupies) creates numerous problems even from its own perspective. For instance, the Commission falls prey to the major "moderate" defect of not being certain of the nature of the population it wishes to study and generalize about. Are those individuals who are (a) identified as offenders and (b) apprehended and convicted of a crime truly representative of all those who commit crimes? Here, the thorny question of criminal statistics arises—how much do we really know about the crime picture? The Law Enforcement Assistance Administration (LEAA) has noted that its "victimization surveys" (extensive interviews with selected households and businesses involving 500,000 people each year) reveal that at least one-half of all crimes committed never are reported to the police, thus rendering present crime statistics virtually meaningless. Cities such as Philadelphia, it was disclosed, underreport their crime by about 80 percent, while in others there may be twice to three times as much serious crime as is officially acknowledged. The reaction to the LEAA survey (which is a continuing one) was predictable—police chiefs denounced it and the F.B.I. vowed to fight to retain jurisdiction over the Uniform Crime Reports (UCR) rather than surrender authority to any new federal agency.

Thus, we can surmise that many offenders are never even identified, much less apprehended; we can reasonably assume that those who become enmeshed in the criminal-justice system represent a fraction of those who commit crime. How great a fraction is unknown. Although it is likely that those apprehended have committed more than the particular crimes for which they are accused, police "clearance rates" (admissions by suspects of other crimes for which they are never formally tried) have always been suspect; in any event, even assuming the truth of those rates, no more than 30 percent of all known crimes in most categories (except murder) are even "cleared." The Commission was realistic enough to acknowledge, in the light of the foregoing, that even a zero-percent recidivism rate among known offenders may only translate into a minuscule reduction of the overall crime rate. It did not entertain the chilling possibility that the little we know about the psychological and sociological characteristics of known offenders may bear little relationship to the conduct of unknown offenders—so that all treatment proposals may be inadequate.

The Commission mirrored the tendency of "moderate" analysts of the problem to ignore white-collar crime (about which contradictions also abound); it should be remembered that the Report is addressed to the prominent "scare" crimes such as homicide, rape, assault, robbery, and burglary. Yet, there are linkages between lower- and middle-class crimes (although they are complex and often highly speculative ones), and it is conceivable that no substantial reduction of the former can take place without a simultaneous attack on the latter. Why?

Examples of our national lawlessness are common. Even the phrase "law and order" implies the equality of the two, so that achievement of order may often occur at the expense of law, where they conflict, e.g., the 1971 "May Day" mass arrests in Washington, D.C. The attitude that the society is rigged to favor some and disadvantage others is prevalent in both minority and middle-class communities, and that perspective cannot be dismissed as merely a cynical rationalization for lower-class illegality. The relationship between white-collar and blue-collar crime is also significant because organized crime operates to bind the two in a seamless web. People may either steal or embezzle to pay gambling or loan-sharking debts, to feed drug habits, to satisfy blackmail, or to obtain other services (or avoid other penalties) provided by organized crime. The Commission, even from its own perspective, should have devoted more attention to the commonalities between apparently diverse forms of crime. The only substantial analysis occurs in the Community Crime Prevention Report which deals with political corruption and campaign financing, only one part of the subject.

# 4: Decline of the Adversary System of Justice

The Commission's perspective (unwittingly) leads to an endorsement of the most significant trend in our criminal-justice system, the conversion from an adversarial model to an inquisitorial one. The fabled Ideal of our Anglo-Saxon heritage envisages certain images: two competent, well-trained attorneys, the prosecutor and defense counsel, locked in zealous combat to sustain their positions; the presence of certain fundamental rights which protect the defendant; the passive role of the judge and jury who listen to both sides and wait for all the evidence to come in; the judgment of guilty only if the evidence convinces beyond a reasonable doubt. Other images reflect the Ideal: the defendant has the right not to testify and not to have adverse inferences drawn from his silence; the drama of the all-powerful state with its immense investigative resources and its public credibility pitted against the individual armed only with his rights and a dedicated defender.

Of course, the Ideal is rarely realized in our beleaguered criminal justice system, especially in urban areas, although it does establish the framework and provides a meaningful measuring rod for all activities within the system. The prevalence of plea-bargaining of course undercuts the Ideal, since the defendant is required both to admit his guilt and to waive most of those precious constitutional rights which allegedly constitute the essence of the system. Often, the bargaining process, as several studies have shown, is initiated by the defendant's own (dedicated?) lawyer and the name of the game is to tactically admit *something* in return for the promise of either charge reduction or favorable sentence recommendation by the prosecutor. The bargain has become the norm in perhaps 90 percent of all criminal prosecutions, and the skills of defense counsel become mediatory, rather than adversarial, ones.

If the Ideal hasn't been battered enough by the reality of urban criminal justice, then both law and judicial decision accelerate its diminution by compelling the defendant to reveal much of his case prior to trial without infringement upon his constitutional right not to testify. Thus, the defense may be required to notify the prosecution prior to trial whether certain defenses (alibi or insanity) are to be offered, or the defendant may have to supply a witness list to the prosecution (and vice versa). In addition, the defendant may be required to submit to various "tests" to obtain (nontestimonial) evidence of his guilt. He can be compelled to furnish blood and handwriting samples or to try on pieces of evidence (hats, gloves, etc.) before the jury. Although the use of voiceprints is presently unclear, the present obstacle to their introduction involves their scientific validity rather than their tendency to compel the defendant to convict himself.

The Commission's perspective clearly accelerates the trend. As treatment becomes the new Ideal, as pretrial diversion out of the criminal-justice system becomes the predominant mode of procedure, as the mentally ill and the drug addict are to be treated by other agencies, "cooperation" between the accused, "his" attorney, "his" social worker and other components of the criminal-justice system will inevitably increase. Although the Commission warns against any element of coercion in these programs, it acknowledges that extant "voluntary" release programs have been suspect and agrees that the pressures generated by the criminal-justice process itself can never be entirely abated. Most defense attorneys will advise their clients to opt for treatment rather than run the uncertain risks of a criminal trial, even in close and dubious cases.

At first glance, the Commission's proposal to abolish plea-bargaining would indicate a resuscitation of the adversarial Ideal. But it should be remembered that the other proposals are designed to reserve the criminal-justice process for those few who are truly dangerous to society; essentially, for most, the bargaining will occur under another rubric—and more of it will be required.

Other proposals indicate the Commission's disenchantment

with the adversarial concept of justice. Thus, the essence of the inquisitorial system is disclosure—the abandonment of surprise and other "sharp" trial tactics which hamper the pursuit of truth. The Commission recommends the extension of the present limited obligation of the prosecutor to disclose to the defendant before trial evidence which might tend to exonerate him. As the Courts Task Force Report states, "The prosecution should disclose to the defendant all available evidence that will be used against him at trial." The same disclosure requirement would apply to the contents of presentence reports so that the defendant can contest their accuracy and relevance. Both proposals are valuable to any realization of the Ideal of due process of law, because, for instance, it is unthinkable that a man may be sentenced on the basis of inaccurate and unknown information. Yet, the duty of the prosecution to tell all may well become the basis for "reform" proposals—already in the hopper—to abolish or limit the scope of the Fifth Amendment (either by court reinterpretation or by a new constitutional amendment) on the plausible ground that it presents a barrier to rehabilitation. The Commission itself viewed the right against self-incrimination as a condition which limited the scope of its "reform" proposals—and even the conservative Supreme Court Justice William Rehnquist warned a criminal-justice conference called to analyze the Report that various Commission proposals came close to the line drawn by that constitutional provision.

Crucial to the functioning of the inquisitorial system in non-common-law countries is the role of the judge. The Commission's Task Force on the Courts argued that judges should play a more activist role at various times, especially during the pretrial interrogation process. Thus, "The supervision [of interrogation] by a judicial officer might be an adequate substitute for the right to an attorney established in *Miranda* [v. *Arizona*]." The Task Force also contended, in disagreement with the American Law Institute, that, under *Miranda,* the defendant's consent to interrogation is not necessary, provided that his attorney is present. Other proposals, contained in either the main Report or Task Force additions thereto, further contemplate the extension of the inquisitorial model and dilution of the adversarial one.

The trend, both within and without the Commission, may well be socially beneficial, especially if the new leitmotif is rehabilitation and reintegration instead of punishment. But suspicions linger. Will the Commission's laudable proposals constitute newer and more sophisticated means for dealing with "troublemakers," without the inconveniences and difficulties of an adversarial battle? The history of the juvenile-court system—its initial purpose was to remove the stigma of criminal conviction but its nonadversarial development contributed to that stigma—engenders pessimism. Must not law-enforcement agencies themselves undergo significant political and ideological change to insure that the Commission's reforms are carried out in spirit as well as letter? To trade the benefits of the adversarial Ideal for more sophisticated means of social control over individuals may not be the answer, although it is the risk. If plea-bargaining severely undermines the adversarial Ideal, it must be remembered that the defendant is benefiting (many say he is the only one so benefiting) because the presence of that Ideal is what compels the prosecutor to participate in the bargaining process. Removal of that impetus, even under the treatment rubric, may have serious, deleterious effects upon our very notions of justice.

In its pursuit of the twin Ideals of truth and rehabilitation, the Commission overlooks certain intangible, though real, values of the present system. Those values involve the system's predisposition (though not always its ability) to ferret out, expose, and limit law-enforcement excesses and abuses—and it is certainly conceivable, if not inevitable, that increased corner-cutting by police and others will occur when and if truth replaces fairness as our guiding Ideal. James Madison's warning in Federalist #51 that the duty of government is twofold—to control the people and to control itself—is well taken in this context. Whatever the defects of our combat image of criminal justice, it has allowed for a continual monitoring at least by the judiciary of the entire law-enforcement process. It has encouraged new and just claims to be raised and has expanded the scope of constitutional liberty for all of us. If one trusted our criminal-justice personnel and processes more, if one believed that police and prosecutors were as zealously committed to protecting the innocent (or to rehabilitating the marginally guilty) as they are to prosecuting and punishing the socially dangerous, if one could accept the ability of various criminal-justice agencies to truly check and balance each other's powers, the inquisitorial model might be acceptable, indeed even admirable. The suspicions linger.

Indeed, in many respects they are enhanced. For instance, the problem of gross police misconduct in violating the Fourth Amendment by illegally seizing evidence has continually plagued our courts. The judicial response came in 1961 in the landmark case of *Mapp* v. *Ohio,* a Supreme Court decision which penalized police violations of the right to be secure in one's home, person, and effects by forbidding the use of evidence so acquired. Often, that evidence is extremely good and relevant in a criminal case. Unlike compelled confessions, for instance, it is reliable. The *Mapp* decision was engendered by the adversarial system of justice because, quite simply, attorneys were willing to litigate and relitigate that issue. (*Mapp* reversed a 1947 decision which had held that no state was required by the federal Constitution to exclude such evidence.) Although it is conceivable that an inquisitorial system would continue to apply the exclusionary rule, it is not probable—it must be remembered that truth is the touchstone for such a system. How does the Commission deal with the rule?

Tucked away in the Courts Task Force Report is a section which argues that the rule may be inappropriate to eliminate or limit police misconduct. Further study of its effectiveness is recommended. Many students of the system have argued that the rule should be abolished because it (a) defeats successful prosecution of the obviously guilty and (b) is ineffective to control such misconduct. Police often seize evidence illegally to harass and intimidate miscreants rather than to prosecute them. Other means of deterring illegal police conduct, it is argued, are necessary. Perhaps civil suits for monetary damages against policemen, departments, and municipalities which engage in or tolerate such misconduct could be undertaken; civil-rights suits, including injunctions, against illegal practices might be appropriate (and effective); effective internal disciplinary procedures against offending police officers could be utilized. (The last proposal would be rendered virtually nugatory by the Commission's own conclusion that civilian review boards are ineffective and undesirable and that intradepartmental controls are the only acceptable means of dealing with police misconduct.)

At least four Justices of the Nixon Supreme Court have expressed misgivings about the rule, and undoubtedly the pressures to reverse the *Mapp* decision will grow, both within and without the high Court. Yet, as Justice Brennan pointed out in a 1973 case, the rule exists not only to deter misconduct but as an "enforcement tool to give content and meaning to the Fourth Amendment's guarantees." He tied the rule to prevention of judicial participation in illegal activities and argued (quoting from a famous opinion of Justice Brandeis) that government should not play an "ignoble part" in using its vast police powers. Both sides—and the Commission—ignore the most potent social reason to maintain the rule: its abolition may well encourage the police illegally to search the homes and persons of *innocent* people for no reason or for bare suspicion.

# 5: The Two Crime Commissions

The National Advisory Commission resembles its predecessor, the 1967 Crime Commission, in at least one respect—a shared addiction to homiletics. The current Report takes the upbeat theme that "Every citizen can live without fear of being brutalized by unknown assailants," and such hortatoriness can only recall some of the painful absurdities of the earlier study. Its earnest reminder of the "need for all elements of the criminal justice system to plan and work together" is a tribute to goodwill which does not reflect the disorganization of the system, or more importantly, the profound reasons underlying such disorder. Its belief that "If the people of this country are committed to reducing crime, its rate will decrease dramatically" misses the point; crime can be reduced dramatically only if there is a commitment to ameliorate its social roots—and, depressingly, even that may not be enough. The assumption that good faith will reign occasionally verges on the ludicrous. For instance, the Report enjoins prosecutors not to plea bargain (while the system remains) simply because they have weak cases, and not to "overcharge" (bring numerous charges of serious crimes to induce a bargain more favorable to themselves) for the simple purpose of pressuring a guilty plea. Prosecutors, until either they or the system are overhauled, will do everything they can to keep the calendar moving, including perpetuation of the "unfair" practices condemned by the Commission.

Both the 1967 and 1973 reports treat the police gingerly. Bromides should not replace analysis in this critical area, but, for some reason which seems endemic to the jargon of reports, they do. Thus, the Police Task Force calls for unexceptional measures such as increased police-community relations and public airing of police policies; it then blandly recommends that the police join faculties of junior and senior high schools, presumably to serve as "resource personnel." One study, referred to in the excerpted material following the police chapter, claimed that police counseling led to "some deterioration of student attitudes" but not as much as had occurred in another school lacking such an ideal program. The police have often used the rubric of "police-community" relations as a one-way street to inform the public of favorable information and to resist public disclosure of threatening or embarrassing data; the Commission apparently made no independent survey to ascertain how much "resource" input as against how much (doubtlessly clumsy) "brainwashing" occurs in these school programs. If education is designed to enable students to acquire critical thinking skills and to act independently, it borders on farce to regard anything but the most rigorously controlled police education program as pedagogical.

Fortunately, the present Report is comparatively freer of either blandness or misplaced beneficence than was the 1967 document. It does assume that its "action" proposals will be instantly recognized as meritorious and will be carried out with dispatch. It is not a philosophical discussion of crime and does not contain the wide-ranging, unfocused, discussions of needed reform, without a sense of priorities—all of which characterized its predecessor Report. Also, the present document is much more wary of technological innovation to aid crime control than was the considerably more sanguine Katzenbach study. There is little discussion of improved antiburglary equipment, Mace, scooters, and other paraphernalia, and no obvious enchantment with the "fortress" mentality that pervaded the 1967 report. Of course, both reports emphasize the need for modern radio and other communications equipment to shorten police-response time to citizen complaints, an uncontroversial subject.

The National Advisory Commission's Report was substantially more specific, imaginative, and sensitive to the problem of the computer and criminal justice than was the rather skimpy treatment of the subject in 1967. The recommendations for the keeping and compiling of criminal justice files are impressive and comprehensive. Fortunately, for the Commission and for the society, the issue became a lively public one soon after the Report (perhaps in part because of it, though largely, one suspects, because of Watergate), and Congress is now considering several bills of great political sophistication. Since the issue has aroused such substantial public concern, generous excerpts from the Commission's recommendation (contained in its Criminal Justice System Task Force Report) are included herein.

The Commission's task was formidable. One study reported that as of November 1972, California alone had 139 criminal-justice computer information systems. The Law Enforcement Assistance Administration is rapidly funding the creation of others, and the F.B.I. has been urging the states to connect ("interface" is the technocratic term) with its system (Massachusetts has, thus far, refused to participate in the bureau's computerized criminal-history file because it feared that too many agencies, including nongovernmental ones, had access to it and that it recorded and disseminated arrest information without any follow-up about convictions).

The history of criminal-justice files has not been an inspiring one. J. Edgar Hoover, it will be remembered, wanted to fingerprint every American—and World War II nearly gave him the opportunity to do so—and the bureau has been negligent about separating its noncriminal fingerprint files from its criminal-justice records. The bureau favored, but Congress rejected, a National Data Bank, and the implications of such a scheme (which may yet be revived) are staggering for a nation which keeps so many records containing so much information upon virtually all of its citizens.

The Commission proposed that three basic types of files be kept within the criminal-justice system; they would serve different purposes and would be kept by different levels of the system. They would consist of (a) individual criminal-history records; (b) records of treatment of individuals by the criminal-justice system; and (c) data about general occurrences of crime in various geographic areas. Standards relating to safeguarding of the systems, limited access to them (by both criminal-justice and some governmental noncriminal-justice agencies, often on a "need-to-know" basis), verification of their accuracy, and the purging of outdated information (especially of first-conviction records of nonrepeaters) are fundamental to the Commission's concern for both security and privacy. The Commission also recommends that the individual have access to the data and be allowed to contest it. Attorney General Saxbe opposed the latter proposal in January, 1974, and two months later the F.B.I. announced its opposition to the "sealing" (a lesser act, it should be noted, than purging) of any criminal-justice information. The Commission is opposed to the traditional law-enforcement concept that all criminal-justice information is potentially valuable for its own sake, and it has incurred the wrath of many practitioners in the system for that precise reason.

Congress has been more receptive and, as of the date of this analysis, several bills are pending to regulate federal and federally financed criminal justice computer systems. Congressional concern ranges from Senator Henry Jackson's proposal for a joint Congressional Committee on Surveillance to determine, among other things, how much and what type of surveillance is necessary and what standards should govern the relationship between federal and local criminal-justice record sharing to Senator Ervin's bill to seal records after a period of seven years (after a convicted felon has been released from incarceration; five years in the case of a misdemeanant), to forbid the compilation of pure "intelligence files," and to forbid the dissemination of arrest records only (with certain exceptions). The bill would create a new nine-member board (not controlled by criminal-justice practitioners) to supervise the bill's standards. The Justice Department introduced a bill containing some similar provisions (it, however, contained no restriction on dissemination of arrest records) and vesting regulatory authority in the Attorney General. It is noteworthy that Clarence Kelley, Director of the F.B.I., refused to support even the administration's bill. Pending passage of a final comprehensive measure, the Justice Department has proposed the creation of interim standards to govern the operations of criminal-justice computers.

Although the Commission performed a noble and yeomanlike task in formulating standards and passionately arguing for an extensive right of privacy in the collection and distribution of potentially explosive materials, it made no detailed recommendations on the equally thorny and complex subject of intelligence files. Indeed, it explicitly endorsed maintenance of such files without apparent restriction as to subject matter, although it did state that they should be kept by a special unit of the police department operating independently of any investigations branch, with safeguards as to access.

# 6: Overhauling the System

The Commission's proposals are important not necessarily because they will reduce crime, but because they are humane and fair. If adopted, those attributes themselves, and their underlying values, may help to ameliorate some of those persistently destructive social conditions that conduce toward crime. The essence of the Commission's argument is that the system must be devoted to assessing the needs of the individual offender and to meeting those needs. For many, the Commission stresses, the needs are simple enough—jobs, housing, training. The Commission calls for increased community involvement by agencies such as Youth Service Bureaus (about which, more later), employer groups, and even religious organizations. Criminal justice must be removed as far as possible from the professionals, not only those in the law-enforcement agencies, but also their "scientific" advisers. The average criminal—if he exists and if we know anything about him—is not very different from his law-abiding counterpart, and we do not need vast hordes of psychiatrists and social workers to experiment endlessly with the lives of those caught up in the criminal-justice system. For many offenders, social and economic betterment (it is hard to make a dollar as a criminal; as one sociologist has observed "crime is work," often unremunerative work) is sufficient. Perhaps, the Commission gently suggests, it is time for the professionals to lay aside their pet theories about deviance and crime and allow the community to take over.

Some may find the Commission's correlation to be simplistic (I do, but from another perspective). After all, the crime rate increased most dramatically in the sixties, a decade of little unemployment. While this is apparently true, that boom period obscured some critical transformations in the nature of work and the changing forms of unemployment. The overall unemployment rate is not nearly as significant as the differential rate—the rate for various groups in the economy. The changing nature of American employment, the shift from an industrial to a service economy, the diminution of marginal businesses which hired the unskilled and trained them to become semiskilled, the greater skills increasingly becoming required for even blue collar employment, the shift of jobs from city to suburb, the unreality of official unemployment indices (which measure only those working or actively in the job market rather than those who have simply given up) all created a jumbled picture. As might have been expected, during the sixties, the black unemployment and underemployment rates were significantly higher than the white, and the unemployment rate for black teen-agers was astronomically so.

This is not to argue that "crime" will be significantly reduced by full employment or by general economic and social rejuvenation of the ghettos and slums of the nation. It is right to undertake antipoverty programs (like Christianity, they were never really tried, despite LBJ's rhetoric) for their own sake; more significantly, *any* reduction in crime will doubtlessly convince many skeptics that treating crime as a problem of the society rather than of individual or group pathology will be more productive. One recent study found that, ironically enough, fear of danger and violence in and about school created much truancy and subsequent delinquency; its conclusion did not differ vastly from that of the Commission: "Income maintenance and improved neighborhood life seem to be reasonable recommendations, although of course they are not novel ideas."

The Commission mentions two demographic factors that may play a greater role in the crime rate than do all the activities of the criminal-justice system put together. The ratio of teen-agers to the general population may be the critical determinant of the crime rate. In 1971, juveniles accounted for 25.8 percent of all arrests and 50.8 percent of all arrests for crimes against property. The fact that the proportion of juveniles to the rest of the population in the next decade will diminish may in itself account for a reduction of the crime rate. There may well be some correlation between rising suburban crime and the increasing percentages of juveniles in the suburban population, although analysis of several comparative urban crime rates indicates that the correlation does not exist. Given both high American crime rates in general and the disproportionate incidence of juvenile participation in particular, a few intercity discrepancies may not be very significant. For the society as a whole, much crime may be simply a reflection of the postwar baby boom which created a vast number of juveniles in the sixties.

Another demographic factor over which our criminal-justice institutions have no control is population density, and the Commission notes that there is an "historical association between population density and crime rate." The Commission recognizes that "Pervasive movement produces rootlessness which in time leads to a sense of anonymity. . . ." Factors such as density, mobility, transiency of neighborhoods, inability of neighborhood institutions to develop, all strongly correlate with crime (again, these factors seem to be strongest now in certain suburban areas).

Since Americans and the Commissions which stand as surrogates for them are a peculiarly unhistorical people, they simply fail to recognize that urban living has always been socially disorganized, in this country as well as others. From the scanty evidence available, the nineteenth-century crime rates in our heavily populated, slum-ridden cities were much greater than those prevailing even in the sixties. One historian, speaking of his analysis of New York City's archives for the late eighteenth century (when only 75,000 people resided there) observed that "The people who complain about life today ... wouldn't have lasted a week then." A long-term rather than myopic view of our national experience might better aid any analysis of how much crime is truly a product of our society and how much can be controlled by the criminal-justice system or even by political change. Perhaps a national commission of historians should seriously study the problem of "criminality"; their conclusions could serve as a background for a more informed (and more broadly based) analysis.

# 7: Establishing Priorities

The Report establishes four priorities; they are both sane and sensible. Probably the most urgent of the four is the reduction of juvenile delinquency. If crime is often—if not primarily—a juvenile activity, if criminal careers commence at that time, and if, as the Commission notes, "The further an offender penetrates into the criminal-justice process, the more difficult it becomes to divert him from a criminal career," then the Report's concern is not misplaced.

The Commission concludes that juveniles should not come into contact with the juvenile-court system, wherever possible. It estimates that as many as 50 percent of juvenile-police contacts are disposed of by referral to other agencies; probably, another 50 percent of the remainder should be similarly treated. Juvenile court jurisdiction over so-called "status" offenses (minor in need of supervision, homelessness) should terminate, since no antisocial conduct is involved. Presently, disposition of cases involving "status" is the main business of the juvenile courts: the Task Force Report on Corrections found that, in California, only 17 percent of juvenile arrests were for acts which would be equivalent to felonies if committed by adults and 20 percent of such arrests involved conduct resembling misdemeanors. Many detained juveniles (often in centers which are filthy and understaffed) have done nothing—literally nothing—to warrant such forced detention. The Commission's recommendations—including a critical one that *all* detention decisions be made by nonpolice juvenile-court personnel—are amplified by the excerpted material following Chapter IV.

Commission recommendations concerning "diversion" (channeling of those charged to special agencies, while holding in abeyance criminal or juvenile charges) are particularly critical in the case of juvenile offenses. There are approximately fifty pretrial diversion programs operating within American cities (at the end of 1973), and many are limited to first offenders, to those who voluntarily choose to enter, and to those accused of nonviolent offenses. Many bar addicts. The paucity of diversion resources is pointed up by a study of the Baltimore program, which manages to take only 400 of the 10,000 teen-agers eligible each year. The Commission recommends expansion of present, and the development of new, community treatment facilities.

One institution which receives the Report's unqualified approbation is the youth services bureau. This agency maintains liaison with all community social agencies to deal with problems of youth, both delinquent and nondelinquent. Although the track record of the bureaus is not clear (in 1972, only 150 bureaus existed and they received only $25 million in federal funds), the Commission is undoubtedly correct in pressing for "Legislation . . . to mandate the use of Y.S.B.s as a voluntary diversion resource by agencies of the criminal justice system."

Police response to youth services (taken generically) has been guarded, and the Commission notes that "Unfortunately, existing youth services bureaus have been underutilized as a diversionary resource by law enforcement." The most intractable problem of the juvenile-justice system involves the vast discretion of police to refer matters either to court or to social agencies (or to ignore or informally dispose of them altogether). Although the statistics quoted above indicate that much police discretion operates in favor of informal referral, the Commission is aware that many more cases could and should be disposed of by such methods if the police were more sensitive to juvenile needs and the reasons for their often hostile demeanor. Studies have demonstrated that the decision to formally invoke judicial processes against juveniles in nonserious situations by the police is most often governed by (a) the local social culture (suburban juvenile "troublemakers" are treated more tenderly than are their urban counterparts) and (b) the demeanor (defiance instead of contrition) of the offender. The Commission rightly argues for increasing the limitations upon police discretion in this vital area, even to the extent of requiring a written report in cases where the officer refuses to divert, and granting superior officers the authority to countermand such decisions. In addition, as previously mentioned, the "intake" decision—the formal acceptance by the court of jurisdiction over the juveniles—would always be made by a court officer, and *all* detention of juveniles would be determined by the court or its personnel.

Although these suggestions are helpful and even invaluable, it is time to consider whether the Commission's concept of "community treatment" should not be extended in both juvenile and family-dispute cases. The model posited by the Commission would abolish juvenile courts, transfer all juvenile-related proceedings into a new family court, and would promote diversion as both a preintake and pretrial mechanism. Yet, the overhauled system still retains its "criminal justice" origins. The basic model of even a family court is that of the criminal court, and, although the language changes ("petition" instead of criminal complaint, "hearing" instead of trial), the underlying perceptions of all those participating are still the same. Indeed, the Supreme Court in 1967 found that juvenile courts still rendered essentially criminal judgments in the guise of "delinquency determinations" and that such proceedings required a modicum of due process. Nothing the Commission proposes would fundamentally alter the image.

Perhaps it is time to consider whether, at least in juvenile cases, the courtroom itself could be transformed into a therapeutic environment emphasizing community concern for helping the troubled offender. If the first contact with juvenile court is the critical one in terms of subsequent criminal careers, then the last vestiges of legal adjudication should be abolished. Merely requiring judges to doff their robes is clearly not the answer, especially when many juvenile judges through the nation sit also as criminal-court jurists and attitudes attributable to that function readily carry over to their more sensitive role. European criminal courts commonly require that judges and jurors sit together in criminal cases, juvenile and adult, thus adding vital communal input into the legal system, and there is no reason why this should not occur in our allegedly compassionate juvenile proceedings. Even more significantly, why should a legally trained judge have any greater expertise about intrafamily quarrels and difficulties than do other community representatives? If business disputes are often removed from the courts and referred to arbitrators who understand the complex problems involved, and whose proceedings are more informal than those of conventional courts, why do family disputes remain in the "legal" realm?

The public interest in maintaining its criminal laws and practices intact against adult offenders may well justify use of state tribunals to determine guilt and punishment, but the same alleged state interest in juvenile and family matters simply does not exist. The juvenile court system itself is a theoretical tribute to the commitment of the society to helping rather than judging the individual. One solution might involve the creation of an alternative form of community, nonjudicial, arbitration panel to the processes of a state-created court. As with arbitration generally, the juvenile (depending upon his age, alone or with parental consent) would have to consent. That "body" might consist of, let us say, a businessman, a clergyman, and a lawyer, sitting informally and rendering a disposition which could be appealed to the family court in cases of gross arbitrariness. Such an institution now exists precisely for family problems which do not come to the attention of formal state agencies in the form of the so-called "Jewish Court" (actually an arbitration body composed of a businessman, a rabbi, and an attorney) which is perceived by many as a humane and acceptable alternative to more formal proceedings. If the "model" is to be created by the state, there are substantial problems of jurisdiction, eligibility for panel membership, and relationship to other state agencies. Those problems are not insurmountable, and such a model would be entirely consistent with other Commission objectives such as "community participation"; indeed, there is good reason to believe that it would go further toward fulfillment of those objectives than would a revamped family court.

# 8: The Task Force Reports

The major aspects of the National Advisory Commission's Report are its informal style, lack of analysis, and liberal (almost random) sprinkling of suggestions. Many of its conclusions are so startling—and novel, at least to the public—that fuller explanation is owed, at least in this popular edition of the document. Accordingly, relevant excerpts from the Task Force Reports have been appended to each appropriate chapter of the main Report. The materials have been chosen for several reasons (some already discussed), including the need to amplify some of the newer suggestions, to fill in where the main Report's materials are cursory or confusing, and also, it must be admitted, to emphasize those aspects which I find particularly (and perhaps peculiarly) fascinating.

Some vital subjects, only briefly discussed in the main Report, require amplification. I have already noted that the question of criminal-justice files has become a "hot" public issue recently, so that substantial addition to the Report in this area certainly is warranted. Another important Commission (and public) concern is that of drug abuse and crime, and appropriate explanatory additions are included. The question of the relationship between drugs and crime is a complex one, and has engendered great public misunderstanding. Do drug abusers, especially heroin addicts, commit crimes of violence (rather than crimes against property) to pay for their habits? If so, which comes first—the criminality or the drug abuse? Is there an escalation in the forms of dangerous criminality perpetrated by those who need drugs? Has there been a fall-off in heroin addiction and addiction-related crimes in the last few years and, if so, can such fall-off be attributable to tougher laws, to greater regulation of opium production internationally, or to changes in drug-abuse patterns, or all three? What works to rehabilitate the drug abuser, and what form of treatment does not? Perhaps the drug problem (at least insofar as heroin is concerned) is not as serious now as it was three years ago, but there are signs that a resurgence of heroin use is in the offing. (The Drug Enforcement Administration, housed in the Justice Department, recently reported that Mexican heroin is replacing the Near Eastern brand; but the Customs Bureau has taken issue with the estimate that 50 percent of the heroin trade is now attributable to Mexican smuggling—thus demonstrating once again that the "drug problem" is in part a political and bureaucratic one.)

The main Report presents a few bare conclusions, endorses methadone maintenance, decries heroin maintenance ("After careful consideration, the Commission has concluded that heroin maintenance is a potentially harmful method of treatment both to the individual and to society as a whole"), and broadly advocates the use of therapeutic communities for addicts without analyzing their substantial failure rate. Which addicts are more suited for which types of programs? Should "narcotic antagonists" (drugs that block craving for heroin) be encouraged, despite their apparent danger and their strong resemblance to behavior-modification experimentation? Without the supporting material that has been provided, the Commission's suggestion that "effective drug abuse prevention programs be established" has little meaning.

# 9: The Police

I have already mentioned that the Commission treated the police gingerly, and the main and Police Task Force reports raise (and often do not address) some fundamental problems relating to both police work and conduct in a democratic society. One major problem—deeper than the Commission either realizes or is willing to admit to—is that of effectiveness. The Commission views that issue in fairly conventional terms, such as better deployment of police resources, upgrading the patrol function, technological improvements, "team policing" and other new patrol concepts. Implicit within this range of concerns is the assumption that more effective use of present methods and incremental (i.e., modest) improvement will contribute to crime reduction.

In broader perspective, though, proposals for improving police effectiveness may be lamentably irrelevant. The conventional wisdom assumes that "preventive patrol" is the first line of police response to crime. Eighty-five percent of all police work directly related to crime prevention and detection and one-half of the $4.5 billion spent on the police involves patrol. Yet, recent studies have indicated that there may be absolutely no relationship between the number of police officers per capita and the (known) crime rate. For one year, Kansas City, Missouri, experimented with three patrol systems in sectors of approximately the same social and demographic characteristics. One group of these areas had no patrol cars (car would be sent only in response to citizen complaints), another was serviced by one car, and the third was "saturated" with four or five patrol cars. The only areas where the crime rate was negatively (though insignificantly) affected were those with *no* patrol services.[4]

The public's belief that somehow crime will be reduced by expansion of the police force has also been tested and found wanting. A report in 1974 about "New York's finest" showed that only about 1,000 men out of a total force of 31,000 were available for patrol duty at a given time. Between 1953 and 1973, the New York City Police force grew by 55 percent, but the number of officers actually patrolling the streets remained steady. In addition to the few patrolmen available, the total number of police officers "on the street" (supervising sergeants, plainclothesmen, officers occupying fixed posts) and therefore theoretically available to civilian calls for help never exceeded 8 percent of the force. One may conclude that an increase in police personnel may well be "counterproductive" because it creates greater public expectations which cannot be fulfilled. (Another factor which limits the ability of

[4] The Kansas City study prompted an Assistant Chief of Police in that city to acknowledge that "We just went out, and proved that the liberal cliché is correct: Crime is caused by social conditions. . . ."

patrolmen to detect crime is the fact that much criminal activity occurs indoors; in New York City, for instance, 54 percent of all known serious crimes occurred out of the view of those thousand foot soldiers.)

The major result of an increase in the force appears to be a corresponding—or disproportionate—growth of the police bureaucracy. The political disputes within the bureaucracy may also operate to limit effectiveness even further and to imbalance police resources. In the spring of 1974, another myth, that of detective effectiveness in solving robberies, was laid to rest by an extensive study which concluded that those vaunted heroes only made 10 to 30 percent of all robbery arrests and suggested that "major detective forces might not be required except in the largest cities," and that specialized detective squads may be necessary in none. The report recognized the bureaucratic difficulties involved in any major overhaul of extant police work patterns by observing that "In no other area of police operations do there appear to be so many myths of so much resistance either to change or serious self-examination."

Given this background, it is no wonder that the Commission's recommendations concerning effectiveness and measurement of effectiveness is inconclusive. Some Task Force materials have been included simply to show that "measurement" is almost a primitive concept (perhaps, as I have indicated, it is also a meaningless one). Even the Commission's cautious endorsement of "team policing"—the combining of patrol and investigative work in a single unit responsible for a certain geographic area—may be irrelevant. Although team policing has received much favorable publicity, there are, as the Commission recognizes, certain inherent difficulties—and in Aberdeen, Scotland, where it was first introduced in 1948, it was abandoned fifteen years later. The Commission hesitates to draw the obvious conclusion: that police work has little to do with crime. Where team policing or some other nostrum is (often, temporarily) effective in one area, it may simply mean that criminal activity shifts to another region. In the end it is the social composition and climate of the community that determines the amount of crime.

Although much of the Police Task Force Report is devoted to numerous and well-taken suggestions for "housekeeping" reforms, better planning, and increased training (400 hours), some proposals are more controversial than is apparent on their face—and, hopefully, the excerpted material will help the reader to understand more about the implications of these seemingly innocuous calls for reform.

For instance, the Commission and the Police Task Force endorse what has by now become almost a universal call for a college degree for policemen (by 1983). Only one reasonably large police department (Ventura, California) presently requires a B.A. degree for entrance, while others formerly mandating it have returned to the ranks of what liberal critics refer to as "stumblebum" operations. Police education has become a popular form of academic pastime, especially since Law Enforcement Assistance Administration funding is available and criminal-justice programs, employing part-time police faculty, are cheap and profitable for hard-pressed academic institutions. The academic respectability of many "police science" programs is questionable, and it is arguable that a true liberal education, rather than a fanciful extension of training-school subjects, is necessary for the human development of a police officer. How it will enhance his "professional" abilities is still an open question. There is some evidence that well-educated police more often avoid public complaint but, beyond that, there is no visible link between education and performance.

But there are other difficulties. Education may be the wedge, the rubric by which "professionalism" becomes a credible argument, and the history of the growth of police "professionalism" is not uncontroversial or reassuring. The police have sought to use the aura of professionalism throughout the twentieth century as a shield against political interference with first the police function, then police autonomy. As the worst excesses of political partisanship (appointment and promotion by recommendations from political leaders, nonenforcement of certain laws against political favorites) have faded, the professionalism movement has sought to convince the public that police work is a science (if not an art) that outsiders are ill-equipped to judge. Thus, adapting the rubric which operates to protect other professional groups from public scrutiny, the police have sought to protect their own autonomy and definition of their role from review, oversight, and even criticism. Police education, certainly in an attenuated, uncritical form, may operate to increase police isolation and power.

Apart from the question of education, the Commission offers little analysis of the real issues involved in professionalization. The argument as to whether police work is a profession akin to law and medicine or merely an elevated craft (with certain skills in the social sciences required of some policemen) will undoubtedly continue, without resolution or clarification. But a legal system which vests so much power in an agency such as the police, which confers upon the police a virtual monopoly over force, and which professes a belief that democratic control and check of all power is necessary should not readily accept that same group as the final arbiter of its own actions. The absence of any tradition of ethical standards and effective internal review procedures also lessens police claims to professionalization (or, at least, requires the development of these attributes *before* society confers the benefit of professionalization). To an extent, the issue might be irrelevant since elected officials such as mayors or city managers have the authority to fire and hire police chiefs, and thus to hold them accountable to public standards of performance. Unfortunately, professionalism is being abetted by another trend, unionization, which may so completely attenuate the supervisory powers of police chiefs that even the indirect controls may be rendered ineffective.

Public accountability will be eroded by the increasing inability of the chief to manage internal police operations; unionization has already extended far beyond job security and economic enhancement. Unions have begun to demand a greater voice in police operations and, simultaneously, freedom from oversight. In New York City a few years ago, a more rational allocation of police resources was stymied by the opposition of the Patrolmen's Benevolent Association to a "fourth shift" during high-crime hours. That powerful lobby also played upon public fears in 1966 to abolish civilian presence on the department's Review Board—in opposition, it should be noted, to the position of most of the city's and state's elected officials. In the spring of 1974, an insurgent slate triumphed in a New York P.B.A. election on a platform which derided attempts to "civilianize" the department (by hiring nonpolicemen to perform clerical functions) and to bring more women into police work (the Commission favors both). Inevitably, police autonomy will not only increase but will drift downward toward the lower ranks, and the priorities of the department and the union (which, for many practical purposes, may become the department) will supersede those of the mayor or city council. Unionization is not the evil; its effects in an area of peculiar public sensitivity may well be. The Commission has little to say about either professionalization or unionization in this critical context.

The Report and the Task Force supplement barely analyze

other critical public police issues. (To be fair, some of these concerns did not surface until after the Report was in.) I have previously alluded to the Report's unconcern with the nature of police intelligence files. The Task Force recommends that any agency with more than seventy-five employees create a full-time intelligence capability, but adds nothing about what kinds of information this capability should collect or, more critically, what tactics (infiltration, agent provocateurism, creation of an informant system) should be either encouraged or forbidden in the gathering of such information.

The Commission commends the use of undercover "decoy" squads to apprehend street crimes—particularly the Detroit STRESS ("Stop the Robberies, Enjoy Safe Streets") program. Unfortunately, STRESS has been disbanded because of community fears that the decoys would engage in wholesale bloodbaths and in particular because of a notorious incident involving a shoot-out between white STRESS officers and black policemen from the Wayne County Sheriff's office. Perhaps it is unfair to single out STRESS and to apply 20-20 hindsight to the Commission's uncritical endorsement of decoy programs, but it should have been sensitive to the need for strong internal controls of such potentially volatile police endeavors.

The STRESS problem and the professionalism-unionism problem blend into the overriding critical issue of review of police misconduct—and here the Commission's reasoning is simply tortured. After admitting (in the Task Force Report) that "Review mechanisms and investigative units have continuously been advocated or discussed by national commissions," the Task Force concludes that (a) "there has been little success" with present review bodies and (b) "there has been virtually no . . . experimentation with alternatives. . . ." To "explain" this failure, the Report argues that "A review board cannot perform adequately the function it is assigned because it cannot demand change." Presumably, adjudicatory bodies—up to and including the Supreme Court—cannot "demand change," but their rulings (and suggestions) can induce those with authority to institute change to exercise such authority (especially if the judges are prestigious and their rulings are publicized). The reasoning here seems to be, charitably put, a bit lame.

The Task Force's conclusion that even the addition of a strong and independent staff to aid a review board "would [not] result in a successful . . . operation" is supported by nothing more than the cynical statement that the police don't like review boards. The entire matter is both trivialized and whitewashed by statements such as

> A public complaint must not be regarded as a dispute between two people but rather as criticism that the delivery of police service did not meet the complainant's expectations.

Complaints, of course, can involve either or both of the above types of dissatisfaction, and to reduce the controversy to one resembling a dispute between a department store and a buyer is demeaning as well as inaccurate.

The final conclusion that the "effective use of the many governmental agencies already legally empowered to review police agency activities is a better solution" is inadequate, and the example chosen to support that generalization, the appointment of the special prosecutor in New York City, is particularly ingenuous. That office was created after an independent commission found widespread police corruption (apparently unknown to the department itself), was created for a limited period of time, and its mandate is to investigate corruption (among all criminal-justice agencies) and not to function as a review board to determine the myriad forms of complaints that do not relate to corruption.

I have suggested in another context[5] that the most feasible solution to problems of police misconduct is to place the department, at least for purposes of complaint-resolution, under the jurisdiction of the local prosecutor's office and to institute prosecutorial review. The prosecutor, unlike the police chief, is an attorney and an officer of the courts, and his conduct, including the performance of his office, is reviewable in turn by the local bar association or the courts. Whatever the jurisdictional problems inherent in subjecting the department to varying duties to differing public officials, there is no question that lawyers—who are (theoretically) bound to certain canons of ethics, who are subject to review by other agencies, and who are trained to establish and operate procedures (such as review mechanisms) which are both fair and firm and do not interfere with ongoing activities—are best equipped to handle matters of police review. The local prosecutor who shares certain duties with the police is also well equipped to understand police problems and procedures and would be immune to any criticism that he is an outsider. As an elected

[5] "Restraining the Police," *Massachusetts Review*, Summer 1970.

official, he could be held accountable to the public for his conduct in this respect as well as in others. An idea such as this may be necessary because the simple truth of our experience with the subject demonstrates that internal review does not work, and that sporadic external review is too unstructured and too limited to be meaningful.[6]

One Commission proposal which has startled civil libertarians would allow the police to obtain search warrants by telephone in emergency situations. The concern is misplaced, for the fundamental problem resides in the willingness of judges to grant warrants liberally in the first place, no matter how unpersuasive the underlying reasons. When police apply for warrants, judges do not often ask about the source of the information (often the product of a mysterious and perhaps nonexistent "previously reliable informant") and have even been known to sign warrant authorizations in blank. The judiciary is more critical when the warrant is attacked in the course of a later criminal proceeding (assuming that the warrant turned up something; we don't know about the number of cases that never develop because nothing incriminating was found) and only then do judges carefully scrutinize the affidavit submitted by the police officer to support issuance of the warrant. Theoretically, it should not have been issued unless the facts stated therein would lead a reasonable man to believe that incriminating evidence will probably be found, but the initial issuance of the warrant is regarded by most judges as routine, technical act.

The problem requires that judges be more sensitive to the Fourth Amendment's protection against unwarranted entry; perhaps such sensitivity can be attained when judges regard the issuing process with more solemnity than now occurs. A warrant issuance panel of three judges (with the concurrence of two being necessary) in multi-judge districts might be helpful. Indeed, the Commission itself makes the valuable suggestion that prosecutorial advance approval be obtained before application for a warrant can be initiated (the proposal does not deal with the problem of the "emergency" telephone warrant). In essence the telephonic warrant issue is not particularly germane to the Fourth Amendment problems that plague both current and proposed warrant practices.

---

[6] One criticism of internal review—that it was too harsh—was voiced by the "insurgent" slate which won the New York City PBA election referred to earlier; the winners described the large numbers of officers devoted to investigating other policemen.

# 10: The Courts

The Report's chapter on the Courts and the Task Force supplement are intriguing for several reasons. Since the Commission was composed of practitioners, it understandably sought to inject efficiency into the criminal-justice system. Often, though, efficiency has a price, and that price was not always recognized by the Commission (interestingly enough, the only formal dissents to the whole Report and its five Task Forces occurred in connection with both this subject, the courts, and its treatment, efficiency). Clearly, the reduction of court time will be substantial if matters such as drunkenness, vagrancy, and minor traffic offenses are to be decriminalized. The Commission offers little in detail on the question of how society is to deal with these occurrences (some of which are harmful to the individual involved, some to others), especially since the criminal-justice system did perform a certain social function for inebriates (as the Commission notes, many of the functions of the system have little to do with protecting the state or the citizenry but rather with serving private ends). Is the community willing to spend to create new facilities to replace the "jailhouse cure" (usually thirty days) and to provide proper (and expensive) social and psychological treatment to the denizens of Skid Row? Although the Commission takes the matter in stride, its Corrections Task Force found that the St. Louis and Washington, D.C., detoxification centers were essentially "holding areas." Although it may be true that "Therapy may, in long run, prove to be the most practical means of dealing with the problem," will true therapeutic facilities ever be developed?

The Courts chapter endorses screening (the decision not to bring someone into the system) and diversion (discussed earlier) as "important means of reducing caseloads." One hopes that efficiency is not the sole justification for these reasonable (and necessary) innovations. Some of the excerpted material from the Courts Task Force Report deals with proposed guidelines for screening by police officers, their superiors, and even prosecutors serving at the station houses. The Commission is beguiled by the necessity of imposing restrictions upon the discretion of power-holders such as police, but, of course, can find only the vaguest language to express its concern. Cases, we are told, should be screened where there is "bad evidence" (a commendable, though not very specific criterion), to "further justice," and to preclude "high costs." If these are the criteria used by the Philadelphia prosecutor's office when it throws out one-third of all arrests at the station house, one wonders whether screening is used for its own sake, for the purposes of statistical pride (Philadelphia, it may be recalled, is the worst offender in the underreporting of crime), or because prosecutors in the city of brotherly love are genuinely compassionate. The Commission might have given us a clearer picture of the process had it interviewed both prosecutors and police to ascertain what the real, as distinct from the formal, criteria are.

The Commission's equanimity extends to its "diversion" analysis. Diversion is a decent alternative, as has been previously discussed, but the Commission may be trapped if it believes that it will significantly aid in the reduction of crime. If diversion does not produce significantly less recidivism (assuming it is widely instituted) than do probation and incarceration, then public backlash may be strong. Obviously, no self-respecting establishment group can simply say that something is right and may be effective; rather, it must declaim that the proposal will work—and must inevitably run into the strange truth that very little seems to work within the criminal-justice system. The Commission singles out Project Crossroads for youthful first offenders in Washington, D.C. as a successful diversion program and notes that during the first two and one-half years of the program, only 283 accused were returned to court for continued prosecution while 487 defendants had their cases dropped. Also, allegedly, the recidivism rate for those who entered the program was considerably lower than it was for those incarcerated after trial. Unfortunately, the story is more complicated than that, and the appropriate material about Project Crossroads is included in the Task Force excerpts following Chapter VI.

The quest for efficiency is often breathtaking—accused felons should go to trial within sixty days of arrest, omnibus pretrial motions should be heard at one sitting (and the judge should have a checklist to make sure that all possible issues have been raised), and appeals should be equally brisk. Certainly the Commission has much to complain about, and, by now, every American must be aware of the lengthy delays, the endless pretrial bickering, the spate of preliminary proceedings and even preliminary appeals, the incredible length of jury selection, and the dilatory pace of the trials themselves in many cases. Appeals continue endlessly and state and federal judges continually bicker over jurisdiction—or so it seems. Were it not for plea-bargaining (and, it must be remembered, the Commission opposes this) the system would break down instantly. The Commission evidently assumes that, after decriminalization, screening, diversion, and the like have flushed out most defendants, anyone left must either be pretty innocent or pretty dangerous. In either case, it believes plea-bargaining is inappropriate; in either case, a brisk and efficient and rapid trial should "bring out the facts" and lead to a just disposition. For those remaining, the Commission envisages giving them if not short, then shorter, shrift.

Perhaps the most startling proposal proffered in the name of expediency would reduce the number of jurors in a case not involving either the death penalty or life imprisonment to six. Although the twelve-member jury was a historical accident, it has functioned for six centuries as a people's check upon unwarranted or venal prosecutions, and the Commission did not explain how six would be able to reject and retain the presumed benefit of community input into the system as well as twelve. (In light of the Commission's recommendations for greater community participation in corrections, the idea is ludicrous and even outlandish; as one expert put it, "Our jury system is too precious to play around with.") The experience of the State of Connecticut with six-member jury panels for serious cases has engendered a pervasive feeling that the broad spectrum of the community is not represented, the verdicts are unpredictable and often hasty, and that the intangible value of fundamental fairness has been reduced. The only apparent virtues of the Commission's recommendation is a reduction of the number of hung juries—but when liberty is at stake, perhaps some minimal margin should be accorded to the defendant (it should also be noted that hung juries may well contain a majority in favor of acquittal). Everything we know about the subject of small-group dynamics supports the belief that pressures to change beliefs will be more intense in a six-member group than in larger one. The proposal is so un-thought-out that it prompted the Vice-Chairman of the Courts Task Force to dissent, and his reasons are set forth in the excerpts following Chapter VI (as is the Commission's scanty reasoning).

The Commission casts a baleful eye on defense counsel who seek to "improperly" persuade the (obviously susceptible) jury. Thus, it recommends that only the trial judge—and not opposing counsel—conduct the *voir dire* (questioning of jurors to determine bias). That system—the federal model—would undoubtedly expedite jury selection and subsequent trials, but it would also severely undercut the jury's "informal" role, its ability to mitigate unduly harsh criminal statutes or to restrain vindictive prosecutions. Trials are indeed prolonged (how often this occurs the Commission does not venture to tell us) by the jockeying for position, but there is a considerable social value to the process. In some notorious political cases of recent vintage, the defense has boldly attempted to use the *voir dire* to "educate" the jury (with some success), and in all cases the function of defense counsel requires him to humanize the defendant and to overcome the general jury belief that the government would not be prosecuting the case unless the accused were guilty. A trial is not only a dispassionate search for truth; it is a social ritual and drama which pits the machinery of the state against an accused under circumstances where truth is often ambiguous. The symbolic uses of the criminal trial have been a staple of serious (and popular) literature and drama for centuries, although they have received little formal academic analysis, and jurors know this. Neither the Report nor the Courts Task Force study explain why we would be better off abolishing one vital aspect of the drama.

The Courts Task Force extends the Commission theme that trials should be businesslike. It derides "orations" by defense counsel during summation which "are made at the expense of defendants awaiting trial and of the public interested in seeing criminal justice rendered promptly." Thus, it reduces an American criminal trial to the status of an arbitration session between businessmen and ignores its ritual role of reaffirming fundamental community values (or choosing between contradictory ones). It is true that the current system is "permissive" and the defendant does not always benefit (such permissiveness often engenders flamboyant prosecutorial tactics which may unduly influence a jury toward conviction), but excesses on both sides can be controlled by the patient trial judge.

The Commission's concern for efficiency also pervades its recommendations for abolition of the grand jury and limitation upon the number of appeals. The grand jury is the subject of considerable public debate and distrust; most states have either abolished it or provided alternatives to it, and all have recognized that this once august body of citizens which protected fellow citizens against overweening state power[7] has become little more than a rubber stamp for prosecutors today. Civil libertarians who have been appalled by the experience of grand-jury "abuse" by Richard Nixon's

[7] In reality, its historic function in England was to screen out malicious or unfounded prosecutions brought by private persons.

Justice Department in political cases have been joined by conservatives who deplore leaks, immunity dealings by prominent public officials in return for testimony against others, and "fishing expeditions" by a body whose mandate is virtually limitless. In addition, it is costly.

The Commission argues that the jury throws out very few cases recommended for indictment by the prosecutor (20 percent in Washington, D.C.), so that the return on the community's investment is low. Others may believe that 20 percent is a substantial rate (while conceding that judges in states using the device of a preliminary hearing, where the prosecution must present some evidence to warrant trial, actually dismiss more cases) but may inquire whether that citizen's body performs other valuable functions. For instance, how many charges originally brought by prosecutors are reduced by the grand jury? How many dubious cases are presented by district attorneys who are not sure of community sentiment and seek guidance by the jury?

Perhaps it is too late to restore the grand jury's protective function, but measures short of abolition may help. For instance, why should the prosecutor, a member of the executive branch seeking indictments, simultaneously act as an advisor to a judicial body? If the grand jury is theoretically an arm of the court and not of the prosecutor, it should have its own attorney-advisor and this would undoubtedly eliminate many of the abuses. Ironically, Richard Nixon, as a congressman, proposed just such an innovation, long before he began to experience his own difficulties with that "citizen's body."

It must be remembered that the ability to compel testimony will be lodged elsewhere if the grand jury is abolished. The Commission proposes to vest it in the prosecutor himself, so that there is no insurance that abuses inherent in secret compulsion of testimony will end. They may well increase, given the prosecutor's self-image. Indeed, the Commission recognizes that the grand jury serves a valuable function in investigating political corruption and organized crime conspiracies; it would be retained for these purposes and indeed could be used for any purpose desired by the prosecutor. The issue is not free from doubt and certainly cannot be resolved by the Commission's ukase that the grand jury is a failure. Again, ironically, the Commission generally proposes greater community participation in the criminal justice process but abjures it in this vital area.

The Courts Task Force impressively analyzes the problem of judicial qualification and selection, another currently controversial issue. Should judges be elected or selected (and, if the latter, how)? The evidence that a better brand of judge is produced by one or the other method is inconclusive. Many have persuasively argued that the elective process merely insures that political machines, rather than the voters, will select the candidates; there is also little doubt that the worst judges are produced by the elective system. In contrast, there is evidence that the "Missouri System," whereby the governor appoints judges from a list submitted by a nonpartisan panel, merely changes the politics of the situation to insure that establishment types are chosen. The Commission wisely opts for the creation of a judicial nomination commission not subject to elitist influence; the proposed commission would include public members and its legal members would be appointed by the governor where no "unified bar association" (one encompassing all lawyers within the state) exists. Thus, it is hoped, elite bar associations would not have the same power they presently wield in Missouri and eight other states.

The well-publicized dichotomy between the polar opposites, election and selection, has so mesmerized our thinking that we do not consider alternatives. In Europe, of course, judges are regarded as professionals in fully the same sense many believe the police should be, and the traditions of the Continental law system require training and civil-service examinations. Although our customs differ, they would not necessarily preclude a requirement that those aspiring to judgeships be educated in a postlegal program in the humanities, social sciences, and ethics. The major objection to this (as well as to any merit system) involves our belief that elected judges somehow are equipped to comprehend the problems of the little man or minority groups. The presence of some 300 black judges (of the 17,600 full-time jurists in the country) is believed to have had a beneficial effect upon our legal system. The Commission recommends continuous education and training after appointment in lieu of preappointment prerequisites. If we are not prepared to rethink the question, then the Commission's proposals are by far the best available, and one would hope that judicial training (whenever it occurs) would be devoted as much to the cultivation of the liberal mind as the law.

# 11: Corrections

The current public interest in Corrections has prompted the extensive use of supplementary Task Force materials following Chapter VII. In the main, they are self-explanatory, if not particularly novel (other studies, including an excellent one conducted by the American Bar Association, have largely paved the way for the Commission's work in this area). Court decisions which directly and substantially affect the administration of the corrections systems have obviously had their effect upon the Commission's findings. The primary orientation of the Corrections Task Force Report emphasizes prisoners', parolees' and probationers' rights to due process in various forms.

The Report's call for a "substantial and rapid change" and its finding that "There is no evidence that prisons reduce the amount of crime" are both amply supported by dismal statistics. Within the first six months of release on parole in the federal prison system, 9 percent return as violators; within five years, 64.5 percent are returned. The Commission also notes that there is no significant difference in the recidivism rate between those who have received special treatment within institutions and those who have not. Clearly, the system is inadequate to aid anyone, and the Commission is being realistic, rather than woolly-headed, in recommending that only the truly dangerous be sent to prison, that their terms be relatively short (no more than five years, with some exceptions), that the law not impose any mandatory minimum terms or deny parole for any fixed periods, that there be a moratorium on the building of new prisons, and that juvenile reformatories be phased out. The Commission's call for establishment of community corrections centers which should "replace the prison" for most purposes is sensible and sound, although far in advance of public attitudes.

For the prisons that remain to house dangerous offenders, "Adult institutions should revamp their programs so that, among other things, the job training they offer trains for real jobs, using skilled supervision and modern machinery." The Commission also recommends individualized treatment of offenders based upon valid classification of their problems and character types (a subject still clouded by much vagueness) and substantial reforms in the parole process.

For all of the excellent and comprehensive work performed by the Commission in the realm of corrections, it must be faulted for devoting little analysis to public attitudes.

Reluctance to "coddle" prisoners will create insuperable difficulties for lasting change. The problem of public attitudes is relegated to a pithy comment:

> Reform in corrections will also require changes in public values and attitudes. The public must recognize that crime and delinquency are related to the kind of society in which offenders live. Reduction of crime may therefore depend on basic social change.

# 12: The Relevance of History

One reason for incorporating Task Force materials into the main Report is to give the reader some insight into the history of our criminal justice system, institutions, and modes of thought. Unfortunately, as I have said, the Report is not particularly enlightening on the subject of how and why we have arrived where we are. History may not demonstrate much (Henry Ford probably expressed the prevailing American attitude toward Clio by calling it bunk), but it does compel us to realize that institutions often develop as reflections of new modes of thought.[8] The Enlightenment gave us the mental asylum because men could be (and, more important, should be) made perfectible (with "treatment" to free him from his internal demons); "science" has also been applied (often haphazardly) to our criminal-justice institutions because Americans pride themselves on their realism—and science, to us, is real.

History also demonstrates often—and this is especially true of our criminal-justice system—that advances do not replace outmoded institutions, but merely supplement them. The tenacious ability of institutions to remain, and to function in conjunction with inconsistent supplementary ones, the reliance on faddism in various forms (the history of the "science" of criminology is largely a history of faddism), and a paradoxical jumble of new and old ideas and ideologies have characterized the development of our criminal-justice system.

[8] For a brilliant exposition of the thesis that both Enlightenment perfectionism and a (paradoxical) apprehension that society was becoming increasingly disorganized and dangerous account for the rise of both the insane asylum and the prison in early nineteenth-century America, see David Rothman, *The Discovery of the Asylum* (Boston: Little, Brown, 1971).

If the early nineteenth-century prison movement and the late nineteenth-century juvenile-court innovation represent the best of American idealism, the administration of these programs has aimlessly wandered between rehabilitation and punishment (and, too often, sheer neglect). Parole and probation were either created or brought to fruition in America and, as the Commission points out, they have been beset by conflicting images about the offender. One historian has perceptively called us a "People of Paradox," and nowhere has this paradox been more evident than in our treatment (and very definition) of the criminal. Some of the excerpted material deals with this checkered history. Unfortunately, it is not enough to educate us about the difficulties of allowing us to break away from that history's dead hand.

History should also render us more sensitive to the flaws of faddism in the Commission's own thinking. In perspective, the Commission has taken a leap of faith, faith in the ability and willingness of what it calls the community to deal humanely with the offender. If crime is a fundamental attribute of our national character and our national experience (the latter can affect the former), the problem may be more intractable than the Commission perceives. Can "serious crime" really be reduced by 50 percent within ten years? (In the year since the Commission reported, the rate of increase of known crime has again risen substantially.) The Commission is typically American in its optimism. History should teach us to temper our own inclination to concur.

One particular example of the Commission's own faddism should be mentioned. Considerable public controversy has been aroused by behavior-modification experiments upon (allegedly) socially dangerous prisoners. The Corrections Report calmly notes that certain youth centers use "counseling and therapy, including operant conditioning and behavior modification." The Task Force calmly concluded that "The explorations conducted so far furnish a basis for continued study of an ancient correctional problem: the usefulness of incentives and punishment in changing behavior patterns." An appreciation of the history of attempts to change behavior patterns—including the endorsement of solitary confinement (to permit meditation on one's sins)—might have given the Commission a basis for critically judging behavior-modification programs with more insight (and foresight) than it demonstrated.

A knowledge of history might also have given the Commission a greater appreciation of the role of criminal-justice agencies in recruiting public support to achieve their own ends and, in the process, molding attitudes toward vital public issues. For instance, politically potent groups such as the former Bureau of Narcotics (now a part of the Drug Enforcement Administration in the Justice Department) and the American Medical Association have profoundly affected our beliefs about drug abuse. One Task Force report deals with the growth of opposition to clinical treatment (by heroin maintenance programs) of addiction in the 1920s and notes, "Records of the clinics' experience, and the precise reasons why they were closed, are unknown." Behind this brief statement lies a fascinating story involving the interplay of public attitudes (fear of the heroin user, especially of the black user), the bureaucratic needs of the Bureau of Narcotics, and the liaison between the bureau and the AMA, all of which resulted in the replacement of the traditional belief that addiction was a medical problem by a newer one that the law should deal punitively with the addict. That change in fundamental belief still haunts us to this day—and may yet affect acceptance of some of the Commission's recommendations— but the Report has little to say about that background.

# 13: Conclusions

Governor Peterson's introduction to the Report stresses its "clear statement of priorities, goals and standards. . . ." By emphasizing priorities such as prevention of juvenile delinquency, improvement of social services, prompt adjudication of criminal charges, and greater citizen action, the Report does partially fulfill the ambitious proclamation of its title. Perhaps the Commission is a bit too sanguine about the capacity of those priorities (assuming they are implemented) to reduce crime[9] and perhaps there is some confusion between strategic goals and tactical means for their realization. Perhaps the Commission has overemphasized the differences between its goal—specific proposals for crime reduction—and that of the 1967 Crime Commission (at least half the proposals of the two groups overlap).

The Report must be analyzed as a whole, for its plea-bar-

[9] Its pride in the fact that it has overcome the tendency of other reports to deal with "improvement" of institutions rather than to demonstrate how those improvements will reduce crime is certainly misplaced, for it can show no real correlation between the two phenomena.

liv

gain recommendations cannot be severed from the accompanying calls for decriminalization of such status offenses as alcoholism and vagrancy, limitation of penalties for several categories of victimless crime, screening, diversion, and probation, and prison sentences (sharply curtailed ones at that) for only the most dangerous offenders. The Report acknowledges that society (in its terms, the community) is responsible for both the conditions that cause crime and the remedies required to reduce it. The Commission's recommendations in general make sense—at least in the abstract.

The Commission's assumptions about the willingness of middle (and middle-class) America to accept radical changes may be too optimistic, although numerous peripheral recommendations (especially those involving technology and science) may be adopted precisely because they are "innovative." If the possibility for profound change exists—and our national ambivalence indicates that it may—a reevaluation of our perception of social justice is necessary. Our criminal-justice system is but a reflection (often a confused one) of our jumbled social values, for our beliefs about crime and criminality tell us more about ourselves than they ever will about our "criminal class."

We have thus far shown little inclination to make the hard choices called for by this and other commissions, and have not given sufficient thought to the underlying premises of our beliefs about the complex and perplexing phenomenon of crime in our "crime-ridden" society. We have demanded of "professionals" that they reflect both public indignation about the crime rate and public compassion for the underlying social conditions that produce much criminality. Perhaps our dilemmas are best exemplified by our contradictory attitudes toward bail. Several release-on-recognizance projects (involving no bail) have clearly demonstrated that there is little risk of either (a) default and bail-skipping or (b) repeated criminal acts by those so released. But, we (and the Commission) are ambivalent about preventive detention. Even without that particular issue, the dilemma remains: as one Task Force report puts it, "Bail reform substantially reduces the inequities of a jailing system. . . ." but release projects have been "instituted in only a fraction of the nation's courts." The Commission's avoidance of any discussion of capital punishment, by its own perspective a useless and probably disastrous penalty, reflects our own ambivalence on the subject.

The Commission was "soft" not about criminals, but about the willingness of spokesmen for our leading criminal-justice institutions to accept change. Although there are discussions in the Report about "strategies for change," it contains only fleeting comments about the scope and intensity of resistance to change by those who have a stake—economic or ideological—in the extant system. Although many criminal-justice agencies profess to be frustrated by and concerned about contemporary realities, they fear change more. The chorus of resistance to the Commission's recommendations about gun control and delimitation of the penalties for victimless-crime offenses is only a pale reflection of the profound distrust of certain forms of innovation. This Commission, composed not of idealists and quacks (or out-of-office politicians), has made little impact upon the system.

The Commission has taken a large step (but so have many of its predecessors), but future steps will be hazardous, for no society relishes the task of close self-examination, especially when it threatens certain fundamental and cherished beliefs. Crime is the inevitable concomitant of how we have chosen (or been influenced) to arrange our institutions; it is part of the price we pay for what we are and have become. This truth has rendered the work of previous Commissions nugatory, and may yet abort the valuable work performed by the National Advisory Commission. Already much of the Report reads as if it were written a century ago for a society that never existed. If the price of the study, $1.75 million, succeeds only in radicalizing twenty-two people, then we may well ask how much it will cost to engender change in both the society and its criminal-justice institutions. It appears that *that* price will be too much to pay, but, if so, it is imperative that we comprehend both the value of what we have not obtained as well as that which we retain in our social accounting. If, as one eminent authority put it, "Every society gets the crime it deserves," we should at least understand why we get it and why we deserve it.

—ISIDORE SILVER

John Jay College of Criminal Justice
New York
*June, 1974*

# A Note on the Avon Edition

Every word of the Commission's Report, *A National Strategy to Reduce Crime*, is reprinted here. In addition, extensive excerpts from the Commission's five Task Force reports—over 2200 pages in the originals—have been included after the appropriate chapters of the main Report. The main Report's synopses of the Task Force recommendations and standards have been interwoven with the excerpted material, so the reader may have a clear idea of the relation of the excerpts to the originals, and may readily refer to the full Task Force reports for amplification of any points of particular interest.

Notes and bibliographies have been omitted from the excerpts for reasons of space. The original numbering of the recommendations and standards has been retained. Internal references to chapter numbers within the Task Force excerpts refer to the subsections headed with arabic numerals (e.g., 1: Planning for Crime Reduction); the chapters mentioned in the main text are now numbered with Roman numerals (e.g., Chapter II, National Goals and Priorities). It seemed most practical to leave the wording of the text intact, and it is hoped this consideration outweighs any momentary inconvenience to the reader.

—*Ed.*

Report by the National Advisory
Commission on Criminal Justice
Standards and Goals

# A National Strategy
# to Reduce Crime

# Foreword

This volume, *A National Strategy to Reduce Crime*, is one of six reports of the National Advisory Commission on Criminal Justice Standards and Goals.

The Commission was appointed by the Administrator of the Law Enforcement Assistance Administration (LEAA) on October 20, 1971, to formulate for the first time national criminal justice standards and goals for crime reduction and prevention at the State and local levels.

The views and recommendations presented in this volume are those of a majority of the Commission and do not necessarily represent those of the Department of Justice. Although LEAA provided $1.75 million in discretionary grants for the work of the Commission, it did not direct that work and had no voting participation in the Commission.

Membership in the Commission was drawn from the three branches of State and local government, from industry, and from citizen groups. Commissioners were chosen, in part, for their working experience in the criminal justice area. Police chiefs, judges, corrections leaders, and prosecutors were represented.

Other recent Commissions have studied the causes and debilitating effects of crime in our society. We have sought to expand their work and build upon it by developing a clear statement of priorities, goals, and standards to help set a national strategy to reduce crime.

Some State or local governments may already meet standards or recommendations proposed by the Commission; most in the Nation do not. In any case, each State and local government is encouraged to evaluate its present status and to implement those standards and recommendations that it deems appropriate.

The precise standards and recommendations of the Commission are presented in the other Commission reports. Those

3

five volumes, entitled *Criminal Justice, Police, Courts, Corrections,* and *Community Crime Prevention,* are addressed to the State and local officials and other persons who would be responsible for implementing the standards and recommendations. Synopses of all Commission standards and recommendations are presented in this volume to provide an overview of that material.

A seventh volume, *Proceedings of the National Conference on Criminal Justice,* is being published by the Commission. The *Proceedings* do not constitute a statement of the Commission, but they are included with the reports of the Commission for the convenience of the interested reader. They contain the edited transcripts of the National Conference on Criminal Justice, sponsored by LEAA and held in Washington, D.C., on January 23-26, 1973.

The purpose of *A National Strategy to Reduce Crime* is to present a broad picture of the Commission's work and its strategy for the reduction of crime in America. Many of the chapters of this volume are based on the companion reports. This volume also contains a substantial amount of material that does not appear in any other Commission report, including material in the chapters entitled National Goals and Priorities, Criminal Code Reform and Revision, Handguns in American Society, and A National Commitment to Change.

This Commission has completed its work and submitted its report. The Commission hopes that its standards and recommendations will influence the shape of the criminal justice system in this Nation for many years to come. And it believes that adoption of those standards and recommendations will contribute to a measurable reduction of the amount of crime in America.

The Commission thanks Jerris Leonard, Administrator of LEAA, and Richard W. Velde and Clarence M. Coster, Associate Administrators, for their efforts in authorizing and funding this Commission and for their support and encouragement during the life of the Commission.

The Commission expresses its sincerest gratitude to the task force chairmen and members and to the many practitioners, scholars, and advisers who contributed their expertise to this effort. We are also grateful to the Commission staff and to the staffs of the task forces for their hard and dedicated work.

On behalf of the Commission, I extend special and warmest thanks and admiration to Thomas J. Madden, Executive Director, for guiding this project through to completion.

(signed) RUSSELL W. PETERSON
Chairman

Washington, D.C.
January 23, 1973

# National Advisory Commission on Criminal Justice Standards and Goals

## Chairman

Russell W. Peterson

### Vice Chairman

Peter J. Pitchess

# Task Force Chairmen

**Police**

Edward M. Davis

**Courts**

Daniel J. Meador

**Civil Disorders**

Jerry V. Wilson

**Community Involvement**

George B. Peters

**Drug Abuse**

Sterling Johnson

**Education, Training, and Manpower Development**

Lee P. Brown

**Corrections**

Joe Frazier Brown

**Community Crime Prevention**

Jack Michie

**Information Systems and Statistics**

John R. Plants

**Juvenile Delinquency**

Wilfred W. Nuernberger

**Organized Crime**

William L. Reed

**Research and Development**

Peter J. McQuillan

# Commission Staff

**Executive Director**

Thomas J. Madden

**Deputy Director**

Lawrence J. Leigh

**Associate Director**

Robert H. Macy

**Assistant Directors**

Hayden Gregory
Marilyn Kay Harris
Thomas M. O'Neil, Jr.

**Special Assistant to the Chairman**

Joseph M. Dell'Olio

7

8

# Overview: A National Strategy to Reduce Crime

## Goals and Priorities

### Goals for Crime Reduction

The Commission proposes as a goal for the American people a 50% reduction in high-fear crimes by 1983. It further proposes that crime reduction efforts be concentrated on five crimes. The goals for the reduction of these crimes should be:

- Homicide: Reduced by at least 25% by 1983
- Forcible Rape: Reduced by at least 25% by 1983
- Aggravated Assault: Reduced by at least 25% by 1983
- Robbery: Reduced by at least 50% by 1983
- Burglary: Reduced by at least 50% by 1983

### Priorities for Action

The Commission proposes four areas for priority action in reducing the five target crimes:

- Juvenile Delinquency: The highest attention must be given to preventing juvenile delinquency and to minimiz-

9

ing the involvement of young offenders in the juvenile and criminal justice system, and to reintegrating juvenile offenders into the community.

- Delivery of Social Services: Public and private service agencies should direct their actions to improve the delivery of all social services to citizens, particularly to groups that contribute higher than average proportions of their numbers to crime statistics.
- Prompt Determination of Guilt or Innocence: Delays in the adjudication and disposition of criminal cases must be greatly reduced.
- Citizen Action: Increased citizen participation in activities to control crime in their community must be generated, with active encouragement and support by criminal justice agencies.

# Key Commission Proposals

## Criminal Justice System

The Commission proposes broad reforms and improvements in criminal justice planning and information systems at the State and local levels. Key recommendations include:

- Development by States of integrated multiyear criminal justice planning.
- Establishment of criminal justice coordinating councils by all major cities and counties.
- Establishment by each State of a Security and Privacy Council to develop procedures and recommendations for legislation to assure security and privacy of information contained in criminal justice information systems.
- Creation by each State of an organizational structure for coordinating the development of criminal justice information systems.

## Community Crime Prevention

The Commission proposes that all Americans make a personal contribution to the reduction of crime, and that all Americans support the crime prevention efforts of their State and local governments. Key recommendations include:

- Increased citizen contribution to crime prevention by making homes and businesses more secure, by participating in police-community programs, and by working with youth.

- Expanded public and private employment opportunities and elimination of unnecessary restrictions on hiring ex-offenders.
- Establishment of and citizen support for youth services bureaus to improve the delivery of social services to young people.
- Provision of individualized treatment for drug offenders and abusers.
- Provision of statewide capability for overseeing and investigating financing of political campaigns.
- Establishment of a statewide investigation and prosecution capability to deal with corruption in government.
- Development in the schools of career education programs that guarantee to every student a job or acceptance to an advanced program of studies.

## Police

The Commission proposes that the delivery of police services be greatly improved at the municipal level. Key recommendations include:

- Consolidation of all police departments with fewer than 10 sworn officers.
- Enhancement of the role of the patrolman.
- Increased crime prevention efforts by police working in and with the community.
- Affirmative police action to divert public drunks and mental patients from the criminal justice system.
- Increased employment and utilization of women, minorities, and civilians in police work.
- Enactment of legislation authorizing police to obtain search warrants by telephone.

## Courts

The Commission proposes major restructuring and streamlining of procedures and practices in processing criminal cases at the State and local levels, in order to speed the determination of guilt or innocence. Key recommendations include:

- Trying all cases within 60 days of arrest.
- Requiring judges to hold full days in court.

- Unification within the State of all courts.
- Allowing only one review on appeal.
- Elimination of plea bargaining.
- Screening of all criminal cases coming to the attention of the prosecutor to determine if further processing is appropriate.
- Diverting out of the system all cases in which further processing by the prosecutor is not appropriate, based on such factors as the age of the individual, his psychological needs, the nature of the crime, and the availability of treatment programs.
- Elimination of grand juries and arraignments.

## Corrections

The Commission proposes fundamental changes in the system of corrections that exists in States, counties, and cities in America—changes based on the belief that correctional systems usually are little more than "schools of crime." Key recommendations include:

- Restricting construction of major State institutions for adult offenders.
- Phasing out of all major juvenile offender institutions.
- Elimination of disparate sentencing practices.
- Establishment of community-based correctional programs and facilities.
- Unification of all correctional functions within the State.
- Increased and expanded salary, education, and training levels for corrections personnel.

## Criminal Code Reform and Revision

The Commission proposes that all States reexamine their criminal codes with the view to improving and updating them. Key recommendations include:

- Establishment of permanent criminal code revision commissions at the State level.
- Decriminalization of vagrancy and drunkenness.

## Handguns in American Society

The Commission proposes nationwide action at the State

level to eliminate the dangers posed by widespread possession of handguns. The key recommendation is:

- Elimination of importation, manufacture, sale, and private possession of handguns by January 1, 1983.

# Chapter I

# A National Strategy to Reduce Crime

This report presents a national strategy to reduce crime. After almost 2 years of study and research, the National Advisory Commission on Criminal Justice Standards and Goals concludes that this Nation can markedly reduce crime over the next ten years.

The Commission foresees a time, in the immediate future, when:

• A couple can walk in the evening in their neighborhood without fear of assault and robbery.
• A family can go away for the weekend without fear of returning to a house ransacked by burglars.
• A woman can take a night job without fear of being raped on her way to or from work.
• Every citizen can live without fear of being brutalized by unknown assailants.

America can and should make its cities and neighborhoods,

its highways and parks, and its homes and commercial establishments safe places for all persons at all times.

America can and should begin to reduce crime of all sorts, and to erase those social conditions associated with crime and delinquency—poverty, unemployment, inferior education, and discrimination.

This can be done.

The National Advisory Commission concludes that this Nation can and should reduce the rate of "high-fear" crime by 50 percent in the next 10 years. These are the crimes of murder, rape, aggravated assault, robbery, and burglary, when committed by strangers.

# The Need for a Plan

Americans know that crime reduction is imperative. They know the costs and consequences of crime. They know the fear of crime. They have been the victims of crime.

In early 1973, Dr. George Gallup released a poll showing that more than one of every five people across the Nation had been victimized by crime between December 1971 and December 1972. The figures for center cities showed that one of three people had been victims of crime. Respondents listed crime as the worst problem in their community. Fifty-one percent of the people questioned by Dr. Gallup said there was more crime in their area than there was a year ago. Only 10 percent said there was less crime.[1]

There has been considerable study of the criminal justice system in this Nation in recent years. Congress has examined the problems and developed laudable programs. The Department of Justice, the Department of Health, Education, and Welfare, and the Special Action Office for Drug Abuse Prevention—to name just a few Federal agencies—have studied the crime situation and begun to move toward solutions. State and local governments have reacted to the growing public desire for crime reduction, and the press has focused attention on many of the most neglected areas of the criminal justice system.

What has been needed, however—and what this Commission now offers—is a plan of action that States, cities, and citizens can implement to reduce crime, protect society, and increase public safety.

The Commission's plan begins with the selection of

[1] The Gallup Poll, January 13, 1973, and January 15, 1973.

goals—including the goal of reducing "high-fear" crime by 50 percent in 1983.

The Commission's plan emphasizes four basic priorities:

- Prevent juvenile delinquency.
- Improve delivery of social services.
- Reduce delays in the criminal justice process.
- Increase citizen participation.

The plan also emphasizes the need for all elements of the criminal justice system to plan and work together as a system and to plan and work together with the social service delivery system. The plan emphasizes the need for the police patrolman to strengthen his ties to the community and to be given greater responsibility and authority for preventing and reducing crime in the community. The plan emphasizes the need for the prosecutor, defender, and judiciary to work toward insuring speedier trials while still protecting fundamental rights. The plan also emphasizes the need for corrections to develop effective programs and procedures for reintegrating offenders into the community as soon as possible consistent with the protection of the community.

To reach these goals, the Commission offers hundreds of standards and recommendations. These standards and recommendations establish performance levels for operation of the criminal justice system as a whole, for police, for courts, for corrections, and for service agencies of government.

The details are presented in this volume and in five companion volumes—*Community Crime Prevention, Criminal Justice System, Police, Courts,* and *Corrections.*

The six volumes were developed by the 22 members of the National Advisory Commission on Criminal Justice Standards and Goals and by the more than 180 members of its task forces as well as by an even greater number of advisers, consultants, and staff members. Represented on the Commission and task forces were men and women with practical working experience in the criminal justice and crime prevention fields who have direct knowledge of the crime problems facing America and insight into contemporary society.

This volume contains summaries of the other volumes, as well as new material that does not appear in the other reports. The new sections cut across the entire subject matter of the Commission's work and include National Goals and Priorities, Criminal Code Reform and Revision, Handguns in American Society, and A National Commitment to Change.

A seventh volume contains the proceedings of the National Conference on Criminal Justice, where the basic plan of the

Commission was introduced to and critiqued by more than 1,500 members of the criminal justice community.

# Principles Guiding the Commission's Work

The first principle guiding the Commission's work is that operating without standards and goals does not guarantee failure, but does invite it.

Specific standards and goals enable professionals and the public to know where the system is heading, what it is trying to achieve, and what in fact it is achieving. Standards can be used to focus essential institutional and public pressure on the reform of the entire criminal justice system.

In setting standards and goals for the prevention and reduction of crime, this Commission was not constrained by the limits of the traditional criminal justice system, usually defined as comprising police, courts, and corrections. In addition to setting standards for police, courts, and corrections, it established a broad range of standards and recommendations for citizen action, for improving governmental integrity, and for improving and expanding the delivery of social services to the community.

In undertaking its work, the Commission began with an acceptance of the scope and extent of crime and the damaging effects it has on the social structure of America. These matters had been well documented by other commissions, including the Commission on the Causes and Prevention of Violence and the President's Commission on Law Enforcement and Administration of Justice. The reports of this Commission go directly to the beginning of a solution, to workable practical standards.

In developing its standards, the Commission directed its research in large part to existing programs and practices, to criminal justice planning documents, and to articles and reports on crime prevention and reduction programs.

Because the Commission was developing standards, the emphasis of its efforts was placed not only on what was desirable but also on what was workable and practical. Many standards are based upon successful models that are operational in one or more places in the country. Many models were found that had never been documented before. Where no model existed, standards were based upon concepts that

17

the task forces and the Commission felt were necessary for crime reduction.

The scope of the Commission's work did not extend to the setting of standards and recommendations for agencies of the Federal Government. The reason is that the Commission's work was funded by LEAA, which is charged with improving law enforcement and criminal justice at the State and local levels. The Commission's membership therefore consisted of citizens from public and private life at the State and local levels; the one Federal official on the Commission had no voting participation.

The role of the Federal Government is discussed, however, in instances where Federal programs impact on or coincide with the law enforcement and criminal justice efforts of State and local agencies. In its *Report on Police,* for example, the Commission recommends that law enforcement agencies cooperate in the establishment of task force efforts with other criminal justice agencies on the local, State, and Federal levels. The organized crime strike forces operated by the United States Department of Justice are another activity in which local and Federal cooperation is encouraged.

Finally, some of the standards, upon initial reading, may not appear to be directly related to crime reduction. Examples include standards dealing with expansion of the constitutional rights of convicted offenders, elimination of plea bargaining, expansion of the right to counsel, the use of summons in lieu of arrest, and integrity in government. In setting such standards, it was the opinion of the Commission that to foster respect for the criminal laws and to win the respect and cooperation of all citizens, the agencies and officials of the criminal justice system and the governing authorities of this country must themselves respect the law and must act fairly and justly toward all citizens.

# Need for a National Commitment

This Commission calls for the establishment of a national strategy to reduce crime through the timely and equitable administration of justice; the protection of life, liberty, and property; and the efficient mobilization of resources.

Implementation is inherent in the development of any strategy. Central to the work of this Commission is the belief that crime in America can be reduced, that the goals in this report can be met if the standards and recommendations proposed in the reports on *Community Crime Prevention, Police,*

*Courts, Corrections,* and *Criminal Justice System* are implemented.

The Commission is aware that the cost of implementing the standards could be substantial, at least in the short term. Yet, when the cost of crime reduction is weighed against the cost of crime itself, it is clear that the additional outlays by the system are more than justified. In addition, less crime will mean fewer victims of crime and will result in genuine, demonstrable savings, both to potential victims and to the whole society.

A critical step in the implementation process is a comprehensive evaluation of all standards and recommendations considered applicable in a given jurisdiction. Through careful evaluation, needless frustration and wasted time and effort can be avoided, as inevitably some measures that appear desirable are found after further study to be too ambitious, too costly, or otherwise inappropriate. The Commission's program for implementation and evaluation is presented in Chapter X.

There are signs that leadership at the State level around the Nation is interested in the concept of establishing standards for law enforcement and criminal justice agencies. A majority of States already have plans to review and examine formally the standards and recommendations of this Commission with a view to implementing those that are appropriate. Details on these developments are provided in the Postscript to Chapter X.

A commitment to change is vital to implementation. The citizens of this country and the agencies of government, individually and collectively, must work to bring about the necessary changes both inside and outside the criminal justice system. If the people of this country are committed to reducing crime, its rate will decrease dramatically.

19

# Chapter II

# National Goals and Priorities

Crime is not a new phenomenon in American life. Scholars and commissions before this one have documented the growth and complexity of the crime problem in the United States, its causes, and its destructive effects on national life. The damage to persons, property, and spirit, and the fear of unprovoked, unpredictable violence are more than familiar.

This Commission does not offer easy solutions to those problems. But it does offer a beginning.

## Goals for the Decade Ahead

The Commission believes that the American people can reduce the social and economic damage caused by all forms of crime. The Commission also believes that there are certain crimes that threaten the very existence of a humane and civilized society and that the rate of these crimes can be assessed and controlled. These are the violent crimes of murder and nonnegligent manslaughter, forcible rape, robbery, aggravated assault, and the property crime of burglary.

These five crimes are particularly serious when committed by a stranger on the streets and highways of the Nation. In such cases, an extra dimension is present—the dimension of fear. Thus, when these crimes are committed by strangers, the Commission labels them "high-fear" crimes and proposes a sharp reduction in their rate.[1]

Violent crime and burglary, however, are also serious when committed by relatives and acquaintances.

Generally, the Commission proposes a two-level attack on these five crimes:

First, the rate of "high-fear" (stranger-related) crimes should be cut in half by 1983.

Second, whether the crime is committed by a relative or acquaintance, or a stranger, the crime rates should be cut by 1983 as follows:

• Homicide (murder and nonnegligent manslaughter)—at least 25 percent.
• Forcible rape—at least 25 percent.
• Aggravated assault—at least 25 percent.
• Robbery—at least 50 percent.
• Burglary—at least 50 percent.

The Commission is aware that the selection of these crimes and percentages of reduction[2] will arouse the doubts of skeptics, but the Commission submits that the proposed crime reduction goals are aspirations, not predictions. They define what could be, not what necessarily will be. To reach these goals will require a concentration of the national will and the best application of our capabilities. The Commission is confident that by improved effort, including use of the standards and recommendations presented elsewhere in its reports, the goals can be attained.

[1] The National Commission on the Causes and Prevention of Violence pointed out in 1969 that, although violent crimes form a relatively small percentage of all crimes known to the police, their effect is out of proportion to their volume. "In violent crime man becomes a wolf to man, threatening or destroying the personal safety of his victim in a terrifying act. Violent crime (particularly street crime) engenders fear—the deep-seated fear of the hunted in the presence of the hunter." National Commission on the Causes and Prevention of Violence, *To Establish Justice, To Insure Domestic Tranquility* (1969), p. 18.

[2] Crimes are defined and trends noted in Federal Bureau of Investigation, *Crime in the United States: Uniform Crime Reports—1971* (1972), pp. 6-21. Publication is referred to hereinafter as *UCR*, with the appropriate date. The rate of commission of these crimes is the number of actual and attempted offenses per 100,000 inhabitants.

## Why These Crimes?

The Commission decided to focus attention on the five target crimes because of their cost to society—economic cost to some degree but, more importantly, their cost to citizens in fear, psychic damage, and mistrust.

The economic loss resulting from the five crimes amounts to hundreds of millions of dollars.[3] According to the FBI, money and property taken from victims of robbery and burglary in 1971 totaled $87 million and $739 million respectively.[4] These figures do not show the undoubtedly large losses resulting from unreported offenses.

To add up economic costs alone would be to underestimate seriously the total cost of crime in America. No price tag can be put on the fear that, as much as any other factor, is speeding the exodus from the cities, strangling businesses, and causing people to mistrust each other.

Polls conducted by the Gallup organization indicate that fear may have become more widespread since the Violence Commission reported. In 1968, 31 percent of Gallup survey respondents said they were afraid to walk in their own neighborhoods at night. By the end of 1972, the number had risen to 42 percent.

Considerations similar to those above caused the Commission to include burglary among the target crimes. A Gallup poll late in 1972 found that one person in six does not feel safe in his own home at night.[5] While burglary is technically classified as a property crime rather than a crime of violence and might perhaps be expected to occasion less fear, widespread apprehension about personal safety in the home certainly indicates that fear of being burglarized is the subject of acute concern among many Americans.

By focusing attention on the target crimes, the Commission does not wish to suggest that other crimes are not serious problems for the Nation. Yearly arrests for shoplifting, fraud, embezzlement, forgery and counterfeiting, arson, and vandalism far exceed in number the arrests for the target crimes.

---

[3] For discussion of several methods of estimating costs of crime, see Donald J. Mulvihill and Melvin M. Tumin, *Crimes of Violence,* a report of the National Commission on the Causes and Prevention of Violence (1969), pp. 394-404.

[4] *UCR—1971,* pp. 15, 21. These figures do not indicate how much stolen property was recovered.

[5] The Gallup Poll, "The Dimensions of Crime" (January 14, 1973), p. 3.

Nor do the target crimes produce the greatest direct economic loss. The President's Commission on Law Enforcement and Administration of Justice (the President's Crime Commission) estimated that in 1965 direct losses through crimes against persons, crimes against property, and the cost of illegal goods and services, amounted to about $15 billion a year. Of this loss, violent crimes and burglary were estimated to account for little more than $1 billion, or 7 percent of the total.[6]

The estimate of the President's Crime Commission did not include losses from crimes where victimization is often secondary, diffuse, and difficult to measure, such as violations of antitrust laws, building codes, pure food and drug laws, and statutes relating to the public trust (prohibiting bribery of public officials, for example). Whatever the cost of these crimes, it is certainly greater than direct economic losses from violent crimes and burglary.

The true cost of the target crimes lies in their capacity—their increasing capacity—to inspire fear. It is this fear that, in the words of the Violence Commission, "is gnawing at the vitals of urban America."

## Why Set Quantitative Goals?

The use of numerical values gives a dimension to goal-setting that has been lacking in earlier proposals for reducing crime.

Previously, government reports and political leaders have spoken in broad terms, such as: crime should be controlled and reduced; administration of the criminal justice system should be improved; public expenditures on the system should be increased; Americans should redouble their efforts to eliminate the causes of crime, such as poverty, discrimination, urban blight, and disease; planning should be improved; additional research should be undertaken; citizens should become more involved; and so on.

Unfortunately, these broad statements are not easily translated into action. What, for example, does it mean to say that crime should be reduced? Which crimes? What is to be reduced—the rate, the actual number, the economic and social impact, or something else? How great a reduction is possible? How great a reduction is acceptable? How do State

[6] President's Commission on Law Enforcement and Administration of Justice, *Task Force Report: Crime and Its Impact—An Assessment* (1967), pp. 44, 46.

and local governments, criminal justice agencies, and citizens go about realizing these goals? And how is it possible to tell if a goal has been achieved?

These are not academic questions. They have practical implications in time, dollars, and lives. Goals are most useful when they are measurable, when at the end of a given period achievements can be compared with expectations and an assessment of the reasons for discrepancies made. For citizens, goals to reduce crime provide benchmarks for judging the effectiveness of criminal justice operations and other public programs. For legislators, they are guides to funding. For operating agencies, they are focal points for the allocation of men and equipment.

# Basic Factors in
# Setting Goals for Crime Reduction

In making its judgments on goals for crime reduction, the Commission considered in depth many factors. Although it is impossible to enumerate all of the factors, the Commission believes that among the most important are the following:

- Characteristics of the target crimes.
- Socioeconomic changes.
- Changes in public attitudes.
- Public support for the criminal justice system.
- New methods of measuring progress.

## Characteristics of the Target Crimes

In 1971, more than 3 million violent crimes and burglaries were reported to the police in the United States (see Table 1). Since victimization surveys conducted by LEAA and the Crime Commission indicate that at least as many unreported violent crimes and burglaries occur as are reported,[7] it is

---

[7] A preliminary national survey of several thousand households was conducted by LEAA to determine the extent and nature of victimization in 1970. The survey, a developmental step in preparation for a continuous national victimization survey, polled the population 16 years of age or older for forcible rape, robbery, aggravated and simple assault, burglary, larceny, and auto theft. Murder and nonnegligent manslaughter were not covered. The responses were for personal, not business, victimization. Hereinafter the survey will be referred to as LEAA 1970 Survey. For victimization data see also *Crime and Its Impact*, p. 17.

**Table 1: Violent Crime and Burglary Reported to the Police, 1960 and 1971**

| | Murder and nonnegligent manslaughter | Forcible rape | Robbery | Aggravated assault | Burglary | Total |
|---|---|---|---|---|---|---|
| **Number of Offenses:** | | | | | | |
| 1960 | 9,030 | 17,030 | 107,340 | 152,580 | 900,400 | 1,186,380 |
| 1971 | 17,630 | 41,890 | 385,910 | 364,600 | 2,368,400 | 3,178,430 |
| Percent Change 1960-1971 | +95.2 | +146.0 | +259.5 | +139.0 | +163.0 | +168.0 |
| **Rate per 100,000 Inhabitants:** | | | | | | |
| 1960 | 5.0 | 9.5 | 59.9 | 85.1 | 502.1 | 661.6 |
| 1971 | 8.5 | 20.3 | 187.1 | 176.8 | 1,148.3 | 1,541.0 |
| Percent Change 1960-1971 | +70.0 | +113.7 | +212.4 | +107.8 | +128.7 | +132.9 |

Source: Federal Bureau of Investigation, *Crime in the United States: Uniform Crime Reports—1971* (1972) p. 61. Publication referred to hereinafter as *UCR 1971*.

highly probable that at least 6 million violent crimes and burglaries occurred in 1971.

## Trends in Crime Rates

From 1960 to 1971, numbers of reported offenses and crime rates increased greatly in all five target crime categories. Except for the rate for murder and nonnegligent manslaughter, which increased 70 percent from 1960 through 1971, the rates for all of the target crimes more than doubled over the 12-year period.

Studies of reported crimes show wide fluctuations in rate from decade to decade. If the period prior to 1960 is any guide, Americans do not necessarily have to expect ever-increasing crime rates.

Although it is difficult to assess the period prior to 1933, when the FBI first began to compile national statistics, the available evidence indicates that rises and declines in crime have occurred since the beginning of the Nation. Probable peaks of violent crime in the late 19th century and the early 20th century have been identified in earlier studies.[8]

At this point it is necessary to enter a caution about the data on which the Commission based its conclusions on the extent of crime. The only source of overall information on crime on a continuing basis is the FBI's Uniform Crime Reports (UCR), which tabulate and analyze the reports of local police departments about crime in their areas. Because the FBI has succeeded in securing better local reporting over the years, it is essential, in the words of the President's Crime Commission, to "distinguish better reporting from more crime."[9] In considering trends, it is also important to note changes in public attitudes toward reporting crime. Possibly some of the increase in the figures on forcible rape is due to the fact that women are not as reluctant as they once were to report rape.

Having said this much, the Commission points out what the UCR does show: that the number of crimes reported has risen much faster than the population. It may be assumed that the target crimes, which are widely regarded by the public as more serious, are better reported than many others. It

---

[8] Mulvihill and Tumin, *Crimes of Violence*, p. 52.
[9] President's Commission on Law Enforcement and Administration of Justice, *The Challenge of Crime in a Free Society* (1967), p. 3.

26

therefore seems appropriate to make use of the UCR for basic data, with reference also to victimization surveys.

According to the UCR, the current "crime wave" did not get under way until the mid-1960's. From 1933 to 1940, the rate for one of the target crimes, forcible rape, rose 41 percent. Rates for all the others declined: criminal homicide by 14 percent, robbery by 51 percent, aggravated assault by 13 percent, burglary by 21 percent.[10] In view of the state of the early UCR figures, which have been questioned more vigorously than current statistics, no extensive conclusions can be drawn except that the crimes experiencing the greatest decreases in reported rates—robbery and burglary—probably did decrease.

From 1940 to 1963 the rates for rape, assault, and burglary rose gradually; the rate for robbery showed very little increase; and the rate for homicide declined appreciably. Beginning in the early 1960's, however, the rates for all five crimes rose steeply and continuously through 1971 (see Figures 1-5).

Preliminary data for 1972 released by the FBI indicate that violent crimes increased by only 1 percent over 1971. Robberies, which make up the largest number of crimes in the violent category, showed a 4 percent decrease. Murder was up 4 percent, aggravated assault 6 percent, and forcible rape 11 percent. Burglary was down 2 percent.

It thus appears that the Nation might be reaching the peak of a crime cycle, but it is quite possible that crime rates will rise again. The past does not necessarily foreshadow the future.

## Types of Offenders and Victims

In 1969, the Violence Commission noted several chief characteristics of violent crime, which, with one or two exceptions, are linked to burglary as well:

- Violent crime in the United States is primarily a phenomenon of large cities.
- Violent crime in the city is overwhelmingly committed by males.
- Violent crime in the city is concentrated especially among the youths between the ages of 15 and 24.
- Violent crime in the city is committed primarily by individuals at the lower end of the occupational scale.

[10] Crime rates from 1933 furnished by the FBI.

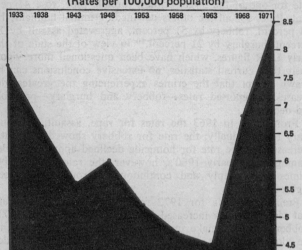

**FIGURE 1. MURDER AND NONNEGLIGENT MANSLAUGHTER KNOWN TO THE POLICE, 1933-1971**

(Rates per 100,000 population)

Source: Data from the Federal Bureau of Investigation.

- Violent crime in the city stems disproportionately from the ghetto slums where most Negroes live.
- The victims of assaultive violence in the cities generally have the same characteristics as the offenders; victimization rates are generally highest for males, youths, poor persons, and blacks. Robbery victims, however, often are older whites.
- By far the greatest proportion of all serious violence is committed by repeaters.[11]

Current statistics on arrests and offenses reported in the 1971 UCR generally support the Violence Commission's find-

[11] *To Establish Justice, To Insure Domestic Tranquility*, pp. 20-24, 26. (The Violence Commission defined repeaters as persons with prior contacts with police.)

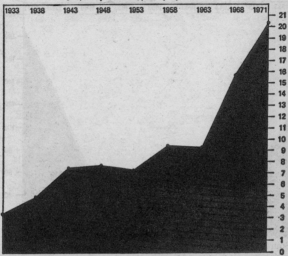

**FIGURE 2. FORCIBLE RAPE**
**KNOWN TO THE POLICE, 1933-1971**
(Rates per 100,000 population)

Source: Data from the Federal Bureau of Investigation.

ings on violent crime. They also indicate that burglary, which is a property crime, is less confined to central cities and less likely to be committed by nonwhite offenders than is violent crime.

Almost three-fifths of the violent crimes and almost two-fifths of the burglaries reported in 1971 took place in cities with populations of more than 250,000, where just over one-fifth of the U.S. population lived.[12] Since 1968, however, violent crime and burglary rates have risen faster in the suburbs than in cities with populations greater than 250,000 (see Table 2). Serious crime is becoming less a central city phenomenon.

In 1971, almost 60 percent of the arrests for violent crimes and more than 80 percent of the arrests for burglary involved young people, 24 years or younger.[13]

More than 90 percent of those arrested for violent crimes and burglaries in 1971 were males.[14] While there has been an

[12] *UCR—1971*, pp. 100-101.
[13] *UCR—1971*, pp. 122-123.
[14] *UCR—1971*, p. 126.

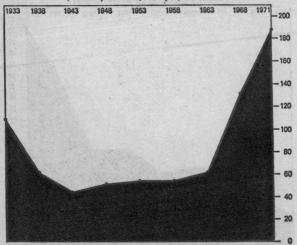

**FIGURE 3. ROBBERY KNOWN TO THE POLICE, 1933-1971**
(Rates per 100,000 population)

Source: Data from the Federal Bureau of Investigation.

overall increase since 1960 in the number and proportion of arrestees who are female, the percentage increase of males arrested for violent crimes has grown even faster. This has not been true of females under 18, where there was an increase of 229 percent. However, the priority crimes remain clearly the actions of males.

More than one-half of those arrested for violent crimes in 1971 were nonwhites, mostly blacks. One-third of those arrested for burglary in 1971 were nonwhites, again mostly blacks.[15]

Within a group of persons arrested in 1971 on Federal charges of violent crime or burglary, from 65 percent to 77 percent had been arrested at least once before for violations of Federal or State law.[16] While FBI rearrest statistics include only those charged under Federal authority, available evidence indicates that similar high rearrest rates are the norm for States and localities as well. A reminder should be made

[15] *UCR—1971*, p. 127.
[16] *UCR—1971*, p. 38.

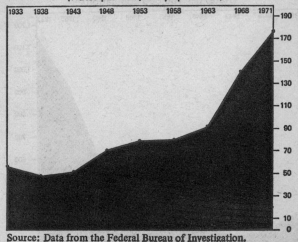

**FIGURE 4. AGGRAVATED ASSAULT KNOWN TO THE POLICE, 1933-1971**
(Rates per 100,000 population)

Source: Data from the Federal Bureau of Investigation.

here: arrest statistics show who has been arrested, not necessarily who committed an offense.

A national victimization survey made in 1970 by LEAA also shows that the persons most likely to be victims of violent crimes are males, youths, poor persons, and blacks.

The survey data do not indicate the sex or age characteristics of the heads of households victimized by burglary. They do show that the rate of victimization by burglary is more than one and one-half times as high for black families as for white ones. They also reveal no significant difference in the rate of victimization between households with incomes under $10,000 and those above $10,000.

This latter finding conflicts with the conclusion of the President's Crime Commission in 1967: "The risks of victimization from . . . burglary, are clearly concentrated in the lowest income groups and decrease steadily at higher income levels."[17] Because the President's Crime Commission also based its findings on a representative national survey, further research will have to be undertaken to resolve the inconsist-

[17] *Crime and Its Impact,* p. 80.

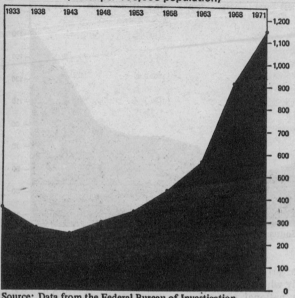

**FIGURE 5. BURGLARY KNOWN TO THE POLICE, 1933-1971**
(Rates per 100,000 population)

Source: Data from the Federal Bureau of Investigation.

ency in the two sets of data. But it is likely that a shift in the pattern of victimization has occurred since 1966.

### Other Characteristics of Offenders and Victims

Additional characteristics of offenders, victims, and places of occurrence of the five priority crimes suggest important contrasts in factors associated with each offense.

Murders, assaults, and rapes tend to be "crimes of passion," a label that indicates the spontaneous and non-economic elements of these crimes. It is known, too, that victims of criminal homicide and assaults frequently precipitate attacks by using insulting language or physical force in quarrels and disagreements.[18]

Studies of homicide and aggravated assault show that a substantial percentage of offenders and victims had been drink-

---

[18] Mulvihill and Tumin, *Crimes of Violence*, pp. 224-228. Precipitation was defined as first resort to insults or force.

## Table 2: Violent Crime and Burglary Known to the Police (Rates per 100,000 Population)

|  | Urban (cities over 250,000) | Suburban | Rural |
|---|---|---|---|
| Crime Rate 1968: |  |  |  |
| Violent Crimes | 773.2 | 145.5 | 108.4 |
| Burglary | 1,665.8 | 761.0 | 387.2 |
| Crime Rate 1971: |  |  |  |
| Violent Crimes | 1,047.5 | 205.7 | 133.4 |
| Burglary | 2,026.1 | 974.5 | 484.9 |
| Percentage Increase: |  |  |  |
| Violent Crimes | +35 | +41 | +23 |
| Burglary | +22 | +28 | +25 |

Sources: *UCR—1968–1971*, "Crime Rate by Area."

## Table 3: Offender-Victim Relationships

|  | Status of Offenders | |
|---|---|---|
| Offense [1] | Previously known to victim (percent) | Stranger [2] to victim (percent) |
| Forcible Rape | 35 | 65 |
| Aggravated Assault | 34 | 66 |
| Noncommercial Robberies | 15 | 85 |

Source: LEAA

[1] Attempts and actual offenses.

[2] Stranger means that the victim stated that the attacker was a stranger, or that he could not identify the attacker, or that the attacker was known by sight only.

ing before the event and one study of criminal homicides revealed that either the victim or the murderer had been drinking in almost two-thirds of the cases.[19]

[19] Data on the role of alcohol in violent crimes are summarized in Mulvihill and Tumin, *Crimes of Violence*, pp. 641-649. The homicide study is reported in Marvin E. Wolfgang, *Patterns in Criminal Homicide* (Wiley, 1966).

Alcohol appears to be only a minimal factor in robbery, according to another study. When there was evidence of alcohol, at least as many victims as offenders were drinking. The study pointed out that "this somewhat reinforces the image of the robbery offender as an individual who rationally plans his act against an unsuspecting victim, in contrast to the offender in the other major violent crimes, who often acts more passionately and impulsively."[20] No comparable information on the role of alcohol in burglaries is available.

A popular explanation of the recent rise in reported crimes has been the use of drugs, especially heroin. There is considerable evidence that heroin-dependent persons frequently engage in theft, burglary, and robbery to support their habits. There is little evidence, however, that points to heroin as a significant factor in non-income-producing violent crime.[21] From an in-depth study of the relation between drug abuse and crime, the National Commission on Marihuana and Drug Abuse reported in 1973 that heroin-dependent persons usually commit crimes against property, principally shoplifting and burglary, though occasionally when desperate they will commit an assault, mugging, or robbery.[22]

### Time and Place of Criminal Acts

The target crimes vary considerably as to where, when, and how they are committed.[23]

Victimization surveys and reported crime statistics answer many questions about where and when crimes are committed. Assaults occur about equally inside and outside buildings.[24] The home and various other inside locations are the likeliest locations for forcible rapes and homicides.[25] Sixty percent of

[20] Mulvihill and Tumin, *Crimes of Violence*, pp. 644-646.

[21] For a discussion of the relationship between drug abuse and crime, see Harwin Voss and Richard Stephens, "The Relationship between Drug Abuse and Crime," to be published in *Drug Abuse;* Richard Stephens and Stephen Levine, "Crime and Narcotic Addiction," to be published in Raymond Hardy and John Cull (eds.), *Applied Psychology in Law Enforcement and Corrections* (Thomas, 1973); and James A. Inciardi, "The Poly-Drug User: A New Situational Offender," in Freda Adler (ed.), *Politics, Crime, and the International Scene: An Inter-American Focus* (San Juan, P.R.: North-South Center Press, 1972), pp. 60-69.

[22] National Commission on Marihuana and Drug Abuse, *Drug Use in America: Problem in Perspective* (1973), p. 175.

[23] *UCR—1971*, p. 21.

[24] Mulvihill and Tumin, *Crimes of Violence*, p. 302.

[25] *Ibid.*

reported burglaries occur in residences, as opposed to commercial establishments.[26] Possibly 60 percent of all burglaries and noncommercial robberies occur at night, as do two-thirds of the aggravated assaults and one-half of the rapes.[27]

Many persons are victimized more than once within relatively short time periods. About one in six robbery and assault victims during 1970 were victimized twice during the 12-month period, according to the LEAA victimization survey.

Eighteen percent of the households burglarized in 1970, according to the survey, were burglarized more than once in that year, 3 percent of them three times or more in the same year. About two in five of the burglaries reported in the survey in 1970 involved entries without force through unlocked doors, unlatched windows, or other means of access. These findings have particular relevance for crime prevention efforts by police and citizens.

## Relationship Between Criminal and Victim

A critical factor differentiating the five target crimes is the relationship between the criminal and his victim. It has long been assumed that a majority of murders are committed by someone known to the victim, and the same theory has been held in regard to aggravated assault and forcible rape. However, victimization surveys are indicating that the proportion of these crimes committed by strangers is increasing.

A special survey, conducted by the FBI in 1960 in cities where 38 percent of the U.S. population lived, reported that about one-third of all aggravated assaults were committed by strangers.[28] But the 1970 LEAA survey showed that nearly two-thirds of rapes and aggravated assaults were committed by strangers—i.e., the victim stated that the attacker was a stranger, or that he could not identify the attacker, or that the attacker was known by sight only (see Table 3). Almost all noncommercial robberies are committed by strangers.

Accurate information on relationships between burglars and their victims is not available, principally because burglars are rarely confronted by the persons they victimize. Many

[26] *UCR—1971*, p. 21.

[27] Data on all burglaries, residential and commercial, are taken from *UCR—1971*, p. 21. Data on residential burglaries in LEAA 1970 Survey indicate that roughly 60 percent of these are committed at night. Data on noncommercial robbery, forcible rape, and aggravated assault are taken from LEAA 1970 Survey.

[28] *UCR—1960*, p. 11.

## Table 3.1. Criminal Justice Functions Performed by Automated Information Systems

| POLICE: FUNCTION | COURTS: FUNCTION | CORRECTIONS: FUNCTION |
|---|---|---|
| Activity Reporting | Administration/Finance | Administration/Finance |
| Administration/Finance | Assignment—Attorneys | Corrections Personnel |
| Alphabetical Index | Assignment—Courtroom | Inmate Accounting |
| Arrests | Assignment—Judges | Inmate Records |
| Command and Control | Calendaring/Scheduling | Menu Planning |
| Communications—Message | Case Control | Performance Evaluation |
| Switching | Case Disposition Reports | Physical Goods Inventory |
| Communications—On-Line | Citation Control | Planning |
| Inquiry | Courts Personnel | Prison Industries |
| Communications—Other | Criminal History | Prisoner Behavior Models |
| Computer-Assisted Dispatch | Defendant Control | Rehabilitation |
| Crime Lab | Docketing | Research/Statistics |
| Crime Trend Analysis | Evidence Control | Trust Fund Accounting |
| Criminal Associates | Fines, Collateral, Bail | |
| Criminal History | Jury Management | |
| Evidence Control | Juvenile Records | |
| Field Contact Reporting | Probation Control | |
| Fingerprint Processing | Process Service Control | |
| Juvenile Index | Research/Statistics | |
| | Simulation/Modeling | |

36

**Table 3.1. Criminal Justice Functions Performed by Automated Information Systems (Cont.)**

Licensing/Registration
Missing Persons
Modus Operandi
Narcotics Control
Organized Crime
Performance Evaluation
Planning
Police Personnel
Research Statistics
Resource/Allocation
Simulation/Modeling
Stolen Licenses
Stolen Property—Guns
Stolen Property—Vehicles
Stolen Property—Other
Subjects-in-Process
Training
Uniform Crime Reporting
Vehicle Maintenance
Warrants/Wanted Persons
White Collar Crime
Workload Analysis

Summons Control
Warrant Control
Witness Control

Source: United States Department of Justice, LEAA, *Computer Summaries from the Directory of Automated Criminal Justice Information Systems (1973)*, pp. 37, 45, 53.

burglaries—probably a majority—are committed by habitual offenders—individuals who are involved in dozens, and in some cases hundreds, of offenses. For example, interviews with Dallas County inmates held by the Texas Department of Corrections in 1972 found that 48 repeat offenders admitted to an average of 65 burglaries per inmate.[29] Obviously, such persons are unlikely to confine their activities to residences and establishments of persons with whom they are acquainted.

The relationship of the offender to the victim for the five target crimes has important implications in selecting crime reduction strategies. This relationship takes on additional meaning when put in the context of possible changes in general social and economic conditions.

## Socioeconomic Changes

Every serious study of crime has noted the association between fluctuations in crime rates and changes in population, social values, and economic conditions. Among the societal conditions most frequently linked with the problem of crime are the following:

- The proportion of young people in the population.
- Metropolitan area population growth.
- Population mobility.
- Family stability.
- Income distribution.

The Commission is sure that relationships exist between crime and social justice, technological progress, and political change, although the nature of such relationships remains exceedingly ill-defined. The long-term effect of greater personal and national affluence, for example, may well depend on what type of criminal behavior is being addressed. In setting crime reduction goals, therefore, the Commission considered these two questions:

1. What significant changes will occur in society during the next decade?
2. How will societal changes affect violent crime and burglary?

The following discussion covers the factors the Commission considered most pertinent in answering these two questions.

### Proportion of Young People in the Population

One important crime-related factor is the changing age

[29] Dallas Police Department, *Repeat Offender Study: Summary Report* (July 1972), p. 5.

structure of the population. This is especially true for young males—the group noted above as most likely both to commit crime and to be victimized by crime. Calculations made by the Commission indicate that the proportion of the population aged 15 to 24 will decrease. (See Figure 6.)

Whereas young males increased as a percentage of the total population, and in absolute numbers, during the 1960's, their group will stop increasing—indeed will actually decline in both numbers and proportion of the population—by the late 1970's. The group increased by one-third—from 6.6 percent to 9.0 percent of the population—between 1960 and 1970. Its share of the population will peak around 1976 (9.5 percent) and decrease to about 8.5 percent in 1983.[30] This is about the same level as in 1968.

A similar change will take place in the youth population as a whole, including both males and females. The 15-24 age group will stop increasing relative to the total population in about 1976 and will decline in absolute numbers beginning about 1980.

Thus, the pressures recently felt by the criminal justice system due to the unusually large numbers of youths resulting from the postwar "baby boom" will be substantially lessened during the 1970's and 1980's.

### Metropolitan Area Population Growth

A quite different influence on crime may be expected from other changes in American demographic patterns in the decade ahead. Projections prepared by the National Commission on Population Growth and the American Future indicate that the United States will continue to become more urbanized over the next several decades. In 1970, about 71 percent of all Americans lived in metropolitan areas. By the year 2000, the Population Commission expects 85 percent of the population to be living in metropolitan areas. The increases

---

[30] Calculations derived from estimates and projections published by the Bureau of the Census. The projected percentages shown here for 1976 and 1983 are the medians of the calculated percentages of the four projections used by the Bureau of the Census. See *Current Population Reports*, Series P-25, No. 493, "Projections of the Population of the United States, by Age and Sex: 1972 to 2020" (1972); and P-24, No. 483, "Preliminary Estimates of the Population of the United States, by Age and Sex: April 1, 1960 to July 1, 1971" (1972).

## FIGURE 6. PERCENTAGE OF MALES, 15-24, IN POPULATION, 1960-1985

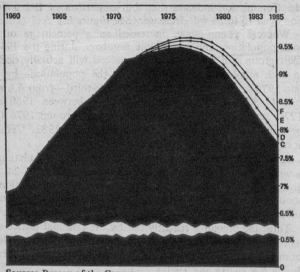

Source: Bureau of the Census.

Note: Lines F, E, D, and C are high, intermediate, and low projections of the percentage of males in the population. The median of the four projections for 1983 is about 8.5%.

in most metropolitan areas will be in suburbs rather than in central cities.[31]

While estimates of the magnitude of population changes may vary as projections are updated, the direction is clear. The population density of central cities will not change drastically, and parts of surrounding suburbs will become more dense. This is significant in light of the historical association between population density and crime rates. Robbery, bur-

[31] Commission on Population Growth and the American Future, *Population and the American Future* (1972). The term "metropolitan area" refers to the Commission's definition: "Functionally integrated areas of 100,000 population or more, composed of an urbanized area or central cities of at least 50,000 people, and the surrounding counties." See also Patricia Leavey Hodge and Philip M. Hauser, *The Challenge of America's Metropolitan Population Outlook—1960-1985*, Research Report No. 3 for the National Commission on Urban Problems (1968), pp. 15-16.

glary, and other property crime rates are considerably higher in central cities than in suburbs or rural areas. As shown in Table 2, however, violent crime and burglary rates have been rising faster in the suburbs than in central cities. It is probable that the suburbs already are beginning to feel criminogenic effects of steadily increasing urbanization.

## Population Mobility

The move to urban areas will bring with it not only pressures and opportunities for antisocial behavior but also the loss of a sense of community that comes with widespread mobility.

The extent and impact of transiency in the population has been explored recently by Vance Packard, who estimates that "at least a fifth of all Americans move one or more times each year, and the pace of the movement of Americans is still increasing." He considers this widespread and constant movement to be a factor "contributing to the social fragmentation we are witnessing. . . ."[32] Pervasive movement produces rootlessness which in turn leads to a sense of anonymity that is felt by segments of large urban populations.

A lack of common experience in a crowded but transient populace makes the organization of citizen crime prevention efforts more difficult. It also hinders the development of close police-community relations.

Rootlessness or mobility may also be a factor leading to criminality. A longitudinal study of delinquent males in Philadelphia, Pa., found that one of the variables significantly associated with police contacts, especially repeated contacts, was degree of school and residential mobility—the more mobility, the more police contacts.[33] Although there may be several explanations for this association, one of the most likely is that high mobility lessens ordinary community ties that restrain delinquency-prone youths from illegal acts.

In short, increasing population mobility is likely to contribute to America's crime problems during the next decade.

## Family Stability

Society has long depended on the authority of the family as a major instrument of social control and thus of crime

[32] Vance Packard, *A Nation of Strangers* (McKay, 1972), pp. 6, 8.

[33] Marvin E. Wolfgang, Robert M. Figlio, and Thorsten Sellin, *Delinquency in a Birth Cohort* (University of Chicago Press, 1972), p. 246.

prevention. Whether it can continue to rely so strongly on the family is open to serious question. The next 10 years will probably witness declines in traditional family stability. Steeply rising trends in illegitimate births and divorces over the last 3 decades point to weaker family ties than in the past.

## Income Distribution

Few developments will have greater influence on American life than changes in national income distribution. The proportion of the population in lower income brackets decreased throughout the sixties.[34] While increasing affluence is not assured, current projections are encouraging.

One analyst has estimated that by 1980 more than half of the Nation's households will have incomes of more than $10,000 a year, as against two-fifths in this category in 1970.[35] (Estimates are in 1970 dollars.) At the same time, the proportion of households with incomes of $7,000 or below will decrease to less than one-third (see Figure 7). Thus the average will be rising and affluence will be spreading.

As these changes take place, the relationship of wealth, poverty, and crime becomes more difficult to assess. Greater affluence for the majority of the people means more valuable targets for burglary and robbery, possibly with less caution exerted by owners to protect possessions that can readily be replaced. Rising general affluence may mean that frustration and envy will in fact increase for persons in the lowest income brackets—one out of every nine families will have incomes below $3,000 a year, according to Linden's estimates—and this may lead to more attempts to supplement income by illegal acts.

On the other hand, greater affluence should mean that more citizens will have more of their basic wants satisfied than at any previous time in our Nation's history. The basic

[34] The proportion of persons in the poverty bracket declined from 22.4 percent in 1959 to 12.6 percent in 1970, and total numbers also declined. (Bureau of the Census, *Statistical Abstract of the United States, 1972*), p. 329. There was a reversal in the trend in the year 1970 as compared with 1969. But most opinion and historical experience point to a return to the trend of declining numbers of persons living in poverty and their proportion of the population.

[35] Fabian Linden, "The Expanding Upper Income Brackets," *The Conference Board Record* (November 1971), p. 15.

## FIGURE 7. THE CHANGING PYRAMID OF INCOME DISTRIBUTION
(Total households each year = 100%; based on 1970 dollars)

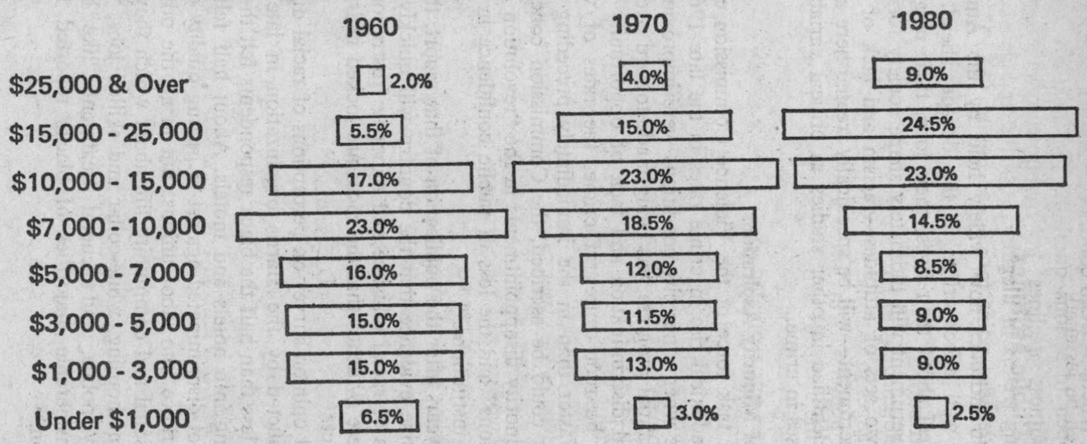

|  | 1960 | 1970 | 1980 |
|---|---|---|---|
| $25,000 & Over | 2.0% | 4.0% | 9.0% |
| $15,000 - 25,000 | 5.5% | 15.0% | 24.5% |
| $10,000 - 15,000 | 17.0% | 23.0% | 23.0% |
| $7,000 - 10,000 | 23.0% | 18.5% | 14.5% |
| $5,000 - 7,000 | 16.0% | 12.0% | 8.5% |
| $3,000 - 5,000 | 15.0% | 11.5% | 9.0% |
| $1,000 - 3,000 | 15.0% | 13.0% | 9.0% |
| Under $1,000 | 6.5% | 3.0% | 2.5% |

Source: Fabian Linden, "The Expanding Upper Income
Brackets," The Conference Board Record
(November 1971), p. 51.

43

economic pressures that lead to stickups, break-ins, and violence may well be lessened.

## Changes in Public Attitudes

Changes in attitudes now widely held by the American public may well affect crime in the decade ahead. How Americans feel about their lives, their jobs, their neighbors, and their government will ultimately shape society for better or worse. Two sets of attitudes—racism and lack of confidence in government—will be specifically treated here as they have been identified in other studies as critical variables in the recent rises in crime.

### Frustration of Minority Aspirations

In 1969 a task force of the Violence Commission considered the paradoxical rise in crime rates in the late 1960's at the very time when inner city conditions were improving. Although substantial progress was being made toward overcoming the racial discrimination and lack of opportunity which appeared to be root causes of crime, the rates of violent crime rose faster than in the immediately preceding years. The paradox could be ascribed, the Commission concluded, mainly to minority disappointments in the "revolution of rising expectations" and the loss of public confidence in social and political institutions.[36]

Today, 4 years after the publication of that report, there is little conclusive evidence that the country will quickly solve the problems of racial injustice and minority frustration. But neither is there evidence that the races are locked in irreconcilable conflict.

A national opinion survey on perceptions of racial discrimination conducted by the Harris organization in late 1972 showed that less than half the black respondents felt they had trouble getting into hotels and motels. About half felt their group was not discriminated against in getting quality education and entrance into labor unions. But in all the other aspects of personal and community life about which they were asked—decent housing, white-collar and skilled jobs, wages, treatment by police, and general treatment "like human beings"—considerable majorities of blacks reported feeling discrimination.[87]

[36] *To Establish Justice, To Insure Domestic Tranquility,* pp. 38-43.
[87] The Harris Survey, January 15, 1973.

44

Significantly, however, when compared with a survey on the same subject in 1969, fewer black respondents perceived discrimination on the job and in the community in 1972. In some areas the percentage drop was substantial. In 1969, for example, 83 percent of the black respondents felt discrimination in housing; the percentage in 1972 was 66. When two-thirds of the blacks still feel discriminated against in so important an area as housing, American society has a long way to go yet toward racial justice. But, at least in the opinion of some, progress is being made.

Another interesting point about the Harris surveys is that, in some key areas, the white residents in 1972 perceived more discrimination against blacks than they had in 1969. In the earlier year, for example, 19 percent of the whites thought blacks were discriminated against by the police; 25 percent of the whites thought so by 1972. Discrimination against blacks in housing and education was also more apparent to whites in 1972 than in 1969.

Finally, it should be mentioned that in another national survey taken in mid-1972 black respondents "were significantly *more* optimistic about their personal futures" (emphasis in original) than whites.[38]

These may appear to be small gains. But if disappointment of minorities in the revolution of rising expectations is a cause of violent crime, they have some importance for the future.

Whether they have permanent significance remains to be seen. The dismal heritage of years will not pass quickly. Bold and sustained government action is essential to progress.

## Mistrust in Government

In contrast to the encouraging, though small, shifts in public opinion regarding racial problems, national surveys indicate that lack of public confidence in political institutions is reaching crisis proportions.

In 1970, the University of Michigan's Survey Research Center found that between one-third and one-half of those surveyed in a national sample responded affirmatively to questions asking whether they believed (1) that their government can be trusted only some of the time; (2) that the government is run for the benefit of a few big interests; and (3)

[38] William Watts and Lloyd A. Free (eds.), *State of the Nation* (Universe Books, 1973), p. 25.

45

that many officials are "a little crooked."[39] The percentages of respondents expressing these beliefs have increased significantly since the Center began periodic surveys in the late 1950's.

These findings are of great significance to the reduction of crime. In this society, citizens do not obey the law simply in response to threats by the authorities but because they acknowledge the right of the lawmaking institutions to lay down the rules and the right of the law enforcement agencies to enforce them. In other words, citizens recognize the legitimacy of the country's political institutions. As the Violence Commission put it, "what weakens the legitimacy of social and political institutions contributes to law-breaking, including violent crime."[40]

The findings are also encouraging in the light of the need for close cooperation between citizens and officials in crime-fighting efforts. Few citizens will long be willing to cooperate with officials whom they believe to have a hand in the till or to be "on the take" from illegal enterprise. Indeed, the impact of the Watergate problem and other aspects of the 1972 presidential election on the confidence of the people in this country in their government has yet to be assessed.

It cannot be said with certainty whether public cynicism about government is a deepening chronic malaise or whether it will abate along with the domestic turbulence of the 1960's and American military involvement in Southeast Asia. The Commission is hopeful, however, that public confidence will be restored by public leadership that is honest and fair.

## Public Support for the Criminal Justice System

The fourth major factor that the Commission took into consideration in setting its goals for crime reduction in the decade ahead was public support for the criminal justice system.

In mid-1972 a national survey conducted by the Gallup organization showed that violence and crime were the domestic problems that most worried the respondents. And the respondents were willing to put their money where their worries were. A larger proportion of them were willing to approve government spending to combat crime than spending for any

[39] "Election Time Series Analysis of Attitudes of Trust in Government" (Center for Political Studies, University of Michigan, 1971).
[40] *To Establish Justice, To Insure Domestic Tranquility,* p. 42.

46

other activity, including air and water pollution, education, and mass transportation.[41]

As a matter of fact, the share of the Gross National Product (GNP) devoted to expenditures for the criminal justice system has been rising steadily for nearly 20 years. From 1955 to 1965, criminal justice expenditures rose from one-half to two-thirds of 1 percent of GNP, with an estimated annual increase since 1966 of more than five times that shown in the 1955-65 period.[42] Although percentage increases have undoubtedly been influenced by expanded Federal spending, all levels of government have spent more for the criminal justice system. Preliminary estimates by the Law Enforcement Assistance Administration and the Bureau of the Census indicated total spending of $10,513,358,000 in 1971.[43]

The other major evidence of public support for the criminal justice system lies in the increasing participation of citizens in the operation of the system. No hard statistics are available, but, beginning in the late 1960's, there was an upsurge of citizen activity directly aimed at reducing crime. This took the form of working for better streetlighting, setting up neighborhood security programs, and other activities. Hundreds of local projects emerged in communities across the country. Citizen participation is one of the Commission's priorites for action, and it will be discussed in detail in this chapter. The reader should also refer to the chapters on community crime prevention and on corrections, as well as to the separate reports on these subjects.

# New Methods in Measuring Progress

The establishment of crime-specific goals is a meaningless exercise if the rate of progress cannot be accurately assessed. One factor in the Commission's conclusions, therefore, was the ability to measure crime.

There are now two tools for measuring national crime

[41] Discussed in Watts and Free (eds.), *State of the Nation,* pp. 35, 117-118. Interestingly, the means most favored to reduce crime was "to clean up the slums." Improvements in the criminal justice system received from one-third ("more police") to two-thirds ("improve jails") the number of mentions made of slum clean-up.

[42] Data from *Statistical Abstract of the United States* for appropriate years.

[43] "Expenditure and Employment Data for the Criminal Justice System, 1970-1971" (LEAA, unpublished).

rates: the UCR compiled annually by the FBI, and the national victimization survey developed by LEAA.

The UCR has the inherent limitations of being based on reports from police departments. Hence it includes only those crimes known to the police.

Victimization surveys made since 1966 in various cities indicate that at least half of all crimes against persons and property are not reported to the police. Moreover, there have been findings that police departments have not recorded fully the extent of crimes that are reported by citizens, or have not accurately classified and defined reported offenses.[44] Consequently, the victimization survey is widely believed to give a more precise estimate of the volume of crime and other dimensions of criminal activity, such as cost, than the UCR.

LEAA, in conjunction with the Bureau of the Census, is now conducting an annual victimization survey of a representative national sample of households and commercial establishments.[45] Local data will be provided by supplemental sample surveys in about 35 of the Nation's largest cities. These local surveys will be updated periodically. For the five largest cities—New York, Chicago, Los Angeles, Philadelphia, and Detroit—survey information will be provided biennially.

The surveys, which are expected to continue under Federal auspices, should provide a fairly reliable estimate of the true level of rape, aggravated and simple assault, robbery, burglary, larceny, and auto theft. Attempted crimes will be counted as well as crimes actually committed.

Homicide will not be included in the LEAA victimization survey. There is, however, probably little disparity between the actual incidence of homicide and that recorded by police.

In the case of rape, the resulting picture from victimization surveys may not be as clear as for other offenses, owing to

[44] The usefulness of officially reported crime statistics has been widely debated. Doubts have been expressed as to how accurately UCR data can show the extent of and changes in crime. After careful study, a task force of the Violence Commission concluded, "For individual acts of violence covered by national police statistics, limitations on the accuracy of the data are apparent." Such limitations affect understanding of the levels, trends, incidence, and severity of crime. Mulvihill and Tumin, *Crimes of Violence*, pp. 16-38.

[45] The survey is described in detail in the Commission's *Report on the Criminal Justice System*, Appendix A. Information for the present brief description was also supplied by the National Criminal Justice Information and Statistics Service in LEAA.

the reluctance of victims to identify incidents. However, the interview technique may be more successful in eliciting information than the official reporting process. Discreet and indirect approaches to the incident are expected to overcome a good deal of the reporting problem. The fact that rapes are comparatively small in number will undoubtedly mean that it will take longer to establish a significantly reliable measure of change for this offense than for others which occur with far greater frequency.

The LEAA survey will ascertain the amount of property lost and recovered, attitudes toward police, fear, age and race characteristics of offenders, place of occurrence, and weapons used by assailants. Unlike UCR statistics, the LEAA survey will indicate offender-victim relationships. This will make it possible to measure progress towards reducing "high-fear" (stranger-related) crime which the Commission has set forth as a national goal.

In sum, the LEAA survey will make it possible to achieve a more precise record of the volume and rate of crime. The first complete annual picture of victimization will emerge for 1973. Preliminary tabulations of annual survey results will be available approximately 8 months after the end of each year.

It should be noted that victimization surveys also present some problems. First, victimization surveys may be interpreted as showing an increase in crime. The data should show higher numbers and rates of crime than the public is accustomed to reading and hearing. This is attributable to greater accuracy, but citizens may find it difficult to distinguish between accuracy in reporting and actual increases in crime.

Second, victimization surveys are expensive. Therefore reliance on victimization surveys to assess national progress cannot mean discarding traditional police statistics. Surveys are too costly to be run on a continuous basis by LEAA in every jurisdiction.

Most States and localities will have to continue to rely on official police statistics to determine directions of change in their crime rates. Even those cities that are surveyed yearly by LEAA will need to use information on crimes known and reported to the police. Such data are essential to effective allocation of police manpower. They are an irreplaceable indicator of the extent to which citizens are willing to bring crimes to the attention of the police. Unlike the LEAA victimization survey, most police departments do not collect statistics on offender-victim relationships. The Commission, however, urges that departments expand their statistical coverage to do so.

It is unrealistic to expect any measure of crime to be 100 percent accurate. Victimization surveys should be useful in evaluating reported crime statistics and vice versa. Not only will such cross-comparisons lead to more accurate data, but they should also encourage public confidence in official estimates of the crime problem. A lessening of public debate as to whether crime has gone up or down in the Nation and communities may be a byproduct of the development of victimization surveys.

# A Look Ahead with Priorities for Action

The crime reduction goals proposed in the preceding pages are not the result of using some heretofore unknown formula. Nor were they the result of abstract or wishful thinking. They were decided upon after considering the nature of the target crimes and some of the social and governmental developments—past and future—that will affect them. The Commission believes that reductions of the magnitude proposed are not unrealistic.

The Commission was led to this belief by the several signs discussed above, signs that point to the possibility of reducing the priority crimes. Among them are the probable reduction in the proportion of the population who are in the crime-prone 15-to-24 age bracket. Increasing national prosperity is an encouraging sign if it eliminates absolute poverty. Recent formation of citizen crime-prevention organizations and public willingness to approve increased government spending for the criminal justice system also augur well for progress toward the goal of reducing crime.

Among the priority crimes of murder, rape, assault, robbery, and burglary, the Commission has concluded that the greatest reduction is most likely to occur in the rates of the latter two. These differ in several key ways from the other priority offenses. Robbery and burglary are acquisitive crimes, committed for material gain, and often they are calculated and planned carefully. Usually, they are committed by persons who are strangers to the victims. They occur in environments that can be altered to reduce the opportunities open to the criminal. Large numbers of burglaries and robberies are vulnerable to relatively easily implemented deterrent strategies: police patrols, street lighting, citizen crime prevention activities, and speedy and effective court dispositions.

In addition, the Commission is convinced that society and the criminal justice system are capable of directing many delinquent youths and ex-offenders to lawful avenues of economic gain so that the attraction of the "easy money" of holdups and break-ins will be less important.

In short, there are solid grounds for optimism in deterring the acts themselves and in reducing the potential number of offenders.

The fact that the Commission has set lower percentage goals for reducing murder, assault, and rape does not mean that they are less important. Indeed, murder, rape, and assault are probably feared by the average citizen more than any other crimes.

The proposed percentage of reduction is lower for these so-called crimes of passion because they are less easily controlled than the other target crimes by conventional criminal justice methods. Many of these crimes are committed by acquaintances and are impervious to ordinary deterrent strategies. Victims of assault and homicide frequently show little inclination to avoid criminal attacks. Indeed, they often incite assailants by their own speech and actions. Alcohol—a drug that has proved consistently resistant to efforts to lessen its abuse—is an important catalyst in homicides, assaults, and, to a lesser extent, rapes. To reduce there crimes, a change in values is needed—an increased respect for others and a willingness to settle disputes by means other than violence.

The Commission proposes four priorities for action for reducing all of the target crimes. These are:
• Preventing juvenile delinquency.
• Improving delivery of social services.
• Reducing delays in the criminal justice process.
• Securing more citizen participation in the criminal justice system.

The Commission submits that many of the standards set forth in subsequent chapters are easily categorized within these priorities and lead to the accomplishment of the numerical goals established earlier in this chapter.

## Priority: Preventing Juvenile Delinquency

The highest attention must be given to preventing juvenile delinquency, to minimizing the involvement of young offenders in the juvenile and criminal justice system, and to reintegrating delinquents and young offenders into the community. By 1983 the rate of delinquency cases coming before courts that would be crimes if committed by adults should be cut to half the 1973 rate.

Street crime is a young man's game. More than half the persons arrested for violent crime in 1971 were under 24 years of age, with one-fifth under 18. For burglary, over half of the 1971 arrests involved youths under 18.[46]

There is strong evidence that the bulk of ordinary crime against person and property is committed by youths and adults who have had previous contact with the criminal justice or juvenile justice system. Recent evidence in support of this assumption is a study of delinquency in all males born in 1945 who lived in Philadelphia from their 10th to their 18th birthdays. Specifically the study concluded that the more involvement a juvenile had with the police and juvenile justice authorities, the more likely he would be to be further involved.[47] Of the 9,945 subjects, 3,475 (35 percent) came in contact with police at least once. Of this delinquent group, about 54 percent had more than one contact with police. This 54 percent was responsible for 84 percent of all police contacts in the group. Eighteen percent of those having repeated contact with the police had five or more contacts and were responsible for 52 percent of all police contacts in the delinquent group.

Increased efforts must be made to break this cycle of recidivism at the earliest possible point. One approach is to minimize the involvement of the offender in the criminal justice system. Minimized involvement is not a fancy phrase for "coddling criminals." It means simply that society should use that means of controlling and supervising the young offender which will best serve to keep him out of the recidivism cycle and at the same time protect the community. It is based on an easily justified assumption: the further an offender penetrates into the criminal justice process, the more difficult it becomes to divert him from a criminal career.

People tend to learn from those closest to them. It is small wonder that prisons and jails crowded with juveniles, first offenders, and hardened criminals have been labeled "schools of crime."

People also tend to become what they are told they are.

[46] *UCR—1971*, p. 121.
[47] Wolfgang, Figlio, and Sellin, *Delinquency in a Birth Cohort*, chs. 6, 14.

52

The stigma of involvement with the criminal justice system, even if only in the informal processes of juvenile justice, isolates persons from lawful society and may make further training or employment difficult. A recent survey conducted for the Department of Labor revealed that an arrest record was an absolute bar to employment in almost 20 percent of the State and local agencies surveyed and was a definite consideration for not hiring in most of the remaining agencies.[48]

For many youths, as noted above, incarceration is not an effective tool of correction. Society will be better protected if certain individuals, particularly youths and first offenders, are diverted prior to formal conviction either to the care of families or relatives or to employment, mental health, and other social service programs. Thus a formal arrest is inappropriate if the person may be referred to the charge of a responsible parent, guardian, or agency. Formal adjudication may not be necessary if an offender can be safely diverted elsewhere, as to a youth services bureau for counseling or a drug abuse program for treatment. Offenders properly selected for pretrial diversion experience less recidivism than those with similar histories and social backgrounds who are formally adjudicated.

To assure progress toward the goal is minimizing the involvement of juveniles in the juvenile justice system, the Commission proposes that the 1973 rate of delinquency cases disposed of by juvenile or family courts for offenses that would be crimes if committed by adults be cut in half by 1983.

The Department of Health, Education, and Welfare, which collects information on juvenile courts, estimates that a little less than 40 percent of cases disposed of by courts are cases of running away, truancy, and other offenses that would not be crimes if committed by an adult.[49] These are the so-called juvenile status offenses.

The remaining 60-odd percent of cases estimated to be disposed of by juvenile or family courts are nonstatus crimes, those that would be crimes if committed by adults. It is the rate of these cases which the Commission would propose to cut in half.

[48] Herbert S. Miller, *The Closed Door: The Effect of a Criminal Record on Employment with State and Local Public Agencies,* report prepared for the U.S. Department of Labor (February 1972), p. 100.
[49] Estimates from U.S. Department of Health, Education, and Welfare.

Meeting the goal, the Commission believes, should result in significant decreases in crime through preventing recidivism and might also prove to be far less costly than dealing with delinquents under present methods. To process a youth through the juvenile justice system and keep him in a training school for a year costs almost $6,000.[50] There is no reason to believe that the cost of a diversionary program would exceed this figure, since most such programs are not residential. Indeed, diversion might prove to provide significant savings.

One final note should be added. Minimizing a youth's involvement with the criminal justice system does not mean abandoning the use of confinement for certain individuals. Until more effective means of treatment are found, chronic and dangerous delinquents and offenders should be incarcerated to protect society. But the juvenile justice system must search for the optimum programs outside institutions for juveniles who do not need confinement.

## Priority: Improving Delivery of Social Services

**Public agencies should improve the delivery of all social services to citizens, particularly to those groups that contribute higher than average proportions of their numbers to crime statistics.**

There is abundant evidence that crime occurs with greater frequency where there are poverty, illiteracy, and unemployment, and where medical, recreational, and mental health resources are inadequate. When unemployment rates among youths in poverty areas of central cities are almost 40 percent and crime is prevalent, it is impossible not to draw conclusions about the relationship between jobs and crime. The Commission believes that effective and responsive delivery of public services that promote individual and economic well-being will contribute to a reduction in crime. The rationale for the value of a variety of services is well expressed in the Commission's *Report on Community Crime Prevention*. Having called for citizen action on such priorities as employment, education, and recreation, the report points out:

> This is not to say that if everyone were better educated or more fully employed that crime would be eliminated or even sharply reduced. What is meant is

[50] Derived from "Youth Service System: Diverting Youth from the Juvenile Justice System," paper prepared by the U.S. Department of Health, Education, and Welfare.

that unemployment, substandard education, and so on, form a complex, and admittedly little understood amalgam of social conditions that cements, or at least predisposes, many individuals to criminal activity.

Thus a job, for example, is just one wedge to break this amalgam. Increased recreational opportunities represent another. Though one wedge may not have much effect on an individual's lifestyle, two or three might.

The Commission is aware that improvement of social services to a degree necessary to have an impact on crime will take time. Building career education programs into elementary and secondary school curriculums, for example, cannot be accomplished in the next 2 or 3 years. But it must begin now if society is to realize benefits at the end of 10 years and beyond.

The Commission particularly wishes to call attention to the provision of drug and alcohol abuse treatment. Communities must recognize the diversity of drug abuse and alcohol problems and the need for a number of alternative treatment approaches. Citizens must be willing to make the investment that such treatment requires, not merely because it will reduce crime but because adequate treatment is essential to deal with an increasingly serious national health problem.

## Priority: Reducing Delays in the Criminal Justice Process

**Delays in the adjudication and disposition of cases must be greatly reduced and the period between arrest and trial must be reduced to the shortest possible time.**

In recent years, backlogs in the courts have become a well-publicized symbol of inefficiency in the entire system. In large cities, many cases have been subject to delays of 300 to 1,000 days from arrest to trial and final disposition. Legislatures and other parts of the criminal justice system, as well as judges, defense attorneys, and prosecutors, must bear some of the responsibility for the problem. Delay in the criminal justice process frustrates law enforcement efforts and develops a sense of injustice in offender, victim, and citizen alike.

The negative byproducts of judicial delay are many. The number of defendants incarcerated and awaiting trial is reaching alarming proportions in many large cities, and detention facilities are dangerously overcrowded. The LEAA

55

National Jail Census in 1970 revealed that 52 percent of the jail inmates were awaiting trial.[51] Pretrial incarceration is costly to the individual, for it denies him income and, in fact, may cause him to lose his job. Extended incarceration resulting from judicial delay is also costly to the public, since pretrial detainees must be fed and supervised.

Alternatives to incarceration such as bail and release on recognizance present another set of problems in cases of long delays between arrest and trial. A 1968 survey in the District of Columbia found ". . . an increased propensity to be rearrested where the release period extends more than 280 days."[52]

The pressures of heavy backlogs contribute to the notorious practice of plea bargaining. Faced with an overwhelming caseload, prosecutors seek to avoid time-consuming trials by disposing of felony indictments through negotiated guilty pleas to less serious felonies and misdemeanors. Whether viewed from a rehabilitation or deterrence perspective, workload-motivated plea bargaining is an undesirable practice that can be gradually eliminated if accompanied by less burdensome court backlogs.

Speeding up the criminal justice process may not reduce crime by itself, but when coupled with effective treatment alternatives and intelligent correctional decisions, it should have a significant impact. Additional judges will undoubtedly be needed in many jurisdictions, but much can be done to improve the adjudicatory process by streamlining court procedures.

## Priority: Increasing Citizen Participation

**Citizens should actively participate in activities to control crime in their community, and criminal justice agencies should actively encourage citizen participation.**

The criminal justice system depends on citizen participation. Most crimes do not come directly to the attention of police; they are reported by citizens. Without active cooperation of citizen jurors and witnesses, the judicial process cannot function. Institutional education and training programs

[51] Law Enforcement Assistance Administration, *1970 National Jail Census* (1971) p. 1.

[52] J. W. Locke and others, *Compilation and Use of Criminal Court Data in Relation to Pre-Trial Release of Defendant: Pilot Study Report* (National Bureau of Standards, 1970), p. v.

will not be useful to the offender if he cannot find employment in the community in which he is released. The best-trained and equipped police force will fare poorly in the battle against crime if the citizens it serves do not take basic precautionary measures to protect themselves and reduce criminal opportunities.

Citizens in many communities are organizing to form block crime prevention associations and court-watching groups, and to furnish volunteers to work in the criminal justice system. One striking example is a nationwide program that began with the involvement of a few citizens in Royal Oak, Mich. The Volunteers in Probation program grew from eight citizens in 1959 to an estimated quarter of a million nationwide in 1972.

The Royal Oak concept utilized volunteers and professionals together and statistics indicate that volunteers and professionals working together can provide intensive probation services that are three times more effective than those provided by a probation officer working alone.[53]

Citizen cooperation with police also has great potential, but it is largely unrealized. In 1970, 18 percent of the households in America took some form of home protection—special locks, lights, alarms, watch dogs, and/or weapons.[54] Whether the measures adopted were the most effective that could have been chosen is another matter. Certainly every police department could perform a useful service by actively disseminating its crime-prevention knowledge to citizens. It is not necessary to sell self-protection to many persons, certainly not to those who have been victimized before. Yet, in many jurisdictions, aggressive outreach programs for crime prevention are nonexistent. The Police chapter of this report identifies in greater detail what some departments have done in this area.

All criminal justice agencies can do much in their operations to encourage citizens' involvement. They first must organize their operations to increase acceptability to the citizens they serve and to encourage these citizens to their activities. This means, for example, that police must process complaints efficiently and courteously; that courts must minimize the time lost by jurors and witnesses; that corrections must

[53] Information from project director, Judge Keith Leenhouts, Sept. 11, 1972. For details on the Royal Oak project, see the Commission's *Report on Community Crime Prevention,* chapter on Citizen Action.
[54] Data from LEAA 1970 Survey.

57

run its institutions to permit the community reasonable access to those incarcerated. These are minimums. Criminal justice agencies can do much more, if they actively seek to explain their role to citizens' groups and show how citizens themselves may participate in community crime prevention. Above all, criminal justice agencies must understand and know the communities they serve. Active personnel recruitment from all facets of the community is essential if citizens and the criminal justice system are to work together as a team.

# Conclusion

This chapter has dealt with the Commission's research and findings involving the factors affecting the reduction of crime.

In succeeding chapters of this book, the Commission proposes its broad outline for action by State and local units of government and by citizens to reduce crime.

In addition, the complete standards and recommendations of the Commission are set out in its volumes on *Criminal Justice System, Police, Courts, Corrections,* and *Community Crime Prevention.*

# Chapter III
# Toward a System of Criminal Justice

"Fragmented," "divided," "splintered," and "decentralized"'
are the adjectives most commonly used to describe the American system of criminal justice.

The sheer number of independent agencies is the most visible evidence of fragmentation. According to a 1970 survey,
there are 46,197 public agencies in the criminal justice system that are administered at the State or local government
level in towns of over 1,000 population. Most States have
hundreds of criminal justice agencies. For example, in Wisconsin, a medium-sized State whose criminal justice structure
is typical of other States, there are 1,075 separate criminal
justice agencies. These include 458 law enforcement agencies,
221 courts, 197 prosecution offices, five defenders offices, 98
adult and juvenile corrections departments, 72 probation offices, and 24 other criminal-justice-related agencies.[1]

Words such as fragmented and divided, however, refer not
only to demarcations in authority, but to differences in states

[1] Law Enforcement Assistance Administration, *Criminal Justice
Agencies in Wisconsin* (1972), pp. 1, 10.

of mind, and not only to physical distances, but to distances in philosophy and outlook.

In a recent study of conflict within a large urban criminal justice system, police, courts, and corrections personnel were asked what problems were caused for them by other criminal justice agencies. A sample of the responses reveals the different perspectives of those interviewed.

• Criticisms of law enforcement: "Police are disrespectful and tend to harass parolees." "Most of them believe in a police state and if one doesn't agree with their values, etc., they classify that person as the enemy."

• Criticisms of the public defender: "Excessive use of technical legal points to free an obviously guilty person." "Oftentimes this agency will attempt to stall a case by using questionable techniques in court."

• Criticisms of city and district attorneys: "Tend to overcharge by filing too many charges of greater severity than offense calls for." "Go-it-alone attitude—entire division created for juvenile justice work with no discussion or involvement of probation people."

• Criticisms of municipal and superior courts: "The sentences have little or no relation to the crimes charged." "Entirely too many cases dismissed due to minor technicalities."

• Criticisms of departments of corrections and probation: "They take a soft approach to criminals." "Has no real rehabilitation—sends problems back to the community."

These perceptions are not surprising. Criminal justice agencies are highly dependent upon one another. What particular law enforcement, courts, and corrections agencies do in handling offenders and processing information affects all the rest. Yet attorneys, patrolmen, and corrections officers frequently have quite different on-the-job experiences, constitutional responsibilities, educational backgrounds, professional objectives, and social class origins.

In addition, crime is an emotional issue. Its causes and solutions are the subject of intense disagreement among police, courts, and correctional personnel. General consensus among professionals can rarely be reached on basic questions such as:

• Which crime problems should receive greater criminal justice attention? Which ones should receive less?

• Which criminal offenses should be removed from the books? Which ones should be added?

• Which arrestees should be diverted before trial? Which ones should not?

- Which offenders should be channeled into community-based corrections? Which ones should not?
- Which aspects of the criminal justice process need to be improved immediately? Which ones can afford deferred action?

Lack of agreement on answers to these basic questions presents criminal justice with its most difficult dilemma. If criminal justice professionals cannot reach a consensus on what to do about crime and criminals, it is unrealistic to expect the public and political leaders to do so. The most enduring problems facing the criminal justice system are not technical or financial—they are political. The consequences of lack of professional agreement are deadlock, inaction, and confusion in making public policy.

## Major Recommendations

Discussed in this chapter are three concerns common to the total criminal justice system: criminal justice planning, criminal justice information systems, and criminal justice education. Major recommendations call for:
- Development by States of a general system of multiyear criminal justice planning.
- Establishment of criminal justice coordinating councils by all major cities and counties.
- Creation by each State of an organizational structure for coordinating the development of criminal justice information systems.
- Establishment by each State of a Security and Privacy Council to oversee security and privacy of information contained in criminal justice information systems.
- Establishment of strict security and privacy procedures to protect the integrity of criminal history files.
- Establishment by agencies of higher education of criminal justice system curriculums and programs to prepare persons to work in the criminal justice systems.

Action on the Commission's standards in each of these areas should bring greater consensus on common goals and priorities. Another byproduct should be more meaningful relations in the day-to-day contact among police officers, judges, defense attorneys, prosecutors, and corrections officers.

The areas of planning, information systems, and education are crossroads at which the various components of the criminal justice system come together. They present joint endeavors that can assist professionals in overcoming the unnecessary friction that currently characterizes the system.

# Criminal Justice Planning

A community has received $250,000 in additional funds for law enforcement and crime prevention purposes. How should this money be spent?

In an urban city, it will pay 10 policemen for 1 year, including salaries, uniforms, training, equipment, overhead, and fringe benefits. The same money would pay for eight new prosecutors together with their necessary support services. It might also pay for 3 months of special training in prerelease centers for each of 120 offenders or pay for an entire year of noninstitutional aftercare for 70 people in the system. The same money might greatly aid narcotics treatment centers, or maintain for 1 year two or three youth services bureaus that provide help for delinquent and troubled youth.

With such highly diverse alternatives as those discussed above, it is exceedingly difficult for executives, budget chiefs, and legislators to make intelligent choices.

The decisionmaking process, however, can be made more rational by improved planning techniques. The Commission recommends:

• Multiyear planning in each State, taking into account all available Federal, State, and local resources.

• Metropolitan area coordinating councils to plan across county and city boundaries.

• Expanded membership from non-criminal-justice sources on criminal justice planning councils.

• Formalized exchanges of ideas and personnel between planning and operating agencies.

## State Planning Under the Law Enforcement Assistance Program

In the past 4 years, a beginning has been made toward establishing a network of institutions that will define appropriate goals and crime control strategies for State and local criminal justice activities. The Omnibus Crime Control and Safe Streets Act of 1968 requires each State wishing to receive Federal law enforcement assistance funds to create a State Criminal Justice Planning Agency (SPA) and to develop an annual State comprehensive plan.

Upon approval of the comprehensive plan by the Law Enforcement Assistance Administration, a block action grant is awarded. The grants are called block action because they are awarded as a lump sum rather than on a categorical program-by-program basis, and because they provide direct support to State and local police, courts, corrections, and other criminal justice programs. Smaller "block planning" grants also are awarded to support the planning and grant administration efforts of the SPA's and whatever regional planning councils the SPA's establish.

Since the passage of the Safe Streets Act, all 50 States, American Samoa, Guam, the District of Columbia, Puerto Rico, and the Virgin Islands have established SPA's. Overseeing the policymaking of the SPA's are supervisory boards whose members represent State and local criminal justice offices, citizen groups, and non-criminal-justice public agencies. Although an SPA director is administratively responsible to his Governor, the comprehensive plan that he and his staff have designed usually must be approved by the SPA supervisory board. In most cases the Governor formally appoints members of the SPA supervisory board and the boards of any regional planning councils the State might establish.

The States have been receiving planning and action grants in increasingly larger amounts. In 1969, $43.65 million was made available to the States. In 1972, this had increased to $497.44 million in planning and action grants.[2]

Criminal justice is still an activity funded primarily through State and local sources.[3] The Federal block grant contribution is far less than 10 percent of the combined State and local criminal justice expenditures, which in 1971 totaled $9,302.23 million.

The actual funds received from the Federal Government under the Safe Streets Act may be less important in the long run than the stimulus the Act provided to criminal justice planning. For the first time, State governments have a staff arm for closely examining criminal justice problems from a systemwide perspective. In a number of States, SPA's are becoming useful instruments for policy analysis and comprehensive reform.

In Nebraska, for example, the legislature's Judiciary Committee and the Nebraska Crime Commission (SPA) in 1971 cooperated in the examination of such problems as court reform, law enforcement consolidation, changes in bail prac-

[2] Source: LEAA.
[3] Source: Bureau of the Census and LEAA.

tices, and prison and parole reform. In Kentucky, in 1972, the SPA recommended to the General Assembly a 12-point legislative package that included: revision of the criminal laws, State support of police educational and training incentives, authorization of work and educational release for misdemeanants and felons, and establishment of a public defender system. Much of the recommended legislation subsequently was passed.

While SPA activities such as those described above are signs of emerging planning capabilities, the role of SPA's as conduits for Federal funds has received the most attention in the press and in the halls of Congress. Faced with the need in the late 1960's and early 1970's to provide operating agencies with the resources to deal with crime, many SPA's became preoccupied with funding.

Due to a variety of intergovernmental problems, in the first 3 years of the Safe Streets Act program SPA's experienced great difficulty in disbursing their action grants to State and local police, courts, corrections, and other criminal justice agencies. Data released in 1972 indicate time lags of more than a year between congressional appropriation and SPA disbursement of funds in some instances. At the end of fiscal year 1972, for example, 10.2 percent and 47.9 percent of the block action funds appropriated during fiscal years 1970 and 1971, respectively, still had not been disbursed.[4]

SPA's were attacked by critics of the Safe Streets Act program for disbursing funds too slowly. They also were criticized for not establishing adequate fiscal controls for the awarding of subgrants. Specific instances of mismanagement of funds by SPA's led to congressional charges of inefficiency and waste. In more than one SPA, fiscal control personnel replaced planners, as executive directors acted to insure the financial integrity of their programs.

As attention to the funding role of the SPA's increased, the concept of total criminal justice planning was given a low priority by both LEAA, which required plans for Safe Streets funds, and by the States that produced them. Within guidelines furnished by LEAA, SPA's produced weighty and lengthy volumes that often had questionable information value for the executive, legislator, administrator, technician, and concerned citizen. A major deficiency of the plans to date is their frequent inability to address the question of State and local agency priorities for reducing crime. States

4 Source: LEAA.

64

have just begun to define their crime problems and make decisions about the patterns of criminal activity in their jurisdiction. A Commission staff survey of the 1972 plans revealed that:

• Four States did not cite any crime statistics in their plans.
• Only 19 States cited data in their plans on the nature and extent of juvenile delinquency. These data usually were based on either police arrests or referrals to juvenile court.
• Many States did not cite common criminal justice performance statistics that relate to crime control; e.g., apprehension rates, recidivism rates, and court processing rates.

The absence of basic crime-oriented statistics in formal planning documents raises questions as to whether many SPA's see themselves as planners or simply grant administrators. A quantitative assessment of State crime problems and criminal justice system response is an obvious first step in even the most basic planning process.

A second deficiency of the plans is that they generally attempt only to specify what use will be made of the funds available from LEAA and other Federal sources. In its 1972 planning grant application to LEAA, the Wisconsin Council on Criminal Justice succinctly stated the problem:

> A reality that the Safe Streets planning concept does not take into account ... is that Safe Streets funds represent only a small fraction of local government moneys available for law enforcement improvement. Regional plans [and state plans] cannot be realistic until the improvement strategy takes into account revenue for law enforcement improvement from all sources inclusive of local and state moneys.

If criminal justice planning is to have full impact upon the system, the scope of planning needs to be broadened to include the entire budgetary picture for criminal justice at the State and local levels.

**The Commission recommends that SPA's develop by 1978 a general system of multiyear planning that takes into account all funds directed to crime control activities within the State.**

This system would include all sources of Federal funds as well as State general and capital funds; State subsidy funds to local governments; local government funds; and private donations, endowments, and contributions.

Under a broadened planning process, proposed statewide changes in criminal justice programs would be analyzed and set forth by SPA's for Governors, legislators, budget directors, agency heads, local officials, and the public. Priority problems calling for significant changes in State policy would receive special staff attention. Consideration of funding sources would not be limited to Safe Streets money.

Such a planning process would have several benefits. A truly comprehensive multiyear plan for criminal justice would make planning, programing, and budgeting more visible. It would encourage much needed question-asking by legislators and the press. It would provide a statement of crime-oriented goals and standards to which the public could hold elected leaders accountable. A multiyear plan would provide a reference point for budget and appropriations decisions.

Presently, the Michigan Council on Criminal Justice (SPA) is developing an expanded formal planning process. While it may take several annual cycles to define it, the Michigan objective is to develop a multiyear plan for the prevention, control, and reduction of crime and delinquency in the State to be carried out through the allocation of resources at the Federal, State, and local levels as well as through private resources. The experience in Michigan may provide a useful case study for other States.

## Metropolitan and Regional Planning

The systemwide perspective that SPA's can provide at the State level must also be provided at the local level. Large cities and counties in most States now are receiving direct planning money either from the State or from regional planning councils. A movement toward local criminal justice coordinating councils (CJCC's) has taken place in large metropolitan areas. A main objective of these CJCC's is to plan and coordinate local criminal justice activities. Many CJCC's receive Safe Streets assistance. At the end of 1971, 33 of 50 of the Nation's largest cities had CJCC's.

CJCC's are creations of local government. They may derive formal authority from a resolution or ordinance adopted by the city council and/or county board of supervisors, or from an executive order by the mayor and/or the county chief executive. On the other hand, CJCC's may operate informally at the request of the mayor and/or the county chief executive and by the agreement of the various participating agencies.[5]

Usually headed by local chief executives, CJCC's are more than mere funnels of Safe Street funds. With broad-based representation of various elements of the criminal justice system and competent staffs, they can suggest and plan for programs that have nothing to do with Federal funding.

The oldest and one of the most successful CJCC's is that of New York, N.Y. Planning is accomplished through a 74-member council comprised of representatives of the criminal justice system, other public agencies, and citizens, and a 16-member executive committee headed by the mayor. A staff of 20 professionals supports the council's activities. The NYCJCC has been designated by the State as the regional planning council for New York City, and administers State and Federal subgrants and grants. It also submits proposed legislation to the State legislators. It engages in program development with every agency in the city that bears directly upon criminal justice and the levels of crime. Acting as an occasional mediator in interagency conflicts, it permits police, prosecutors, and corrections officials to plan for the effects of one part of the system upon another.

The primary purpose of CJCC's is to coordinate local criminal justice planning efforts, and to serve as a staff for local authorities by exploring alternatives for crime control programing. In New York City, for example, the local jail was overcrowded. The CJCC analyzed the costs and benefits of various alternatives including construction of a new facility, release-on-recognizance projects, diversion projects, and speed-up of court processing. The research done by the CJCC and the consideration given to this research by the mayor and city council were critical in making an informed decision.

CJCC's may assume additional responsibilities such as reviewing the planning for Safe Streets funds from the State and the Federal Government. As with any local agency they would be subject to statewide regulations and legislation. CJCC's are no longer experimental institutions, but essential parts of the criminal justice system.

[5] National League of Cities and United States Conference of Mayors, *Criminal Justice Coordinating Councils* (1971), p. 3.

**The Commission recommends that all major cities and counties establish criminal justice coordinating councils under the leadership of local chief executives.**

Metropolitan cities and counties should be encouraged to consolidate criminal planning and coordinating operations. In metropolitan areas with a population of more than 250,000, a criminal justice planning office should be established with a minimum of one full-time position for a professional planner to aid chief executives and the CJCC in developing priorities and programs.

## Participation in the Planning Process

Criminal justice planning must reach beyond traditional police, courts, and corrections processes. Crime control requires participation by persons who are not criminal justice practitioners. It is important to have the involvement of locally elected officials, non-criminal-justice public agencies, labor unions, business associations, and citizen groups.

The participation of minority members on planning agency supervisory boards and councils is also critical. Boards that wish to concentrate efforts on urban street crime cannot afford noninvolvement or mere token involvement of minority populations, since these groups contribute disproportionately to both offender and victim statistics.

Criminal justice planning agencies and councils should seek the participation of criminal justice operating agencies, government departments, and private citizens and groups in the planning process.

**The Commission recommends that at least one-third of the membership of State and local planning agency supervisory boards and councils be from officials of non-criminal-justice agencies and from private citizens.**

Many boards of SPA's already reflect a non-criminal-justice emphasis. A 1971 internal LEAA survey indicated that twenty-two States had more than one-third of their board membership from non-criminal-justice sources.

The concept of participation should also be extended to operating agencies. It serves no purpose to establish a superstructure of state and local criminal justice planners if police departments, prosecutors, public defender offices, courts, and corrections systems do not themselves take part in planning. Planning must begin from the ground up. Setting goals and priorities, developing programs, and defining performance measures must be undertaken in the greatest detail at the agency level.

In a number of states, law enforcement, courts, and corrections agencies are invited by the SPA to submit their positions on the development of needs and priorities for the state plan. The agency submissions are reviewed by the SPA and, where appropriate, are incorporated into the plan.

To avoid being insulated from concerns of other parts of the criminal justice system, operating agencies and planning agencies have initiated temporary staff exchanges. Exchanged personnel contribute to the spread of new ideas and innovation throughout the system. The NYCJCC, for example, has drawn upon various criminal justice agencies in developing its plans and programs.

**The Commission recommends that criminal justice planning agencies request direct written communications from operating agencies to assist them in defining the jurisdiction's objectives, needs, problems, and priorities. Temporary exchanges of personnel between criminal justice planning agencies and operating agencies should be undertaken on a regular basis.**

The criminal justice planning standards suggested by the Commission are not radical, nor entirely novel. Planning is so basic an activity that a person not aware of the chaos of large urban criminal justice systems would scarcely think it need be mentioned. Unfortunately, it must be. In the United States a monolithic criminal justice system is unthinkable. The judiciary is staunchly independent; Federal, State and local legislators and other elected officials jealously guard their independence as well. If the imbalances and conflicts of the present system are to be reduced, a comprehensive and participatory planning effort of the type described in this chapter is essential.

## CRIMINAL JUSTICE INFORMATION SYSTEMS

Organizing the Nation's criminal justice information into a useful body of knowledge was talked about for decades but little was done. Recently, however, the urgency of the nation's crime problem, and the availability of computers and data processing equipment, have made integrated State and National information systems a possibility.

Along with many other disciplines, criminal justice has been experiencing an "information explosion" since the late 1960s.

Its characterstics are steadily increasing demands for more capability in gathering, processing, and transmitting information, and steadily increasing information needs.

More frequent use of the computer and other automated technology is a national trend. In 1968, according to LEAA, only ten States in the nation had automated state-level criminal justice information systems. By 1972, forty-seven States had operational automated information sytems serving at least one component of the system.

The uses of information and computers vary from jury selection to police manpower allocation to correctional program placement. A recent survey of States by LEAA identified thirty-nine different police functions, twenty-three court functions, and thirteen different corrections functions performed by automated information systems in one or more States or cities (see Table 3.1 pp. 36-37).

Criminal justice agencies—like most public and private agencies—are voracious consumers of information. As the pace and complexity of change in the criminal justice system quickens, police, courts, and corrections agencies will seek more information and a faster response in its delivery.

To avoid duplication of effort and to facilitate effective collection and proper dissemination of information during this period of rapid expansion, the Commission recommends that:

• State offices coordinate development of information systems.

• High priority be given to development of criminal history and offender-based transaction statistics systems.

• Each State establish a Security and Privacy Council to prevent improper use of information.

## Development of Information Systems

Decisions must be made as to which information systems deserve priority attention and which ones are less important. Choosing the right jurisdictional level at which to apply and use the developing criminal justice information systems technology is also a critical decision.

At the present time, local, State, and Federal agencies are spending considerable moneys for the hardware and impedimenta of incompatible and duplicative information systems. Money is being wasted and the human resources, technical talents, and skills available for development of a criminal justice information system are being diffused in many redundant development efforts.

The availability of Federal funds has contributed to the diffusion of effort. Most State criminal justice planning agencies have been faced with decisions on a project-by-project basis where all projects appear to be reasonable and no setting of priorities is possible. As funding expands, the demand increases. Nearly every State is in the position of having a plethora of information systems which cannot be integrated into a usable network. The price of neglected planning is often high; millions of dollars are spent by State and local governments in large urban States without obtaining the necessary information in its most usable form.

**The Commission recommends that each State create an organizational structure for coordinating the development of criminal justice information systems.**

Such a structure would: (1) prepare a master plan for the development of an integrated network of criminal justice information systems; (2) provide technical assistance and training to all jurisdictions in data collection methods, system concept development, and related areas; and (3) arrange for audit and inspection of State and local information systems.

Proper jurisdictional responsibilities in an integrated network of criminal justice information systems are set forth in the Commission's *Report on the Criminal Justice System.* Standards define State, local, and component system roles based on several principles of system integration.

The most important principle of system integration is that identical records should not be contained within two separate repositories unless there are strongly overriding considerations of total system efficiency to be gained thereby. In practice, this means that there should not be, for example, criminal histories kept at the local level unless the State is temporarily unable to provide this service. In a time of rapid automated information technology, duplicative systems are usually unnecessary and wasteful.

In 1971, the FBI's National Crime Information Center (NCIC) began operating a nationwide system for the exchange of criminal histories among States. This system is the result of an LEAA-funded program of intergovernmental cooperation on information systems among Federal, State, and local governments called Project SEARCH. Since the Commission's work is confined to State and local governments, it

71

set no standards for the FBI, LEAA, or any other Federal agency. However, because State and local governments are primary data sources for the NCIC, implementing the Commission's report would affect the national level as well.

Various other operational and management needs of criminal justice agencies are discussed in the Commission's *Report on the Criminal Justice System*. Standards, for example, are set for improving the collection and processing of local police crime statistics. In addition, the Commission identified two information needs that merit the highest priority attention—criminal histories and offender-based transaction statistics (OBTS).

## Criminal Histories and OBTS

The criminal history record is a major thread in tying the criminal justice system together. It shows, as no other document or record does, the actions of the total system on individuals. It describes the official actions of police agencies, judicial and supportive agencies, and all correctional components.

The uses of criminal histories are varied. A police detective may use a criminal history to indicate whether a suspect is likely to have committed the crime under investigation and also the suspect's possible whereabouts. A district attorney may find an arrestee's criminal history invaluable in making recommendations on the question of bail and its amount. Most judges who face the choice of placing a convicted defendant on probation or sending him to prison realize that a criminal history is vital to intelligent sentencing.

Closely allied to the need for criminal history data on a given offender is the need for aggregate data on offenders processed through the system, namely, offender-based transaction statistics (OBTS). OBTS data have come to be thought of as "derivative" from individual criminal histories since many data elements are the same. Statistics on what happens to offenders at each significant step in the criminal justice process can provide answers to questions such as these:

What percentage of those arrested are prosecuted?

What percentage of those prosecuted are acquitted or dismissed?

What is the average length of time between arrest and final disposition?

What percentage of arrestees wait more than 1 year before the final disposition of their cases?

What percentage of offenders in institutions and community-based corrections programs are rearrested and reconvicted upon release?

The evaluation of whether a part of the system is meeting its basic objectives must have its roots in the statistics describing the passage of offenders through the system. Without OBTS data, planners and legislators frequently find themselves relying on the uncertain grounds of good intentions and the often ill-founded assumptions of conventional wisdom.

In spite of need for particular and statistical data derived from individual criminal histories, most criminal justice systems find it difficult to produce, rapidly and easily, complete criminal history information. Local police department files are still the most important sources of criminal history information. Known as "rap sheets," summary criminal history records are kept by police and commonly shared with other criminal justice agencies. In most jurisdictions there is no immediately available substitute to the rap sheet; indeed they are vital to the functioning of urban criminal justice systems.

Nevertheless, there are major difficulties in relying totally on local information. Rap sheets are often not complete; followup on the disposition of the offender after he has been arrested for offenses in other cities and counties without the arrests ever showing up on the records of the original jurisdiction. Some offenders are highly mobile. For instance, a New York study of 869 persons arrested in a 2-month period revealed that one in five had been arrested at least once before in another jurisdiction.[6]

In most localities criminal history information is in manual files, impeding fast retrieval. Yet, police conducting investigations and judges setting bail cannot tolerate long delays. Retention of criminal history data in many files makes the compilation of offender-based transaction statistics on a continual basis all but impossible.

The need for States to become repositories for criminal history information is clear; this need coincides with other needs requiring statewide attention, such as on-line files on wanted persons, stolen autos, and other identifiable stolen items.

[6] New York State Identification and Intelligence System, *System Development Plan* (1967), p. 58.

73

**The Commission recommends that all state criminal justice information systems provide computerized criminal history files and collection and storage of additional data elements to permit collection of offender-based transaction statistics.**

Advisory committees representing information users from all parts of the criminal justice system should be established to assure compatibility of systems designs. National requirements such as the FBI's National Crime Information Center (NCIC) specifications must be considered in the design of information systems.

## Privacy

The permanent storage, rapid retrieval, and national coverage of a computer-based criminal justice information system can deprive a citizen of his "right to privacy"—his right to be free from unwarranted intrusion in his affairs.

The problem in establishing a criminal justice information system is to determine who should have access to the files or computer terminals, who should be eligible to receive information from these files, and under what circumstances.

For these reasons, the collection and dissemination of criminal history information and other criminal justice information should be carefully supervised.

**The Commission recommends that each State adopt legislation to establish a Security and Privacy Council which is vested with sufficient authority to adopt and administer security and privacy standards for criminal justice information systems.**

Fifty percent of each Council's members should be private citizens.

In its *Report on the Criminal Justice System* the Commission establishes a number of standards that it recommends should be enacted into legislation and enforced by Privacy and Security Councils. Among those adopted were key standards on the purging, access, and dissemination of criminal history information and the individual's right to review official records.

Criminal justice files contain information that may be useful to a wide range of agencies outside the criminal justice system, for background investigations of potential employees of public agencies and private firms, for determining eligibility for occupational licenses, for credit evaluation, and for general public information supplied by news media.

The potential damage to privacy is increased when the information in criminal justice files is inaccurate, incomplete, misleading, and unnecessarily disseminated to persons outside the criminal justice system.

**In view of the sensitivity and content of criminal history files, the Commission recommends that strict security and privacy procedures be established to insure that there be no dissemination outside the government.**

Credit bureaus, news media, employers, employment agencies, and other seekers of information should be denied access to criminal histories. Although items in a criminal history file are for the most part matters of public record, the government should not compile the items and turn the composite over to persons outside of government. This recommendation may appear to be an exception in freedom of information laws and practices, but the Commission believes the protection of individual privacy to be of paramount concern in this instance.

Files should be reviewed periodically to eliminate inaccurate, incomplete, misleading, unverified, and unverifiable information. Individuals should be accorded the right to inspect criminal history files pertaining to them and to challenge the validity of inaccurate or misleading entries. In addition, information that, because of its age, is no longer a reliable guide to the subject's present attitudes or behavior should be purged from the files.

Information concerning individuals convicted of serious crimes should be purged from active files 10 years after the date of release from supervision by the criminal justice system. For less serious crimes, the period should be 5 years. Exceptions to this purging rule should be made in the case of wanted persons, persons under indictment, and multiple offenders.

The principle of purging should also apply to simple arrest records. The economic and personal damage resulting from an arrest that does not lead to conviction is unnecessary yet often substantial. Although the existence of an arrest record is neither an indication of guilt nor a reliable guide to a person's character, it may become an automatic disqualification for employment.

The Commission recommends that all copies of informa-

75

tion filed as a result of an arrest that is legally terminated in favor of the individual should be returned to that individual within 60 days of final disposition, upon order of a court, or if requested by the agency that disposed of the case. Exceptions should be made in the case of persons against whom a criminal action or proceeding is pending or who have previously been convicted of a crime.

In its *Report on the Criminal Justice System,* the Commission acknowledges that purged information may be removed from active files and still retained for internal recordkeeping and bona fide research purposes. Information that is purged, but not returned or destroyed, should be held in confidence, in separate files, and not disseminated except under several narrowly defined cases specified in the Commission's report.

Legislation should be enacted that limits questions about arrests on applications for public and private employment and licenses, and that specifies other civil rights and privileges applicable to those arrests. (See the chapter in this report on Community Crime Prevention for a further discussion of removing employment barriers resulting from arrests and convictions.)

Few persons doubt the necessity for the criminal justice system to be aware of community conditions and potential criminal activity. Controversy occurs, however, on what information should be gathered, how it should be obtained, and who should have access to it. The threat to individual rights from unrestricted intelligence operations is direct. Leaks occur. Details that should be strictly private become public news. Reputations may be destroyed and careers ruined. The Commission wishes to discourage the retention of demonstrably inaccurate and unnecessary intelligence information and to prevent its dissemination.

In no instance should criminal history files be linked with intelligence files. To minimize the threat to privacy, criminal history files must contain only information concerning formal contacts with the criminal justice system such as arrest, charge, and release information. Unproven allegations, rumors of illicit associations, and subjective opinions have no place in criminal history files which of necessity will be used by the entire criminal justice system and possibly by other government agencies.

All of the privacy standards discussed above and others specified in the Commission report would be promulgated and enforced by the State Privacy and Security Councils in the absence of controlling national legislation.

Developing adequate information systems that safeguard basic rights is not a police problem or a courts problem or a corrections problem, it is a criminal justice problem. Issues surrounding such areas as criminal history exchanges, offender-based transaction statistics, and privacy and security requirements must be decided on a multiagency basis. The Commission information systems standards present a suggested course of action that will unify the criminal justice community in this critical area.

# Criminal Justice Education

Higher education in criminal justice has been stimulated by a number of trends in recent years: increasing monetary support for criminal justice education through LEAA, increasing emphasis on career preparation in higher education, and rising pay scales making criminal justice attractive as a career. An indication of the rapid advances that have been made is that, in 1972, 515 institutions of higher education offered full-time degree programs in law enforcement, compared to only 65 a decade earlier.[7]

A characteristic of contemporary higher education in criminal justice is that, like the criminal justice system itself, its roots lie in a number of different disciplines and programs: law, criminology, sociology, public administration, political science, police science, and social work. A serious disadvantage of the present educational structure is that it does not provide common approaches to the problems of crime and justice that currently divide the system.

Legal education historically has deemphasized criminal justice. In many law schools a single course in criminal law is sufficient for graduation. Outside of law schools, most professionally oriented higher education programs have dealt with police only, neglecting a core curriculum that could apply equally to police, courts, and corrections agencies. Law enforcement programs have focused on training-type courses that can be more effectively provided outside of universities and colleges. Some colleges and universities, for example, have courses in such obvious training areas as officers' notebook procedures, first aid, defensive tactics, and weapons instruction.

[7] International Association of Chiefs of Police, *1972-73 Directory of Law Enforcement and Criminal Justice Education* (1972), p. 2.

Only a few colleges and institutions of higher education offer useful graduate programs in criminal justice to middle and upper management personnel who wish to upgrade their professional skills. College catalogs have scarcely acknowledged the emerging discipline of criminal justice planning in their course offerings in spite of the serious need for skilled planners in the hundreds of jurisdictions throughout the country.

By failing to treat criminal justice as a whole, many institutions of higher education have overlooked an opportunity to help unify a frequently divided and unnecessarily competitive system.

**The Commission recommends that criminal justice system curriculums and programs be established by agencies of higher education to unify the body of knowledge in law enforcement, criminology, social science, criminal law, public administration, and corrections, and to serve as a basis for preparing persons to work in the criminal justice system.**

Possible models for criminal justice education programs are presently available from the community college to the graduate level. In California, core curriculums have been developed for criminal justice education in the community college system. The State University of New York and the University of Southern California have pioneered in the development of graduate curriculums in criminal justice. Classes in subjects of common interest to police, courts, and corrections personnel, such as the prevention and control of crime and the administration of justice, reflect the systemwide perspective of such schools.

One of the reasons that criminal justice education is in such an unsettled state is that practitioners and academicians have not tried to define jointly what role higher education is to play in career development. A national survey of law enforcement programs by LEAA found that most curriculum development has proceeded independent of systematic analysis of the roles police, courts, and corrections personnel are expected to perform.

The Commission urges that criminal justice education programs be developed with the active contribution of practitioners. If criminal justice education is to be effective, practitioners must understand the purpose of new programs and education must be familiar with the everyday concerns of practitioners. The Commission standards provide for the systematic development of both education and training curriculums according to a general statewide policy. State planning agencies, standards and training councils, criminal justice agencies, and agencies of higher education would all participate in the formation of the State's policy.

In proposing its standards, the Commission realizes that education alone cannot mold behavior. However, when combined with exposure to different interests in the criminal justice system and the community, it can be an important catalyst for change.

# Conclusion

At the conclusion of this chapter, a judgment made at its beginning bears repeating: "The most enduring problems facing the criminal justice system are not technical or financial—they are political."

No one agency alone has been given the societal responsibility of reducing crime. Questions of major policy in criminal justice require agreement among police, courts, corrections, and other public and private agencies. The Commission's standards on criminal justice planning, criminal justice information systems, and criminal justice education present avenues for reaching agreement. Planning agency supervisory boards and college classrooms are forums where various parts of the system and the non-criminal-justice community may come together to discuss particular concerns and ultimate objectives. Criminal justice information systems that are centrally planned and organized can provide data badly needed in understanding the problems of the criminal justice process.

The standards proposed in this chapter will take time to implement. Their impact will not easily be measured by immediate decreases in crime. Yet they are among our most important recommendations. They provide for a rational future of crime control.

# Excerpts from the Task Force Report on the Criminal Justice System

## A: Criminal Justice System Planning

### 1: Planning for Crime Reduction

THE SAFE STREETS ACT AND CRIMINAL JUSTICE PLANNING

**The LEAA Comprehensive State Plans**

... States have just begun to define their crime problems and make decisions about the patterns of criminal activity in their jurisdictions. A Commission staff survey of the 1972 plans revealed:

1. Four States did not cite any crime statistics in their plans.

2. Only eight State plans had any substantial information on white collar crime—embezzlement, fraud, forgery, and bribery. The statistics in these cases were from traditional sources (crimes reported to the police and police arrests).

3. Only 14 State plans contained statistics on the number of drug-related arrests or cited estimates of the number of addicts within their State.

4. Only 19 States cited in their plans data on the nature and extent of juvenile delinquency. This data usually was based on either police arrests or referrals to juvenile court.

5. Many States did not cite criminal justice performance statistics that relate to crime control; e.g., apprehension rates, recidivism rates, and court processing rates.

The absence of basic crime-oriented statistics in formal planning documents raises questions as to whether many SPA's see themselves as planners or simply grant administrators. A quantitative assessment of State crime problems and criminal justice system response is an obvious first step in even the most basic planning process.

Program funding decisions may change drastically depending on whether the crime problem given top priority is white collar crime, burglary, or various types of violent crime. Critics of the block grant approach have noted that funds frequently are dispersed among many recipients, thus diluting the impact of Federal money. This situation often accompanies a lack of consensus on crime reduction goals, priorities, and action strategies. The criminal justice system has such a widespread need for resources that it is hard to find an undeserving project.

Another deficiency in the planning efforts of SPA's has been lack of evaluation. Although States have attempted to include evaluation in their funding activities at the project and program levels, the evaluation undertaken is relatively primitive. It is difficult to find evidence in many State plans that evaluation of past projects and programs has had any effect on planning. Few activities are evaluated in terms of their direct impact upon crime, primarily because of the extreme difficulty in measuring impact.

If all projects and programs were evaluated with methodological rigor, a great deal more time and money would have to be invested than at present. Programs and projects that clearly represent important advances in criminal justice have to be singled out for detailed evaluations. While SPA's continue to seek the proper balance in this area, it is nevertheless clear that too little evaluation has been undertaken in the past. . . .

BARRIERS TO EFFECTIVE CRIMINAL JUSTICE PLANNING

In the foreseeable future, planners will continue to be hampered by legal, constitutional, and political conditions beyond their control. Locally, systemwide planning frequently stops at the city limits. Police, courts, and corrections planners are limited by their agency's responsibilities. Responsibility for the crime problem in most urban areas remains fragmented. Formerly, local police chiefs and ultimately their mayors took responsibility for peacekeeping in cities. The day has come, however, when the police alone cannot make a decisive impact on crime. More and more police chiefs and mayors are recognizing that what corrections, courts, schools, and social welfare agencies do in relation to their clients affects crime as much as police activity. In most cities, more-

81

over, these agencies are either controlled or significantly influenced by nonlocal policies and funding.

The separation of powers presents another obstacle to coordinated planning. Legislatures often appropriate funds and enact criminal statutes without considering effects on the administration of justice. The courts, whose primary purpose is justice, also sit astride the flow of offenders. Their traditional independence leads them to be very cautious in engaging in planning activities with the executive branch. In several States this has lead to friction with criminal justice planning bodies.

Another problem is traceable to the newness of the planning process. Twenty years ago few criminal justice agencies had planners; many agencies do not even today. Most systemwide criminal justice planning agencies were established in States, regions, and counties only after the 1968 Safe Streets Act. It was inevitable that planners would encounter the same skepticism from established interests that early master planners encounter in the zoning/land use field. The latter assumed that their solutions provided the best of all possible worlds, and that mere publishing of the plans would summon the support needed for implementation. Naturally this did not happen.

When a new bureaucracy is created, it must prove itself. The first 5 years of operation usually are spent gaining a sense of the problem. Confidence is won only gradually. In a field as divided as criminal justice, this is especially true.

Perhaps the most serious problem facing planners is the lack of any firm understanding of the control of crime. It is impossible for planners to identify programs that will absolutely guarantee crime impact. Moreover, the probability of immediate breakthrough is unlikely due to the difficulty in using traditional experimental techniques to evaluate crime control programs. Thus knowledge will be accumulated only gradually and in piecemeal fashion. . . .

**Standard 1.1: Crime-Oriented Planning**

Every criminal justice planning agency and coordinating council should:

1. Analyze the crime problems in its jurisdiction;

2. Identify specific crimes deserving priority attention;

3. Establish quantifiable and time phased goals for the reduction of priority crimes;

4. Evaluate and select alternative strategies and programs for reducing priority crimes;

5. Allocate its own funds and staff resources in accordance with the crime goals, strategies, and programs chosen;

6. Maintain close working relationships with criminal justice and other public agencies to implement crime reduction goals and objectives; and

7. Assume responsibility for the effective evaluation of its planning and funding decisions, and the use of evaluation results to refine goals, strategies, and programs.

These planning agencies, during their initial years of operation concentrated almost totally on analysis of the criminal justice system and identification of priorities for system improvement. Indeed, an explicit assumption of the Safe Streets Act was that strengthening criminal justice capabilities at all levels would reduce crime. So strong was the belief that better personnel, facilities, and equipment would lead to decreases in crime rates that the focus on crime reduction as an ultimate objective was blurred.

LEAA plan guidelines, moreover, encouraged States to concentrate only upon criminal justice system improvements. Instead of defining crime as the problem that criminal justice planning agencies must address, LEAA took the view that the immediate objective should be to improve or upgrade the agencies of criminal justice. Nothing reveals the emphasis on "systems improvement" better than the language of LEAA *Guidelines for 1973 Comprehensive Law Enforcement Plans.* In discussing an appropriate basis for development of the Multi-Year Plan, the guidelines urge that: ". . . the general statement should seek to define the kind of law enforcement system deemed 'ideal' yet attainable for the State and its localities in terms of manpower, training, equipment, facilities, workloads, operational standards, and services provided. . . ."

In short, LEAA has laid heavy emphasis upon planning improvements to the criminal justice system, using some concept of an ideal system as a guide to resource allocation and program development.

In many ways this approach was a sensible one for the initial years. The State and local planning agencies' analysis of local problems indicated that the criminal justice stystem had many serious deficiencies—its management was poor and untrained, its equipment was outdated, it failed to plan its response to problems, and in many cases its approach was ineffective. Thus, before more sophisticated approaches could be taken to deal with crime and to improve the criminal justice system, a basic foundation first had to be established. It is now time for criminal justice planning agencies to take a more critical view of this assumed positive relationship between the overall system improvement and crime reduction. Much more attention must be paid to the nature of crime itself. This fact has been recognized by LEAA, which already has developed a detailed crime-oriented planning methodology.

A number of diverse activities are labeled as criminal in the United States. Smoking a marijuana cigarette is against the law; so is the theft of a bicycle. An apartment break-in, a forged check, and a premeditated homicide are all illegal acts. The Crime Index of the Federal Bureau of Investigation's *Uniform Crime Reports* includes criminal homicide, forcible rape, aggravated assault, robbery, burglary, larceny, and auto theft. There are important differences between these crimes in offender motivation, victim response, and environmental risk. These factors may call for different control and reduction strategies. If a jurisdiction experiences a sharp rise in serious assaults and rapes, for example, planners must examine a number of crime control alternatives. Basic questions must be answered from available data. Do the majority of victims know their assailants? Is there a rapid increase in the proportion of assaults that involve strangers? Is there evidence that arrestees are frequent users of alcohol or drugs? What proportion of the arrestees are juveniles? And so on.

During the course of such question asking, some general strategies for dealing with the problem may begin to suggest themselves. These strategies can take the form of prevention, deterrence, apprehension, and reintegrative programs depending upon what is known about the characteristics of the offenses committed.

Crime oriented planning rests on several key assumptions. First, chief executives assisted by planners must make conscious choices as to what offenses should receive special attention. The empire of crime is too large and diverse to be attacked on all fronts simultaneously.

Second, crime reduction goals and objectives must be quantified wherever possible and set for specific time periods. The value of goal-setting in public accountability and professional evaluation is readily apparent. It presumes the common sense notion that a person should know his destination before he begins his journey. By defining goals by time periods an assessment may be made of the various reasons for the discrepancies between the ideal and the actual. Admittedly, serious problems exist in the development of reliable crime indicators. Quantified goal-setting may not be possible for all offenses.

Third, an effective crime-oriented planning process requires a careful analysis of specific types of crime environments, victims, targets, and offenders. The response of the criminal justice system to particular offenses also must be considered. These activities must occur before any new departures in programing.

Fourth, criminal justice planners must focus in greater detail on State and local criminal justice funding patterns if they are to allocate their resources effectively. The Commission is acutely aware of the difficulties in asking State planning agencies and regional planning agencies to broaden their concerns beyond the allocation of Federal funds. Standard 1.2 addresses this problem in greater detail.

Fifth, attention must be paid to governmental, social, and economic developments outside police, courts, and corrections agencies. Environmental trends found to be associated with the incidence and costs of crime should be examined and anticipated. Planning personnel should be the last to assume a static society. A recent LEAA-funded study by Oscar Newman, for example, has clearly established a relationship between crime and the physical design of public housing. The study is particularly critical of large high rise public housing in which the anonymity of the intruder is preserved and the isolation of the resident from his neighbors is accomplished. In the future, criminal justice planners must make certain that physical, environmental, and social planners understand the crime prevention implications of their proposals before they are acted upon.

Sixth, crime-oriented planning and evaluation are inseparable activities. For communicating this basic fact, the evaluation standard adopted in 1972 by the National Conference of State Criminal Justice Planning Agencies ((NCSCJPA) provides a concise and useful model:

Each SPA shall assume responsibility for undertaking effective evaluation of its funding decisions. Evaluation shall be defined as whether the project or program accomplished its objective, in terms of either preventing, controlling, or reducing crime, or of improving the administration of criminal justice within the context of the State comprehensive plan.

**Standard 1.2: Improve the linkage between criminal justice planning and budgeting.**

**Standard 1.3: Set minimum statewide standards for recipients of criminal justice grants and subgrants.**

**Standard 1.4: Develop criminal justice planning capabilities.**

**Standard 1.5: Encourage the participation of operating agencies and the public in the criminal justice planning process.**

... Planning agency supervisory boards exist as a result of an administrative regulation of the Law Enforcement Assistance Administration. The present role of such boards appears clouded by their limited success in the development of State plans. The question may then be asked: Should these boards have the authority to approve the Comprehensive plan? Many staff directors of the SPA's might prefer eliminating the policymaking powers of their supervisory boards, if only because of the considerable time that must be spent by staff working with board members to insure their understanding, agreement, and support for staff activity. Many SPA staff members can cite examples of a well-advised program having been thwarted by lack of support from its board members.

One major defect of the supervisory board is that comprehensive planning often is confused with comprehensive funding. A tendency exists for the component parts of the system to stake claims in the allocation of funds contrary to what an objective analysis of needs might dictate.

On the other hand, such incidents may supply the strongest argument for retention of policy boards at State and local levels. The demand for reform, which led to the Safe Streets Act, intended to bring about an evolution in the criminal justice system. If planning is to be realistic, a precondition may be that the agencies affected by such plans participate fully in their preparation. The administrator of an operating agency must be able to support a plan in its formulation if he is later to provide resources or policy direction in its eventual implementation.

No definite conclusions on this controversy are made in this report. The Commission urges LEAA and State and local governments to examine closely the proper role of supervisory boards. ...

Recommendation 1.1: Urge the Federal Government to apply these standards in its own planning.

# B: Criminal Justice System Information Systems

## INTRODUCTION

Organizing the Nation's criminal justice information into a useful body of knowledge has been talked about for decades but little has been done. Recently, however, the urgency of the Nation's crime problem, the availability of computers and data processing equipment, and the emergence of highly skilled professionals have made integrated local, State, and national information systems a possibility.

Along with many other disciplines, criminal justice has been experiencing an "information explosion" since the late 1960's. Its characteristics are steadily increasing capabilities for gathering, processing, and transmitting information, and steadily increasing information needs.

More frequent use of the computer and other automated technology is a national trend. In 1968, according to LEAA, there were just 10 States in the United States with automated State-level criminal justice information systems. By 1972, 47 States had operational automated information systems serving at least one component of the system.

The uses of information and computers vary from jury selection to police manpower allocation to crime-oriented planning to correctional program placement. A recent survey of States by LEAA identified 39 separate police functions, 23 separate court functions, and 13 separate corrections functions performed by automated information systems in one or more States or cities.

As more sophisticated and expensive systems develop, it is essential that their testing, implementation, and use proceed in an efficient and orderly manner. The Commission's standards on information systems represent a series of specific guidelines not only to professionals, but to elected officials and interested citizens as well.

## Information Needs

Criminal justice information needs involve data on offenders, crime events, and statistics on the operation of the criminal justice system.

For the effective administration of justice, information must be rapidly available on the identity, location, characteristics, and description of the known criminal offender. To this end, there is a continuing national effort to develop computerized criminal history (CCH) files that will be stored centrally and will be instantly available to any qualified agency in the law enforcement and criminal justice system in any State.

A second need is information about the event, the crime itself. At the Federal level, the National Crime Information Center (NCIC) is a rapid-response system that can provide local agencies with information on wanted felons plus identification numbers for stolen weapons, vehicles, and serial-numbered properties.

Collecting this information on criminals and stolen property and making it almost instantly available to the criminal justice system nationwide is itself not enough to mount or support a successful campaign to reduce and prevent crime. Planners in criminal justice have learned that they also need working information about what the police do, what occurs in courts and in the prosecutors' offices, and what are the events of importance occurring during the corrections phase of the criminal justice system. Moreover, planners found that they would like to assemble and integrate the information about these various separate activities so that criminal justice could indeed be looked at as a single entity, an operating system.

To this end, the Offender Based Transaction System (OBTS) has been developed and is recommended for use in all States and localities. No new information is required for OBTS, but rather a reordering and restructuring of currently available information. The OBTS follows the arrested person through the criminal justice system from the first encounter with the arresting officer until the final disposition of the case. The OBTS is not simply an assembly of facts; it is also an accounting of events, relationships, and time. When operative, the OBTS will be as informative about the criminal justice system as the NCIC is about crimes, and the CCH about criminals. . . .

INFORMATION SYSTEMS AND STATISTICS IN CRIMINAL JUSTICE

. . . On the national level, the pioneering efforts of the International Association of Chiefs of Police (IACP), in cooperation with the Federal Bureau of Investigation, led to the establishment in 1924 of the Uniform Crime Reporting Program (UCR) and in 1966 of the National Crime Information Center (NCIC). The NCIC was designed to supply an almost instantaneous response to inquiries about fugitives, wanted persons, stolen cars, stolen guns, and similar items. Thus, names and descriptions of persons and properties wanted by the police in one jurisdiction would be immediately available to law enforcement agencies elsewhere.

The next national effort was the System for Electronic Analysis and Retrieval of Criminal Histories (Project SEARCH), which was funded in 1969 by a grant from the Law Enforcement Assistance Administration. SEARCH initially developed pilot computer operations in seven cooperating States, and eventually extended the prototype system into 20 States.

The success of SEARCH led to the decision in December 1970 to establish a national operational system coordinated by the FBI. Under the FBI, the operational system has become the Computerized Criminal History (CCH) system, a part of the NCIC. When fully implemented, the CCH system will be able to supply criminal histories to any requesting agency anywhere in the country.

An increasing number of State and local agencies are acquiring or improving systems for collecting, processing, and disseminating data. Concerted efforts are being made to overcome the kind of traditional parochialism that for many years has hampered efforts to establish intra- and interagency information and statistics systems. It will still be several years before State and local legislation can be passed that will enable existing information systems technology to be applied to the criminal justice system throughout the country. . . .

## 2: Requirements for Criminal Justice Information

Contains no standards or recommendations.

## 3: Jurisdictional Responsibility

Standard 3.1: Coordinate the development of criminal justice information systems and make maximum use of collected data.

Standard 3.2: State Role in Criminal Justice Information and Statistics
Each State should establish a criminal justice information system that provides the following services:
1. On-line files fulfilling a common need of all criminal justice agencies, including wanted persons (felony and misdemeanor), and identifiable stolen items;

89

**2.** Computerized criminal history files for persons arrested for an NCIC-qualified offense, with on-line availability of at least a summary of criminal activity and current status of offenders;

**3.** Access by computer interface to vehicle and driver files, if computerized and maintained separately by another State agency;

**4.** A high-speed interface with NCIC providing access to all NCIC files;

**5.** All necessary telecommunications media and terminals for providing access to local users, either by computer-to-computer interface or direct terminal access;

**6.** The computerized switching of agency-to-agency messages for all intrastate users and routing (formating) of messages to and from qualified agencies in other States;

**7.** The collection, processing, and reporting of Uniform Crime Reports (UCR) from all law enforcement agencies in the State with report generation for the Federal Government agencies, appropriate State agencies, and contributors;

**8.** In conjunction with criminal history files, the collection and storage of additional data elements and other features to support offender-based transaction statistics;

**9.** Entry and updating of data to a national index of criminal offenders as envisioned in the NCIC Computerized Criminal History file; and

**10.** Reporting offender-based transaction statistics to the Federal Government.

**Standard 3.3: Local Criminal Justice Information Systems**

Every locality should be serviced by a local criminal justice information system which supports the needs of criminal justice agencies.

**1.** The local criminal justice information system (LCJIS) as defined in the commentary should contain information concerning every person arrested within that locality from the time of arrest until no further criminal justice transactions can be expected within the locality concerning that arrest.

**2.** The LCJIS should contain a record of every local agency transaction pertaining to a criminal offense concerning such persons, the reason for the transaction, and the result of each such transaction. A transaction is defined as a formal and public activity of a criminal justice agency, the results of which are a matter of a public record.

**3.** The LCJIS should contain the present criminal justice status for each individual under the cognizance of criminal justice agencies.

4. The LCJIS should provide prompt response to inquires from criminal justice agencies that have provided information to the data base of LCJIS.

5. If the LCJIS covers a geographical area containing contiguous jurisdictions, it should provide investigative field support to police agencies within this total area.

6. LCJIS should provide a master name index of persons of interest to the criminal justice agencies in its jurisdiction. This index should include identifying information concerning persons within the locality under the cognizance of criminal justice agencies.

7. The LCJIS should provide to the proper State agencies all information concerning postarrest offender statistical data as required.

8. The LCJIS should provide to the proper State agencies all postarrest data necessary to maintain a current criminal history record on persons arrested and processed within a locality.

9. If automated, LCJIS should provide telecommunications interface between the State CJIS and criminal justice agencies within its locality.

**Standard 3.4: Criminal Justice Component Information Systems**

Every component agency of the criminal justice system (police, courts, corrections) should be served by an information system which supports its intra-agency needs.

1. The component information system (CIS) should provide the rationale for the internal allocation of personnel and other resources of the agency.

2. The CIS should provide a rational basis for scheduling of events, cases, and transactions within the agency.

3. The CIS should provide the agency administrator with clear indications of changes in workload and workload composition, and provide the means of distinguishing between short-term variations (e.g., seasonal variations) and long-term trends.

4. The CIS should provide data required for the proper functioning of other systems as appropriate, and should retain only that data required for its own specific purposes.

5. The CIS should provide the interface between LCJIS and individual users within its own agency. This interface provision should include telecommunications facilities as necessary.

6. The CIS should create and provide access to files needed by its users that are not provided by the State or local criminal justice information systems to which it is interfaced.

7. The CIS should support the conduct of research and program evaluation to serve agency managers.

## 4: Police Information Systems

**Standard 4.1:** Define the proper functions of a police information system.

**Standard 4.2:** Utilize information to improve the department's crime analysis capability.

**Standard 4.3:** Develop a police manpower resource allocation and control system.

**Standard 4.4:** Specify maximum allowable delay for information delivery.

**Standard 4.5:** Insure that all police agencies participate in the Uniform Crime Reporting Program.

**Standard 4.6:** Expand collection of crime data.

... Arrest data used in conjunction with incident reports can produce specific area crime estimates of offender characteristics. Arrest rates must be used with extreme care. For example, an arrest is largely irrelevant to the deterrence of crime if the arresting officer fails to make a case to warrant prosecution. Thus, a primary measure should be "effective arrests"—those which result in prosecutable cases. Arrests which do not result in a defendant being "bound over" should not be used to evaluate the effectiveness of the police.

**Standard 4.7:** Insure quality control of crime data.

**Standard 4.8:** Establish a geocoding system for crime analysis.

## 5: Courts Information Systems

**Standard 5.1:** Provide background data and case history for criminal justice decisionmaking.

**Standard 5.2:** Provide information on case flow to permit efficient calendar management.

**Standard 5.3: Provide capability to determine monthly criminal justice caseflow and workloads.**

**Standard 5.4: Provide data to support charge determination and case handling.**

**Standard 5.5: Create capability for continued research and evaluation.**

**Standard 5.6: Record action taken in regard to one individual and one distinct offense and record the number of criminal events.**

## 6: Corrections Information Systems

**Standard 6.1: Define the needs of a corrections information system.**

**Standard 6.2: Apply uniform definitions to all like correctional data.**

**Standard 6.3: Design a corrections data base that is flexible enough to allow for expansion.**

**Standard 6.4: Collect certain data about the offender.**

**Standard 6.5: Account for offender population and movement.**

**Standard 6.6: Describe the corrections experience of the offender.**

**Standard 6.: Evaluate the performance of the corrections system.**

## 7: Operations

**Standard 7.1: Provide for compatible design of offender-based transaction statistics and computerized criminal history systems.**

**Standard 7.2: Develop single data collection procedures for offender-based transaction statistics and computerized criminal history data by criminal justice agencies.**

**Standard 7.3: Develop single data collection procedures for offender-based transaction statistics and computerized criminal history systems.**

**Standard 7.4: Restrict dissemination of criminal justice information.**

**Standard 7.5: Completeness and Accuracy of Offender Data**

Agencies maintaining data or files on persons designated as offenders shall establish methods and procedures to insure the completeness and accuracy of data, including the following:

1. Every item of information should be checked for accuracy and completeness before entry into the system. In no event should inaccurate, incomplete, unclear, or ambiguous data be entered into a criminal justice information system. Data is incomplete, unclear, or ambiguous when it might mislead a reasonable person about the true nature of the information.

2. A system of verification and audit should be instituted. Files must be designated to exclude ambiguous or incomplete data elements. Steps must be taken during the data acquisition process to verify all entries. Systematic audits must be conducted to insure that files have been regularly and accurately updated. Where files are found to be incomplete, all persons who have received misleading information should be immediately notified.

3. The following rules shall apply to purging these records:

   a. General file purging criteria. In addition to inaccurate, incomplete, misleading, unverified, and unverifiable items of information, information that, because of its age or for other reasons, is likely to be an unreliable guide to the subject's present attitudes or behavior should be purged from the system. Files shall be reviewed periodically.

   b. Purging by virtue of lapse of time. Every copy of criminal justice information concerning individuals convicted of a serious crime should be purged from active files 10 years after the date of release from supervision. In the case of less serious offenses the period should be 5 years. Information should be retained where the individual has been convicted of another criminal offense within the United States, where he is currently under indictment or the subject of an arrest warrant by a U.S. criminal justice agency.

   c. Use of purged information. Information that is purged but not returned or destroyed should be held in confidence and should not be made available for review

94

or dissemination by an individual or agency except as follows:

(1) Where necessary for in-house custodial activities of the recordkeeping agency or for the regulatory responsibilities of the Security and Privacy Council (Chapter 8);

(2) Where the information is to be used for statistical compilations or research studies, in which the individual's identity is not disclosed and from which it is not ascertainable;

(3) Where the individual to whom the information relates seeks to exercise rights of access and review of files pertaining to him;

(4) Where necessary to permit the adjudication of any claim by the individual to whom the information relates that it is misleading, inaccurate, or incomplete; or

(5) Where a statute of a State necessitates inquiry into criminal offender record information beyond the 5- and 10-year limitations.

When the information has been purged and the individual involved is subsequently wanted or arrested for a crime, such records should be reopened only for purposes of subsequent investigation, prosecution, and disposition of that offense. If the arrest does not terminate in conviction, the records shall be reclosed. If conviction does result, the records should remain open and available.

Upon proper notice, a criminal justice agency should purge from its criminal justice information system all information about which a challenge has been upheld. Further, information should be purged by operation of statute, administrative regulation or ruling, or court decision, or where the information has been purged from the files of the State which originated the information.

... For a variety of reasons, some of which are related to privacy considerations, it is sometimes desirable to eliminate entries or whole records from files. Various terms are used to describe this elimination process such as "expunging," "purging," or "closing" files. For our purposes the word "purge" will be used, meaning the elimination of an entry or a file from active storage and dissemination. The data may be physically retained under special controls but it is eliminated from current circulation.

To insure privacy, purging is desirable when information is potentially ambiguous or misleading, or when its continued active use would subvert other important values. Another goal affects rehabilitation. Having a criminal record carries with it a substantial social stigma and is a handicap to employment. In some circumstances the individual should be relieved of the burden of his past mistakes.

Under the legal doctrine of presumed innocence, mere initiation of a criminal proceeding against an individual without conviction or other adverse action does not warrant the stigma of a criminal record. Finally, entries or records should be purged when their reason for being ceases, e.g., a wanted person is found; a stolen car is recovered. Continuation of such entries in an automated information system exposes people to needless risks.

People change with time. Files which contain information about them, however, do not change unless someone changes them. Often old data presents an unreliable guide to a person's present attitudes and behavior. When such data becomes misleading, it should be removed from the system.

Certain types of information warrant special attention. Arrest data is potentially damaging to an individual and its retention in the information files should be carefully limited. In many cases it should not be kept at all.

From the point of view of privacy, retention of this data in ordinary (as opposed to intelligence) files imposes an undue burden. The possible harm to the individual outweighs the benefits to the criminal justice community of retaining arrest data without dispositions attached.

Sections b and c of this standard are derived from the Project SEARCH document entitled *Model Administrative Regulations for Criminal Offender Record Information.* The authors point out that the 5- and 10-year record retention periods were their reasonable assessment of what might constitute an adequate period of rehabilitation for various classes of offenders. The definition of what constitutes a "serious" and "less serious" crime is also open to interpretation. Each State administering such a standard would have latitude in establishing the definition.

If records are purged, it does not mean that they disappear in all cases for all time. In some instances, such as an arrest without a conviction, the records probably ought to be physically destroyed. In other instances, such as lapse of time, it may be enough to keep the records confidential. In some circumstances these records ought to be available for inspection and/or dissemination.

### Standard 7.6: Separation of Computerized Files

For systems containing criminal offender data, the following protections should apply:

1. All criminal offender record information should be stored in a computer dedicated solely to and controlled by criminal justice agencies.

2. Where existing limitations temporarily prevent the use of a solely dedicated computer, the portion of the computer used by the criminal justice system should be under the management control of a criminal justice agency and should be dedicated in the following manner.

   a. Files should be stored on the computer in such a manner that they cannot be modified, destroyed, accessed, changed, purged, or overlaid in any fashion by non-criminal-justice terminals.

   b. The senior criminal justice agency employee in charge of computer operations should write and install, or cause to have written and installed, a program that will prohibit inquiry, record updates or destruction of records from any terminal other than criminal justice system terminals which are so designated.

   The destruction of records should be limited to specifically designated terminals under the direct control of the criminal justice agency responsible for maintaining the files.

   c. The senior criminal justice agency employee in charge of computer operations should have written and installed a classified program to detect and store for classified output all attempts to penetrate any criminal offender record information system, program, or file.

   This program should be known only to the senior criminal justice agency, and the control employee and his immediate assistant, and the records of the program should be kept continuously under maximum security conditions. No other persons, including staff and repair personnel, should be permitted to know this program.

3. Under no circumstances should a criminal justice manual or computerized files be linked to or aggregated with non-criminal-justice files for the purpose of amassing information about a specified individual or specified group of individuals.

97

... While law enforcement generally argues for dedication, administrative agencies and data processing units generally promote consolidated or shared computer systems for economic reasons.

## The Protection of Personal Privacy

The case for dedicated systems is usually based on arguments related to insuring security of data and protecting personal privacy. Such arguments were rejected prior to the recent accumulation of criminal offender record files. Until about 1969, most criminal justice computer systems providing remote terminal access to computerized files contained fairly harmless data with regard to individual rights of privacy. These files, including wanted persons, stolen vehicles, etc., held very little potential for a damage due to unauthorized disclosure.

The computerized criminal history is a different issue. The potential for misusing a criminal record has been amply demonstrated in court cases involving nonautomated records, particularly affecting employment eligibility. Thoughtful law enforcement officials recognize the danger which comes with automation and the interstate exchange of records. The potential problems arising from disclosure, whether authorized or not, are increased many times over those existing in the manual systems.

Most modern law enforcement officials seriously desire to protect the individual's reasonable right to privacy, particularly in those cases where inclusion in the file may have been a mistake or an unjustified result of the formality of criminal justice processes.

There is, however, another concern. The consequences of improper disclosure are not well-known. It is possible, for example, that enough violations could cause the Congress to severely restrict these vital files. Congress has already made clear its opposition to a national data bank, and if it should appear that the criminal history file were a similar threat, similar action might be taken. This uncertainty is a serious concern of law enforcement officials.

To protect the individual, two points are relevant in a discussion of system dedication. First, by legislative authority the control of and responsibility for the collection, storage, and dissemination of criminal history records lies with law enforcement agencies. When a computer system storing such records is not dedicated to criminal justice, its control is not under a proper agency and, therefore, the complete control of the records has been disestablished. Lacking management control over system operators and programers, law enforcement officials cannot assure legislators that the data is properly protected. Few States have statutes providing sanctions for the improper disclosure of such records, so that the only control mechanisms are administrative.

Second, several questions arise from the interstate aspects of the system. A law enforcement agency in one State may be able to exercise inspection and control over a nondedicated system. However, to be sure that released data is properly controlled in other States having nondedicated systems, the agency would have to determine the exact treatment being afforded the data by all other States. While State law enforcement agencies are willing to protect data from counterpart agencies, they do not extend that willingness to agencies and persons outside law enforcement.

It should be pointed out that the concern for management control is more pertinent than the concern for dedication, but both could be satisfied if total management control would cover both hardware and personnel.

Dedication, commonly thought of as implying a totally separate system, can be further argued as a defense against the possible compiling of files—a procedure strongly opposed by the Congress and various other groups. If the system is dedicated, there is less chance that the efficiency-minded systems developer could create a single "dossier" on persons by linking welfare, tax, health, criminal justice, and other files. As long as criminal justice data is separately maintained, it is unlikely that coterminous files will be generated. While that threat could be neutralized simply by requiring file seperation, professionals in this field believe that the existence of coterminous files makes it hard to resist linking. Eagerness for more data about people and for cost reduction may endanger the individual's right to privacy.

Many of the concerns over nondedicated systems could be resolved through a combination of law and technical system design procedures. System security can be instituted as well in a nondedicated system as in a dedicated one. However, there is very little evidence that non-criminal-justice agencies will necessarily adopt the proposed protections, or that the criminal sanctions against misuse will be enacted. Law enforcement officials generally view the lack of statutory action as a noncredible response to the need for protection.

The uncertainty concerning the actual implications of the system, and the absence of proper statutory and administrative controls, raise unresolved arguments. These arguments may not be sufficient to justify a dedicated system to the extent that the security and privacy concerns can be otherwise satisfied. However, even if the security and privacy arguments can be dismissed, there is a second basic and meaningful justification for dedicated systems. For those installations having the workload to justify it, the fundamental reason for a dedicated system is responsiveness.

Criminal justice agencies, especially police and courts, have unique needs for information as opposed to most other government agencies. Their needs range from immediate to short-term (within hours). The failure to respond can impair the lives of officers and cause substantial variances in the administration of justice.

Criminal justice information systems are highly distributed systems, i.e., access to the system is generally by physically remote terminals relying on telephone line connections to the central computer. State criminal justice information systems tend to have hundreds of such remote terminals; multiagency systems at the local level have at least dozens of remote terminals.

The distribution of the system and the varying requirements imposed upon it tend to make criminal justice information systems unique. A number of features distinguish these systems from other governmental computer installations. A criminal justice information system serving police, courts, and corrections is perhaps the only governmental system where access is required 24 hours a day every day. The required response time, to return information to the user, is in the range of seconds for some users (especially police officers on the street).

The availability of the system, from the perspective of the user, must be very high. When operational personnel rely on the computer for their information about suspects or offenders as a basis for action (ranging from arrest to adjudication), the demand placed on the system is for almost perfect availability. This demand is complicated by the increasing tendency to link computers together, such as from the local police systems to a State system and then to NCIC. As computers are linked, reliability problems increase and require redundancy to assure that the total system availability is maintained. Because of this increased interface, it is difficult to consider individual local systems as isolated.

There is also a broad range of priorities concerning inquiries within a criminal justice information system. Response to an inquiry to determine whether a person is wanted or dangerous must be almost instantaneous, while an inquiry made by a prison official to obtain a criminal history as a routine part of a new prisoner's file is obviously not as urgent.

The uniqueness of criminal justice information systems, particularly those serving the police, can also be seen in the trend to use "front-end" or communications handling computers. The communications computer is essentially a minicomputer designed expressly for handling and routing of inquiries and messages in conjunction with a larger general purpose computer. Most major law enforcement information systems installations, including NCIC, are moving toward the use of these machines to handle the immense communications problems caused by the highly distributed nature of the information systems.

Because criminal justice information systems are unique and demand a higher level of service than other governmental users, it is possible that a dedicated system is a more logical alternative when cost and effectiveness are used as determinants for system design.

Even if some additional cost is required, it is the position of the Commission that the extra cost is justified by the improved potential for responsiveness that is possible with dedicated or decentralized systems. Ignoring cost, there is no question that dedicated systems can be more responsive to user needs.

The pursuit of responsiveness, even when supported by concern for security and privacy, does not dictate that every criminal justice computer installation should be dedicated. Even if cost and effectiveness analyses can generally show that dedicated systems are justified for criminal justice, there are limitations on how far such arguments can reach. An obvious constraint is agency size, which would prohibit justification of a computer installation—particularly one in which numerous remote terminals are involved.

Second, if the system or installation under consideration is not highly distributed, i.e., serves a single agency with a few terminals, or highly used, the arguments for uniqueness tend to be diffused. For example, a dedicated system serving a single police department in a small city, or a court installation serving only a few courts would not easily be justified on the basis of cost and effectiveness.

Further, for single-agency systems and perhaps even for local or regional multiagency systems, the security and privacy arguments lose some of their force. If systems develop as now envisioned, it will be State level systems which actually collect, store, and disseminate criminal history information. If this is the case, then the various local systems will contain, at most, temporary storage of criminal offender record information considered to be potentially hazardous. Under this mode of operation, computers at the local level are largely message routing or switching mechanisms connecting the user terminals with State systems.

The rationale for dedicated systems, then, appears to be strongest when statewide criminal justice information systems are used to contain criminal offender records (as stated in the standard).

If the State system, as the repository of criminal offender data, is dedicated, and is so controlled as to satisfy security and privacy concerns while providing needed responsiveness, it would then appear that local systems could reasonably be shared instead of dedicated. Under such circumstances the State level controlling agency must have the authority and capability to inspect and audit the shared systems to insure that the security and privacy procedures are adopted and effective. The resulting system, composed of dedicated computers at the State level and shared computers at the local level, would appear to satisfy most of the concerns regarding privacy and cost.

Dedication, of course, does not restrict the processes of procurement and computer equipment responsibility. A department of general services or other non-criminal-justice agency can "own" the computer and service it as a dedicated system, provided that the criminal justice agency which "owns" the data has sufficient management control over programers, operators, terminals and other input-output devices, and the storage media.

**Standard 7.7: Establish computer interfaces for criminal justice information systems.**

**Standard 7.8: Insure availability of criminal justice information systems.**

# 8: Privacy and Security

The past several years have witnessed a substantial growth in both the number and the size of criminal justice information systems. Some of these systems are manual, but most of the larger ones are automated in whole or in part. The criminal justice community now collects, stores, and disseminates millions of items of information about crimes, arrests, charges, prosecutions, convictions, sentences, correctional supervision, accused persons, stolen property, motor vehicle licenses and registrations, and similar data.

As the scope of the systems increases and as they become more automated, new problems arise. First, the increased dependence of criminal justice personnel on automated files leads to a greater awareness of the need to protect these files from accidental or intentional invasion or injury. A lapse in the security of an information system could cause serious damage to law enforcement operations.

Security is seriously compromised when unauthorized persons can add to, change, or delete entries in the information system, when authorized persons can make extracts of information within the system for private motives or personal gain, or when the contents of the system or some portion of the contents can be made known to unauthorized personnel. Some of the ways in which the system can be compromised are discussed later in the section on Security.

In this report, "privacy" refers to the protection of the interests of the people whose names appear for whatever reason in the contents of a criminal justice information system. "Security" refers to the protection of the system itself against intended or accidental injury or intrusion.

The protection of individual privacy is a highly important concern in the development of a national criminal justice information system. This protection of privacy can occur in part by ensuring that the information in the system is valid—in other words, no entries save those which are justified and accurate in every detail. But the greater protection will be provided by a complete assurance that the information in the system will not be freely distributed to all comers, but will be available only to law enforcement agencies with both the right and the need to know it.

In the past, a law enforcement agency's capacity to collect, store, process, access, and disseminate personal data was severely limited. The very inefficiency of the then-available systems was one of the chief protections of individual privacy. Scattering of data in many manual files, no linking of files, poor access, and storage problems all served to reduce the scope and effectiveness of pre-computer information systems. . . .

## Standard 8.1: Security and Privacy Administration

1. **State Enabling Act.** Each State should adopt enabling legislation for protection of security and privacy in criminal justice information systems. The enabling statute shall establish an administrative structure, minimum standards for protection of security and privacy, and civil and criminal sanction for violation of statutes or rules and regulations adopted under it.

2. **Security and Privacy Council.** Each State shall establish a Security and Privacy Council. Fifty percent of the members named to the Council shall be private citizens who are unaffiliated with the State's criminal justice system. The remainder shall include representatives of the criminal justice information systems and other appropriate government agencies. The Security and Privacy Council shall be vested with sufficient authority to adopt and administer security and privacy standards for criminal justice information systems.

The Council should further have authority to establish rules and regulations in this field and to sanction agencies which fail to comply with them.

Civil and criminal sanctions should be set forth in the enabling act for violation of the provision of the statute or rules or regulations adopted under it. Penalties should apply to improper collection, storage, access, and dissemination of criminal justice information.

3. **Training of System Personnel and Public Education.** All persons involved in the direct operation of a criminal justice information system should be required to attend approved courses of instruction concerning the system's proper use and control. Instruction may be offered by any agency or facility, provided that curriculum, materials, and instructors' qualifications have been reviewed and approved by the Council.

Minimum course time should be 10 hours for operators, with 15 hours required of immediate supervisors. Each operator or supervisor shall attend a course of instruction within a reasonable period of time after assignment to the criminal justice information system.

The Council should conduct a program of public education concerning the purposes, proper use, and control of criminal justice information. It may make available upon request facilities, materials, and personnel to educate the public about the purposes, proper use, and control of criminal justice information.

## Standard 8.2: Scope of Files
An item of data may be collected and stored in a criminal justice information system only if the potential benefits from its use outweigh the potential injury to privacy and related protected interests.

. . . One useful procedural limitation on data collection might be public disclosure and justification. Sometimes data is collected in a criminal justice information system without any well-defined uses for it. Open disclosure and justification of each item of information and how it will be used will tend to force a weighing of utility as against privacy considerations. . . .

## Standard 8.3: Access and Dissemination
1. General Limits on Access. Information in criminal justice files should be made available only to public agencies which have both a "need to know" and a "right to know." The user agency should demonstrate, in advance, that access to such information will serve a criminal justice purpose.

2. Terminal Access. Criminal justice agencies should be permitted to have terminal access to computerized criminal justice information systems where they have both a need and a right to know. Non-criminal justice agencies having a need or right to know or being authorized by statute to receive criminal justice information should be supplied with such information only through criminal justice agencies.

3. Certification of Non-Criminal-Justice Users. The Security and Privacy Council should receive and review applications from non-criminal-justice government agencies for access to criminal justice information. Each agency which has, by statute, a right to such information or demonstrates a need to know and a right to know in furtherance of a criminal justice purpose should be certified as having access to such information through a designated criminal justice agency.

4. Full and Limited Access to Data. Criminal justice agencies should be entitled to all unpurged data concerning an individual contained in a criminal justice information system. Non-criminal-justice agencies should receive only those por-

tions of the file directly related to the inquiry. Special precautions should be taken to control dissemination to non-criminal-justice agencies of information which might compromise personal privacy including strict enforcement of need to know and right to know criteria.

5. Arrest Without Conviction. All copies of information filed as a result of an arrest that is legally terminated in favor of the arrested individual should be returned to that individual within 60 days of final disposition, if a court order is presented, or upon formal notice from one criminal justice agency to another. Information includes fingerprints and photographs. Such information should not be disseminated outside criminal justice agencies.

However, files may be retained if another criminal action or proceeding is pending against the arrested individual, or if he has previously been convicted in any jurisdiction in the United States of an offense that would be deemed a crime in the State in which the record is being held.

6. Dissemination. Dissemination of personal criminal justice information should be on a need and right to know basis within the government. There should be neither direct nor indirect information to nongovernmental agencies or personnel. Each receiving agency should restrict internal dissemination to those employees with both a need and right to know.

Legislation should be enacted which limits questions about arrests on applications for employment, licenses, and other civil rights and privileges to those arrests where records have not been returned to the arrested individual or purged. Nor shall employers be entitled to know about offenses that have been expunged by virtue of lapse of time (see Standard 7.5).

7. Accountability for Receipt, Use, and Dissemination of Data. Each person and agency that obtains access to criminal justice information should be subject to civil, criminal, and administrative penalties for the improper receipt, use, and dissemination of such information.

The penalties imposed would be those generally applicable to breaches of system rules and regulations as noted earlier.

8. Currency of Information. Each criminal justice agency must ensure that the most current record is used or obtained.

This standard must be tempered by the current state of the law throughout the Nation. Any number of licensing boards, for example, have, by statute, the right and duty to review past criminal history information about prospective licenses. It would be difficult to justify such access on the grounds that a criminal justice purpose is being furthered. If this standard is to be followed, there must be legislative changes at the State level to limit access of agencies such as licensing boards.

Access can be direct or indirect in computer-based systems. In simple terms an agency can have a direct terminal hookup to a data base which it can access in whole or in part. To ensure security and privacy it would be advisable to limit such access to the most reliable terminal users. These, presumably would be criminal justice agencies. Non-criminal-justice agencies that are eligible to receive information would have to initiate inquiries and receive responses through criminal justice agency terminals.

The slight inconvenience that this roundabout method of access imposes on non-criminal-justice users is more then offset by the increased level of control over access. Agencies should require proof of right and need to access data before permitting use of their terminals by non-criminal-justice users. To simplify the process somewhat it would be helpful if some single State body could review eligibility for access to criminal justice data and certify non-crimininal-justice governmental users. . . .

Certain types of information warrant special attention. Arrest data is potentially very damaging to an individual and its retention should be carefully limited. In most instances it should not be kept in criminal justice information files.

From a privacy point of view, retention of this type of data in ordinary files imposes an undue burden. The possible harm to the individual outweighs the benefits to the criminal justice community of retaining arrest data without dispositions attached.

The economic and personal damage resulting from an arrest that does not lead to a conviction is unnecessary. The principle of presuming an individual's innocence until he is proven guilty should guide not only the criminal justice system, but other public and private systems as well. Confining questions on employment and other application forms to arrests where there are unreturned or unpurged records safeguards individual privacy. . . .

From a security and privacy perspective, there should be no dissemination outside the government. The media, credit rating services, and the like should not receive from criminal justice agencies, either directly or indirectly, any information from criminal justice information systems. It is virtually impossible to monitor and restrain the use of data once it passes out of the government. Where State law permits or even requires such dissemination, every effort should be made to repeal these statutes. The potential harm to the individual outweighs the benefit that private agencies receive from this type of information. Where security checks or clearances are required as a condition of employment on a government-funded job, the check or clearances should be made by government personnel. All security clearance decisions should also be made by government personnel and not private employers. . . .

## Standard 8.4: Information Review

1. **Right to Review Information.** Except for intelligence files, every person should have the right to review criminal justice information relating to him. Each criminal justice agency with custody or control of criminal justice information shall make available convenient facilities and personnel necessary to permit such reviews.

2. **Review Procedures.**

   a. Reviews should occur only within the facilities of a criminal justice agency and only under the supervision and in the presence of a designated employee or agent of a criminal justice agency. The files and records made available to the individual should not be removed from the premises of the criminal justice agency at which the records are being reviewed.

   b. At the discretion of each criminal justice agency such reviews may be limited to ordinary daylight business hours.

   c. Reviews should be permitted only after verification that the requesting individual is the subject of the criminal justice information which he seeks to review. Each criminal justice agency should require fingerprinting for this purpose. Upon presentation of a sworn authorization from the individual involved, together with proof of identity, an individual's attorney may be permitted to examine the information relating to such individual.

   d. A record of such review should be maintained by each criminal justice agency by the completion and preservation of an appropriate form. Each form should be completed and signed by the supervisory employee or agent present at the review. The reviewing individual should be asked, but may not be required, to verify by his signature the accuracy of the criminal justice information he has reviewed. The form should include a recording of the name of the reviewing individual, the date of the review, and whether or not any exception was taken to the accuracy, completeness, or contents of the information reviewed.

e. The reviewing individual may make a written summary or notes in his own handwriting of the information reviewed, and may take with him such copies. Such individuals may not, however, take any copy that might reasonably be confused with the original. Criminal justice agencies are not required to provide equipment for copying.

f. Each reviewing individual should be informed of his rights of challenge. He should be informed that he may submit written exceptions as to the information's contents, completeness or accuracy to the criminal justice agency with custody or control of the information. Should the individual elect to submit such exceptions, he should be furnished with an appropriate form. The individual should record any such exceptions on the form. The form should include an affirmance, signed by the individual or his legal representative, that the exceptions are made in good faith and that they are true to the best of the individual's knowledge and belief. One copy of the form shall be forwarded to the Security and Privacy Council.

g. The criminal justice agency should in each case conduct an audit of the individual's criminal justice information to determine the accuracy of the exceptions. The Council and the individual should be informed in writing of the results of the audit. Should the audit disclose inaccuracies or omissions in the information, the criminal justice agency should cause appropriate alterations or additions to be made to the information, and should cause notice of such alterations or additions to be given to the Council, the individual involved, and any other agencies in this or any other jurisdiction to which the criminal justice information has previously been disseminated.

3. Challenges to Information.

a. Any person who believes that criminal justice information that refers to him is inaccurate, incomplete, or misleading may request any criminal justice agency with custody or control of the information to purge, delete, modify, or supplement that information. Should the agency decline to do so, or should the individual believe the agency's decision to be otherwise unsatisfactory, the individual may request review by the Security and Privacy Council.

b. Such requests to the Council (in writing) should include a concise statement of the alleged deficiencies of the criminal justice information, shall state the date and result of any review by the criminal justice agency, and shall append a sworn verification of the facts alleged in the request signed by the individual or his attorney.

c. Each Council should establish a review procedure for such appeals that incorporates appropriate assurances of due process for the individual. . . .

**Standard 8.5: Adopt a system of classifying criminal justice system data.**

**Standard 8.6: Protect criminal justice information from environmental hazards.**

**Standard 8.7: Personnel Clearances**

1. The Security and Privacy Council shall also have the responsibility of assuring that a personnel clearance system is implemented and complied with by criminal justice agencies within the State.

2. Personnel shall be granted clearances for access to sensitive places and things in accordance with strict right to know and need to know principles.

3. In no event may any person who does not possess a valid sensitivity clearance indicating right to know have access to any classified places or things, and in no event may any person have access to places or things of a higher sensitivity classification than the highest valid clearance held by that person.

4. The possession of a valid clearance indicating right to know does not warrant unconditional access to all places and things of the sensitivity classification for which the person holds clearance. In appropriate cases such persons may be denied access because of absence of need to know.

5. In appropriate cases, all persons in a certain category may be granted blanket right to know clearance for access to places and things classified as restricted or confidential.

6. Right to know clearances for highly sensitive places and things shall be granted on a selective and individual basis only and must be based upon the strictest of personnel investigations.

7. Clearances shall be granted by the head of the agency

concerned and shall be binding only upon the criminal justice agency itself, except that right to know clearances for members of the Council shall be granted and shall be valid for all purposes where a need to know exists.

8. Clearances granted by one agency may be given full faith and credit by another agency; however, ultimate responsibility for the integrity of the persons granted right to know clearances remains at all times with the agency granting the clearance.

9. Right to know clearances are executory and may be revoked or reduced to a lower sensitivity classification at the will of the grantor. Adequate notice must be given of the reduction or revocation to all other agencies that previously relied upon such clearances.

10. It shall be the responsibility of the criminal justice agency with custody and control of classified places and things to prevent compromise of such places and things by prohibiting access to persons without clearances or with inadequate clearance status.

11. The Council shall carefully audit the granting of clearances to assure that they are valid in all respects, and that the categories of personnel clearances are consistent with right to know and need to know criteria.

12. Criminal justice agencies shall be cognizant at all times of the need periodically to review personnel clearances so as to be certain that the lowest possible clearance is accorded consistent with the individual's responsibilities.

13. To provide evidence of a person's sensitivity classification clearance, the grantor of such clearance may provide an authenticated card or certificate. Responsibility for control of the issuance, adjustment, or revocation of such documents rests with the grantor. In any event, all such documents must have an automatic expiration date requiring affirmative renewal after a reasonable period of time.

**Standard 8.8:** Establish criteria for the use of criminal justice information for research.

# 9: Technical System Design

**Standard 9.1:** Insure standardized terminology following the National Crime Information Center example.

**Standard 9.2:** Establish specific program language requirements for criminal justice information systems.

**Standard 9.3: Assure adequate teleprocessing capability.**

## 10: Strategy for Implementing Standards

**Standard 10.1:** Take legislative actions to support the development of criminal justice information systems.

**Standard 10.2:** Establish criminal justice user groups.

**Standard 10.3:** Establish a plan for development of criminal justice information and statistics systems at State and local levels.

**Standard 10.4:** Consolidate services to provide criminal justice information support where it is not otherwise economically feasible.

**Standard 10.5:** Consider conformity with all standards of this report as a condition for grant approval.

## 11: Evaluation Strategy

**Standard 11.1:** Monitor the criminal justice information system analysis, design, development, and initial steps leading to implementation.

**Standard 11.2:** Monitor the implementation of the system to determine the cost and performance of the system and its component parts.

**Standard 11.3:** Conduct evalutions to determine the effectiveness of information system components.

# C: Criminal Justice System Education and Training

## 12: Development, Implementation, and Evaluation of Education Curriculums and Training Programs for Criminal Justice Personnel

**Standard 12.1:** Develop, implement, and evaluate criminal justice education and training programs.

**Standard 12.2:** Establish criminal justice system curriculums.

112

# D: Criminal Justice System and the Law

## 13: Criminal Code Revision

**Standard 13.1: Revise criminal codes in States where codes have not been revised in the past decade.**

**Standard 13.2: Complete revision of criminal codes.**

... Every existing criminal statute should be examined to determine its utility in current law enforcement. If a statute can be combined with others into a single statute of broader coverage, this should be done. When administrative or civil remedies can meet the underlying need as well as or better than a criminal statute, the criminal section should be repealed and replaced by appropriate civil provisions. Law that prohibits conduct that a substantial minority, or majority, of the citizens finds tolerable or acceptable, could be considered for abolition, particularly if identifiable victims are not apparent. The objective should be a cohesive code that responds to current law enforcement needs—one that is free from vestiges of needs from a different era.

Removal of certain offenses from the criminal statutes is appropriate when the harms governed will be controlled properly by civil regulatory authority. In this category are the lesser vehicle-related offenses, violations of building codes, zoning ordinances, health and safety regulations, and evasion of State taxes. Revision of law in these areas is best left to a separate, specialized drafting group for each category.

On drug abuse, which includes the use of alcohol, commonly discussed approaches to repealing unobserved and unenforced penal provisions are tied to the existence of treatment centers for drug users and alcoholics. Although drug treatment centers and alcoholic detoxification centers can be expected to free the criminal justice system to deal with other pressing law enforcement needs, it must be recognized that such programs are not yet widespread.

Other widely unobserved and unenforced penal laws relate to consensual homosexual activity, patronizing of prostitutes, pornography, abortion, adultery, and gambling not organized for profit. Controversy frequently rages over attempts to remove such laws from the penal statutes. Because a consensus is needed in order to revise a criminal code, a drafting commission should initially avoid the detracting issues and establish the revisions on which there is agreement. Issues on which there will be no general agreement may be left for later consideration.

Suggested practical techniques for structuring a revision that is complete include: (1) initial preparation by a reporter of a projected table of contents; (2) the rating of offenses within a given chapter by a degree gradation, with the first degree category bearing the heaviest penalty; (3) use of clear language free of inherited legal jargon; (4) development of indexing and cross-referencing; and (5) creation of separate provisions for exceptions from coverage.

To insure that the revised code will be well structured, code draftsmen should be instructed on the drafting commission's express objectives. Acts that the commission wishes to penalize should be enumerated, along with indications of specific exclusions from coverage.

## Standard 13.3: Penalty Structures

**A revised substantive code should simplify the penalty structure, impose procedural controls on the exercise of discretion in sentencing, and encourage use of probation where circumstances so warrant.**

... Moreover, the law in many States authorizes or requires high maximum and minimum terms of imprisonment and imposes limitations on probation or parole eligibility for certain classes of offenders. Thus release from imprisonment is controlled not by the character and needs of the convict as determined by a paroling authority after a period of supervision, but by the arbitrary decision of a criminal court judge at the time of conviction. That decision in itself might almost guarantee the return to crime by an offender who has been imprisoned so long that he lost the ability to function normally in society. Conversely, even the most dangerous criminal has to be released at the expiration of the statutory maximum period, less good conduct allowances.

The new codes avoid mandatory minumum sentences and other statutory restrictions on the discretion of paroling authorities to release a convict at an optimum time to prevent the commission of repeated crimes. Under new codes, administration of penal fines and court costs is also geared to the economic realities of the defendant's abilities and family responsibilities so that a defendant is not imprisoned and his family forced onto the welfare rolls because the criminal law system imposes on him an impossible financial responsibility. . . .

## Capital Punishment

Consideration of the scope of aggravated murder and the extent of nonculpability because of mental disease or disorder will be more difficult in a State with the death penalty than in one in which the death penalty has been abolished. However, the character of the debate is markedly different today in light of the Supreme Court's decision that capital punishment in its present form constitutes a denial of equal protection and a form of cruel and unusual punishment. The only option open to a legislature appears to be to require capital punishment for all persons convicted of the crime to which it attaches, without any exercise of discretion. Whether any State will adopt so draconian a punishment for any crime remains to be seen.

## Concurrent Terms

Some jurisdictions have long permitted the trial judge a choice between concurrent sentences, in which separate penalties imposed for different crimes run at the same time, and consecutive sentences, in which case sentence maxima and minima are added together to a total that in some instances is the functional equivalent of a life sentence (and may be so intended). Parole eligibility will accrue much earlier under concurrent sentencing.

Revised criminal codes frequently adopt concurrent sentencing as the standard. This reflects in part the belief that most cumulated crimes arise from one transaction or set of transactions, so that the most serious offense committed is likely to provide a satisfactory maximum term of imprisonment. In part, the assumption is that early parole eligibility is needed if rehabilitation is even a slight possibility. If some defendants must be segregated for longer periods, the appropriate statutory alternatives are higher maximum sentences for dangerous crimes or recidivism statutes authorizing increased maximum penalties for confirmed criminals.

Only one special context seems to call for the possibility of cumulated sentences: crimes committed during imprisonment, the crime of escape from prison, and crimes committed during escape. If most of or the entire term of imprisonment assessed for these crimes is to be served concurrently with a sentence imposed earlier, there is little deterrent to prison crime or escape efforts, particularly on the part of those sentenced originally for long prison terms. Cumulative sentences are standard in the escape context. However, even cumulated terms mean nothing to a convict under a mandatory life sentence; in this case one confronts again the question of the death penalty. . . .

## Standard 13.4: Revise Correction Laws

. . . Classic criminal law theory identifies four purposes of criminal sanctions: (1) retribution against the offender for the harm he has done, the so-called lex talionis; (2) deterrence of future criminal acts, which may be either special deterrance against the defendant to prevent him from committing crime again, or general deterrence aimed at other unidentified persons who might be tempted to do what the defendant has done; (3) segregation of a dangerous offender so that he has no opportunity to harm again; and (4) rehibilitation of the offender so that he will not commit future crimes. Two of these objectives—deterrence and segregation—are not necessarily mutually exclusive. However, there is inevitable polarity between retribution and rehabilitation, and this is the source of disagreement in a drafting group.

Another source of division is that citizens not only must be protected by the criminal law, but must feel protected. If citizens believe that the criminal code fails to punish sufficiently, they will oppose it even though an objective observer would note complete safety from harm. Ultimate acceptance or rejection of the proposed code may depend on whether or not legislators and citizen constituents believe the new code will afford greater protection from harm. The same feelings of uneasiness or confidence also tend to determine the reactions of drafting commission members to the reporters' drafts. An underlying distrust will not always surface; however, a reporter should expect to encounter it at any time, since there is no way to forecast which proposed action may cause an emotional volcano to erupt.

## Standard 13.5: Create a drafting body to carry out criminal code revision.

## Standard 13.6: Revise criminal procedure laws.

## Standard 13.7: Support drafted criminal law legislation with interpretive commentaries.

**Standard 13.8: Assure smooth transition to the new law through education.**

**Standard 13.9: Continue law revision efforts through a permanent commission.**

# Chapter IV

# Community Crime Prevention

The term "community crime prevention" can mean citizens patroling their neighborhoods or conducting campaigns to improve streetlighting and reduce auto thefts. The term also can mean the renovation of slums, the improvement of schools, jobs for the unemployed, and the counseling of troubled young people.

These and many other activities are part of community crime prevention. Any public or private activity outside the conventional criminal justice system which is directed toward reducing crime is, in fact, community crime prevention.

## Major Recommendations

The Commission's standards and recommendations regarding community crime prevention cover such diverse but critical areas as:

- Citizen volunteers in criminal justice.
- Expanded public employment programs in areas of high unemployment.
- Career education in elementary and secondary schools.
- Individualized community drug abuse treatment services.
- Physical design of buildings, parks, and thoroughfares to reduce criminal opportunities.
- Ethical codes of conduct for governmental officials.

These varied approaches to community crime prevention are based on the assumption that there is no single solution to the crime problem. Indeed, actions designed to combat one type of crime may have no impact on another. A methadone maintenance program, as an example, might be useful in preventing shoplifting by addicts but may have no significant effect on the murder rate. A streetlighting campaign may prevent auto theft and vandalism but may not reduce aggravated assault.

Similarly, one type of program may not be beneficial to all offenders. Alternative strategies must be designed to deal with particular cases—treatment programs for the addict and the alcoholic; special counseling for the addict and the alcoholic; special counseling for the young offender; and job training and placement for the unemployed offender.

The following synopsis of the Commission's *Report on Community Crime Prevention* focuses on three areas of activity outside the traditional criminal justice system that can contribute significantly to reducing serious, high-fear crime. These areas are citizen action, the delivery of public services, and the reduction of criminal opportunities. In a fourth and final area, integrity in government, the Commission presents recommendations for reducing another serious crime problem—official corruption.

# Citizen Action

Action by private citizens is at the heart of community crime prevention.

Citizens can improve education, employment, and recreation; citizens can devise programs to reduce criminal opportunities by designing safer buildings; citizens can insure the integrity of elected and appointed officials.

In recent months, citizens in many communities have contributed directly to the prevention and reduction of crime by:

• Conducting campaigns to improve streetlighting.

• Serving as volunteers in probation departments or corrections institutions.

• Providing employment and training for ex-offenders, disadvantaged young people, or ex-addicts.

• Counseling young people on such diverse problems as drug abuse, alcohol, and family disputes.

• Reporting crime to the police and serving as volunteers in neighborhood security programs.

No national inventory exists of the time and effort Americans freely give to others and to their communities. The Commission's staff, however, reviewed hundreds of accounts of successful citizen action projects reported in daily newspapers, magazines, professional newsletters, and scholarly journals. It followed up the most promising projects with hundreds of discussions with people who have knowledge and experience in these areas, and, in the case of several, with onsite visits. The staff also interviewed dozens of community leaders, some heading local efforts and others affiliated with national organizations such as the U.S. Chamber of Commerce, the National Council on Crime and Delinquency, the Junior Chamber of Commerce, and the National Alliance for Safer Streets.

The Commission drew two important conclusions from its investigation. First, private group activity specifically directed at preventing crime is increasing. Although no hard statistics are available, during the late 1960's and early 1970's hundreds of local projects emerged in communities across the country. Second, most citizen efforts are designed to complement, not supplant the existing operation of the criminal justice system. Although occasionally given wide publicity, extralegal vigilante efforts are not characteristic of most citizen crime prevention activity.

The benefits of responsible citizen action appear to be many. A community spirit often develops when neighbors join together to solve common problems. Volunteers frequently can provide more personal attention and care to a particular problem or individual than can a harried professional. Citizen involvement also can plug many holes in the delivery of needed community services that otherwise would be unavailable because of lack of funds, personnel, or other resources.

Citizen action crime prevention efforts often fall into three general areas: neighborhood security, volunteers in criminal justice, and multipurpose community improvement activities. Each of these types will be discussed below.

## Neighborhood Security

In many communities the only response to crime has been a retreat behind locks, bars, alarms, and guards. Although these prophylactic measures may be steps in self-protection, they can lead to a lessening of the bonds of mutual assistance and neighborliness.

Other communities, however, have developed collective means of protection in addition to traditional self-protection measures. The principle behind neighborhood security efforts

120

is group action to make blocks, apartments, streets, and parks safer from and less vulnerable to crime.

In some areas, citizens have banded together to report crimes in progress or suspicious activities in their neighborhoods. Organizations offer rewards to those reporting criminal activity or hold special crime prevention clinics to reduce robbery and burglary. Citizens have initiated campaigns to educate people to the seriousness of shoplifting or to give tips on preventing auto theft.

In Roxbury, Mass., residents joined a self-help program by signing house-watch contracts under which they agree to be alert to and report to the police suspicious behavior in the neighborhood. To combat increased burglaries, thefts, and robberies in the area, they refused to buy or even tolerate the sale of stolen goods. They also marked belongings with social security numbers, so that stolen goods could be identified and returned. This evolving sense of community was in evidence in early 1972 when the planned opening of a bar by alleged organized crime elements was successfully opposed by the neighborhood.

Often the byproduct of group action is a heightened sense of security. Tenants in a New York City apartment building, for example, called a meeting in response to a series of burglaries. They not only resolved to watch out for each other but found that getting to know each other had enhanced their safety. As one tenant remarked, "... we now have friends to run to, not just faceless, nameless neighbors.... I now know when to be suspicious of people I pass in the halls and when to smile and say hello."[1]

## Volunteer Programs in Courts and Corrections

While some citizen efforts are designed to increase the safety of persons and property or to prevent certain crimes, other efforts are aimed at strengthening agencies in the criminal justice system.

Perhaps the largest group of citizens assisting the system are volunteers who work in the courts or in corrections institutions. In the early 1960's, a few pioneer courts began to use volunteers to provide desperately needed probation services. The idea spread quickly and the national director of Volunteers in Probation estimates that today there are about 250,000 volunteers working in courts, prisons, and juvenile

[1] "The Cities Lock Up," *Life Magazine* (November 19, 1971), p. 32.

institutions. These volunteers, most of whom work individually with offenders, provide services and counseling not otherwise available.

Volunteers in San Diego County, Calif., contributed more than 30,000 hours of service to probationers in 1971; in Royal Oak, Mich., some 500 individuals furnished more than $250,000 a year in services on a $17,000 budget from the city. When probationers from Royal Oak were compared with probationers from a nonvolunteer court, it was found that Royal Oak probationers were less hostile and had substantially lower recidivism rates: approximately 15 percent of the Royal Oak probationers committed subsequent offenses, compared with nearly 50 percent of the other group.[2] Massachusetts, noting the success of these programs, has passed a law that requires the commissioner of probation in that State to initiate and develop volunteer programs.

Studying the court system is another effective citizen action approach. Groups of housewives, professionals, and businessmen have undertaken court-watching programs, studies of the pretrial process, or surveys of courtroom efficiency. Based on these studies, citizens have recommended more efficient methods of selecting judges, reducing court backlog, and improving juvenile care procedures.

The Washington, D. C., Pretrial Justice Program, for example, is concerned with practical alternatives to pretrial detention. Studies and reforms have been suggested to minimize the use of pretrial detention consistent with public safety. The group has helped those detained in jail by reporting and attempting to resolve cases of error and delay, and by securing the admission of some defendants into community programs. Other citizen groups have implemented projects to divert defendants from the criminal justice system at a point between arrest and trial, thereby reducing caseloads.

Citizens now are also a part of a substantial movement for correctional reform. Many citizen groups such as the National Council on Crime and Delinquency (NCCD) are concerned with educating the public and legislators to the potential benefits of work release programs, community-based corrections, and other diversion measures.

Citizen organizations are promoting correctional reforms by conducting jail studies, by informing others about the problems faced by offenders while in prison and after release,

---

[2] National Institute of Mental Health, "Royal Oak, Michigan, Municipal Court Research Study," p. 3.

by encouraging the construction of halfway houses and community-based facilities, and by supporting reform legislation.

In one project, citizen volunteers inspect jails in Jefferson City, Mo., and report their findings to the county court. As a result, 12 antiquated jails have been closed; the citizens' group has recommended that they be replaced with new regional facilities.

## Community Improvement

Successful citizen programs have been directed against the building blocks of crime—unemployment, substandard education, drug abuse, and inadequate or nonexistent recreational opportunities. Programs include encouraging dropouts to stay in school, tutoring students with learning problems, and offering alternative educational experiences such as street academies or vocational programs.

In Philadelphia, Pa., for example, the Urban Coalition has developed a vocational program for inner city youth. In this program, the business community and the school system cooperate to train a youth for a specific job in a specific industry. Other citizens counsel youths, establish scholarship funds, or work to familiarize students with the law.

Many businessmen have assumed responsibility for crime prevention by hiring disadvantaged youths and by employing ex-offenders. Some businesses have agreed to fill a certain percentage of their openings with the hard core unemployed. The JOBS program of the National Alliance of Businessmen had placed almost 1 million disadvantaged youths in businesses, unions, and industry.

The religious community, with its concern for human dignity and justice, has much to offer in crime prevention resources. Some congregations have contributed their buildings, facilities, and equipment for community programs, especially those for children and youth.

In Chicago, Ill., for example, an inner city parish has become over a period of years a service center to the entire community. A child care center and Head Start program in the church have helped neighborhood children through their preschool and school years, while also allowing mothers to obtain job training and employment in lieu of welfare assistance. A drug awareness center has been opened in the basement of the rectory, and sports and social activities are supervised in the parish community center.

There are also multipurpose citizen groups that become en-

123

gaged in a wide variety of neighborhood security, criminal justice volunteer, and general community improvement activities.

In one example of effective citizen mobilization, the Indianapolis Crime Crusade has organized 80,000 women who have been instrumental in the return of more than 1,000 dropouts to school, formed a court-watching program, supported increases in police salaries, and, with the Jaycees, initiated a campaign for improved streetlighting.

In the area of government reform, the Better Government Association in Chicago, Ill., has investigated instances of waste and inefficiency, as well as corruption, in government. The group estimates that up to 60 percent of their investigations are effective and result in the passage of new laws, changes in regulations, or indictments of corrupt officials. Group representatives claim that these investigations saved taxpayers up to $50 million in 1970.

The importance of citizen involvement at the neighborhood level is reflected in the 1974 New York City budget, which carries a $5 million proposal for a block security plan. Under the program, block associations and tenant groups would develop their own crime prevention plans and the city would provide the funds to implement them. Such support might involve direct funding, as in New York City, or it might mean making public facilities available for group meetings or providing public recognition for outstanding service to the community.

The Commission recommends that every citizen contribute to local community crime prevention efforts. Government agencies should encourage and support citizen action programs to prevent and reduce crime. Existing community organizations should explore ways they can relate their activities to crime prevention.

# Government Responsiveness

Some of the problems faced by the criminal justice system can be alleviated to some degree by responsive action on the part of other segments of government.

Open, responsive governments can encourage citizen involvement in crime prevention. When citizens find government complex, confusing, and uninviting, a chasm can develop between city hall and the community. The burden of cutting through the red tape of an impersonal bureaucracy falls primarily on those most dependent on its services and least equipped to deal with its complexity—the elderly, the poor, the uneducated, those with language barriers, and minority and ethnic populations unfamiliar with governmental structures.

To maximize government responsiveness, the Commission recommends that government units open neighborhood offices and that local governments develop complaint centers. These programs, together with a greater flow of information, can bring the community together.

**City governments should establish neighborhood facilities, such as multiservice centers and "little city halls," to aid in dispensing government services and to improve communication between citizens and government agencies.**

In this way citizens can receive effective services close to their homes with a minimum of bureaucratic red tape. A neighborhood center can help to convince citizens that government is concerned about their needs. The objectives of decentralization are a more citizen-oriented service delivery system and increased citizen participation in government.

The concept of decentralized municipal services is not new. Since the late 1920's, branch city halls that provide most city services have been operating in Los Angeles, Calif., to reach more conveniently more than 40 subcommunities in the city.

Before community involvement in governmental processes can become a reality, community members must be able to obtain information on which government decisions and programs are based. Informing citizens about the activities of the local government will help assure the public that the government is working in its best interest.

The Commission believes that local governments should provide access to such information by:

● Enacting "right to know" laws that provide citizens with open and easy access to agency regulations, audits, minutes, and other pertinent information.

● Permitting local radio and television stations to cover official and public meetings on a regular basis.

● Holding public hearings to acquire an understanding of the real concerns of the community.

An orderly and effective mechanism for general redress of citizen grievances will also bring local government closer to its citizens. Individual agencies often do not have the time or personnel to respond to complaints. In addition, citizens sometimes find bureaucracy so confusing they are unable to locate or identify the department that could help them. Citi-

125

zens' attitudes toward government are adversely affected when local governments rely solely on haphazard procedures to respond to citizen complaints, and when there is no regular monitoring to insure the public is served adequately.

Municipal governments should establish a central office of complaint and information to improve government effectiveness and to permit citizens to obtain information and direction on any problem with a minimum of "red tape."

The Commission also proposes the establishment of mass media action line programs that will assist government officials to respond to citizen requests and complaints. Direct exchange can allow the public to become familiar with city officials and to gain insight into the complexities of governmental processes. It also will help insure greater accountability to the public of elected and appointed officials.

The remoteness of government and a declining sense of community have been noted as two significant characteristcs of urban America. They are undoubtedly linked, but they need not become permanent conditions. There are signs of a renewed interest among citizens in the problems—including crime—of their cities and towns. A responsive government can help sustain this interest.

# Delivery of Public Services

The need to deliver all public services in a comprehensive fashion is becoming increasingly apparent in urban areas. Education, employment, health, sanitation, and criminal justice agencies frequently have found themselves addressing mere segments of larger problems. An illustration of the fact that social ills rarely occur in isolation comes from the Model Cities Program of the Department of Housing and Urban Development. What follows is a profile of a 1970 neighborhood typical of many depressed areas in cities and towns across the country.

Unemployment in the low-income model neighborhood (MN) is 6.2 percent, compared with 3.4 percent for the entire city. Ten of the 11 schools in the target area have mental maturity, reading, and arithmetic norms one and two grades below the national average. The high school dropout rate is 16 percent, compared with 9 percent for the school system as a whole. Only 4 percent of the model area housing is "standard." Existence of outside toilets attests to primitive conditions.

Overcrowding is characteristic in the model neighborhood. Since 1960, the population has increased but the number of housing units has decreased. The target area has only three supervised playgrounds with a combined area of 2.6 acres. Thus 5.9 percent of the total city-supervised playground area serves 15 percent of the city's population. There are 8 miles of unpaved streets and sidewalks in the MN, in sharp contrast to the historic section of the city, with its beautiful old buildings and well-kept parks and gardens.

Health conditions in the MN are below the city and county rates. In 1968, infant mortality rates per 100,000 persons were 42.5 in the county and 60 in the MN; tuberculosis rates were 42 in the county and 105 in the MN; infectious syphilis rates were 27.6 in the county and 115 in the MN.

Dependence on public welfare is heavy, yet few social service agencies are located within the MN or have outreach services there. Residents complain of inadequate coordination between the public and private agencies that provide social services.

Finally, life in the target area is threatened by a high incidence of crime. With only 15 percent of the population, the MN experiences 33 percent of the homicides and rapes and 27 percent of the felonious assaults. Juvenile delinquency, as represented by the number of arrests, is also high. The arrest rate of persons under 18 years of age in the target area is 48.2 per 1,000, compared with 33.8 per 1,000 for the whole city.

As the Model City example suggests, public services are not always adequate to meet the pressing needs of many individuals. Those in need of public services are likely to have multiple problems: youths involved in crime are often dropouts and unemployed; a drug-dependent person may require not only medical treatment, but employment counseling and skill training as well.

In some neighborhoods important services are simply not available or are severely deficient. Low income areas often suffer while middle- and upper-class neighborhoods receive a high level of service.

**The Commission believes municipal services should be allocated to neighborhoods on the basis of need.**

Achieving this end will require the expenditure of sufficient funds to maintain equally effective services in all areas of the city or jurisdiction. Also needed is a means of coordinating

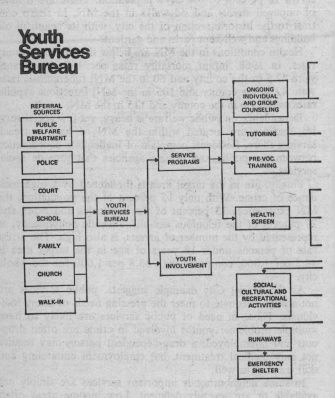

# Youth Services Bureau

REFERRAL SOURCES

- PUBLIC WELFARE DEPARTMENT
- POLICE
- COURT
- SCHOOL
- FAMILY
- CHURCH
- WALK-IN

YOUTH SERVICES BUREAU

SERVICE PROGRAMS

- ONGOING INDIVIDUAL AND GROUP COUNSELING
- TUTORING
- PRE-VOC. TRAINING
- HEALTH SCREEN

YOUTH INVOLVEMENT

- SOCIAL, CULTURAL AND RECREATIONAL ACTIVITIES
- RUNAWAYS
- EMERGENCY SHELTER

Source: Derived from material developed by the
Youth Development and Delinquency Prevention
Administration, U.S. Department of Health, Education, and Welfare

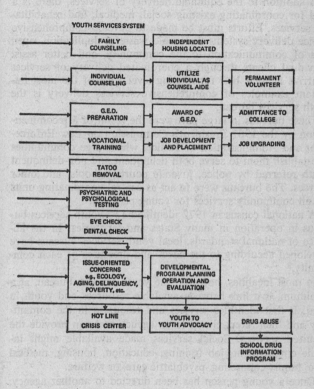

YOUTH SERVICES SYSTEM

FAMILY COUNSELING → INDEPENDENT HOUSING LOCATED

INDIVIDUAL COUNSELING → UTILIZE INDIVIDUAL AS COUNSEL AIDE → PERMANENT VOLUNTEER

G.E.D. PREPARATION → AWARD OF G.E.D. → ADMITTANCE TO COLLEGE

VOCATIONAL TRAINING → JOB DEVELOPMENT AND PLACEMENT → JOB UPGRADING

TATOO REMOVAL

PSYCHIATRIC AND PSYCHOLOGICAL TESTING

EYE CHECK DENTAL CHECK

ISSUE-ORIENTED CONCERNS e.g. ECOLOGY, AGING, DELINQUENCY, POVERTY, etc. → DEVELOPMENTAL PROGRAM PLANNING OPERATION AND EVALUATION

HOT LINE CRISIS CENTER → YOUTH TO YOUTH ADVOCACY → DRUG ABUSE → SCHOOL DRUG INFORMATION PROGRAM existing social, medical, and rehabilitative services so that persons may be treated comprehensively.

## Social Service Delivery Mechanisms: Youth Services Bureaus

In addition to the equitable delivery of services, there is a need for coordinating existing social, medical, and rehabilitative services. Efforts must be made to develop comprehensive service delivery systems that avoid wasteful duplication, open lines of communication to the community, and better assist individual clients through a coordinated delivery of services to arrive at their best functioning level. One of the most important examples of comprehensive services delivery is the youth services bureau.

These bureaus in large part were the result of a recommendation by the 1967 President's Commission on Law Enforcement and Administration of Justice, which urge communities to establish them to serve both delinquent and non-delinquent youth referred by police, juvenile courts, schools, and other sources. The bureaus were to act as central coordinating units for all community services for young people.

A national census in 1972 identified 150 youth services bureaus in operation in many States and territories. In the absence of national standards, local youth services bureaus have developed according to the needs and pressures of each community.[8]

In most localities, however, the youth services bureau, at a minimum, is a link between available resources and youth in need. It first identifies services and resources in the community and then refers clients to an agency that can provide the required services. Social services made available might include employment, job training, education, housing, medical care, family counseling, psychiatric care, or welfare.

Once a young person has been directed to another agency, the youth services bureau follows up to assure that adequate services are being provided. The bureau acts as a services broker, matching the young person with the service he or she needs. When services are not available through governmental

8 William Underwood, *A National Study of Youth Service Bureaus*, U.S. Department of Health, Education, and Welfare, Youth Development and Delinquency Prevention Administration (December 1972).

or volunteer sources, they may be purchased from private agencies or independent professionals.

In Worcester, Mass., for example, coordination of services for individual youths is taking place through case conferences. Representatives of all agencies involved with a young person meet to gain a complete view of the youth's problems and to develop a comprehensive plan to meet his needs. In some instances, the youth or the youth and his parent attend the case conference. In order to strengthen the youth's responsibility, he is encouraged to contribute to the decisions that will affect him. After the youth is referred to another agency, the bureau systematically follows up to assure that services are being provided.

Specialized services often are needed to help a child and to keep him out of trouble with the law. A child might need services that are not available in the community, such as an alternative educational experience, career training, drug treatment, a group residence, or psychiatric services. It is frequently the responsibility of the youth services bureau to identify these gaps in service and to promote the development of needed resources.

The Youth Development Service in Billings, Mont., as an example, provides little direct service to youth. Instead, it brings agencies together to develop community priorities, to eliminate service duplication, and to redirect resources when current projects are inappropriate. The Youth Advocacy Program in South Bend, Ind., attempts to influence youth-serving agencies to develop innovative programs. Field workers are assigned to five agencies—the recreation department, schools, a family and child agency, city government, and Model Cities—with the task of making them more responsive to youth.

Youth services bureaus sometimes provide specific services themselves when the services are not easily available through other public or private agencies. A number of bureaus, for example, provide temporary shelter for runaways. In Los Angeles County, Calif., the Basset Youth Service Bureau sponsors a free clinic in conjunction with other community groups, staffed primarily with volunteers. The clinic includes a counseling center in addition to an outpatient medical clinic. Venereal diseases, unwanted pregnancies, and drug use are the most frequently treated medical problems.

Clients come to youth services bureaus from a variety of sources. Individuals may be referred to bureaus by schools or other community agencies, or young people may come to the bureau on their own seeking help. The police and juvenile court can also be major sources of referrals. A nationwide sample of more than 400 cases from 28 youth services bureaus showed that 13 percent of the referrals were from law enforcement; 30 percent were referred by self, friend, or family; and the remainder were referred by schools and other public and private agencies.[4] (See Youth Services Bureau Chart.)

Enough information has now been gathered on existing youth services bureaus for the Commission to recommend that bureaus be established in communities experiencing serious youth problems. Each year a vast number of young people become involved in the justice system for acts that are not crimes for adults: incorrigibility, truancy, running away, and even stubbornness. In addition, many youths are processed through the juvenile justice system for minor offenses that are neither recurring nor a serious threat to the community. Such behavior is often an indication that a young person needs special attention, but not necessarily punitive treatment.

Many of what are now considered delinquency or predelinquency problems should be redefined as family, educational, or welfare problems and diverted from the juvenile justice system. Such diversions can relieve overburdened probation offices and courts and allow them to concentrate on offenders that need serious attention. In addition, diversion through youth services bureaus can avoid the unnecessary "delinquent" label that frequently accompanies involvement with the juvenile court.

Unfortunately, existing youth services bureaus have been underutilized as a diversionary resource by law enforcement. In many communities, police seldom refer young people to community agencies. In 31 interviews with juvenile officers in one large metropolitan area, fully one quarter of the officers could name no community resources and only two of the 31 used direct referral practices. Some police agencies have a policy of no diversion—all arrested juveniles are processed in the system.[5]

Youth services bureaus should make a particular effort to attract the diversionary referrals from the juvenile justice system. At the same time, law enforcement agencies and courts

[4] *Ibid.*

[5] Malcolm W. Klein, "Issues in Police Diversion of Juvenile Offenders: A Guide for Discussion" (unpublished paper, University of Southern California), pp. 7, 16.

should make policy changes that would allow for the diversion of every juvenile who is not an immediate threat to public safety and who voluntarily accepts referral to a youth services bureau.

The Youth Service Project in San Antonio, Tex., provides an example of how an administrative policy change in bringing about diversion in that city. The police chief has ordered his officers to deliver to one of the three neighborhood youth centers in the city juveniles picked up for such offenses as glue or paint sniffing, liquor violations, and running away.

Accessibility of the bureaus' offices to law enforcement is another asset in encouraging diversion. Until recently, the Youth Service Bureau of Greensboro, Inc., in Greensboro, N.C., was across the street from the police department. Not only did this enable bureau staff to pick up "paper referrals" each day from the police department, but it also increased understanding between the police department's juvenile officers and the bureau staff during the youth services bureau's developmental stages.

Legislation is another means of overcoming the reluctance of law enforcement and court personnel to utilize diversionary alternatives. Legislation accompanied by State funding also would increase awareness of the youth services bureau concept and could stimulate the creation of bureaus in the less affluent and less powerful communities of each State.

**Each State should enact enabling legislation that encourages local establishment of youth services bureaus throughout the State and that provides partial funding for them. Legislation also should be enacted to mandate the use of youth services bureaus as a voluntary diversion resource by agencies of the juvenile justice system.**

**To avoid misunderstanding, criteria for referrals should be developed jointly and specified in writing by law enforcement, courts, and youth services bureau personnel.**

Diversion can take place only if there is cooperation and communication between concerned parties.

In California, some of the criteria presently considered by juvenile justice agencies in diverting youth to youth services bureaus include: nonprobation status, first offense, age, minor offense that does not threaten the public safety, residence in the project area, cooperative attitude toward voluntary referral, and the need for additional services the bureau can provide.

In a few communities, what masquerades as a youth services bureau is actually a field office for probation surveillance. Where the probation services are particularly limited, court referrals ordering youths to participate in the bureau's programs may seem to be an expeditious alternative. But such action negates the role of the bureau as a program in which young people participate by choice. The bureau becomes part of the traditional enforcement machinery by deciding, in effect, whether or not a youth must be returned to juvenile court. Thus, the stigma of a coercive officially mandated service remains, without the legal safeguards currently emerging in the justice system itself.

**Referrals to the youth services bureau should be completed only if they are voluntarily accepted by the youth. Youths should not be forced to choose between bureau referral and further justice system processing.**

In making this recommendation, the Commission departs from the original recommendation of the President's Crime Commission. In its report, that Commission said that the youth services bureau could be vested with the authority to refer back to court with 30 to 60 days "those with whom it cannot deal effectively."

Such a practice can result in an extension of control over the youth by community institutions, without providing the legal safeguards of the justice system. Sherwood Norman, writing in *The Youth Service Bureau: A Key to Delinquency Prevention*, stated that to refer to court upon a young person's failure to cooperate ". . . would be a clear indication to him that the youth services bureau was not a voluntary agency but rather part of the justice system and therefore coercive."

The essence of any social service delivery system is the marshaling of resources in a coordinated way to bring clients to the best functioning level. As stated earlier, the youth services bureau provides a useful model for delivery of service systems which should be applied to adults as well as young persons.

## Employment

There is a definite association between unemployment or underemployment, and crime. Some individuals who cannot find satisfactory jobs or who are discriminated against in the labor market will turn to illegal activity as a source of income. The President's Commission on Crime in the District of Columbia in 1965 found that of adult offenders surveyed, 60 percent had no history of regular employment at the time

134

of arrest and the majority, whether employed or not, were in unskilled occupations. Among the offenders about whom income information was available, 69 percent earned less than $3,000 annually and 90 percent earned less than $5,000.[6]

A 1972 study comparing national youth arrest rates, unemployment rates, and labor-force participation rates over two decades concluded that lack of employment opportunities among white and black youths was a key factor in generating property crime.[7]

Assisting those with severe employment problems is, in the Commission's judgment, an important way to prevent crime. As in other areas, particular attention must be given to programs for young persons. Unemployment among young people became gradually more serious during the 1960's. In 1960, the unemployment rate for teenagers aged 16 to 19 was three and one-third times the adult rate; in 1971, it was more than four times the adult rate.[8] The problem is even more critical among minority youths in cities. In 1971 the unemployment rate among nonwhite teenagers aged 16 to 19 in low income urban areas was 38 percent compared with an overall unemployment rate for all teenagers of 16.9 percent.[9]

Ex-offenders are another group that has traditionally experienced difficulties in the labor market, particularly in periods of rising unemployment. Evidence from manpower programs suggests that in slack labor markets, training, placement, and job development tend to be less effective than when there are many unfilled jobs. In the Manhattan Court Employment Project, which has continued up to the present time, placements have dropped from 270 in the first year to 135 in the third, even though, judging by placements per referral, efforts have apparently improved. The problem is that fewer employers are willing to talk to or hire ex-offenders as long as qualified candidates without criminal records are available.

[6] *Report of the President's Commission on Crime in the District of Columbia* (1966), pp. 127, 130.

[7] Llad Phillips, Harold L. Votey, Jr., and Darold Maxwell, "Crime, Youth and the Labor Market," *Journal of Political Economy* (May/June 1972), pp. 491-504.

[8] *Manpower Report of the President,* U. S. Department of Labor (March 1972), p. 79.

[9] *Manpower Report of the President,* U. S. Department of Labor (March 1972), Table 1, p. 78, and U. S. Department of Commerce, Bureau of the Census, *Statistical Abstract of the United States,* 93rd edition (1972), Table 356, p. 223.

It is increasingly doubtful that the private sector alone can provide enough jobs to produce satisfactory changes in unemployment rates among urban youths and ex-offenders. Even in the best of times, meaningful public employment will be needed if the chronically unemployed are to be put to work.

**The Commission urges expanded public employment programs in areas of high unemployment. Programs should offer full-time, part-time, and summer employment.**

Most likely, these programs will require joint cooperation and funding from two or more levels of government. There are a number of different public employment strategies whose adoption depends upon community priorities: transitional jobs that would serve as stepping stones to permanent jobs in the public sector; permanent jobs that would provide a program of education, experience, and training needed for advancement; temporary job slots for offenders immediately after their release from confinement; and jobs that would serve as an alternative to incarceration for misdemeanants.

In the private sector, the Commission urges employers and unions to institute or accelerate efforts to expand job or membership opportunities to the economically and educationally disadvantaged. Various employment approaches could include work-study programs, summer and after-school employment, and job training and development for out-of-school youths.

In its *Report on Community Crime Prevention*, the Commission notes outstanding examples of private initiative. One of the most successful summer programs was developed by the Philadelphia Urban Coalition's High School Academy in 1970 and repeated in the summer of 1971. This effort provided work for students under 17 who were too young to get regular summer jobs. Under the auspices of the Urban Coalition and with the assistance of Junior Achievement, the students formed their own company, the Edison Electric Shop. The youths earned $1.75 an hour, and functioned under their own management with the help of a teacher-director, whose salary was paid by the Coalition.

Youth for Service in San Francisco, Calif., developed jobs for inner city youth by contracting with urban development and community action programs to build, repair, and maintain mini-parks in the blighted areas of the city. A similar group in Chicago, Ill., is running a food store, a boutique, a paper recycling program, and a restaurant.

The success of public and private efforts to expand employment opportunities depends to a large extent on general economic conditions. The close relationship between poverty area unemployment and national economic conditions suggests that a high national employment rate is essential if inner city unemployment is to be reduced. From 1968 through 1971 unemployment rates in urban poverty areas dipped below 5.5 percent only twice,[10] a level that most economists and politicians decry as unacceptable. At both times the national unemployment rate was around 3.5 percent.[11] The increase from 3.5 percent total unemployment at the end of 1969 to 5.9 percent in 1971 was accompanied by a rise in urban poverty area unemployment from 5.5 to 9.7 percent.[12]

**The Commission recommends that economic policy be concentrated on maintaining aggregate employment at a high level. The Commission believes that the ultimate goal of such policy should be to assure that the unemployment rate in poverty areas is no greater than the national rate.**

Consideration must also be given to changing credit, taxation, and expenditure policies that may have an impact on unemployment.

## Criminal Records and Employment

Surveys estimate that approximately 25 percent of the national population may have nontraffic arrest records. The chances that a black male from an urban area will be arrested have been estimated at from 50 to 90 percent.[13]

There is little doubt that arrest records are a barrier to employment. In the private sector, few firms exclude former offenders as a blanket policy, but often selection criteria tend to have this effect in practice.

In a survey in New York City, 75 percent of the employment agencies contacted said they would not recommend an

[10] Bureau of Labor Statistics, U.S. Department of Labor, *Handbook of Labor Statistics—1971*, p. 104, and *Handbook of Labor Statistics—1972*, p. 113. The poverty neighborhood classification used is based on a ranking of census facts according to 1960 data on income, education, skills, housing, and a proportion of broken homes. The poorest one-fifth of these tracts are considered poverty neighborhoods.

[11] *Handbook of Labor Statistics—1970*, p. 125.

[12] *Handbook of Labor Statistics—1972*, pp. 113, 129.

[13] Herbert S. Miller, *The Closed Door* (prepared for the U. S. Department of Labor, February 1972), p. 147.

individual with an arrest record, regardless of the disposition of the charges against him.[14]

Barriers to employment are at least as forbidding in the public sector as they are in the private sector. Most States, counties, and cities ask questions about prior arrest records when hiring. Few of the applications state that a record does not automatically bar the applicant. Civil service statutes that govern hiring often use language that could be and apparently is grounds to exclude large numbers of individuals with mere arrest records.[15]

Responses from employers indicate that employees with criminal records are not different from other employees. Agencies in a national survey were asked whether employees with criminal records were better than, the same as, or worse than other employees in each of eight categories: punctuality, attendance, honesty, judgment, initiative, cooperativeness, accuracy, and industriousness. There was little difference between employees with criminal records and other employees. What little difference there was in the reports was favorable toward employees with records.[16]

The Commission's standards on information systems (see Chapter 3) prohibit the dissemination of criminal records to private employers, provide for the return of arrest records of individuals not convicted of a crime, and direct the purging of criminal records after certain periods of time.

**To eliminate arbitrary barriers to employment, legislation should be enacted prohibiting employers from inquiring about an applicant's criminal history after records have been purged or returned.**

Government civil service regulations, moreover, should specify that no person can be barred automatically from taking a civil service test because of a criminal record.

## Education

Schools are the first public agencies that most children contact. For this reason, the schools inevitably have been

---

[14] Albert G. Hess and F. Le Poole, "Abuse of the Record of Arrest Not Leading to Conviction," *Journal of Research on Crime and Delinquency* (1967).

[15] Miller, *The Closed Door*, pp. 4, 6, 7.

[16] *Ibid.*, pp. 100-101.

proposed as vehicles for the solution of a host of public problems including the problem of crime. In making its recommendations, the Commission is well aware of crushing demands already placed upon local schoolteachers, principals, and school boards.

Nevertheless, individuals sometimes come to the attention of the criminal justice system because the educational system has not met their personal needs. The fact that the public schools have not helped a large portion of young people is reflected in high youth unemployment rates and high dropout rates. Twenty percent of those who now enter grade five leaves before high school graduation, and only 28.7 percent of 1971 high school graduates went on to college. Yet 80 percent of the effort in schools is structured to meet college entry requirements.[17] Too often classroom instruction is not related to life outside. Undoubtedly many of the 850,000 students who left elementary and secondary schools in 1970 and 1971 did so because they felt their educational experiences were irrelevant.[18]

The Commission believes that the primary goal of American education should be to prepare and interest people in satisfying and useful careers.

**Schools should plan programs that will guarantee that every child leaving school can obtain either a job or acceptance to an advanced program of studies, regardless of the time he leaves the formal school setting.**

The San Mateo, Calif. school district, for example, formally accepts responsibility for insuring that students are employable whenever they choose to leave school—whether as dropouts from the 10th grade or with advanced degrees.

If schools are going to make guarantees of this kind there must be a shift to career education. In career education programs, instruction is related to the world of work and opportunities are provided to explore or receive training in a career. Career education may begin in first grade or earlier and continue beyond high school graduation. It should bring

[17] Statistical data abstracted from: (1) Kenneth B. Hoyt, R. Evans, Edward Mackin, and Garth Mangum, *Career Education: What It is and How to Do It* (Olympus Publishing Co., 1972); (2) U.S. Department of Health, Education, and Welfare—Office of Education Materials; (3) U.S. Bureau of Census, *Statistical Abstract of the United States—1972.*
[18] National School Public Relations Association, "Dropouts: Prevention and Rehabilitation" (Washington NSPRA, 1972), p. 3.

an awareness to students of the wide range of jobs in American society and the roles and requirements involved.

The Seattle, Wash., public school system has a prototype career education program that offers occupational information to students at all grade levels, from kindergarten to grade 12, and integrates materials into every subject of the curriculum. Another program inverts the curriculum. Students choose preparatory trade areas as electives, staying in each long enough to become oriented to the occupation, explore it, or be trained in it. A core of general education courses—communications and humanities—accompanies the program.

A significant approach to career education is a cooperative education program, Project 70,001, operating since 1969 in Wilmington, Del. The program provides on-the-job work experience and related classroom instruction to students unable to participate in or benefit from regular programs of education and training. Similar programs have been started in Dover, Del.; Harrisburg, Pa.; Kansas City, Mo.; and Hartford, Conn. The Wilmington project combines the efforts and resources of a large shoe manufacturer, the Distributive Education Clubs of America, the Delaware Department of Public Instruction, and the Wilmington Public Schools.

In the Education chapter of the Commission's *Report on Community Crime Prevention*, additional approaches designed to make school systems more responsive to the individual student are recommended.

**Varied alternative educational experiences should be provided to students who cannot benefit from classroom instruction. School counseling and other supportive services should be available. There should be bilingual programs for young people who are not fluent in English. There should be a guarantee of functional literacy to every student who does not have serious emotional, physical, or mental problems.**

Aside from fulfilling the primary objective of preparing young people for adult life, school systems may also contribute to community crime prevention by serving as centers for community activities. The traditional school operating 5 days a week for 39 weeks a year is an unaffordable luxury. Schools can become total community opportunity centers for the young and the old, operating virtually around the clock, 365 days a year.

In Flint, Mich., schools are used for a wide variety of community services: adult education and retraining recreation and counseling; civic meetings; health clinics;

YMCA, YWCA, Boy and Girl Scouts, Big and Little Brother activities; job counseling and placement; senior citizen activities; and parent aid in developing curriculums. Members of the community are represented by a neighborhood council that advises the school and expresses the desires of the residents. There are 92,000 people per week using schools after hours; 80,000 adults enroll in classes each year. The accessibility of the school and the wide variety of programs offered there have greatly increased citizen involvement in the community. Special programs for men and women in trouble with the law have been tremendously successful in Flint schools. Among the total population, there are indications of decreasing rates of juvenile crime, dropping out of high school, and parole recidivism.

The Flint experience and others like it provide positive examples of the multipurpose use of educational facilities. The Commission urges authorities to make schools available to all citizens as centers for community involvement and adult education.

## Drug Abuse Treatment and Prevention

During the past decade, the nonmedical use of drugs by increasing numbers of people has become an urgent problem. In addition to the familiar alcohol and nicotine, doctors, researchers, and criminal justice professionals have had to become better acquainted with other types of drugs—amphetamines, heroin and other narcotics, barbiturates, hallucinogens, and antidepressants.

A link between some drugs, particularly heroin, and criminal behavior does exist, although many myths and inaccuracies surround that link. Drug abuse does not automatically cause crime. Many heroin or multidrug users were involved with crime before drug use and would continue their illegal activities whether addicted or not. Many recent heroin-dependent persons have grown up in a subculture in which both criminal and addict lifestyles are common. Crime and addiction can be two sides of the same coin.

The National Commission on Marihuana and Drug Abuse in 1973 reported that recent estimates on the daily cost of supporting a heroin habit range from $20 to $100, fluctuating accordingly to availability and location. Assuming that a heroin-dependent person had a daily habit of $20, the cost of his habit could amount to $7,300 per year.

It seems relatively safe to assume that most addicts cannot

support their habits without supplementing their income through illegal means since judging from available evidence, cited by the National Commission on Marihuana and Drug Abuse, a majority of heroin-dependent persons have below-average incomes.

This illegal activity usually takes the form of property crime—primarily burglary and shoplifting—rather than crimes against persons. Pimping, prostitution, and drug dealing are also major sources of income for heroin-dependent individuals.

To combat drug-related criminal activity, communities must take steps to prevent further drug abuse or addiction and to offer treatment to those individuals already involved with drugs.

**The Commission urges the establishment of multimodality drug treatment systems that would provide a comprehensive range of services in communities with a significant number of drug abusers.**

Nonmedical drug use involves different kinds of people who are drug-dependent in varying degrees and ways, who live in a variety of cultural settings, and who use drugs for different reasons. A multimodality approach enables the drug abuser or user to be treated in a program suited to his individual needs so that he may regain his position as a functioning member of society. Some of the recommended elements of multimodality treatment systems include crisis intervention and drug emergency centers, methadone treatment programs, therapeutic communities, and narcotics antagonist programs.

The Commission does not recommend the inclusion of heroin maintenance in a multimodality treatment system. After careful consideration, the Commission has concluded that heroin maintenance is a potentially harmful method of treatment both to the individual and to society as a whole.

## Modality: Crisis Intervention Centers

Basic to any system of care are the lifesaving, hospital-based emergency room forms of service designed to treat overdoses, toxic drug reactions, transient psychotic episodes, and severe withdrawal illness. These centers, located in a hospital or community clinic, should offer both medical aid and psychological services, such as hotline telephone help and various types of counseling.

## Modality: Methadone Treatment Programs

Methadone is a synthetic narcotic that is being distributed to an estimated 80,000 of this country's several hundred thousand heroin addicts. When administered in maintenance doses, methadone permits some chronic compulsive heroin users to become law-abiding, productive members of society. Opportunities can be provided to addicts to withdraw completely from methadone maintenance when they have made a satisfactory adjustment to a heroin-free existence and when they express a desire to end all involvement with drugs.

Methadone treatment has passed through a phase during which many observers felt it represented the solution to the heroin problem. However, a more moderate position seems to be indicated at present. The rate of those retained in treatment was once thought to be as high as 80 percent or more, but studies over a period of time indicate it actually approaches 50 percent.

High-dose methadone maintenance, nevertheless, is viewed today as an important treatment method for heroin addicts. It retains in treatment, on a voluntary basis, a much larger percentage of patients than other approaches. Evaluations performed on individuals undergoing methadone maintenance indicate that their rearrest record is low and that, in time, significant numbers find their way back to employment, school, or training.

## Modality: Therapeutic Communities Staffed in Part with Ex-addicts

Therapeutic communities are -drug-free environments in which the drug user is treated as an underdeveloped, immature personality. The existence of a community prepared to accept or reject the individual is at the core of the process. Banishment from this "family" group is a severe punishment.

Therapeutic communities are drug-free environments in cessful approach than methadone maintenance but one that may be effective for certain individuals. The treatment is wholly free of drugs and is often demanding and difficult. Few individuals "graduate" into self-sufficiency outside the therapeutic community. Residents are expected to remain in the community for extended periods of time ranging from 18 months to 2 years or more. In many program settings, there are no nonaddict representatives establishing limits or rules of conduct. Rather, participants are confronted by ex-addicts who themselves abstained from further drug use. In cases in which primary responsibility for operating the program does rest with ex-addicts and paraprofessional staff, the Commission believes that backup services of psychiatrists, teachers, and employment specialists should also be readily available.

143

## Modality: Narcotics Antagonist Programs

When taken in adequate amounts, narcotics antagonists such as cyclazocine and naloxone block the effects of heroin and other narcotic drugs. Although some success with narcotics antagonists has been achieved, it has been with relatively small numbers of patients. Many of the drugs used as antagonists produce undesirable side effects. Cyclazocine, a long-acting antagonist first used in 1966, is not well received by many narcotics addicts who complain they feel uncomfortable while taking the drug. In addition, patients are able to interrupt its use for a day in order to experience the euphoric effects of heroin. Naloxone, another drug utilized, has few side effects, but its short duration of action has limited its usefulness.

A major effort is now underway to find a safe long-acting antagonist. Should such research be successful, a much more extensive use of antagonists in treatment will be possible than now is the case. The Commission does not necessarily endorse the narcotics antagonist concept, but only recommends that this concept be considered and carefully evaluated as one more potential element of a multimodality approach.

## Modality: Variations in Treatment Approach

Communities might also consider variations in the four treatment approaches discussed above. For example, they might consider low-dosage methadone programs, or closed or open residential centers and halfway houses. A closed facility provides a therapeutic environment in which addicts can live free of their drug use with the help of constraints while an open facility operates without physical and other restraints.

## Compulsory Drug Treatment

Many drug-dependent individuals live from day to day, experience one crisis after another, and are unable to relate to any kind of treatment on a voluntary basis. Probation, deferred prosecution, and civil commitment all can and are used to structure compulsory treatment for such individuals. When compulsory treatment is indicated, individuals should be assigned to a coordinating body that is capable of making appropriate treatment decisions. Courts should be encouraged to rely on these coordinating committees through statutory action or through procedural means. Due process should always be assured. Compulsory treatment by deferred prosecution, probation, or civil commitment need not be equated with institutional confinement. Rather, all possible treatment

144

options should remain open and existing public and community resources, including private treatment agencies, should be brought to bear on the treatment process.

## Drug Abuse Prevention

In addition to treatment modalities, the Commission also recognizes the importance of drug abuse prevention. Past prevention efforts, however, often have been misdirected. Scare tactics have been used to stress the dangers of drug use. These efforts were discredited by many young people who had tried one or more drugs, and who find antidrug representations not substantiated by their own experiences. Prevention programs frequently failed to point out that each individual will respond to a drug in a different way, depending on such factors as the amount taken and the frequency of use.

The Commission believes that each community should implement a carefully designed program to prevent drug abuse. When information on drugs is misrepresented to young people, it can often discredit an entire prevention effort.

**Drug education should begin in the home before the child enters school. Teachers in the school should receive special training in drug education and prevention. Programs also should concentrate on helping the individual solve the problems that led him to drug use and should provide him with constructive alternatives.**

The Commission urges that effective drug abuse prevention programs be established. Such programs should present information objectively on drugs and drug abuse.

## Coordinating Prevention and Treatment Efforts

**Both prevention and treatment activities should be coordinated through a central State agency and local coordinating agencies.**

These agencies should assume responsibility for setting priorities for delivery of services, avoiding duplication, and determining the extent to which funded programs are effective. Basic standards on training, staffing, administration, and programming also should be adopted by such agencies. Coordinating agencies should work closely with the Special Action Office for Drug Abuse Prevention, the Federal agency charged with overall responsibility for Federal drug abuse prevention programs.

145

# Reducing Criminal Opportunity

An important assumption throughout the delivery of services section is that the provision of lawful alternatives to crime—satisfying employment and drug abuse treatment, for example—will persuade some persons to abandon or avoid criminal careers. But as this chapter emphasized at the outset, it is unrealistic to expect an improved delivery of service strategy to be effective in all cases. The Commission believes that protective measures taken by public authorities, commercial establishments, and private homeowners can also play an important role in deterring criminals.

Of all the things a citizen or community can do to reduce crime, the most immediate and most direct approach is to eliminate obvious opportunities for criminals. Locked cars, well-lighted streets, alarm systems, and properly designed and secure housing make crime, particularly acquisitive crimes such as larceny, burglary, auto theft, and robbery, more difficult to commit.

The following section contains the Commission's general recommendations for security precautions that can be taken by both individuals and public officials.

## Building Design

The physical design of residential complexes and housing can increase or decrease the probability that crime will occur. A housing complex designed so that all areas may be easily and frequently observed by tenants, passers-by, and police patrols can discourage criminal behavior. On the other hand, elevators, fire stairs, and underground parking garages that are hidden from public view easily mask the activities of unlawful intruders.

In *Death and Life of Great American Cities*, Jane Jacobs describes the loneliness and apprehension that large, anonymous housing projects evoke in many city dwellers:

> The corridors of the usual high rise low income housing buildings are like corridors in a bad dream: creepily lit, narrow, smelly, blind. They feel like traps and they are. These traps are what people mean when they say, time and again, "Where can we go? Not to a project! I have children, I have young daughters . . ."[19]

[19] Jane Jacobs, *The Death and Life of Great American Cities*,

In a recent book, partially funded by LEAA and entitled, *Defensible Space*, Oscar Newman has identified spatial arrangements that improve the security of buildings by opening certain areas to public view. He recommends that: (1) semipublic areas such as stairways and halls be visible to residents and passers-by; (2) front entrances be positioned along the street; (3) lobbies be well lit and designed so that all activity is visible from the street; (4) semiprivate areas such as paths and hallways be easily seen by tenants from apartment windows; and (5) elevators be monitored with electronic surveillance devices.

Newman's findings confirm the beliefs of those who fear massive housing complexes. Public housing projects with more than 1,000 units and seven or more stories were found to have crime rates almost one and one-half times higher than similar projects with less than 1,000 units and fewer than seven stories.[20] Newman also found that feelings of anonymity and lack of community pervade many large projects.

There are, however, positive actions that can be taken to make even the largest projects safe. By subdividing the interiors of these buildings (so that certain stairways and halls serve only small groups of families), small social groups are formed whose members jointly maintain and survey this shared area. Small walkup or garden apartments that are subdivided this way have lower crime rates.

Unfortunately, most public housing is planned and designed without considering the security system that should be built in. The placement of elevators, doors, or windows, or the installation of locks and burglar-resistant glass can be costly once a building is constructed. Many architects and physical planners are not aware of crime prevention construction techniques, and the information and experiences available through law enforcement agencies are rarely utilized.

**Law enforcement agencies, criminal justice planners, and professions involved in architectural design and physical planning should coordinate their efforts to reduce criminal oppor-**

---

as quoted in the Rand Institute, *Improving Public Safety in Urban Apartment Dwellings: Security Concepts and Experimental Design for New York City Housing Authority Buildings* (Rand: 1971), p. 105.

[20] Oscar Newman, *Defensive Space* (Macmillan, 1972) p. 28.

tunity through improved design of buildings, thoroughfares, parks, and other public places.

## Security Codes

Many communities are attempting to reduce residential and commercial burglaries by adopting security codes or by revising building codes to include security measures. The usual approach is to set specification standards for security devices and hardware in terms of specific styles and materials to be used. Thus a code might prescribe the thickness of a door or the type and design of locks. The materials and devices specified by such standards frequently become obsolete as better products are developed. Such codes also provide little incentive to manufacturers to develop better products. They divert attention from what security devices can accomplish to how they are made.

**Security requirements should be included in building codes and stated in terms of effectiveness, not design.**

The test of lock systems, for example, would not be their construction, but the degree of force and the length of time needed to overcome particular systems.

The formulation of these requirements or standards should be primarily the task of building, fire, and public safety departments. There should also be consultation with community criminal justice planners, transportation and sanitation departments, architectural firms, and proprietors.

At this writing, California is considering statewide standards for buildings. The standards would be based on performance and effectiveness of security hardware rather than design.[21]

## Lighting

Reports from a number of urban cities and counties generally support the use of lighting as one means of achieving safe streets.

In St. Louis, Mo., as an example, a program of improved streetlighting was initiated in 1964. The first area completed involved the downtown business district, which consists of

[21] State of California, Office of the Attorney General, Attorney General's Building Security Commission, "Preliminary Report to the California Legislature: Building Security Standards" (1973).

large department stores, brokerage firms, investment companies, and comparable business establishments.

In a comparison of crime in 1963, the last full year before improvements, and in 1965, the first full year after improvements, it was found that crimes against persons in the improved lighting area decreased by 40.8 percent. Auto thefts decreased by 28.6 percent and business burglaries decreased by 21.8 percent.[22]

Other reports of crime reduction associated with improved streetlighting have come from New York City, Detroit, Mich., and Washington, D. C. Proponents of streetlighting argue that it deters would-be criminals and increases the chances that actual offenders will be seen, recognized, and apprehended. Streetlighting also reportedly encourages nighttime use of the streets, itself an important deterrent to street crime.

Even the most enthusiastic advocates of streetlighting, however, admit a need for further evaluation and research. Factors such as police patrol levels, displacement of criminal activity, and seasonal change must be taken into account in rigorous studies so that the advantages and disadvantages of lighting will be more completely known.

**On the basis of available evidence, the Commission recommends that units of local government consider the establishment of improved streetlighting programs in high crime areas.**

The wishes of the residents and property owners should be considered at the outset of such programs and the experiences of comparable jurisdictions should be reviewed before such programs are begun.

## Other Considerations

In addition to security measures already mentioned in this chapter, other measures such as alarms and intruder detection devices, legislation to aid police in tracing stolen cars, anti-shoplifting programs, and multimedia campaigns to encourage motorists to lock their cars must be considered.

One program common to many measures designed to reduce criminal opportunities is that of the displacement of crime or the "mercury effect." Simply put, this term refers to

---

[22] J. Parker Heck, "Light Up for Safety" (prepared for the Street and Highway Safety Lighting Bureau, Cleveland, Ohio), pp. 9-10.

the shifting of criminal activity from relatively secure high-risk areas to unprotected low-risk areas. Skeptics of the usefulness of security measures argue that they merely move criminals around, rather than reduce crime. There are two responses to such arguments. First, many crimes are crimes of opportunity; locking cars and removing keys can prevent spontaneous joy-riding; secure doors and windows will discourage the casual burglar. Second, criminals are not infinitely mobile; their area of operations can extend just so far before robberies, thefts, and burglaries become less profitable and not worth the trouble or risk.

The Commission is persuaded that systematic programs to reduce criminal opportunity will reduce crime if they are implemented with the joint cooperation of public agencies, citizens, and police.

# Integrity in Government

Although many of the recommendations in this report are directed toward reducing street crime, the Commission also considers official corruption to be one of the most damaging forms of criminal activity in society.

The Commission recognizes that most people in public service are honest and dedicated. Official corruption, nevertheless, does exist, and in some jurisdictions has involved the highest elected and appointed officials.

Charges of corruption, some of which have led to convictions, have been brought against officials throughout the United States. Since 1969, more than 60 elected or appointed officials in a large Eastern State have been indicted or convicted on Federal or State criminal charges. In another, smaller State, similar charges have been brought against at least 24 officials, including a former Governor, two State senators, a State attorney general, and several other State and local officers or employees.

Corruption, as defined in this report, is not limited to its most egregious and sensational form—cash purchase of official favor. Corruption includes all of the circumstances in which the public officeholder sacrifices or sells all or part of his judgment on matters within his official purview in return for personal gain. Corruption thus defined includes a direct or tacit agreement between the official and the person requesting action that would benefit the official (cash, securities, a share in a business venture, or the promise of a future job on the outside) in exchange for official action or inaction.

## Conflict of Interest

Certain types of activity are clearly incompatible with the responsibility of public employment. A conflict of interest exists when an official intentionally disregards the public's interest in return for personal gain, or when, because of financial interest or outside pressures, he is unable or unwilling to perform his duties impartially.

The Temporary Commission of Investigation of the State of New York included in its report to the 1971 State Legislature the story of a resident engineer in the city of Yonkers Engineering Department. In that position, the man (Mr. S.) was responsible for verifying compliance with his department's specifications for all contractors doing business with the city.

In the course of the commission's investigations, testimony revealed that Mr. S. and at least two construction inspectors also employed by the city were privately employed by the contractors whose work they were charged with inspecting. The three city employees were moonlighting in the largest sewer project ever handled by Yonkers, a contract totaling $916,431; at the same time they were acting in their official capacity to insure the project's compliance with city regulations.[23]

Conflicts of interest can be a problem whenever public officials exercise power and discretion over decisions that affect many citizens. Because of the enormous impact such measures can have on special interest groups and individuals, public officials are approached continually by people who want to influence official action.

A proper system of conflicts regulation and a code of ethical principles to guide officials are needed. Present conflict of interest regulations are inadequate at the State and local levels. As of 1969, only 26 States had any laws on this subject, and none of these States included local government employees within the scope of the law's coverage.[24] Among the

[23] *Thirteenth Annual Report of the Temporary Commission of Investigation of the State of New York* (March 1971), pp. 96-109.
[24] All statistics are taken from *Assembly of the State of California, Ethical Conduct of Government Integrity: The Conflict of Interest Issue* (1970).

States that have enacted laws, only a few approach the requirements of an adequate safeguard.

Another failing of current legislation is that it often does not deal with borderline or minor cases of official misconduct that do not warrant criminal prosecution. The purchasing agent who accepts a dinner invitation or a small gift from a supplier should be subjected to a reprimand rather than criminal prosecution. The Commission believes that no single law or type of law is sufficient to deal with the gamut of ethical problems that underlie an official's conduct. A system of various types of provisions—criminal laws, ethical guidelines, and an enforcement body—is essential to assure the public that officials will act with integrity.

**The Commission recommends that States, in addition to criminal sanctions, adopt provisions for an ethics code and an ethics board to enforce and interpret the provisions of the code and to apply administrative sanctions.**

This code should require that public officials disqualify themselves from taking official actions when a conflict of interest might exist; should prohibit acceptance of gifts, favors, services, or promises of future employment that might influence their performance of official duties; and should prohibit acceptance of positions of employment that might involve conflicting duties.

**States also should adopt provisions requiring public officials to disclose fully and openly their financial and professional interests.**

This is perhaps the most effective method of conflict of interest regulation; it seeks to deter wrongful conduct by giving the public access to information on areas of an official's professional and private life that offer the greatest potential for conflict.

## Political Campaign Financing

A potential for corruption or conflict of interest exists when a candidate for political office is forced to rely on large contributions from special interest groups. Such contributions might be made as an attempt to purchase goodwill and influence future decisions or they might be payment for favors or preferred treatment already received. These practices are certainly widespread. Various studies have estimated that 15 percent of the money for State and local campaigns comes from persons engaged in illegal gambling and racketeering who seek protection for their illegal activities.[25] If correct, this would mean that well over $15 million might have come from criminal elements in the 1972 State and local elections.

In order to reduce opportunities for corruption in campaign financing, the Commission recommends that States impose and enforce realistic campaign spending limitations, require full disclosure of financial contributions to all parties and candidates for local and State office, and prohibit contributions from significant government contractors, labor unions, trade associations, and corporations.

## Government Procurement, Zoning, Licensing, and Tax Assessment

Government procurement, zoning, licensing, and tax assessment are functions of State and local governments often known for inefficiency, mismanagement, and corruption. Commercial enterprises and individuals dealing with government have a tremendous stake in these areas and the opportunity for graft exists when explicit and precise standards are not adhered to.

In the competitive area of governmental purchasing, the unethical vendor needs only a slight edge to beat the competition on a given contract. With the cooperation of the corrupt government employee, the vendor can utilize various devices to maximize his profits at the expense of the purchaser. The losers in such transactions are the government and ultimately the taxpayer, who will pay more than the

---

[25] According to Alexander Heard, this estimate "embraces funds given in small towns and rural areas by individuals operating on the borders of the law who want a sympathetic sheriff and prosecutor, but who are not linked to crime syndicates. This estimate applies chiefly to persons engaged in illegal gambling and racketeering. It does not extend, for example, to otherwise reputable businessmen who hope for understanding treatment from building inspectors and tax assessors." Alexander Heard, *The Costs of Democracy* (University of North Carolina Press, 1960), p. 165, fn. 73, also pp. 154-168; see also Harold D. Laswell and Arnold Rogow, *Power Corruption and Recititude* (Prentice Hall, 1963), pp. 79-80; and Donald R. Cressy, *Theft of the Nation: The Structure and Operations of Organized Crime in America* (Harper and Row, 1969), p. 253.

goods or services are worth or who will purchase materials that cannot be used.

Most States have taken steps to upgrade the integrity of the government procurement function by creating centralized State purchasing agencies. Centralization has encouraged efficiency and economy in purchasing as well as the professionalization of purchasing agents.

**States should adopt formal procedures for setting and disseminating commodity specifications, handling complaints, encouraging competition, and insuring timely delivery of goods and services. A State purchasing agency should be established with an advisory board composed of the heads of the finance committees of the legislature, the purchasing director, and the heads of the various sections of the purchasing agency.**

Some of the corruption in zoning, licensing, and tax assessment occurs because otherwise honest citizens become so frustrated with government bureaucracy and red tape that they are willing to offer bribes and kickbacks just to get action in governmental decisions. In New York City, there are at least 40 different licenses or permits required to construct a new building. A construction delay of several days resulting from a pending permit would cost contractors substantially more than they lose in payoffs to officials to speed up permit processing. According to one estimate, as much as 5 percent of the total construction costs in the city are attributable to graft paid to city employees.[26] Five percent of the estimated $1.5 billion annual construction bill amounts to $75 million.

Cash payments for zoning changes are not uncommon in some communities. A favorable zoning decision can boost the value of certain pieces of land and may mean substantial profits. Corruption in tax assessments also involves large sums. For example, when the assessor of a large metropolitan area discovered he was being investigated by a local citizen group for "arbitrary and manipulative" operation of his office, he "reassessed" nine high rise properties in the city. The reassessment of those nine buildings added $34 million to the city's tax base.[27]

The Commission believes that the greatest single cause of

[26] "5 Percent of Building Costs Are Laid to New York Graft," *Washington Post* (October 20, 1971).

[27] *Moore et al.* v. *Cullerton*, 72-c-680 filed in U.S. Dictrict Court for the Northern District of Illinois. See also "A $16 Million U. S. Steel 'Tax Break' Charged," *Chicago Daily News* (May 18, 1971), and "Charge Loop Bank Gets Big Tax Break," *Chicago Today* (July 13, 1971).

corruption in these three areas of government operation is the availability of excessive discretion involving significant sums of money. Vague and improperly stated decision guidelines invite attempts at manipulation and fraud and are, at a minimum, indicative of sloppy management.

**Each jurisdiction should develop explicit criteria for use by officials in making decisions in zoning, licensing, and tax assessment.**

## Investigation and Prosecution of Corrupt Officials

An essential part of eliminating corruption and the influence of organized crime in government is a firm commitment on the part of State and local government to seek out and prosecute vigorously all types of corrupt practices in which the government is involved.

The first step is for State and local units of government to assess the nature and extent of their corruption problems. Because each jurisdiction has different statutory powers, administrative organizations, and social and political makeup, the Commission was unable to propose a single set of standards for investigation and prosecution of corruption cases. However, it has set out broad, general guidelines that State and local governments can use in developing their anticorruption approaches.

The Commission strongly believes that the first line of defense against illegal conduct by government officials is a local prosecutor's office staffed by well-compensated and adequately trained personnel. It is recognized, however, that there are cases where local authorities are technically not prepared or are unwilling to handle corruption problems.

**States having a history of public corruption at State and local levels should establish an ongoing statewide capability for investigation and prosecution of governmental corruption and organized crime.**

This capability might take the form of a corruption investigation unit under the State attorney general, a special grand jury convened when needed by legislative act or executive order, or a State investigation commission created by constitutional amendment. The experiences of New York and New Jersey with investigation commissions provide useful models for other States.

One of the most vital attributes of an anticorruption unit (and one that currently is absent in all existing State investigation commissions) is its power to prosecute the case as it develops. The Commission recommends that this power be granted to the anticorruption unit.

# Implementing Community Crime Prevention Activities

Many of the programs and activities discussed in this chapter will require financial underwriting. In many instances, sufficient funds should be available at the State or local level, or in the case of many citizen activities, from private sources.

Under certain circumstances, some crime prevention programs might qualify for support from funds provided by LEAA. LEAA makes its funds available to States, which in turn fund projects at the operational level.

In other circumstances, funds might be available from other Federal agencies, including the Department of Health, Education, and Welfare (HEW). Aid in the form of information, speakers, films, and expert assistance might be available from such agencies as the Special Action Office for Drug Abuse Prevention and the Bureau of Narcotics and Dangerous Drugs, to name only two.

Citizens, groups, and organizations should inform themselves fully about the availability of funds for the particular kind of program they have in mind. Congress has directed how the funds can and cannot be used. In some cases, there may be uncertainty about the propriety of using funds for certain projects.

# Conclusion

The local community is one of the Nation's most underdeveloped and underutilized crime fighting resources. It is a resource that needs to be utilized by everyone concerned about the incidence of crime in his community.

A community may translate its concern about crime into action through the individual and group efforts of its citizens, through its local institutions such as schools, youth services bureaus, and religious organizations, and through the responsible and responsive efforts of its governing bodies.

Neither in this chapter, nor in its *Report on Community Crime Prevention,* has the Commission exhausted the possible approaches that a community may take to reduce and prevent crime. Indeed, there are as many viable approaches to community crime prevention as there are citizens who deplore the conditions that are known to cause crime. What is needed is a positive commitment to action.

# Excerpts from the Task Force Report on Community Crime Prevention

## A: Crime Prevention and the Citizen

### 1: Citizen Action

... Crime prevention as each citizen's duty is not a new idea. In the early days of law enforcement, well over a thousand years ago, the peacekeeping system encouraged the concept of mutual responsibility. Each individual was responsible not only for his actions but for those of his neighbors. A citizen observing a crime had the duty to rouse his neighbors and pursue the criminal. Peace was kept, for the most part, not by officials but by the whole community.

With the rise of specialization, citizens began to delegate their personal law enforcement responsibilities by paying others to assume peacekeeping duties. Law enforcement evolved into a multifaceted specialty as citizens relinquished more of their crime prevention activities. But the benefits of specialization are not unlimited. Criminal justice professionals readily and repeatedly admit that, in the absence of citizen assistance, neither more manpower, nor improved technology, nor additional money will enable law enforcement to shoulder the monumental burden of combating crime in America. ...

Attacking Crime's Infrastructre

Citizens can prevent crime by focusing their attention on the social factors that lead to crime, e.g., unemployment, poor education, and lack of recreational opportunities. Because subsequent chapters discuss these subjects in greater detail, this section only outlines some of the opportunities available for citizen action.

**Education**

Many citizens are involved in encouraging school dropouts to complete their education. The "Keep a Child in School" program in Charleston, W.Va., attempts to meet this objective by working with students on a one-to-one basis, and insuring that they have adequate clothes and supplies. This program also provides tutors for students who have fallen behind in their work or need special help.

Other groups have found it necessary to offer alternative educational opportunities, such as street academies or vocational programs. New York City's Harlem Prep is one of the best known and most successful street academies. It is supported by contributions from foundations and industry and its purpose is to prepare dropouts for college. The Philadelphia Urban Coalition has developed a vocational program to serve the needs of the inner city high school youth with poor reading skills who is planning to drop out. The school system and the business community will cooperate to give the youth the training he needs for a specific job in a specific industry. . . .

# B: Delivery of Government and Social Services

## 2: Citizen Involvement and Government Responsiveness in the Delivery of Services

. . . A survey by Louis Harris, released in June 1972, confirms the fact that the levels of alienation in 1 year increased from 40 percent to 47 percent among those surveyed. The survey questions dealt with the individual's perceptions of his own power and importance, and his perceptions of the essential justice of our economic and political system. Harris points out:

> The sense of alienation is broadest concerning economic complaints as represented in the nearly seven out of 10 who agree with the statement that "the rich get richer and the poor get poorer." But perhaps even more intense is the social and political isolation expressed in admissions such as "what you think doesn't count very much" and "the people running the country don't really care what happens to people such as yourself." This revival of the "forgotten man" runs deep in America today.

... The Commission believes that the immediate priorities for improving the responsiveness of government must center on the aspect of government that will enable citizens to view government in a positive light; namely, the delivery of services. To that end, this chapter proposes standards and recommendations consistent with the following broad goals:

- To achieve equitable and more effective municipal services;
- To improve methods of access to government services and program information;
- To improve citizen complaint and grievance response mechanism; and
- To promote maximum community involvement and participation in the governmental process.

The methods for achieving these goals are reflected in the following standards and recommendations, which include proposals for: reallocating resources, establishing complaint and information offices, utilizing the public media more effectively, improving channels of communications, decentralizing city halls, establishing multiservice centers, and developing partnership citizen councils.

**Recommendation 2.1: Distribute public service on the basis of need.**

**Recommendation 2.2: Decentralization Mechanisms.**

The Commission recommends that neighborhood facilities, such as multiservice centers and "little city halls," be established to facilitate the dispensing of government services and to improve communications between citizens and government agencies. These centers should provide a variety of government services in one location, so that local residents can receive effective services close to their homes with a minimum of bureaucratic entanglement.

1. Need and Geographic Jurisdiction: Establishment of neighborhood facilities should be based on at least the following factors relating to the needs of a particular area:

    a. Density and nature of the population, i.e., number of service recipients;

    b. Degree of citizen alienation; and

    c. Extent of ineffectiveness of present service delivery systems.

2. Types of Services:

    a. Multiservice centers should provide a wide variety

of services in one location. The specific services should depend on the needs of the population in the area being served. Services might include: welfare processing, food stamps, legal aid, day care, head-start programs, health care, employment and family counseling, housing code enforcement, and assistance to senior citizens.

b. Little city halls should provide services similar to those provided at the main city hall. Services might include: city and court clerk assistance, complaint processing, tax and water bill collection, license and permit issuance, voter registration, birth certificate assistance, and information dispensing. . . .

3. Coordination:

a. Internal. The center director should hold regular meetings, bringing together staff and representatives of each agency functioning in the facility.

b. External.

1. The facility director should make arrangements, through the chief executive or chief administrative officer, to hold mini-cabinet meetings in the area of jurisdiction of the little city hall or multiservice center operation. The mini-cabinet should consist of the district heads of city departments and agencies that have responsibilities in the jurisdiction. Meetings should be held regularly and should focus on neighborhood problems. The participation of agency and department officials should be mandated by ordinance or agency regulation.

2. Insofar as practicable, the lines of service delivery should be correlated with local district lines, thereby creating coterminous districts that align all governmental services in a given neighborhood.

**Recommendation 2.3: Enact public right-to-know laws.**

**Recommendation 2.4: Broadcast local government meetings and hearings.**

**Recommendation 2.5: Public Hearings**

The Commission recommends that public hearings be held on issues of citywide and neighborhood interest, so that government officials may receive citizen input on the real concerns of the community.

1. Subject Matter: Hearings should be scheduled to con-

161

sider such issues as the city budget, setting of priorities for allocating city resources, public housing and urban renewal site selection, zoning changes, location of park and public works facilities, and neighborhood security.

2. **Timing:** Prior to official designation of projects and priorities, citizens should have the opportunity to determine the projects most suitable to them, and to make their views known through public hearings. Once a project has been designated, it is important that public hearings be held during various stages of project development. In some cases this may be in the preplanning stages, but in all cases it should occur during the planning process.

3. **Convenience:** To ease transportation problems and encourage maximum participation, hearings should be convened in a facility as close as possible to the affected population, e.g., in neighborhood schools, community centers, churches, or other local facilities. Hearings should be scheduled when most of the affected citizens are available (usually evenings and weekends).

4. **Official Interest:** The principal elected and administrative officials should conduct the hearings so that there is an exchange of first-hand, accurate information between the public and those who have authority to make decisions.

COMMUNITY INVOLVEMENT IN GOVERNMENTAL PROCESSES

. . .The real need is to allow neighborhood groups to control their own destinies, to participate in the systems affecting their daily lives, and to create and manage their own policies. It is no longer satisfactory to appease neighborhood organizations with an illusory form of participation of the type that involves rubber-stamp advisory committees or advisory boards intended to manipulate community support. Nor is it totally satisfactory to include citizens on decisionmaking panels and policy committees without a corresponding relinquishment of the government's superior bargaining position. In either situation, there is serious danger of co-opting the very people that these forms of involvement are designed to serve. It is essential that citizens be afforded a genuine opportunity to share in the administration of issues that directly concern them, and that they be granted a mode of access to centers of decisionmaking that currently exclude them.

**Neighborhood Governments**

One attempt to make government more responsive to the needs of its constituents, and to involve a greater number of residents in policymaking, involves the establishment of little city halls and multiservice centers, as discussed earlier in this chapter. This decentralization has potential for expediting the administration of public services in neighborhood areas. However, little city halls and multiservice centers do not respond to the problems of apathy and distrust that tend to greet agents of the system. To achieve realistic and effective citizen participation, the Commission recommends that consideration be given to the creation of politically decentralized systems, in addition to the administrative decentralization recommended earlier in this section.

One of the best-known methods of political reorganization is the metropolitan federation, roughly patterned after the structure of the Federal government. Power is divided between the central metropolitan government and the units of local government, primarily municipalities, with legally prescribed interrelationships and a specified distribution of functions between the two levels. The metropolitan government exercises those powers essential to providing solutions to metropolitanwide problems, while the local units retain powers related specifically to local matters. Further, the local government is represented at metropolitan level of government. The federation advocates "a partial disannexation of neighborhoods, as a counterweight to central power, to ensure that those who have been left out of the political decision-making system are given a role to play." . . .

Neighborhood governments could insure responsiveness and accountability through their optimum size, central location, and local membership.

> It is not unreasonable to conclude that by facilitating more citizen inputs into the decision-making process in a larger city, a system of neighborhood government will make local government more responsive to the special needs of citizens in different neighborhoods. With respect to the functions exclusively assigned to neighborhood governments, uniform city-wide policies would be replaced by policies custom-tailored to the conditions prevailing in each neighborhood.

The representative nature of neighborhood governments could fulfill the dire needs for shared decisionmaking and distribution of power; neighborhood governments could offer political and economic clout to otherwise powerless communities and also a basis for healthy competition and cooperation with city officials. Neighborhood governments should be granted certain policymaking and discretionary authority, as well as program, fiscal, and personnel autonomy. . . .

**Recommendation 2.6: Establish neighborhood governments.**

COMPLAINT AND GRIEVANCE RESPONSE MECHANISMS
. . . With a centralized complaint reception and information system, citizens can call a single number and learn whether a complaint should be lodged with a department of the county, city, or State government. Dialing one number puts citizens in contact with a responsible government employee whose specific job is to receive complaints, refer the complaint to the proper office, and make any necessary followup calls. A central information office that provides these services should help dispel some of the public's cynicism about the performance of government offices, and should help convince the public that giant government superstructures can—and want to—provide service to the people. . . .

**Recommendation 2.7: Create a central office of complaint and information.**

**Recommendation 2.8: Broadcast local Action Line programs.**

# 3: Youth Services Bureaus

YOUTH SERVICES BUREAUS: A MODEL FOR THE DELIVERY OF SOCIAL SERVICES
. . . Youth Services Bureaus in large part were the result of a recommendation of the 1967 President's Commission on Law Enforcement and Administration of Justice, which urged communities to establish these bureaus to serve both delinquent and nondelinquent youth referred by the police, juvenile courts, schools, and other sources. That Commission envisioned these bureaus as central coordinating units for all community services for young people.

In its recent report, The Challenge of Youth Services Bureaus, the California Youth Authority stated that youth services bureaus serve as models for developing direct service to children and youth. The report indicated that these bureaus are a pioneer example of a service delivery component of a comprehensive youth services delivery system. . . .

Social services are made available to clients who have a need for such services, which include employment, job training, education, housing, medical care, psychiatric care, family counseling, or welfare. At present, these services for adults as well as for youth are fragmented. A family with multiple problems is often seen by several agencies at the same time. Often one agency does not know what another is doing, and it is not uncommon for agencies to be working at cross-purposes with one another.

The service delivery system would solve this problem by integrating the services available to the individual through a central intake unit, which analyzes the individual's needs and refers him to the appropriate agency. It is critical to the success of these programs that the clients are involved in the actual development and operation of the programs, both in an advisory role and as employees. . . .

## YOUTH SERVICES BUREAUS TODAY

Since 1967, youth services bureaus have been established across the Nation in large cities and small, in overcrowded inner city neighborhoods, middle income suburbs, and sprawling rural counties—joining the few pioneering youth services bureaus that had preceded the Commission's recommendations.

A national census in 1972 identified 150 youth services bureaus currently in operation in many States and territories throughout the country.

## GOALS FOR YOUTH SERVICES BUREAUS

The goals for youth services bureaus suggested by the President's Commission in 1967 were principally to provide and coordinate programs for young people. As bureaus have come increasingly into operation, these basic goals have been expanded. At the present time, youth services bureaus have at least five goals. These include: (1) diversion of juveniles from the justice system; (2) provision of services to youth; (3) coordination of both individual cases and programs for young people; (4) modification of systems of services for youth; and (5) involvement of youth in decisionmaking, and the development of individual responsibility.

The discussion that follows examines the rationale for each of these goals, presents some of the most effective decisionmaking structures for each, and looks at some of the programs that are oriented toward attaining these goals.

## DIVERSION

. . . At each decision point, there is a selective reduction of young people who penetrate to the next stage of the juvenile justice system. For example, estimates for 1973 indicate that almost four million juveniles had a police contact during that year; two million of these contacts resulted in arrests; and over one million of the arrests resulted in referral to the juvenile court. Of the cases referred to juvenile court throughout the Nation, nearly 500.000 were handled judicially. Thus, roughly one out of eight police contacts resulted in a court appearance.

Although some of these cases were closed for lack of evidence, a large part of this reduction in cases is based on the overreferral for service. For example, many more young people are referred to court by police, parents, schools and others than could realistically be processed by the justice system at the present time. . . .

*Juvenile Court*

. . . There are, therefore, many reasons for developing youth services bureaus with a diversionary objective, and with a focus on providing an alternative to the justice system for young people in trouble. Planners for youth services bureaus need to consider these flaws in the justice system as they attempt to create workable, effective alternatives to this system.

Two alternatives to justice system processing merit consideration: (1) some of the actions of children and parents now subject to definition as delinquency or unfitness should be considered as part of the inevitable, everyday problems of living and growing up; and (2) many of the problems considered as delinquency or predelinquency should be defined as family, educational, or welfare problems, and diverted away from the juvenile court into other community agencies, such as youth services bureaus. In this manner, ". . . problems will be absorbed informally into the community, or if they are deemed sufficiently serious, they will be funneled into some type of diversion institution, staffed and organized to cope with problems on their own terms rather than as antecedents to delinquency." . . .

*Underuse*

Where youth services bureaus are in operation, have police forces made full use of them? Have the bulk of referrals to youth services bureaus come from police and juvenile court intake staff, as the President's Commission on Law Enforcement and Administration of Justice anticipated?

Overall, the answer is no. In many communities with youth

services bureaus, police seldom or never refer young people there. A nationwide sample of more than 400 cases from 28 youth services bureaus showed that only 13 percent of the referrals were from law enforcement, while 30 percent were referred by self, friends, or family, and 21 percent were referred by schools. Findings from California's nine pilot bureaus reveal a slightly larger proportion of referrals from law enforcement (21 percent), with referrals from probation accounting for an additional 11 percent of the cases served. . . .

There are many reasons that police officers have not made greater use of the youth services bureaus. These reasons include negative attitudes of individual policemen toward diversion and the likelihood of juveniles' participation in a voluntary program, lack of support from the department's policymakers, perceptions that the community is content with the existing dispositions, real and imagined legal restrictions, and by no means least often, negative opinions held by policemen of the youth services bureau itself.

### Relationship with Criminal Justice Agencies

Although many recommend that a youth services bureau should not be operated by any agency of the juvenile justice system, it appears that the bureaus most genuinely capable of diversion are those with a linkage to the juvenile justice system. The most successful bureaus maintain immediate communication but are not coopted by the justice system, its traditionally most powerful leaders, or its existing practices. . . .

Some of the criteria presently considered by juvenile justice agencies in diverting youth to youth services bureaus in California include: nonprobation status, first offense, age, minor offense that does not threaten public safety, residence in the project area, cooperative attitude of youth (or youth and parents) toward voluntary referral, and the need for additional services the bureaus can provide, as perceived by the referring agency. . . .

### Accessibility to Law Enforcement

. . . Detaching law enforcement officers from the juvenile division to work full time in the bureau is another method of increasing the confidence of the police department and thereby enhancing diversion. It should be noted that this method of staffing could defeat the confidential, noncoercive stance of the bureau if the role of these officers is not clearly defined in advance.

This system, however, has worked well in the youth services bureaus in San Diego and San Jose, Calif., where the officers working in the bureaus make no arrests, gain a better understanding of youth problems by counseling youth and their parents, and are rotated back to the police department after several months to provide broader police department exposure to the benefits of diverting youth to the bureau. . . .

Recent guidelines for youth services bureaus indicate that bureaus should accept referrals from all law enforcement agencies on the condition that the authoritative agency close its case upon bureau acceptances of referrals.

In addition, these guidelines note that the youth referred to a bureau should not be subject to court action unless he subsequently commits an offense warranting court referral by police or is the subject of neglect. To refer to court upon the young person's failure to cooperate ". . . would be a clear indication to him that the youth services bureau was not a voluntary agency but rather part of the justice system and therefore coercive."

It appears that many youth services bureaus are providing probation supervision. In communities where probation services are particularly limited, court referrals ordering youth to participate in the bureaus may seem to be an expeditious alternative. The same is true of informal probation referrals to bureaus. But this action negates the role of bureaus as programs in which young people participate by choice.

## PROVIDING SERVICES FOR YOUTH

. . . An area of controversy in the youth services bureau movement is whether a bureau should develop and provide services itself or should function principally as an information and referral service, following up with individual advocacy or case coordination for the young people it refers. . . .

One set of standards for youth services bureaus states explicitly that bureaus should not provide service directly: "The Bureau strengthens existing agencies by performing an enabling function rather than itself attempting to fill gaps in services." It ". . . bridges the gap between available services and youth in need of them by referral and followup. It acts as an advocate of the child to see that he gets the service he needs." In short, "The youth service bureau is not itself a service agency so much as an agency for organizing the delivery of services to children and their families." . . .

## Drawbacks

There are, however, many drawbacks to operating a youth services bureau primarily as an information and referral program. Among the handicaps in referring substantial numbers of youth to other services are: the expectations of the youth or his family when they are referred to the bureau; the expectations of the agency referring them to the bureau; the availability of other services for youth in the community; the bureau staff's knowledge of community resources; and the style of delivery of existing services in the community. . . .

There are two strong arguments for youth services bureaus to provide services without the necessity of parental permission: (1) many youth services bureaus increasingly are becoming advocates for the child or youth. When the best interests of the parent and of the youth are in conflict, bureaus must select the interests of one as a priority. Because the bureaus' focus is service for youth, the youth's interests should be their first choice; and (2) in an era of increasing youth responsibility, the choice to participate in a needed service should be increasingly theirs. . . .

The fundamental strength of most bureaus has been in their provision of a variety of innovative services for youth—services that include counseling, tutoring, job referrals and other employment services, crisis intervention, crisis shelter care, and medical services. A basic element of these services it that they are generally provided at accessible locations and hours and in an appealing manner to their clients. Moreover, several of the bureaus that primarily provide direct service also provide referral services—followup, individual advocacy, and service brokerage. . . .

**Standard 3.1: Coordinate youth services through youth services bureaus.**

**Standard 3.2: Operate youth services bureaus independent of the justice system.**

**Standard 3.3: Target Group**

Youth services bureaus should make needed services available to all young people in the community. Bureaus should make a particular effort to attract diversionary referrals from the juvenile justice system.

1. Law enforcement and court intake personnel should be strongly encouraged, immediately through policy changes and ultimately through legal changes, to make full use of the youth services bureau in lieu of court processing for every juvenile who is not an immediate threat to public safety and

who voluntarily accepts the referral to the youth services bureau.

2. Specific criteria for diversionary referrals should be jointly developed and specified in writing by law enforcement, court, and youth services bureau personnel. Referral policies and procedures should be mutually agreed upon.

3. Diversionary referrals should be encouraged by continual communication between law enforcement, court, and youth services bureau personnel.

4. Referrals to the youth services bureau should be completed only if voluntarily accepted by the youth. The youth should not be forced to choose between bureau referral and further justice system processing.

5. The juvenile court should not order youth to be referred to the youth services bureau.

6. Cases referred by law enforcement or court should be closed by the referring agency when the youth agrees to accept the youth services bureau's service. Other dispositions should be made only if the youth commits a subsequent offense that threatens the community's safety.

7. Referring agencies should be entitled to and should expect systematic feedback on initial services provided to a referred youth by the bureau. However, the youth services bureau should not provide justice system agencies with reports on any youth's behavior.

8. Because of the voluntary nature of bureau services and the reluctance of young people who might benefit from them, the youth services bureau should provide its services to youth aggressively. This should include the use of hotlines and outreach or street workers wherever appropriate.

In a few communities, what masquerades as a youth services bureau is in actuality a field office for probation surveillance. In these communities, the procedures of due process may be circumvented and the stigma of a coercive, officially mandated service still remains.

Reluctance on the part of law enforcement and the courts to accept the concept of noncoercive service for troubled and troublesome youth is an impediment to rapid implementation of diversion on a widespread basis. Immediately instituting policy changes and then legal changes to encourage diversion more strongly will contribute a great deal to realizing widespread diversion. Policy and legal changes, too, will contribute to a rational diversion strategy rather than to a series of individual, idiosyncratic dispositional choices, which may do nothing to further the cause of equitable administration of justice.

Some police may be dismayed that a youth services bureau does not provide justice system agencies with reports of any youth's behavior. Indeed, there will be rare instances when bureau staff may find it necessary to involve the police for the immediate protection of public safety, as would be required of any responsible community resident. However, a capable youth services bureau would have the capacity to minimize and neutralize such incidents. Moreover, the role of the youth services bureau should not be to provide a pipeline to law enforcement on drug users or other offenders.

**Standard 3.4: Provide direct and referral services to youths.**

**Standard 3.5: Hire professional, paraprofessional, and volunteer staff.**

**Standard 3.6: Plan youth program evaluation and research.**

**Standard 3.7: Appropriate funds for youth services bureaus.**

**Standard 3.8: Legislation**

Each State should enact necessary legislation to fund partially and to encourage local establishment of youth services bureaus throughout the State. Legislation also should be enacted to permit the use of youth services bureaus as a voluntary diversion resource by agencies of the juvenile justice system.

# C: Practical Programs for Crime Prevention

## 4: Programs for Drug Abuse Treatment and Prevention

... The multimodality approach to drug treatment should provide a comprehensive range of services to treat all drug users. This approach enables each addict to be treated in a program suited to his individual needs so that he may regain his position as a functioning member of society.

The Commission recommends a number of programs that should be present in a comprehensive drug treatment program but specifically withholds its endorsement from heroin maintenance programs. Among the recommended elements of comprehensive drug treatment systems are:

• Crisis Intervention and Drug Emergency Centers;
• Facilities and personnel for methadone maintenance treatment programs;
• Facilities and personnel for narcotics antagonist programs;
• Therapeutic community programs staffed entirely or largely by ex-addicts; and
• Closed and open residential treatment facilities as well as halfway houses staffed primarily by residents. . . .

## THE FACTS OF DRUG ABUSE

### Types of Drug Users

There are several different kinds of drug-taking behavior. These do not depend on the substance used or the source from which it is obtained. The following is a description of each type:

1. Experimental user. Drugs play no special or regular role in the experimental user's life. Use is episodic and reflects a desire to see what the drugs are like, or to test their effect on other activities ordinarily experienced without drugs.

2. Social or recreational user. Drugs are associated with social or recreational activities in which this type of user would take part whether or not drugs were present. Little or no time and effort are devoted to seeking out drugs or making connections to obtain them. The pattern of drug use is occasional and is situationally controlled.

3. Seeker. Drugs play a significant role in the seeker's life. Time is dedicated to seeking them out or making connections to obtain them. The user cannot enjoy or cope with some situations without drugs. Use of drugs may range from irregular to regular, controlled, or heavy daily use, although the individual may still remain functional and able to meet primary social and physical needs.

4. Self-medicating user. The self-medicator uses legally distributed tranquilizers or stimulants. While this type of use may have beneficial characteristics, it also can become a habitual way of responding to boredom, loneliness, frustration and stress. The precise incidence of such chemical coping is unknown, but existing data suggest that it is extensive. It is necessary to learn more about the situations and experiences that move the self-medicator to dysfunctional use. At present

it is only assumed that some type of emotional difficulty or problem underlies such use.

Both self-medicators and seekers are attempting to deal with anxiety, depression, or other problems, and both often use drugs as a kind of self-therapy among other reasons.

5. Dysfunctional drug user. Drugs begin to dominate the life of the dysfunctional drug user. The process of securing and using them interferes with essential activities.

## Factors That Affect Drug Experiences

In the past, policymakers and program planners often were preoccupied with tolerance and withdrawal illness to the exclusion of other factors. This is no longer true. Emphasis now is placed appropriately on the drug user and the circumstances under which the drug is taken. This underlines the point that heavy involvement with drugs depends more upon the person than the drug itself, since any changes in mood, behavior, and emotion will be experienced as pleasurable or alarming depending on psychological or social needs. If a person is stable, he or she may engage in drug experimentation without total involvement. It is the personality of the user that determines how important such drug use becomes—whether it will dominate his life or allow him to be an occasional recreational user. . . .

## Drug Use and Crime

A conventional view of crime and drug addiction is that the first derives from the second. This view holds that addicts engage in illegal activities to obtain money to support their habits. Another view is that the kind of person most likely to start using drugs is the one also most prone to crime, with or without addiction.

According to some social scientists, for certain individuals both crime and drug abuse may be ways of "acting out" emotional needs for danger, excitement, and self-destructive experiences, or they may offer secondary rewards in terms of a subculture's restricted opportunities for legitimate achievement. Finestone and others have noted that criminality, drug use, and drug selling all may be high status forms of behavior in certain subcultures. . . .

There is also ample evidence that many addicts were pursuing criminal lifestyles prior to their drug use. For example, in a random sample of black male adults in St. Louis, Mo., 73 percent of those who became addicted to heroin had police records before addiction.

Another narcotic study has cited several earlier works establishing the existence of illegal activity prior to drug use. Among them was a 1966 study of New York addicts; it found that 57 percent of the sample members treated at the Lexington, Ky., Federal hospital had criminal records before their addiction. (After treatment, the percentages of those who eventually were incarcerated rose to 92 percent.) Similarly, a 1965 study of addicts in the California Rehabilitation Center revealed that only 5 percent had no previous criminal record. . . .

The above figures indicate that the relationship between crime and drugs is not always unidirectional. Some individuals were involved in crime before their drug use, and others apparently chose illegal activity after such use began, in order to secure funds to support their habits. The various interrelationships and patterns are complex and need to be studied further. The drug problem must be dealt with not only for the sake of preventing crime but also to save valuable human resources.

It is important to look at the individual behind the statistics. It is known, for instance, that there is no consistent drug-user personality, and no demonstrated profile for all addicts, but rather a wide range of individuals from different economic, ethnic, and geographical backgrounds. Some of these people may be more closely associated with crime than others, depending on social and economic status or personal makeup. For example, hidden drug abusers have been discovered who are delinquent only in the sense of using heroin, but conventional in other areas. They are steadily employed, support families, have never been arrested or hospitalized for drug usage, and are pursuing conventional goals. . . .

As a further development, crime recently has been associated with the new breed of polydrug users. As contrasted with the traditional street addict, they begin using drugs at an earlier age, became criminally involved earlier, and engage in a more wide-ranging series of offenses. Thus, while the heroin street addict of the past was most likely to commit property crimes of nonpersonal nature such as shoplifting or burglary, these multiple drug users are likely to do whatever is situationally necessary at the spur of the moment to obtain money. However, contrary to much of the popular rhetoric on the subject of crime and addiction, official records still support the contention that drug users, when they do commit crimes, generally participate in nonviolent property crimes to obtain money to purchase drugs. . . .

In the case of 38 male polydrug users interviewed in a 1970 New York study, 6,766 self-reported crimes were committed during a median period of 4 years. These offenses were broken down to 6,290—or 93 percent—property crimes, and 476—or 7 percent—offenses against persons. Burglary was the act most often cited, followed by shoplifting and thefts from vehicles. Crimes such as numbers running, procurement of prostitutes, and drug use or sale were not listed but were assumed to be prevalent in this group. . . .

In conclusion, it is safe to say that many drug addicts were involved in crime before their addiction and would be criminals whether addicted or not. It also is widely accepted that the crimes committed are largely related to things rather than persons. That is, there are clear links between drug addiction and crime in such areas as illegal sale of heroin, shoplifting, burglary, and prostitution.

A COMPREHENSIVE APPROACH TO TREATMENT

. . . The AMA position [of the 1920's] set the tone for the institutional aftercare model of treatment. This called for inpatient detoxification of addicts, including rebuilding their physical health, and providing counseling, vocational rehabilitation, and social services. This inpatient care was followed by supervised aftercare when it was felt the patient could be trusted in the community. The understanding was that if the patient failed and resumed drug use he could be returned to the institution. Abstinence thus became the goal. Indeed, no degree of rehabilitation was considered worthwhile unless the addict could renounce drug use completely and quickly achieve a drug-free state.

For a number of years, abstinence was the primary goal of treatment. During the 1930's, two United States public health hospitals were established. One was located in Lexington, Ky.; the other in Fort Worth, Tex. These facilities did much to carry forward the institutional aftercare approach and quickly became the centers of drug treatment in America, as other levels of government gave up their treatment programs.

Following the end of World War II, there was a resurgence of narcotic use, centered in the deprived socioeconomic areas of the Nation's largest cities. In New York, the problem generated local government response, and Riverside Hospital was opened in New York City in 1950. Programing by the New York State Department of Mental Hygiene followed in 1959. Both programs adopted the institutional aftercare model. In California, a similar program for drug addicts was initiated under the auspices of the State Department of Corrections.

During the 1960's, institutional aftercare programing was expanded in California and New York and under the auspices of the Federal Government. The sixties also saw the advent of therapeutic communities directed by ex-addicts. Their goal closely paralleled that of institutional aftercare, with stress on abstinence and avoidance of all drugs.

The first important change in treatment rationale occurred in 1964 with the development of methadone programing. Up to that time, addicts were frequently viewed as infectious agents. Policymakers frequently advocated quarantine in a drug-free environment for whatever period necessary to quell the "infection"—despite the fact that, following their release, such patients promptly relapsed to drug use once they returned to their former environments.

The methadone approach followed a different line of reasoning. Proponents of this method felt that not every individual could achieve total immediate abstinence. This approach further suggested that it was permissible for narcotic-dependent individuals to be supported by a narcotic drug if this helped them function productively in the community. This thinking was consistent with developments that had taken place elsewhere in medicine, particularly the assistance afforded psychotic patients through the use of tranquilizing drugs.

The desire of several jurisdictions to face their narcotic problem led to the development of still other techniques, including the use of narcotic antagonists, the application of nonpunitive authority concepts, the use of religious approaches, and development of daytime treatment centers, and the opening of special facilities for females. . . .

The gradual accumulation of a variety of treatments has led to a multimodality approach to drug dependence. This approach is advanced through provision at the community level, of a comprehensive range of services that can treat all drug abusers. It is hoped that the largest number of individuals can be helped in this way, even though a particular approach may be applicable to only a small number of people.

**Recommendation 4.1: Adopt multimodality drug treatment systems.**

**Compulsory Treatment**

Many drug-dependent individuals live from day to day, experience one crisis after another, and are unable to relate to treatment on a voluntary basis. Thus the Commission recognizes that the opportunity to curb, through compulsory, nonvoluntary means, the socially disruptive behavior of certain drug users is a necessary part of a comprehensive approach to treatment. Probation, deferred prosecution, and civil commitment procedures all can be and are being used to structure treatment for such individuals. Indeed, most voluntary programs now receive at least some patients through these mechanisms, and find that they can hold them better in treatment as a result of the authority retained and the compulsion applied. . . .

**Recommendation 4.2: Crisis Intervention and Emergency Treatment**

The Commission recommends, as one element of the multimodality treatment program, the establishment of a variety of crisis intervention and drug emergency centers in States and units of local governments that have a significant population of narcotics addicts and other drug-dependent individuals. Although the specific nature of such centers can only be determined after careful study of local conditions, experience indicates that they should include at least some of the following characteristics:

1. Selected centers should be located either in or in close proximity to a hospital emergency room, detoxification facility, or clinic.

2. In patient facilities and beds should be available at selected centers for patients who require treatment on more than a one-time basis; e.g., those withdrawing from heroin, barbiturates, and sedative hypnotics or from the effects of a long run on amphetamines or methedrine.

3. Selected centers should be separated from hospital or medical facilities, be staffed with peer-group individuals backed by the facilities of a nearby hospital, and should provide services to runaways and persons with emotional problems or venereal disease as well as to those with drug involvement.

4. Telephone hotlines, operated in conjunction with walk-in information and referral centers, should be a part of the crisis intervention program in most cities.

5. Counseling centers offering individual and group guidance should be established, and should have effective liaison with other agencies that supply a wide range of services

such as housing, family assistance, vocational training, and job referral.

## Methadone Maintenance Treatment Programs

### Problems of Methadone Maintenance

Methadone maintenance treatment passed through a phase in which many observers felt it represented the solution to the narcotic problem. However, a more moderate position seems to be indicated at present. For example, the rate of those retained in treatment was once thought to be as high as 80 percent or more, but it actually approaches 50 percent or less over time. In addition, it now seems clear that many methadone patients turn to non-narcotic drugs once they have been stabilized. Alcohol and cocaine abuse by such individuals is fairly frequent. Others use barbiturates and amphetamines, and still others a variety of substances. . . .

In spite of these objections, high-dose methadone maintenance is viewed today as an important approach for confirmed heroin addicts. It retains in treatment, on a voluntary basis, a much larger percentage of patients than other approaches. Evaluations performed on patients thus far indicate that their rearrest record is low, and that significant numbers find their way back to employment, school, or training with the passage of time. Further, at least some of those who drop out of the program ultimately come back, and are better assisted the second or third time around.

**Recommendation 4.3: Establish methadone maintenance programs.**

## Narcotic Antagonists Treatment Programs

In the mid-sixties, clinical tests with opiate antagonists were begun. Such substances, when given in adequate amounts, block the effects of heroin and other narcotic drugs. They are useful for treating narcotic overdose situations because they can quickly reverse narcotic coma. However, they also can precipitate a withdrawal illness when given to individuals who are physically dependent on narcotics. In the past, they were utilized only in small amounts to cause minimal withdrawal symptoms for diagnostic purposes.

In 1966, their use took a new direction. Armed with a new, long-acting antagonist, cyclazocine, clinical researchers first detoxified narcotic addicts, then stabilized and maintained them on the new drug. The goal was to create a pharmacological state whereby the effect of any narcotic would be nullified, with the ultimate aim of removing the patient from all drug use. Though some success has been achieved, it has been with relatively small numbers of patients. While this suggests a possible role for these substances, no sweeping claims can be made for them thus far.

**Recommendation 4.4: Establish narcotic antagonist treatment programs.**

### Therapeutic Community Programs

Therapeutic communities are drug-free environments where the drug user is viewed as an underdeveloped, immature personality. This approach is designed to facilitate emotional growth. Central to this concept is the existence of a community prepared to accept or reject the individual, depending upon the behavior shown. Banishment from this "family" group thus emerges as a severe punishment, and is used as a lever for social control. . . .

The vogue for the therapeutic community peaked several years ago and has diminished somewhat since. Growing criticism emanated from the realization that only a small number of residents were being rehabilitated and returned to the community. Directors have been urged to redefine the population they can actually help, and to build in additional components to reinforce the program, either through the use of "rational authority"—that is, drawing upon probation and parole—or by incorporating chemotherapy as Daytop Village in New York City has been exploring recently. It has also been suggested that they use minority group leadership to attract more blacks, Puerto Ricans, and Chicanos for treatment. . . .

### Recommendation 4.5: Therapeutic Community Programs

**The Commission recommends that States and units of local government having a significant population of narcotics addicts and other drug-dependent individuals consider establishing a therapeutic drug-free community program as one element of a multimodality approach to treatment. . . .**

### Residential Programs

. . . The rationale for these programs recognizes that a comprehensive effort must include some use of authority to hold selected patients in treatment long enough to deal with their psychological and social problems. Such programs need to encompass a full range of professional and paraprofessional services within a variety of settings. Once placed in a structured environment, the addict must not be returned to the community abruptly but in stages, with varying kinds of support and supervision provided along the way.

**Recommendation 4.6: Organize residential drug treatment programs.**

**Recommendation 4.7: Encourage broader flexibility in varying treatment approaches.**

### Voluntary Court Referral for Addicts

The Federal Government, through its Special Action Office for Drug Abuse Prevention, currently advocates a program called "Treatment Alternatives to Street Crime" (TASC). This program involves voluntary referral of the addict-defendant to community-based treatment in lieu of prosecution.

TASC uses the lever of the criminal justice system to bring the addict into treatment and to hold him there. At the same time, it reduces processing, custodial, and other burdens on police, courts, and penal institutions. . . .

Results of a voluntary urinalysis and of the interview are sent to the court, to the prosecutor, and to the individual's lawyer or public defender. A judge determines whether to release the individual outright on his own recognizance or on bail, to send the individual to detention, or to order treatment as a condition of release with diversion of the individual to TASC. In either event, if the person is intoxicated on drugs, he is provided with medical assistance during detoxification.

Persons entering TASC are evaluated by a diagnostic unit and sent to a holding facility pending transfer to a community treatment program. While in treatment, the individual is checked by a tracking system to assure that he is meeting conditions of release. If the individual drops out of treatment or fails to comply with other conditions of release, he is treated by the court as if he had violated conditions of release.

When the individual's case is set for trial, the court may take into account his cooperation and success in treatment and may determine that he should remain in TASC in lieu of prosecution.

**Recommendation 4.8: Voluntary Court Referral of Addicts**

The Commission recommends that States and units of local government having a significant population of narcotics addicts and other drug-dependent persons establish procedures for voluntary referral of the addict-defendant to treatment before conviction. Such efforts might be modeled on the TASC program (Treatment Alternatives to Street Crime), and should meet at least the following criteria:

1. Liberal eligibility requirements should be developed to allow a large number of defendants to be screened for participation.

2. Minimal punitive connotations should be incorporated in the program. Undue delays in court procedures, as well as forced concessions from the addict, should be avoided. Supervision should be as nonpunitive as possible and addicts should be advised that the alternatives to diversion—plea, probation, and incarceration—may result in the lasting stigma of a criminal record, as well as delay in receiving treatment.

3. Treatment should be made available as early as possible in the criminal process even, where possible without prejudice to society's right to protection, before a decision to divert has been made. The device of pretrial release on bond could be used, as well as release on personal recognizance upon the addict's acceptance of treatment.

4. Treatment should be flexible enough to allow changes in the length of the predisposition period in diversion. This would minimize the period of time necessarily spent in treatment.

5. Inducements for the defendant who has been diverted to remain in treatment should be provided for effective control. Most, if not all, of the time spent in treatment should be community-based out-patient care, if possible. Dismissal of the charges should be arranged upon successful completion of treatment.

6. Diversion procedures should be developed without losing sight of society's right to be protected or of constitutional safeguards designed to protect the defendant—for example, equal protection under the law, the right to speedy trial, and guarantees against self-incrimination. (See the Commission's Report on Courts for a detailed discussion of this issue.)

**Heroine Maintenance**

... This Commission believes that, as an overall solution to the narcotics problem, heroin maintenance has overwhelming

181

drawbacks. Among those not already mentioned are the following:

1. Heroin maintenance could in time have drastic negative-incentive effects on other voluntary programs, even if intake were initially limited to those who had failed in other programs.

2. The requirements of high dosages to discourage clandestine purchases and multiple visits per day would make regular employment impossible in many cases, overburden the clinic staffs, and increase the possibility of illicit diversion.

3. Heroin maintenance would not be directly relevant to the increasing abuse of amphetamines and barbiturates, except to the extent that heroin is the favored drug among multiple drug abusers. (They would presumably not seek other drugs as long as the free heroin continued to produce highs.)

On the basis of its current understanding, the Commission believes that the heroin maintenance approach has no place in a comprehensive system of care, and is a potentially harmful method of treatment for the reasons cited. . . .

**Recommendation 4.9: Establish training programs for drug treatment personnel.**

DRUG ABUSE PREVENTION PROGRAMING

**Past Prevention Efforts**

It is likely that only a small proportion, approximately 1 percent or less of the 13- through 30-year-old population group, is involved in heavy, dysfunctional drug use. A large proportion, perhaps 22 to 24 percent, is engaged in active drug-seeking behavior and demonstrates regular drug-taking patterns. The remaining three-fourths are most likely either nonusers, self-medicating users, or social-recreational drug users. Prevention therefore must address the predominant group. In short, the great task of drug prevention is to guard against the individual's movement from occasional to serious dysfunctional use.

**Recommendation 4.10: Plan comprehensive, community-wide drug prevention.**

**Recommendation 4.11: Coordinate drug programs through a State agency.**

**Recommendation 4.12: Coordinate Federal, State, and local drug programs.**

## 5: Programs for Employment

. . . Correlations between individual failure in the labor market and criminal behavior, and similar correlations between high local unemployment rates and high local crime rates, suggest that unequal economic status is a major cause of crime. . . .

### ALTERNATIVE APPROACHES

It would be difficult to develop a realistic set of recommendations for reducing criminality by providing greater economic opportunity for every present or potential criminal suffering from economic disabilities. But certain groups in the population, who have economic problems that result in part from unequal opportunities, can be identified as high crime risks and given concentrated attention. One group consists of individuals whose basic problem is economic, and whose failure in the world of work is a primary source of their criminality. This group includes many parolees, probationers, and previous offenders—those who are no longer in the purview of the corrections system. Their employment problems were usually severe before their first contact with the law, and these problems are typically aggravated by the stigma of a criminal record. This group also includes low income inner city youth, especially males in their late teens and early twenties, for whom street life, work, and crime are mixed together, making contact with the law almost inevitable.

Another identifiable high risk group is made up of individuals addicted to drugs or suffering from emotional problems that lead them into crime. The criminal careers of many of these individuals are closely related to their lack of employment or job skills. Many are involved in a vicious cycle: economic exclusion is a root cause of specific patterns of personal deviancy; involvement in these patterns dictates continued economic exclusion and increasing probabilities of criminal activity.

Another group of actual and potential criminals, larger but less easily isolated, can be assisted by aggregate measures designed to change the economic climate of American cities. In this group are individuals not directly and immediately motivated to crime by their own unemployment of their economically related personal deviancies. They are the products of an environment that condones and sometimes rewards criminal behavior, while offering little inducement for avoiding criminal activities. Unless this environment is changed, a continuous stream of offenders will be produced. To reverse this pattern requires across the board upgrading of opportunities for those left out of America's economic, social, and political mainstream. . . .

## Choosing Among the Alternatives

From a short-range point of view, it is far easier to address the employment problems of those who may be disposed to crime than it is to change the economic and social conditions that breed it. Measures can be specifically directed to the individuals who need help most, and can be concentrated on their particular needs. But the impact of these efforts will be severely limited unless opportunities are opened and the effects of unequal economic status are directly attacked. There is no way to know in advance whether the most effective appproach is to concentrate resources on potential criminals with economic handicaps, to direct them to individuals with additional personal problems such as drug addiction, or to try to alter the economic and social system. . . .

ECONOMIC DISADVANTAGE AND CRIME

## The Employment Problems of Offenders

. . . Some of the best available data comes from a comprehensive 1964 survey of males released from Federal prisons. This survey shows that 11 percent of the group had never been employed and more than half had been employed a total of less than 2 years before incarceration, even though their median age was 29 years.

Postrelease experiences were equally dismal. As of June 30, 1964, less than three-fifths of the study's sample were employed full time and 16 percent were unemployed. Comparative figures for the national male civilian labor force showed that four-fifths were employed full time and only 5 percent were unemployed. More than half of those studied in the survey had worked in unskilled or service jobs prior to commitment; more than two-fifths returned to such jobs upon release. The median monthly income of those employed was only $256 in 1964, while average income in the private, nonagricultural sector was $394.

## The Criminal Dimensions of Economic Problems

. . . These data suggest that for every offender with employment problems there are many nonoffenders in equally serious trouble. Many nonoffenders also have motivational

184

problems, low skills, educational deficiencies, and limited opportunities.

... Too often inner city youth find the traditional ways of achieving meaningful work, status, and high income indirect or frustrating, and illegal activities seem to offer an easier road to recognition and economic success.

## Concentration on the Highest Crime Risks

This Commission believes that if more numerous and attractive job opportunities were available many potential offenders would take them. Recent experience in cities shows long waiting lists of people seeking training or job placement assistance. There is abundant documentation of the relationship between the availability of jobs and the level of criminal activity. Glaser and Rice found that property crimes by adults vary directly with the level of unemployment. Fleischer's complex statistical analysis estimated that for every 1 percent increase in unemployment there is an 0.5 percent increase in the rate of delinquency.

A recent study, "Crime, Youth, and the Labor Market," concluded that changing labor market conditions are sufficient to explain increasing crime rates for youth. Crime rates could be explained not only by the unemployment rates but by participation rates which represent the proportion of each age group in the labor force. Other studies have demonstrated that property crimes are more likely to be committed by those in the lower socioeconomic classes. The cause-and-effect relationship cannot be proven beyond question nor quantified precisely, but it is clear that unemployment reduction will have a significant impact on criminal conduct. ...

To identify young inner city males as a target group in fighting crime through employment programs is not an act of discrimination; it is recognition of a fact. At the height of the economic boom in 1969, more than 25 percent of nonwhite 16- to 19-year-olds, and a smaller but still substantial portion of 20- to 24-year-olds in the central cities were unemployed—a rate more than seven times that for adults in the central city. Low income white youth and other minorities had similar problems, which undoubtedly contributed to high rates of crime. ...

## Drug Addiction and Economic Status

Current evidence and theory support the proposition that crime-producing personal deviancies frequently develop in otherwise normal individuals when they experience economic and social exclusion, and the frustration and despair that exclusion generates. Exclusion from the mainstream of community life, economic or otherwise, frequently presents individuals with their first stimulus for deviant behavior. Once even marginally involved in crime, the individual finds himself even further excluded from the community—a process sociologists have termed the "deviancy reinforcement cycle."

Such individuals, including drug abusers and addicts, are a logical target group for special economic attention. Efforts emphasizing integration or reintegration into the world of work are a necessary adjunct to treatment programs and social services designed to change the life pattern of the criminal. This is an approach that recognizes that the deviant is a person who has been gradually compelled to identify with and participate in a subculture which rejects mainstream community values. . . .

## Drug Addiction, Crime, and Unemployment

Getting and using drugs lends goals and structure to the life of the addict; the cycle of self-administering drugs, hustling for cash, and purchasing more drugs is an invariable daily routine. Contrary to the popular image of the idle, self-indulgent life of the addict, the necessities of maintaining a habit generally dictate a demanding and time consuming round of activity. Furthermore, the hierarchical patterns of the drug subculture, based on such factors as the size of an individual's habit or his proficiency at avoiding arrest, reward "success" with status, much as economic and personal achievements are recognized in the context of legitimate work. . . .

SYSTEMATIC ECONOMIC CONSIDERATIONS AND CRIME

## Economic and Social Characteristics of High Crime Areas

. . . Street crimes, the kinds of crime that worry most citizens, are closely associated with a host of social and economic factors that define inner city poverty neighborhoods. Among those factors is the substantial gap between the average family income of whites and minorities in this country.

Factors contributing to delinquency rates include income, family stability, and population density in the residential area. Available data tend to support the idea that delinquency rates are highest in urban slum areas where these socioeconomic conditions are worst. In Washington, D.C., for example, neighborhoods with the highest delinquency rates are those areas that have the highest rate of public welfare recipients, the largest percentage of births without prenatal care, and the greatest population density in the city. . . .

Attempts to isolate cause and effect in these associations between crime, income, race, and social factors are difficult because of circularity. For example, narcotics-related crime in the inner city is certainly affected by the aura of despair resulting from unemployment, low wages, decaying housing, and the dominance of white society. But widespread narcotics abuse aggravates all these problems and contributes to core city deterioration. Even without demonstrations of formal cause-and-effect relationship, this close correlation between crime rates and a complex of other factors suggests that one way to combat crime is to change the social and economic conditions related to it. Street crime is spawned, in part, by the factors that exist in many low income areas.

### National Economic Conditions and Unemployment

. . . Unemployment in inner city neighborhoods is sensitive to conditions in the national economy. From 1968 through 1971, unemployment rates in poverty areas averaged 60 percent above the national unemployment rate. In only 4 of the 16 quarters in these 4 years was the difference below 50 percent or above 70 percent of the national rate. When the core city's underemployment is added to its unemployment, it seems obvious that slackness in poverty area labor markets is roughly 3 to 3.5 times greater than in the entire national economy—assuming national underemployment is less extensive than underemployment in the inner city. . . .

Between 1967 and 1970, aggregate unemployment declined and then rose steeply. In the fourth quarter of 1967, unemployment stood at 3.9 percent; by the fourth quarter of 1968, it had fallen to a low of 3.4 percent; but with the subsequent recession it rose to 5.8 percent in the fourth quarter of 1970. Black inner city youths were at the tip of the whiplash of these changes. The 0.5 percentage point drop in aggregate unemployment between the fourth quarter of 1967 and the fourth quarter of 1968 was accompanied by a 9 percentage point decline in the rate, not seasonally adjusted, for black teenage males, and a smaller but still significant decline for those in their early twenties. Conversely, while the aggregate unemployment rate rose 2.4 percentage points between the fourth quarter of 1968 and the fourth quarter of 1970, the rate of black teenagers' unemployment increased 15 percentage points. . . .

## The Dual Labor Market Hypothesis

... Today, for example, a black high school graduate has little more chance of finding a job than a black with only an eighth grade education, and a much lower probability of being employed than a white high school graduate. Among those who are employed, black high school graduates' incomes are far below whites, and not significantly higher than the incomes of blacks with less education. Among whites the value of a high school diploma is much greater, both in terms of finding a job and the wage rate that the job offers.

... The studies described above show that education by itself does not increase the welfare of minorities or make them more competitive with whites in labor markets. In the slack economic conditions of the past few years, seniority rules and the scarcity of jobs have kept racial occupational patterns stable. High black unemployment rates at all educational levels are consistent with black access to dead-end jobs only. If racial discrimination is a persistent, structural characteristic of the American economy, then new, more aggressive strategies will be required to eliminate this type of discrimination.

## The Flight from the City

... The population shift of higher income groups to the suburbs and lower income groups to the central cities has led to the deterioration of the urban property tax base and the increase of tax rates on remaining property. As tax rates have risen, maintenance costs on the older physical plants in the cities also have increased. Overall data on the extent of industrial shifts are not available, but even large corporations that may have the most to gain from locating in business and financial centers have now begun to leave central cities such as New York, N.Y., and Washington, D.C., for suburbs like Stamford, Conn., and Alexandria, Va.

OVERCOMING THE EMPLOYMENT PROBLEMS
OF HIGH RISK POTENTIAL OFFENDERS

## Helping Inner City Youth

... Available research on dropouts indicates that little is gained by forcing these students back to school as the school is presently structured. Compulsory education laws created part of the problem. Dropouts frequently are delinquent, but their delinquency invariably begins when they are in school. Rather than force youngsters to endure school failure and frustration, the school should provide a more meaningful education in relation to the probable career objectives of the student, and, together with the community, should assist these youth in making the transition into the world of work.

For example, subsidies based on the real costs of employing initially less productive workers can be given for hiring and training the unskilled and semiskilled. Since black and other minority youths are often found in these groups, such a subsidy program can operate as a positive incentive to eliminate discriminatory practices, leaving the employer with no excuse to turn down a minority member because he is less educated or experienced. . . .

## Combating Discrimination

. . . The Nation's record of fighting discrimination has not been impressive. There have been many Federal efforts, but they have had little impact. Efforts under State and local legislation have generally proved even less effective.

Of all the Federal efforts, the Equal Employment Opportunities Commission (EEOC), created by the Civil Rights Act of 1964, has had the broadest mandate and the feeblest tools. Under that Act the five-person Commission was empowered to investigate complaints of discrimination and, if it found a complaint just, to attempt a voluntary conciliation between employer and employee. When conciliation failed, the Commission had no further recourse in most cases. Under the Equal Employment Opportunity Act of 1972, the EEOC has new powers to bring enforcement actions where conciliation fails. The potential of this new power remains to be tested in practice.

Another agency charged with combating discrimination is the Office of Federal Contract Compliance (OFCC), which has the authority to delay or cancel any Federal contracts with employers who do not take affirmative action to provide equal employment opportunity. Those who are especially recalcitrant can be denied government contracts, If enforced, this power would have far-reaching significance. Executive Order 11246, which gives the OFCC its broad powers, is more inclusive in combating discrimination than the Civil Rights Act of 1964. The order not only precludes discrimination but requires contractors to take positive steps to overcome its effects. In some instances, especially areawide bargaining with builders, this has been interpreted to mean that equal entry is not sufficient, but that quotas or other numerical goals can be required to bring minority participation up to stated levels. However, contractors frequently ignore or postpone contract compliance recommendations because the OFCC is reluctant to use its powers.

## Educating Youth for Employment

... There are a variety of old and new approaches to improving the preparation for work provided by the school system. The oldest is the vocational or career education program. Available evidence indicates that, despite problems, this is effective in helping minority youths. Academic courses generally concentrate on preparation for college, although less than half of high school graduates will attend college. The large proportion of youth are in general studies programs that are typically without direction, providing little more than a weak exposure to academic subjects. Only in career education courses are students likely to acquire useful occupational skills and exposure to the demands they will encounter outside of school.

More experimental educational reforms may also be in order. For example, the private sector might become directly involved, with large corporations offering a wide range of assistance to schools in low income neighborhoods. Cooperative education, in which the student's curriculum is adapted to his vocational needs in a particular career, is another possibility. The Opportunities Industrialization Center (OIC) has had substantial success with this approach in many cities. Central to its program are periodic skill shortage surveys to determine the future manpower needs of an area. Vocational curricula are then devised in cooperation with local unions and employers to satisfy entry level requirements in a variety of trades. The OIC experience demonstrates that involving potential employers in program design frequently results in a higher rate of successful job placements and fewer trainees frustrated by job shortages.

## Expansion of Job Opportunities

*Job Corps*

The Job Corps concentrates on a clientele with even more needs, residential and nonresidential basic education and other intensive services to youths aged 16 to 21. In 1970, almost 66 percent of enrollees were black—61 percent male and 39 percent female. Among the blacks, only 4 percent of the boys and 25 percent of the girls had completed high school.

Working intensively with such a group, often providing room and board, the Job Corps is inevitably expensive. Annual costs still average about $6,500 per enrollee despite drastic cost cutting. Unfortunately, the results to date have not demonstrated that the investments are justified. Innovative educational techniques have not proved as effective as had been hoped. The enrollees who had trouble with conventional academic programs have had almost as much difficulty in the Job Corps. Followup studies suggest that the gains in earnings of former enrollees, both white and minority, were slight in comparison with a control group and that the incidence of unemployment among the minority youth was not noticeably affected by the Job Corps experience. . . .

**Recommendation 5.1: Expand job opportunities for disadvantaged youth.**

**Recommendation 5.2: Broaden after-school and summer employment programs.**

### Pretrial Intervention Programs

Along with youth, another target group for crime prevention through employment aid consists of those who are or have been involved in the police, courts, and corrections systems. Efforts to upgrade employability are needed as an adjunct to probation, parole, and rehabilitation in prison, but they are also needed for those who have left the purview of the criminal justice system.

One approach is to provide individual manpower services to those arrested, prior to court disposition. Examples of such efforts are the Manhattan Court Employment Project, established in New York City by the Vera Institute of Justice, and Project Crossroads, operated in Washington, D.C., by the National Committee for Children and Youth. These programs provide employment-oriented services to young men and women in the pretrial stage of the criminal process, concentrating on those without serious prior records. The courts suspend judgment for three months in the cases of participants, and agree to consider dropping charges upon successful completion of the project. This approach can be effective in solving employment problems and reducing recidivism.

For instance, Project Crossroads worked with a clientele that was 84 percent male and had 87 percent minority group representation. Three-fifths were aged 18 to 29, and 63 percent had less than a high school education. Fewer than half the participants were employed at the time of intake, while most of these earned less than $1.75 an hour at unskilled jobs.

Despite these handicaps, participants benefited in their employment status, their wages, and their occupation distribution. A year after the project, 44 percent of a participant sample had an average wage of $2.00 or more per hour compared with 20 percent at intake, though some of this gain is due to aging. In the year prior to the project, 30 percent worked at least 80 percent of the year; in the year following, nearly 50 percent worked that long. Overall recidivism was reduced, though the benefits diminished after the project was over. Only 29 percent committed further crimes during the three months of the project, compared with 50 percent of the control group; but 71 percent committed further crimes in the 11 months following the project, compared with 50 percent of the control sample. . . .

The Manhattan and Crossroads projects demonstrate that pretrial manpower programs can help arrestees by improving their employment and diverting them from jail. Society benefits to the degree that increased output and reduced correction expenses outweigh the cost of the program. From available evidence, modest expansion is warranted to test the concept fully. . . .

**Recommendation 5.3: Establish pretrial intervention programs.**

**Recommendation 5.4: Expand job opportunities for offenders and ex-offenders.**

**Recommendation 5.5: Remove ex-offender employment barriers.**

**Recommendation 5.6: Create public employment programs.**

EMPLOYMENT ASSISTANCE IN
DEALING WITH DRUG PROBLEMS

. . . All available studies indicate that improved employment status among methadone maintenance patients is intimately related to decreased criminality and continued participation in the drug program. A patient who is already employed at intake is more likely to remain than one who is not, because he has more at stake. One followup study of Methadone Maintenance participants showed that fully 88 percent of those employed at intake remained in treatment for at least 2 years. No similar statistics are available on the retention ratio of participants who find work after enrollment, but there is reason to believe that, with employment the motivation to continue treatment increases markedly.

## Employment Opportunities for Former Drug Users

In the next few years, existing methadone maintenance programs will be under considerable pressure to expand rapidly and serve the estimated 35 to 50 percent of the addict population that can benefit from this therapeutic approach. During the same period, hundreds of new programs will be created. Since the cost of methadone maintenance ranges from $500 to $2,500 per patient per year, depending largely on the range and quality of ancillary services, an informed judgment of the necessity of these services will be required before rational program expansion can occur. . . .

According to Dr. Alan Freedman's widely accepted eclectic view of addiction and treatment, the proper goal of any therapeutic program is not total abstinence from heroin use by participants. Instead, it is a reduction in the damage caused to themselves and others by their destructive personal life styles. Low cost, high volume methadone maintenance treatment will, in the short run, have the greatest impact on aggregate heroin use. But, in the longer run, it will have a less favorable impact on patient behavior than higher cost, lower volume programs offered by therapeutic communities. Patients who do not receive supportive services, particularly in the area of employment, will drop out of maintenance programs and resume heroin use in greater numbers. Similarly, they will be more likely than fully supported patients to attempt the combination of methadone maintenance and continued criminality. . . .

Perhaps the most promising alternative is to attempt to integrate methadone maintenance programs more completely with existing vocational education, skill training, and job development programs. If adequate referral mechanisms were developed, and if existing manpower programs were sufficiently funded to accept large numbers of referrals from methadone treatment centers, a full range of supportive employment services might be made available to many former addicts at substantial total cost savings. . . .

**Recommendation 5.7: Expand job opportunities for former drug abusers.**

**Recommendation 5.8: Target employment, income, and credit efforts in poverty areas.**

**Recommendation 5.9: Require employers' compliance with antidiscrimination laws.**

**Recommendation 5.10: Increase support of minority businesses.**

### Housing and Transportation Services

... All the programs just discussed can be grouped under the title of "ghetto gilding," for all are designed to improve economic and social conditions in inner city minority neighborhoods. A different approach to the web of interrelated social and economic factors that produce inner city crime, poverty, unemployment, and despair is to eradicate ghettos as distinct entities, integrating the residents into the rest of the metropolitan areas economically, socially, and culturally. This strategy of ghetto dispersal has been highly controversial. Militant minority groups have attacked it as cultural genocide designed to cover up the socioeconomic problems of minorities rather than overcome them. In particular, they claim, ghetto dispersal ignores the hard core unemployable who cannot benefit from access to a job because his school, job, and criminal histories prevent any employer from hiring him. Therefore, it is argued, ghetto dispersal simply results in taking economic and social leaders out of the inner city and leaving it smaller but even more desperate.

Nevertheless, ghetto dispersal programs have staunch defenders who argue that inner city problems have been impervious to many of the attempted solutions. For example, attempts to upgrade housing through urban renewal have led to actual reductions in the availability of low income housing in many places such as Washington, D.C.'s Southeast area. In other cities, low income public housing construction has resulted in disasters like the Pruitt-Igoe project of St. Louis, Mo. Land values in most cities now are so high that private low income housing is economically infeasible, and public budgets are too small to permit redevelopment on the vast scale needed.

Because of the economic cost and social failure of large low income housing projects, attention has focused on scatter site housing in metropolitan areas. Scatter site housing usually entails public construction of a few units of low income housing in a middle class residential area, although the concept may be extended to as large a development as the Forest Hills project in Queens, N.Y., where over 200 apartments are planned. A similar program consists of giving rent supplements to families eligible for public housing, and letting them use their own public housing rents plus public supplements to obtain commercial housing. In both programs, inner city residents can move closer to jobs, better schools, or safe streets. But opposition from prospective neighbors and inadequate government budgets so far have limited these programs to small scale tests.

**Recommendation 5.11: Alleviate housing and transportation discrimination.**

## 6: Programs for Education

... The conclusion of the Commission is that we are doing very little in the schools as a direct, intentional effort to discourage young people from criminal careers. Moreover, there is the strong suggestion that some of the basic conditions of schools which we take for granted actually create the animosities, frustrations, and despair that lead people eventually to violence.

In the first place, the school system shows an almost absolute imperviousness to change. Schools have changed little in the past hundred years. Although changes in values, customs, life styles, technology, and knowledge have been extensive, schools seem unable to adapt to people's needs. This inability must be considered a major contribution to the frustrations that breed crime. Jerrold Zacharias' contention that "it is easier to put a man on the moon than to reform the public schools" is a tragic historical fact. ...

To develop realistic goals and recommendations for an educational system that will contribute to the reduction and prevention of crime, one can pursue two major alternatives. One can conclude, first, that the educational system in the cities is defeated, and that the system as a whole requires radical restructuring and change. As a second alternative, one can identify certain features, components, or practices of the system as contributors to criminal behavior and suggest programs to improve these.

The difficulty with the first alternative is that a total restructuring of education is impossible, even if it were necessary. The problem with the second alternative is that it is remedial. It is an attempt to repair defects whose causes we leave unaffected. Moreover, it is costly, and in most cases where it has been tried, it has not proven very effective. The point of view adopted by the discussion and recommendations presented here represents a composite of the two alternatives. ...

## THE HOME AS A LEARNING ENVIRONMENT

The human organism adopts permanent basic organizations of stimuli from the environment quite early in life. There is evidence of the fact that by the time children reach age 7, half the basic response strategies have been imprinted for life. Certainly by the time the child reaches the end of puberty, most of his habits of emotional response, patterns of thinking and problem-solving, and basic physical response patterns are virtually impervious to change, except under new and—depending upon the age level of the individual—fairly powerful environments. . . .

Differences in early childhood learning are caused by different home environments and are not overcome by normal schooling. This is one of the pathbreaking findings of the Coleman Report, confirmed by similar findings in England.

Fifty percent of the child's intelligence as measured at age 17 develops between conception and age 4.

Fifty percent of academic achievement that children will have attained at age 18 develops by the end of the third grade (age 9).

Thirty-three percent of the variability at adolescence of intellectual interest, emotional dependence, and aggression is predictable by age 2. At about age 5, as much as one-half of the variance at adolescence is predictable. . . .

This research appears to indicate that the home and surrounding neighborhood are such powerful factors that the schools can make little impact on the deterrence or encouragement of any behavior. Indeed, the Jencks' study has shown that the school has far less impact in selected areas than most people suspected. The study asserts that "variations in what children learn in school depend largely on what they bring to school, not on variations in what schools offer them. . . ."

. . . The [Homework House Project in Berkeley, California] is organized with a home as the center of seven ever-widening circles of surrounding resources and support. Each home in the first circle has a parent who is regarded as a synergist, or cooperator. The second circle is the neighborhood-community parent organization, which provides parents to work as teachers, aides, tutors, materials developers, or in other roles. Neighbors comprise the third circle and classroom teachers, the fourth. In the fifth circle are members of the Berkeley Unified School District staff, and in the sixth, resource people from throughout the Bay Area. The final circle is characterized by an incentive program—the provision of awards, such as books, games, clothing, and tickets to sports events, to either parents or students for exceptional achievement. . . .

**Recommendation 6.1: Adopt teacher training programs for parents.**

THE SCHOOL AS A MODEL OF JUSTICE

. . . Children develop concepts of justice, law, and good citizenship primarily from continual first-hand experience with the realities those concepts embrace. School children should understand the reasons for law and order in their surroundings; students should have a part in formulating the rules of behavior derived from these reasons; and these rules should be in accord with practices of justice and fairness that students encounter outside the school.

To the extent that democratic practices are lacking in the formulation and enforcement of school rules and regulations, school authorities should design alternatives. . . .

**Recommendation 6.2: The School as a Model of Justice**

**The Commission recommends that school authorities adopt policies and practices to insure that schools and classrooms reflect the best examples of justice and democracy in their organization and operation, and in the rules and regulations governing student conduct.**

**Recommendation 6.3: Guarantee literacy to elementary school students.**

**Recommendation 6.4: Provide special language services for bicultural students.**

**Recommendation 6.5: Develop career preparation programs in schools.**

**Recommendation 6.6: Provide effective supportive services in schools.**

**Recommendation 6.7: Offer alternative education programs for deviant students.**

USE OF SCHOOL FACILITIES FOR COMMUNITY PROGRAMS

When cities and schools were smaller, teachers and neighborhood residents met often in both formal and informal situations. However, as cities became larger, community living became more complicated. This situation isolated staff from students and the school from the community. Although the schools received the financial support of the community, they tended to ignore almost completely the problems of the community as a whole.

The school calendar was originally built around an agrarian lifestyle—classes were scheduled so that schools would close during the planting and harvesting periods. The economy was dependent on the availability of children and young adults to work in the fields, and the schools regulated their hours and weeks around this principle. World War I and the industrial revolution of the early twenties, followed by rapid technological development, turned the basic economic posture from farming to industry. The workweek was reduced to 40 hours, in most cases, yet the school paid little attention to the change in either the economic system or the general lifestyle. Schools still operated as they did in the 19th century—6 hours a day, 5 days a week, 180 days a year.

The community had taxed itself heavily to provide a facility that was being used 25 percent of the time for a small percentage of the total population—those aged 6 to 16. . . .

A school that fails to provide opportunity for people to participate actively in meaningful educational programs and in decisionmaking functions is obsolete, and does not deserve continued support.

School experiences must be relevant to life experiences and employment opportunities. Schools must become accessible to every resident, young and old, on a 7-day a week, year-round basis. The school is a public instrument and must be used to train and serve all the people. Since it is the principal training institution, it is imperative that the school be provided with the resources to operate on a fulltime basis. . . .

*Inventory of Facilities*

The first step is to take a community inventory of facilities available for educational and recreational purposes. Once this is done, plans can be made for using all available space, equipment, and staff. It might be discovered, for instance, that there is no need for a new wing on an existing building or that planned buildings can be delayed indefinitely.

There is a need to consider use of the facilities on a 12-month basis. Teachers and administrators would be given an opportunity to work a 12-month year (1-month vacation), or a conventional 9-month year, and be paid accordingly. Students would be scheduled to attent in different time-frames so that they can select a vacation period consistent with family wishes and interests.

The school cafeteria would provide service 7 days a week to those in need. The elderly, those on welfare, and the children of working mothers would all be eligible.

The school buses that now run for an hour or two in the morning and again in the afternoon would be used as needs arise: to take young people to summer camps or on weekend trips; to provide transportation for the elderly; to move students from suburban to urban settings and vice-versa.

School libraries would be accessible to the entire family and open until 9 or 10 o'clock at night.

The occupational spaces would be used during the day by students and in the evenings and weekends to provide additional education and training to their families. These same laboratories could be used by nearby reformatories for the special training of those incarcerated.

Child care centers should be operated in the schools as part of those courses dealing with family living. Extended day care should be provided for children of working mothers.

A variety of day, night, and summer classes should be conducted to assist families in managing their home responsibilities, and to provide self-improvement opportunities for adults and out-of-school youth. For example, classes could be conducted in budgeting and income tax, smoking clinics, child growth and development, alcohol and narcotic abuse, sex education, teacher training for parents, sewing and upholstering, judo and body building, home remodeling, small business opportunities, appliance and automobile repair, or cooking and baking.

Many adult residents in the community have not completed the requirements for a high school diploma and are, therefore, handicapped in securing satisfactory employment and promotion. Through the services of the schools, a wide range of high school credit and high school equivalency classes should be offered both during the day and in the evenings. . . .

Schools make excellent community centers because they are centrally located; their facilities are adaptable to broad community uses; they are owned and supported by the public; and they are nonpolitical.

The traditional school, operating 6 hours a day, 5 days a week for 39 weeks each year is a luxury this era cannot afford. Too many Americans are lost in their leisure time.

Wasted talent and unfulfilled lives are a blight on the Nation. . . .

**Recommendation 6.8: Open schools for community activities.**

**Recommendation 6.9: Adopt merit training and promotion policies for teachers.**

## 7: Programs for Recreation

USE OF RECREATION TO PREVENT DELINQUENCY

A recreation-oriented delinquency prevention program must confront the major influences in the lives of young people. Empey points out that, "juveniles, and especially delinquents, exist within a narrow life space centering around the family, school, and peers. Consequently, an especially difficult situation is created for any individual who is cut off from two of these three major sources of support. . . ."

Special emphasis must be placed on programs that reach out to youths who traditionally reject or avoid established recreation programs, and the effectiveness of such efforts needs to be assessed. Youths whose behavior typically precludes their participation in recreation programs should be permitted to take part in programs designed to deal with disruptive behavior in the recreation setting. Counseling may be necessary to help change that behavior, and thus should be closely associated with the program either as part of it or as a referral option. . . .

**The Roving Leader**

Ever since Thrasher's study of the gang (1927-1931), there has been particular interest in one of his recommendations:

> The common assumption that the problem of delinquency will be solved by the multiplication of playgrounds and social centers in gang areas is entirely erroneous. The physical layout of gangland provides a realm of adventure with which no playground can compete. The lack is not of this sort. The real problem is one of developing in these areas or introducing into them leaders who can organize the play of boys, direct it into wholesome channels and give it social significance. Ganging is merely one symptom of deepening community disorganization.

200

Out of this and similar findings by other researchers have come the concepts of the detached worker and the roving recreation worker or roving leader. The U.S. Office of Education has published a guide to assist agencies in developing leadership through an effective preservice training program for roving leaders. The roving leader is described therein as:

> ... a worker generally assigned to a specific geographic area within a community for the purpose of strengthening, extending, and stimulating participation of hard-to-reach youth in wholesome recreation programs. A prime example of this outreach service is to help delinquency-prone and disadvantaged youth to use their free time constructively. ...

### The Youth Services Bureau

... In one community, the Youth Service Bureau held workshops on the need for a citywide recreation program planned on the basis of greatest need. The first workshop found that the inner city had no public recreation programs because the trained adult leadership had never worked solely with minority groups and was afraid to do so. A second workshop dealt with finding facilities and recreational equipment for the inner city area.

As a result of these workshops and other activities, a total recreation plan for the entire community was developed. Youth from all areas of the community participated in the decisionmaking. School facilities were opened during evenings, weekends, and vacations; group discussions and cultural activities for youth were held; and volunteers were recruited to make it possible to extend the recreational activities to all cultural and ethnic groups, particularly to those living in the most deprived areas.

**Recommendation 7.1: Develop recreation programs for delinquency prevention.**

## 8: Programs for Religion

### Fear and Isolation

There is some indication that the fear of crime in America is more widespread than the actual incidence of crime. Such fear foments an environment that may be as dangerous as crime itself, for it distorts the facts and diverts resources.

Fear of crime is focused on the physical violence that often accompanies property loss, particularly in the case of street crime. This fear has manifested itself in a fortress or seige mentality—a retreat behind multiple locks, elaborate alarm systems, and guest screening devices.

According to some crime watchers, this kind of response may actually perpetuate some of the conditions that encourage criminal acts: near-empty streets, lack of trust in police power, and the absence of a broad sense of community.

In citing the dangers of an overemphasis on the fortress mentality, it is not the intention of this Commission to minimize the importance of reasonable caution in the safeguarding of one's person or property. Indeed, a separate chapter of this report contains specific recommendations to that end. The Commission believes, however, that measures designed to promote and enhance a sense of community offer a better hope of lasting reduction in crime than do elaborate security precautions.

Fear also places greater pressures upon the government to deal with symptoms rather than causes, and compels a disproportionate investment of limited resources in ineffective programs. Academic studies, legislative proposals, corporate decisions, and agency programs that arise primarily out of fear frequently are characterized by faulty conclusions, inadequate planning, and repressive strategies. . . .

### Affluence, Materialism, and Poverty

There is a tendency in our affluent Nation to measure personal worth by the amount of money earned and the number of material possessions acquired. This measurement receives much emphasis through the communications media, which even the poor have access to, and which raise their hopes and expectations of participating in the society's affluence. The educational and economic mechanisms for fulfilling those hopes are unavailable to many people, who thus may become alienated and turn to illegal mechanisms.

The religious community can emphasize the value of persons as independent of and greater than the value of property. In addition, religious leaders and others can show concern for eliminating poverty and other social ills, and that concern should match their interest in preventing crime and rehabilitating offenders. . . .

**Recommendation 8.1: Enlist religious community participation in crime prevention.**

### Informed Constituencies

If religious people are to become involved in crime prevention, they must understand the crime problem. Crime is a social problem and the concern of the entire community. The law enforcement effort is limited to those factors within its control; such social problems as unemployment, discrimination, poverty, illiteracy, and poor housing are not within the control of law enforcement and must be solved within the community.

There are key education services that the religious community can provide to involve its members in crime prevention efforts. One is an attempt to promote acceptance of the citizenry of needed criminal justice reforms. This may mean, for example, urging individuals to accept a halfway house or drug treatment center in their neighborhood. The religious community can also inform members of programs designed to alleviate the social conditions linked to crime. . . .

Advocates of various religions also may want to consider taking on some of the functions they have previously expected the criminal justice system to perform. This could be done, for instance, in the case of crimes which cause no injury to another person. Examples of such crimes are drunkenness and vagrancy. Acts such as these result in a great proportion of arrests, and consequently place a great burden on police, courts, and corrections systems.

Historically, the disapproval of certain kinds of personal behavior by the religious community may have caused these acts to be legally classified as crimes. Now religious institutions can take the lead in removing such acts from the legal codes, so that the criminal justice system can deal with serious crimes that cause injury and loss. . . .

**Recommendation 8.2: Encourage religious institutions to educate their constituencies about the crime problem.**

**Recommendation 8.3: Enlist religious institution support of crime prevention.**

**Recommendation 8.4: Open church facilities for community programs.**

*Service to the Community*

In addition, religious groups could involve themselves in no-strings-attached services to the families of those who are incarcerated. Many such programs are now in progress. In Lewisburg, Pa., where a Federal prison is located about 2 miles outside of town, a number of churches initiated a special program when they discovered that the families of inmates experienced real inconveniences in visiting prisoners.

203

They found that, on weekends, there was only one bus in and out of town, and that taxi fare from the bus station to the prison was beyond the means of those visiting. Area churches, on a rotating basis, now provide committees that meet the bus on Sunday mornings, serve breakfast, and furnish transportation to the prison.

**Recommendation 8.5: Promote religious group participation in the justice system.**

## 9: Programs for Reduction of Criminal Opportunity

**Recommendation 9.1: Design buildings that incorporate security measures.**

**Recommendation 9.2: Include security requirements in building codes.**

STREET LIGHTING PROGRAMS FOR HIGH CRIME AREAS

The implementation of an adequate lighting system has been shown to have some correlation with the reduction and deterrence of crime.

A program of improved street lighting was first begun in St. Louis, Mo., in 1964. The first area completed involved the downtown business district, which consists of large department stores, brokerage firms, investment companies, hotels, and comparable business establishments.

In a comparison of criminal acts in 1963, the last full year before improvements, and in 1965, the first full year after improvements, it was found that crimes against persons in the improved lighting area decreased by 40.8 percent. Auto theft incidents decreased by 28.6 percent, while business burglaries decreased by 12.8 percent.

The Park Department of New York City relighted some of its playgrounds, in the hope of reducing vandalism. Within a year after relighting, vandalism in Staten Island's play areas had been virtually eliminated; in Brooklyn, it was down 86 percent; in Manhattan, down 81 percent; and in the Bronx and Queens, down 50 percent. . . .

It must be noted, however, that these statistics cannot be interpreted as proof of the efficacy of lighting programs in reducing crime. Although a number of cities that have implemented multimillion dollar programs for relighting high crime areas have announced significant drops in crime rates in those areas, additional scrutiny of these results is necessary. Such study will have to take into account the effects of such variables as police patrol levels, displacement of criminal activity to other times and places, and seasonal changes in crime patterns. Until all evidence is sifted, it should be assumed that lighting is only one of the factors that help reduce crime. . . .

**Recommendation 9.3: Improve streetlighting in high-crime areas.**

**Recommendation 9.4: Adopt shoplifting prevention techniques in retail establishments.**

**Recommendation 9.5: Legislate car theft prevention programs.**

**Recommendation 9.6: Involve citizens in law enforcement.**

# Integrity in Government

These chapters are based on three postulates, which the Commission believes are supported by ample evidence: (1) the corruption of public officials at all levels of government—Federal, State, and local—is perceived as widespread by the American public; (2) such corruption results in a staggering cost to the American taxpayer; and (3) the existence of corruption breeds further crime by providing for the citizen a model of official lawlessness that undermines any acceptable rule of law.

Corruption, as the Commission defines it, is not limited to its most egregious and sensational form—cash purchase of official favor. Corruption includes all of the circumstances in which the public officeholder or government employee sacrifices or sells all or part of his judgment on matters within his official purview in return for personal gain. Corruption thus defined includes a direct bargain—cash (or securities, a share in a business venture, or the promise of a future job on the outside)—in exchange for official action or inaction.

. . . No wonder, then, that a 1971 Harris poll revealed that 80 percent of the American people believe that "organized crime has corrupted and controls many politicians in the country."

Charges of corruption, some of which already have led to convictions, have been brought against many officials throughout the United States. Since 1969, in one large eastern State at least 57 elected or appointed officials have been indicted or convicted on Federal or State charges based on Federal investigations. These officials include 10 mayors, two judges, three State legislators, various local officials, and several State officials including two secretaries of state. Not all officials were charged while still in office. In another, smaller State similar charges have been brought against at least 24 officials, including a former Governor, two State senators, a State attorney general, and several other State and local officers or employees.

## 10: Conflicts of Interest

... Conflict of interest is an issue that comes occasionally to public view—usually when sensational headlines appear in the newspapers. But the problem is one that public officials and students of government confront every day. Where does one draw the boundary between private interest and public duty? Who is to determine standards for ethical conduct? What body can be entrusted to judge very complex cases involving a public official's outside income and employment? ...

### Conflicts of Interest and Organized Crime

Organized crime can thrive only through the acquiescence or active assistance of public officials. Because public officials act on measures that affect the regulation and conduct of State agencies and businesses, they are prime targets for organized crime influence.

Recent methods of influence have become more indirect than outright bribery:

> As syndicates have grown and evolved they have come to employ more varied and sophisticated means. They may encourage the promotion of a co-operative, or they may arrange for him [the official] to receive shares of stock dominated by organized crime. The goal is nullification of government, whether the means be bribes [or] more subtle rewards. ...

These more subtle forms of conflict of interest as well as the continued existence of bribery give organized crime access to the political process. ...

**Standard 10.1: Adopt an Ethics Code for public officials and employees.**

**Standard 10.2: Ethics Board**
States should create, by legislative enactment, an Ethics Board to enforce the provisions of the Ethics Code, and

should advise public officials and State and local employees covered by the Ethics Code on all ethical matters.

1. The members of the Ethics Board should be chosen from the public at large and should not include any individuals who hold public office. The Governor (the mayor or head of local government for a local government unit) should select the members from a list of individuals submitted by the State bar association, civic and professional associations, civil rights groups, minority organization, and other citizen groups. Appointment of the members should be subject to approval by the State senate or other independent body already empowered to pass upon the fitness of persons nominated for high public office. No more than a simple majority of the members should be of the same political party.

2. The duties of the Ethics Board should be:

a. To initiate complaints against officials over whom it has jurisdiction when the board has information establishing the possibility of an official's ethical misconduct for purposes of personal gain;

b. To investigate all complaints against officials over whom the board has jurisdiction. Action on such complaints must be initiated within 30 days, and completed within reasonable time; . . .

3. The Ethics Board should have the power to subpena witnesses and documents.

Standard 10.3: Disclosure of Financial Interests by Public Officials

States should adopt provisions requiring public officials to disclose their financial and professional interests, and should establish a procedure to determine which public officials on the State, county, and local levels will be included under its provisions. Such disclosure should provide the general public and the Ethics Board with reliable information upon which to judge the propriety of official conduct.

1. Each public official shall, within 10 days from assuming office, and annually on January 31, file a financial disclosure statement with the Ethics Board, and the statement shall be open to the public for inspection. All candidates for public office shall, in addition, file a disclosure statement at least 2 weeks prior to the date of the election in which they wish to participate. The statements should include at least the following information:

a. The identity and amount of all assets legally and constructively owned;

207

  b. The original sources and amounts of all income, including but not limited to outside employment, consultant fees, or other services performed during the preceding reporting period;

  c. The nature and amounts of all debts owed in excess of $1,000 and the names of the persons or institutions to whom such debts are owed;

  d. The identity of all businesses, agencies, or corporations with which one is associated as a partner, director, or officer;

  e. If a partner in a law firm, a list of all clients whose annual fees exceed $2,000 or comprise 5 percent or more of the firm's remuneration per annum and the amounts of such fees;

  f. The original source of all gifts received and the type of gift;

  g. The nature of all interests in any business, either legally or constructively owned; and

  h. The original source and amount of all honoraria.

2. Each public official shall disclose to the Ethics Board any conflict of interest that exists in respect to specific action of an official nature prior to acting on such official matters.

One obstacle to widespread acceptance of disclosure requirements has been the contention that mandatory disclosure is an invasion of privacy not imposed on others in society. However, when a person assumes public office he voluntarily opens some of his private affairs to public scrutiny, and what was previously only of personal concern enters, in part, into the public domain. This is not a novel proposition; it has been recognized in the law since the landmark Supreme Court ruling in *N.Y. Times* v. *Sullivan.*

Another contention is that disclosure requirements are too burdensome and thus will keep qualified men out of office. However, every taxpayer undergoes a similar burden every year, and disclosure statements are less time-consuming than tax statements.

It should be noted that the suggested disclosure standard, 10.3, includes no exceptions for interests of a de minimis nature whose threat to the public interest is minimal. These exceptions are advisable, but due to the great disparity among existing exceptions, any attempt to suggest a uniformly appropriate de minimis level would be arbitrary. . . .

Paragraph g does not limit disclosure of business interests to those businesses regulated by the State or city, as some disclosure provisions do. Any business interest, whether or not directly regulated by a State agency, may be affected by legislation, and it in turn may affect an official's judgment. In Section h the word "original" indicates that if a gift or money was directly given by an agency of the donor or by an intermediary, the donor, not the intermediary, is to be disclosed.

## Standard 10.4: Criminal Penalties

States should define as violations of their criminal codes certain situations involving conflicts of interest, and should assign meaningful penalties when such violations constitute a serious and substantial abuse of public office. State criminal codes should include the following minimum provisions:

1. No public official shall use confidential information for the purpose of financial gain to himself or to any other person. This provision shall continue to be applicable for 2 years after an official leaves office.

2. No public official shall accept compensation, gifts, loans, privileges, advice and assistance, or other favors from private sources for the performance of tasks within the scope of his public office.

3. No public official shall represent another person before a court, or before a government agency or commission, when such client is claiming rights against the government.

4. No public official, and no business in which a public official has a substantial interest (including but not limited to substantial financial investments, directorates, and partnerships) shall enter into a contract with the government or with a business regulated by the government, unless the contract has been awarded through a competitive bidding process with adequate public notice. This provision shall continue to be applicable for 1 year after the official leaves office.

5. No public official or candidate for public office shall fail to file a disclosure statement by the date established by the Ethics Board, and no public official or candidate for public office shall knowingly file a false financial statement.

6. Any official or candidate for public office alleged to be in violation of the above criminal provisions shall be granted a prompt preliminary hearing. If tried and convicted, he shall be guilty of a felony.

7. Any elected official convicted of any felony or misdemeanor involving moral turpitude shall be removed from office. Any appointed official likewise convicted shall be suspended from his duties.

In the past, two deficiencies have impeded the effectiveness of criminal laws and led to infrequent enforcement. First, the laws intended to offer ethical guidance to officials were written in vague and general terms. Such vagueness violates the individual's right to due process under the fourteenth amendment to the Constitution. Because criminal sanctions can be applied only against predetermined wrongs, the laws should be written in specific terms.

## 11: Regulation of Political Finances

... Corruption in political financing not only increases public cynicism about political money but also affects basic citizen attitudes toward politicians and the entire political process. To the degree that unhealthy attitudes persist, parties and candidates have difficulty raising sufficient funds from legitimate sources, and hence may be forced to turn to funds from questionable sources.

To combat these negative impressions and questionable practices, the Commission believes that State and local governments should strive:

• To curb excessive campaign spending and unacceptable disparities in the financial resources of competing candidates and parties;

• To sustain significant political activities performed by candidates, parties, and others;

• To assure political competition for all public offices;

• To encourage participation by broadening the base of campaign contributors;

• To assure the representative quality of campaign constituencies; and

• To improve public confidence in politics by reducing the influence of campaign contributors.

... In this context, public demonstrations and acts of violence are considered because they may gain for dissenters the attention—some of it free—that dollars buy for politicians using traditional means. Our democratic system guarantees free speech, but effective speech to reach large audiences is expensive if purchased through broadcast time and newspaper advertising. An economical way to reach large audiences is through demonstrations, picketing, and other events that are reported by the media as news but convey the content and the context of the protest. The impact of 25 protesters on a street corner may well be greater than the influence of 25 signatures on a petition that will receive little public or official attention. Unfortunately, demonstrations sometimes lead to violence and crimes that need to be understood in terms of the ineffectiveness and unresponsiveness of the political system.

An incumbent always has a public forum (in the White House, the State house, etc.). To the alienated person or the dissenter, who has access neither to a governmental forum nor to funds with which to propagandize, it is easy to take to the streets to gain media attention and thereby an audience. Given the cost of politics, plus the slow processes of American government, one may be led readily to extratraditional methods of accomplishing goals.

Protest movements are much less expensive than regular politics. In 1968, once the antiwar forces were channeled into established institutional processes by the candidacies of Senators Eugene McCarthy and Robert F. Kennedy, the costs of effective dissent rose considerably. More than $15 million was spent between the time candidacies were announced and the conclusion of campaigns. Thus it is clear that the costs of challenge within the system need to be kept within reasonable bounds.

EXAMPLES OF CORRUPTION

... It is impossible to measure the amount of political money contributed with expressed or tacit obligations, but the amount undoubtedly is greater at the State and local levels than at the Federal level. Not only criminal elements, but respectable businessmen and professionals, use campaign contributions to obtain favor and preferment in contracts, jobs, taxation, zoning, and numerous other areas of government. Some relationships are acknowledged openly. In many places, those who benefit from the system are solicited systematically. For example, it was reported that, in Indiana, members of the Two Percent Club, composed of certain government employees, were assessed at the rate of 2 percent of their salary as a formal means of financing the party in power. ...

The American system of government is rooted in the egalitarian principle of "one man, one vote," but like all democracies it is confronted with an unequal distribution of economic resources. The attempt to reconcile the inequalities lies at the base of the problem of money in politics. In a sense, broadly based political power, as effected through universal suffrage, was conceived and has been used to help compensate for inequalities in economic resources. But the people's voice cannot be heard if special interests get undue preferment from candidates and parties forced to depend on them because alternative sources of adequate funds are not available.

Coincident with the extension of the franchise and the democratization of the institutional framework, has been the increasing concentration of wealth—the economic element that generates political power. The great industrial, financial, labor, criminal, and other interests seek to dominate the political as well as the economic environment. They do this directly—through lobbies and the contribution of money—and indirectly—through access to the public in both election and nonelection activities.

... Various scholars have estimated that 15 percent of the money for State and local campaigns is derived from the underworld. ... If such money is concentrated in nonfederal campaigns, legislation would be desirable to help remove financial pressures on candidates and political parties—by reducing costs, by encouraging or providing alternative sources of funds, by having government provide certain campaign services that are now a burden on campaigners, or by some combination of the above.

### The Need for Meaningful Regulation

At the same time, it is desirable to work for regulations that are realistic, meaningful, administrable, and enforceable. Part of the problem is that too often the present system of financing politics invites criminal offenses. Where statutes are loosely drawn, practices will develop to evade or avoid them; in any case, such statutes are not enforced vigorously. Many laws are unrealistic and thus invite noncompliance; for example, excessive limitations on amounts that can be contributed or spent in campaigns virtually force all participants, winners and losers alike, to violate the law. Limitations that do not take into account the requirements or the high stakes of winning, lead readily to noncompliance. ...

Unlike previous, loosely drawn laws, the Federal Election Campaign Act of 1971 lists specific duties of supervisory officers responsible for administering the law. Vigorous prosecution of key practitioners who violate the law will help encourage future compliance, as will the knowledge that government agencies are alert, serious, evenhanded, and persevering in their efforts to enforce the law.

Government prosecutors have shown that they can be successful even in enforcing laws that contain loopholes and ambiguities. For example, criminal charges were filed in 1968-70 against about 18 corporations alleged to have violated the Federal prohibition of corporate contributions. All defendants pleaded guilty. But none of the defendants so charged was a candidate or finance manager who accepted the corporate gifts.

It may be assumed that until some candidates and campaign managers, treasurers, and contributors are punished severely for white-collar violations of election laws, the old habits of laxity will persist. ...

Excessive Campaign Spending

Although there seems to be strong public sentiment that campaign expenditures are too high and should be curbed, the emphasis on cost is mainly misplaced. ...

Americans pay a high price for the democratization of the nomination process. The adoption of primaries forces candidates to spend heavily in their quest for nomination. The spending is greatest in the prenomination period, when voters get their cues from wide personalized advertising and instant grassroots organization rather than from party affiliation or habit. Generally, Democrats spend much more heavily than Republicans in internecine contests. In any case, it is difficult to devise satisfactory policy remedies in the initial selection process without restricting many of the candidates who want to compete.

The decline of traditional party organizations, which formerly carried the main burden of campaigning, has forced candidates to finance intensive media campaigning and voluntary organizing. Even the mass volunteer campaign generates new political costs—for numerous storefronts, for the preparation of computerized canvass lists, for postage and telephones, for transporting and feeding workers from distant locales, and for millions of pamphlets and brochures.

*Decline in Party Affiliation*

More vigorous competition has replaced one-party control in the formerly Republican strongholds of the Midwest and Great Plains and in the formerly Solid South, and this, too, has led to increased spending. Similarly, reapportionment causes candidates to spend great sums of money wooing voters in areas where campaigns previously were mere formalities. Redoubled campaigning also has been caused by the recent erosion of strong party affiliation among voters in general and by the uncertain partisan loyalties of millions of young voters. More independents, more ticket-splitters, and a large "floating" vote all demand more strenuous appeals.

Structural factors also add to the total cost of American elections, although they do not inflate spending in particular campaigns. Federalism requires the election of officials at three levels—national, State, and local. Separation of powers requires the election of officials of two branches at the Federal levels and three in most States. America's commitment to large bicameral legislatures adds still more offices and higher political costs. The American long-ballot tradition—more than 500,000 public officers are filled at elections—necessitates additional campaign expenditures in contests for many nonpolicy positions. . . .

Expenditure limitations may be relevant to certain kinds of political activities; at some point additional media advertising becomes excessive by popular judgment, adds only marginally to the information flow, and serves mainly to escalate campaign spending because other candidates feel compelled to keep pace. Curbs on spending for particular activities may therefore be appropriate, especially if such spending can be monitored and regulated readily. This was the intent of Title I of the Federal Election Campaign Act (§ 104), which imposed on campaigns for Federal office a media limit of the greater of $50,000 or 10 cents per constituent who has reached 18 years of age, and a broadcast media limit of 60 percent of those amounts.

## POLITICAL COMPETITION FOR PUBLIC OFFICE

At present, the disparity in political resources between opposing candidates and parties often is so great that competition is only nominal. Incumbents ordinarily have vast advantages over challengers. Conservative candidates usually command more resources than liberals. But most important, candidates and parties in districts where the electoral balance is strongly in their favor usually are able to amass substantially more political resources than their opponents. More than two-thirds of the seats in the United States House of Representatives are filled in such electorally noncompetitive districts. Patterns in State, county, and municipal legislatures vary, but most are characterized by one-party dominance.

The minority party tends to atrophy in one-party districts; indeed, it often fails even to file candidates for office there. Even when a candidate is recruited, he often is so impoverished that he is unable to wage a viable campaign to identify himself, his qualifications, and his programs. Nor can he subject the incumbent's record to the scrutiny and criticism that are necessary if public officials are to be held accountable. When disadvantaged candidates and parties cannot afford to compete with the party in power, electoral checks on public officials will deteriorate.

Because responsive government depends in part on vigorous, creditable competition in elections, finance regulation should encourage and support the activities of all major parties and candidates.

## REPRESENTATIVE CAMPAIGN CONSTITUENCIES

... As a rule, candidates and parties do not move so rapidly that they lose their base of support. They temper decisions with considerations of how a given action would affect existing relationships with financial or other supporters. A law of anticipated reactions is at work. Politicians learn to estimate the boundaries of acceptable behavior, and thus tend to circumscribe their actions even when no expressed commitments have been made for contributions. The need to continue and expand fundraising appeal, even to smaller contributors, limits the pace of acceptable change. ...

## REDUCING THE INFLUENCE OF CAMPAIGN CONTRIBUTORS

... Public funding of parties and candidates at a minimum level would seem to insure creditable and adequate campaigns while reducing the role of special-interest money. Under this system, the amount of money contributed by an individual to a given campaign could be limited. Such limits would encourage politicians to seek assistance from many small contributors. Hence, public subsidization could be considered as a means of assuring limited access to the electorate for legally qualified candidates and parties, with remaining funds collected privately to the extent of the candidate's appeal and popularity.

On the other hand, a subsidization system requires arbitrary definitions of eligibility and utility. Broad eligibility may help bring some dissenters into the system, but it would create new problems in defining what constitutes responsible candidacy. Subsidies in the prenomination period might encourage frivolous candidacies. Many incumbents would oppose the enactment of a system of subsidies that assures financing of certain unpalatable opposition. Thus it is hard to achieve a system that is politically viable and yet attractive enough to channel the voices of opposition and dissent into regularized party activities. ...

Alternative plans exist. President Kennedy's Commission

on Campaign Costs recommended a system of grants under which the government would match small private contributions, perhaps up to $10 each. This would provide public money for campaigns, encourage candidates to broaden their financial base, make small contributions a more efficacious way of paying for campaigns, permit citizens to choose freely who would benefit from the contributions and the matching grants generated by them, and draw more citizens into campaign activity. Another plan calls for the government to distribute vouchers worth a small sum to all citizens. Candidates or political parties that were recipients of the vouchers contributed by citizens could redeem them for cash at the Treasury. However, voucher distribution is a costly endeavor for a mobile population. . . .

Tax incentives have long been advocated as an alternative to direct subsidies, and as a means for encouraging public participation in campaign funding. Ten States have adopted some form of tax incentive for political contributions. The U.S. Congress enacted an incentive plan in the Revenue Act of 1971, which permits a tax credit of one-half of contributions up to $25, or a tax deduction of $50. (Both sums are doubled on joint returns.)

There are no studies on the effectiveness of tax incentives in increasing participation and improving the representativeness of financial constituencies. Tax incentives are a means for government to assist candidates and parties in their solicitations, but they require that the candidates and parties do the soliciting themselves and thus remain active and in touch with various constituencies. . . .

Public funding also might take the form of providing campaign services—through assumption of greater responsibilities in registration and election-day activities, provision of cheaper or free mailing rates, use of airwaves, preparation of voters' pamphlets, provision of transition costs between election day and inauguration day, payment for vote recounts if the vote is very close (e.g., within 1 percent)—in short, in whatever ways will reduce costs for candidates and parties and thereby remove some of the financial burden from them. . . .

**Standard 11.1: Disclosing the Role of Money in Politics**

**All significant receipts and expenditures by every candidate and organization seeking to influence any election should be disclosed periodically before and after elections and between elections in a manner that insures transmission of these dis-**

closures to the public. A registration system for qualifying political committees is necessary. All disclosures should be made to a bipartisan Registry of Election Finance that is isolated from political pressures.

Disclosure should be considered as the cornerstone of a larger regulatory scheme. Disclosure should be as accurate and complete as possible, should occur at times when voters can use the information most effectively to judge candidates and parties, should be readily available to those interested, and should be given as wide coverage as possible.

1. To insure uniformity, State disclosure regulations should be at least as stringent as those of the Federal Election Campaign Act of 1971, which requires: (1) candidates for nomination or election to Federal office; and (2) committees raising or spending in excess of $1,000 for candidates, to register and disclose their finances periodically. . . .

5. Reports should meet a test of substantial completeness. They should provide all reasonably pertinent information, while at the same time avoiding such bulk and volume as to be difficult to use. Under the Federal Election Campaign Act of 1971 (Title III, §302 and 304), only receipts and expenditures in excess of $100 must be itemized; others must be reported in totals and retained on candidate and committee account books, which are subject to inspection and audit.

Reports should be cumulative, so that the latest report provides all necessary information for a calendar year or electoral phase such as pre- or post-nomination. This reduces the volume of reports an examiner must scrutinize, and summarizes data as much as feasible. Summaries of major categories of receipts and expenditures should be included in the report.

6. To insure full disclosure, there should be established a bipartisan agency, isolated from political pressures to the greatest extent possible, and having responsibility to (1) receive, examine, tabulate, summarize, publish, and preserve registrations and campaign fund reports: (2) prescribe the forms in which reports are to be made; and (3) determine how the data in the reports can best be disseminated both before and after elections.

7. The agency should be vested with authority to audit any books kept separately by candidates and committees; it should perform sample audits and should have subpena powers and all other means necessary to conduct compliance investigations.

8. Enforcement of the regulations should be vested first in

217

the agency. Criminal prosecution should be undertaken by the agency itself and civil redress should be permitted. Citizens also should be provided an opportunity to seek enforcement of the regulations. If the agency, candidates, and citizens can go directly to court, it should be possible to bypass partisan enforcement agents and achieve strict enforcement.

At present, only nine States require candidates and committees to file reports detailing sources of funds and types of expenditures both before and after primary and general elections. But in some of these cases, the information filed is incomplete—for example, contributors may be disclosed but without full name or complete mailing address. Currently nine States are without any laws whatsoever requiring disclosure of political funds. Substantially fewer than half the States require officials to report delinquents, incorrect filings, or violations of expenditure limits to the prosecutor. This practice further erodes the already weak statutory provisions for enforcement of disclosure laws.

## Standard 11.2: Limiting Political Spending

With due regard for constitutional rights, selective limitations should be imposed on the sums that can be spent to advance the candidacy of any aspirant for office and to conduct the affairs of any political party or other organization that aids candidates or otherwise participates in election campaigns. Such limits should be reasonable and enforceable, so that they will not go unobserved or breed disrespect for the law.

2. All expenditures on behalf of a candidate, except those of his political party, should be channeled through a single committee he designates. To protect the constitutional rights of those wishing to express political views, but whose expenditures the candidate does not wish to accept as his own, the requirement that all expenditures be channeled through the candidate's authorized committee should exempt individuals or committees spending less than a certain designated amount, provided that their intended activity has been offered to and rejected by the candidate. Such expenditures should not be regarded as part of the sum that the candidate is permitted to spend. Negative advertising should be permitted without charge to any candidate's limit if it is not authorized by opposing candidates.

In recent years, expenditure limitations have fallen into disfavor with political commentators, academic students of politics, and lawmakers. Many States have repealed spending limits in favor of other regulatory approaches. Twenty-three States include expenditure limits in their corrupt practices laws, but most of the provisions are so loosely drawn that they are easily and readily evaded. It is better to have no limitations than unenforceable ones that breed disrespect for the law.

The Federal Election Campaign Act of 1971 takes a new approach to expenditure limitations: it aims only at certain media expenditures that are easily monitored. Further, the Federal law explicitly provides that States may, by legislation, bring themselves under the Federal media expenditure limits and take advantage of the Federal mechanism for monitoring such expenditures. New experimentation with realistic limitations is called for at the State level.

### Standard 11.3: Curtailing Conflicts of Interest in Campaign Finance

State laws should prohibit campaign contributions, and other spending relating to politics or campaigns for State and local offices, by persons who transact an annual business of more than $5,000 with those units of government, or who are directors or shareholders owning or controlling 10 percent or more of a corporation, business, or association engaged in such transactions. Further, those who own or operate any corporation, business, or association regulated by the State, or who are directors or shareholders of 10 percent or more of stock in it, should similarly be prohibited from making political contributions. Labor unions and their officers having contracts with the unit of government should be similarly prohibited from making campaign contributions. Such laws should carry criminal penalties and should provide procedures for initiation of citizen complaints.

### Standard 11.4: Prohibiting Corporate and Labor Contributions

In addition to prohibiting government contractors from contributing, State law should prohibit other corporations, labor unions, and trade associations from contributing or making expenditures for political purposes. Corporations, unions, and associations should be treated alike. Statutes should require disclosure of all corporate or union or association resources used directly or indirectly for or against political parties, candidates or ballot issues, including educational, registration and fundraising activities conducted in the name of education or citizenship.

## 12: Government Procurement of Goods and Services

. . . As State purchasing agencies become larger and more centralized, they also become more professionalized. Fourteen States presently require a competitive examination for appointment to the position of purchasing agent. Fifteen States use a civil service or merit system; 35 States have directors who are politically appointed. Salary ranges for director of purchasing vary from $9,600 to $34,064. The availability of adequate salary enables the unit to obtain and retain competent employees and is as important in purchasing as in other professional fields. A professional, adequately salaried staff increases the efficiency and integrity of the State purchasing agencies by reducing pressures "to make a little on the side," and by lessening the temptation to seek other, more lucrative employment.

. . . Too often, procurement personnel are not selected on the basis of any demonstrated ability or experience in the procurement process. States recognized as leaders in the field are those that have instituted training programs, in which young men and women move through successive training stages learning to deal with contracts that involve hundreds of thousands of dollars. . . .

There is also much to be said in favor of opening the records of a State purchasing agency to public review, as has been done in Florida. If all bid proposals and bid awards were made public, the publicity alone would be sufficient to deter most criminal activity in purchasing. . . .

Perhaps the most obvious means by which a procurement official can repay a bribe is to select arbitrarily the vendor who is to receive the bid. The official may or may not later attempt to justify the award of the bid to a vendor who was, perhaps, the highest bidder. When an official who is in a position to award the bids has accepted bribes, even advertising of bids is of little value; no matter how many legitimate bids are received, the corrupt official will still select the vendor who has bribed him.

A practice known as "specing out"—the establishment of arbitrary requirements and specifications—is also a common form of corruption. This practice can take several different forms. For example, the specifications required in the contract may be established so that they describe in detail one specific brand of equipment, thereby automatically eliminating from consideration vendors of all other brands.

Various other requirements—that only one vendor can fulfill—may be set. The official who has been bribed naturally would determine in advance that other vendors could not meet these requirements, which may take the form of arbitrary delivery dates, the need for stocking an unreasonable quantity of spare parts, the requirement of the presence of a local company representative, or the availability of certain warehouse or display facilities. . . .

**Standard 12.1: Establish a State procurement agency.**

## 13: Zoning, Licensing, and Tax Assessment

The target areas—government land-use zoning, tax assessment, and licensing control activities—were chosen because of their economic importance to groups outside of government. For the most part, these functions involve relatively small public expenditures to cover the cost of personnel and other administrative services. Consequently they tend to receive somewhat less public attention than public safety, sewers, parks, or any of the larger, more direct services of local governments. Nevertheless, government decisions in these areas are of substantial economic importance to private interests. The same incentive for corruption exists here as in other areas of government operation. . . .

THE TARGET AREAS

In 1968, the National Commission on Urban Problems wrote:

> In some communities, there is a very real problem of corruption in zoning decisions. A property owner who could build a shopping center or a high-rise apartment suddenly discovers that his property is worth many times as much as the property owner who is relegated to low-density development. The values at stake are enormous, so it is not surprising, therefore, that the zoning system is subject to enormous pressures by landowners and developers and that outright corruption is more than simply an occasional exception.

In 1973, the problem not only remains but shows every prospect of growing. The Commission on Urban Problems estimated that more than 18 million acres of land would come into new urban use between 1970 and 2000. The land, now in farm and randomly owned semiurban parcels, will be subjected to increasingly attractive purchase options by developers speculating against future urban growth. In fact, the race is already on in many major urban areas. In 1968, farmland in Frederick County, Md.—more than 30 miles from Washington, D.C.—was selling for as little as $100 per acre and seldom for more than $1,000 per acre. In 1971, Frederick County acreage having reasonable access to Interstate 70S was selling for $2,000 per acre and more. . . .

Pressures on zoning officials as well as on private sector groups involved in the urbanization process are enormous. While zoning does not create land values, it determines whether landowners—and which landowners—will reap the benefit of increased values. It does this by setting up development goals, presumably in the public interest, that take precedence over the real estate market as the arbiter of land uses. It follows, therefore, that those who control the zoning decision control the land values.

Zoning, however, is only the first element of concern to urban developers. Building and construction codes and tax assessment policies of local jurisdictions affect costs and are integral parts of corporate and development planning. Favorable regulatory and tax environments are as important as favorable purchase arrangements, and developers tend to seek out jurisdictions responsive to their interest for the best arrangement possible on taxes and services. . . .

The Commission to Investigate Alleged Police Corruption in New York City (Knapp Commission) heard testimony in October 1971 that as much as 5 percent of the total construction costs in the city are attributable to graft paid to city employees. Five percent of the estimated $1.5 billion annual construction bill amounts to $75 million in that city alone, or just slightly less than the expected 1972 general fund revenues of Cleveland, Ohio. The contractors pay—and through various "budgetary arrangements" pass the costs on to tenants—because there are at least 40 licenses or permits required to construct a new building in the city. A construction delay of several days resulting from a pending permit would cost contractors substantially more than they lose in payoffs.

In Chicago, the Justice Department and the Internal Revenue Service are investigating reported cash payoffs for city zoning changes. Cash payments for as much as $3,000 allegedly have been made to "officials" for allowing specific variances to the city's code. In 1966 in one large eastern county, the outgoing County Council—in its final 48 hours of life—made several hundred changes in the county's carefully developed master plan. Although no collusion was ever proven between the outgoing council members and the land developers in whose favor the changes were made, over 5 years and thousands of dollars in court costs were required to reverse those decisions.

## Property Tax Abuse

The most sensational abuses and perhaps the most complex ones occur in the area of property taxation. The prevention of corruption in tax assessments is more than a legal or moral issue—it involves the financial solvency of already hard-pressed cities.

In 1966, property taxes and revenues from local user charges (licenses, permits, etc.) accounted for more than 51 percent of the general revenue of America's 25 largest cities. For all American cities in 1968-69, the amount was just under 70 percent. A "reasonable" tax break on one or two principal commercial locations can cost individual taxpayers tremendous sums either in increased taxes or lost services. When the assessor of Cook County, Ill. (which includes the city of Chicago), discovered he was being investigated by a local citizens' group for "arbitrary and manipulative" operation of his office he "reassessed" nine high-rise properties in the city. The reassessment of those nine buildings alone added $34 million to the city's tax base. . . .

### How Corruption Occurs

. . . Much of this problem could be prevented through the simple expedient of sound management. Applications should be centrally controlled with review deadlines specified for the various evaluations; evaluations (specific review element approval/disapproval) should be required in writing from the reviewing official; and the application pipeline should be audited regularly by an external agency, particularly field inspection reports.

The need for external audits is critical. Public surveillance of zoning, licensing, and tax decisions is hampered by secrecy, technical obfuscation of both regulations and decisions, and a too-frequent unwillingness of public officials to relinquish their "flexibility" by publicizing detailed decision criteria. Regular audits by external agencies would go a long way toward protecting the public from venal public officials and their private corruptors.

**Standard 13.1: Develop equitable criteria for zoning, licensing, and tax assessment.**

**Standard 13.2: Formulate specific criteria for government decisionmaking.**

**Standard 13.3: Publicize zoning, licensing, and tax assessment actions.**

# 14: Combating Official Corruption and Organized Crime

HISTORY AND STRUCTURE OF
STATE AND LOCAL LAW ENFORCEMENT

... Whether at the State or local level, practical considerations usually dictate some degree of partisan political commitment on the part of the law enforcement officer or agency. Complete independence from political influence is rare in the case of a law enforcement unit; pressure may be felt directly through election or appointment, or indirectly through budget control. The political histories of local jurisdictions within a given State, therefore, are also important for analysis. Such factors as whether local prosecuting attorneys are elected or appointed, whether electoral districts are highly competitive or areas of one-party control, whether prosecuting attorneys who have been in office for a number of years have kept their offices free from political influence and favoritism, and what trends in priorities operate in such jurisdictions—all contribute to the development of an environment that is favorable or unfavorable to successful prosecution of corruption cases. The courageous prosecutor who wants to attack the corruption problem in his jurisdiction must know the forces he will confront. If a favorable law enforcement environment does not exist, he may have to create one by initiating theretofore unthinkable cases. ...

**Nature or Level of the Government Service Compromised**

Corruption involving local-level functionaries may be handled effectively by the local prosecutor without extraordinary tools at his disposal. This may be true even if the problem is within police ranks, but here absence of prosecutor initiative is a greater risk. The interdependency of police and prosecutor is enormous. It would be easy merely to decry the social and professional relationships that make prosecutions of police corruption difficult. Where this is the case, the Commission does condemn the nullification of law enforcement that results. But for the prosecutor who is anything less than courageous in bringing corruption cases against the police or other agencies within the criminal justice system, there must be found some prosecutorial mechanism that is insulated from or independent of the agencies or officials accused. The standards that follow this discussion suggest such remedies.

When the nature or level of government service compromised has made it politically difficult for corruption cases to be prosecuted vigorously, either within or outside the criminal justice system, other remedies must be developed. In many cases, the most serious or most important corruption cases fall into this category. Political cowardice cannot be the guidepost in dealing with situations that determine the fundamental integrity of the law enforcement process. . . .

## VISIBILITY OF THE CORRUPTION ISSUE
## WITHIN CRIMINAL JUSTICE AGENCIES

The political pressures a local prosecutor faces when he decides whether or not to bring a corruption case require critical analysis. On the one hand, it is good politics to make a name for oneself by successful prosecutions of officials corruption cases. The crusading D.A. is one who is respected and feared in a community. On the other hand, many people fail to realize that there are tremendous political risks involved in bringing such cases, with the reward coming only at the time of conviction. A district attorney can find no better way to destroy his effectiveness than by earning a reputation for witch hunting. Nor is it unlikely that a prosecutor's charges of corruption will be labeled as political maneuvers and met by rebuttals from those charged. Allegations concerning a prosecutor's political motivations sometimes have credence with the American public.

The interdependence of members of the criminal justice system often makes it unlikely that even the most blatant corruption within the system will surface. Local prosecutors, though otherwise honest and competent, are often loathe to deal with the problem aggressively.

Their dilemma, for example, extends into the area of investigating police corruption. In many cities, the police are the sole investigative arm of the prosecutor's office. Virtually every case brought to the district attorney's office each year is dependent in some part on police testimony. A cooperative relationship thus inevitably develops between the prosecuting attorney and the police department. The district attorney can abrogate his responsibility to eradicate corruption among police, if he rationalizes that the police department is best equipped, by staff and experience, to keep its affairs in order.

The police department, then, is permitted through its internal affairs division to handle inhouse virtually all corruption matters. To preserve his relationship with the police department, a prosecutor may react only to specific complaints charging wrongdoing by a named officer. Even if there are reports of widespread corruption in a particular division (e.g., narcotics or gambling enforcement), the prosecutor may maintain an attitude of caution, avoiding sweeping investigations of systematic corruption.

Other partnership relationships develop within the criminal justice system that also tend to obscure corruption. In communities where the prosecutor, police, public defender, courts, and judges are thought of as one unit, operating in an atmosphere of cooperation and mutual support, the whole adversary process can break down. In many such instances, corruption, even within a single agency, has low visibility. Where there is a lack of accountability in any criminal justice agency, corruption finds a favorable breeding ground. . . .

### Standard 14.1: Maintaining Integrity in the Local Prosecutor's Office

1. States should redefine their law enforcement districts so as to combine smaller jurisdictions into districts having sufficient workload to support at least one full-time district attorney.

2. States should devise training standards for prosecution service, and should provide prosecutors' salaries that will attract the best-qualified personnel.

3. All local prosecutors and their staff attorneys should be prohibited from engaging in partisan political activity. Local prosecutors who are elected should be elected in nonpartisan elections.

4. All local prosecutors should be required to publish and make available annual reports detailing the deployment of personnel and resources during the preceding reporting period. Such reports should disclose the number of cases pending, hours spent in court and before the grand jury, and other details cataloging the number and kinds of cases handled by the prosecutor and their status at the time of reporting. Reports should be available for public inspection.

### Standard 14.2: Statewide Capability to Prosecute Corruption

States having a history of concern regarding the existence of public corruption and organized crime, both within and outside the criminal justice system, should establish an ongoing statewide capability for investigation and prosecution of corruption.

1. The office charged with this responsibility should have clear authority to perform the following functions:

    a. Initiate investigations concerning: the proper conduct and performance of duties by all public officials and employees in the State, and the faithful execution and effective enforcement of the laws of the State with particular reference but not limited to organized crime and racketeering;

    b. Prosecute those cases that are within the statutory purview and that the State unit determines it could most effectively prosecute by itself, referring all other evidence and cases to the appropriate State or local law enforcement authority;

    c. Provide management assistance to State and local government units, commissions, and authorities, with special emphasis on suggesting means by which to eliminate corruption and conditions that invite corruption;

    d. Participate in and coordinate the development of a statewide intelligence network on the incidence, growth, sources, and patterns of corruption within the State; and

    e. Make recommendations to the Governor or State legislature concerning: removal of public officials, government reorganization that would eliminate or reduce corruption and encourage more efficient and effective performance of duties and changes in or additions to provisions of the State statutes needed for more effective law enforcement.

2. The office should have the following minimum characteristics and powers:

    a. Statewide jurisdiction;

    b. Constant capability to obtain and preserve evidence prior to the filing of formal complaints;

    c. Power to compel testimony for purposes of investigation and prosecution; authority to subpena witnesses, administer oaths, obtain grants of immunity, and have access to the sanction of contempt; ability to hold private and public hearings; and power to prosecute cases in court;

    d. Adequate budget, protected from retaliative reduction;

    e. Specialized staff: investigators, accountants, and trial attorneys, with access to others as needed;

**f.** Consulting services available to all units of State and local government, commissions, and public corporations for counsel on means of maximizing the utilization of available staff and resources to meet workload demands, with special priority for service to licensing, regulatory, and law enforcement agencies; and

**g.** Annual disclosure of financial interests to the State Ethics Board by all persons performing regular duties in fulfillment of the above. Legislation should be enacted to authorize these and other powers as needed.

... A statewide office to investigate and prosecute corruption could have a variety of beneficial effects. Aside from the immediate benefits of developing new evidence and new cases to prosecute, the agency would encourage local prosecutors and others charged with responsibility in this area to give a higher priority to official corruption cases. The agency would in no way detract from the existing jurisdiction of local prosecutors. In fact, pressures created by the successes of the State agency would encourage the local prosecutor to be more aggressive in his jurisdiction.

Reform also will come from within city, county, and State agencies, as well as from within the criminal justice system itself, when the anticorruption unit brings integrity problems to the attention of these agencies and the public. Likewise, the State unit will provide the public with an unimpeachable, sympathetic forum to which complaints of official misconduct might be brought with confidence. The accompanying restoration of the public's faith in city and State government would be no small benefit.

The power to prosecute in court is the singularly absent criterion in all existing State investigation commissions. The same political forces that make the creation of the State agency essential often make it impossible for corruption cases to be brought at the local or State level, even if the cases are referred by the anticorruption agency. The Commission urges that this vital power be granted, lest the best efforts of the agency fail when it cannot prosecute the cases it develops. ...

... Many conspiracies engineered by corrupt officials cannot be investigated or prosecuted without the assistance of the extraordinary skills of accountants, management systems specialists, tax experts, and others. Thus, these cases are best developed by an office with statewide jurisdiction, and continuity of powers and staff. ...

Adequate appropriations to support this sensitive investigative service are an obvious necessity. Experience has shown that effective performance of these duties has caused public officers and citizens to react with anger. It is reasonable to expect retaliation by legislators in the form of attempts to slash the budget. One means of budget protection is to require a two-thirds vote of the legislature to reduce the appropriation below the level of the previous fiscal year. Another way might be to offer the protection within the State's constitution, even specifying a fixed percentage of the State's general fund as an absolute floor to the annual funding of the office. . . .

### State Attorney General's "Strike Forces" or Special Corruption Investigation Units

A strike force is a self-contained investigative and prosecutorial anticorruption unit with potential for genuinely independent action. This calls for a group, gathered by the State attorney general and responsible either to him or to an "organized crime and corruption prevention council," with personnel drawn from several State departments, often actively assisted by agents of several Federal law enforcement agencies. It is assumed that, lacking certain legal powers for obtaining evidence, the unit will utilize a citizens' grand jury with statewide jurisdiction. The possible applicability to other States of Michigan's organized crime investigation service which exists within the department of the attorney general, merits study and adaptation. Rhode Island, Wisconsin, and Illinois also have units working within the attorney general's office and with grand juries to investigate organized crime and corruption. Many of these efforts have been funded by the Law Enforcement Assistance Administration under the Safe Streets Act of 1968.

### Special Grand Juries or Special-Purpose Commissions

These are bodies convened to investigate identified public problems and bring prosecutions where violations of law are found. Although they are armed with the legal powers listed earlier, the duration of their existence is limited, from several months to as long as 2 years. Special grand juries are authorized and operate upon a judicial order; special commissions are convened by legislative act or executive order. The attorney general or local prosecutor may be counsel to the grand jury, or the jury may have authority to hire its own attorneys. Provision should be made in jurisdictions desiring this form of investigatory unit for independent response to a two-thirds vote of the grand jury.

In cases of official corruption reaching into higher levels of local government, use of the grand jury permits the prosecutor to isolate himself from direct responsibility for the decision to charge. . . .

Implementing Goals and Standards for
Community Crime Prevention Programs:
A Strategy for Change

### Intervention in Social Processes as a Mechanism for Change

In order to achieve both the necessary climate and the institutionalization of changes in attitude and behavior in community crime control, two difficulties that have characterized previous attempts must be overcome. Past attempts to bring about structural changes in the relationship between the community and crime prevention have been uncoordinated and scattered. In both the private and public sectors, individuals and organizations have developed programs of crime prevention using a variety of ideas and techniques. Some have been successful at the local level and some have won national notice, but generally their effects have been noncumulative and short-lived.

A second difficulty has been the tendency to develop programs that have a direct impact on the individual. Such programs fail because they do not build opportunities for change in the groups, structures, and systems that influence and support the behavior of the individuals who are members. Thus, the individual may be motivated to change his behavior but he is unable to find the necessary reinforcement and support in society. The cycle of recidivism, which has troubled the courts, the corrections system, and society, is testimony to the need for individuals to find some means of joining with others if the structure of their attitudes and behavior is to change. . . .

Multi-purpose Crime Prevention Organizations

### National Council on Crime and Delinquency

. . . Volunteers in Probation (VIP) has merged with NCCD and will become a part of the organization's citizen action program. VIP, established by a judge in Royal Oak, Mich., will work with NCCD's field staff to promote the volunteer service concept.

The formation and development of VIP is a story of unusual success. Due to the lack of funds, citizens were asked to serve as volunteer probation officers. The group grew from eight volunteers in 1960 to approximately 500 in 1965. The current director of VIP states that: "the program was giving about $250,000 a year in services on a very small budget from the city ($17,000) by and through the use of volunteers and the services which the volunteers inspired from ... retirees, who administered the program very carefully, psychiatrists, psychologists, . . . lawyers, doctors, marriage counselors, recovered alcoholic and many others."

Research conducted at Royal Oak, Mich., indicates that the volunteer and the professional working together can provide very intensive probation services that are said to be three times more effective than those provided by a probation officer working alone. Psychological tests and measuring devices showed that in two sample groups of youthful offenders, the hostility of defendants was reduced in 74 percent of the cases in Royal Oak and only 18 percent in another, nonvolunteer court. Success also was recorded in terms of recidivism between probationers in the two courts. Of all the 1965 probationers in Royal Oak, only 14.9 percent subsequently committed other offences during a study period of almost 5 years. In the other court, the comparable figure was 49.8 percent.

As a result of the success of the Royal Oak program, the Board of Christian Social Concerns of the Methodist Church in Washington, D.C., provided funds to spread the idea throughout the country. By 1969, the concept had been accepted by about 125 courts. Since 1969, the idea has spread to approximately 2,090 courts, prisons, and juvenile institutions. Judge Keith Leenhouts, present director of the program, estimates that about 250,000 volunteers now are involved, and that "within 5 years there will be a million citizens involved as volunteers mostly on a one-to-one basis, in courts and correctional institutions throughout the United States." (The Law Enforcement Assistance Administration provides consultants on volunteer court rehabilitative services at no cost to the community, court, or agency requesting the service.)

One-to-one volunteers are selected carefully. They must be either experts in counseling or probation personnel, or the judge must believe that they possess the natural talent, sincerity, and warmth of personality that would make them inherently good counselors and friends. Many fall into both

231

categories. Those who do not must be willing to go through a psychiatric-psychological screening process.

Treatment for probationers at Royal Oak is provided by 30 psychiatrists in private practice, each of whom takes one patient in continuing therapy. These doctors donate several hours a month to the program. The treatment is not necessarily free for the probationer; the fee is adjusted according to his financial status.

Employment counseling is an important aspect of rehabilitation. This program was first directed by a retired citizen, who administered aptitude tests and advised probationers on how to find jobs.

The Royal Oak VIP program also has a Women's Division and its own chapter of Alcoholics Anonymous. . . .

# Chapter V

# Police

In the decade that just passed, the American people witnessed massive riots and demonstrations and experienced widespread fear of crime and personal violence. The people sought answers and demanded solutions.

The police were at the center of controversy and the pressure to change was immense. Fortunately, this pressure was accompanied by support never before experienced by American law enforcement practitioners. One chief of a large city termed 1968 the "year of the policeman." Others looked to the seventies and predicted that it would be the "decade of the policeman."

The police have responded to the call for change. Progress in many areas is evident. Law enforcement agencies throughout the land have taken steps, some small and unsteady, others large and bold, to come to grips with their problems and to assume roles previously shunned by police administrators. These efforts portend more effective police service.

## Major Recommendations

In this chapter the Commission highlights some of the more important changes taking place in law enforcement and calls on every police agency to work toward their implementation. In its *Report on Police,* the Commission sets forth in even greater detail specific standards for improving the effectiveness of the police function.

The Commission's recommendations are directed toward increasing the effectiveness of the police in reducing crime. The recommendations and standards recognize the patrolman as the primary force in reducing and preventing crime. They seek to enhance his role. Major recommendations call for:

- Active crime prevention efforts by the police working with the community.
- Diversion of juveniles, drunks, and mental patients from the criminal justice system.
- Use of the patrolman as the primary investigator for crimes which come to his attention.
- Consolidation or elimination of police departments with fewer than 10 full-time police officers.
- Increased use of civilians.
- College education entrance requirements for employment of police officers.
- Legislation authorizing police officers to obtain search warrants by telephone.
- Continuing analysis of crime trends and deployment of special units to react to developing crime trends.
- Establishment of different classification and pay levels within the basic patrolman category.
- Development of units within police departments to work with prosecutors, courts, and corrections officials and to follow specific cases and individuals through the criminal justice system.

# The Police Role

Maintenance of order and enforcement of law are the two traditional missions of the police. As society has become more complex, many and varied demands have been put upon the police because of their unique authority. In developing its recommendations the Commission recognized the many functions which police agencies perform, including:
- Prevention of criminal activity.
- Detection of criminal activity.
- Apprehension of criminal offenders.
- Participation in court proceedings.
- Protection of constitutional guarantees.
- Assistance to those who cannot care for themselves or who are in danger of physical harm.
- Control of traffic.
- Resolution of day-to-day conflicts among family, friends, and neighbors.
- Creation and maintenance of a feeling of security in the community.
- Promotion and preservation of civil order.

These functions represent the core elements in the contemporary role of police. However, controversy exists as to the emphasis which should be placed on each of these functions. The Commission has recognized that local governments and citizens are in the best position to determine their needs, and the ultimate definition of the police role and the degree of emphasis to be placed on each function should be consistent with the laws and needs of the community that is being served.

It also is crucial that the police role be defined within the legal limits of authority. There are numerous laws that set out the authority under which the police must operate. In addition to and in accord with the pertinent law, guidelines should be developed for handling such problems as the resolution of family disputes and neighborhood altercations; the taking into custody of adults and juveniles, alcoholics, drug offenders, and the mentally ill; and the control of civil disorders.

Every police agency should write out a detailed statement of its role. The statement should be consistent with the United States Constitution and the laws of its State or city and the policies of the government the agency serves. The statement should identify the absolute limitations on the use of force by police and should establish guidelines for the use of discretion in making arrests and maintaining order.

## Working with the Community

The communities of this Nation are torn by racial strife, economic chasms, and struggles between the values of the old and the viewpoints of the young. These circumstances have made it difficult for the policeman to identify with and be identified as part of a community of citizens. As communities have divided within themselves, there has been a breakdown in cooperation between the police and the citizens.

The problem is particularly acute in large urban population centers. Here, the fibers of mutual assistance and neighborliness that bind citizens together have grown precariously thin.

Yet it is a fact that cooperation between the police and the community is the first step in effective crime control. As an essential ingredient to cooperation, every police agency should formally recognize the importance of communication with the public and constantly seek to improve its ability to determine the needs and expectations of the public, to act upon these needs and expectations, and to inform the people of the resulting policies developed to improve the delivery of police services.

The police must obtain information from the community as to its needs, and the public also must be informed of the police agency's roles so that it can better support the police in their efforts to reduce crime. Toward this end, the Commission recommends that:

• Police agencies should participate in educational efforts at the elementary, secondary, and college levels, and in youth programs aimed at improving the community's cooperation with and understanding of the police.

• Agencies should encourage public speaking engagements by police officers and should hold open houses and tours of police facilities.

• Police agencies should publish annual reports and periodic bulletins on significant crime trends and developments in police operations.

Many police agencies have used the schools to increase public understanding of the police role. "Officer Friendly" programs at the elementary school level have been particularly effective. The programs teach children traffic and bicycle safety and encourage them to accept policemen as their friends.

Programs at the secondary level require more careful structuring to be effective. They must delineate between the officer's enforcement role and his educational role. The Commission's examination of these programs indicates that an officer's primary assignment should include teaching classes on the role of the police and serving as a counselor. The assignment should not include law enforcement duties except as related to counseling.

In one program instituted by a major metropolitan police department, officers were assigned to selected schools with full-time faculty status and limited law enforcement duties. During 1970-71, approximately 2,000 students were given attitude tests that showed that the program created favorable changes in student attitudes toward the law and the police.

Programs of adult education and college education involving personnel from local police agencies also have been implemented effectively.

In addition to school activities, many agencies have found that police-supported recreational programs aid development of better relationships between the officers and young people of the community. Some departments, for example, have provided funds from their budgets to send children to summer camp. Other departments have established and supplied equipment for Police Athletic Leagues and Police Boards for Youth. These programs are all established on the principle that they are an effective force in crime prevention because they encourage youths to view police as a positive force and help them to understand their own responsibilities toward the law.

## Community Relations

The Commission recommends that police agencies in major metropolitan areas establish a specialized unit responsible for maintaining communication with the community. In smaller agencies, the police chief executive should assume direct responsibility for maintaining communication.

The unit should be no more than one step removed from the chief executive in the chain of command. It should identify impediments to communication within the community and devise methods of overcoming these impediments, including the use of public opinion polls, neighborhood meetings, and radio and television to elicit public opinion.

## Reducing Criminal Opportunity

The vital role the police can play in educating the public to take self-protective measures and reduce criminal opportunity must be recognized by police departments. Direct police crime prevention efforts include the security profile program conducted by the Michigan State Police, in which residences and commercial establishments are compared and rated against a comprehensive checklist of security measures by the police. Insurance companies are then encouraged to give discounts in burglary and robbery insurance premiums to those who get a high rating by the police.

The California Criminal Justice Council has funded a series of burglary prevention programs which reduced burglary by significant amounts in 1973 in the affected areas. These programs include publicity campaigns on how to prevent burglary, voluntary door-to-door inspection of residences and commercial establishments by specially trained police officers, encouragement of the establishment of neighborhood security programs in which people in the community work with the police to report crime and alert their neighbors to developing crime trends, and establishment of special telephone numbers for citizens to report anonymously crimes in progress or crimes about to be committed.

The single most successful crime prevention program instituted in recent years is the Operation Identification program established originally by the Monterey Park, Calif., police department and implemented since by a number of police departments and citizen groups across the country. In this program citizens use engraving tools to put an indelible marking, such as a social security number, on their personal belongings. A list of marked property is then filed with a central agency such as the police department and warning stickers are placed on the outside of residences. Participating residences are rarely, if ever, burglarized.

Yet another example of neighborhood self-protection and police cooperation is provided by the tenant patrols of the New York City Housing Authority, in which more than 11,000 volunteers in more than 600 apartment buildings act as the eyes and ears of the police department, reporting suspicious persons or circumstances to the police.

**Every police agency should establish programs that assist and encourage members of the public to take an active role in preventing crime. Police agencies should assist actively in the establishment of volunteer neighborhood security programs, and police agencies in major metropolitan areas should establish crime prevention units to work with the community in reducing criminal opportunities.**

## Police and the News Media

The relationship between the police and the news media in a democratic society is characterized by complementary interests. The news media have a legitimate need for information about police activities and they offer an excellent channel for informing the public about the nature of police tasks and problems.

As long as individual freedom is protected in all cases, agency policy should give the media the right to receive information upon request. There should be a basic presumption that information will be supplied upon request unless the released information would be improper due to court order. Policy should express respect for the news media, their role in a democratic society, and their value to effective police service.

In addition to responding to requests for information, police agencies should establish policy and procedures that provide for notifying the media about newsworthy events. In one metropolitan area, departments use special police radio broadcast channels to inform newspapers and broadcasting organizations of significant or unusual occurrences. In another area, police departments have established a newswire teletype circuit over which subscribing news media agencies routinely receive notification of serious or unusual events in which the police agency is involved.

**Every police agency should acknowledge the important role of the news media in reporting on police activities and the need for the police agency to be open in its relations with the media.**

Agencies should:

• Establish policies which protect and foster the right of the press to obtain information for dissemination to the public.

• Establish a regular news liaison function for responding to inquiries from the media and for disseminating information on police activities.

## Minority Community Needs

A critically important community problem confronts the police in urban areas with significant minority populations. A disproportionate amount of crime often occurs in these areas. Inhabitants of these areas frequently feel that they have less influence on police enforcement policies and practices than do other community residents. They are not convinced that the police serve them or respect them as citizens.

Some police departments, therefore, have established programs that seek the views of the minority community on police service. Other departments have provided training for their officers in race relations, community awareness, and ethnic history.

For example, the Dayton, Ohio, police department developed a training program in which new recruits were assigned as professional assistants to 14 different social action agencies during the first 4 weeks of training. This was followed by a training and service program that combined community awareness and role identification.

In Kansas City, Mo., recruits trained in role identification and social awareness were the subject of substantially fewer complaints during the first 6 months of service than were their associates who had not received this training.

The most encouraging development has been the efforts of some major city departments, working with organizations

239

such as the Urban Coalition, to recruit minority citizens as police officers. These efforts have produced encouraging results and the police chief of Washington, D.C., in response to a question from a reporter on how his department had reduced crime in Washington, cited the increase in minority officers on the police force as a major factor.

The Commission recommends that every police agency that has racial or minority groups of significant size in its jurisdiction insure that the needs of minorities are actively considered in the establishment of police policy and the delivery of police service. Affirmative action should be taken to achieve a proportion of minority group employees that approximates their proportion in the population of the area.

Recruit and inservice police training programs should provide explicit instruction in community culture. The training should be general as to the whole community and specific as to significant minority or ethnic groups in the community. Training programs should stress interpersonal communications and should rest on a single standard of fair and equal treatment for all persons.

Further, every police agency should insure that recruitment, hiring, assignment, and promotion policies do not discriminate against minority groups. Every police agency should engage in positive efforts to employ ethnic or minority group members.

## Citizen Grievances

All efforts to establish effective relations with the community will fail if the police agency is not responsive to complaints from the community about general police services and about individual officers. Accordingly, it is imperative that police agencies establish procedures for insuring that complaints about police service are handled in an expeditious and fair manner. The procedures should insure that every police agency inform the public on a continuing basis of its complaint reception and investigation procedures. Complaint forms should be developed and made available to the public.

The procedures should insure that the making of the complaint is not accompanied by fear of reprisal or harassment. Complete records of complaint reception, investigation, and adjudication should be maintained in a central record and statistical center. Complaints should be chronologically recorded. Information based on these records should be published regularly and made available to the public.

Every police agency should insure that all allegations of service misconduct and all complaints are investigated by a specialized unit or individual in the agency.

**The Commission recommends that every police agency establish procedures to facilitate full and fair processing of complaints about general police services and about individual officer's conduct. Every person making a complaint should receive written verification that his complaint is being processed by the police agency. Every person who files a complaint should be notified of its disposition and personal discussion regarding this disposition should be encouraged.**

## Patrol and Crime Prevention

Of all the functions performed by the police, there is none more important than the day-to-day job of the patrol officer. The patrol officer is the community's first line of defense against crime.

In its simplest terms, patrol is the deployment of police officers in a given community to prevent and deter criminal activity and to provide day-to-day police services to the community.

**Every police chief executive should insure that all elements within the agency provide maximum assistance and cooperation to the patrol officer and patrol officers should be relieved of minor tasks in order to increase their capability to reduce crimes.**

A survey done for the 1967 President's Crime Commission found that almost 48 percent of all arrests are made within 2 hours of the commission of the crime and 36 percent of all arrests are made within an hour. The Commission then went on to conclude that "ways should be found of getting persons with investigative experience to crime scenes with the greatest possible rapidity—before crimes, in police terms, are cold."

In the view of the National Advisory Commission an important way is to enlarge the patrol officer's investigative role. Too often the patrol officer's involvement in a criminal investigation is limited to taking reports. He is expected to interview witnesses and victims, conduct a preliminary investigation, formulate a report, and return to service, all within 30 minutes. The result is usually a hastily prepared report, a cursory preliminary investigation, and an unsolved crime.

**Patrolmen should receive training in conducting investigations and in gathering evidence. Patrol officers should be utilized to conduct the complete investigation of crimes which do**

241

not require extensive followup investigation and patrol officers should be utilized to follow up and close out investigations of these crimes.

## Geographic Policing

The Commission has been encouraged by the efforts of police departments in recent years in developing policing programs that insure stability of assignment of individual patrol officers within a given neighborhood and community. Under these programs, police agencies require patrol officers so assigned to meet on a regular basis with persons who live and work in the area to discuss and identify crime problems and the proper solution to these problems.

The "Basic Car Plan" initiated by the Los Angeles City Police Department and followed by other departments utilizes the geographic policing concept. It has been successful in involving thousands of citizens in a direct effort to make their neighborhood safe and is built on two major premises. The first premise of the program is that an officer assigned to a given area and given primary responsibility for reducing crime in that area can prove more effective than an officer randomly assigned to an area and given no specific crime reduction responsibility. This can be even more true when the patrolman's investigative role is expanded as recommended earlier.

The second premise is that support of citizens living and working in the community is essential for successful policing and is the best method of reducing crime; this support can best be obtained through long-term assignment of officers to a neighborhood and through police efforts to communicate with citizens.

In many respects, the program is an update of the concept of the police "walking the beat," which was generally abandoned in the late 1940's and early 1950's because reformers were concerned that the officer on the foot beat could be corrupted by his familiarity with local residents and was slow to respond to the scene of an emergency. To solve the latter problem, they put him in a radio car; to solve the former, they transferred him frequently so that he would not have a chance to become corrupt.

There are better means available to police departments to control corruption, including departmental audits of police arrests and the use of internal discipline investigative units. Police need to return to patrol programs that establish stronger ties to the community while maintaining the flexibility and speed of response provided by the patrol car.

**The Commission recommends that every police agency adopt policing programs that insure stability of assignment in a given geographic area for individual patrol officers who are operationally deployed.**

Every police agency should insure that officers assigned to geographic policing programs meet regularly with persons who live or work in their area. Every patrol officer assigned to the program should be responsible for control of crime in his area and should, within the framework of the agency's objectives and policy, be granted authority to determine the means he will use to fulfill that responsibility.

## Team Policing

Team policing incorporates the concept of geographic policing and carries it even further. First experiments in team policing took place in Europe and certain aspects of it were recommended in the President's Commission on Law Enforcement and Administration of Justice. Since the issuance of that Commission's report, team policing has become one of the most popular forms of police reorganization and innovation. It has been practiced in different ways in different agencies and has received considerable publicity. However, no definitive study has yet been made of its effectiveness and the changes to be achieved. Total team policing can be defined as:

1. Combining all line operations of patrol, traffic, and investigation into a single group under common supervision;

2. Forming teams with a mixture of patrolmen, investigators, and specialists in such areas as juvenile delinquency and drug abuse;

3. Permanently assigning teams to geographic areas; and

4. Charging the teams with total responsibility for all police services within their respective areas.

Most team policing systems have not taken this total approach, but from the experience of cities that have implemented various aspects of team policing programs, the Commission is satisfied that these programs have a significant potential for crime control.

**The Commission recommends that every police agency examine and test the team policing concept to determine its value in improving the agency's efforts to reduce crime, im-**

prove the quality of police service, and enhance police-community cooperation.

## Police Community Reserves

Many police agencies in this country utilize citizen reserve officers to supplement the regular force of officers. Many reserves are authorized to make arrests and perform all of the routine police functions. Reserves operate on a part-time basis and can be used to provide backup manpower, increase police-community cooperation, and perform many valuable volunteer services.

Utilization of reserves is an extension of a tradition that precedes the existence of structured police forces. The early use of reserves in this country is a sordid history of the misuse of police power beginning with deputized posses and vigilantes in the West in the 19th century, and carrying through to the American Protective League that was established as a citizens' auxiliary to the United States Department of Justice in 1917. The league, operating without legal authority, conducted mass roundups of suspected draft dodgers, enemy aliens, and deserters.

This history has produced many opponents to the police reserve concept. However, it is the opinion of the Commission, based on an analysis of modern-day programs, that properly structured and standardized civilian reserve programs can make a valuable addition to a police force.

One excellent modern-day use of reserves is the Reserve Deputy Sheriff's Program conducted in Los Angeles County, Calif., which uses reserve patrolmen and reserve specialists who are specially trained and selected.

Reserve personnel donated 374,867 man-hours of police service to the County of Los Angeles during fiscal year 1970-71, resulting in a total cost savings to the county in police salaries of over $2 million.

If reserve officers are used, there must be clear standards for their training and use. Police agencies should furnish the reserve officer with the uniform and equipment of a regular sworn officer upon completion of all training requirements. Until the reserve has completed training requirements, his uniform should readily identify his as a reserve officer, and he should perform his duties under the direct supervision of a regular sworn officer. The Florida State Police Standards Board has developed a set of standards that could provide a sound basis for utilization of police reserves.

Every police department should consider employment of police reserve officers to supplement the regular force of officers and increase community involvement in local police service.

## Diversion

It is becoming increasingly clear that every suspect need not be arrested and that every suspect should not be processed through the courts and correction processes. Juveniles, alcoholics, the elderly, the mentally ill, drug users, the physically sick or handicapped frequently need help outside the criminal justice system. The police can and should assist in bringing to light community resources, in opening new avenues of help to people coming to their attention, and in diverting these people out of the criminal justice system.

These efforts have two main advantages: by relieving the burdens both on courts and on corrections of processing individuals who could be more appropriately handled outside the criminal justice system, they free valuable criminal justice resources and provide more effective help to the individual. In the case of juveniles, counseling and informal referral are often more effective than formal procedures. Detoxification treatment, therapy, and counseling are clearly more appropriate for alcoholics than traditional confinement and release.

Some police agencies are reluctant to engage in diversion, particularly diversion with referral to welfare agencies. As an example, the vast majority of juveniles taken into custody in 1971 (over 1.2 million) were either referred to juvenile court or handled within the police department and released. Less than 2 percent were referred to welfare agencies.[1]

Diversion does not take place in many departments because police are either not familiar with private and public resources or such resources are simply not available. These problems can and should be corrected by cooperation among police, criminal justice planners, and community officials.

Some agencies eschew diversion in the belief that they will be accused of selective and unequal law enforcement. This difficulty can be avoided, however, if police agencies will develop written criteria specifying who can be diverted and under what circumstances.

**Every police agency should establish formal criteria for deverting from the criminal and juvenile justice system all in-**

[1] Federal Bureau of Investigation, *Uniform Crime Reports— 1971* (1972), p. 112.

dividuals coming to their attention for whom processing into the justice system would be inappropriate or for whom the use of resources outside the criminal and juvenile justice system would be more appropriate.

These guidelines are to be developed after consultation with prosecutors, judges, and other criminal justice personnel. States and units of local government should enact legislation and ordinances authorizing diversion and authorizing and funding alcohol detoxification, drug treatment, youth services bureaus, and other appropriate diversion-oriented programs.

# Planning and Organizing for More Effective Law Enforcement

Proper planning for effective use of resources necessarily begins with the collection and analysis of data that reflect the community's needs for police services, and the type of activities performed by the police. Reported crimes, arrests, and calls for service must be analyzed by type, date, time, and location. The amount of police time expended on these functions, on preventive patrol, on traffic enforcement, and on nonemergency and noncriminal matters must be analyzed.

The extent of the analysis required should be consistent with the volume and nature of the local demands for police services and the size and resources of the agency.

**Every police agency should conduct workload studies on a regular basis; information obtained from the workload studies should form the basis for establishing patrol and investigation operational objectives and priorities.**

## Deployment

Crime and workload data may indicate the advisability of special task forces to deal with particular crimes or series of crimes.

In one city, for example, reported crime and arrest data are collected by each precinct on each shift. These data are transmitted to the headquarters crime analysis unit, which records and analyzes them. When the unit detects significant trends, it dispatches officers from a special headquarters tactical squad to selected areas of the city to provide increased patrol investigative capability. The tactical squad includes uniformed officers, plainclothes officers, and officers in disguise. The department credits this technique with having a substantial impact on the reductions in reported crime it has recorded in recent years and similar experiences have been reported in other departments.

The Commission recommends that police departments in major cities establish tactical squads for flexible, highly mobile, and rapid deployment against special crime problems. The tactical squad should be deployed on the basis of current crime pattern analysis and projected criminal activity. A full-time tactical force should include an analytical staff element.

## Responsibility for Police Service

Almost all local governments can benefit from some form of combined police service. At one extreme, local government can get out of the police business entirely by contracting for all police services from another government or agency, or State and local police agencies may simply develop ways to assist and reinforce each other.

Consolidation can frequently upgrade police service and lower its costs. Because it is larger, the consolidated agency usually has superior resources. Because it eliminates much duplication, citizens get more for their money.

Local governments should analyze the various methods of combining police services, compare the cost effectiveness of each to that of its own operations, and develop applications to its own operations.

The most comprehensive combined service is total consolidation of local government. One type of total consolidation took place in 1965 when personnel of the North Sacramento, Calif., police department were absorbed into the Sacramento police department.

A second type of total consolidation is the merger of a city government with a county government. In 1968 in Florida the 474-man Jacksonville police department merged with the 260-man Duval County sheriff's office under the office of the sheriff. In January 1973, the city of Lexington and Fayette County Ky., merged under a charter establishing the Lexington-Fayette Urban County Government with a single police department.

A further method of providing consolidated police services includes contracting for police service. The most frequent type of contract is the city-county contract. In Los Angeles County, approximately 29 cities ranging in population from 1,000 to 100,000 contract with the county to provide total police services. Each jurisdiction contracting with the county can, through the contract process, establish the amount of police service to be provided.

There are also advantageous arrangements between States and local jurisdictions. In New Jersey and Kentucky, State police departments provide contract services to certain jurisdictions in their respective States.

A number of agencies have also undertaken to provide consolidated support and operative services in selected areas. In the Kansas City, Mo., metropolitan area, a metro squad composed of personnel assigned by the various participating agencies in the metropolitan area assists in investigating major cases (primarily homicides) deemed likely to constitute a metropolitan threat. Arrests have been made in more than 70 percent of the cases investigated by the metro squad. Additionally, numerous arrests for offenses other than those being investigated have been made by the metro squad. The squad functions throughout the multijurisdictional geographic area, even transcending the Missouri-Kansas State line.

In 1972, the Jefferson County and Louisville, Ky., police departments merged seven major functional areas: training, records, information systems, fingerprinting and identification, photo laboratories, planning and research, and communication systems. This has resulted in greater efficiency and effectiveness of these services and the operations of the two police departments.

## Total Consolidation of Small Police Departments

It is the view of the Commission that 10 police officers should be considered the minimum level required for an agency to operate as an independent entity.

The facts are as follows: approximately 80 percent of the 25,000 police agencies in the United States have fewer than 10 full-time commissioned officers, yet they account for less than 10 percent of the total full-time police officers in the United States.

Small agencies often are not able to serve their communities efficiently. The Advisory Commission on Intergovernmental Relations in its 1971 report on *State-Local Relations in the Criminal Justice System* noted:

> Small police departments, particularly those of ten or less men, are unable to provide a wide range of patrol and investigative services to local citizens. Moreover, the existence of these small agencies may work a hardship on nearby jurisdictions. Small police de-

partments do not have adequate full-time control in preliminary and investigative services and may require the aid of larger agencies in many facets of their police work. Moreover, lack of adequate basic police services in one locality can make it a haven for criminals and thus impose social and economic costs on the remainder of the metropolitan community.

Other studies show that five sworn police officers are required to provide one sworn police officer on a full-time, around-the-block basis, allowing for days off, vacation and sick time, and other variables. To provide for the full-time employment of two policemen, a local government would ideally need to hire 10 police officers. If fewer than 10 sworn personnel are employed, the employment is usually not cost effective and often results in inadequate services.

**The Commission recommends that any police agency employing fewer than 10 sworn officers combine with one or more other agencies to improve efficiency in delivering police services. In remote areas where there is no nearby local agency, combined or contract programs with county or State agencies should be established.**

# Maximum Use of Human Resources

Of all the resources committed to the law enforcement process, manpower is at once the costliest and the most important. Nationally, more than 80 percent of all police budgets is committed to salaries.[2] It is imperative that police obtain maximum productivity from available manpower.

## Recruitment

The first step in obtaining an effective police force is the recruitment and selection of competent personnel. It is imperative that police agencies engage in forceful, active recruiting to bring their departments to authorized strength.

The Commission recommends that every police agency aggressively recruit applicants when qualified candidates are not readily available. In recruiting applicants, a variety of techniques should be implemented, including use of professional recruiters and central government personnel agencies, development of cooperative personnel systems with other police

[2] Kansas City Police Department, "1970 Survey of Municipal Police Departments," (1970).

agencies, and utilization of all agency personnel in the recruitment process.

**Police recruitment efforts should concentrate on college-educated applicants. Recruitment resources should be applied according to the agency's needs for personnel with varied ethnic and minority characteristics. Residency should be eliminated as a prerequisite for employment and decentralized application procedures should be utilized.**

## Education

More than half of the Nation's young people now go on to college. In terms of education norms, an undergraduate degree today is equivalent in prestige to a high school diploma at the turn of the century. Yet most police agencies have failed to take notice of this change and for many agencies the minimum required education level is the same as it was 40 years ago, a high school education.

Police agencies have lost ground in the race for highly qualified employees. College graduates look elsewhere for employment, and police work has often come to be regarded by the public as a second-class occupation. It is ironic that this is taking place when studies are showing that police officers with a college background perform at a significantly higher level than police officers without a college degree.

A 1972 study by the Rand Institute in New York, N.Y., revealed that men who had college degrees demonstrated better on-the-job performance than the average policeman and had a low incidence of misconduct.[8] These findings are similar to the results of a 1968 Chicago study, which revealed that the highest rated group of tenure officers were those with significantly high levels of education.[4] Upgrading the educational level of police officers is one of the more important challenges facing the police service in the 1970's.

**The Commission recommends that every police agency require immediately, as a condition of initial employment, completion of at least 1 year of education at an accredited college or university and that by 1983, every police agency require, as a condition of initial employment, completion of at**

[8] Bernard Cohen and Jan M. Chaihen, *Police Background Characteristics and Performance Summary* (Rand Institute, May, 1972).

[4] Melany E. Baehr, *Psychological Assessment of Patrolman Qualifications in Relation to Field Performance* (Government Printing Office, November 1968).

least 4 years of college-level education or a baccalaureate degree at an accredited college or university.

It is imperative that police agencies upgrade the educational levels of their present officers as well as their recruits, since many of these officers will be performing police services for some years to come. Police agencies therefore should establish incentives to encourage police officers to achieve a college-level education. Officers' assignments should be made, where possible, to accommodate attendance at local colleges, and financial assistance to defray educational expenses should be provided. Increased pay should be provided for the attainment of specified levels of academic achievement.

## Training

There is a serious flaw in the police profession—the insufficiency of initial and inservice training given to most policemen. Perhaps no other profession has such lax standards, or is allowed to operate without firm controls and without licensing.

The average barber receives 4,000 hours of training. The average policeman receives less than 200 hours.

In 1931, the National Commission on Law Observance and Enforcement (Wickersham Commission), impressed by what it saw taking place in larger police agencies, predicted that the time for thorough police training had come and that within 15 years high quality police training would be all but universal in the United States. What that Commission perhaps failed to see is that only large agencies have the resources to provide adequate police training. Smaller agencies cannot develop the needed programs.

Yet this training must be made available to all policemen in all agencies. The people have a right to expect high quality police professionalism everywhere.

Every State should enact legislation that establishes mandatory minimum basic training of 400 hours for police; that establishes a representative body to develop and administer programs for police; and that establishes financial support for local police training.

This legislation should prohibit any individual from performing the police function unless he is certified as having met the minimum standards.

In addition to traditional basic police subjects, training should include instruction in law, psychology, and sociology, and should involve assigned activities away from the training academy to enable the employee to gain insight into the community and the criminal justice system of government. Remedial training should be provided for individuals who are deficient in performances but have the potential to perform satisfactorily.

In calling for 400 hours of minimum training, the Commission is supporting a basic recommendation of the 1967 President's Crime Commission. A survey conducted in 1970 by the International Association of Chiefs of Police disclosed that only 19 States required more than 200 hours of instruction, and that the number of required hours ranged from 72 to 400. Basic police training programs reflect to a large degree both the police agency's commitment to quality police service and the complexity of police responsibilities. Thus, in major cities a few police agencies require more than 1,000 hours of training as a minimum for all employees.

The representative body for setting training standards could also set selection standards. Presently 33 States have commissions charged with the responsibility for setting police standards in the areas of selection and training.[5]

## Development, Promotion, and Advancement

Development, promotion, and advancement of personnel are necessary activities in achieving successful and efficient policing. Promotion and advancement of employees should be based on demonstrated ability and proven performance. Police agencies should adopt the policy of promoting to higher ranks and advancing to higher paid grades only those personnel who successfully demonstrate their abilities to assume increased responsibilities and to perform the duties of the position to which they are promoted or advanced. Police agencies should screen all personnel to identify their individual potential and guide them toward achieving full potential.

Police agencies should offer comprehensive and individualized programs of education, training, and experience designed to develop the potential of every employee.

**The Commission recommends that every police agency implement programs designed to aid employees' professional growth and increase their capacity for their present and future roles within the agency.**

Such programs should include, where feasible:

[5] Advisory Commission on Intergovernmental Relations, *State-Local Relations in the Criminal Justice System* (1971), p. 30.

- Provision for internships with other police, criminal justice, and governmental agencies.
- Provision for the temporary assumption of the position, responsibility, and authority of an immediate superior.
- Provision for selective and individualized rotation of personnel to develop patrol and specialist expertise.
- Provision for rotation to areas of varying crime incidence, and to major administrative assignments.

## Lateral Entry

The development of incumbent personnel is the most effective manner in which to fill senior advanced positions, but it is not the most practical or expeditious technique for every agency. Because of inattention to personnel development, it is not unusual for individual police agencies to have vacancies for which qualified replacements are unavailable within that agency. Conversely, it is not unusual for the more professional police agencies to develop what amounts to a surplus of managerial and administrative talent.

If the opportunity for lateral movement within the law enforcement profession were enhanced, manpower would be used more efficiently with commensurate benefit accruing to individual agencies and professions as a whole. Lateral entry is particularly promising in selecting the police chief executive and in adding minority officers to the ranks.

Before the full benefits of lateral mobility can be realized, certain dynamic changes must be made within the police service. Among the necessary changes is the elimination of overly restrictive residency requirements and of civil service restrictions on eligibility for entry-level and advanced positions. Additionally, State and national provisions must be made for transferring retirement pensions and other fringe benefits so that those who desire to move laterally do not suffer financially.

**Personnel should be recruited for lateral entry at any level from outside police agencies when it is necessary to do so in order to obtain the services of individuals who are qualified for a position or assignment.**

Every State should provide a statewide police retirement system for all sworn personnel within the State. Reciprocal agreements should be formulated among independent, local, State, and interstate agencies to allow any police officer in the country to accept any law enforcement position available within any State and still retain his accrued retirement benefits.

## Classification and Pay

Increased professionalization of the police service depends on the caliber of the people it can recruit and retain.

Many police agencies are unable to attract the officers they need because of unreasonably low salaries. The police must offer salaries to recruit and retain the caliber of personnel necessary to perform the police function.

**The Commission recommends that every State and local government establish and maintain salaries that attract and retain qualified personnel capable of performing the police function.**

**Every State should set minimum entry-level salaries for all State and local police officers and should reimburse the employing agency for a portion of the guaranteed salary.**

A salary review procedure should be established to insure the automatic annual adjustment of police salaries to reflect the prevailing wages in the local economy.

As noted earlier in this chapter, the Commission feels that the patrolman is the most vital element of the police function and that police departments should make every effort to attract and retain highly qualified patrolmen. The policies of many police agencies, however, encourage the best patrol officers to seek other assignments.

These agencies make no provisions for officers who desire to advance and earn more pay while remaining in the patrol function. As a result, qualified patrol officers often seek promotion to supervisory positions or transfer to specialist positions in order to obtain greater status and pay. In most police agencies, no distinction is made between the duties and responsibilities of the patrol officer with 1 year of service and the officer with 15 years. As a result, a highly qualified, well-motivated officer feels that he is not progressing unless he transfers from the patrol force.

A system (the Jacobs Plan) recently adopted in the Los Angeles City Police Department provides multiple pay grades within the basic patrol rank, granting well-qualified patrol officers greater responsibilities and pay while they remain on the patrol force. The Commission would carry this plan even further and allow a patrol officer to advance to a salary level equal to that of an investigator or any other police officer at the nonsupervisory level.

The Commission also feels that proficiency pay should be given to patrol officers who train recruits in patrol duties, who coordinate activities of a patrol team, or who acquire specialist skills or experience that contribute to patrol efficiency. Competent patrol officers with greater responsibility should receive appropriate and distinctive uniform insignia.

**Every local government should expand its classification and pay system to provide greater advancement within the basic patrol rank.**

The system should provide:

• Multiple pay grades within the basic patrolman rank.

• Opportunity for advancement within the basic patrolman rank.

• Parity in top pay grades between patrol officers and nonsupervisory officers assigned to other operational functions.

• Proficiency pay for patrol personnel who have demonstrated expertise in specific field activities that contribute to more efficient police service.

## Women in Policing

The role of women in the police service has been based largely on traditional and often outmoded ideas. Some misconceptions concerning women's ability to perform certain "masculine" tasks have been dispelled as a result of changing social attitudes. The police service should keep current with social changes and legal requirements by reexamining the function of female police officers.

Just prior to the turn of the century, a movement to employ women as regular police officers gained support among several social action groups and culminated in the hiring of the first regularly appointed policewomen in the country. By the end of World War II, more than 200 cities employed policewomen. These women, however, have been assigned mainly to duties that do not involve patrol. Most policewomen work in clerical jobs or in jobs related to juvenile delinquency, family crises, missing persons, runaways, and sex offenses.

Within the past 2 to 3 years, police departments in some major cities have been moving toward using policewomen in all functions performed by the police and particularly in patrol. More and more departments are assigning women to patrol duties and some departments have developed promotional policies requiring that when a vacancy occurs the next eligible person be elevated, regardless of sex.

The Commission recommends that every police agency immediately insure that there exists no agency policy that discourages qualified women from seeking employment as sworn or civilian personnel or that prevents them from realizing their full employment potential.

Agencies should institute selection procedures to facilitate employment of women and should insure that recruitment, selection, training, and salary policies do not discriminate against women.

Agencies should require career paths for women, allowing each individual to obtain a position commensurate with her particular degree of experience, skill, and ability.

## Use of Civilian Employees

Police agencies traditionally have staffed the majority of positions with sworn police officers. Policemen have been assigned clerical tasks, general maintenance, and even construction duties.

The term "sworn police officers" refers to those individuals in a police department who are authorized to make arrests and who have peace officer status under applicable provisions of State and local laws. Civilian or nonsworn personnel include all other individuals employed by a police department.

Civilian personnel can be an important addition to the operations of a police agency. They can free police from routine tasks for more effective assignment in line operations.

Additionally, civilians capable of performing routine tasks often do not command the salaries of trained policemen and often have specialized skills needed in police work.

The Dallas, Tex., Police Department, for example, has made extensive use of civilian personnel. It has established the positions of "police service officer" and "community service officer" to perform nonenforcement functions. Civilians are used by Dallas as helicopter pilots, radio dispatchers, communications aides, property control and supply officers, and jail aides, and are used for issuing traffic citations and for performing traffic patrol and control duties.

Police agencies should explore all possible uses of civilians and should be innovative in determining the functions they could perform.

In addition to the functions set out above, in some departments civilians are employed as evidence-gathering technicians, lab technicians, personnel specialists, and photographers.

## Employee Relations
## and Police Employee Organizations

The police chief executive is usually held more accountable by the public for the activities of his personnel than are most other public agency officials. The conduct of police employees depends, in turn, upon the attitudes and programs of the police chief executive. His reaction toward employees encourages their cooperation.

The police chief executive must promote an atmosphere of effective cooperation and employee relations. He must create an atmosphere that encourages an employee to do a good job, and the employee must feel that he is contributing to the agency's success.

**Every police chief executive should develop methods to obtain information from police employees who have daily contact with operational problems in order to assist him in reaching decisions on personnel and operational matters.**

In addition, every police chief executive should develop fair and effective grievance procedures to consider the complaints of all police employees. Every police chief executive should have employee relations specialists available to him. He must be prepared for collective negotiation and must establish effective working relationships with employee organizations.

The Commission notes that one of the most innovative methods of employee participation is occurring in Kansas City, Mo. The police department has established numerous task forces directed by patrolmen and other line personnel to explore and develop new methods for crime reduction. Funds are provided for the work of the task forces, and police employees are involved in planning and designing projects.

The Commission recommends that every police chief executive acknowledge the right of his agency's officers to join employee organizations.

**Legislation should be enacted to authorize every police agency and all employees to engage in collective negotiations in arriving at terms and conditions of employment, police service effectiveness, and equitable representation for police employees and management. Such legislation should specifically prohibit strikes, work stoppages, and concerted job actions, and should provide for the retention of management rights including the setting of management policies, the direction of employees' work, and the setting of hiring, firing, and promotion policies.**

# Maximum Use of Technology and Support Services

In addition to allocating human resources in the most efficient manner possible, police agencies need to concentrate on obtaining and applying sophisticated technological and support resources. Communications systems, information systems, and criminal laboratories are tools that multiply the effectiveness of police officers.

Only token progress has been made in the application of available modern technology in police work. Another surge of technological innovation is needed if law enforcement is to respond adequately to the increasing sophistication of the criminal element.

## Communications Systems

The time it takes a patrol car to respond to a call for service is critical to successful apprehension of criminals. Police communications systems are vital to improving this response time.

The elapsed time in the communications center is a significant part of the total time it takes for police to respond to a call for service. A study done by the 1967 President's Crime Commission showed that patrol cars took an average of 3.8 minutes to reach the scene of a crime after the initial call was placed. The communications center delay thus accounted for as much as 50 percent of the total delay.

Many police communications systems are actually chaotic assemblies of independent radio networks that somehow manage to move a monumental volume of radio traffic despite considerable inefficiency. They operate on the threshold of collapse, with radio traffic overloads the rule rather than the exception. In a major civil disorder, disaster, or other massive emergency, most police communications systems will break down.

The first element of a police communications system is the telephone. Substantial improvements are needed in telephone systems linking police to the community. To most people in the United States, the policeman is usually no farther away than the telephone. Yet police agencies often fail to give enough thought to the importance of a successful telephone call and a prompt response. Inefficient telephone and radio communications can result in serious injury or loss of life to the victim of a crime or accident and can hamper apprehension of criminal offenders. In an emergency, the public should be able to contact the police immediately by making a single telephone call.

States and units of local government should undertake to provide a single universal telephone number for all calls for emergency, police, and other municipal services in a given geographic area.

The second element of a communications system is the radio system. The degree to which agencies achieve communications with their field units is critical. It affects the success of the agencies' efforts to preserve life and property and increases the potential for apprehension of criminal suspects.

**The Commission recommends that every police agency immediately establish command and control centers for the operation of their communications systems and provide a 24-hour, two-way radio capability for continuous communications between the command and control communications center and the field units.**

Where necessary smaller agencies should contract for services or consolidate operations with those of larger agencies. The elapsed time between receipt of a complaint emergency call at the communications center and the time of radio message transmission should not exceed 2 minutes. As soon as possible, this elapsed time should not exceed 1 minute. Upon receiving an emergency call patrol cars should reach the scene of the call within a minimum of three minutes.

All patrol cars should be equipped with two-way radios, and every police agency should equip all on-duty uniformed officers with a portable two-way radio capable of being carried with reasonable comfort on the person of the officer.

Research has shown that digital communications may have the potential for vastly increasing the efficiency of police operations. Digital communications systems can provide instantaneous dispatch of routine operational messages and can provide field units with direct access to computer data banks. They can reduce frequency congestion and can allow field units to query computer-based information systems directly, without going through a dispatcher. They also can be used to inform dispatchers whether field units are available for assignment.

In a system tried in Oakland, Calif., police officers utilized a "touch map" mounted on a police vehicle dashboard. This device allowed the policeman to touch a specific point on the map, which automatically, by a digital communication, activated a light showing his unit number and location on a similar map in front of a dispatcher.

The components of a fully automated digital communications system have been used independently or in various combinations but never have been brought together in an integrated system. The individual development of these sophisticated and complex devices should not continue on a random and uncoordinated basis. Coordinated research and development will result in considerable savings of time and money.

**The Commission recommends that the Law Enforcement Assistance Administration (LEAA) initiate a competitive research and development effort for the study, design, manufacture, and operation of pilot digital communications systems.**

The systems should include the use of vehicular visual display devices with printed computer readouts, automated vehicle locater devices, and real-time unit status reporting devices.

## Evidence Gathering and Crime Laboratories

An efficient and productive crime laboratory can be an invaluable aid to the police investigation process. Forensic science applies the principles of physical and biological disciplines to solving crimes. Few police agencies have taken full advantage of developments in this field. Police services need to become more familiar with the extent to which an efficient forensic science program can contribute to police effectiveness.

In order to solve many crimes the police agency must be able to identify, collect, and preserve physical evidence at the crime scene. In recent years, court decisions and more effective criminal defense have placed a stronger burden on police agencies to prove their cases. Greater efficiency in gathering evidence is necessary.

**The Commission recommends that every police agency provide all incoming police personnel with a formalized basic training course in forensic science and evidence-gathering techniques, and that every police agency also develop and deploy specially trained personnel to gather physical evidence 24 hours a day.**

Every State should establish a consolidated criminal laboratory system composed of local, regional, or State facilities capable of providing the widest possible range of forensic science services to police agencies.

# Coordination with Other Criminal Justice Agencies

Success in protecting society is not measured by the length of time it takes the police to respond to a crime scene, by the number of arrests they make, or by the number of arrestees successfully prosecuted or sentenced. Rather, success or failure is determined by the degree to which society is free of crime and disorder.

This is but another way of saying that no element of the criminal justice system completely discharges its responsibility simply by achieving its own immediate objectives. The police, the prosecutor, the courts, and probation, parole, and corrections agencies must cooperate with each other if the system is to operate effectively. This requires an effort on the part of each element to communicate with the other elements, even though this is sometimes difficult because of legal and administrative separation of powers and responsibilities.

## Case Preparation Unit

An essential element in cooperation between the police and prosecutor is the development of evidence necessary to obtain the conviction or acquittal of arrested individuals. The police department in Detroit, Mich., has found that by establishing a special unit for case preparation it could relieve precinct investigators from spending excessive time in court and on court-related activities. This unit has also considerably improved the quality of court case preparation and improved the working relationship among the police, the prosecutor's office, and the courts. The case preparation unit has saved the department almost 875 man-hours per month in patrol and investigative measures.

**The Commission recommends that police departments in major metropolitan areas utilize case preparation specialists to insure that all evidence that may lead to conviction or acquittal of defendants is systematically prepared and presented for review by the prosecutor.**

Procedures for case preparation should be developed in cooperation with the representatives of the local prosecutorial and judicial systems to establish a format and procedure beneficial to all agencies. Procedures should include the establishment of case files which clearly document all legal action on the case from the first police action to final disposition. The files should constitute a firm foundation upon which police agency recommendations on diversion, bail, release on recognizance, sentencing, probation, and even parole can be based.

## Major Violations and Criminal Case Followup

Police agree that the sequential processing of defendants through the criminal justice system has contributed to the common but erroneous belief that, except for police appearances as witnesses, their function ends when a criminal complaint is issued. Police agencies, however, have undertaken a more active role in the disposition of criminal cases.

Police departments in New York and Washington, D.C., have initiated Major Violator Programs to focus attention on suspected offenders who they believe are responsible for a large amount of crime. An example of a major violator might be an individual who has been found to be responsible for a large number of burglaries or robberies in a given area. By concentrating on those individuals the police departments, in cooperation with prosecutors and the courts, have been able to pinpoint and concert prosecution efforts on individuals who might pass unnoticed through congested courts. Prosecution agencies in New York and Washington, D.C., have generally agreed to cooperate in avoiding plea negotiations in cases involving major offenders and to give them priority handling.

In determining major violators many factors are considered, including police expenditure of resources to solve the crime, defendant's alleged responsibility for a number of crimes, and seriousness of the offense or the situation in the area where the crime occurred. Additionally, police departments in New York and Washington have established followup procedures to correct improper handling of cases in cooperation with the local courts and prosecuting agencies.

Every police agency in cooperation with local courts, prosecutors, and corrections agencies should provide for the adequate followup of criminal cases.

**Police agencies should identify major violators and should follow the progress of these individuals through the criminal justice system. Police agencies should review all major criminal cases that prosecutors refuse to prosecute or later cause to be dismissed, in order that administrative action may be taken to correct any police actions that may have weakened the case. The review procedure should also serve to inform the prosecuting office of deficiencies that the police may feel**

the prosecution has made in the case in order that the prosecutor may correct those inconsistencies.

The programs described above may be more effective in the court systems of large urban areas. Every police agency may, however, use the case followup procedure to encourage outside evaluation of the quality of case preparation and courtroom demeanor and testimony. Police agencies should be receptive to external evaluation by prosecutors and courts and should take steps to correct reported deficiencies.

## Formal Consultation with Other Criminal Justice Agencies

Among the agencies in the criminal justice system, the police are in the best position to observe the tangible effects of crime on the victim and possible disruption of order. It is rare, however, for the police to be consulted formally by other criminal justice elements attempting to arrive at decisions concerning screening, diversion, plea negotiation, probation, or parole.

This problem was highlighted in a survey of more than 3,-400 criminal justice practitioners.[6] The survey showed that 2,274, or 66 percent, said that it was undesirable for the prosecutor to engage in plea negotiations without consulting the arresting officer. Yet 2,393, or 70 percent, said that this was either very probable or somewhat probable.

**Information from the police regarding such matters as the effect of crimes upon the victims and the likelihood of future crimes by an arrested individual or convicted offender should be made available to and utilized by other criminal justice agencies for reference in making screening, diversion, plea negotiation, sentencing, and parole recommendations. Uniform standards and procedures should be established for making such recommendations.**

## Summons in Lieu of Arrest

The 1970 National Jail Census, conducted by the U.S. Bureau of the Census for the Law Enforcement Assistance Administration, found that on a given day more than 50 percent of those in the Nation's jails were awaiting trial.

These numbers can be significantly reduced and the crimi-

[6] Project STAR, *Survey of Role Perceptions for Operational Criminal Justice Personnel Data Summary* (California Department of Justice, 1972), p. 179.

nal justice system better served if, in lieu of arrest and detention, police issue a citation requiring the person to attend a court hearing. In Oakland, Calif., for example, more than 10,000 misdemeanants have been issued citations in lieu of arrest by police since 1970 and recent figures show a failure-to-appear-at-trial rate of less than 5 percent.

**The Commission recommends that every police agency issue, where legal and practical, written summons and citations in lieu of physical arrest. Police should establish procedures to seek out expeditiously and take into custody individuals participating in these programs who fail to appear in court.**

## Telephonic Search Warrants

The question of searches and seizures presents a critical problem to effective operation of the criminal justice system. The fourth amendment prohibits unreasonable searches and seizures by the police. Evidence obtained pursuant to an unreasonable seizure cannot be used against an individual and many otherwise valid criminal prosecutions fail.

Judicial decisions have tended to equate a reasonable search with one conducted pursuant to a properly issued warrant. For example, *Katz* v. *United States*, 389 U.S. 347, 357 (1967), held: "Searches conducted outside the judicial process, without prior approval by judge or magistrate, are per se unreasonable under the fourth amendment subject only to a few specifically established and well delineated exceptions."

In justifying exceptions to the rule requiring warrants, police officers often mention the long delay required to obtain them from the courts. However, while this delay frequently extends up to 10 hours the courts have been reluctant to accept delay as an exception under *Katz*.

To resolve this problem, California in 1970 and Arizona in 1971 enacted legislation that allows a search warrant to be issued during a recorded telephone conversation with a judge in which the requesting officer orally makes a sworn affidavit to the judge. This affidavit is later transcribed. The requesting officer then may be permitted to sign the judge's name on a duplicate original warrant, which then serves as the officer's search warrant. Following the conversation the judge signs and files the original warrant with the court clerk. Under this procedure the issuing authority remains with the judge and the officer's role is ministerial in executing the search ordered by the judge. Following execution of the warrant and completion of the search, the officer files the duplicate original warrant, an inventory of seized property, and a transcription of the recording with the court.

The efforts of these two States are an attempt to employ technology in carrying out the intent of the law. The procedure has been held to be constitutional by the California Supreme Court. (See the Commission's *Report on Police* for a more detailed discussion of this subject.)

**The Commission recommends that every State enact legislation that provides for the issuance of search warrants pursuant to telephone petitions and affidavits from police officers.**

## Court-Authorized Electronic Surveillance

The use of electronic surveillance by law enforcement agencies has been a controversial subject because of its potential for abuse of individual rights of privacy.

Efforts to enact Federal legislation in this area culminated in 1968 with the passage of Title III of the Omnibus Crime Control and Safe Streets Act. This legislation permitted limited and narrowly circumscribed court-authorized electronic surveillance. The act prohibited private electronic surveillance.

Reports filed by the Attorney General with the Administrative Office of the United States Courts indicate that Title III-authorized electronic surveillance has been used on a limited basis and that it has proved to be productive in terms of arrests and indictments of organized crime figures. The offenses investigated through the use of electronic surveillance frequently involved dangerous drugs and narcotics, gambling, and larceny. In 1971, 816 intercepts were authorized; these resulted in 2,818 arrests.

The figures quoted above include intercepts authorized by State court judges as well as those authorized by Federal judges. Title III authorized electronic surveillance by State enforcement officials if the State enacts statutes meeting the standards for intercept orders set forth in the Federal law. According to a 1972 report of the Administrative Office of the United States Courts, 19 States had enacted such legislation.

This legislation substantially strengthens the police resources utilized in the fight against bribery, corruption, organized crime, and narcotics distribution and can be a vital tool to reduce crime.

**The Commission recommends that each State enact legisla-**

tion prohibiting private electronic surveillance and authorizing court-supervised electronic surveillance by law enforcement officers, consistent with the provisions of Title III of the Omnibus Crime Control and Safe Streets Act of 1968.

# Conclusion

Police decisions—whether to arrest, to make a referral, to seek prosecution, or to use force—have profound and visible effects. Many of these decisions must be made within the span of a few moments and within the context of the most aggravated social problems. Yet the police officer is just as accountable for these decisions as any other public official.

The Commission's standards are designed not only to make police decisions more rational, but also to make them more understandable to the average citizen. The standards are based on the broad currents of reform generated by other professional and governmental efforts.

The police profession has made important advances in recent years. The pace of progress should continue and accelerate.

# Excerpts from the Task Force Report on Police

## Introduction

... American culture combines factors that contribute to crime and disorder. Widely varying beliefs and changing life styles mark the structure of this complex and competitive society. Extremes in ideals, emotions, and conduct are trademarks of life in the United States. ...

# A: Police Service in America

## 1: The Police Role

... The police in the United States are not separate from the people. They draw their authority from the will and consent of the people, and they recruit their officers from them. The police are the instrument of the people to achieve and maintain order; their efforts are founded on principles of public service and ultimate responsibility to the public. ...

Currently, the relationship in most communities between the police and the public is not entirely satisfactory. Members of the public frequently do not notify the police of situations that require enforcement or preventive action. Often, they avoid involvement in averting or interfering with criminal conduct, and many are suspicious of the police, the criminal justice system, and the entire political process.

During the 20 years following World War II, the police became increasingly isolated from their communities. Reasons for this isolation include urbanization, rapidly changing social conditions, greater demands for police services, increased reliance by the police on motorized patrol, police efforts to professionalize, and reduce police contact with non-criminal elements of society. These factors, combined with public apathy, caused many police agencies to attempt to combat rising crime without actively involving their communities in their efforts. . . .

### Standard 1.1: The Police Function

Every police chief executive immediately should develop written policy, based on policies of the governing body that provides formal authority for the police function, and should set forth the objectives and priorities that will guide the agency's delivery of police services. Agency policy should articulate the role of the agency in the protection of constitutional guarantees, the enforcement of the law, and the provision of services necessary to reduce crime, to maintain public order, and to respond to the needs of the community.

1. Every police chief executive should acknowledge that the basic purpose of the police is the maintenance of public order and the control of conduct legislatively defined as crime. The basic purpose may not limit the police role, but should be central to its full definition.

2. Every police chief executive should identify those crimes on which police resources will be concentrated. In the allocation of resources, those crimes that are most serious, stimulate the greatest fear, and cause the greatest economic losses should be afforded the highest priority.

3. Every police chief executive should recognize that some government services that are not essentially a police function are, under some circumstances, appropriately performed by the police. Such services include those provided in the interest of effective government or in response to established community needs. A chief executive:

    a. Should determine if the service to be provided has a relationship to the objectives established by the police agency. If not, the chief executive should resist that service becoming a duty of the agency;

    b. Should determine the budgetary cost of the service; and

    c. Should inform the public and its representatives of the projected effect that provision of the service by the police will have on the ability of the agency to continue the present level of enforcement services.

    d. If the service must be provided by the police agency, it should be placed in perspective with all other agency services and it should be considered when establishing priorities for the delivery of all police services.

**e.** The service should be made a part of the agency's police role until such time as it is no longer necessary for the police agency to perform the service.

**4.** In connection with the preparation of their budgets, all police agencies should study and revise annually the objectives and priorities which have been established for the enforcement of laws and the delivery of services.

... Police administrators must make the difficult determination of which reported crimes will be actively investigated and to what extent, and which unreported crimes will be sought out and to what degree. A determination must be made as to whether a reported theft warrants the same investigative resources as a crime of violence. Police must also assess the extent to which police resources should be used to suppress gambling, prostitution, and liquor law violations.

The law provides only general guidance. In their sterile statutory form, laws define crimes; classify them as felonies or misdemeanors; and assess penalties for them. But the law does not provide sufficient criteria to guide enforcement resource allocation, particularly at the local level.

In determining enforcement policies and priorities, police agencies should identify and direct primary attention to those crimes which are "serious": those that stimulate the greatest fear and cause the greatest economic losses. Beyond that, police agencies should be guided by the law, collective police experience, the needs and expectations of the community, and the availability of resources. . . .

### Standard 1.2: Limits of Authority

Every police chief executive immediately should establish and disseminate to the public and to every agency employee written policy acknowledging that police effectiveness depends upon public approval and acceptance of police authority. This policy at least:

**1.** Should acknowledge that the limits of police authority are strictly prescribed by law and that there can be no situation which justifies extralegal police practices;

**2.** Should acknowledge that there are times when force must be used in the performance of police tasks, but that there can be no situation which justifies the use of unreasonable force:

**3.** Should acknowledge that in their exercise of authority the police must be accountable to the community by providing formal procedures for receiving both commendations and

269

complaints from the public regarding individual officer performance. These procedures at least should stipulate that:

a. There will be appropriate publicity to inform the public that complaints and commendations will be received and acted upon by the police agency;

b. Every person who commends the performance of an individual officer in writing will receive a personal letter of acknowledgment; and

c. Every allegation of misconduct will be investigated fully and impartially by the police agency, and the results made known to the complainant or the alleged victim of police misconduct.

4. Should provide for immediate adoption of formal procedures to respond to complaints, suggestions, and requests regarding police services and formulation of policies. These procedures at least should stipulate that:

a. There will be appropriate notice to the public acknowledging that the police agency desires community involvement;

b. The public will be involved in the development of formal procedures as well as in the policies that result from their establishment; and

c. Periodic public surveys will be made to elicit evaluations of police service and to determine the law enforcement needs and expectations of the community.

## Standard 1.3: Police Discretion

Every police agency should acknowledge the existence of the broad range of administrative and operational discretion that is exercised by all police agencies and individual officers. That acknowledgment should take the form of comprehensive policy statements that publicly establish the limits of discretion, that provide guidelines for its exercise within those limits, and that eliminate discriminatory enforcement of the law. . . .

2. Every police chief executive should establish policy that guides the exercise of discretion by police personnel in using arrest alternatives. This policy:

a. Should establish the limits of discretion by specifically identifying, insofar as possible, situations calling for the use of alternatives to continued physical custody;

b. Should establish criteria for the selection of appropriate enforcement alternatives;

c. Should require enforcement action to be taken in all

270

situations where all elements of a crime are present and all policy criteria are satisfied;

d. Should be jurisdictionwide in both scope and application; and

e. Specifically should exclude offender lack of cooperation, or disrespect toward police personnel, as a factor in arrest determination unless such conduct constitutes a separate crime.

3. Every police chief executive should establish policy that limits the exercise of discretion by police personnel in conducting investigations, and that provides guidelines for the exercise of discretion within those limits. . . .

. . . In their exercise of administrative discretion, police chief executives may determine that enforcement of certain laws under some circumstances would be contrary to legislative intent and intolerable to a majority of the public. Such laws are those without complaining victims or witnesses; those which have become antiquated; and those which, although not stated as such, were intended for unusual situations. Determinations in such cases are based most frequently upon police experience in past enforcement activity, and policies established by prosecution agencies.

While it would be desirable to have the criminal law clearly express effective and enforceable limits of conduct, the fact that it does not always do so requires the police to establish enforcement policies that provide some clarification to the meaning of the law. As long as those policies are openly adopted, reduced to writing, and applied in a nondiscriminatory manner, the public and governing bodies are assured that the law enforcement is being administered properly by the police. . . .

In determining discretion guidelines, it is important that situations as well as particular crimes be identified. For example, both drinking in public, and drunkenness short of incapacity or in the absence of a disturbance, might be situations where discretion could be limited. Another example might be assault when the victim declines to prosecute. An arrest would be required in all other assaults where legal cause is present, but if the victim refuses to prosecute, an officer cannot make an arrest. On the other hand, an agency might require arrests in all assault cases, as in the Oakland Police Department. Another situation where discretion might be limited involves crimes where the victim's interest in reimbursement may be greater than his desire to prosecute—for example, shoplifting, vandalism, and passing bad checks. . . .

271

Arrest criteria may be particularly beneficial to an officer confronted with a person who, while making a speech in a public park, may be fomenting violence in his audience. Whether the officer should protect the first amendment rights of the speaker, disperse the crowd, arrest the speaker, or do nothing, is a policy decision that properly should be made in advance, not by him but by his agency.

Once policy guidelines are established, they should be applied uniformly by all line operations personnel. If an arrest is made by a field policeman and it complies with agency policy, investigators should not thwart policy by failing to seek a criminal complaint. . . .

Leniency is commonly used by the police to secure cooperation, as in "narcotic-buy" cases or in exchange for information, on grounds that not to prosecute will further the objective of public order. Such determinations should be a matter of agency policy and not left to the discretion of individual officers. In setting nonenforcement policy for such cases, police agencies must balance the benefits of the practice against the disrespect for the law that it might engender. . . .

Police guidelines governing criminal investigations have other advantages. By taking the initiative, police agencies can provide courts with thoroughly considered policies expressing police investigative needs that courts may recognize when ruling on the propriety of police investigations. The Washington, D.C., Circuit Court of Appeals, in a case involving an eyewitness identification said:

> We also note that, after this case arose, the Metropolitan Police Department put into operation a regulation restricting on-and-near-the-scene identification confrontations to suspects arrested within 60 minutes after the alleged offense and in close proximity to the scene. We see in this regulation a careful and commendable administrative effort to balance the freshness of a confrontation against the need to pick up the trail while fresh if the suspect is not the offender. We see no need in interposing at this time any more rigid time standard by judicial declaration.

When courts recognize that police agencies are preventing violations of constitutional rights by enforcing policies internally, the courts may decide that an effective alternative to the exclusionary rule exists. As stated by Judge Carl

McGowan of the Washington, D.C., Court of Appeals in *Rule-Making and the Police:*

> The judges might say in effect to the police: If you can satisfy us that you are doing everything you can to reduce the incidence of violations through meaningful disciplinary action, we will no longer need to seek deterrence through the indirect sanction of exclusion.

... It is desirable to consult the public in developing police policy. While developing general orders on eyewitness identifications and automobile searches, the Metropolitan Police Department in the District of Columbia consulted informally with members of the judiciary and criminal lawyers. The Los Angeles Police Department conferred with citizen experts while researching and drafting its policy manual. A more direct approach is being considered by the Dayton, Ohio, Police Department; enforcement policy there is being developed by police-citizen task forces. ...

**Standard 1.4: Improve communication and relations with the public.**

**Standard 1.5: Enhance police officers' understanding of their role.**

*Employee Participation in Role Identification*

Officers' attitudes cannot be altered by administrative decree. The way an officer views his role depends on many factors, and the desire to achieve his agency's objectives is only one of them.

Like everyone else, an officer needs self-respect. When he finds that his contacts with the public are frequently antagonistic, and that some people slight his role, he may begin to feel alienated. This feeling of isolation often leads to development of a police subculture to which officers turn for comfort and respect.

Officers frequently need to be persuaded that the official concept of their role is a proper one. Now, especially, when employee groups representing officers are becoming more aggressive, basic changes will be resisted. Short term successes may be achieved through revised recruit training programs, but long term advances require continuing in-service training of officers.

The most effective and sensible way to overcome employee resistance to policy defining the police role is to enlist the cooperation of officers at all levels. Their varied experience can contribute to making the policy realistic and acceptable. An officer's self-respect is enhanced when he realizes that his superiors value his opinion.

*Evaluation of Role Adherence*

The police role not only must be taught to policemen, but incentives must be developed to encourage each officer to adopt that role. If a stronger service orientation is desired, an agency must assure an officer that service will be rewarded, not ridiculed. An officer who takes time to learn how to refer persons in need to the proper agency deserves recognition as much as one who makes an arrest. The degree of recognition should be determined by the priorities established within the police role. Therefore, there must be a means of evaluating compliance. Too often the police service measures performance solely by the number of arrests made, traffic citations issued, or radio calls answered. Such performance measures are replete with abuses. More sophisticated supervision techniques must be developed to measure the degree of community responsiveness or of courtesy in citizen contacts....

## Standard 1.6: Public Understanding of the Police Role

Every police agency immediately should establish programs to inform the public of the agency's defined police role. These programs should include, but not be limited to, the following:

1. Every police agency should arrange for at least an annual classroom presentation by a uniformed officer at every public and private elementary school within its jurisdiction.

a. The content of the presentation should be tailored to the learning needs of the students; however, each presentation should include a basic description of the police role.

b. Every agency should work through the school to develop a basic study unit to be presented by the teacher prior to the officer's arrival, and every officer assigned to a school visit should be provided with prepared subject matter to be reviewed prior to making his visit.

2. Every police agency with more than 400 employees should, dependent upon securing the cooperation of local school authorities, assign a full-time officer to each junior and senior high school in its jurisdiction.

a. The officer's assignment should include teaching classes in the role of the police, and serving as a counselor. His assignment should not include law enforcement duties except as related to counseling.

b. Course content should be developed in cooperation with the schools and should include discussion of the police role, juvenile laws, and enforcement policies and practices relating to juveniles.

3. Every police agency, where permitted by local conditions, should participate in government and civic classes offered in local evening adult schools and community colleges.

4. With agency resources, where available, or in cooperation with employee organizations or local civic groups, every police agency should develop or participate in youth programs including scouting and other athletic or camping activities.

a. All such programs should be designed to provide officers and young people with the opportunity to become personally acquainted with each other.

b. Every officer participating in youth programs should be provided with written material describing the objective of the program and its relationship to the police role.

5. Every police agency should accept invitations for officers to speak to business and civic organizations. Efforts should be made to provide speakers in response to every reasonable request and to coordinate the speaker's ability and background with the intended audience. Every opportunity should be taken to describe the police role and the agency's objectives and priorities.

6. Every police agency with more than 150 employees should publish a statement of the police role, the agency's objectives and priorities in filling that role, and the agency's activities to implement its role. An annual report should be used for this purpose. In addition, periodic statistical reports on crime, arrests, and property loss due to crime should be disseminated to the public. These reports should include an evaluation of significant trends and other interpretations.

7. Every police agency should inquire into the availability of public service resources from advertising and communication organizations to assist in developing support for the agency and its programs.

8. Every police agency should hold an annual open house and should provide other tours of police facilities and demonstrations of police equipment and tactics when appropriate to create greater public awareness of the police role.

275

... As part of their public education programs, several police agencies assign officers full-time to junior and senior high schools. These programs are of two basic types. School Resource Office programs, pioneered by the Cincinnati, Ohio, Police Department in 1967, assign officers to certain schools where they have both law enforcement and teaching duties. Officer Instructor programs of the type developed by the Los Angeles Sheriff's Department and the Los Angeles Police Department assign officers and deputies to selected schools where they have full faculty status and limited law enforcement duties.

**Standard 1.7: Promote police relations with the media.**

As long as individual freedom is protected in all cases, agency policy should mandate that the media have the right to receive information upon request. There should be a basic presumption that individual employees are under an obligation to supply information upon request unless there are specific reasons why this would be improper. Policy should express respect for the news media, their role in a democratic society, and their value to effective police service. ...

## 2: Role Implementation

**Standard 2.1: Develop workable agency goals and objectives.**

**Standard 2.2: Establish written policies to help employees attain agency goals and objectives.**

**Standard 2.3: Establish a formal police inspection system.**

## 3: Developing Community Resources

**Standard 3.1: Establish geographic team policing.**

**Standard 3.2: Involve the public in neighborhood crime prevention efforts.**

## 4: Criminal Justice Relations

**Standard 4.1: Coordinate planning and crime control efforts with other components of the criminal justice system.**

**Standard 4.2: Develop cooperative procedures with courts and corrections agencies.**

**Standard 4.3: Formalize diversion procedures to insure equitable treatment.**

276

**Standard 4.4: Utilize alternatives to arrest and pretrial detention.**

**Standard 4.5: Develop court followup practices for selected cases.**

**Recommendation 4.1: Divert drug addicts and alcoholics to treatment centers.**

**Recommendation 4.2: Telephone Search Warrants**
It is recommended that every State enact legislation that provides for the issuance of search warrants pursuant to telephoned petitions and affidavits from police officers.

... Lengthy delays in obtaining search warrants are the chief reason that police officers rely upon exceptions to the rule requiring warrants. It is one thing to say, as the court did in *Chimel,* that officers having probable cause may wait at the scene until another officer returns with a warrant, and another to deal with the legal and practical problems presented when the delay extends 7 to 10 hours, as it frequently does in many jurisdictions.

It was to resolve this problem that California in 1970 and Arizona in 1971 enacted legislation that allows a search warrant to be issued during a recorded telephone conversation in which the requesting officer makes a sworn affidavit that is later transcribed. The requesting officer then is permitted to sign the judge's name on a duplicate original warrant, which is deemed a search warrant. The judge signs and files the original warrant with the court clerk. The issuing authority remains with the judge, and the officer's role is ministerial in executing the search ordered by the judge. Following execution of the warrant, the officer files the duplicate original warrant, inventory, and recording transcription with the court.

The efforts of these two States are an attempt to employ existing technology in carrying out the intent of the law. Every State should adopt similar legislation.

**Recommendation 4.3: Enact State legislation prohibiting private surveillance and authorizing court-supervised electronic surveillance.**

... These reports—there have now been four of them—indicate that electronic surveillance has been used on a limited basis, but that these intercepts have proved to be productive in terms of indictments and arrests or organized crime figures.

In 1971 (the latest period for which statistics are available as of the date of this writing) there were 816 applications made to State and Federal judges for intercept orders. None was denied as 285 were signed by Federal judges and 531 were signed by State judges. The 816 applications filed in 1971 compare with 596 filed in 1970 and 301 in 1969.

Of the 792 applications that resulted in intercepts, 753 involved telephone wiretaps. The offenses involved were bribery (16), burglary (7), dangerous drugs and narcotics (126), loansharking and usury (5), gambling (570), homicide (18), larceny (31), and robbery (17).

At least six out of every 10 conversational intercepts produced incriminating evidence. Most of the cases in which there were interceptions were still under investigation at the time of the report. A total of 2,818 arrests had been made in 1971 as compared with 1,874 arrests in 1970. At the time of the report, there had been 322 convictions reported as a result of the interceptions installed in 1971, and based upon the nature of the offenses and the normal pretrial delays, it is logical to assume that a large number of the cases had not reached the trial stage. These statistics demonstrate, as stated earlier, that electronic surveillance is an effective law enforcement tool. . . .

# B: The Control of Crime

## 5: Planning and Organizing

**Standard 5.1: Establish a police service that meets the needs of the community.**

**Standard 5.2: Consolidate police agencies for greater effectiveness and efficiency.**

**Standard 5.3: Implement administrative and operational planning methods.**

**Standard 5.4: Assign responsibility for agency and jurisdictional planning.**

**Standard 5.5: Participate in any community planning that can affect crime.**

**Standard 5.6: Assign responsibility for fiscal management of the agency.**

**Standard 5.7: Develop fiscal management procedures.**

**Standard 5.8: Derive maximum benefit from government funding.**

**Recommendation 5.1: Formalize relationships between public and private police agencies.**

... Despite the large investment of manpower and money in private security forces, licensing regulations and other government controls are inadequate. Consequently, private police agencies generally employ individuals who are older, less educated, and lower paid than public officers. These employees lack training and experience in police-related duties, usually leaving them unprepared to deliver effective police service when the need arises.

Limited research has revealed that private security forces have a variety of other shortcomings. These include excessive force, false arrest and imprisonment, illegal search and seizure, impersonation of a peace officer, trespass, invasion of privacy, and dishonest or subprofessional business practices. Existing controls are insufficient to deal with such problems.

Remedies must be found for the ills that plague private police. Their acceptance by public police as a productive force within the criminal justice system will be enhanced if standards of performance and regulatory controls are implemented.

All private agencies should be required to obtain State licensing as a prerequisite for engaging in police-related security functions. Licensing requirements would allow State control of important considerations such as the selection standards of private police personnel, the educational criteria for employment, and the minimum training necessary for private police forces. States would then be able to control the activities of security forces by revoking or withdrawing licenses when minimum performance standards are not met.

Legal remedies should also be sought to elevate the quality of private security agencies. Current civil, criminal, and constitutional laws are inadequate in controlling private police problems. Legislation should be drafted to alleviate such police problems and provide recourse for private citizens victimized by illegal or unscrupulous police practices...

The 1971 report of the Advisory Commission on Intergovernmental Relations, *State-Local Relations in the Criminal Justice System,* disclosed that by 1966, 41 States had agreed to the Uniform Law on Interstate Fresh Pursuit, yet not all

States had enacted legislation granting intrastate extraterritorial police powers. The independence of elected law enforcement officers makes modernization and interagency coordination of police activities difficult. Sheriffs are still elected in 47 States, constables in 29 States, and coroners in 26 States. Many State police agencies operate under excessive functional and geographic restrictions and cannot provide supplementary and coordinated services to local agencies. For example, in 1970, 26 State police agencies were generally restricted to highway patrol functions.

Widespread fragmentation of public police services prevails in this country. Complicated police agency interrelationships often result in overlapping services across jurisdictional boundaries. While consolidation or regionalization of agencies or agency services may be feasible alternatives for local agencies, they may not be feasible for agencies differing greatly in size or function. . . .

Without taking control from local agencies, each State should bear responsibility for coordinating interagency law enforcement efforts within its boundaries. The Advisory Commission on Intergovernmental Relations, in its 1971 report, urged that States assure effective interstate and intrastate crime control. It recommended that States authorize the creation of special task forces to operate throughout multicounty or interstate metropolitan areas to deal with extralocal and organized crime.

It further recommended that States enact legislation and enter into interstate compacts giving local agencies carefully circumscribed extraterritorial police powers relating to "close pursuit" of felony offenders and to geographically extended powers of arrest. The Commission also suggested that local agencies, unable to provide full-time police services to residents, provide such services through intergovernmental cooperation with States, counties, and other local agencies. . . .

**Recommendation 5.2: Form a National Institute of Law Enforcement and Criminal Justice Advisory Committee.**

**Recommendation 5.3: Develop standardized measures of agency performance.**

. . . The percent of arrests leading to convictions is a measurement that involves the adjudication phase of the criminal justice system more than the police role. It is recommended that convictions on both the original or a reduced charge be used to judge the ultimate effectiveness of arrests. This would aid in neutralizing any residual effects of plea barbaining which might distort the true conviction rate. Another indicator of the quality of arrests is the percent of arrests that are upheld by the first court to hear the case before appeals. At this point in the judicial process, the police role is still predominant and any case dismissal would be connected with poor police work.

Because response to calls for service within minutes of the commission of a crime results in a higher arrest probability, the average response time should be used as an indicator of increased productivity in the apprehension of offenders. It would be necessary for police agencies to adopt comparable techniques in recording the times of the original complaint, the dispatch of a unit, and the arrival of the first officer at the scene. The longer a criminal is allowed to remain free, the greater the likelihood of his committing more crimes. Therefore, some measure should be taken of the amount of time spent in clearing specific crimes. Due to the variety of techniques required in investigating different types of crime, data should be collected and analyzed separately for each type of crime. . . .

Many other measures might be useful as indicators of police effectiveness. These include the cost of crime, the percent of police time spent in productive pursuits, police workloads, personnel complaints, innocent persons arrested, and stolen goods recovered. These and the measures mentioned previously will be useful only if considered in the light of the particular traits of the jurisdiction being examined. Regardless of the measurement used, police productivity must be related to the particular characteristics of the city or county, the size of the population, socioeconomic factors affecting the police, the crime mix of an agency's workload, and the amount of resources available to the agency.

## 6: Team Policing

. . . Team policing requires considerable individual initiative and responsibility. Many patrolmen are reluctant to exercise such authority. There are other situations that require quick, military orders and obedience. How can this be reconciled with team member equality?

These are the problems that are being worked out and answered in pilot programs now in progress. One definite benefit is that team policing concepts are rich in fresh thoughts; they stir police agencies to reexamine many assumptions about police procedures. Even when team policing is not adopted, examining other agency programs can prove beneficial to overall police thinking.

So far, even where team policing has proved most beneficial, programs are still in the experimental stage. This chapter advises any agency considering team police work to plan carefully before going ahead.

Larger agencies have the advantage of being able to try programs in certain precincts while carrying on routine police work in others. Smaller agencies have no such option. For the smaller agency, it is all or nothing.

The benefits of team policing, primarily greater police-public cooperation, are not automatic. Team policing only affords the opportunity for such benefits. It is up to the participants to go out into the community and foster the cooperation needed. The police agency must let the public know about its new program and what it hopes to achieve.

Just as importantly, in agencies where a team policing experiment is being prepared, all employees—not just those to take part—must understand and support the program. . . .

## Standard 6.1: Determine the applicability of team policing.

### Syracuse Crime Control Team

Syracuse, N.Y., was the first police agency to combine the patrol and investigative function into one unit with a geographic responsibility for crime control. The crime control team was implemented in July 1968, and consisted of a team leader, deputy leader, and eight policemen. The team was relieved of many routine, noncriminal duties and given responsibility for controlling serious crime, apprehending offenders, and conducting investigations in a small area of the city.

The team leader, a lieutenant, was given considerable discretion in directing the activities and operations of the team. The program was decentralized and operated independently of the rest of the agency. The crime control team concept was later extended to other agency operations after the project report on the experiment indicated considerable success in reducing crime and increasing crime clearance rates.

### Dayton, Ohio, Team Policing

Dayton designed its team policing project to test the generalist approach to police work, to produce a community-based police structure, and to change the police organization from its traditional military structure to a neighborhood-oriented professional model. All specialized assignments in the test

282

area were eliminated. Discretion was allowed in the wearing of uniforms, modes of operations, and program development.

The experiment began in October 1970, in a district covering about one-sixth of the city area. The personnel consisted of 35 to 40 officers, 12 community service officers, a lieutenant in charge, and four sergeants who acted as leaders for teams of 10 to 12 men. The lieutenant was selected by the chief and approved by neighborhood groups. The officers selected by vote their team leaders from a slate of sergeants.

The Dayton team project is probably the most fundamental attempt to change police field operations. Most internal matters are settled democratically among team members. The project decentralized authority and function, and concentrated upon community participation in achieving its goals. . . .

**Standard 6.2: Plan, train for, and publicize implementation of team policing.**

## 7: Unusual Occurences

**Standard 7.1: Plan for coordinating activities of relevant agencies during mass disorders and natural disasters.**

**Standard 7.2: Executive Responsibility**
Every police chief executive should be given responsibility immediately to command all police resources involved in controlling unusual occurrences within his jurisdiction. This authority should be preempted only when a state of emergency is declared by the Governor, local authority breaks down, or command authority is transferred by prior agreement. In carrying out this responsibility, the police chief executive should direct all police activities within the affected area, and he should insure that at least minimum services are provided to the remainder of the jurisdiction.

1. Every local government should provide by law that the police chief executive be responsible for all law enforcement resources used to control unusual occurrences within the jurisdiction. The police chief executive immediately should establish a system designating executive command in his absence. . . .

**Standard 7.3: Develop an interim control system for use during unusual occurrences.**

*The Intelligence Organization*
A common failure in the control of unusual occurrences is

283

neglect of the intelligence function, including failure to require operational feedback. Manpower is often deployed to solve problems that no longer exist, while new problems go unattended. Successful unusual occurrence control administration is founded on planning, intelligence, and control (PIC): intelligence data is gathered, plans are made and executed, and control is continuously exercised to call back and reassign missions to meet new problems.

Two important types of intelligence information are covert or strategic intelligence, and overt or tactical intelligence.

Covert intelligence is continuous activity that precedes an occurrence and does not end with its termination. It includes information gathered from all available sources about community tensions, rumors, and planned or ongoing activities. . . .

Intelligence gathering is a sensitive function, especially in maintaining a preparedness for mass disturbances. The police chief executive should be personally aware of the range of intelligence-gathering activities. These activities should be a staff rather than enforcement function and directly under the police chief executive or an assistant chief, depending upon the size of the organization. The intelligence function should be managed to insure that agency priorities, goals, and policies are observed. This management should provide scrupulous security. All files should be kept within the intelligence unit and maintained separately from other agency records. Access to these files should be limited to members of the intelligence unit or members of the agency approved by the police chief executive.

Many police officials feel that the intelligence function is the most important aspect of riot control. Preparedness through intelligence-gathering can save lives. Without such intelligence there is no basis for determining the manpower and equipment required to control an occurrence. . . .

### Standard 7.4: Mass Processing of Arrestees

Every police agency should immediately develop a system for the arrest, processing, transportation, and detention of large numbers of persons. The agency should seek alternatives to mass arrests, but if it is determined that mass arrests are necessary, a system should be available to provide adequate security for prisoners and officers and to insure that the arresting officer is returned to his field assignment as quickly as possible. The system should facilitate the restoration of order by means of lawful arrest, and preservation of all available evidence.

1. The mass arrest system should insure that arrestees are processed as rapidly as possible. The system should provide:

a. A procedure for gathering and preserving available evidence to connect the arrestee to the crime he is to be charged with. The evidence may include photographs, recordings, videotapes, statements of witnesses, or other evidence;

b. A procedure for receiving each prisoner from the arresting officer and facilitating the officer's return to his field assignment as soon as possible;

c. Positive identification of the arrestee and the arresting officer;

d. A procedure for receiving and maintaining continuity of evidence;

e. Rapid removal of arrestees from the affected area. Security should be provided en route to prevent attempts to free prisoners;

f. A secure detention area to prevent escape or attempts to free prisoners. The facility should be adequate to maintain custody of a number of prisoners in safety;

g. Prearranged interagency agreements to facilitate the assimiliation of the arrestees into the jail system when the arresting agency is not the custodial agency;

h. Defense counsel visitations after processing. These visitations should not be permitted under field conditions or at temporary detention facilities unless adequate security is provided. Prisoners should be transported to a secure detention facility without delay; and

i. Liaison with local courts and prosecutors to determine procedures and temporary court sites for speedy arraignment of arrestees.

2. The mass arrest system should make the name and charge of persons arrested available to public inquiry as soon as possible after the arrestee has been processed. A current list of arrestees should be communicated to the agency command center as the information becomes available. Inquiries should be directed to one central location.

## Standard 7.5: Legal Considerations

Every State and local government should immediately review existing law and consider new legislation to permit necessary action by all control agencies and afford each individual all his constitutional guarantees during an unusual occurrence.

1. Full-time protection should be afforded every community by permanent legislation to provide for:

    a. Federal and State reimbursement of local law enforcement agencies required to react to Federal and State events, such as conventions, campaigns, or VIP visits, and extraordinary costs incurred in responding to mutual aid requests;

    b. Mutual aid agreements between local, county, and State police, and the National Guard;

    c. The prohibition of unnecessary force or violence in making arrests;

    d. The prohibition of any sanctuary by providing police access to any area, public or private, within the jurisdiction or close enough to constitute an immediate threat to public order within the jurisdiction;

    e. The prohibition of interference with or attacks upon firemen or other emergency personnel;

    f. The prohibition against failure to disperse any unlawful assemblies;

    g. Prohibition of impeding pedestrian or vehicular traffic;

    h. Strict controls on the manufacture, possession, transportation, or distribution of incendiary or explosive devices; and

    i. Permits for parades, assemblies, and public events and regulation of the size and material used in picket signs and sign handles or any other device used in a public demonstration.

2. Emergency statutes specifically designed to cope with unusual occurrences should be enacted to provide for:

    a. The arrest powers of county and State police and National Guard forces when engaged with or without the local police agency's assistance in control operations within a local jurisdiction;

    b. Emergency police authority enabling local police to maintain public order by suspending due process where a clear and present danger exists that mob action will render ineffective any local police agency's ability to maintain order;

    c. Restrictions upon sales of gasoline, liquor, and weapons;

    d. The restriction of public access to certain geographic areas under specifically defined circumstances;

e. Curfew, loitering, and other crowd control measures;

f. The restriction of public use of schools, places of amusement, water, and private aircraft; and

g. Control of the storage of firearms, firearms parts, and ammunition.

... Few States have laws giving State military forces the arrest powers of peace officers. This lack of authority is not critical if police officers are designated to accompany National Guard troops when arrests are to be made. The arrest powers of mutual aid forces, State Police, and National Guard troops when engaged in control operations, with or without the local police agency's assistance, should be reviewed during the planning process. If arrest authority is given to National Guard troops, then appropriate guidelines for the use of such authority must also be provided. Emergency statutes should be written clearly and carefully to prescribe the authority and relationships necessary for agencies to interact effectively in coping with unusual occurrences.

Restrictions on police authority in effect under normal conditions should be less restrictive when the police agency's ability to maintain order is threatened. Legislation should provide for temporary suspension of due process to permit reasonable processing of arrestees and seizing of contraband where an emergency exists. In some situations, caches of guns, incendiaries, or explosives may elude seizure because of legal restrictions on searches. If dangerous contraband is illegally seized by the police to protect themselves and the community, there can be no successful prosecution of serious offenders for possession of such contraband.

In mass disorders deviations from normal arrest procedures may be necessary. Some agencies have confronted law violators in groups so large that, during mass arrest and processing, normal rights to bail, telephone calls, and attorney visitation could not possibly be carried out within the time that would have been reasonable under ordinary conditions. Providing food and sanitary facilities are examples of more immediate concerns. ...

**Standard 7.6: Implement training programs for unusual occurrence control procedure.**

.. The Department of the Army instituted a civil disturbance orientation course in 1967. The military police school at Fort Gordon, Ga., conducts the course, titled SEADOC—

an acronym for Senior Officers Civil Disturbance Orientation Course. The mission of the school is to provide senior members of Federal, State, and municipal agencies, both military and civilian, with a general knowledge of civil disturbance control, planning, and operations. The instruction discusses interagency planning and coordination but places emphasis on civil disorder management concepts and techniques. It is an excellent course to enable top and middle management to develop an awareness of preventive and preparatory measures and functional management techniques for civil disturbance control.

SEADOC has a counterpart on the West Coast in the California Specialized Training Institute. The Institute is operated by the State Military Department. It is approved as a Sixth United States Army Area school and is accredited by the California Commission on Peace Officer Standards and Training. It conducts the California Civil Disorder Management Course at Camp Luis Obispo, Calif. The course consists of 5 days of civil disorder management training for middle management employees of law enforcement agencies, government public utilities, universities, and the military.

The program is designed to study the causes and manifestations of organized dissent and the methods for preventing or reducing disorders in scope and intensity. It offers control and management techniques and operational procedures to be employed during a civil disorder. Emphasis is placed on the necessity for advance joint planning by all echelons of authority involved in control of disorders.

A valuable byproduct of these schools is the feedback and exchange of ideas that is made possible by bringing together the varied experiences of those attending. The schools are effective in promoting among the participants a mutual understanding of the responsibilities, policies, capabilities, and limitations of the various agencies involved in civil disorder operations. This type of training also prepares the military response units to cooperate with local police agencies in assigning and accomplishing missions.

These are two examples of programs that can be offered by the State or Federal Government to assist local government agencies in preparing for civil disorders. The State must assume responsibility for training members of local police agencies when the local governments lack the resources for this training. The State must face its obligation to insure that adequate numbers of local police personnel are trained in unusual occurrence control for response to local emergencies. . . .

# 8: Patrol

... Police textbooks refer to the patrol officer as "the backbone of the police department," yet the policies of many police departments seem to deny this. The patrolman is usually the lowest paid, least consulted, most taken for granted member of the force. His duty is looked on as routine and boring. In another portion of this chapter, agency policies are analyzed to show why the patrol force often consists of "the inexperienced and the mediocre." This situation, where it exists, must be changed.

The importance of police patrol and the standards in this chapter cannot be understated. The patrol officer in any city is the most visible representative of government. He responds to calls for services, enforces the law, and maintains order in the community. Many changes have taken place in police departments over the past 20 years, but the patrolman's role has changed only incrementally and this role will continue with little change into the foreseeable future. ...

**Standard 8.1: Establishing the Role of the Patrol Officer**

Every police chief executive immediately should develop written policy that defines the role of the patrol officer, and should establish operational objectives and priorities that reflect the most effective use of the patrol officer in reducing crime.

1. Every police chief executive should acknowledge that the patrol officer is the agency's primary element for the deliverance of police services and prevention of criminal activity.

2. Every police chief executive should insure maximum efficiency in the deliverance of patrol services by setting out in written policy the objectives and priorities governing these services. ...

3. Every police chief executive should insure that all elements of the agency, especially the patrol and communications elements, know the priority placed upon each request for police service.

4. Every police chief executive should implement a public information program to inform the community of the agency's policies regarding the deliverance of police service. This program should include provisions to involve citizens in crime prevention activities.

... The patrol officer is the first interpreter of the law and in effect performs a quasi-judicial function. He makes the

289

first attempt to match the reality of human conflict with the law; he determines whether to take no action, to advise, to warn, or to arrest; he determines whether he must apply physical force, perhaps sufficient to cause death. It is he who must discern the fine distinction between the civil and a criminal conflict, between merely unorthodox behavior and a crime, between legitimate dissent and disturbance of the peace, between the truth and a lie. As interpreter of the law, he recognizes that a decision to arrest is only the first step in the determination of guilt or innocence. He is guided by, and guardian of, the Constitution.

## Standard 8.2: Enhancing the Role of the Patrol Officer

Every local government and police chief executive, recognizing that the patrol function is the most important element of the police agency, immediately should adopt policies that attract and retain highly qualified personnel in the patrol force.

1. Every socal government should expand its classification and pay system to provide greater advancement opportunities within the patrol ranks.

   a. Multiple pay grades within the basic rank;

   b. Opportunity for advancement within the basic rank to permit equality between patrol officers and investigators;

   c. Parity in top salary step between patrol officers and nonsupervisory officers assigned to other operational functions;

   d. Proficiency pay for personnel who have demonstrated expertise in specific field activities that contribute to more efficient police service.

2. Every police chief executive should seek continually to enhance the role of the patrol officer by providing status and recognition from the agency and encouraging similar status and recognition from the community. The police chief executive should:

   a. Provide distinctive insignia indicating demonstrated expertise in specific field activities;

   b. Insure that all elements within the agency provide maximum assistance and cooperation to the patrol officer;

   c. Implement a community information program emphasizing the importance of the patrol officer in the life of the community and encouraging community cooperation in providing police service;

**d.** Provide comprehensive initial and inservice training thoroughly to equip the patrol officer for his role;

**e.** Insure that field supervisory personnel possess the knowledge and skills necessary to guide the patrol officer;

**f.** Implement procedures to provide agencywide recognition of patrol officers who have consistently performed in an efficient and commendable manner;

**g.** Encourage suggestions on changes in policies, procedures, and other matters that affect the delivery of police services and reduction of crime;

**h.** Provide deployment flexibility to facilitate various approaches to individual community crime problems;

**i.** Adopt policies and procedures that allow the patrol officer to conduct the complete investigation of crimes which do not require extensive followup investigation, and allow them to close the investigation of those crimes; and

**j.** Insure that promotional oral examination boards recognize that patrol work provides valuable experience for men seeking promotion to supervisory positions.

... Police agencies should not limit their use of patrol officers to uniform patrol in marked police vehicles at fixed hours within artificial boundaries. For example, apprehension rates can be increased by using patrol officers in surveillance and undercover assignments and in plain clothes and unmarked cars in an area experiencing numerous burglaries or robberies. These and other unconventional approaches can reduce crime and raise morale among patrol officers.

Because crime varies within jurisdictions and districts, a police agency should be able to shift its patrol officers accordingly. Some police agencies successfully employ a tactical squad in high crime areas. Saturating a problem district with such a squad, however, usually results in only a temporary reduction in crime. In a few weeks, the patrol officer is faced with the same crime problem as before. By using regularly assigned patrol officers to cope with variations in criminal activity, the agency benefits from their experience and training and enhances their role. ...

Allowing patrol officers to conduct followup investigations on some minor incidents relieves the burden on investigators, who usually have time only for major incidents. When no further investigation is possible, the patrol officer should close the case. When necessary, such closed cases can be reopened by the investigative branch of the agency. ...

## Standard 8.3: Develop a responsive patrol deployment system.

... In recent years the pressure on police agencies to make changes and implement new programs, particularly in community relations, has caused a disproportionate increase in the number of personnel assigned to administrative and staff support functions. The practice in many agencies is to expand administrative and staff support activities by drawing personnel from other units within the agency. Because of their relatively large personnel strength, line operations usually provide a convenient source of manpower for administrative assignments. Even when the personnel are drawn from other sources, the ripple effect ultimately produces a vacancy in the line operations, often in the patrol force. One promising solution to this problem, discussed in Chapter 10, is the assignment of civilian police personnel to certain staff and administrative positions. . . .

There is no universally accepted scientific methodology for determining the number of police personnel needed in a given jurisdiction or the percentage distribution of personnel within an agency's organizational structure. Officer to population ratios are often used to indicate total manpower needs. There have been no compelling arguments in support of police to people ratios; and these ratios differ widely from one jurisdiction to another.

Formulas to determine the percentage distribution of personnel functions within police agencies are similarly lacking in rules or guidelines. The typical agency deploys approximately 80 percent of its total sworn strength in patrol, traffic, and detective assignments. The remaining 20 percent are divided among the staff and auxiliary service functions. Within the line operations, patrol accounts for approximately 70 to 80 percent of available line personnel. The remaining 20 to 30 percent are in traffic and investigative assignments. . . .

There are differing opinions and a lack of empirical research on the extent to which patrol deters crime. Theere are evidence that some so-called crimes of passion are not deterred by police presence. However, even if a particular crime is considered nonrepressible, its repetition indicates a police problem. Aggravated assaults are to a certain extent repressible, especially those occurring in public places. Murders and rapes indicate the need for patrol personnel in those areas with a higher proportion of crimes of violence. Additionally, the location and time of nonrepressible crimes are to a certain extent predictable when considered in bulk. These crimes can be reduced by special crime control techniques, particularly community interaction programs that encourage citizen involvement in neighborhood anticrime campaigns.

Calls for services are included in an allocation system index because they represent a recognizable and readily measurable demand for police services. Apprehending suspected offenders and processing arrestees are included because these activities provide a separate and distinct measure of the need for patrol manpower.

Experience shows that using the number of calls for service and the number of arrests without regard for time expended is of little or no value in determining workload. For example, the same number of service calls and arrests may occur on two different shifts. All the activities on one shift, however, may take twice as long as on the other shift. Therefore, using only the number of incidents would indicate falsely that the workload was the same on both watches.

Service calls and arrests should be weighted on the basis of the average elapsed time by watch for each of the activities. Selected repressible crimes should not be so weighted, because they involve no expenditure of field time.

Another factor in establishing an allocation system is the frequency of tabulation of the various factors. In most agencies, a quarterly tabulation provides the information required, with reports issued in January, April, July, and October. The factors are calculated by category for these 4 months and then totaled. In agencies with more than one precinct or division, a percentage allocation should be determined for each geographic division and applied to the allotted patrol personnel. A certain number of fixed posts must be manned in each patrol division regardless of the number of officers on patrol duty in the field. That is the overhead or basic operating manpower for the division. It includes jailers, desk officers, and other fixed posts and specialty assignments. These positions are deducted from the total number of personnel to determine the final number available for field patrol deployment. . . .

Shift hours should begin at the periods when the incidence of crime is greatest. When the times have been selected, the average percentage of the problem during each 8-hour period should be plotted on the chart. The chart is used only as a guide—there are several considerations in determining shift hours. For example, establishing certain shift hours may require changing from two-man cars to one-man cars, or the reverse on a specific watch. Another possibility is that a correct choice of shift hours may eliminate the necessity for a midwatch (a fourth overlapping shift). A midwatch should be considered only when the incidence of crime from the average line within one or two shifts is serious enough that the carryover of the problem would require additional personnel for the last part of one watch and first part of another. The human element must also be considered. People do not like to go to work at 3 or 4 a.m. ....

## 9: Operations Specialization

**Standard 9.1: Authorize only essential assignment specialization.**

**Standard 9.2: Specify selection criteria for specialist personnel.**

*Rotation of Personnel*

The potential for legal and ethical compromise and corruption exists throughout the police service. It is probably greatest in those areas where the criminal activity provides illicit services to willing customers.

Each agency should identify those areas of special assignments where the potential for compromise and corruption are greatest, such as vice, narcotics, and all types of undercover assignments. To minimize the potential for officer compromise written policy and procedure should cover the orderly rotation of personnel from high risk assignments to other special assignments with a different type of criminal clientele, or to positions where the potential for compromise is low.

Different policies for supervisory and administrative personnel and execution level positions should be established. The potential for officer compromise at the supervisory and administrative level is considerably less than at the street or execution level. Each agency should consider the two elements separately and should permit supervisory and administrative personnel to remain in one assignment longer than execution level personnel.

Exceptions to this procedure are sometimes necessary, particularly on the execution level, to insure the successful completion of current investigations. The rotation system must be flexible enough to permit the conclusion of current activities with specific approval of the chief executive.

Orderly procedure provides a continuing high level of operational competence through systematic changes in personnel in the various specialized assignments. . . .

**Standard 9.3: Review agency specializations annually.**

**Standard 9.4: Provide State specialists to local agencies.**

**Standard 9.5: Formulate policies governing delinquents and youth offenders.**

A juvenile becomes a delinquent when he commits an act which, if he were an adult, would be a crime. The activities of police in connection with juveniles who are not yet delinquent is a matter of controversy and concern. Some believe that the police should have no contact with a juvenile unless he commits a crime. This belief, however, precludes the assistance of law enforcement agencies in the identification of neglected and dependent children; from deterring the delinquency of children who persistently refuse to obey the reasonable directions of parents and school authorities, or are beyond the control of these authorities; or are otherwise in clear and present danger of becoming delinquent.

In California children fitting the latter description are within the jurisdiction of the juvenile court, and may be made wards of the court. This provision of law allows police in California to take an active part in preventing delinquency. Police officers throughout the Nation are in a position to do this, because they confront juvenile problems 24 hours a day and are trained and experienced in those problems.

To suggest that law enforcement abrogate its preventive responsibilities concerning juvenile delinquency is to recommend that police merely enforce the law through the apprehension process. . . .

**Standard 9.6: Control traffic violations through preventive patrol and enforcement.**

**Standard 9.7: Train patrol officers to conduct preliminary investigations.**

**Standard 9.8: Create a mobile unit for special crime problems.**

**Standard 9.9: Establish policy and capability for vice operations.**

Vice operations in many agencies include a wide variety of enforcement activities; the principal activities, however, are directed against illegal gambling, traffic in liquor, prostitution, pandering, pornography, and obscene conduct.

Vice enforcement poses special problems. First, these offenses involve a consensual act between the person that desires the service and the person who provides the service. In many jurisdictions the individual who seeks out or receives the illegal services is also violating the law. Second, community attitudes often reflect a high level of tolerance toward certain vice activities. . . .

Sensitive units—such as vice, narcotics, and intelligence—have a tendency to isolate themselves from other elements of the agency and from each other, particularly in larger agencies. It is imperative that a continual exchange of information and coordination of effort be maintained between the vice operation and all other elements within the agency. Vice activities often are directly connected with narcotics abuse, robbery, theft, and similar crimes. Therefore, specialized elements should work as a team. Moreover, it is essential that the patrol force be used to suppress vice activity. Uniformed patrol officers can significantly deter offenses in areas of high crime incidence. This exchange of information and coordination of effort should also extend, wherever practicable, to Federal, State, and county agencies with similar operations. . . .

### Standard 9.10: Narcotic and Drug Investigations

**Every police agency should acknowledge the direct relationship between narcotic and drug offenses and other criminal activity, and should have available a narcotic and drug investigation capability based on that acknowledgment.**

**1.** Every police agency should provide fundamental narcotic and drug investigation training to every officer during basic training.

**2.** Every police agency should cooperate in and, where necessary, establish narcotic and drug abuse public awareness programs such as school system educational programs, civic group programs, multi-agency community programs, and Analysis Anonymous programs.

**3.** Every police agency employing more than 75 personnel should have a full-time narcotic and drug investigation capability. Personnel in smaller agencies may be assigned where justified by the local problem.

    **a.** The number of personnel assigned to the narcotic and drug operation should be determined by the local problem.

    **b.** Where appropriate in agencies with 75 or less personnel, drug and narcotic operations may be consolidated with vice operations.

c. Drug and narcotic operations should be decentralized to the extent that the agency is; however, a central drug and narcotic unit should be maintained to coordinate the decentralized operations.

4. Every police agency should insure coordination and the continual exchange of information between officers assigned to narcotic and drug enforcement, vice enforcement, intelligence, and uniformed patrol.

5. Every chief executive should establish written policies and procedures requiring that every narcotic and drug complaint will be reported in writing and thoroughly investigated. These policies and procedures should provide that:

a. All narcotic and drug complaints be distributed to the chief executive or his delegate, and to the central narcotic and drug unit;

b. A written followup report of every open drug or narcotic investigation be prepared every 30 days to indicate the progress of the investigation;

c. Individual, team, and unit narcotic and drug investigation reports and activity summaries be inspected and reviewed continually;

d. Individual, team, and unit performance measures continually be applied to drug and narcotic operations. These measures should include arrests and dispositions; number of purchases by type of drug or narcotic, quantity and quality of seized narcotics and drugs, other crimes cleared, and working caseload.

6. Every police agency should provide narcotic operations with special funds and specialized equipment such as vehicles, electronic equipment, and vision devices necessary to conduct effective narcotic and drug operations.

... To the maximum extent possible, every police agency should actively participate in programs designed to make the community aware of the narcotic and drug problem and its effect on the total crime problem within the community. These programs should be sponsored by local educational, business, professional, and social welfare organizations, both public and private. In communities where sponsorship cannot be readily obtained from these sources, however, the police agency should undertake it.

Programs should be varied. They should be factual and oriented toward prevention and community awareness.

These programs should be available to school systems and to civic and professional groups, particularly those involved

297

in education and medicine. These programs are usually more effective when members of all law enforcement agencies— Federal, State, county, and municipal—participate to provide different insights.

In 1969, the Detroit Police Department implemented the Analysis Anonymous Program, which has since been utilized by other jurisdictions. Under this program, an individual may anonymously request the analysis of suspected narcotics or drugs by taking the substance to the nearest police station. It is then sent to a laboratory. After a 5 day waiting period, the anonymous sender can call the narcotics section, give an assigned identification number, and receive the results of the analysis by telephone.

Safeguards to avoid improper use are built into this program, which is primarily designed to provide parents with a method of determining whether or not suspicious behavior patterns of their children result from drug abuse. When illegal drugs are detected, police will meet with parents and children, at the parents' request, to determine the best procedure for handling the problem. The arrangements are made without the stigma of an arrest. . . .

## Standard 9.11: Intelligence Operations

Every police agency and every State immediately should establish and maintain the capability to gather and evaluate information and to disseminate intelligence in a manner which protects every individual's right to privacy while it curtails organized crime and public disorder.

1. Every State should establish a central gathering, analysis, and storage capability, and intelligence dissemination system.

    a. Every police agency should actively participate in providing information and receiving intelligence from this system.

    b. Every police agency should designate at least one person to be responsible for liaison with the State intelligence system.

    c. Every State intelligence system should disseminate specific intelligence to local agencies acording to local needs and should disseminate general information throughout the State.

2. Every local agency should participate, where appropriate, in the establishment of regional intelligence systems. Every regional intelligence system should participate actively in the State system.

3. Every police agency with more than 75 personnel should have a full-time intelligence capability.

a. The number of personnel assigned to this operation should be based on local conditions.

b. The intelligence operation should be centralized; however, intelligence specialists may be assigned, where appropriate, to major transportation centers.

c. When the size of the intelligence operation permits, organized crime intelligence should be separate from civil disorder intelligence.

d. In smaller agencies the intelligence specialist should be required to take direct enforcement action only where limited agency resources make it absolutely necessary. In larger agencies the intelligence specialist should be required to take direct enforcement action only where a serious threat to life or property makes it absolutely necessary.

e. The intelligence operation should include an independent and well-secured reporting and record system.

4. Every police agency should insure exchange of information and coordination between the intelligence operation and all other operational entities of the agency and with other government agencies.

5. Every police agency should supply its intelligence operation with the funds, vehicles, vision devices, and other specialized equipment necessary to implement an effective intelligence operation.


... The State systems should be responsible for evaluating information received from local agencies, storing it, and disseminating specific intelligence to local agencies on a need basis and general information throughout the State. The system should employ procedures that insure security and privacy.

Effective State intelligence systems vary in structure and authority. Florida's Bureau of Law Enforcement is a statewide law enforcement agency that also engages in extensive intelligence activities. The Organized Crime Intelligence Branch of the Division of Law Enforcement of the California Department of Justice provides excellent support services and intelligence functions on the State level.

A unique situation exists in Michigan, where the Michigan Association of Chiefs of Police, the Michigan Sheriff's Association, and the Michigan State Police established the Michigan Intelligence Network (MIN), designating the Michigan

State Police as the central processing and information repository. More than 300 law enforcement agencies throughout the State now belong to MIN. . . .

## Centralization of Intelligence Operation

Even if an agency's other operations are run on a decentralized geographic basis, the intelligence operation should remain basically centralized. Decentralized intelligence operations require considerably more manpower; surveillance capability is decreased; efforts become fragmented due to the wide distribution of manpower; and effective communication of situations and criminal activities is hampered. If additional manpower is assigned, an agency in effect creates as many intelligence operations as it has precincts or areas, but it still should maintain a central intelligence unit to coordinate, evaluate, and disseminate intelligence data. It is frequently advantageous to assign intelligence personnel to major transportation centers—particularly airports—to observe the movements of persons under surveillance.

The management, personnel, records, and operations of the organized crime intelligence organization should be separate from those of the civil disorder intelligence operation. Staff and records should be separate to assure the proper emphasis and integrity of each. Both intelligence operations should include a fixed staff element to provide for rapid analysis of important issues. The police chief executive should be advised and consulted regularly to facilitate the formulation of workable tactics to resolve crisis situations.

Two current philosophies of intelligence operations exist. Under the first, which is enforcement oriented, the intelligence operation develops the case, makes the arrest, and follows through on the prosecution. Under the other, which stresses "pure" intelligence, the information is developed, evaluated, and delivered to the appropriate enforcement element of the agency.

In the intelligence survey cited above, 31 of the 38 respondents recommended that members assigned to intelligence operations not take part in direct enforcement activities except in situations involving a serious threat to life or property. In smaller agencies, this policy may not be feasible. However, to protect the identity of intelligence personnel and the integrity of the unit's techniques, direct enforcement action should be undertaken only when absolutely necessary.

Because of the type of activity and the nature of the information within the system, intelligence operations dealing with organized crime and civil disorder each should have its own reporting and record system, independent of the total agency system. This system requires safeguards for security and privacy. . . .

## 10: Manpower Alternatives

. . . Most police agencies that have some form of police reserve provide . . . training. In California, more than 90 percent of all reserves have been given instruction. Most police agencies require reserves to participate in regularly scheduled drills.

The importance of reserve training lies in the power reserve officers may exercise. A reserve police officer is a sworn nonregular member of a police agency who has regular police powers while functioning as the agency's representative. He, like other police officers, may be confronted with life-and-death situations and required to make quick decisions. An untrained reserve officer poses a liability to a police agency. . . .

. . . Agencies must be careful to distinguish between trained reserves and untrained reserves. Standards 10.2 . . . of this chapter warns:

> . . . (police agencies) should furnish the reserve officer with the same uniform and equipment as a regular sworn officer only upon his completion of all training requirements. Until he has completed all training requirements, his uniform should readily identify him as a reserve officer, and he should perform his duties only under the direct supervision of a regular sworn officer.

Once trained, reserve police should receive the same inservice training given regular police officers to insure they remain at a high level of competence.

The use of police reserves is traditional in this Nation. It is a tradition that remains alive and can be useful to agencies needing help. The romance of police work reaches beyond police officers. It touches others who know them. Wives and children are usually proud of the role their husbands and fathers carry out when they participate in police functions. Police reserves broaden the base of community support.

Police chief executives should take these benefits into consideration when considering a police reserve. And police chief executives should recognize the dangers. A police reserve must be organized and administered on a professional basis. Just as a good reserve can broaden public support, a badly trained, badly disciplined police force can diminish it. It is up to the police chief executive to insure that his civilian employees and his police reserve add to the efficiency of his agency.

## Standard 10.1: Assignment of Civilian Police Personnel

Every police agency should assign civilian personnel to positions that do not require the exercise of police authority or the application of the special knowledge, skills, and aptitudes of the professional peace officer. . . .

. . . The traditional role of the civilian in most police agencies has been restricted to clerical or secretarial duties, maintenance or sanitation work, jail security or booking tasks, and motor pool assignments. Although the civilian may be a highly qualified, educated, and capable individual, his stature within most police agencies is diminished by the relative insignificance of his function in the total police effort. In larger agencies with significant numbers of civilian employees, this situation has resulted in conflicts between sworn and civilian workers.

In some agencies, police officers and civilian employees have expressed a degree of mutual distrust. Some civilian employees may harbor a negative attitude toward police officers, an attitude developed prior to joining the service. Inadequate selection policies may fail to identify such attitudes. Police absorb criticism from all levels of society and often assume defensive postures in relationships with those outside the service. . . .

The selective use of civilian personnel also may contribute to raising police educational standards. Some who oppose requiring a college degree for sworn police personnel argue that many officers still perform nonprofessional, routine tasks. If such tasks are assigned to civilians, reservists, or paraprofessionals, sworn officers can concentrate on duties that require a high degree of professionalism. . . .

The Ventura, Calif., Police Department uses three community services officers to cite parking violations and impound vehicles. Ventura has required a college degree for new officers since 1966; it appeared a waste of manpower to use sworn officers, paid more than $1,000 per month, for such tasks. The program has resulted in significant salary savings since CSOs receive a starting salary from $533 to $649 per month. Savings in time also have been realized. Sworn personnel have more time to devote to basic police functions. . . .

### Standard 10.2: Employ reserve officers.

. . . The hazards of police work were major considerations in the development of the Los Angeles Reserve Corps training program. A city ordinance specified that reserves take a minimum of 200 hours of training. The present course calls for 268 hours, which exceeds the minimum established by the State. Instructors who teach regular recruits are used so that uniformity in training standards is maintained. Training, which lasts approximately 7 months, includes subjects ranging from criminal law and human relations to physical defense and firearms procedures. Classes are held two nights each week and two Sundays each month.

The Reserve Deputy Sheriff program in Los Angeles is perhaps the best example of the selective training of reserve generalists and specialists. The bulk of the Uniform Reserve Unit, comprising about 75 percent of the reserve force, receives 300 hours of training in all phases of county police operations. However, highly specialized units, such as the Photographic Reserve Unit, the Mounted Posse, and the Mountain Rescue Team, receive only a 56-hour indoctrination course outlining the duties of a reserve, and pertinent county and State laws. Each member of these specialized units already possesses the necessary expertise. . . .

Lending reservists on a short-term basis to vice, narcotics, and intelligence units may be warranted. Adequately trained and well-screened reserves as "new faces" can assist regular undercover officers in gathering intelligence information, uncovering vice activity, or identifying narcotics dealers. Another innovative idea is the use of female reservists to supplement juvenile units and provide expertise in juvenile matters. Using reserve officers in duties involving jail, property, and deskwork would result in the direct release of sworn personnel for other duties. . . .

Some police administrators have considered forming reserve units to perform riot control duties. This use of reserves might prove more beneficial than calling for outside agencies or Federal troops. They would be more familiar with the general area and would probably elicit less criticism than outside forces. In 1969, the Cook County, Ill., Sheriff formed such a unit, which functions only as a supplement to regular forces and is not intended to be the primary defense force during civil disturbances. . . .

# 11: Professional Assistance

**Standard 11.1: Establish working relationships with outside professionals.**

*Behavioral Science Resources*

Traditionally, police departments have emphasized hardware and technology in attempting to stay in the forefront of change and in increasing effectiveness. Unquestionably, modern equipment is essential to law enforcement; however, there is a need to balance technology with human variables, since police work is basically an enterprise dealing with people.

Top police administrators currently are more aware of the importance of behavioral science factors in the many areas of police work, and modern departments are beginning to employ the appropriate kinds of expertise.

Psychological evaluation of police applicants is considered an essential part of the overall selection process and is discussed in Chapter 13, "Recruitment and Selection," Standard 5, "The Selection Process." It is one of the most important contributions the behavioral science professional can make to a police agency.

Recruit training academies are increasing emphasis on psychological and human relations subjects. This is based on the realization that the police officer is more a social science specialist than a hardware technologist: approximately 80 percent of his time is spent in activities that involve keeping the peace rather than making arrests. Because policemen deal with mentally ill, suicidal, criminal, and emotionally disturbed citizens on a daily basis, it is imperative that they have some working knowledge of abnormal psychology.

Because police work is a high stress occupation that involves considerable provocation on a day-to-day basis for policemen on the street, it is desirable that new officers be conditioned to respond at an acceptable level of performance when confronted by critical field situations. Since shoot, no-shoot situations are extremely critical in police work, the training in this area should involve decision-making under stress as well as an exposure to those situations likely to be encountered on the street that often lead to shootings.

Police administrators should have the benefit of consultation with behavioral science specialists in regard to developing training programs in the areas of human relations, mental health, minority group relations, provocation, stress training, and group disturbances.

Police work is an occupation requiring a high level of emotional stability. Because personal, family, or job-related problems are likely to interfere with optimal performance on the job, it is important that professional counseling and therapy services be made available to policemen and families. This can be financially justified by the reductions in disability pensions with emotional basis; lawsuits against the city because of psychological disturbances in the policemen; and lost man-hours through sick time, psychosomatic ailments, and hospitalization.

Policemen's wives have an enormous effect not only on their husbands' efficiency on the job but also on their general well-being. Adequate orientation and ongoing group counseling programs help new policemen's wives adapt to the requirements of their husbands' occupation.

Inevitably, critical events such as questionable shootings, suicides, homicides, and other emotional incidents generate press coverage and arouse community interest. Behavioral science consultation in many of these situations might elicit the underlying psychological factors and help to develop modifications in the system to prevent future incidents.

Because counseling and therapy provided by the police department must necessarily be limited in scope, an adequate referral network for police personnel should be established both inside and outside the department.

In the *Task Force Report: The Police* (1967), the President's Commission on Law Enforcement and Administration of Justice recommended: "Civilian experts in such fields as psychology, sociology, and urban problems should be recruited as full-time employees of units in large police departments." The need for increased behavioral science capability in police departments today is obvious.

Those police agencies not having the benefit of behavioral scientists within their agencies should at least implement working relationships to use behavioral science resources in selection, training, counseling, and to assist in referrals. . . .

**Standard 11.2: Acquire legal assistance when necessary.**

**Standard 11.3: Create a State police management consultation service.**

# 12: Support Services

**Standard 12.1:** Train technicians to gather physical evidence.

**Standard 12.2:** Consolidate criminal laboratories to serve local, regional, and State needs.

**Standard 12.3:** Establish a secure and efficient filing system for evidential items.

**Standard 12.4: The Detention System**
Every police agency currently operating a detention facility should immediately insure professionalism in its jail management and provide adequate detention services. Every municipal police agency should, by 1982, turn over all its detention and correctional facilities to an appropriate county, regional, or State agency, and should continue to maintain only those facilities necessary for short term processing of prisoners immediately following arrest.

1. Every police agency that anticipates the need for full-time detention employees after 1975 should immediately hire and train civilian personnel to perform its jail functions.

2. Every municipal police agency currently operating its own detention facility should immediately consider using an easily accessible State or county facility for all detention except that required for initial processing of arrestees. Every agency should also consider using State of county facilities for the transfer of arrestees from initial processing detention to arraignment detention.

Although almost all local police agencies maintain detention facilities, most are not adequate according to modern penological standards. A 1970 Jail Census revealed that local jails held 160,000 persons—8,000 were juveniles, and over half had not been convicted of a crime. The survey reported that in counties and municipalities over 25,000 in population, 85 to 90 percent of the jails offered no educational or recreational facilities, 50 percent provided no medical facilities, and 25 percent had no provisions for visitation. Additionally, over 25 percent of the jails were housed in buildings over 50 years old and 6 percent in buildings over 100 years old.

Standards for jails and detention centers are set out in the Commission report on Corrections. These standards cover in great detail the operation of jails and detention centers, and the reader is referred to this report for more information.

The public cost of incarceration is extremely high, with the minimum salary outlay for continuous supervision of prisoners estimated at $30,000 annually.

**Recommendation 12.1: Establish crime laboratory certification standards.**

# C: Toward Effective Police Service

## 13: Recruitment and Selection

**Standard 13.1: General Police Recruiting**

Every police agency should insure the availability of qualified applicants to fill police officer vacancies by aggressively recruiting applicants when qualified candidates are not readily available.

1. The police agency should administer its own recruitment program. . . .

2. The police agency should direct recruitment exclusively toward attracting the best qualified candidates. In so doing it:

    a. Should make college-educated applicants the primary targets of all recruitment efforts.

    b. Should concentrate recruitment resources according to the agency's need for personnel from varied ethnic backgrounds.

3. Residency should be eliminated as a preemployment requirement.

4. The police agency should provide application and testing procedures at decentralized locations in order to facilitate the applicant's access to the selection process. . . .

. . . A 1972 Rand Corporation study of the New York Police Department—*Police Background Characteristics and Performance*—revealed that college-educated police officers were rated as superior performers and received fewer civilian complaints. Similarly, a 1968 study of the Chicago Police Department—*Psychological Assessment of Patrolman Qualifications*—revealed that the highest rated group of tenured officers had achieved significantly higher levels of education than had those rated lower. . . .

Once a police officer has accepted employment; . . . the value of his living within the community in which he works should not be overlooked or underestimated. Mutual understanding between the officer and other citizens results from the officer's assuming an active private role in addition to his professional role in the community. This rapport, in turn, helps the officer understand local problems and needs, while destroying the false and damaging stereotyped image many people have of their police. Such understanding develops when police officers become, for example, scout leaders or members of such groups as PTA, Optimists, or Kiwanis.

In any situation in which there is a good reason, such as an economic one, for an officer's not living within the community where he works, he should be required to live within a reasonable distance of it. At a minimum the "reasonableness" should be predicated upon time necessary to respond to an emergency call. . . .

**Standard 13.2: Recruit college-educated personnel.**

**Standard 13.3: Insure nondiscriminatory recruitment practices.**

**Standard 13.4: State Mandated Minimum Standards for the Selection of Police Officers.**

Every State, by 1975, should enact legislation establishing a State commission empowered to develop and enforce State minimum mandatory standards for the selection of police officers. This legislation should provide that the commission represent local government.

1. The majority of this commission should be composed of representatives of local law enforcement agencies to insure responsiveness to local needs. Police practitioners, other members of the criminal justice system, and local government officials should be selected as commission members for a fixed term.

2. This commission should insure that standards are met by inspecting for local compliance, and certifying as competent to exercise police authority, only those police officers who have met the mandated standards. The commission should establish minimum standards for:

    a. Age, with consideration given to lowering the present minimum age of 21 and to establishing a maximum recruitment age that reflects the physical demands placed upon a police officer and the retirement liability of police agencies;

    b. Physical health, strength, stature, and ability, with consideration given to the physical demands of police work;

    c. Character, with consideration given to the responsibilities of police officers and the need for public trust and confidence in police personnel;

d. Personality profile, with consideration given to the need for personnel who are psychologically healthy and capable of enduring emotional stress; and

e. Education, with consideration given to the mental skills and knowledge necessary to perform the police function properly.

3. The commission should establish minimum standards that incorporate compensating factors such as education, language skills, or experience in excess of that required if such factors can overcome minor deficiencies in physical requirements such as age, height, or weight.

4. Every State should provide sufficient funds to enable this commission:

a. To employ a full-time executive director and a staff large enough to carry out the basic duties of the commission; and

b. To meet periodically.

**Standard 13.5:** Formalize a nondiscriminatory applicant-screening process.

**Standard 13.6:** Encourage the employment of women.

**Recommendation 13.1:** Develop job-related applicant tests.

**Recommendation 13.2:** Develop an applicant scoring system.

## 14: Classification and Pay

. . . Career incentives within the police service have been directed exclusively toward the recruitment and development of management personnel. All financial and personal rewards are reserved for individuals pursuing careers as police managers. Vertical development is limited to management personnel, with little opportunity for horizontal development. If this practice of steering all the most talented and ambitious individuals into management positions continues, the quality of personnel in basic line functions will obviously decline. Multiple career paths must be provided so needed expertise will remain at the operational level. Nonmanagerial career paths should progress to a level of compensation beyond that of management. This will provide appropriate incentives for officers who choose to perform line functions.

This type of classification plan offers advantages beyond its obvious benefits as a recruitment and incentive tool. It

309

creates a competitive climate among young police officers and encourages advancement both within the basic ranks and to higher classification levels. It also offers a wider range of sanctions in matters of internal discipline. In most jurisdictions, it will be easier to discipline an individual by reducing his salary level, or pay grade with a particular rank, than to demote him to a lower classification. Finally, the plan may be psychologically advantageous in that it provides for advancement of all personnel, regardless of their career interests, rather than limiting promotional opportunities to a special few. . . .

**Standard 14.1: Maintain salaries competitive with private business.**

**Standard 14.2: Establish a merit-based position classification system.**

*Career Paths*

Historically, promotional opportunities within police agencies have existed almost exclusively in supervisory or managerial positions. Officers whose interests lay in nonmanagerial functions were either denied promotion opportunities or forced to compromise their career interests for salary considerations.

Adherence to the principle of a wide salary range within a classification is essential to the establishment of nonmanagerial career paths. Career opportunities such as these will be realized by advancement through various pay-grade positions rather than by promotion to a management or supervisory position. A patrol officer who chooses to remain in basic patrol functions without assuming a supervisory position should be afforded the opportunity to advance in position and salary as he becomes more proficient in his work. Similarly, a neophyte investigator should be able to progress in his particular occupational pursuit even if he decides to forego a supervisory role. There are clear benefits to the agency when the classification system is structured to encourage such alternative career goals for employees who possess a significant degree of expertise in certain nonmanagerial functions. . . .

*Promotions and Assignments*

All the inherent advantages of a multilevel classification system will probably be lost unless equitable promotion and assignment procedures are established in conjunction with the system. To derive the greatest benefit from any classification plan, it is imperative that police agencies base promotion and advancement policies on the merit principle. In any system based on merit, each individual is judged according to his particular attributes as they relate to the job that he seeks. The purpose of this procedure is to identify the truly capable individual; to evaluate his abilities; and to select him on the basis of his demonstrated performance, his potential for growth, and, to an extent, his level of experience. It is the ultimate responsibility of the police chief executive to devise methods by which such attributes can be accurately measured, and to insure that procedures for the selection of qualified personnel are standardized and consistent. A workable merit system should enable every candidate for advancement to comprehend the particular qualifications he must possess to progress up the career ladder.

Many agencies traditionally have used a rigid civil service classification system in upgrading their employees. Civil service has always been considered the safest method of avoiding favoritism, bribery, and other forms of corruption in promotional policies. Although civil service procedures provide some external safeguards to police agencies, their innate rigidity often inhibits flexibility in assignments and encourages mediocrity in job performance. Most civil service systems are based on job tenure testing procedures intended to measure individual capabilities. Consequently, many individuals, upon promotion, immediately begin to prepare for the next promotional examination with little concern for the caliber of work they do in the meantime.

Most agencies also fail to make provision for moving someone out of a promotional position because of sub-par performance. For these reasons, civil service procedures should be applied only in promotions to broad position classifications and not to advancement between pay-grade positions within those classifications. . . .

## 15: Education

. . . The standards contained in this chapter would require all police officers to have an undergraduate degree or its equivalent no later than 1982. In the meantime, the standards propose: immediately, all police officers should have at least 1 year of college or obtain 1 year of college within 36 months; by 1975, 2 years of college; and by 1978, 3 years of college. . . .

**Standard 15.1: Upgrade entry-level educational requirements.**

**Standard 15.2: Implement police officer educational incentives.**

In such a program prime consideration must be given to the type of classes, majors, or degree for which financial assistance should be provided. Such assistance should be directed toward the education of police officers and their retention as police practitioners, not toward preparing police officers for other careers. However, the exact form of education that produces the best police officers has not yet been determined. It has never been satisfactorily proved whether a liberal arts or a police science education is more appropriate. Obviously, some courses offer little value to police personnel. Home economics, nursing, industrial arts, art, and some of the sciences are of questionable value in police work, although even within nonrelated majors many general education credits may be valuable.

LEEP has taken a liberal position on this question and extends financial aid to students pursuing degrees or certificates "in areas related to law enforcement or suitable for persons employed in law enforcement." These areas include liberal arts, the humanities, behavioral and social sciences, as well as programs in law enforcement and criminal justice. Perhaps until research provides better educational criteria, this broad policy should serve as a suitable guide to local agencies in administering their own programs of financial assistance. . . .

It is true that the implementation of an education incentive pay plan can initially create personnel problems. New recruit officers with a higher level of education may earn more than veteran officers who did not progress beyond high school. Two options are available to alleviate this problem—make the incentive pay applicable only when a recruit officer has reached the top pay step for that rank, or grant seniority credit to experienced officers on a temporary basis while allowing them to return to school and qualify academically for the extra pay. Madison, Wis., among many other agencies, has adopted the latter system. . . .

**Standard 15.3: College Credit for the Completion of Police Training Programs**

Every police agency should pursue the affiliation of police training programs with academic institutions to upgrade its level of training and to provide incentive for further education.

1. All police training courses for college credit should be academically equivalent to courses that are part of the regular college curriculum.

2. Every member of the faculty who teaches any course for credit in the police training curriculum should be specifically qualified to teach that course.

> a. The instructor in a police training course, for which an affiliated college is granting credit, should be academically qualified to teach that course.

> b. Police personnel not academically qualified to teach a course in the regular college curriculum may, if otherwise qualified, serve as teaching assistants under the supervision of an academically qualified instructor.

... Affiliation of police academies with colleges often upgrades the level of training given to police officers and encourages police personnel to continue the pursuit of a college education. Police chief executives should examine such programs carefully to insure their legitimacy and quality. ...

**Recommendation 15.1: Outline police curriculum requirements.**

... While variety in police education may be beneficial, it does appear to cause some confusion. There is no master plan for education. Instead, educational programs for the police have arisen from local and individual perceptions of police needs and philosophies of education. As a result, persons engaged in the same occupation often pursue widely divergent educational courses. Considering the difference between rural and urban law enforcement, and the variety inherent in the patrol, specialists, and managerial functions, this may be valid—but no one is certain.

There is an obvious need to identify the true educational needs of the police service.

## 16: Training

... Once State legislation is passed and a funding system established, training programs must be developed. The first step is to insure that the program includes the instruction and basic material necessary to make a good police officer. This is not easy. The science of police training is still in its infancy. Studies of the role of the police officer, and what he must know and be able to do to perform his job well, are still incomplete. The role of the police officer is constantly changing and varies from region to region, even from one neighboring town to the next. ...

## Curriculums

Basic police training falls into six broad categories: law, the criminal justice system, patrol and investigation, human values and problems, police proficiency, and administration. The commentary in section 16.3 provides a suggested percentage breakdown of each category, developed primarily from the curriculums of the Dayton, Ohio, Oakland, and Los Angeles, Calif., and Seattle, Wash., training programs.

The patrol and investigation function is the foundation of police training. Human values and problems is a relatively new field; psychology, sociology, and community relations are in this category. Instruction usually must come from outside the training center. Long Beach, Calif., and Dayton, Ohio, require police officers to attend local college courses. Chicago, Ill., brings in qualified instructors. Many agencies use role playing and other modern training methods. Seattle, Wash., credits workshop sessions with helping policemen on and off the job. ...

The Commission recommends that new police officers complete a minimum of 400 hours of formal training followed by 4 months in a field training and development program. Each graduate of a basic course should be given coached field training in a variety of field assignments, and his training should include conferences among patrolman, coach, and supervisor. In addition, the new police officer should be given additional instruction in police functions, by correspondence courses if appropriate. At the end of the first 6 months and again at the end of the first year, the new police officer should return to formal training for a 2-week period. ...

## Standard 16.1: State Legislation and Fiscal Assistance for Police Training

Every State, by 1975, should enact legislation establishing mandatory minimum basic training for police, a representative body to develop and administer training standards and programs for police, and financial support for mandated training for police on a continuing basis to provide the public with a common quality of protection and service from police employees throughout the State. By 1978, every State should certify all sworn police employees.

1. Every State should enact legislation that mandates minimum basic training for every sworn police employee prior to the exercise of authority of his position.

2. Every State should enact legislation establishing a State commission to develop and administer State standards for the training of police personnel. The majority of this commission should be composed of representatives of local law enforcement agencies. Other members should be from the criminal justice system, local government, and criminal justice education and training centers. The State should provide sufficient funds to enable this commission to meet periodically and to employ a full-time staff large enough to carry out the basic duties of the commission. In addition to any other duties deemed necessary, this commission should:

    a. Develop minimum curriculum requirements for mandated training for police;

    b. Certify police training centers and institutions that provide training that meets the requirements of the State's police training standards;

    c. Establish minimum police instructor qualifications and certify individuals to act as police instructors;

    d. Inspect and evaluate all police training programs to insure compliance with the State's police training standards;

    e. Provide a consulting service for police training and education centers; and

    f. Administer the financial support for police training and education.

3. Every State should reimburse every police agency 100 percent of the salary or provide appropriate State financed incentives for every police employee's satisfactory completion of any State mandated and approved police training program.

4. Every State, through the police training body, should, by 1978, certify as qualified to exercise police authority every sworn police employee who satisfactorily completes the State basic police training and meets other entrance requirements.

... The Advisory Commission on Intergovernmental Relations, in State-Local Relations in the Criminal Justice System, identified some arguments against State-legislated police training standards. Small agencies could not afford to participate because of fiscal and personnel limitations. The quality of police work in small and rural agencies does not warrant minimum requirements because State or county forces would handle serious incidents. Larger police agencies generally exceed minimum training requirements, and mandatory State training could tend to bring down the level of training afforded by these agencies. State basic police training would not be responsive to local needs. Lastly, any State program would take funds away from local training efforts.

With few exceptions, the experience of the many States that have such legislation has dramatically refuted these arguments. State-legislated mandatory minimum police training standards have been recommended by many groups and study commissions, including the IACP, the President's Commission on Law Enforcement and Administration of Justice, the Council of State Governments, the American Bar Association (in 1952 and 1972), and the Advisory Commission on Intergovernmental Relations.

*Minimal Training Level*

. . . Policemen should not be allowed to exercise the full authority of their position until they successfully complete the State-mandated basic police training program. The powers of arrest and the potential for injury and death are too great to allow policemen to practice their profession without adequate training. . . .

**Standard 16.1: Establish State minimum training standards.**

**Standard 16.2: Develop effective training programs.**

**Standard 16.3: Provide training prior to work assignment.**

. . . In New York City, in its 1969 *Police Training and Performance Study* of 60 various size police training programs, compared the percentage of time allocated to nine basic training areas. The study identified the 15 agencies allocating the highest and lowest percentages in each category. In most cities a comparatively high percentage of the curriculum was devoted to patrol, traffic training, criminal law, evidence, and investigation. The subjects of community relations and human relations, cooperation with other agencies, and first aid were uniformly low. However, the study found no consensus on proper distribution of training curriculum.

The study did prove to be a useful evaluation tool, particularly in identifying topic areas receiving inordinate attention. For example, the differences between the 15 high and low agencies in each category illustrate the divergence of thought on basic police curriculum:

| | Percent of Time | |
| --- | --- | --- |
| | High | Low |
| Patrol and Traffic Training | 42.9 | 16.0 |
| Criminal Law, Evidence, and Investigation | 34.3 | 12.3 |
| Cooperation with other Agencies | 9.0 | 1.3 |
| Physical Training | 18.2 | 4.5 |
| Firearms Training | 12.9 | 3.9 |
| Department Orientation, Policy, and Procedure | 19.5 | 5.4 |
| Community Relations and Human Behavior | 10.9 | 2.4 |
| First Aid | 8.0 | 2.3 |
| Miscellaneous | 6.6 | 0.0 |

Questionnaire responses, however, may have been based on course titles rather than course content. . . .

**Standard 16.4: Provide interpersonal communications training.**

**Standard 16.5: Establish routine inservice training programs.**

**Standard 16.6: Develop training quality-control measures.**

**Standard 16.7: Develop police training academies and criminal justice training centers.**

## 17: Development, Promotion, and Advancement

**Standard 17.1: Offer self-development programs for qualified personnel.**

**Standard 17.2: Implement formal personnel development programs.**

**Standard 17.3: Review personnel periodically for advancement.**

**Standard 17.4: Authorize police chief executive control of promotions.**

**Standard 17.5: Establish a personnel information system.**

## 18: Employee Relations

### Structures of Employee Organizations

The ideal employee organization from the point of view of many—including police managers, professional employees, and persons unwilling to accept organized labor in law enforcemen—has generally been an independent, incorporated,

317

professional association with membership open to all ranks. The organization should be free of outside influence; under State restrictions intended to retain control in the membership; genuinely interested in professional police work; and pledged to a policy of open membership that provides depth and influence to the organization's activities.

But, in the end, it will be the choice of each police employee to decide if his personnel interests will be guided by an independent police organization or an organized labor affiliate. Though the latter has played an increasingly strong, yet still relatively minor, role in police employee organizations during the past several years, indications are that organized labor is not the road police organizations wish to travel. . . .

### Collective Negotiation

. . . Experience has shown, however, that management prerogatives are subjected to the negotiation process only if the police chief executive allows them to be. It is generally felt that management under collective negotiation processes does change, but for the better. It becomes more careful, more responsible, and more responsive.

Civil service systems are affected by collective negotiation. Initially they were created to protect the merit system in government employment and to overcome the problems of political patronage. Through the years, civil service bodies have enlarged their scope of responsibilities and have become, in essence, the personnel department of most government entities. It is this enlarged scope of activities that will probably become subject to collective negotiation, as has been demonstrated in many agreements reached by police agencies.

The National League of Cities has recommended that civil service laws and practices should be revised where they restrict effective employee relations.

Collective negotiation in the police employment field is misunderstood and poorly defined. Political power remains an essential element as well as a block to effectiveness. There is a sufficient degree of confusion and variation in State and local collective negotiation legislation. As a result, a need for standard Federal legislation to overcome the lack of effective State legislation has been expressed. Legislation could be accomplished easily by a minor change in the Taft-Hartley Act, which controls private sector labor relations. The likelihood of this intervention is real if the States do not respond by enacting effective legislation. . . .

**Standard 18.1: Maintain effective employee relations.**

**Standard 18.2: Formalize policies regulating police employee organizations.**

**Standard 18.3: Allow a collective negotiation process.**

**Standard 18.4: Prohibit work stoppages by policemen.**

## 19: Internal Discipline

### External Review

Review mechanisms and investigative units have continuously been advocated or discussed by national commissions. The President's Commission on Law Enforcement and Administration of Justice, and the National Advisory Commissions of Civil Disorders and the Causes and Prevention of Violence, all documented the performance of external review agencies and all came to the conclusion that to date there has been little success. There has been virtually no documentation or experimentation with alternatives proposed by these commissions, such as the ombudsman and Executive Appeal Commission.

Since these reports, the civil review board in Washington, D.C., has voluntarily ceased its operation to protest its lack of a supportive staff. A similar unit in New York City was voted down after a heated campaign against it by the police employee organization.

One reason for the failure of civilian review boards is that the police chief executive cannot give away his authority and accountability, and without that authority and accountability, a review board cannot perform adequately the function it is assigned because it cannot demand change.

Another reason for their failure has been the lack of support from the police, local government and the public. None of the civilian review boards has been given a truly sufficient and independent investigative staff. However, it is unlikely that even the addition of these elements would result in a successful civilian review board operation.

A public complaint must not be regarded as a dispute between two people but rather as criticism that the delivery of police service did not meet the complainant's expectations.

The clamor for civilian review is caused not by the innocence or guilt of the accused employee, but by the system which the police agency uses to investigate and adjudicate the complaint. To end this debate, the police chief executive must constantly review and monitor his agency's administration of internal discipline or let others do it.

External review of police conduct is already readily available through existing institutions of government. However, these legally provided review mechanisms are seldom used. They may include a civilian police commission, the chief administrator of the jurisdiction, the legislative body, the various levels of prosecuting attorney offices, the FBI, and the State and Federal court systems.

Creating another review agency on a model that has usually failed is not the answer. The effective use of the many governmental agencies already legally empowered to review police agency activities is a better solution. The Knapp Commission, after studying the New York City Police Department, recommended that the Governor simply use his legally constituted authority to appoint a special deputy attorney general to investigate and prosecute police corruption. ...

**Standard 19.1: Formulate internal discipline procedures.**

**Standard 19.2: Complaint Reception Procedures**
Every police agency immediately should implement procedures to facilitate the making of a complaint alleging employee misconduct, whether that complaint is initiated internally or externally.

**1.** The making of a complaint should not be accompanied by fear of reprisal or harassment. Every person making a complaint should receive verification that his complaint is being processed by the police agency. This receipt should contain a general description of the investigative process and appeal provisions.

**2.** Every police agency, on a continuing basis, should inform the public of its complaint reception and investigation procedures.

**3.** All persons who file a complaint should be notified of its final disposition; personal discussion regarding this disposition should be encouraged.

**4.** Every police agency should develop procedures that will insure that all complaints, whether from an external or internal source, are permanently and chronologically recorded in a central record. The procedure should insure that the agency's chief executive or his assistant is made aware of every complaint without delay.

**5.** Complete records of complaint reception, investigation, and adjudication should be maintained. Statistical summaries

320

based on these records should be published regularly for all police personnel and should be available to the public.

## Standard 19.3: Create a specialized internal discipline investigative unit.

... The need for a specialized unit is most evident in larger police agencies. The public tends to believe—sometimes with justification—that the large police agency is remote and unresponsive to public complaints. In these larger agencies the task of administering internal discipline is greatest. Until recently, the chief executives of these agencies have been able to maintain an internal discipline system free from internal and external hindrance of pressures for change. During the last few years, demands for change in the system have been heard from community elements and police employees.

One advantage of a specialized internal discipline investigation unit is that investigators can devote all their time to the specific task without distraction from other duties.

In addition, investigators can be selected individually, trained especially for this type of investigation, and through concentrated experience can become expert in the requirements of this investigative specialty. Even though a strong fraternal bond usually exists between an investigator and an accused employee, greater objectivity is possible than if that investigator were a current coworker of the accused.

Previous national commission reports on police have indicated greater public confidence in investigations by specialized units than by line supervisors, although the basis for such confidence was not documented.

The majority of public complaints against police officers fall into two categories: use of excessive force and conduct unbecoming an officer. These are serious allegations and of patent concern to the public. They should be investigated thoroughly and all evidence gathered that will contribute to proving or refuting the charge. A specialized investigating unit is more likely to have the time and expertise to achieve this objective. ...

## Standard 19.4: Investigation Procedures

Every police agency immediately should insure that internal discipline complaint investigations are performed with the greatest possible skill. The investigative effort expended on all internal discipline complaints should be at least equal to the effort expended in the investigation of felony crimes where a suspect is known.

1. All personnel assigned to investigate internal discipline complaints should be given specific training in this task and should be provided with written investigative procedures.

2. Every police agency should establish formal procedures for investigating minor internal misconduct allegations. These procedures should be designed to insure swift, fair, and efficient correction of minor disciplinary problems.

3. Every investigator of internal discipline complaints should conduct investigations in a manner that best reveals the facts while preserving the dignity of all persons and maintaining the confidential nature of the investigation.

4. Every police agency should provide—at the time of employment, and again, prior to the specific investigation—all its employees with a written statement of their duties and rights when they are the subject of an internal discipline investigation. . . .

. . . Recently, police employee associations have questioned certain internal discipline procedures, including the duties and rights of employees who are subjects of internal discipline investigations. It is believed, however, that police employees simply want to know what will be expected of them in this process.

Most of these duties and rights are recognized by police agencies but they have seldom been put into writing. Police chief executives should establish employee duties and rights, then publish and circulate them to all employees. Some agencies that have not done this have had restrictive procedures established for them during employee contract negotiations. The New York State Police were severely hampered in investigation procedures through such a negotiation. They were restricted from using the polygraph and breathalyzer. Yet current case law has upheld the use of these investigative aids in administrative investigations.

Buffalo, N.Y., and New York, N.Y., have established written procedures for employee conduct. These procedures, duties, and rights cover the manner of interview, the requirement to submit to investigative processes, and the type of assistance and representation a subject of an internal discipline investigation should receive during the process. Police agencies have great legal latitude in investigative methods. A police agency need not give away any of these rights.

Being the subject of an internal discipline investigation can be an extremely disturbing experience. In nearly all States the employee has no legal right to counsel during the investigative phase of an administrative matter. Police agencies should allow the employee a reasonable opportunity to secure advice concerning the investigation from someone he respects and in whom he has confidence. A police agency should encourage the employee to seek this assistance from another member of the agency. What the employee wants to know is what he might expect to happen to him. A police agency should not allow this to impede the progress of the investigation unnecessarily.

**Standard 19.5: Authorize police chief executive adjudication of complaints.**

**Standard 19.6: Implement positive programs to prevent misconduct.**

... The Bakersfield, Calif., Police Department instituted an unusual preventative program 5 years ago. To defend employees against the one-to-one verbal complaints so frequent in traffic enforcement contacts, this agency supplied traffic employees with cassette tape recorders for their equipment belt. Approximately 1 year later similar equipment was issued to all uniformed field personnel. The necessity for complaint investigation has been nearly eliminated. Persons still initiate verbal complaints either in person or by telephone: however, they often drop the complaint after listening to the taped recording of the incident.

The agency requires officers to use the recorder in all official contacts and disciplines those who do not. The knowledge that incidents are being recorded serves as a deterrent to misconduct. Although there was some initial resistance to the program, employees have become convinced of its benefits. Tape recorders have also proved useful in the areas of training, investigation, and court presentation. ...

**Recommendation 19.1: Study in Police Corruption**

It is recommended that a national police-supported organization such as the International Association of Chiefs of Police be commissioned by the Law Enforcement Assistance Administration to study the conditions that have led to reduction or elimination of corruption in policy agencies that have been successful in dealing with this problem. This research should not focus on police agencies where corruption is currently widespread.

## 20: Health Care, Physical Fitness, Retirement, and Employee Services

**Standard 20.1:** Require physical and psychological examinations of applicants.

**Standard 20.2:** Establish continuing physical fitness standards.

**Standard 20.3:** Establish an employee services unit.

**Standard 20.4:** Offer a complete health insurance program.

**Standard 20.5:** Provide a statewide police retirement system.

**Recommendation 20.1:** Compensate duty-connected injury, death, and disease.

## 21: Personal Equipment

**Standard 21.1:** Specify apparel and equipment standards.

**Standard 21.2:** Require standard firearms, ammunition, and auxiliary equipment.

**Standard 21.3:** Provide all uniforms and equipment.

## 22: Transportation

**Standard 21.1:** Evaluate transportation equipment annually.

**Standard 22.2:** Acquire and maintain necessary transportation equipment.

**Standard 22.3:** Conduct a fleet safety program.

**Recommendation 21.1:** Test transportation equipment nationally.

## 23: Communications

**Standard 23.1:** Develop a rapid and accurate telephone system.

**Standard 23.2:** Insure rapid and accurate police communication.

**Standard 23.3:** Insure an efficient radio communications system.

**Recommendation 23.1:** Conduct research on a digital communications system.

**Recommendation 23.2: Set national communications equipment standards.**

**Recommendation 23.3: Evaluate radio frequency requirements.**

## 24: Information Systems

**Standard 24.1: Standardize reports of criminal activity.**

**Standard 24.2: Establish an accurate, rapid-access record system.**

**Standard 24.3: Standardize local information systems.**

**Standard 24.4: Coordinate Federal, State, and local information systems.**

# Chapter VI
# Courts

The criminal court system in the United States, which should bring swift and sure justice, has broken down under the burden of increased business while trying to operate under outmoded procedures.

The Commission, in its research and deliberations, sought to identify the underlying causes of the breakdown and to propose standards that provide realistic, meaningful solutions to the problems that plague the courts and that will be instrumental in reducing crime in the United States. Before discussing specific solutions, the complexities of the problems and the role and function of the criminal courts need to be defined.

Within the criminal justice system, the criminal court system ideally should perform the following functions:

• Swiftly determine the guilt or innocence of those persons who come before it.

• Sentence guilty offenders in such a way that their rehabilitation is possible, and that others are deterred from committing crimes.

• Protect the rights of society and the offender.

What problems cause the courts to fall short of the ideal? The Commission sees them as inconsistency in the processing of criminal defendants, uncertainty as to the results attained, unacceptable delays, and alienation of the community.

## Uncertainty and Inconsistency

To many observers, it appears that the court processes produce inconsistent treatment in similar cases. They observe that a few defendants go to trial while the vast majority "cop pleas" to lesser charges, are placed in treatment programs without prosecution, or are handled by other nontrial procedures. The system thus appears to be unequal and suspect.

Over the years, nontrial procedures undoubtedly have been used inconsistently and without explanation to the public. Often only experts in criminal justice have understood some of the distinctions. There have been no accepted standards and few written policies against which the equality of the system could be measured.

In addition to nontrial procedures, inconsistency in sentencing has caused controversy. Sentencing disparities in many jurisdictions are pronounced.

## Delay

Delay in the judicial process is harmful to both the accused offender and society at large. Delay also results in unavailable witnesses, forgotten circumstances, and dismissal of prosecutions because the defendant did not receive the speedy trial guaranteed by the Constitution.

Insofar as the apprehension and punishment of offenders have a deterrent effect upon the offenders themselves and others, the Commission believes that the more closely punishment follows a crime, the greater its deterrent value will be; the longer the delay, the smaller the deterrent effect will be. Finally, delay thwarts society's interest in incapacitating those who have committed crimes.

Examples of the effect of delay are plentiful. On January 18, 1973, as the result of a 36-month pretrial delay in one major metropolitan court, charges were dismissed against six men accused of a $128,000 robbery. And on February 2, 1973, a man who had been held in jail in a large city for more than 2 years awaiting trial was acquitted by a jury.

## Public Alienation

A special poll conducted for *Newsweek* magazine by the Gallup organization found that many Americans have little faith in their courts:

"It's not the courts of justice any more."

"Lawyers use every loophole to free the guilty and the innocent suffer more than the lawbreakers."

"Convicted criminals are let off easily. I don't think all people are treated fairly by the law. The judges, the juries and the lawyers are biased."

The statistics from the *Newsweek* poll indicate that only 35 percent of blacks and 53 percent of whites believe that juries produce correct verdicts most of the time. Seventy percent of blacks and 39 percent of whites believe that a Negro suspected of a crime is more likely than a white man to be convicted and sentenced. Eighty-four percent of blacks and 77 percent of whites believe that poor people are more likely to be convicted and sentenced than those who are wealthy.[1]

These statistics and statements clearly suggest that the American public is alienated from or at best suspicious of the criminal court system. Cynicism is replacing respect.

Some criticism of the court system is well taken, as the studies of the Commission made clear and this report strives to reflect. Other criticism, however, stems from a lack of information. Many of the processes followed by judges, prosecutors, and defenders are not visible to the public. Policies, if they exist, are not published. Public perceptions of the court system are gained through the news media or through infrequent service as jurors or witnesses. Valid judicial decisions, when announced without explanation of the legal basis or rationale, are a constant source of public concern and generate further criticism.

## Major Recommendations

The need to avoid unnecessary delay in criminal processing from arrest to final appeal is emphasized throughout this chapter and in the Commission's *Report on Courts*. But efficiency and speed are not advocated to the detriment of just and equitable treatment for every person coming within the jurisdiction of the Nation's judicial system.

Accordingly, the Commission's major proposals call for:
- Establishment of objective criteria for screening.
- Diversion of certain offenders into noncriminal programs before formal trial or conviction.
- An end to the practice of plea negotiation.
- Elimination of inefficient and unnecessary pretrial proceedings.
- Pretrial processing period not to exceed 60 days from arrest to trial in felony cases and 30 days in misdemeanor cases.
- Affording every convicted offender the opportunity to obtain full and fair judicial review of his conviction.
- Abolition of the trial de novo system.
- Unification of all trial courts within a State into a single

[1] *Newsweek* (March 8, 1971).

court of general jurisdiction, under administrative authority of the State's highest appellate court.

• Establishment of a State court administrator responsible for setting policies for the administration of the entire State court system.

• Employment of qualified full-time prosecutors provided with the necessary personnel, fiscal resources, and support services.

• Provision of public representation to all eligible defendants from arrest to exhaustion of all avenues of relief from conviction.

• Improvement of court-community relations.

• Establishment of family courts to handle juvenile cases.

• Reform of juvenile handling procedures.

# Priorities

The Commission has assigned priorities to the standards, according to the importance of each in reducing crime.

First priority is given to the standards dealing with the litigated case and the review of trial court proceedings. Attaining speed and efficiency in the pretrial and trial processes and achieving prompt finality in appellate proceedings should result in increased deterrence of crime and earlier and more effective rehabilitative treatment of offenders.

As a second priority, the Commission believes that the prosecution and defense functions must be upgraded. The public prosecutor must be able to perform fairly and adequately the screening, diversion, plea negotiation, and case preparation duties of that office. Similarly, a public defender must have the ability and the resources to handle his clients fairly and competently. High-caliber personnel in both these functions would help reinforce public faith in the American system of justice.

Third priority should go to insuring the high quality of the judiciary. Again, competent and dedicated judges would insure the proper functioning of the court system and upgrade that system in the minds of the public.

These priorities should be viewed in terms of the recommended allocation of effort. However, the Commission believes that immediate and concentrated effort should be expended on complex, high-priority actions that may require constitutional amendment or legislation. However, those standards easy to implement should be implemented quickly, regardless of priority.

The Commission's priorities pervade all the standards relating to court processes and procedures, court organization and administration, court-community relations, and juveniles. These major topics are covered in succeeding sections.

# Court Procedures and Processes

Uncertainty, inconsistency, and delay in the court system frequently have their origin in outmoded or inappropriate procedures and processes. The Commission, therefore, believes that major changes must be made in pretrial, trial, and appellate processes. Two objectives, reducing criminal caseloads and insuring a fair disposition of cases, are the motivating forces behind the Commission's proposed reforms.

## Reducing Caseload

Achieving efficiency in the criminal court system involves more than setting time limits. Decriminalization, screening, and diversion are important methods of reducing caseloads. The Commission endorses all three methods. Decriminalization of drunkenness and vagrancy and the administrative disposition of traffic offenses are discussed in the chapter on criminal code reform. Screening and diversion are discussed in this chapter.

Screening is a critical step in increasing the efficiency of the system. It consists of a decision by the prosecutor or the police to release the accused unconditionally prior to trial or plea. The decision often occurs before the filing of charges.

In Philadelphia, Pa., the district attorney initiated a system of placing prosecutors in police precinct stations around the clock to review every criminal complaint prior to arrest and every search warrant prior to execution. As a result, one-third of the cases filed by the police were screened out.

Screening occurs because the evidence of guilt is insufficient to bring the accused to trial, because the evidence was improperly obtained and could not be used at trial, or because prosecution would not serve the interests of justice.

The standards encourage careful screening at the earliest possible stage of the proceedings. To assure fair and equitable screening, the Commission proposes establishment of policy guidelines. There should be a uniform basis for the screening decision—a basis that will assure decisions in the interests of society and the accused.

The Commission recommends that prosecutors establish objective criteria for screening and that police consult with the prosecutor to develop guidelines, based on these criteria, for arresting and taking persons into custody. After a person is taken into custody, the decision to proceed with formal prosecution should rest with the prosecutor.

Screening criteria should include:
- Whether the evidence is sufficient to convict.
- Whether prosecution would further the interests of the criminal justice system.
- Whether the value to society of prosecution and conviction would be commensurate with financial, social, and individual costs.

Diversion is a second means of relieving the court system of inappropriate cases. In diversion, by the prosecutor or by the court, prosecution is stopped short of conviction in exchange for the defendant's agreement to do such things as enroll in a rehabilitation program, make restitution to the victim of his crime, or enter a mental institution. Although the court may enter into the decision to divert, the agreement is usually a product of negotiation between the prosecutor and the defendant.

Project Crossroads illustrates the advantages of a diversion program.

Project Crossroads is a pretrial intervention program which began in the District of Columbia in 1968. It was designed to divert youthful first offenders from the justice process. The offender had to meet certain criteria for enrollment including offense, age, residence, employment status, and prior record. To offer an alternative to a criminal career the staff tutored, counseled, and found jobs for those enrolled in an effort to give them an alternative to a criminal career. After 90 days with the program, a defendant's case was dismissed if he had completed program requirements, extended if the staff and court determined that he needed further assistance, or resumed if he had failed in the program.

From April 1968 to September 1970, 824 individuals were referred to Project Crossroads. Of those, 74 were still enrolled in the program, charges against 467 had been dropped, and 283 had been returned to court for prosecution. A year after release from Project Crossroads, participants experienced a doubling in their employment rates. Former participants were earning more money in better jobs and staying in jobs longer than before, and had a lower rate of recidivism than a control group of nonparticipants.[2]

Programs utilizing the same principle were established for drug addicts in a number of cities in 1972 with the assistance of the President's Special Action Office for Drug Abuse Prevention and the Law Enforcement Assistance Administration (LEAA). The program, called "Treatment Alternatives to Street Crime" (TASC), provided community-based treatment for addicts. After police processing, TASC representatives and the prosecutor test all arrestees for addiction. A judge determines whether to release the individual outright on his own recognizance or no bail, to send the individual to detention, or to order treatment as a condition of release with diversion of the individual to TASC.

Multimodality treatment clinics throughout the community serve clients, mostly outpatients, near their homes. Failure to cooperate with these programs' regulations causes expulsion from the program and criminal prosecution. Full program participation is viewed favorably by the court and can result in dismissal of pending criminal charges against the participant.

A properly administered diversion program with full cooperation of the court offers many benefits. A court can save time and money better devoted to more serious criminals. An offender can find gainful employment and avoid a criminal record, and the community can gain contributing residents.

**The Commission recommends that in appropriate circumstances offenders be diverted into noncriminal programs before formal trail or conviction.**

Diversion decisions should be made as soon as adequate information is available. Diversion should be made when there is a substantial likelihood of conviction and when the benefits to society of diversion are expected to outweigh the potential dangers of nonprosecution. However, precise decision guidelines should be established and made public by the deciding agency—police or prosecutor. When the diversion program would involve substantial deprivation of liberty, a formal, court-approved diversion agreement should be executed.

[2] John Holahan, *A Benefit-Cost Analysis of Project Crossroads* (National Committee for Children and Youth, 1970).

# Plea Negotiation

In many courts in this country, more than 90 percent of criminal convictions are obtained by pleas of guilty, not by the verdict of the jury or the decision of a judge.

Many of these guilty pleas are the result of an express agreement between the defendant and the prosecution, in which the charge and the sentence are negotiated in a process of mutual advantage-taking.

Associate Justice William Rehnquist of the U.S. Supreme Court in a commentary of plea negotiation noted:

> It should be recognized at the outset that the process of plea bargaining is not one which any student of the subject regards as an ornament to our system of criminal justice. Up until now its most resolute defenders have only contended that it contains more advantages than disadvantages, while others have been willing to endure or sanction it only because they regard it as a necessary evil.[3]

In the past 10 years more and more prosecutors have come to rely upon plea negotiation to dispose of the vast majority of their cases. This is in part attributable to the dramatic increase in the amount of crime reported to the police and prosecuted in the courts. The large metropolitan courts are inundated and have unmanageable backlogs of criminal cases. The resources for prosecution, defense, and the courts simply are not adequate for handling these cases. The prosecutor with a serious case backlog and limited resources to try cases is faced with the prospect of negotiating a plea or dismissing the case.

Further, in many large cities, persons accused of crime are anxious to plead guilty rather than languish in jails for months awaiting trial. Often the time spent awaiting trial is longer than the sentence. Consequently, there is a tendency, especially among the poor and ignorant, whether innocent or guilty, to plead guilty, start serving time, and get out of jail quickly. Persons receiving this treatment understandably may lose their faith in the criminal justice system. This distrust is carried over into society through their families and associates.

[3] Speech before the National Conference on Criminal Justice, Washington, D.C. (January 25, 1973).

The public is also getting shortchanged. According to Arlen Specter, District Attorney of Philadelphia:

> The bitter experience of our criminal courtrooms has demonstrated that the bargained plea is really no bargain. We should not settle for a system which simultaneously deprives the innocent defendant of the forum where the prosecutor is compelled to prove his case, and the public is victimized by excessive leniency for hard-core criminal repeaters.
>
> Experience with plea bargaining in many jurisdictions has taught us the painful lesson, again and again, that the violent criminal who secures his freedom through plea bargaining is often encouraged to rob or rape again. The practical effect of plea bargaining unquestionably results in the violent receiving less than an adequate prison sentence.[4]

The experience in New York is illustrative. The *New York Times* reported in the fall of 1972 that the number of persons serving time in State prisons dropped from 18,000 in 1966 to 12,500 in 1972 and that suspects brought before New York City's overflowing courts received lighter sentences than those convicted of the same crime in upstate New York. The reasons for this, the *Times* states, were the judges' loss of faith in the prison system and "massive plea bargaining," in which a defendant is offered a light sentence in return for a guilty plea.

There is also a threat to defendants' rights in the plea negotiation process. A recent survey of more than 3,400 criminal justice practitioners in four States—California, Michigan, New Jersey, and Texas—reveals the potential threat to defendant rights inherent in the plea negotiation process. Sixty-one percent of the survey respondents agreed that it was very probable or somewhat probable that most defense attorneys "engage in plea bargaining primarily to expedite the movement of cases." Thirty-eight percent agreed that it was very probable or somewhat probable that most defense attorneys in plea bargaining negotiations "pressure clients into entering a plea that [the] client feels is unsatisfactory."[5]

[4] Speech before the National Conference on Criminal Justice, Washington, D.C. (January 24, 1973).

[5] Project STAR, *Survey of Role Perceptions for Operational Criminal Justice Personnel Data Summary* (California Department of Justice 1972), pp. 238, 243.

Despite the dangers posed by plea negotiations, many experts have concluded that plea negotiation is inevitable, desirable, or both, and that efforts should be directed at improving rather than eliminating the practice. The Commission does not agree.

In the view of the Commission, the high volume of court business and the lack of resources should not and need not cause the perpetuation of undesirable practices. Neither is the plea bargain necessary to avoid the harshness of some laws or to obtain the informant's cooperation.

The experience in Philadelphia, Pa., illustrates methods of handling large caseloads without undue plea negotiation. In Philadelphia the criminal backlog has been steadily reduced in recent years from its 1965 peak. The reduction in backlog has been made possible by careful screening and diversion of cases and by a streamlined trial process. It has been achieved in the face of a firm policy against wholesale disposition through plea negotiation. Contrasted with some other major American cities where more than 90 percent of the cases are concluded by guilty pleas, Philadelphia has disposed of only 32 percent of its cases through the guilty plea. The Philadelphia experience is substantial evidence that American court systems can function effectively without heavy reliance on the negotiated plea.

It should be made clear that the Commission does not condemn the entry of guilty pleas. There is a distinction between negotiation of a plea in which the prosecution makes some concessions and the entry of a plea where there are no reasonably contestable issues.

Further, if prosecutors and defense attorneys were convinced that plea bargaining would not occur, the charges filed by prosecutors would correspond more closely to what the prosecutor reasonably thinks he can and should get as a result. (This is often not the case today.) If the defendant and his attorney agree that this is the likely result—as the Commission believes will more often be the case than under existing practice—they can and should enter a plea of guilty. If they do not agree that this is the likely result, they can and should litigate the disagreement.

In addition, if other recommendations of the Commission are followed, there should be more resources available. If the unnecessary and duplicative proceedings are eliminated and procedures are streamlined, the existing judicial personnel and facilities could properly process more criminal cases. Similarly, if pretrial discovery is expanded, many more cases should be resolved early in the proceedings, thus freeing additional judicial resources.

The Commission flatly rejects the idea that plea negotiations are needed to give flexibility to the criminal justice system and to avoid unjustifiably harsh provisions of substantive law. This Commission has recommended a reasoned, rational penalty structure. Further, if there appears to be harsh effect, a prosecutor can alleviate the problem in his selection of initial charge. To the extent that greater flexibility is desired, it should be made available as a matter of formal law, either by changes in the definitions of substantive crimes or in a modification of dispositional alternatives available to sentencing courts.

Finally, as to the value of negotiation to law enforcement, the elimination of plea negotiation need have little effect upon the exchange of leniency for information and assistance. Since the prosecutor can alter initial charge and sentence recommendations in return for law enforcement assistance, the elimination of plea negotiations will have little impact upon this situation.

**The Commission condemns plea negotiation and recommends that as soon as possible, but not later than 1978, negotiations between defendants and prosecutors concerning concessions to be made in return for guilty pleas be abolished.**

Until plea bargaining is eliminated, standards should be adopted that will reduce its potential for abuse, and the Commission therefore recommends that:

• The agreement on which a negotiated guilty plea is based should be presented in open court, and the record should show the judge's reasons for its acceptance or rejection.

• Each prosecutor's office should develop and publish uniform policies on plea negotiations.

• Prosecutors should be barred from making unfair inducements on threats to gain a plea of guilty.

• A time limit should be set for plea negotiation in order to avoid hasty, last-minute pleas and to permit sound management of a trial docket.

• In determining sentence, the court should not consider the fact that the defendant has entered a plea of guilty.

# Pretrial Proceedings

Pretrial delay has been the subject of considerable writing and litigation. Commission review of the problem identified several factors which contribute to pretrial delay. These are:

• Failure to present arrested persons promptly before a judicial officer. This in turn delays appointment of counsel, bail setting, and scheduling of other processes by the court.

• Use of preliminary hearings as evidence discovery devices and the concomitant failure to initiate informal evidence discovery without resort to formal pretrial motions.

• Use of grand jury indictment processes which do not justify the delay and inconvenience inherent in the use of a grand jury.

• Formal arraignment procedures which only duplicate the presentment process after grand jury indictment.

• Excessive filing of formal pretrial motions practice which could be avoided by rules for mutual discovery and omnibus pretrial hearings.

**The Commission recommends that steps be taken immediately to eliminate inefficient and unnecessary pretrial proceedings or procedures and speed up pretrial processing so that the period from arrest to the beginning of trial of a felony generally should not be longer than 60 days. In a misdemeanor prosecution, the period from arrest to trial generally should be 30 days or less.**

The Commission recommends that:

• In misdemeanor prosecutions, preliminary hearings should be eliminated.

• Grand jury indictment should not be required for any criminal prosecution, but the grand jury should be retained for its investigative functions.

• An arrested person should be brought before a judicial officer within 6 hours after arrest.

• The preliminary hearing in felony cases should be held within 2 weeks after arrest, with evidence limited to that relevant to a determination of probable cause.

• Formal arraignment (as distinguished from presentment) befose a judicial officer should be eliminated.

• Disclosure of prosecution evidence to the defense in felony proceedings should take place within 5 days after the preliminary hearing and disclosure of most defense evidence to the prosecution should immediately follow resolution of pretrial motions. Strict rules should limit the admissibility at trial of undisclosed evidence.

# The Litigated Case

SUMMARY OF
COMMISSION
RECOMMENDATIONS
FOR STEPS TO ACHIEVE
TRIAL IN A FELONY CASE
WITHIN 60 DAYS OF ARREST.

Pretrial delay in a criminal prosecution is a major concern of this Commission. In its *Report on Courts*, the Commission proposes standards that would structure the procedural framework for the formal processing of accused persons to achieve trial in felony cases within 60 days of arrest. This chart outlines those proposals. The time frames shown are derived from figures contained in Standards 4.5, 4.8, 4.9, and 4.10 of the *Report on Courts*; and the interested reader is referred to that report for details.

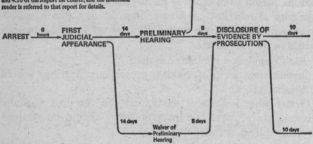

In some felony cases, the Commission recommends that a summons or citation be issued in lieu of arrest. In such instances, there would be no first judicial appearance and the Commission calls for a preliminary hearing within 14 days of the issuance of citation or summons.

In felony cases in which there is a grand jury indictment, the Commission recommends that no preliminary hearing be held. The time limits and steps shown above as following the preliminary hearing become applicable upon apprehension of the indicted individual or service of a summons following the indictment.

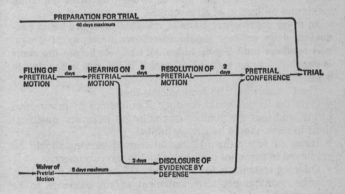

**PREPARATION FOR TRIAL**
46 days maximum

**FILING OF** —5 days→ **HEARING ON** —3 days→ **RESOLUTION OF** —2 days→ **PRETRIAL** → **TRIAL**
**PRETRIAL**      **PRETRIAL**      **PRETRIAL**      **CONFERENCE**
**MOTION**      **MOTION**      **MOTION**

         3 days   **DISCLOSURE OF**
**Waiver of**     5 days maximum  → **EVIDENCE BY**
**Pretrial**      **DEFENSE**
**Motion**

# Trial

Although most public attention has been directed to pre-trial delay, valuable time also is wasted during the actual trial of many cases. This not only prolongs the final disposition of the case on trial, but also ties up court facilities and personnel, preventing the trial of other cases. In a recent trial, 4 months were consumed selecting a jury; 1,035 prospective jurors were examined in the process. Less spectacular—but more frequent—delays result from early adjournments of court during routine trials, preparation of instructions, and similar matters. Similarly, there is substantial delay in the sentencing process.

The standards recommended by the Commission are directed toward insuring a fair and impartial trial while obtaining maximum utilization of all resources.

**In every court where trials of criminal cases are being conducted, daily sessions should commence promptly at 9 a.m. and continue until 5 p.m. unless all business before the court is concluded at an earlier time and it is too late in the day to begin another trial.**

The Commission also recommends that:

• Only the judge should conduct examinations of prospective jurors, and that the number of challenges to jurors' qualifications to serve should be strictly limited.

• Juries of fewer than 12 but at least 6 persons should be employed in cases not punishable by life imprisonment.

• Opening statements to the jury should be limited to a clear, concise, nonargumentative statement of the evidence to be presented.

• Evidence admitted should be limited to that which is directly relevant and material to the issues being tried.

• Instructions to juries should be standardized to the extent possible and clearly conveyed to the jury.

• With a view toward the development of future standards, studies should be made of the use of the exclusionary rule and of the use of video-taped evidence.

# Review of the Trial Court Proceedings

Because of the social stigma and loss of liberty associated with a criminal conviction, many people believe that determining guilt and fixing punishment should not be left to a single trial court. The interests of both society and the defendant are served by providing another tribunal to review the trial court proceedings to insure that no prejudicial error was committed and that justice was done. Review also provides a means for the ongoing development of legal doctrine in the common law fashion, as well as a means of insuring evenhanded administration of justice throughout the jurisdiction. Functionally, review is the last stage in the judicial process of determining guilt and fixing sentence. Like the trial proceeding, it should be fair and expeditious.

The review stage, like other aspects of the criminal process, is in trouble. Several decades ago appeals were taken only in a minority of cases, and collateral attacks on convictions were relatively rare. Today, in some jurisdictions more than 90 percent of all convictions are appealed, and collateral attack is almost routine in State and Federal courts. Courts are handling appeals under procedures used for the past hundred years. The process is cumbersome, fragmented, and beset with delay. Both State and Federal courts are threatened with inundation. Even now, the vast increase in workload is making it increasingly difficult for appellate courts to give to substantial questions the careful, reflective consideration necessary to the development of a reasoned and harmonious body of decisional law.

For a State criminal case, review may have as many as 11 steps, some of which can be repeated. Although not every case goes through each of these steps, they are all potentially available, and it is not uncommon for a defendant to pursue four or five. They are:

1. New trial motion filed in court where conviction was imposed;

2. Appeal to State intermediate appellate court;

3. Appeal to State supreme court;

4. Petition to U.S. Supreme Court to review State court decision on appeal;

5. Postconviction proceeding in State trial court;

6. Appeal of postconviction proceeding to State immediate appellate court;

7. Appeal to State supreme court;

8. Petition to U.S. Supreme Court to review State court decision on appeal from postconviction proceeding;

9. Habeas corpus petition in Federal district court;

10. Appeal to U.S. court of appeals; and

11. Petition to U.S. Supreme Court to review court of appeals decision on habeas corpus petition.

The actual operations and interplay of review proceedings

341

are more complex than this listing suggests. Some convictions are not appealed at all; others are subject to a number of these steps several times over; and with respect to some convictions, review may proceed simultaneously in both State and Federal courts.

Curiously, despite all the variations of review available, the sentence itself—often the most important feature of the case—cannot be reviewed at all in most American jurisdictions.

The result of these limitations and fragmentations is a drawn-out, almost never-ending review cycle. This in turn brings the criminal process into public disrepute and leaves convicted defendants with feelings of injustice mixed with illusory hopes that another round of review will overturn the conviction.

What is needed, in the view of the Commission, is not merely an effort to accelerate the existing review machinery. Rather, it is necessary to experiment with a restructuring of the entire process of review.

The Commission believes that there should be a single, unified review proceeding in which all arguable defects in the trial proceeding can be examined and settled finally, subject only to narrowly defined exceptional circumstances where there are compelling reasons to provide for a further review.

This is a far-reaching and controversial proposal but the Commission recommends it as a reasonable response to an escalating problem.

**The Commission recommends that every convicted defendant be afforded the opportunity to obtain one full and fair judicial review of his conviction and sentence by a tribunal other than that by which he was tried or sentenced. Review in that proceeding should extend to the entire case, including errors not apparent in the trial record that might heretofore have been asserted in collateral attacks on the conviction or sentence.**

The reviewing court should have a full-time professional staff of lawyers, responsible directly to the judges. The function of this staff would be to supplement the work of the attorneys representing the prosecution and defense in each case.

Review procedures should be flexible so as to afford the greatest possible fairness, expedition, and finality. The court also should have the authority to confirm a conviction despite the existence of error if to do so would not amount to a miscarriage of justice.

342

A criminal case should be ready for initial action by the reviewing court within 30 days after the imposition of sentence. Cases containing only insubstantial issues should be finally disposed of within 60 days of imposition of sentence. Cases presenting substantial issues should be finally disposed of within 90 days after the imposition of sentence.

After reviewing court disposition, or after a fair opportunity to gain review, a conviction and sentence should not be subject to further State or Federal review except in such limited circumstances as the following: (1) further review would serve the public interest in the development of legal doctrine or in the maintenance of uniformity in the application of decisional or statutory law; (2) newly discovered evidence raises substantial doubt as to the defendant's guilt; or (3) issue arises as to a constitutional violation which, if well founded, would undermine the basis for or the integrity of the trial or review proceeding.

A review court should always state its reasons for its decision in a criminal case, but formal publication of reasons should be allowed only if the opinion would be significant to the development of legal doctrine or if it would serve other important institutional purposes. Reducing the number of published opinions would speed adjudication by freeing for other purposes the time judges use to write opinions and by reducing the time lawyers and judges need to prepare and decide cases.

The Commission further recommends that funds be devoted to technological innovation in the field of transcript production, such as computer-aided stenotyping, sound recording, and videotaping, in order to expedite preparation of the trial record for review purposes.

The Commission also recommends that the trial de novo system, which permits an offender convicted in a lower court to demand a full retrial in a court of general jurisdiction, be abolished. All courts should be courts of record and all should follow the same appellate practices.

# Court Organization and Administration

In opening the first National Conference on the Judiciary in March 1971, President Nixon called for "genuine reform" of the Nation's courts—"the kind of reform that requires imagination and daring." At the same conference, Chief Justice Warren E. Burger emphasized that "the challenges to our system of justice are colossal and immediate and we must assign priorities." "I would begin," he said, "by giving priority to methods and machinery, to procedures and technique, to management and administration of judicial resources even over the much-needed reexamination of substantive legal institutions."[6]

Essential to "efficient management and administration of judicial resources" is the unified court system. Centralized administrative authority is the unified court system's most important feature.

Under a unified court system, issues which are systemwide in nature may be resolved in a uniform fashion; for example, through the establishment of general rules of procedure, judicial training programs, and information systems. Temporary transfer of personnel to meet changes in workloads is also made possible by a unified court system.

Progress toward complete unification varies from State to State. Lower courts, which process minor criminal offenses and city and county ordinance violations, are often the last to come under State organization and administration. In most cases, there is no coordination of lower courts within the same State. It is not unusual, for example, for a rural justice of the peace to have little or no work while a nearby municipal judge must hold evening sessions to keep his calendar current.

The Commission believes that all courts in a State should be organized into a unified judicial system financed by the State and administered by a statewide court administrative judge under the supervision of the chief justice of the State supreme court. This fully unified court system should consolidate all trial courts into a single court of general jurisdiction. All courts within a State would be unified under the administrative authority of the State's highest appellate court.

A matter of high priority in any reexamination of court processing of criminal defendants is court administration—the management of the nonjudicial business of the court.

Court management and administration has as its goal relieving judges of some nonjudicial functions and enhancing their performance of judicial functions.

Although court administration is one of the newer fields of public administration, it has already proved itself to be a valuable tool in maximizing the efficiency of the courts. A

[6] *Proceedings, National Conference on the Judiciary,* Williamsburg, Va., March 1971 (West Publishing Co.).

survey undertaken by the Commission and reproduced in its *Report on Courts* shows that the Nation already has 43 State court administrators and an undetermined number of regional and trial court administrators.

The Commission believes that professional court administration is an essential function in the reform of American courts. Nevertheless, improvements are needed. More courts need professional court administrators and the manner in which administrators serve their courts needs to be upgraded. The standards in this chapter are designed to stimulate and guide these improvements.

**The Commission recommends that each State have a State court administrator responsible for establishing policies for administration of the entire State court system, including budgets, personnel, information compilation and dissemination, fiscal operations, court system evaluation and remediation, assignment of judges, and external liaison. The court administrator should establish operational guidelines for local and regional trial court administrators.**

Local administrative policies should be established by the judges of each trial court within guidelines set forth by the State's highest appellate court. A presiding judge should have ultimate administrative authority over such matters.

Each trial court with five or more judges should have a full-time administrator. Trial courts with caseloads too small to justify a full-time administrator should combine into administrative regions for that purpose.

# Improving the Quality of the Prosecution, Defense, and Judiciary

A system is only as good as the people who work within it. The quality of personnel working in the court system is particularly important since it has a direct impact on the quality of justice.

Significant efforts must be made to upgrade and make more professional the performance of prosecution, defense, and judicial personnel.

## Prosecution

The prosecutor occupies a critical position in the criminal justice system. His office combines legal, administrative, and judicial functions which require experienced, professional personnel and a rational and efficient organizational structure. Efforts to deal with the problem of crime in America are unlikely to be successful if prosecutors' offices are poorly funded, understaffed, and ineffective.

The personnel policies, size, and organization of many prosecutors' offices are not conducive to meeting the complex demands of the criminal justice system. Most of the Nation's 2,700 prosecutors serve in small offices and have only one or two assistants. Frequently, both prosecutor and assistants are part-time officials who have outside law practices. The salaries of prosecutors and their assistants are still considerably lower than those of private-practice lawyers with similar background and experience.

The President's Crime Commission observed that "a talented attorney, even one dedicated to public service, cannot be expected to remain long in such a position if it is his only source of income." A survey conducted by the National District Attorneys Association indicated that most assistant prosecutors obtain higher paying positions in private law firms after serving an average of 2 to 4 years.[7] Because of low salaries prosecutors therefore are faced with the continuing problem of replacing experienced assistant prosecutors with inexperienced ones.

It is thus inperative that substantial additional resources be devoted to the training and continued education of prosecutors and their assistants. Similarly, every prosecutor's office should systematically develop and review the policies and practices to be followed by all staff attorneys. Only through training and policy guidelines can the requisite standard of performance be achieved.

The Commission believes that prosecutors' offices must be alert to good management and should undertake some new duties. For example, every office should have effective filing procedures and sound statistical systems. In many jurisdictions, the prosecutor's role in criminal investigation should be enlarged to cover consumer fraud complaints, municipal corruption, and organized crime activities, and the prosecutor should specifically develop his relationships with the police and the community.

**The Commission recommends that the prosecutor be a full-time professional selected on the basis of demonstrated**

[7] *Report on Proceedings, Recommendations, and Statistics of the National District Attorneys Association Metropolitan Prosecutors' Conference, pp. 43-44 (1971).*

competence and personal integrity. The prosecutor's office should be provided with the necessary personnel, fiscal resources, and support services to deal effectively and fairly with all cases coming before it and to allow proper preparation of all cases at all levels of the criminal proceeding including screening and diversion.

The Commission also recommends that:

• The prosecutor should serve for a minimum term of 4 years and be compensated on a scale equal to the presiding judge of the trial court of general jurisdiction.

• Assistant prosecutors should be actively recruited from all segments of the population and should possess demonstrated legal ability.

• Professional staff size and scheduling should permit proper preparation of cases.

• The State should establish and support an independent agency or specialized unit in the attorney general's office to provide technical assistance and supplemental support services to local prosecutors.

• Formal national and statewide educational and training programs and local in-house orientation and training programs should be established and utilized for assistant prosecutors.

• The prosecutor should have at his disposal investigatory resources sufficient to assist in case preparation, supplement police investigations, and conduct initial investigations of official corruption, organized crime, and consumer fraud.

## Defense

The task of providing legal defense representation for those accused of a crime has grown tremendously, in part because of the increased functions that defense counsel must perform as a matter of constitutional mandate. The right to representation at trial no longer is confined to those defendants charged with more serious criminal offenses. In *Argersinger* v. *Hamlin,* the U.S. Supreme Court held that no indigent person may be incarcerated as the result of a criminal trial at which he was not given the right to be represented by publicly provided defense counsel.

In considering the provision of defense services to those accused of a crime, the Commission addressed itself almost entirely to the provision of defense services at public expense. This was done because most defense services are provided by

347

public representation and because there is substantial controversy over the adequacy of public representation.

The best available estimates are that about 60 percent of felony defendants, and 25 to 50 percent of misdemeanor defendants, cannot pay anything toward their defense, and therefore must be represented at public expense.[8] However, the proportion of defendants who are actually represented at public expense varies from jurisdiction to jurisdiction. One recent study of several Arkansas counties, for example, found that the percentage of felony defendants represented by appointed counsel ranged from 18.2 percent to 59.5 percent.[9]

With respect to the adequacy of public representation, there has been public criticism. For example, the Administrative Office of the United States Courts issued a report in 1969 that showed that defendants who could not afford private counsel received much harsher sentences than those who had privately retained counsel.[10]

However, the Commission found no evidence that public representation is always, or even generally, worse than private representation. Nevertheless it recognizes widespread suspicion and concludes that this suspicion is itself a major problem.

After study, the Commission drew these conclusions:

• Lawyers provided at public expense should be experienced and well educated.

• More professional staff resources, supporting resources and staff, and education are needed.

• The entire bar should be involved in the provision of public defense services.

• Provision of defense services should be prevented from becoming the realm of a limited clique of practitioners, whether in a public defender's office or a private capacity.

There is also need to deal with the special problems raised by the provision of public defense services. The lawyer rendering services at public expense is liable to be caught between public resentment at having to pay for the defense of

[8] Lee Silverstein, *Defense of the Poor in Criminal Cases in American State Courts* (American Bar Foundation, 1965), pp. 8-9.

[9] Morton Gitelman, *The Relative Importance of Appointed and Retained Counsel in Arkansas Felony Cases—An Empirical Study,* 24 *Ark. L. Rev. 442* (Winter 1971).

[10] Administrative Office of the United States Courts, *Federal Offenders in United States District Court* (1969), p. 49.

348

guilty criminals and defendants' resentment at not having available as effective a defense as those with private counsel.

The Commission recommends that each eligible defendant be provided public representation from arrest until all avenues of relief from conviction have been exhausted.

Each jurisdiction should maintain a full-time public defender organization and a coordinated assigned counsel system involving the private bar, and should divide case assignments in a manner that will encourage participation by the private bar. The standard for eligibility for public representation should be based upon ability to pay for counsel without substantial hardship. Defendants should be required to pay part of the cost of representation if they are able to do so.

The Commission further recommends that:

• The right of a defendant to represent himself should be severely limited.

• If the defendant has no attorney and no request for counsel has been made, the judicial officer at the initial appearance should provide counsel for any eligible defendant who has not made an informed waiver of the right.

• Counsel should be available to convicted offenders for appeals or collateral attacks on convictions and at proceedings concerning detention or early release, parole revocation, and probationary status.

• Organization and administration of defender services should be consistent with local needs.

• The public defender should be selected on the basis of demonstrated and high personal integrity and should serve on a full-time basis at a salary not lower than that of the presiding judge of the trial court of general jurisdiction. A regional office should be established, if necessary to warrant a full-time defender.

• Public defenders should be appointed for a term of not less than 4 years and should be eligible for reappointment. Selection and discipline should be vested in the judicial nominating commission and the judicial conduct commission.

• Staff attorneys should be recruited from all segments of the population and should be hired, retained, and promoted on the basis of merit qualifications.

• Staff size and scheduling should be regulated to insure manageable caseloads.

• All attorneys who represent the indigent accused should participate in comprehensive national, local, and office training programs designed to impart basic and extended skills in criminal defense.

• The public defender should be sensitive to the problems of his client community, and should strive to educate the community about his role.

• The public defender should have available adequate support services including investigative and social work assistance.

## Judiciary

The role of the judiciary in the Nation's efforts to reduce crime is to provide a system of unquestioned integrity and competence for settling legal disputes. If the courts are to fulfill this role, the judicial processes must use effective and up-to-date management methods. In addition, the courts must strive to preserve the American heritage of freedom and to deal thoroughly with all cases that come before them—no matter how minor or routine they may be. Procedures and court systems can be no better than the judges who administer the procedures and render the decisions.

Unless the courts reflect all of these qualities, they will be viewed with disdain, fear, or contempt. Such attitudes are incompatible with the respect for law essential to a free society.

The Commission believes that courts exercising criminal jurisdiction meet these criteria inadequately, and that the American public shares this view. The inadequate quality of some judicial personnel, especially those who exercise trial jurisdiction, is partly responsible for this situation. Rules and methods also are important, but they cannot insure a highly regarded system. Judges exercise enormous discretionary power and trial judges function with almost no direct supervision. The quality of judicial personnel thus is more important than the quality of the participants in many other systems.

The Commission views the selection process as a matter needing attention, but it also believes that other aspects of the court system contribute to the poor quality of judicial personnel. Inadequate compensation is one factor. Judicial tenure also may account for some difficulty in obtaining and retaining capable judicial officers.

These factors—selection, compensation, and tenure—relate primarily to the need to maintain high quality judges. A somewhat different aspect of the problem concerns the behavior of judges. The public loses confidence in the court system when it sees examples of gross misconduct or obvious incompetence, especially when no remedial action is taken. But even if a trial judge commits no overt act of misconduct, his demeanor can have a significant impact upon the public's opinion of the courts.

There is a need for a more effective system of discipline and removal to deal with misbehavior and incompetence among the judiciary. In less extreme situations, the Commission sees the problem as one of inadequate judicial education. The need is not for a means of imposing sanctions on offending judges but rather for a means of developing programs of educating judges and of sensitizing them to the fact that their behavior affects the entire criminal justice system.

**The Commission recommends that judges be nominated by a judicial commission appointed by the Governor, and that judges stand for periodic uncontested elections in which they run against their record. The judicial commission should consist of private nonlawyer citizens and members of the legal profession.**

The Commission further recommends that:

• Retirement at age 65 should be mandatory, but retired judges should be assigned to sit for limited periods at the discretion of the presiding judge of the jurisdiction.

• State and local judges should be compensated at rates commensurate with salaries and retirement benefits of the Federal trial judiciary. When appropriate, salaries and benefits should be increased during a judge's term of office.

• A judicial conduct commission staffed by judicial, legal, and lay members should be established and empowered to discipline or remove judges for sufficient cause.

• Every State should establish and maintain a comprehensive program for continuing judicial education. Participation in the program should be mandatory.

# Court-Community Relations

Because court operations are subject to public scrutiny, court-community relations inevitably exist. The quality of these relations relates directly to the courts' ability to perform their functions effectively. A law-abiding atmosphere is fostered by public respect for the court process. Public scrutiny should not result in public dissatisfaction.

The community's perception of the court system also may have a direct impact on court processes, as when it affects the willingness of members of the community to appear as witnesses, serve as jurors, or support efforts to provide courts with adequate resources.

Court-community relations cannot and should not be avoided. The Commission believes that favorable court-community relations cannot be accomplished without a vigorous and well-planned program to insure that courts deserve to be and are, in fact, perceived favorably by the public.

## Information and Education

There are several areas of serious deficiency in present court-community relations. The first involves information and education. Courts operate in a manner which frequently leaves the public uninformed. Inadequacies here can be traced to several causes. The use of specialized terminology and procedures makes legal proceedings particularly difficult for the public to understand. Added to this is the reluctance of courts to undertake informing the public about their procedures. Courts rarely issue news releases or make public reports.

Apart from the general lack of information, there are also problems of informing participants in the process and the Commission notes the need for courthouse information services. Participation in the criminal justice process often is a confusing and traumatic experience that leaves the witness, juror, or defendant with an unfavorable impression of the system.

## Use of Witnesses

Another area of deficiency involves the methods and procedures by which witnesses are used. Witnesses often are required to make appearances that serve no useful purpose. Police officers, for example, often must be present at a defendant's initial appearance, although they serve no function at this proceeding.

Witnesses often are not compensated for time spent testifying and traveling, or they are compensated inadequately. In Connecticut and South Carolina, for example, witnesses are paid 50 cents for each court appearance. In Alabama, the fee is 75 cents. In Texas courts, witnesses (other than those called as experts) receive no fee for their court appearances.

## Facilities

A most serious deficiency in court-community relations involves court facilities. A study of New York civil courts, conducted by the National College of the State Judiciary, found a correlation between the adequacy of a court's physical facilities and its public image in the community.

Facilities for witnesses sometimes are inadequate or nonexistent. Testifying can be an exhausting experience, as witnesses are frequently subjected to grueling examination. The Courts Task Force of the President's Commission on Law Enforcement and Administration of Justice observed that "sensitivity to the needs of witnesses who are required to return to court again and again, often at considerable personal sacrifice, is usually lacking."

**The Commission recommends that immediate steps be taken to enhance court-community relations through systematic programs of public information and education, through improved treatment of witnesses, and through provision of adequate court facilities.**

The Commission specifically recommends that:

• Courthouses should be designed and placed with careful attention to function. The ability to see and hear the proceedings should be a primary design consideration.

• Comfortable waiting rooms should be provided for jurors. The jury's waiting room should be separate from the one used by prosecution and defense witnesses.

• Courthouse information desks should be provided, and manned by informed staff who are fluent in the languages of the area.

• Court personnel should be representative of the community served, especially with respect to minority-group employment.

• The court should pursue a systematic program of public information and education that includes issuance of news releases and reports, speaking appearances, and public tours.

• Judges and court personnel should participate in criminal justice planning activities.

• Provision should be made for witnesses to be on telephone alert rather than present in court.

• Witnesses should be compensated at more realistic rates than now prevail.

# Juveniles

The general rise in crime throughout the United States in the last decade has brought increasing burdens to all courts, particularly the juvenile courts. In 1960, there were 510,000 delinquency cases disposed of by juvenile courts; in 1970 there were 1,125,000 delinquency cases disposed of by juvenile courts.[11]

The question is whether or not the present juvenile court system is an effective method of controlling juvenile crime. Throughout the country, the juvenile courts vary widely in structure, procedure, and quality. In the main, however, they reflect an understanding that special treatment for the young offender is desirable.

After considerable study, the Commission concurs that the juvenile offender should have special treatment. However, the present juvenile court systems are not providing that special treatment in an adequate, fair, and equitable manner.

The Commission believes that major reform of the juvenile justice system is needed. The juvenile justice system has not obtained optimum results with young people on their first contact with the system. Further, it is the conclusion of the Commission that juvenile courts must become part of an integrated, unified court system; that the jurisdiction of the juvenile courts must be narrowed and that the relationships between the courts and juvenile service agencies must be broadened in a manner which maximizes diversion from the court system. In addition there must be reform of the procedures for handling those juveniles who are referred to court.

### Reorganization of Juvenile Courts

The existence of the juvenile court as a distinct entity ignores the causal relationship between delinquency and other family problems. A delinquent child most often reflects a family in trouble—a broken family, a family without sufficient financial resources, a family of limited education, and a family with more than one child or parent exhibiting antisocial behavior. The family court concept as now utilized in New York, Hawaii, and the District of Columbia permits the court to address the problems of the family unit, be they civil or criminal.

Further, in the past juvenile courts have, by their jurisdictional authorization, intervened in areas where alternative handling of the juvenile is more successful. It is the view of the Commission that the delinquent child—the child who commits an offense which would be criminal if committed by an adult—should be the primary focus of the court system. The Commission takes no position with respect to extension

[11] U.S. Department of Health, Education, and Welfare, *Juvenile Court Statistics* 1971 (1972), p. 11.

of jurisdiction to the "person in need of supervision" (PINS). The PINS category includes the runaway and truant. Jurisdiction, however, should not extend to dependent children—those needing economic, medical, or other social assistance through no fault of their parents. Dependent children should be handled outside the court system through other social agencies. Of course, provision in the court system must be made for the neglected child who must be taken from his parents and cared for due to abusive conduct of the parent, failure of the parent to provide for the child although able to do so, and those circumstances where parents are incarcerated, hospitalized, or otherwise unable to care for their children for protracted periods of time.

**The Commission recommends that jurisdiction over juveniles be placed in a family court which should be a division of a trial court of general jurisdiction. The family court should have jurisdiction over all legal matters related to family life, including delinquency, neglect, support, adoption, custody, paternity actions, divorce, annulment, and assaults involving family members. Dependent children—those needing help through no fault of their parents—should be handled outside the court system.**

### Reform of Court Procedures

*In re Gault*[12] clarified the constitutional rights of juveniles to due process. The juvenile can no longer be deprived of his basic rights by adherence to a *parens patriae*, "best interests of the child" doctrine.

Reform of court procedures, however, must not be limited to the areas identified in *Gault*. There is much, much more to be done in the juvenile justice system to minimize recidivism and control juvenile crime. Reforms are needed in the areas of intake proceedings, detention of juveniles, disposition of juveniles, and transfer of juveniles to the adult system when juvenile resources are exhausted.

### Intake, Detention, and Shelter Care

There are a number of studies which suggest that many children mature out of delinquent behavior. If this is true, the question is whether it is better to leave these persons alone or put them into the formal juvenile justice system. Because there are no satisfactory measures of the effectiveness of the juvenile justice system, there is a substantial body of opinion

[12] *In re Gault,* 387 U.S. 1 (1967).

which favors "leaving alone" all except those who have had three or four contacts with the police.

Each jurisdiction should consider this phenomenon, conduct studies among its juveniles charged with delinquent behavior, and establish intake criteria. Each court system should have an intake unit which should determine whether the juvenile should be referred to court. This intake unit should have available a wide variety of informal dispositions including referral to other agencies, informal probation, consent decrees, etc. In addition, this intake unit should have criteria for determining the use of detention or shelter care where formal petitions are filed with the court.

**The Commission recommends that each family court, in accord with written criteria, create an intake unit which should determine whether the juvenile should be referred to court or dealt with informally, and should determine whether the juvenile should be placed in detention or shelter care. In no event should a child be detained for more than 24 hours pending determination of the intake unit.**

### Transfer of Juveniles to Adult Court

There are some instances in which the juvenile process is not appropriate. These include instances where the juvenile has previously participated in the rehabilitative programs for juveniles; instances where the juvenile justice system has no suitable resources; and instances where the criminal sophistication of the juvenile precludes any benefit from the special juvenile programs.

It is the view of the Commission, however, that transfer of juveniles should be limited. The Supreme Court in *Kent* v. *United States*[13] has given direction on the procedures to be used and on the substantive issues to be resolved in any transfer to adult court. The procedures must meet due process standards.

**The Commission recommends that family courts have authority to order the transfer of certain juveniles for prosecution in the adult courts, but only if the juvenile is above a designated age, if a full and fair hearing has been held on the transfer, and if the action is in the best interest of the public.**

## Adjudication and Disposition

A juvenile charged with an act which, if committed by an

[13] *Kent* v. *U.S.*, 383 *U.S.* 541 (1966).

adult, would be a criminal offense is by law entitled to most of the procedures afforded adult criminal defendants. The juvenile is entitled to:

● Representation by counsel.
● The privilege against self-incrimination.
● Right to confront and cross-examine witnesses.
● Admission of only evidence which is competent and relevant.
● Proof of the acts alleged beyond a reasonable doubt.

There remains some question as to whether juveniles should be afforded jury trials. After consideration of *McKeiver* v. *Pennsylvania*[14] and the rationale therein, this Commission concludes that the State as a matter of policy should provide nonjury trials for juveniles. The theoretical protections of a jury trial are outweighed by the advantages of informality, fairness, and sympathy which the traditional juvenile court concept contemplates.

The Commission noted, however, that where the adjudication of delinquency is in a nonjudicial forum, provision must be made for separation of the adjudication and the disposition. The disposition hearing should be separate and distinct so that the determination of guilt will not be tainted by information that should be considered in making a decision on the appropriate rehabilitative program, including the past involvement of the juvenile with the criminal justice system.

**During adjudicatory hearings to determine guilt or innocence, the juvenile should have all of the rights of an adult criminal defendant except that of trial by jury.**

**The disposition hearing to determine a rehabilitative program for the juvenile should be separate and distinct from the adjudicatory hearing and should follow, where feasible, the procedure recommended for the sentencing of convicted adult offenders.**

# Conclusion

The criminal court system of a free nation should conform to the ideal of equal justice under law and should be typified by quality, efficiency, and fairness. These three words exemplify the standards proposed in the Commission's *Report on Courts*. Great emphasis is placed upon upgrading the quality of criminal court personnel and thereby improving the quality of justice dispensed. Efficiency in processing cases from

[14] *McKeiver* v. *Pennsylvania*, 403 U.S. 528 (1971).

arrest to trial to final appellate judgment is a prominent theme. But throughout the report appear standards safeguarding the rights of all persons, including witnesses, jurors, and defendants.

The Commission believes that persons committing infractions of the law should be speedily arrested, tried, afforded appellate review, and given meaningful sentences. If recidivism is to be reduced, these same persons must feel that they have been treated fairly, honestly, and impartially. The standards in the *Report on Courts* provide a mechanism for achieving both of these sets of goals.

# Excerpts from the Task Force Report on Courts

## A: Introduction

*The Role of Courts in the Criminal Justice System*

... It is the view of the Commission that limited use of the full trial procedure is not only inevitable but desirable. Not all cases present issues best solved by traditional full-scale litigation, and such litigation often involves costs to the public and the defendant—both in terms of financial outlay and emotional strain—that are best avoided if possible. The Commission also recognizes, however, that extensive use of informal processes creates a dual danger.

**Dangers**

First, public interest in the most efficient use of the criminal justice system to reduce crime may not be well served. The wastefulness and inefficiency of decisions may be obscured by informality and may become a pattern of an almost institutional nature. The informality of those procedures minimizes the likelihood that they will be scrutinized for efficiency and economy.

The second danger affects those processed by the system. Each person accused of a crime, whether guilty or not, has a legitimate interest in being treated fairly and, if guilty, in a manner most likely to permit his reintegration into the community as a law-abiding citizen, without sacrificing other objectives of the criminal justice system such as deterrence. The informality of many processes creates dangers to those interests as well as to those of the general public.

The Commission recognizes that those who criticize the informal administrative processing of criminal defendants do so primarily because the administrative procedure involves numerous discretionary decisions made by the various participants in the process, especially the prosecutor. It is this discretionary nature of administrative processing—and the actual or potential abuse of the power to make discretionary decisions—that needs attention.

**Two Approaches**

The Commission focused on two approaches to the problem. First, it agrees with Professor Kenneth Culp Davis that emphasis should be placed on minimizing the adverse effects of discretion by structuring the making of discretionary decisions.

One means of structuring is to raise the visibility of discretionary decisionmaking. Discretionary decisions involved in the administrative processing of criminal defendants are ones of low visibility—that is, they are seldom seen by observers of the system or, in many cases, by the participants themselves. As a result, it is difficult to determine what decisions are being made as well as why they are being made.

... Review could be limited here, as it is in other areas, to the determination of a reasonable basis for the decision; if a basis were found, the judge could not then find that another resolution would have been preferable. Even given the limited scope this review could take, the Commission feels that judicial review would be ineffective as a means of controlling administrative discretion. In some areas—such as the administrative discretionary decision to permit a defendant to plead guilty to a lesser charge—judges may rely on review. But generally, the Commission prefers to rely on structuring to avoid abuse of informal processing.

Recognizing that in most criminal cases judges and juries perform only the limited tasks described here does not depreciate the traditional notions of a criminal defendant's rights to a full and complete litigation of his case, with the burden upon the State to establish guilt. The standards assume that this option will always remain open to a defendant, and the Commission recognizes that fundamental principles of American jurisprudence rightfully demand this. Rather, the report asks for recognition that, in most cases, neither the prosecution nor the defense will want the court to perform this function. They will prefer to have, in effect, an administrative disposition. . . .

# B: The Flow of the Criminal Case

## 1: Screening

**Standard 1.1: Criteria for Screening**

The need to halt formal or informal action concerning some individuals who become involved in the criminal justice system should be openly recognized. This need may arise in a particular case because there is insufficient evidence to justify further proceedings or because—despite the availability of adequate evidence—further proceedings would not adequately further the interests of the criminal justice system.

An accused should be screened out of the criminal justice system if there is not a reasonable likelihood that the evidence admissible against him would be sufficient to obtain a conviction and sustain it on appeal. In screening on this basis, the prosecutor should consider the value of a conviction in reducing future offenses, as well as the probability of conviction and affirmance of that conviction on appeal.

An accused should be screened out of the criminal justice system when the benefits to be derived from prosecution or diversion would be outweighed by the costs of such action. Among the factors to be considered in making this determination are the following:

1. Any doubt as to the accused's guilt;
2. The impact of further proceedings upon the accused and those close to him, especially the likelihood and seriousness of financial hardship or family life disruption;
3. The value of further proceedings in preventing future offenses by other persons, considering the extent to which subjecting the accused to further proceedings could be expected to have an impact upon others who might commit such offenses, as well as the seriousness of those offenses;
4. The value of further proceedings in preventing future offenses by the offender, in light of the offender's commitment to criminal activity as a way of life; the seriousness of his past criminal activity, which he might reasonably be expected to continue; the possibility that further proceedings might have a tendency to create or reinforce commitment on the part of the accused to criminal activity as a way of life; and the likelihood that programs available as diversion or sentencing alternatives may reduce the likelihood of future criminal activity;
5. The value of further proceedings in fostering the com-

munity's sense of security and confidence in the criminal justice system;

6. The direct cost of prosecution, in terms of prosecutorial time, court time, and similar factors;

7. Any improper motives of the complainant;

8. Prolonged nonenforcement of the statute on which the charge is based;

9. The likelihood of prosecution and conviction of the offender by another jurisdiction; and

10. Any assistance rendered by the accused in apprehension or conviction of other offenders, in the prevention of offenses by others, in the reduction of the impact of offenses committed by himself or others upon the victims, and any other socially beneficial activity engaged in by the accused that might be encouraged in others by not prosecuting the offender.

... Subparagraph 5 suggests that in some cases formal proceedings might be justified because of their tendency to foster community confidence. It is arguable that reliance upon this as an independent factor constitutes unjustifiable concession to public ignorance. Under these circumstances, prosecution would be of value only where there is no objectively justifiable need for further proceedings, but where a significant segment of the community unreasonably believes such a need exists. Although it is clear that the criminal justice system should work to educate the community as to the reasonable expectations of the criminal sanction and diversionary programs, it is equally clear that in the interim the system often should not reject community demands, even where those demands are objectively unjustifiable. To maintain community confidence, the criminal justice system must respond to community demands. ...

Subparagraph 8 provides that prolonged nonenforcement of the statute on which the offense is based should be considered to favor screening. If nonenforcement has continued for a significant period there is a strong suggestion that the community no longer regards the activity defined by statute as a proper subject for criminal proceedings. Prosecutors and police must guard against the possibility that conviction will be sought for such conduct because of an unprovable belief that the defendant poses a danger to the community for other reasons. Irregular enforcement of a criminal statute creates the danger—or at least the appearance—of arbitrariness and must be avoided. In addition a person may have committed an offense on the assumption that nonenforcement of a statute meant that the community no longer regarded that activity as illegal. Prosecution may be unnecessary if the offender can be made to understand that the community does consider his activity inappropriate and agrees to comply with the law. . . .

## Standard 1.2: Procedure for Screening

Police in consultation with the prosecutor, should develop guidelines for the taking of persons into custody. Those guidelines should embody the factors set out in Standard 1.1. After a person has been taken into custody, the decision to proceed with formal prosecution should rest with the prosecutor.

No complaint should be filed or arrest warrant issued without the formal approval of the prosecutor. Where feasible, the decision whether to screen a case should be made before such approval is granted. Once a decision has been made to pursue formal proceedings, further consideration should be given to screening an accused as further information concerning the accused and the case becomes available. Final responsibility for making a screening decision should be placed specifically upon an experienced member of the prosecutor's staff.

The prosecutor's office should formulate written guidelines to be applied in screening that embody those factors set out in Standard 1.1. Where possible, such guidelines, as well as the guidelines promulgated by the police, should be more detailed. The guidelines should identify as specifically as possible those factors that will be considered in identifying cases in which the accused will not be taken into custody or in which formal proceedings will not be pursued. They should reflect local conditions and attitudes, and should be readily available to the public as well as to those charged with offenses, and to their lawyers. They should be subjected to periodic reevaluation by the police and by the prosecutor.

When a defendant is screened after being taken into custody, a written statement of the prosecutor's reasons should be prepared and kept on file in the prosecutor's office. Screening practices in a prosecutor's office should be reviewed periodically by the prosecutor himself to assure that the written guidelines are being followed.

The decision to continue formal proceedings should be a discretionary one on the part of the prosecutor and should not be subject to judicial review, except to the extent that pretrial procedures provide for judicial determination of the sufficiency of evidence to subject a defendant to trial. Alleged failure of the prosecutor to adhere to stated guidelines or general principles of screening should not be the basis for attack upon a criminal charge or conviction.

If the prosecutor screens a defendant, the police or the private complainant should have recourse to the court. If the court determines that the decision not to prosecute constituted an abuse of discretion, it should order the prosecutor to pursue formal proceedings.

. . . The decision to charge, to screen, or not to charge should, however, be made by the prosecutor or a member of his staff. Although a police officer should have the authority to arrest and book a person suspected of a serious offense without prior prosecutorial approval, the process should go no further than that without formal involvement of the prosecutor's office. . . .

The final paragraph of the standard deals with the allocation of the screening power between the prosecutor and the court—the matter of judicial review of the screening decision. Traditionally, judicial review has been minimal:

> (I)t is widely asserted that in performing his screening function—both in its evidence-sufficiency and discretionary aspects—the prosecutor is more aware of the unique facts which characterize particular cases, and that this general knowledge, coupled with his direct responsiveness to community attitudes, better qualifies him to assess both whether the suspect is probably guilty and convictable and in what manner it is in the public interest to proceed against him if he is.

This should remain the case.

Under the standards in this report an accused would retain his right to a judicial determination of whether adequate evidence is available to justify trial. To this extent, the Commission believes there should be a right to judicial review of the existence of sufficient evidence to charge. Except for this, there should be no judicial involvement in the decision not to screen. Despite the importance of the charging and screening process, judicial participation in this instance would be unworkable and is unnecessary. Given the necessarily subjective nature of the decision, inappropriate judicial interference with prosecutorial discretion would be a real danger. Chalenges—even if they ultimately prove nonmeritorious—to the exercise of his discretion might encourage a prosecutor to minimize the exercise of his discretion or at least to minimize its visibility. This would be directly contrary to the basic thrust of these standards.

## 2: Diversion

... Diversion uses the threat or possibility of conviction of a criminal offense to encourage an accused to agree to do something: he may agree to participate in a rehabilitation program designed to change his behavior, or he simply may agree to make restitution to the victim of the offense. This agreement may not be entirely voluntary, as the accused often agrees to participate in a diversion program only because he fears formal criminal prosecution. ...

Diversion also poses potential threats to the legitimate interests of those charged with criminal offenses. A defendant's decision to participate in a diversion program is voluntary in one sense of the word. But it is clearly not free of influences over which the law has control, and in this sense the decision is involuntary or coerced. Whatever the label attached to the decision, diversion programs involve a significant danger that the criminal justice system will cause unjustified participation in a burdensome program. An innocent individual, because of ignorance or other factors, may agree to participate in a diversion program, even though he does not have to because the prosecution cannot establish his guilt. The extent to which this occurs under existing diversion programs is unknown. Nevertheless, the possibility that it could occur requires that care be taken to minimize its likelihood. The possibility of unjustified diversion must be considered when determining the desirability of such programs.

### Standard 2.1: General Criteria for Diversion

In appropriate cases offenders should be diverted into noncriminal programs before formal trial or conviction.

Such diversion is appropriate where there is a substantial likelihood that conviction could be obtained and the benefits to society from channeling an offender into an available noncriminal diversion program outweigh any harm done to society by abandoning criminal prosecution. Among the factors that should be considered favorable to diversion are: (1) the relative youth of the offender; (2) the willingness of the victim to have no conviction sought; (3) any likelihood that the

365

offender suffers from a mental illness or psychological abnormality which was related to his crime and for which treatment is available; and (4) any likelihood that the crime was significantly related to any other condition or situation such as unemployment or family problems that would be subject to change by participation in a diversion program. . . .

*Delayed Diversion*

. . . 3. Drug Abuse. Given the wide disagreement regarding the appropriate response to drug-related offenses, general statements about diversion programs for such offenders are difficult to make. It is clear, however, that at least some of these offenders are dealt with best through noncriminal programs. At this point, the Commission recommends experimentation with programs limited to situations in which all of the following characteristics apply: (1) the offense does not involve violence to another person; (2) the offender is addicted to the use of drugs and the offense is related to this addiction, either by having beeen committed during drug intoxication or by being part of the offender's pattern of use of drugs (e.g., possession of drugs) or of obtaining drugs (e.g., concealment of drugs, theft of property to obtain money to purchase drugs, sale of drugs as a means of raising money to purchase drugs for own use); (3) the offender does not have a history of serious long-term criminal activity; (4) appropriate treatment programs are available; and (5) the treatment program has agreed to take the offender on a diversion basis. In many situations, the benefits of diversion will outweigh any decrease in the deterrent impact of seeking formal conviction.

4. Youthful offenders. The offender who is too old for juvenile court jurisdiction but too young to deserve the full impact of a criminal conviction has been an especially troublesome problem for the criminal justice system. It is in this area that diversion can provide an especially attractive middle ground. The effectiveness of efforts in this direction can be predicted to some extent on the basis of the results of Project Crossroads, the pilot project in Washington, D.C. Participation in this program was limited to individuals between the ages of 16 and 26 charged with misdemeanors and less serious felonies, who had no previous adult record, and who were either unemployed or whose jobs were in jeopardy as a result of the criminal charges against them. Each participant was given counseling and personal assistance, job training and placement, and remedial educational assistance. Although only 30 percent had been employed during 80 percent of the

12 months preceding participation in the project, more than 50 percent were employed for 80 percent of the year following participation. Moreover, their wages were substantially higher after participation than before.

Most important, the diversion programs apparently had a significant impact upon their criminality. (The recidivism figures are discussed in detail in the introduction to this chapter.) Such experience strongly suggests at least experimental use of diversion programs for relatively young offenders whose criminality is not part of an established lifestyle. Consideration must be given to the possibility that diversion programs have a strong deterrent effect while criminal conviction, by closing employment doors and causing other hardships, may increase the likelihood of future crimes.

5. Unemployed offenders. Many people do not consider the mere unemployment of the offender a mitigating factor. Yet, from a purely pragmatic point of view, the experience of the Vera Institute's Manhattan Court Employment Project suggests that unemployment be considered a major factor favoring diversion, and that specific programs be established for selected unemployed offenders.

**Standard 2.2: Develop guidelines for diversion decisions.**

## 3: The Negotiated Plea

### Danger to Defendant's Rights

Under some circumstances, plea negotiation raises the danger that innocent persons will be convicted of criminal offenses. Underlying many plea negotiations is the understanding —or threat—that if the defendant goes to trial and is convicted he will be dealt with more harshly than would be the case had he pleaded guilty. An innocent defendant might be persuaded that the harsher sentence he must face if he is unable to prove his innocence at trial means that it is to his best interests to plead guilty despite his innocence. If these persons have a realistic chance of being acquitted at trial, a plea negotiation system that encourages them to forfeit their right to trial endangers their right to an accurate and fair determination of guilt or innocence.

A recent survey of more than 3,400 criminal justice practitioners in four States—California, Michigan, New Jersey, and Texas—reveals the potential threat to defendant rights inherent in the plea negotiation process. Sixty-one percent of the survey respondents agreed that it was probable or somewhat probable that most defense attorneys "engage in plea bargaining primarily to expedite the movement of cases." Thirty-eight percent agreed that it was probable or somewhat probable that most defense attorneys in plea bargaining negotiations "pressure client[s] into entering a plea that [the] client feels is unsatisfactory." Included in the survey respondents were police officers, prosecution attorneys, defense attorneys, judges, probation officers, correctional officers, and parole officers.

Offenders, despite their guilt, have a right to access to leniency on the same basis as other defendants. Yet critics of the plea negotiation process argue that it tends to distribute unevenly and in appropriately among offenders the ability to get a "deal" that provides lenient disposition.

The plea bargaining process may place a premium on experience as a defendant, so that it can be expected to benefit older, more experienced defendants. Young defendants, or those with little past experience with the law, may go to trial or plead guilty without a realistic opportunity to gain the advantages that plea bargaining offers. The fact that bargains are sometimes made by a number of staff members also may mean that there will be uneven opportunity to gain advantage by pleading guilty. Thus, a defendant may be denied the opportunity for a particular bargain simply because his case happens to be prosecuted by one member of the prosecutor's staff rather than by another.

There is no information available on the extent to which the actual administration of plea negotiation results in conviction of the innocent or in improper distribution of leniency, if it does at all. Yet despite the lack of specific evidence, the Commission believes that the manner in which plea negotiation is conducted in many jurisdictions creates a significant danger that these interests will be violated.

## Standard 3.1: Abolition of Plea Negotiation

As soon as possible, but in no event later than 1978, negotiations between prosecutors and defendants—either personally or through their attorneys—concerning concessions to be made in return for guilty pleas should be prohibited. In the event that the prosecution makes a recommendation as to sentence, it should not be affected by the willingness of the defendant to plead guilty to some or all of the offenses with which he is charged. A plea of guilty should not be considered by the court in determining the sentence to be imposed.

Until plea negotiations are eliminated as recommended in this standard, such negotiations and the entry of pleas pursuant to the resulting agreements should be permitted only under a procedure embodying the safeguards contained in the remaining standards in this chapter.

. . . Basic to the Commission's position on plea negotiations is its conclusion that lack of resources should not affect the outcome of the processing of a criminal defendant and that it is not unrealistic to expect that the criminal justice system can and will be provided with adequate resources.

Moreover, it is unlikely that the increase in cases tried and the resulting burden upon the court system will be as great as apologists for plea negotiation assert. The Commission does not condemn entry of guilty pleas. It decries only the system by which these pleas are entered: they are the result of an agreement in which the prosecution makes some concessions.

Where there are no reasonably contestable issues in a case, litigation should not be encouraged. But there is no reason to believe that prosecutors are more enthusiastic about unnecessary litigation than are defense attorneys. Consequently, the Commission believes, if prosecutors and defense attorneys were convinced that plea bargaining would not occur, the charges filed by prosecutors would correspond more closely to what the prosecutor reasonably thinks he can and should get as a result. This is often not the case today. If the defendant and his attorney agree that this is the likely result—as the Commission believes will more often be the case than under existing practice—they can and should enter a plea of guilty. If they do not agree that this is the likely result, they can and should litigate the disagreement.

But eliminating plea bargaining will eliminate the incentive for prosecutors to overcharge or otherwise inappropriately charge. It in fact will encourage them to file formal charges that will provide a reasonable basis for a guilty plea. Elimination of plea bargaining is likely to create less of an increase in the number of trials than many believe. It is virtually certain, however, that it will increase the fairness and rationality of the processing of criminal defendants.

Moreover, the increase in the number of litigated cases need not be as expensive as some predict. In Chapter 4 of this Report, a number of recommendations are made for the elimination of costly aspects of criminal trials, including extensive examination of prospective jurors and the 12-person jury. If these standards are implemented, the cost of the increased number of trials is likely to be substantially reduced. . . .

Once the matter of resource insufficiency is surmounted, there is no legitimate function remaining that plea negotiation could serve. Advocates of the process assert that plea negotiations add flexibility to the criminal justice system and permit avoidance of unjustifiably harsh provisions of substantive law. To the extent that this might be true, it is arguable that plea negotiations minimize the likelihood that the unjustifiably harsh provisions of substantive law will be changed. Since many defendants will be able to avoid them by means of plea negotiations, the pressure to change is minimized. The victim, therefore, is the occasional defendant who, for whatever reason, is unable to make effective use of the plea negotiation system to avoid the harsh provisions of law.

But it is by no means clear that negotiation over plea is essential to performance of this function, if it is agreed that the function is a legitimate one. A prosecutor can accomplish the same result by care in his selection of initial charge. To the extent that greater flexibility is desired, it should be made available as a matter of formal law, either by changes in the definitions of substantive crimes or by a modification of dispositional alternatives available to sentencing courts. . . .

But where there are reasonably disputable issues, the law should not provide an incentive for a defendant to avoid a full and fair resolution of those issues in an adversary context. As is discussed below, it is in this situation where the plea negotiation process exacts one of its most important costs—it discourages efforts to assert legal rights that, if asserted, might be enforced. As to the value of negotiation to law enforcement, the elimination of plea negotiation need have little effect upon the exchange of leniency for information and assistance. Since the prosecutor can alter initial charge and sentence recommendations in return for law enforcement assistance, the elimination of plea negotiation will have little impact upon this situation. . . .

By imposing a penalty upon the exercise of procedural rights in those cases in which there is a reasonable likelihood that the rights will be vindicated, the plea negotiation system creates a significant danger to the innocent. Many of the rights it discourages are rights designed to prevent the conviction of innocent defendants. To the extent these rights are rendered nonoperative by the plea negotiation system, innocent defendants are endangered. Plea negotiation not only serves no legitimate function in the processing of criminal defendants, but it also encourages irrationality in the court process, burdens the exercise of individual rights, and endangers the right of innocent defendants to be acquitted. . . .

**Standard 3.2: Document in the court records the basis for a negotiated guilty plea and the reason for its acceptance.**

**Standard 3.3: Uniform Plea Negotiation Policies and Practices**

Each prosecutor's office should formulate a written statement of policies and practices governing all members of the staff in plea negotiations.

This written statement should provide for consideration of the following factors by prosecuting attorneys engaged in plea negotiations:

1. The impact that a formal trial would have on the offender and those close to him, especially the likelihood and seriousness of financial hardship and family disruption;

2. The role that a plea and negotiated agreement may play in rehabilitating the offender;

3. The value of a trial in fostering the community's sense of security and confidence in law enforcement agencies; and

4. The assistance rendered by the offender:

    a. in the apprehension or conviction of other offenders;

    b. in the prevention of crimes by others;

    c. in the reduction of the impact of the offense on the victim; or

    d. in any other socially beneficial activity.

The statement of policies should provide that weaknesses in the prosecution's case may not be considered in determining whether to permit a defendant to plead guilty to any offense other than that charged.

The statement of policies should be made available to the public.

The statement should direct that before finalizing any plea negotiations, a prosecutor's staff attorney should obtain full information on the offense and the offender. This should include information concerning the impact of the offense upon the victims, the impact of the offense (and of a plea of guilty to a crime less than the most serious that appropriately could be charged) upon the community, the amount of police resources expended in investigating the offense and apprehending the defendant, any relationship between the defendant and organized crime, and similar matters. This information should be considered by the attorney in deciding whether to enter into an agreement with the defendant.

The statement should be an internal, intraoffice standard only. Neither the statement of policies nor its applications should be subject to judicial review. The prosecutor's office should assign an experienced prosecutor to review negotiated pleas to insure that the guidelines are applied properly.

... The standard identifies only one factor the Commission believes ought not to be taken into account by the prosecutor in plea bargaining—any potential weakness in his case. Plea negotiation is properly used to arrive at outer limits that should be placed upon the trial court's sentencing discretion. It should not be used to avoid resolving disputed issues of fact or law. If a prosecutor entertains doubt as to his ability to convict, accepting a plea of guilty—even to an offense less serious than that charged—unjustifiably creates a danger that innocent individuals will be convicted through the negotiated plea process. For this reason, the Commission concluded that prosecutors should not consider actual or potential weaknesses in their cases.

**Standard 3.4: Establish a time limit after which plea negotiations may no longer be conducted.**

**Standard 3.5: Provide service of counsel before plea negotiations.**

**Standard 3.6: Prohibited Prosecutorial Inducements to Enter a Plea of Guilty**

No prosecutor should, in connection with plea negotiations, engage in, perform, or condone any of the following:

**1.** Charging or threatening to charge the defendant with offenses for which the admissible evidence available to the prosecutor is insufficient to support a guilty verdict.

**2.** Charging or threatening to charge the defendant with a crime not ordinarily charged in the jurisdiction for the conduct allegedly engaged in by him.

**3.** Threatening the defendant that if he pleads not guilty, his sentence may be more severe than that which ordinarily is imposed in the jurisdiction in similar cases on defendants who plead not guilty.

**4.** Failing to grant full disclosure before the disposition negotiations of all exculpatory evidence material to guilt or punishment.

**Standard 3.7: Acceptability of a Negotiated Guilty Plea**

The court should not participate in plea negotiations. It should, however, inquire as to the existence of any agreement whenever a plea of guilty is offered and carefully review any negotiated plea agreement underlying an offered guilty plea. It should make specific determinations relating to the acceptability of a plea before accepting it.

Before accepting a plea of guilty, the court should require the defendant to make a detailed statement concerning the commission of the offense to which he is pleading guilty and any offenses of which he has been convicted previously. In the event that the plea is not accepted, this statement and any evidence obtained through use of it should not be admissible against the defendant in any subsequent criminal prosecution.

The review of the guilty plea and its underlying negotiated agreement should be comprehensive. If any of the following circumstances is found and cannot be corrected by the court, the court should not accept the plea:

1. Counsel was not present during the plea negotiations but should have been;

2. The defendant is not competent or does not understand the nature of the charges and proceedings against him;

3. The defendant was reasonably mistaken or ignorant as to the law or facts related to his case and this affected his decision to enter into the agreement;

4. The defendant does not know his constitutional rights and how the guilty plea will affect those rights; rights that expressly should be waived upon the entry of a guilty plea include:

    a. Right to the privilege against compulsory self-incrimination (which includes the right to plead not guilty);

    b. Right to trial in which the government must prove the defendant's guilt beyond a reasonable doubt;

    c. Right to a jury trial;

    d. Right to confrontation of one's accusers;

    e. Right to compulsory process to obtain favorable witnesses; and

    f. Right to effective assistance of counsel at trial.

5. During plea negotiations the defendant was denied a constitutional or significant substantive right that he did not waive;

6. The defendant did not know at the time he entered into the agreement the mandatory minimum sentence, if any, and the maximum sentence that may be imposed for the offense to which he pleads, or the defendant was not aware of these facts at the time the plea was offered;

7. The defendant has been offered improper inducements to enter the guilty plea;

8. The admissible evidence is insufficient to support a guilty verdict on the offense for which the plea is offered, or a related greater offense;

9. The defendant continues to assert facts that, if true, establish that he is not guilty of the offense to which he seeks to plead; and

10. Accepting the plea would not serve the public interest. Acceptance of a plea of guilty would not serve the public interest if it:

    a. places the safety of persons or valuable property in unreasonable jeopardy;

    b. depreciates the seriousness of the defendant's activity or otherwise promotes disrespect for the criminal justice system;

    c. gives inadequate weight to the defendant's rehabilitative needs; or

    d. would result in conviction for an offense out of proportion to the seriousness with which the community would evaluate the defendant's conduct upon which the charge is based.

A representative of the police department should be present at the time a guilty plea is offered.

. . . The Commission disapproves of the result in *McMann v. Richardson*, in which the Court found no fatal defect in a guilty plea that had been entered on the erroneous advice of the defendant's attorney to the effect that a confession obtained from the defendant would be admissible at trial.

. . . In *North Carolina* v. *Alford*, the Supreme Court held that there was no constitutional deficiency in the plea of a defendant who asserted his innocence when offering the plea. In 1968, the American Bar Association Standards took the position that there need only be a "factual basis" for the plea. But the commentary suggests that this meant only that the trial judge was not required to demand "an unequivocal confession of guilt." If a defendant specifically denied commission of the offense, "then, notwithstanding the existence of other information tending to verify the accuracy of the plea, it would be inappropriate for the judge to enter judgment on the plea."

In 1972, after *Alford*, the Council of the American Law Institute recommended authorizing acceptance of the plea "even though the defendant does not admit that he is in fact guilty if the court finds that it is reasonable for someone in the defendant's position to plead guilty."

The Commission's position is stronger than that of the American Bar Association. This standard requires that the defendant make a detailed statement concerning the commission of the offense. If this statement does not contain an admission of facts consistent with guilt of the offense to which he is offering a plea, or if it contains assertions of facts inconsistent with guilt, the trial judge should refuse to accept the plea. Acceptance of a plea from a defendant unable or unwilling to recount facts establishing guilt creates an unacceptable risk that those who are guilty will be convicted through the guilty-plea process.

In addition, accepting such a plea tends to bring the entire system into disrepute. The implementation of this standard may mean that some defendants who are innocent but nevertheless convicted may be deprived of the opportunity to use the plea negotiation process to minimize the impact of conviction. But the Commission believes that this factor is outweighed by the dangers of innocent defendants being convicted and the criminal justice system being disparaged.

This position is contrary to that of the Commission's Courts Task Force, which recommended that guilty pleas be accepted from defendants who cannot or will not make a statement establishing guilt, or who assert their innocence. The Task Force believed that the requirements of voluntariness and intelligence, implemented by the procedure provided in the standards, and the necessity of showing a factual basis for the plea adequately protected against the conviction of innocent defendants. . . .

Consistent with the Commission's Police Report, the standard recommends that a representative of the police department be present at the time the plea is offered. This also is designed to maximize the information available to the judge for use in deciding whether to accept the plea and in sentencing. It is contemplated that the police representative could, where appropriate, be called upon to state his reaction to a proposed plea and to explain why the police department may oppose it. . . .

**Standard 3.8: Effect of the Method of Disposition on Sentencing**

**The fact that a defendant has entered a plea of guilty to the charge or to a lesser offense than that initially charged should not be considered in determining sentence.**

The decision to plead guilty often is a tactical one, made with a view towards minimizing the impact of what is seen as inevitable conviction. Although such pleas assist the criminal justice system, they have no direct relevance to the appropriate disposition of an offender. In some cases, the plea may reflect contrition or some other attitude that would justify a lesser sentence than would otherwise be the case. But in such situations, it is certain that there will be other indications of that attitude, and reliance need not be placed upon the willingness to enter a guilty plea. Consequently, the Commission recommends that guilty pleas be given no consideration in sentencing.

The standard is somewhat inconsistent with the analogous American Bar Association standards. Standard 1.8(b) of those standards relating to guilty pleas provides that no sentence "in excess of that which would be justified by any of the rehabilitative, protective, deterrent, or other purposes of the criminal law" should be imposed because the defendant has declined to plead guilty. But the standard also takes the position that "charge and sentence concessions" may be granted to defendants who enter a plea of guilty "when the interests of the public in the effective administration of criminal justice would thereby be served."

Among the considerations expressly listed by the American Bar Association standard as appropriate in considering whether this interest would be served is "that the defendant by his plea has aided in avoiding delay (including delay due to crowded dockets) in the disposition of other cases and thereby has increased the probability of prompt and certain application of correctional measures to other offenders."

Thus the American Bar Association standard would permit sentencing concessions to be offered to a defendant in return simply for a plea of guilty on the basis that the speed and efficiency that is facilitated by the plea aids society in dealing effectively with other offenders.

The Commission feels that to permit such concessions would provide too great an incentive for an innocent defendant to waive his opportunity to avoid conviction at trial, and this standard would not permit a defendant's willingness to speed up the court process by pleading guilty to be considered in imposing sentence.

## 4: The Litigated Case

**Standard 4.1: Assure that the period from arrest to trial**

does not exceed 60 days in felonies and 30 days in misdemeanors.

## Standard 4.2: Citation and Summons in Lieu of Arrest

Upon the apprehension, or following the charging, of a person for a misdemeanor or certain less serious felonies, citation or summons should be used in lieu of taking the person into custody.

All law enforcement officers should be authorized to issue a citation in lieu of continued custody following a lawful arrest for such offenses. All judicial officers should be given authority to issue a summons rather than an arrest warrant in all cases alleging these offenses in which a complaint, information or indictment is filed or returned against a person not already in custody. . . .

. . . Under the procedure outlined in this standard, a considerable savings in time and manpower occurs. In those cases where an officer makes an arrest for a misdemeanor or a less-serious felony, the officer, after ascertaining through the police dispatcher and information system that the offender meets the necessary criteria, serves the alleged offender with a citation and releases him from custody. In many jurisdictions, this will require a broadening of an officer's authority to cite and release persons after making a legal arrest. . . .

Implementation of the standard would avoid many of the undesirable effects on a defendant. There is no need to arrange for pretrial release; defendants sometimes are severely affected by the short period of custody that occurs between arrest and pretrial release. If the defendant was arrested in a motor vehicle, the vehicle may have been towed—at the defendant's expense—to a place of safekeeping. Parents taken into custody may have no opportunity to arrange for care of their children to minimize the effect of the situation upon the children. Taking a defendant from his job, even for a short period of time, may result in inconvenience to his employer or coworkers or in damage to material under his control. All of these situations could be avoided by use of citation.

Summons or citation in lieu of arrest can and should be used in the majority of misdemeanor and minor felony cases where the defendants are known, have local connections or family ties, and normally could be expected to appear for trial. Evidence indicates that failure to appear is unlikely to be a significant problem if care is taken in issuing citations or summons. A study of the use of citations in New Haven, Conn., for example, disclosed that only 14.5 percent of defendants in nontraffic cases failed to appear on the designated date; half of these responded to a simple letter requesting them to appear. . . .

The American Bar Association Standards on Pretrial Release have treated the subject of this standard in detail. In general, this standard is in agreement. The American Bar Association Standards, however, require arresting officers to file a written report in those cases where a citation is not used. Such a requirement is intended to encourage officers to exercise their authority to issue citations in lieu of arrest. However, the time required and paperwork generated by filing a written report in every arrest situation could be a substantial burden upon the officers and the criminal justice system. The Commission recommends that further study and consideration be given to this proposal.

**Standard 4.3: Eliminate preliminary hearings in misdemeanor proceedings.**

**Standard 4.4: Limitation of Grand Jury Functions**

Grand jury indictment should not be required in any criminal prosecution. If an existing requirement of indictment cannot be removed immediately, provision should be made for the waiver of indictment by the accused. Prosecutors should develop procedures that encourage and facilitate such waivers. If a grand jury indictment is issued in a particular case, no preliminary hearing should be held in that case. In such cases, the prosecutor should disclose to the defense all testimony before the grand jury directly relating to the charges contained in the indictment returned against the defendant.

The grand jury should remain available for investigation and charging in exceptional cases.

. . . Empaneling and servicing a grand jury is costly in terms of space, manpower, and money. The members must be selected, notified, sworn, housed, fed, and provided with a multitude of services. It is unlikely that the grand jury is effective as a buffer between the State and a person suspected of a criminal offense. The presentation of evidence is under prosecutorial control and the grand jury merely agrees to the actions of the prosecutor. In Baltimore, Md., for example, the grand jury returned indictments in 98.18 percent of those cases presented to it in 1969, but 42 percent of those indictments were dismissed before trial. A court management study of the Baltimore courts concluded:

"The Grand Jury, which indicts almost all cases presented

to it, has a negligible effect—other than delay—on the criminal process. It seems most reasonable to avoid using the Grand Jury except in cases where a community voice is needed in a troublesome or notorious case."

In most cities where the grand jury is used it eliminates fewer than 20 percent of the cases it receives. In Cleveland, Ohio, the figure is 7 percent; in the District of Columbia, 20 percent; and in Philadelphia, Pa., 2 to 3 percent.

The Special Committee on Crime Prevention and Control concluded that the preliminary hearing was a more effective screen for unfounded prosecutions based on a finding of a lack of probable cause than was the grand jury. According to a 1967 Chicago court study, tlhe preliminary hearing eliminated almost 90 percent of felony cases, while the grand jury eliminated few cases referred to it after a preliminary hearing. . . .

In short, any benefits to be derived from a requirement that all offenses be charged by grand jury indictment are, in the Commission's view, outweighed by the probability that the indictment process will be ineffective as a screening device, by the cost of the proceeding, and by the procedural intricacies involved. The standard therefore recommends that grand jury indictment not be required for initiation of any criminal proceeding.

The Commission recognizes that in many jurisdictions it may require a considerable length of time to eliminate statutory or constitutional requirements of a mandatory grand jury indictment in each criminal case. In such jurisdictions, where it is not already authorized by law, legislation should be enacted that would allow defendants to waive the indictment process. Defendants desiring to plead guilty to criminal charges, or to proceed immediately to trial should be able to without grand jury action.

The standard recommends that if, for any reason, the grand jury indictment process is used, no preliminary hearing be made available. Both the grand jury and the preliminary hearing determine the existence of probable cause to believe the defendant has committed the offense charged, and therefore using both is unnecessary. The Commission recognizes that preliminary hearings may serve a discovery function that grand jury proceedings do not. Consequently, to avoid unfairness to the defendant who has been the subject of indictment, the standard calls for the prosecutor to make available the information that would have been revealed at a preliminary hearing, had one been held.

Despite its views concerning the indictment process, the Commission does believe that the grand jury has a valuable role in the criminal justice process and should not be eliminated entirely. The investigatory powers of the grand jury could be used to reduce crime more effectively than they are today. The grand jury can perform an important role in the investigation and accusation that leads to the prosecution of crime, a role not satisfactorily filled by the prosecutor-information system in some serious, doubtful, or politically sensitive cases.

Standard 12.8 recommends that prosecutors be given power to compel the appearance of witnesses for interrogation. If implemented, this would eliminate one of the major values of the grand jury under present conditions—a source of authority for legally compelling a person to submit to interrogation under oath.

But in some circumstances, especially in areas of widespread public concern, it would be desirable to have grand jury participation in the investigatory function. Allegations of corruption by public figures, for example, should be investigated by someone outside of the administration to preserve the image of impartiality in the investigation and to avoid charges of coverup or whitewash when no incriminating evidence surfaces.

## Standard 4.5: Presentation Before Judicial Officer Following Arrest

When a defendant has been arrested and a citation has not been issued, the defendant should be presented before a judicial officer within 6 hours of the arrest. At this appearance, the defendant should be advised orally and in writing of the charges against him, of his constitutional rights (including the right to bail and to assistance of counsel), and of the date of his trial or preliminary hearing. If the defendant is entitled to publicly provided representation, arrangements should be made at this time. If it is determined that pretrial release is appropriate, the defendant should then be released.

At the initial appearance, the judicial officer should have the authority, upon showing of justification, to remand the defendant to police custody for custodial investigation. Such remands should be limited in duration and purpose, and care should be taken to preserve the defendant's rights during such custodial investigation.

Much of the opposition to prompt presentation before a judicial officer has come from those who assert that such action eliminates any opportunity for in-custody investigation. At the initial appearance the defendant is generally entitled to bail or some other form of pretrial release; once released, he is not subject to custodial investigatorial procedures. Police—or the prosecutor—may want to interrogate the defendant, have him appear in a line-up, have him provide samples of his handwriting, voice, or hair, subject him to a physical examination, or perform various other procedures that require the physical presence of the defendant. Release by the judicial officer makes use of these procedures impossible.

The standard meets this objection to prompt presentation by recommending that the judicial officer be authorized to order the defendant retained in custody for investigation in appropriate cases. The standard deals only with custodial investigation following the initial appearance of the defendant before a judicial officer. The extent to which similar procedures may be performed during custody before initial presentation is a further and complex issue, but it is one that is beyond the scope of this Report. The Report is limited to custodial investigation after the time the defendant enters the court process.

Under existing law, the right of police to detain a suspect for investigation without presentation before a judicial officer is reasonable when it is for the purpose of conducting custodial investigation. Courts have differed on this.

Statutes in several States currently authorize a judicial officer before whom a defendant is presented to remand the defendant to police custody for a limited period.

2. Further in-custody investigation should be permitted by the judicial officer only upon an adequate showing that further custody is necessary to the investigation and that the investigation is likely to be effective. . . .

There is some indication in the case law that when the police or prosecution seek to conduct an in-custody investigation involving an infringement of the subject's privacy, there must be at least some evidence—in addition to probable cause to believe him guilty of the crime—that the investigation would result in evidence of value in the prosecution. In *United States* v. *Bailey,* the court declined to order defendants to give handwriting exemplars where there was no evidence other than a grand jury indictment for conspiracy that the exemplars would be of value in the investigation or trial. And in *United States* v. *Allen,* the court declined to order defendants to submit to the taking of hair samples, blood tests, and X-rays, since there has been no showing that the results of the procedures would be of value to the police or prosecution.

Where the police or prosecution seek to have the defendant retained in custody for investigation, the Commission believes that the existing fourth amendment approach described above should be applied. Such detention and the investigation the police want to conduct should be permitted only upon a showing of evidence tending to establish (a) that the defendant is guilty of the offense, and (b) that the procedure will result in information of value in the investigation or in the proof of the defendant's guilt. The Commission is not prepared to recommend what the standard of proof should be; but no detention should be permitted without some proof of the reasonableness of continued detention for the specific purpose authorized.

The judicial officer also should be satisfied that continued custody is essential to the investigation for which custody is requested. It may be feasible to release the defendant but require him to return briefly at a later point in the procedure. If it appears that this alternative would reduce the amount of time a defendant would be detained or would reduce the inconvenience of the detention, the less burdensome course should be taken. . . .

It seems clear that detentions for investigation remain reasonable under the fourth amendment and do not constitute an unreasonable infringement of the right to bail only if they are limited to that detention essential to the investigation for which they were authorized. This is sound policy as well as good current law. The period of detention should be limited if preparation for the procedure will require some time; continued detention should be authorized only if there is some basis for believing that it is not feasible to release the defendant and compel his appearance at some later time.

The purpose of the detention also should be limited. If, for example, detention for purposes of fingerprinting is authorized, police officers should not be permitted to place the defendant in a lineup or to question him during that detention. To permit unlimited use of detention obtained upon specified grounds would be too great an encouragement of abuse of the process.

4. If interrogation is authorized during detention, special precautions should be taken to assure preservation of the privilege against compelled self-incrimination.

382

Where custody of a defendant is sought for interrogation purposes, the situation is sufficiently unique to justify special attention. Causing an individual to say things that will be used to convict him of a crime traditionally has been viewed with distaste in Anglo-American legal history.

In part, interrogation presents special opportunities for abuse. Because of the nature of a blood test, there is no motive for extensive coercion to compel the subject to surrender blood with the characteristics desired by the investigator; but because a subject has control over his statements, interrogation may create a motive to persuade the subject improperly. In addition, sensitivity concerning interrogation rests upon the view that it is inconsistent with even guilty persons' basic dignity to compel them to participate in their own criminal conviction. These policies have been embodied in the fifth amendment to the United States Constitution, which provides that "no person ... shall be compelled in any criminal case to be a witness against himself." Similar provisions exist in the constitutions of all but two States, and the substance of the provision is accepted in those States as a matter of case law. The provision in the fifth amendment was held to apply to the States as well as the Federal Government in *Malloy* v. *Hogan*. ...

The Court [in *Miranda* v. *Arizona*] suggested—but did not expressly hold—that if an attorney was provided, custodial interrogation was not improper and a statement obtained during such interrogation would be admissible. But in most jurisdictions, the circumstances under which such interrogation may be carried out—if it may at all—remains undefined. The Commission believes this gap should be closed.

The Commission's Courts Task Force entertained significant doubt that custodial interrogation following initial presentation was consistent with current constitutional law or desirable on general policy grounds. But the Commission has concluded that granting judicial officers the authority to remand for interrogation in some cases is not only desirable but defensible under existing interpretations of the relevant constitutional provisions.

Long before the *Miranda* decision, some critics urged that police interrogation be prohibited and instead that police be required to present an arrested person before a judicial officer who would either interrogate the suspect himself or supervise the interrogation. This suggestion was made again shortly before the *Miranda* decision by a leading Illinois State jurist. Such a procedure might provide maximum protection against abuses of the interrogation power. It is even arguable—although by no means clear—that under existing law the supervision of a judicial officer might be an adequate substitute for the right to an attorney established in *Miranda*.

The Commission believes, however, that reliance should continue to be placed upon the right to an attorney during custodial interrogation as a means of avoiding abuse of the interrogation process. Only an attorney, with his loyalty to his client, can provide adequate assurance that the subject's interests will be well served. If this right is respected, the presence of the judicial officer seems unnecessary to the preservation of the subject's underlying rights.

When custody of a defendant is sought for purposes of interrogation, the judicial officer before whom the defendant is presented should, upon an adequate showing, authorize continued—but limited—detention for such interrogation. Such custody should be authorized only upon a showing that there is sufficient basis to believe that it will be successful (that is, sufficient basis to believe that proper custodial interrogation will result in the defendant making statements of value in the investigation or in the conviction of the defendant). The judicial officer also should see that the right to counsel as established in *Miranda* is respected. This requires insuring that the defendant is aware of his right to remain silent and his right to the presence of an attorney—provided by the government, if necessary—and that either an attorney is provided or that the defendant freely waives the right to an attorney with adequate understanding of the significance of that decision.

The Council of the American Law Institute read *Miranda* as permitting custodial interrogation even in the presence of the defendant's attorney only with the consent of the defendant. The Commission, however, does not read existing law to bar custodial interrogation without the consent of the subject, if the right to counsel is respected and adequate steps are taken to avoid abuse of the process. Insofar as existing law might not authorize this, the Commission urges that it be changed. ...

**Standard 4.6: Eliminate private bail bond agencies; utilize a wide range of pretrial release programs, including release on recognizance.**

**Standard 4.7: Nonappearance After Pretrial Release**
Substantive law should deal severely with offenders who fail to appear for criminal proceedings. Programs for the ap-

prehension and prosecution of such individuals should be established to implement the substantive law. . . .

. . . One possible approach would be to provide for the proceeding to continue in the absence of the defendant. In its extreme, this would result in the trial of a defendant in absentia if he did not appear on his trial date. This not only would avoid the scheduling problems created by postponing the trial, but also would avoid the inevitable weakening of the prosecution's case that accompanies delay. There is some indication that even trials in absentia could be conducted within the existing constitutional framework. But such trials are offensive to notions of fairness, and the Commission believes they should be avoided if possible.

The standard substitutes for trial in absentia a proposal that failure to appear be made an independent offense for which the defendant could be tried. If the penalties are made commensurate with that assigned to the crime with which the defendant had been charged, the prosecution would be under no disadvantage if, upon apprehension of the defendant, it chose to prosecute for failing to appear rather than for the offense initially charged. Moreover, since failing to appear would not require proof of the offense charged, the prosecution would not be harmed by the extent to which its initial case may have aged. . . .

**Standard 4.8: Hold preliminary hearings within 2 weeks after arrest; eliminate formal arraignment.**

**Standard 4.9: Pretrial Discovery**
The prosecution should disclose to the defendant all available evidence that will be used against him at trial. Such disclosure should take place within 5 days of the preliminary hearing, of the waiver of the preliminary hearing, or apprehension or service of summons following indictment, whichever form the initiation of prosecution takes in the particular case. The evidence disclosed should include, but should not be limited to, the following:

1. The names and addresses of persons whom the prosecutor intends to call as witnesses at the trial;

2. Written, recorded, or oral statements made by witnesses whom the prosecutor intends to call at the trial, by the accused, or by any codefendant;

3. Results of physical or mental examinations, scientific tests, and any analyses of physical evidence, and any reports

or statements of experts relating to such examinations, tests, or analyses; and

4. Physical evidence belonging to the defendant or which the prosecutor intends to introduce at trial.

The prosecutor should disclose, as soon as possible, any evidence within this description that becomes available after initial disclosure.

The prosecutor also should disclose any evidence or information that might reasonably be regarded as potentially valuable to the defense, even if such disclosure is not otherwise required.

The defendant should disclose any evidence defense counsel intends to introduce at trial. Intent to rely on an alibi or an insanity defense should be indicated. Such disclosure should take place immediately following the resolution of pretrial motions or, in the event no such motions are filed, within 20 days of the preliminary hearing, the waiver of the preliminary hearing, or apprehension or service of summons following indictment, or whichever form the initiation of prosecution has taken in the case. No disclosure need be made, however, of any statement of the defendant or of whether the defendant himself will testify at trial.

The trial court may authorize either side to withhold evidence sought if the other side establishes in an ex parte proceeding that a substantial risk of physical harm to the witness or others would be created by the disclosure and that there is no feasible way to eliminate such a risk.

Evidence, other than the defendant's testimony, that has not been disclosed to the opposing side may be excluded at trial unless the trial judge finds that the failure to disclose it was justifiable. The desire to maximize the tactical advantage of either the defendant or the prosecution should not be regarded as justification under any circumstances. Where appropriate, a person failing to disclose evidence that should be disclosed should be held in contempt of court.

... The standard is broader than many current proposals insofar as it calls for almost complete pretrial disclosure by the prosecutor. Only work products such as investigatory reports and evidence not intended to be introduced at trial generally are exempted, and these are exempted only if they would not be exculpatory or lead to exculpatory evidence. The standard does provide for either side to assert and establish that revealing the identity of a witness would endanger the witness, his family, or some other persons. If the danger can be averted without denying disclosure, such action should be taken. Thus the trial court might limit the manner in which the party would examine the evidence or it might put parties or attorneys under court order not to disclose certain information to others. (It is likely that an exception also should be made for those situations in which disclosure would endanger the national security, but as this is largely a problem of Federal criminal prosecutions, the Commission did not believe that it should be incorporated into a standard intended to be applied generally.) . . .

The standard departs most significantly from other proposals insofar as it provides for extensive discovery by the defendant. The primary danger in requiring disclosure by the defendant is that it violates the principle that a defendant not be required to participate in his own conviction. To some extent this has been embodied in the privilege against compelled self-incrimination; under the fifth amendment to the Federal Constitution, a defendant cannot be compelled, directly or indirectly, to give testimonial evidence against himself. The Commission realizes that potential constitutional as well as policy problems are raised by this standard. But it believes that where such discovery is limited and is a part of an overall procedure that provides for extensive protection for defendants, it is desirable as a policy matter and is compatible with the fifth amendment.

In *Williams* v. *Florida*, the U.S. Supreme Court held that the fifth amendment was not violated by a requirement that a defendant disclose prior to trial his intent to rely upon an alibi at trial. The Court reasoned that this did not require the defendant to say or testify to anything he would not otherwise say or testify to; it merely determined the time at which he would have to assert the matter. The fifth amendment did not, the Court concluded, protect the right to assert an alibi only at the point at which it had maximum tactical advantage i.e., at trial when the prosecutor's opportunity to counter it was minimized.

The Commission believes this approach should be the touchstone of disclosure by the defendant. Generally, a defendant should not be required to reveal in advance of trial anything that he will not reveal at trial; but he should not have the opportunity to take advantage of surprise by revealing his evidence only at a point at which the prosecution's ability to test its accuracy is minimized. If the defense entertains real doubt as to whether certain evidence should be introduced until the middle of a trial, the failure to disclose it would be justifiable within the meaning of the final paragraph of the standard and the failure to disclose it earlier would not bar its admission at trial. . . .

**Standard 4.10: File all motions within 15 days after preliminary hearing or indictment; hear motions within 5 days.**

This standard requires that judges conducting motion hearings utilize a checklist of motions to insure that all proper matters and issues are raised. This is crucial for two reasons. First, it is imperative to effective protection of the rights of the defendant that issues be raised early in the proceeding. The combination of the expanded use of assigned counsel and the expansion and proliferation of criminal law pose a real danger to the rights of the defendant.

It is difficult for an attorney specializing in criminal law to stay abreast of current developments and decisions. It is impossible for a general practitioner, or specialist in another field, to gain the expertise necessary to conduct a first-rate defense without intensive study and assistance from the bench in protecting the rights of the defendant. Motions to set aside indictments or informations, to challenge pleadings, to challenge venue and jurisdiction, to attack impaneling of grand or petit juries, to reduce bail, to sever defendants or offenses, in addition to motions addressed to the suppression of admissibility of evidence, are all potentially vital to a defendant's case. A checklist would insure that the defense counsel considered every possibility.

Such a checklist would protect the record for review. The court of review will have a transcript establishing that all issues have been raised and considered by the trial court. This should serve to reduce greatly the number of collateral attacks following adjudication and bring finality to criminal proceedings.

**Standard 4.11: Establish criteria for assigning cases to the trial docket.**

**Standard 4.12: Limit granting of continuances.**

**Standard 4.13: Jury Selection**

Questioning of prospective jurors should be conducted exclusively by the trial judge. His examination should cover all matters relevant to their qualification to sit as jurors in the case on trial. Attorneys for the prosecution and defense should be permitted to submit questions to the judge to be asked of the jurors concerning matters not covered by the judge in his examination. The judge should put such questions to the jurors unless they are irrelevant, repetitive, or beyond the scope of proper juror examination.

The number of peremptory challenges should correspond to the size of the jury and should be limited to multiple defendant cases. The prosecution should be entitled to the number of challenges equal to the total number to which the defendants are entitled.

### Standard 4.14: Jury Size and Composition

Juries in criminal prosecutions for offenses not punishable by life imprisonment should be composed of less than 12 but of at least six persons. If a 12-member jury has been seated, a reduction in jury size during the course of a trial to not less than 10 members should be permitted where a jury member has died or is discharged for illness or other good cause. Corresponding decreases in size should be permitted in cases where there were less than 12 jurors initially, but no decrease should be permitted that will result in a jury of less than six persons.

Persons 18 years of age and older should not be disqualified from jury service on the basis of age.

The 12-person jury requirement for criminal trials that exists in most jurisdictions is an accident of history. Experience suggests that juries of less than 12 can provide a reliable and competent factfinding body. As suggested by the Supreme Court in *Williams* v. *Florida,* the touchstone should be whether the group is "large enough to promote group deliberation, free from outside attempts at intimidation, and to provide a fair possibility for obtaining a representative crosssection of the community." States such as Utah and Florida have used criminal juries of less than 12, and in *Williams* v. *Florida,* the Supreme Court held that Florida's use of a sixperson jury did not violate the defendants' sixth and 14th amendment rights to trial by jury.

### Standard 4.15: Trial of Criminal Cases

In every court where trials of criminal cases are being conducted, daily sessions should commence promptly at 9 a.m. and continue until 5 p.m. unless business before the court is concluded at an earlier time and it is too late in the day to begin another trial. Jury selection in the next case should start as soon as the jury in the preceding case has retired to consider a verdict.

All criminal trials should conform to the following:

1. **Opening statements** to the jury by counsel should be limited to a clear, nonargumentative statement of the evidence to be presented to the jury.

2. **Evidence admitted** should be strictly limited to that which is directly relevant and material to the issues being litigated. Repetition should be avoided.

3. **Summations or closing statements** by counsel should be limited to the issues raised by evidence submitted during trial and should be subject to time limits established by the judge.

4. **Standardized instructions** should be utilized in all criminal trials as far as is practicable. Requests by counsel for specific instructions should be made at, or before, commencement of the trial. Final assembling of instructions should be completed by support personnel under the court's direction prior to the completion of the presentation of the evidence.

. . . Many attorneys determine, in advance, the number of witnesses they plan to call on a certain day. Due to the uncertainties of trial procedure and the inability to calculate accurately the time required for direct and cross-examination, this is a hazardous procedure. It is not uncommon for an attorney to put on the witness that he has available and then, if it is earlier than normal court closing hours, move to adjourn until the following morning. Court is sometimes adjourned at 2 p.m. This practice is encouraged by those judges who routinely grant such requests. A much better practice would be to require the attorney to call his next witness or rest his case. Attorneys soon would learn to have all witnesses available or on call so they could testify without delaying the proceedings. . . .

In the days of Clarence Darrow and William Jennings Bryan, it was common for attorneys to take days to deliver a closing argument. Crowds would gather to watch and hear the great orators at work. However, today such orations are made at the expense of defendants awaiting trial and of the public interested in seeing criminal justice rendered promptly. Since summation is not a part of the evidence and the jury is so instructed, it is inappropriate for court time to be wasted by attorneys expounding their views on unimpeachable truisms and the various ills plaguing society.

At the close of the evidence, court and counsel should agree upon the amount of time to be allotted for summations. The prosecution and defense should have equal time in a single defendant case and the prosecution should have more time than any single defendant in a multidefendant case.

**Recommendation 4.1: Study of the Exclusionary Rule**
Use of the exclusionary rule as a means of attempting to compel compliance by police and others with judicially promulgated rules of conduct should be studied and modification and alternative courses of action should be recommended as appropriate.

The Commission recommends further an intensive study of the exclusionary rule as a means of attempting to compel compliance by police and others with judicially promulgated rules of conduct. The effectiveness of the exclusion of resulting evidence as a deterrent to others who might engage in the prohibited conduct is open to question; the cost of the exclusionary rule in terms of court time and case delay and confusion is not. Consideration should be given to the proposal of the American Law Institute that exclusion of resulting evidence follow only if there has been a "substantial" violation of the underlying rule. . . .

**Recommendation 4.2: Use of Videotaped Trials in Criminal Cases**
The use of videotaped trials in criminal cases should be studied and pilot projects should be established and funded by Federal, State, and local government agencies.

The Commission recommends experimentation with videotaped trials in criminal cases. The technique for this process (in a civil case) was described in McCrystal, The Video Tape Trial, 11 *Judge's Journal* 51 (July 1972). All proceedings except the empaneling of the jury, opening statements, and closing statements had been recorded previously—out of the presence of the jury—on videotape. The tape was edited and all inadmissible evidence objections, and rulings on matters of law eliminated. Then, each attorney made an opening statement to the jury, the jury was shown the tape on a television screen, and "live" closing arguments were made. The initial taking of the testimony had required 1 day. The tape, as edited, took only 2 hours and 40 minutes to run, and the entire proceedings with the jury took only about 7 hours. The advantages in this method of proceeding include the following:

1. The trial moved rapidly and without distracting interruptions, since all delays or interruptions in the presentation of the evidence had been edited out;

2. Jurors were not prejudiced by, or asked to disregard, questions or answers ruled to be improper, and were thus

391

able to base their judgment solely on proper evidence;

3. The use of a chart by a doctor was more effective on the videotape than if done live because the camera zoomed in on him and his pointer, giving the jurors a closer view than they would have had by viewing the chart from a greater distance;

4. It was fairer and less confusing for the jurors not to hear comments or exchanges between opposing counsel and the court relative to offered evidence; and

5. Some of the witnesses interviewed said they were more at ease giving their testimony in the presence of the two counsel and the camera operator than they would have been in the courtroom in the presence of the judge and jury.

The Commission believes that such techniques hold great promise for expediting the criminal trial process and for making it fairer. Therefore, experimentation in this area should be encouraged.

## 5: Sentencing

**Standard 5.1: Adopt a policy stipulating that all sentencing be performed by the trial judge.**

## 6: Review of the Trial Court Proceedings

... The basic premise of this chapter is that there should be a single, unified review proceeding in which all arguable defects in the trial proceeding can be examined and settled finally, subject only to narrowly defined exceptional circumstances where there are compelling reasons to provide for a further review. Standards 6.1 throught 6.4 establish the concept of a single, unified review: an amalgamation into one proceeding of all issues that are now litigated on new trial motions, direct appeals, and postconviction proceedings. The new trial motion is abolished, and the traditional distinction between direct appeal and collateral attack is abandoned. ...

### Reviewing Courts

This unified review proceeding—the first, and for most cases the last, stage of review—takes place in what is here called the reviewing court. This term is used instead of appeal and appellate court to make clear that many of the traditional notions about appeals are being discarded. The new unified proceeding has unique characteristics, and should not be encumbered with concepts drawn from a different setting. To make such a single review final as well as fair requires a wholly new way of looking at the proceeding. The Commission believes it is possible that traditional American appellate procedures cannot accomplish these objectives since they confine the appellate court to the record made at trial and do not permit the wide-ranging scrutiny of the case that is essential if the single review is to be fair as well as final. . . .

### Standard 6.1: Unified Review Proceeding

**Every convicted defendant should be afforded the opportunity to obtain one full and fair judicial review of his conviction and sentence by a tribunal other than that by which he was tried or sentenced. Review in that proceeding should extend to the entire case, including:**

**1. The legality of all proceedings leading to the conviction;**

**2. The legality and appropriateness of the sentence;**

**3. Matters that have heretofore been asserted in motions for new trial; and**

**4. Errors not apparent in the trial record that heretofore might have been asserted in collateral attacks on a conviction or sentence.**

. . . A major argument made against sentence review is that it would add to the already swollen appellate dockets, since it would open to review those cases in which conviction rests on a guilty plea. But apprehensions over this are exaggerated. In those cases in which review will be sought solely on the sentence, the lack of merit in the challenge often will be readily apparent to the reviewing court upon a brief examination of the crime for which conviction was obtained, the sentence, and the prior criminal record. . . .

*Scope of Review*

The review proposed in subparagraph 4 would extend to errors and defects not apparent in the trial record, which, under existing arrangements, may be litigated only through postconviction or collateral proceedings. If effectively administered, this concept would go far toward reducing later efforts by prisoners to attack their convictions. In the course of the first review the reviewing court would affirmatively discover and dispose of all conceivably arguable defects in the trial proceeding, even though they may not have been asserted by the defendant and do not appear in the record. Giving this novel scope to the initial review is consistent with, and indeed essential to, the concept of the single, unified review proceeding and to the concept of review of the case rather than of the record. This scope is necessary also in order that a high degree of finality can be attached to the reviewing court's disposition of the case without unfairness to the defendant. . . .

### Standard 6.2: Professional Staff

The reviewing court should have a full-time professional staff of lawyers, responsible directly to the judges, to perform the following functions in review of criminal cases:

1. **Monitoring.** The staff should affirmatively monitor each case to insure that the court's rules are complied with and that there is no unnecessary delay in the review process.

2. **Shaping the Record.** The full trial transcript should be expeditiously provided the reviewing court, and the staff should take action to insure that those portions of transcripts, trial court papers, and other matters that are essential to a full and fair adjudication of the issues are put before the judges.

3. **Identification of Issues.** The staff should take affirmative steps to discover all arguable issues in the case, even though not asserted by defendant and not apparent on the record, so that all matters that might be asserted later as a basis for further review can be considered and decided in the initial review proceeding.

4. **Screening.** The staff should review all cases before they are considered by the judges and recommend appropriate procedural steps and disposition; the staff should identify tentatively those cases that contain only insubstantial issues and should prepare recommended dispositional orders so as to permit the court to dispose of them with a minimum involvement of judicial time, thereby leaving for fuller judicial consideration those cases of arguable merit.

The function of this staff should be to supplement rather than replace the work of attorneys representing the prosecution and the defendant in each case.

*Identification of Issues*

The staff should take affirmative steps to identify all potential issues in the case, even though they were not asserted by the defendant and are not apparent on the face of the record. Performing this function effectively is essential if further review is to be limited. As to alleged constitutional defects in proceedings leading up to conviction and sentence, there is a widely accepted notion that the defendant at some point should be provided an opportunity for a hearing. Failure to provide that opportunity in the regular course of trial and appeal has been one of the causes of growth in postconviction

394

litigation. This standard contemplates that once review is sought, the reviewing court, through its staff, will probe the entire case to spot any arguable issues that may be beneath the surface. Such issues then will be resolved in the review proceeding, thereby making it feasible and fair to prelude a later assertion of the same points.

Various procedures might be devised for carrying out this function. The judges and the court staff, for example, might design a checklist type of questionnaire to be submitted to each defendant and his lawyer. The questionnaire would attempt to list all the typical contentions made by defendants in criminal cases—especially those which abound in postconviction proceedings. On every point the defendant and his lawyer could be asked to indicate whether they claim any irregularity or illegality; a space could be provided for them to state the factual basis of any such claim. The form could carry the advice that this was the sole review to which the defendant had a fight and that only in exceptional circumstances would points not asserted be reviewable thereafter. . . .

*Screening*

A screening function should pervade the staff work. Every case coming to the reviewing court would be reviewed by the staff before being seen by any judge. One purpose is to insure completeness in all the papers, as described above in the description of the process of shaping the record. Another purpose is to recommend further steps. For example, if there is an issue on which a decision by the trial judge is appropriate, as contemplated by subparagraph 2, the staff could frame a recommended order to that effect for the reviewing court's action. If written briefs or oral argument (or both) appear desirable, the staff could make that recommendation to the judges with a suggested limitation as to the issues to be treated.

Another purpose is to identify cases where there are no issues of substance; for example, a recommended per curiam affirmance could be prepared. In all these matters, if any judge disagrees with the staff recommendation, additional procedures or steps can be directed. But if the staff is competent and aware of the general views of the reviewing court, there should be a high degree of harmony between staff recommendations and judicial views. . . .

**Standard 6.3: Flexible Review Procedures**
    The reviewing court should utilize procedures that are flex-

ible and that can be tailored in each case by the staff and the judges to insure maximum fairness, expedition, and finality through a single review of the trial court proceeding. The review procedures should provide for:

1. Receiving and considering new evidence bearing on the issue of guilt, or on the sentence, or on the legality of the trial court proceedings, which could not reasonably have been offered at trial;

2. Referral by the reviewing court to the trial judge of those issues that the reviewing court deems appropriate for the trial judge to decide;

3. Means of identifying and deciding all arguable points in the case, whether or not apparent on the record, that heretofore have been grounds for a collateral attack on the conviction or sentence;

4. Internal flexibility permitting the reviewing court to control written briefs and oral argument, including leeway to dispose of the case without oral argument or on oral argument without written briefs on some or all of the issues;

5. Authority in the reviewing court, at its discretion, to require or permit the presence of the defendant at a review hearing;

6. Authority in the reviewing court, for stated reasons, to substitute for the sentence imposed any other disposition that was open to the sentencing court, if the defendant has asserted the excessiveness of his sentence as error; and

7. Authority in the reviewing court, for stated reasons, to set aside the conviction or remand the case for a new trial, even though the conviction is supported by evidence and there is no legal error, if, under all the circumstances, the reviewing court determines that the conviction should not stand. The reviewing court should be given the authority to affirm a conviction despite the existence of error if to do so would not amount to a miscarriage of justice. This power should be exercised more frequently to speed finality.

. . . There will be some wasted effort when issues ultimately addressed to the trial judge are first submitted to the reviewing court and then dispatched to the trial judge for initial action. The occasional use of such a procedure is necessary, however, if the motion for a new trial is abolished. The few remands that will occur under the proposed review procedure are a small trade-off for the elimination of the substantial delay caused under the existing system by the almost inevitable routine motion for a new trial. It is basic to the concept of unified review that there be one court to which all possible grounds for attacking a criminal conviction must be expeditiously presented. . . .

The Commission recognizes the objections to such a position. Defendants given improperly harsh sentences may be deterred from offering this for review by the possibility that they will end up with a worse sentence. Defendants whose sentences are increased may be so embittered that the correctional task of dealing with them may be greatly complicated. There is arguably some unfairness in submitting only those defendants who offer the purported excessiveness of their sentence for review to the danger of an increase in sentence. These objections, however, appear to the Commission to be outweighed by the value to society in having some recourse against unjustified leniency or other inappropriateness in the sentencing process. While it is not convinced that the prosecution should be given the right to seek review of sentences in all cases, the Commission feels that to grant it this right when the defendant himself has raised the matter of appropriateness of sentence is a reasonable middle ground.

*Subparagraph 7*

An American appellate court normally is given the authority to overturn a conviction only if there is legal error in the record or if the evidence is insufficient to support a finding of guilty. Under this practice the court has no power to set aside the conviction or remand the case for a new trial simply to prevent a miscarriage of justice. The consequence is that in a case where the court is convinced that the conviction works an injustice it is driven artificially to find some legal error on which a reversal can respectably be based, even if this necessitates a distortion of legal doctrine. The more straightforward approach embodied in this standard gives to the court the power to deal with the conviction directly in terms of injustice. . . .

**Standard 6.4: Establish time limits for review proceedings.**

**Standard 6.5: Exceptional Circumstances Justifying Further Review**

After a reviewing court has affirmed a trial court conviction and sentence, or after expiration of a fair opportunity for a defendant to obtain review with the aid of counsel, the conviction and the sentence generally should be final and not subject to further judicial review in any court, State or Federal. Further review should be available only in the following limited circumstances:

1. An appellate court determines that further review would serve the public interest in the development of legal doctrine or in the maintenance of uniformity in the application of decisional and statutory law;

2. The defendant asserts a claim of newly discovered evidence, which was not known to him and which could not have been discovered through the exercise of due diligence prior to the conclusion of the unified review proceeding or the expiration of the time for seeking review, and which in light of all the evidence raises substantial doubt as to defendant's guilt; or

3. The defendant asserts a claim of constitutional violation which, if well-founded, undermines the basis for or the integrity of the entire trial or review proceeding, or impairs the reliability of the fact-finding process at the trial.

. . . A second basis for further review is a traditional ground for posttrial attack on convictions—newly discovered evidence. Here the interest of justice in protecting those not guilty is sufficiently strong to justify an exception to finality. The standard carries forward the longstanding conditions that the evidence was not known to the defendant in time to have been offered earlier (up through the review proceeding) and that it was not discoverable by the exercise of reasonable diligence. These limitations are desirable in the interest of orderly procedure and finality; a defendant should bring forward all evidence that he can reasonably obtain in the regular course of trial and review.

Since the primary purpose of this exception to the finality of the review proceeding is to protect the innocent, it is sound to make the availability of review on this ground depend upon the court's finding from all the evidence, the new included, that there is some basis for believing the defendant is not guilty. The formula of substantial doubt as to guilt seems appropriate to express the degree to which the court should be persuaded on this point; it does not require the court to conclude that the defendant is not guilty. . . .

A claim of constitutional violation that, if well founded, is so fundamental that it undermines the basis of the prosecution or undermines the integrity of the trial proceeding should not be foreclosed by the review proceeding. An example of the former is a claim that the statute under which the prosecution was brought is unconstitutional. An example of the latter is a claim that the defendant was not represented at trial by counsel or a claim of mob domination of the trial.

A constitutional violation may not be of that type, yet it may still endanger the reliability of the factfinding process. Thus the conviction may either work an actual injustice or leave the appearance of such injustice. The concept of this type of constitutional violation has been articulated by the Supreme Court. The Court has made the relationship to fact-finding reliability a factor in determining whether to give retroactive effect to some of its decisions. While the issue there is different, this factor seems a useful basis on which to determine whether further review should be made available. Review on this basis would protect the fundamental fairness of the process.

Examples of constitutional claims that would be accorded further review on this reliability-impairing basis are those involving involuntary confessions, unconstitutionally composed juries, and knowing use of perjured testimony by the prosecutor. Examples of claims that would not be open to further review are those raising the use of voluntary confessions allegedly made without constitutionally required warnings, illegally seized evidence, and lineup identification made in the absence of counsel. . . .

The standard also recommends that insofar as defendants convicted in State criminal proceedings have access to Federal courts for further review beyond direct review by the U.S. Supreme Court of the State courts' affirmance of the decision, they should be permitted to challenge their convictions only in the U.S. courts of appeals. This would eliminate further review in the U.S. district courts as is presently available. This is based upon the Commission's view that overturning a conviction that has already been upheld by the State's appellate court system is a step of such seriousness that it should not be performed by a single judge of a court with general trial jurisdiction. The courts of appeals could use any of the methods provided for in Standard 6.3 for resolving any issue of fact that might be presented in such cases, subject, however, to the restraints imposed by Standard 6.7.

**Standard 6.6: Assure that reviewing courts do not readjudicate claims already adjudicated on the merits by a court of competent jurisdiction.**

**Standard 6.7: Further Review in State or Federal Court: Prior Factual Determinations**
When a defendant seeks further review in either a State or
399

a Federal court, claiming a constitutional violation in the exceptional circumstances described in subparagraph 3 of Standard 6.5, determinations of basic or historical facts previously made by either a trial or reviewing court, evidenced by written findings, should be conclusive, unless the defendant shows that there was a constitutional violation that undermined the integrity of the factfinding process.

The possibility in current postconviction practice of relitigating factual matters underlying alleged constitutional violations is another aspect of the failure of courts to apply general concepts of res judicata in criminal litigation. The interests of justice require that a defendant have an opportunity to litigate, through trial and review, every material factual issue. But once a defendant has had a constitutionally adequate determination and review of a factual issue, the intesests in finality and economy of judicial resources outweigh any interest he may claim in further litigation of the issue. This is true even if the fact be one that is determinative of a constitutional right.

Here, unlike Standard 6.6, a State court determination would be conclusive on further review in a Federal Court as well as in a State Court. But the conclusiveness is limited to determinations of basic or historical facts such as the date on which the defendant was taken into custody, whether he was given any warnings, how many hours he was held in custody, and similar matters.

A State court determination would not be conclusive of matters that might loosely be called constitutional facts, such as whether, given the basic or historical facts as found by the State court, a confession was voluntary. Nor, would a prior State determination of a question of Federal constitutional interpretation foreclose a Federal court from deciding such an issue if the circumstances set out in Standard 6.5 governing the availability of further review were present. It would be not be desirable, and probably not constitutional, to foreclose a State decision on a Federal constitutional claim from all Federal judicial review, and these standards do not purport to do so.

### Standard 6.8: Further Review in State or Federal Court: Claim Not Asserted Previously

When a defendant seeks further review in either a State or a Federal court, claiming a constitutional violation in the exceptional circumstances described in subparagraph 3 of Standard 6.5, the court should not adjudicate the merits of the claim if in the trial court or the review proceeding it was not adjudicated because it was expressly disclaimed by the defendant or his lawyer, or it was not asserted at any point, or it was not asserted in accordance with valid governing rules of procedure, unless the defendant establishes a justifiable basis for not regarding his prior actions related to the claim as foreclosing further review.

... The standard does not absolutely foreclose further review of a constitutional claim (in the circumstances specified in subparagraph 3 of Standard 6.5) if it has not been litigated during trial or review. The defendant can obtain further review if he can show a justifiable reason for his previous failure to litigate the issue. The burden is on the defendant. The standard does not attempt to define justifiable reason. The possibilities are so varied that this is best left to the courts to resolve as the issue arises. Examples of what might be justifiable reasons for not asserting points at the proper time are lack of counsel or a reasonable misunderstanding as to the applicable procedure. Where there has been an express disclaimer the burden on the defendant will be heavier; this is appropriate since a party generally should not be allowed to renounce a contention at one point and revive it later.

There is further qualification on foreclosure in the situation where the defendant has made an effort to obtain an adjudication of his claim but the court declined to pass on it because it was not properly asserted under the procedural rules. The standard requires that further review be foreclosed only if those procedural rules are valid. This means that if a procedural rule a court relied on in declining to abjudicate a claim is itself in violation of due process or any other constitutional provision, the claim remains open for review. Under existing law a State rule of procedure applied to shut off a Federal constitutional claim may be invalid, for example, if it is an arbitrary rule, if it was invented for the case at hand, or if it unreasonably impedes assertion of the Federal claim. This existing body of law would be applicable under this standard to determine the validity of State procedural rules.

... In previous years, there may have been some justifiable basis for leaving open for review indefinitely, in the widest possible scope, all potential constitutional defects in a State criminal proceeding. Many jurisdictions did not provide counsel for indigent defendants. Little attention was given, in the bar and in law schools, to criminal practice. Educational programs for judges were in their infancy.

All this has changed substantially in recent years. Counsel must now be provided for all defendants in felony cases and many or most misdemeanor prosecutions. Law schools have begun to devote substantial teaching and research resources to the criminal field. Continuing legal education programs for lawyers have become widespread on State, regional, and national bases, and they regularly include training in criminal law and procedure. Well-staffed public defender offices now exist in many places. The National Defender Project did much to increase competence and interest among the bar in criminal defense work. Bar committees now give substantial attention to the subject.

Similar developments have improved the judiciary. The National College of the State Judiciary was established in 1964. More than 1,700 State trial judges have taken its month-long residence course, and the college has reached many others through short courses. The American Academy for Judicial Education likewise is conducting substantial educational programs for trial and appellate judges. The Section of Judicial Administration of the American Bar Association has many activities aimed at raising the quality of the trial and appellate bench. These judicial education enterprises address themselves to criminal law and practice as well as other subjects.

**Standard 6.9: Assure that a reviewing court always states the reasons for its decision; limit publication to significant cases.**

**Recommendation 6.1: Develop means of producing trial transcripts speedily.**

**Recommendation 6.2: Study causes of delay in review proceedings.**

**Recommendation 6.3: Study reports and recommendations of the Advisory Council for Appellate Justice.**

# C: Personnel and Institutions

## 7: The Judiciary

**Standard 7.1: Judicial Selection**
The selection of judges should be based on merit qualifica-

tions for judicial office. A selection process should aggressively seek out the best potential judicial candidates through the participation of the bench, the organized bar, law schools, and the lay public.

Judges should be selected by a judicial nominating commission. Representatives from the judiciary, the general public, and the legal profession should organize into a 7-member judicial nominating commission for the sole purpose of nominating a slate of qualified candidates eligible to fill judicial vacancies. The Governor should fill judicial vacancies from this list.

With the exception of the judicial member, the members of the commission should be selected by procedures designed to assure that they reflect the wishes of the groups they represent. The senior judge of the highest court, other than the chief justice, should represent the judiciary and serve as the commission's presiding officer. The Governor should appoint three public members, none of whom should be judges or lawyers. No more than two should be of the same political affiliation or be from the same geographic vicinity. Three members from the legal profession should be appointed or elected by the membership of the unified bar association or appointed by the Governor when no such organization exists. A lawyer member of the commission should not be eligible for consideration for judicial vacancies until the expiration of his term and those of the other two lawyer members and three lay members serving with him. Commission members representing the public and the legal profession should serve staggered terms of three years.

For the appointment procedure to function efficiently, the commission staff should maintain an updated list of qualified potential nominees from which the commission should draw names to submit to the Governor. The commission should select a minimum of three persons to fill a judicial vacancy on the court, unless the commission is convinced there are not three qualified nominees. This list should be sent to the Governor within 30 days of a judicial vacancy, and, if the Governor does not appoint a candidate within 30 days, the power of appointment should shift to the commission.

Standard 7.2: Judicial Tenure

Initial appointment should be for a term of 4 years for trial court judges and 6 years for appellate court judges. At the end of each term, the judge should be required to run in

403

an uncontested election at which the electorate is given the option of voting for or against his retention. If the vote is in favor of retention, he should thereby become entiled to another term of the same length as the initial term.

A mandatory retirement age of 65 years should be set for all judges subject to a provision enabling judges over that age to sit thereafter at the discretion of the presiding or other appropriate administrative judge by designation for limited periods of time.

This standard embodies the main features of the Missouri Plan—the requirement that a sitting judge periodically submit himself to the electorate for their approval or disapproval. He is not to run against another candidate; if he is not approved, his successor will be chosen by the method set out in Standard 7.1 for initial selection. He is simply to run on—and against—his own record. This provides for popular participation in the retention of judges, but eliminates most of the problems of the elective system. In most instances, it is likely that the judge will not have to be concerned about receiving popular approval, and extensive campaigning will be unnecessary. But Standard 7.2 also provides the opportunity for popular rejection of a sitting judge in the exceptional case in which he has so offended community sentiments that the electorate is willing to reject him in favor of an unidentified successor.

The Courts Task Force took the position that there was not adequate evidence to justify recommending the specific length of the term after which judges should be required to run against their own records. It found that there were widely varying views as to the appropriate length of judicial tenure, ranging from a few years to life. But the Commission concluded that there was sufficient experience with both long and short tenure to justify recommending the specific terms of office contained in the standard.

The standard provides for different terms for trial and appellate judges. Appellate judges often deal with widely criticized matters of general policy, and judicial independence suggests that they be provided the extra protection inherent in a longer term against popular reaction to a particular decision. The terms are sufficiently long for a judge to develop skill in his job and to establish a reputation. Yet they are short enough to insure that the opportunity to remove an unsatisfactory judge is never too far into the future.

The standard also deals with the problem of disablement

by age by proposing a maximum retirement age. If a judge is still able and willing to function after age 65, he could continue to function upon the approval of the presiding judge. If, on the other hand, age had caused substantial disablement, he could be prevented from functioning as a judge by the administrative action of the presiding judge. It is likely that approval for continued sitting would be withheld in situations where affirmative action to remove a sitting judge would be unlikely. Thus the approach of the standard should result in removal from the bench of more incapacitated elderly judges than would occur if affirmative action were necessary.

**Standard 7.3: Base salaries and benefits of State judges on the Federal model.**

**Standard 7.4: Judicial Discipline and Removal**

A judge should be subject to discipline or removal for permanent physical or mental disability seriously interfering with the performance of judicial duties, willfull misconduct in office, willful and persistent failure to perform judicial duties, habitual intemperance, or conduct prejudicial to the administration of justice.

A judicial conduct commission should be created, composed of judges elected by the judicial conference, lawyers elected by the bar, and at least two laymen, of different political persuasions, appointed by the Governor. Whatever the size of the commission, no more than one-third should be members of the judiciary. The commission should be empowered to investigate charges bearing on judges' competence to continue on the bench, and should be empowered to take appropriate action regarding their conduct.

One well-known commission that deals with judicial discipline and removal without resorting to impeachment or recall is the California Commission on Judicial Qualifications, created in 1960 by constitutional amendment. The commission consists of two appeals court judges, two superior court judges, and one municipal judge, all of whom are appointed to the commission by the State supreme court. In addition, two members of the State bar who have practiced law in the State for at least 10 years are appointed by the governing body of the State bar. Two lay citizens are appointed by the Governor and approved by the State Senate. All commission members serve a 4-year term.

The California commission receives, investigates, and

screens complaints by any person against any judge in the California State court system. If it finds a complaint is justified, the commission may recommend to the State supreme court that a judge be retired for any disability that seriously interferes with his performance and which is or is likely to become permanent. In addition, the commission may recommend that the State supreme court censure or remove a judge for willful misconduct in office, willful and persistent failure to perform his duties, and habitual intemperance or conduct that may be prejudicial to the administration of justice. While the commission's recommendation is pending, the judge is relieved of his duties without loss of salary. The commission also may recommend or move that the supreme court suspend a judge from office without salary when he pleads guilty to or is convicted of any State or Federal felony or of any other crime involving moral turpitude. If the conviction is reversed, the suspension is lifted and the judge receives his salary for the suspension period. If the conviction becomes final, the supreme court removes him from office. . . .

The Commission recommends that the judicial conduct commission itself, rather than the supreme court, have the ultimate authority to discipline, remove, or retire judges. Again, this is based primarily upon the desire to remove any danger that professional relations will impede effective implementation of the discipline and removal process. The assurances of participation by the general public and the bar in the operation of the judicial conduct commission make it more appropriate to leave the ultimate removal power in that body rather than to transfer it to a court whose members themselves are subject to the removal and discipline power. . . .

**Standard 7.5: Create and maintain a comprehensive program of continuing judicial education.**

## 8: The Lower Courts

. . . The lower courts of most States share three problems.

The first is their position on the bottom rung of the judicial ladder, which results in neglect by those forces that should be scrutinizing and aiding the level of court performance—bar associations, the State supreme court, the press, government agencies, and citizen groups. The neglect is so severe that members of the legal profession and of the judiciary often

406

are unaware of the number, names, function, or identity of the judges of the lower courts. The inferior status of the lower courts and the traditional view that their work is ministerial, monotonous, and legally unchallenging also is reflected in the use of part-time support personnel, low salaries, and inadequate facilities. As a result, the lower courts generally tend to attract prosecutors, defense counsel, clerks, and judges of a caliber lower than normally encountered in the courts of general jurisdiction.

The second problem is the volume and nature of the caseload. The overwhelming part of the caseload of the lower courts consists of traffic violations and public intoxication prosecutions. These cases seldom raise any issue that requires consideration and decision and they encourage perfunctory, summary dispositions, often referred to as assembly-line justice. Assembly-line justice minimizes the likelihood that cases will be heard fully and fairly and virtually precludes any meaningful correctional disposition.

The third problem is the trial de novo system. This precludes effective review and monitoring of the work and decisions of the lower courts by appellate tribunals, and enables judges of the lower courts, unlike their general jurisdiction judicial counterparts, to operate with improper procedures and under erroneous assumptions of the substantive law. A recent comprehensive study of the lower courts in the Boston area pinpointed the trial de novo as possibly the most damaging influence on justice in the courts of limited criminal jurisdiction. . . .

If complete unification of the trial courts is politically unrealistic at present, there are two approaches between the initial step described above and a completely unified system. The Commission recommends these as temporary goals.

One is to eliminate all justice of the peace courts and municipal courts and replace them with one statewide system of lower courts. This would replace laymen and part-time judges with full-time judges who are legally trained and who are members of the bar. As this statewide system of lower courts would not be integrated into the courts of general criminal jurisdiction, this step falls short of complete unification and usually is designed as a unified two-tier trial court system.

This approach in many respects is superior to present practice. Current problems of caseload disparity could be solved by encouraging full-time judges in rural areas to ride a circuit of locations, serving the widespread courts of the county or counties within their jurisdiction. State financing of the court system would eliminate the questionable practices of some local justices who view the sentencing process as a major source of local revenue. State administration would increase the supreme court's authority and consequent responsibility for the operation of the lower courts. This, in turn, should serve to raise the level of those courts and encourage them to adhere to the pertinent law and supreme court rules. If these courts are authorized to defer sentence and to grant probation, as well as to fine and to imprison, they will be capable of dealing meaningfully with defendants convicted of minor crimes. . . .

### Standard 8.1: Unification of the State Court System

State courts should be organized into a unified judicial system financed by the State and administered through a statewide court administrator or administrative judge under the supervision of the chief justice of the State supreme court.

All trial courts should be unified into a single trial court with general criminal as well as civil jurisdiction. Criminal jurisdiction now in courts of limited jurisdiction should be placed in these unified trial courts of general jurisdiction, with the exception of certain traffic violations. The State supreme court should promulgate rules for the conduct of minor as well as major criminal prosecutions.

All judicial functions in the trial courts should be performed by full-time judges. All judges should possess law degrees and be members of the bar.

A transcription or other record of the pretrial court proceedings and the trial should be kept in all criminal cases.

The appeal procedure should be the same for all cases.

Pretrial release services, probation services, and other rehabilitative services should be available in all prosecutions within the jurisdiction of the unified trial court.

### Standard 8.2: Dispose administratively of all traffic cases except certain serious offenses.

## 9: Court Administration

### Standard 9.1: Establish policies for the administration of the State's courts.

### Standard 9.2: Vest in a presiding judge ultimate local adminstrative judicial authority in each trial jurisdiction.

408

**Standard 9.3:** Assure that local and regional trial courts have a full-time court administrator.

**Standard 9.4:** Assure that ultimate responsibility for the management and flow of cases rests with the judges of the trial court.

**Standard 9.5:** Establish coordinating councils to survey court administration practices in the State.

**Standard 9.6:** Establish a forum for interchange between court personnel and the community.

## 10: Court-Community Relations

**Standard 10.1:** Provide adequate physical facilities for court processing of criminal defendants.

**Standard 10.2:** Provide information concerning court processes to the public and to participants in the criminal justice system.

**Standard 10.3:** Coordinate responsibility among the court, news media, the public, and the bar for providing information to the public about the courts.

**Standard 10.4:** Assure that court personnel are representative of the community served by the court.

**Standard 10.5:** Assure that judges and court personnel participate in criminal justice planning activities.

**Standard 10.6:** Call witnesses only when necessary; make use of telephone alert.

**Standard 10.7:** Assure that witness compensation is realistic and equitable.

## 11: Computers and the Courts

**Standard 11.1:** Utilize computer services consistent with the needs and caseloads of the courts.

**Standard 11.2:** Employ automated legal research services on an experimental basis.

**Recommendation 11.1:** Instruct law students in the use of automated legal research systems.

## 12: The Prosecution

**Standard 12.1:** Assure that prosecutors are full-time skilled professionals, authorized to serve a minimum term of 4 years, and compensated adequately.

**Standard 12.2:** Select and retain assistant prosecutors on the basis of legal ability; assure that they serve full time and are compensated adequately.

**Standard 12.3:** Provide prosecutors with supporting staff and facilities comparable to that of similar-size private law firms.

**Standard 12.4:** Establish a State-level entity to provide support to local prosecutors.

**Standard 12.5:** Utilize education programs to assure the highest professional competence.

**Standard 12.6:** Establish file control and statistical systems in prosecutors' offices.

**Standard 12.7:** Assure that each prosecutor develops written office policies and practices.

**Standard 12.8:** The Prosecutor's Investigative Role

The prosecutor's primary function should be to represent the State in court. He should cooperate with the police in their investigation of crime. Each prosecutor also should have investigatorial resources at his disposal to assist him in case preparation, to supplement the results of police investigation when police lack adequate resources for such investigation, and, in a limited number of situations, to undertake an initial investigation of possible violations of the law.

The prosecutor should be given the power, subject to appropriate safeguards, to issue subpenas requiring potential witnesses in criminal cases to appear for questioning. Such witnesses should be subject to contempt penalties for unjustified failure to appear for questioning or to respond to specific questions.

The office of the prosecutor should review all applications for search and arrest warrants prior to their submission by law enforcement officers to a judge for approval; no application for a search or arrest warrant should be submitted to a judge unless the prosecutor or assistant prosecutor approves the warrant.

... Several states already permit a magistrate to subpena witnesses for interrogation even in the absence of a grand jury proceeding. The Commission's proposal would be similar: although the prosecutor would have the initial power to issue the subpena, no penalty for failure to comply with it should be permitted without a judicial hearing on the propriety of the subpena and on the recipient's reason for not responding.

Compelled attendance under such a subpena is a "seizure" of the person. Therefore, it should be permitted only when there is a basis for believing that the interrogation would provide valuable information in the investigation or prosecution. This is not only consistent with existing fourth amendment case law but also, the Commission believes, sound policy. Therefore, no prosecutor should issue a subpena unless he has sufficient evidence to conclude that the interrogation would yield information of value.

Moreover, a subject who contests a subpena may be punished only if he still refuses to comply after the judicial hearing has found the subpena valid. For all practical purposes, this would insert a judicial officer between the prosecutor and the subject, and thereby incorporate the safeguard of the independent magistrate that has been stressed in determining whether investigatory procedures are reasonable within the meaning of the fourth amendment.

Steps also should be taken to protect the right of the subjects against self-incrimination. The prosecutor should be required to give the subject an explanation of his rights. These rights should include the right to have an attorney present during the interrogation and to have an attorney at State expense if the subject is unable to provide his own.

If these procedural safeguards are built into the subpena process, the Commission believes that the process will provide a workable and efficient alternative to the grand jury in many criminal cases. Moreover, it will do so at even less danger to the interests of the subjects, who often are inadequately protected by existing grand jury procedures.

Requiring prior prosecutor approval of arrest and particularly of search warrants would increase the likelihood that only appropriate arrests and searches would be made and would avoid the need for judicial officers to consider, but reject, applications for warrants. Prosecutors more often are qualified to determine whether a given set of facts satisfies the probable cause requirement of the fourth amendment. ...

**Standard 12.9: Assure that prosecutors maintain relationships with other criminal justice agencies.**

## 13: The Defense

**Standard 13.1: Availability of Publicly Financed Representation in Criminal Cases**
... The Commission agrees with the assumption underlying this trend in the constitutional case law that early involvement by counsel in the criminal process is necessary to the protection of basic rights of the accused. Consequently, this standard directs that public representation should be made available early in the process. Counsel should be available upon arrest, whether or not interrogation is to take place. If the defendant is compelled to participate in the investigation—for example, by appearing in a lineup—representation should be provided at that point, even if no arrest is made. Even if this representation is not required by the Federal Constitution, the Commission believes that considerations of equal treatment of indigents and preservation of valuable rights require, as a matter of policy, such representation. ...

**Standard 13.2: Assure that any individual provided public representation pay any portion of the cost he can assume without undue hardship.**

**Standard 13.3: Enable all applicants for defender services to apply directly to the public defender or appointing authority for representation.**

**Standard 13.4: Make counsel available to corrections inmates, indigent parolees, and indigent probationers on matters relevant to their status.**

**Standard 13.5: Establish a full-time public defender organization and assigned counsel system involving the private bar in every jurisdiction.**

**Standard 13.6: Assure that defender services are consistent with local needs and financed by the State.**

**Standard 13.7: Assure that public defenders are full time and adequately compensated.**

**Standard 13.8: Assure that public defenders are nominated by a selection board and appointed by the Governor.**

**Standard 13.9: Performance of Public Defender Function**

... Public defender systems supervised in part or in whole by the judges in whose courts the defender is to function are found in various jurisdictions within the United States. The judiciary, which is charged with safeguarding the rights of all, is arguably the most appropriate group to supervise the public defender who, himself, is to safeguard the rights of the indigent criminally accused. Furthermore, the competence or lack of competence of a lawyer is usually first perceived by and most readily apparent to the judges before whom he practices. However, the practical difficulty of such a system of supervision lies in the fact that in most States the judges are themselves elected by a public that tends to feel that judges should be responsive to the will of the majority: judicial independence, or the lack thereof, is already a serious national problem.

A public defender under the policy control and supervision of judges may experience unwarranted judicial interference in the defense of criminal cases. Those aware of the problems faced by defender offices are strong in this opposition to any substantial degree of judicial control of administration or supervision. The realities of criminal practice are such that the adversary system in this arena is not a two-way but a three-way encounter. The mediator between two adversaries cannot be permitted to make policy for one of the adversaries. ...

**Standard 13.10:** Base upon merit, hiring, retention, and promotion policies for public defender staff attorneys.

**Standard 13.11:** Assure that salaries for public defender staff attorneys are comparable to those of associate attorneys in local private law firms.

**Standard 13.12:** Assure that the caseload of a public defender office is not excessive.

**Standard 13.13:** Assure that the public defender is sensitive to the problems of his client community.

**Standard 13.14:** Provide public defender offices with adequate supportive services and personnel.

**Standard 13.15:** Vest responsibility in the public defender for maintaining a panel of private attorneys for defense work.

**Standard 13.16:** Provide systematic and comprehensive training to public defenders and assigned counsel.

# D: Special Problem Areas

## 14: Juveniles

**Standard 14.1: Place jurisdiction over juveniles in a family court, which should be a division of the general trial court.**

**Standard 14.2: Intake, Detention, and Shelter Care in Delinquency Cases**

An intake unit of the family court should be created and should:

1. Make the initial decision whether to place a juvenile referred to the family court in detention or shelter care;

2. Make the decision whether to offer a juvenile referred to the family court the opportunity to participate in diversion programs; and

3. Make, in consultation with the prosecutor, the decision whether to file a formal petition in the family court alleging that the juvenile is delinquent and ask that the family court assume jurisdiction over him.

A juvenile placed in detention or shelter care should be released if no petition alleging delinquency (or, in the case of a juvenile placed in shelter care, no petition alleging neglect) is filed in the family court within 24 hours of the placement. A juvenile placed in detention or shelter care should have the opportunity for a judicial determination of the propriety of continued placement in the facility at the earliest possible time, but no later than 48 hours after placement.

Criteria should be formulated for the placement of juveniles in detention and shelter care. These criteria must be applied in practice.

**Standard 14.3: Processing Certain Delinquency Cases as Adult Criminal Prosecutions**

The family court should have the authority to order certain delinquency cases to be processed as if the alleged delinquent was above the maximum age for family court delinquency jurisdiction. After such action, the juvenile should be subject to being charged, tried, and (if convicted) sentenced as an adult.

An order directing that a specific case be processed as an adult criminal prosecution should be entered only under the following circumstances:

1. The juvenile involved is above a designated age;
2. A full and fair hearing has been held on the propriety of the entry of such an order; and
3. The judge of the family court has found that such action is in the best interests of the public.

In each jurisdiction, more specific criteria should be developed, either through statute or rules of court, for determining when juveniles should be processed as criminal defendants.

If an order is entered directing the processing of a case as an adult criminal prosecution and the juvenile is convicted of a criminal offense, he should be permitted to assert the impropriety of the order or the procedure by which the decision to enter the order was made on review of his conviction. When the conviction becomes final, however, the validity of the order and the procedure by which the underlying decision was made should not be subject to any future litigation.

Standard 14.4: Separate adjudicatory hearings from dispositional hearings; assure that hearings have all the protections of adult criminal trials.

Standard 14.5: Assure that dispositional hearing proceedings are similar to those followed in sentencing adult offenders.

## 15: Mass Disorders

Standard 15.1: Assure that every plan for the administration of justice in a mass disorder contains a court processing section.

Standard 15.2: Subject Matter of the Court Plan

The court plan should be concerned with both judicial policy matters and court management matters. The council of judges should develop the judicial policy aspects of the plan. The court management aspects also should be developed by the council of judges, unless the community has an adequate court management operation to which such planning may be delegated.

1. Judicial Policy Matters. Generally, the following policies should be developed and enunciated. Provision should be made for their institutionalization by the judicial planning body in its mass disorder plan:

a. The court plan, to the extent possible, should be made public and disseminated widely to assure the community and individual arrestees that their security and rights are being protected. Portions of the plan that contain sensitive information should not be made public.

b. Provision should be made for pretrial release procedures normally available to remain available during a disorder.

c. The adversary process should function as in normal times and to this end the defense and prosecution functions should be performed adequately.

d. Persons coming before the bench should be informed of all their rights as in normal times.

e. Arrested persons should be assured speedy presentation before a judicial officer and a speedy trial.

f. Sentencing growing out of a mass disorder should be deferred until the conclusion of the disorder, with the exception of sentencing to time served in pretrial detention or a minimal and affordable fine.

2. Management Considerations. Generally, the following management considerations should be contained in the court component of the mass disorder plan:

a. To insure prompt execution of the plan in the event of a mass disorder, responsibility for its activation should be vested in a single member of the council of judges. An alternate also should be designated, and he should have activation responsibility in the event that the first member is unavailable. Deactivation should take place under the direction of the same council member.

b. The plan should be designed to be activated in phases scaled to the precise degree required by the disorder at hand. In order to activate to that precise degree, a basic processing module formula for both initial appearance and trial should be developed and used.

c. The normal business of the courts should proceed during a disorder unless the disorder is of such a magnitude that sufficient personnel and facilities are unavailable. In that event, normal business should be postponed and rescheduled for the earliest possible time.

d. Plans should be made for the identification, recruitment, and assignment of sufficient judicial personnel from all courts within the municipality and, when necessary, from neighboring municipalities or even neighboring

States. The requisite intrajurisdictional and interjurisdictional compacts should be entered into, and where necessary, legislation or constitutional amendment should be enacted in conjunction with the planning process.

e. Plans should be made for the identification, recruitment, and assignment of sufficient court administrative and clerical personnel for all purposes, drawing such personnel, if necessary, from nonjudicial governmental departments within the municipality or from the entire metropolitan area. Such auxiliary personnel should be identified and recruited as part of the planning process for potential callup in the event they are needed. The list of such personnel should be updated periodically.

f. Court papers should be designed to conform as nearly as possible to the paper forms employed by the police and the prosecution. Sufficient quantities of such forms should be produced in advance so that they will be available in the event of a mass disorder.

g. Attention should be given to the problem of paper flow and mechanical and electronic data flow, to the end that papers and mechanically and electronically retrieved information move smoothly from the police to prosecutors and defense counsel and to the court.

h. Arrangements should be made to identity and secure facilities within the municipality or metropolitan area suitable for potential use as court, prosecutorial, and defense facilities. Such facilities should be used in the event that the usual facilities become insufficient. Other governmental buildings suitable for such use should be considered first, and, if this is inadequate, arrangements should be made for the use of other facilities.

i. Arrangements should be made for sufficient clerical supplies and equipment to be available for use in processing arrestees during a mass disorder. Material should include sufficient business machinery, office equipment, computers, and the like.

j. Provision should be made to maintain adequate security in the regular courthouses and in any other facilities that may be utilized for court purposes. Alternate facilities should be available in the event the regular courthouse is in the disorder zone and security would be difficult or impossible to maintain.

k. Techniques should be developed to pinpoint the location of detained persons during a disorder and to insure that they can be brought before the court on demand and that their attorneys can establish physical contact when required.

At least yearly a simulated implementation of the plan should be attempted, so that deficiencies in it can be identified and corrected.

**Standard 15.3: Assure that a prosecutorial plan is developed by the local prosecutor(s).**

Screening by the prosecution during mass disorder presents special problems. Much of what is said in this report concerning screening during normal times is applicable during disorder. To facilitate screening in a mass disorder situation, however, specific procedures should be developed to give the prosecutorial staff charged with the screening function sufficient data on which to make its decision. This will require development of a method of recordkeeping and a means for transmission of the record to the screening prosecutor. These two matters, relatively simple in normal times, become complex during mass disorder. In times of mass disorder, the police often are unable to take the time to fill out an arrest report or to confer with the prosecutor on each case. Transmission becomes a problem because of the confusion inherent in disorder situations. The development of a simplified multicopy field arrest form would help alleviate these difficulties. But cooperation by the police in filling out the form and transmitting it to the prosecutor and court also is essential.

During the May Day disorders of 1971 in Washington, D.C., the police failed on a wholesale basis to fill out such forms though sufficient forms were provided. As a result, little or no prosecutional screening took place, and many cases later were dismissed by the courts. The availability of such an arrest form also will facilitate the decision as to what offense to charge, because the prosecutor requires information from the police as to the circumstances and nature of the arrest in order to charge appropriately. . . .

Overcharging must be avoided. Charging more offenses during mass disorder than would ordinarily be charged on a given set of facts has been observed; apparently, the objective has been to obtain pretrial detention by stimulating high bail through overcharging. . . .

**Standard 15.4: Assure that the plan for providing defense services during a mass disorder is developed by the local public defender(s).**

## Dissenting View

STATEMENT OF MR. STANLEY C. VAN NESS

I dissent from the Report on Courts on the subject of "Review" and from that portion of the report treating "The Litigated Case" that recommends six-member juries in criminal cases. It is only fitting that I state my reasons for doing so.

### Review

The basic objective of the majority proposal on "Review" is that there should be a single unified review proceeding where all arguable trial defects can be raised at one time and that thereafter a defendant's opportunity to test the validity of his conviction through subsequent direct appeal and/or collateral attack should be sharply curtailed. The reason given to support this radical departure from traditional appellate practice is that the adoption of the proposed standards would reduce the backlog that plagues almost every appellate court in the country. I have tried in vain to understand how the proposals accomplish in any significant way their stated purpose.

As the administrative head of a State agency charged with the responsibility of representing indigents accused of crime (some 32,000 persons in fiscal 1972), I am ever mindful of the backlog in our trial and appellate courts and I am interested in any reasonable response to the problem that would insure fairness to the accused. Putting aside for the moment the question of fairness, the fact remains that should the Courts Task Force standards be implemented in New Jersey, they would have minimal impact. Of the 11,792 appeals filed in New Jersey from September 1, 1967, through June 30, 1972, only 4 percent involved collateral attacks on criminal convictions. Of the 42,680 active cases pending in the trial courts at the end of June 1972, only 0.15 percent were collateral attacks on criminal convictions.

The activity in the Federal courts basically mirrors the experience in New Jersey. Keeping in mind that the Federal courts receive petitions from all 50 States, it is significant that only 8.5 percent of the total appeals docketed in the courts of appeals between July 1, 1971, and December 31, 1971, involved collateral litigation. During the same period only 5.4 percent of the 70,067 cases commenced in the United States district courts were habeas corpus petitions from State petitioners, the vast majority of which were disposed of on the papers with a minimal expenditure of judicial time.

Thus, it appears to me that the unified review proposals cannot be justified on the basis that they offer any meaningful reduction in judicial backlogs. Since one of the proposals calls for an automatic review of sentences—a result that I feel is justified regardless of calendar problems—it may well be argued that the number of appeals filed will increase, not decrease.

Before I could consider approving standards that limit the availability of the writ of habeas corpus and that in large measure remove the Federal courts from the business of determining Federal Constitution questions arising out of criminal cases, as these standards do, I would wish to see a clearer presentation of the benefits to be derived than I believe has yet been made.

It should be noted that the foreclosure of collateral attack on convictions can lead to the stagnation of development in the criminal law. Clearly, many of the landmark decisions in the criminal law field started via the collateral route. It may be that the majority finds that restricting this possibility is a benefit to be found in the proposed statutes. Certainly much of the discussion about finality suggested that such was the case. I, however, do not favor procedures that would hamper the ordinary growth of constitutional law.

Finally, I consider the proposed standards to be potentially unfair to the criminally accused—largely the poor and members of minority groups. The plain intent of the standards is to make it more difficult for a person to challenge the validity of a conviction by narrowing the possibility of constitutional attack upon that conviction. I am not satisfied that a single unified review, placing as it does heavy reliance upon an appellate staff to perform the almost impossible job of locating error that does not appear of record and that lays heavy emphasis on the doctrine of waiver, is an adequate substitute for present direct and collateral avenues of review.

Although the section on "Review" contains certain valuable suggestions to expedite the handling of appeals, such as an appellate staff to screen and monitor appeals and the use of computer techniques for the preparation of transcripts, they are offered only in the context of the single unified proceeding. It is that concept that I find unacceptable and therefore I am constrained to dissent from the adoption of the entire section.

## Six-Member Juries

The majority proposes a national standard of six-member juries in criminal cases. Although it is true that the U.S. Supreme Court in *Williams* v. *Florida* held that a six-member jury was permissible under the Federal Constitution, I do not read that case as expressing a preference for a jury of less than 12. That decision merely reestablished what everybody had believed to be the State's right prior to 1968, when in *Duncan* v. *Louisiana*, the Court held that a jury trial was required by the due process clause in the 14th amendment.

The question before the Courts Task Force, in my judgment, is not whether a 12-man jury is constitutionally required, but rather, whether there are sound policy reasons for establishing a jury of a lesser number as a standard to be followed throughout the United States. Apparently, the justification for the recommendation that six-member juries be instituted is that the procedure would result in a savings of time and money in the jury selection process. No showing was made, however, that in those few States that now require smaller juries that their utilization results in any appreciable savings, and I feel that the abandonment of a practice that has existed for more than 500 years should be supported by more than intuitive judgment.

My concern for the retention of the 12-member jury is not the result of blind adherence to tradition. Rather, I am concerned that the reduction in the number of jurors may work to the disadvantage of persons accused of crime.

A defendant in a criminal trial is entitled to a jury of his peers, one that ideally represents a cross section of the community. It seems obvious that a jury of six will less likely provide a cross section of the community than will one of 12.

Further, I question whether the smaller jury will not have the effect of easing the prosecutor's burden of proof. It would seem that it would be easier for him to convince six rather than 12 that he has met his burden. Moreover, the reduced size of the jury would make the possibility of the hung jury less likely. I am of the opinion that the possibility of a hung jury is an integral part of the concept of reasonable doubt, which, in turn, is the very cornerstone of the criminal process.

I regret that I am unable to join completely in the opinions of the eminent group of persons comprising the Courts Task Force. A great deal of the Task Force Report contains valuable innovative suggestions for the improvement of the judicial system. In other areas where my views differed from the majority I was willing merely to note my informal dissent from those views; however, in the two areas noted above, I cannot in good conscience accept the majority proposals.

# Chapter VII
# Corrections

The American correctional system today appears to offer minimum protection for the public and maximum harm to the offender. The system is plainly in need of substantial and rapid change.

Figures on recidivism make it clear that society today is not protected—at least not for very long—by incarcerating offenders, for many offenders return to crime shortly after release from prison. Indeed, there is evidence that the longer a man is incarcerated, the smaller is the chance that he will lead a law-abiding life on release.

There is also evidence that many persons in prison do not need to be there to protect society. For example, when the Supreme Court's *Gideon* decision[1] overturned the convictions of persons in the Florida prison system who had not had an attorney, more than 1,000 inmates were freed. Such a large and sudden release might be expected to result in an increase in crime. To check this hypothesis, two groups of inmates released at the time were matched on the basis of individual characteristics. The one significant difference was that one group of prisoners was released as a result of the *Gideon* decision and the other group at the expiration of their sentences. Over a period of 2½ years, the *Gideon* group had a recidivism rate of 13.6 percent, and the other group had almost twice that rate, 25.4 percent. Commented Louie Wainwright, director of Florida's corrections system:

[1] *Gideon* v. *Wainwright*, 372 U.S. 335 (1963). The research is described in Charles J. Eichman, *The Impact of the Gideon Decision upon Crime and Sentencing in Florida* (Florida Division of Corrections, 1966). Mr. Wainwright's statement is quoted on pp. 4-5.

The mass exodus from prison may prove that there are many inmates presently in prison who do not need to be there in order to protect society. It may prove that many more people can be safely released on parole without fear that they will commit new crimes. This may well be the most important lesson we can learn from the *Gideon* experience.

It also seems clear that many persons can serve their sentences in the community without undue danger to the public.

There is substantial evidence that probation, fines, public service requirements, and restitution are less costly than incarceration and consistently produce lower rates of recidivism after completion of sentence.

There is also in this country a growing concern for the widespread abuses in the correctional system. Within the past decade, courts have intervened in prison management. Whole state prison systems have been declared unconstitutional as violating the eighth amendment's prohibition against cruel and unusual punishment. In other cases, courts have ruled that prisoners' civil rights have been violated.

As one court stated:

> In the Court's estimation confinement itself within a given institution may amount to cruel and unusual punishment prohibited by the Constitution where the confinement is characterized by conditions and practices so bad as to be shocking to the conscience of reasonably civilized people even though a particular inmate may never be personally subject to any disciplinary action.[2]

Other courts have reached similar conclusions. In September 1972 the U.S. District Court for the Northern District of Mississippi found that the living units in the Mississippi prison system were "unfit for human habitation under any modern concept of decency" and that confinement of prisoners there under the present circumstances was "impermissible." In this case the U.S. Justice Department intervened on the side of the plaintiffs (prison inmates) after the suit was filed and asserted that the prison system was unconstitutionally segregated and violated the prisoners' rights.

The scrutiny of the courts has extended also to local jails

[2] *Holt* v. *Sarver*, 309 F. Supp. 362, 372-73 (E.D. Ark. 1970), *aff'd* 442 F. 2d 304 (8th Cir. 1971).

and to those forgotten people of the criminal justice system—persons detained awaiting trial. Federal Judge Alfonso J. Zirpoli of the Northern District of California felt compelled to visit the unit of the Alameda County jail where plaintiffs were detained prior to trial. "The shocking and debasing conditions which prevailed there constituted cruel and unusual punishment for man or beast ... the court's inescapable conclusion was that Greystone should be razed to the ground."[3]

In 1971-72, the U.S. Supreme Court decided eight cases directly affecting convicted offenders.[4] The offender's contention prevailed in all eight cases, five of them by unanimous vote. Formal procedures are needed to revoke a person's parole, the Court said. Prisoners are entitled to access to legal materials, and prison officials must provide reasonable opportunities to all prisoners for religious worship. A judge may not use unconstitutionally obtained convictions as the basis for sentencing an offender. Prisoners need not exhaust all possible State remedies before pursuing the Federal route in order to challenge conditions of their confinement. Offenders committed under State laws pertaining to defective delinquents or sexually related offenses are entitled to formal procedures if their sentences are to be extended.

# Major Recommendations

The pressures for change in the American correctional system today are intense; it is clear that a dramatic realignment of correctional methods is needed. The Commission has made many recommendations toward that end, including:
• Enactment of laws clearly defining prisoners' rights, rules of conduct, and disciplinary and grievance procedures to be followed by correctional authorities in dealing with offenders.
• Repeal of legislation that deprives ex-offenders of civil rights and opportunities for employment.

[3] *Brenneman* v. *Madigan*, 11 Crim. L. Rptr. 2248 (N.D. Cal. 1972).
[4] *Morrissey* v. *Brewer*, 408 U.S. 471 (1972); *Arciniega* v. *Freeman*, 404 U.S. 4 (1971); *Younger* v. *Gilmore*, 404 U.S. 15 (1971) affirming *Gilmore* v. *Lynch*, 319 F. Supp. 105 (N.D. Cal. 1970); *McNeil* v. *Director, Patuxent Institution*, 407 U.S. 245 (1971); *Wilwording* v. *Swenson*, 404 U.S. 249 (1971); *Cruz* v. *Beto*, 405 U.S. 319 (1972); *Humphrey* v. *Cady*, 405 U.S. 504 (1972); *U.S.* v. *Tucker*, 404 U.S. 443 (1972).

- Elimination of disparate sentencing practices.
- Increased diversion out of the criminal justice system for certain types of offenders.
- Unification within the executive branch of all non-Federal correctional functions and programs for adults and juveniles.
- Active recruitment of corrections personnel from minority groups and among women and ex-offenders.
- Payment of competitive salaries to corrections personnel.
- Recruitment of volunteers, including ex-offenders, for correctional programs.

## Priorities for Action

Recognizing the inadequacies of the Nation's correctional systems, the Commission identified six goals toward which corrections must move with speed and determination. Top priority must be given to action that will achieve these ends:
- Equity and justice in corrections.
- Narrowing of the base of corrections by excluding many juveniles, minor offenders, and sociomedical cases.
- Shift of correctional emphasis from institutions to community programs.
- Unification of corrections and total system planning.
- Manpower development.
- Greater involvement of the public in corrections.

In furtherance of these six goals, the Commission recommends in its *Report on Corrections* 159 specific standards. These are discussed in summary form in this chapter. Many of the standards are implicit in the recent court decisions. Others have grown out of accepted principles of public administration, such as the need for public agencies and agents to be accountable to the public they serve. Still others have come from the experience of correctional administrators across the country. A committee named by the American Correctional Association and members of the Association of State Correctional Administrators assisted the Commission by studying proposed standards and suggesting improvements.

These standards and goals for corrections cover many areas that have not traditionally been considered within the scope of correctional concern. The Commission, however, concluded that such matters as diversion from the criminal justice process, bail, and sentencing have a direct and important impact on correctional systems. These matters, together with the more traditional areas, are addressed in the following pages.

# Equity and Justice in Corrections

Corrections in the United States often has been—and in some areas still is—characterized by inhumane treatment of prisoners. Personnel in various correctional programs have made arbitrary and discriminatory decisions and exhibited a disregard for law. American society cannot tolerate such conditions. Moreover, it is illogical to try to train lawbreakers to obey the law in a system that does not itself respect law.

Further, correctional institutions too often are impeded by the sentencing practices of the courts. The disparity of sentences, as well as their length, determine the extent to which an offender may be rehabilitated. Rehabilitation is rarely achieved unless the offender perceives some justification for his sentence and sees his sentence as equitable—at least in terms of sentences imposed on fellow prisoners.

The Commission, in an effort to achieve equality and justice, thus offers two groups of recommendations relating to offenders' rights and sentencing practices.

## Rights of Defenders

Convicted offenders should retain all rights that citizens in general have except those rights that must be limited in order to carry out the criminal sanction or to administer a correctional facility or agency.

The strategy for correctional reform must be built on a foundation of nondiscriminatory, just, and humane action that honors the legal and social rights of the offender. Moreover, it is imperative that such action be seen by the offender himself as just and fair.

The Commission's standards in the area of offenders' rights are applicable to all persons under correctional control, but many apply with special force to sentenced offenders in prisons and other correctional institutions and to persons detained awaiting trial.

Several standards deal with the right of offenders to seek protection of the law within the judicial system. Each correctional agency should develop policies and procedures to guarantee the offender's right to:

- Access to the courts.
- Access to legal services.
- Access to legal materials.

These three standards are fundamental.

Guarantees of the right of access to the courts were among the first to be recognized by Federal and State courts. The result has been a dramatic increase in the number of petitions filed each year by prisoners.[5] The Commission realized that implementing guarantees of access to legal services and legal materials presents some problems. These are dealt with in detail in the Commission's *Report on Corrections*.

Another group of standards deals with the conditions under which prisoners live and identifies the prisoner's right to:

● Protection against personal abuse at the hands of staff and other inmates.

● Healthful surroundings.

● Medical care.

● Nondiscriminatory treatment.

Among the types of personal abuse by staff which the Commission rejects are corporal punishment and solitary confinement as punishment, except as a last resort and then for not more than 10 days.

To protect prisoners from abuse by other inmates, the standards call for classification to identify violence-prone prisoners and for better supervision throughout the institution.

Courts in Arkansas, California, Mississippi, Pennsylvania, Virginia, and elsewhere have recognized the strip cell, beatings, and similar disciplinary methods as cruel and unusual punishment. Lack of medical care for prisoners was found by a court in Alabama to be "barbarous" as well as unconstitutional.[6]

Other Commission standards deal with the discretionary power which correctional authorities exercise over offenders and how that power is to be regulated and controlled. The Commission recognizes that correctional agencies must have discretionary power, but this power must not be used arbitrarily or capriciously.

Toward this end the proper foundation for disciplinary action is a code which specifies prisoner behavior and which is easily understood. Many codes in use today are stated in terms that call for subjective and often unprovable judgments, such as prohibitions against being "untidy" or "insolent." Often the code is not explained to offenders in terms they understand.

[5] In the Federal courts alone, such petitions have risen from just over 2,000 in 1960 to more than 16,000 in 1970. In the latter year they constituted one out of every six civil filings.

[6] 12 Crim. L. Rptr. 2113 (M.D. Ala., 1972).

Rules of conduct should be limited to dealing with observable behavior that clearly can be shown to have an adverse effect on the individual or corrections agency, with a full explanation to all offenders concerned.

Disciplinary procedures should allow the individual to be informed of the violation with which he is charged and, on serious charges, to have a hearing at which he may present evidence contradicting or mitigating the charge.

Grievance procedures should allow an offender to report a grievance and have it investigated by a person who is not directly involved in the incident and who is in a position to see that action is taken to mitigate grievances that appear to be warranted.

Each correctional system should have a trained person whose major function is to act as ombudsman. He should hear complaints of both inmates and employees and initiate changes to remedy justified grievances.

Recent court decisions have made clear that prisoners, pretrial detainees, probationers, and parolees have continuing rights under the first amendment. Rights to expression and association are involved in:

• Exercise of free speech.
• Belonging to and participating in organizations and engaging in peaceful assemblies.
• Exercise of religious beliefs and practices.
• Preserving identity through distinguishing clothing, hairstyles, and other items of physical appearance.

The only justification for interfering with freedom of expression or association should be the showing of a compelling state interest in so doing. The degree of interference should be as little as is consistent with protecting the state's interest.

Maintenance of control in the face of an incipient riot is one obvious example of a compelling state interest as contemplated by the Commission. A parolee or probationer can be allowed more latitude than a prisoner in a tense maximum security institution. But agencies traditionally have applied a flat rule, regardless of circumstances, and the standard seeks to correct this situation.

Closely associated with freedom of expression and association is the access prisoners have to the public. Standards are provided in connection with:

• Sending and receiving mail.
• Having access to the communications media.
• Receiving visitors.

Offenders should have the right to correspond with anyone

429

and to send and receive any material that can be lawfully mailed, without limitation on volume or frequency. Correctional authorities should have the right to inspect incoming and outgoing mail for contraband but not to read or censor mail.

Except in emergencies such as institutional disorders, offenders should be allowed to present their views to the communications media through confidential and uncensored interviews with media representatives, uncensored letters and other communications with the media, and publication of articles and books on any subject.

Several recent court decisions have recognized both the public's right to know and the offender's right to tell. Moreover, if correctional authorities are willing to allow inmates more access to the public, the Commission believes they will help to lower the walls of isolation that corrections has built around itself. To build public support, correctional authorities should support public awareness of the needs of the institutions and their inmates.

Correctional authorities should not limit the number of visitors an offender may have or the length of the visit, so long as it is in line with reasonable institutional schedules. Indeed, authorities should promote visitation by providing a suitable place for visiting by individuals and families in privacy.

Potential denial of an offender's rights does not end with the completion of his sentence. All States apply indirect sanctions to the ex-offender and most deny him the right to vote, to hold public office, and to serve on a jury. Even more important to him from an economic standpoint is the widespread practice of denying an ex-offender a license to practice occupations regulated by government. The list of such occupations is long, ranging from barber to psychiatrist.

States should adopt legislation to repeal all mandatory provisions in law or civil service regulations that deprive ex-offenders of civil rights and opportunities for employment. Each State legislature should enact a code of offenders' rights. The sentencing court should have continuing jurisdiction over the sentenced offender during the term of his sentence.

If codes are not enacted, the courts will be kept busy for years defining rights which could well be made specific by State legislation. If the one sentencing court had continuing jurisdiction, the offender could apply to the court for relief if he believed his rights were being denied.

# Sentencing

Sentencing practices of the courts are of crucial importance to corrections. The sentence determines whether a convicted offender is to be confined or be supervised in the community and how long corrections is to have control over him.

If the offender is to benefit from time spent under sentence, it is essential that he feel his sentence is justifiable rather than arbitrary. The man sentenced to 10 years who shares a cell with a man convicted of the same offense under similar circumstances and sentenced to 5 years works against a handicap of bitterness and frustration. Such feelings must be accentuated if the men are of different races, or if one had money to hire a lawyer and the other did not.

The *New York Times*, in the fall of 1972, made a study of sentencing practices that highlighted sentence disparity as a major impediment to effective corrections. Among offenders sentenced to Federal prisons in 1970, whites convicted of income tax evasion were committed for an average of 12.8 months; nonwhites for 28.6 months. In drug cases, the average for whites was 61.1 months; for nonwhites, 81.1 months. The forthcoming 1973 report of the Federal Bureau of Prisons shows that in 1972 the average sentence of all persons committed to Federal prisons was 43.3 months for whites and 58.7 months for blacks. While the reader should not infer that these are all direct cause-and-effect relationships, these national statistics obviously raise questions about the equity of current sentencing practices in all jurisdictions.

**Sentencing councils should be established, in which judges in multijudge courts would meet to discuss cases awaiting sentences in order to assist the trial judge in arriving at an appropriate sentence. Appellate review of sentencing decisions should be authorized.**

Sentencing institutes should also be set up under State auspices, at which sentencing judges, other criminal justice personnel, and possibly members of the academic community would meet regularly to discuss sentencing alternatives and criteria and reexamine sentencing procedures.

Sentencing councils were originally developed in the U.S. District Court for the Eastern District of Michigan, where sentences now tend to be less disparate. Sentencing institutes, also first developed for the Federal judiciary, are now used by several States. Appellate review of sentencing, according to the American Bar Association's study of sentencing alternatives, is now "realistically available in every serious case"

431

in only about 15 States.[7] Even in these States, courts have moved cautiously. However, it is widely believed that, where sentence review is not available, a number of appellate courts have reversed trial courts largely because the sentence was inappropriate.

In addition, the Commission recommends the following to achieve greater equity and less disparity:

• Sentencing courts should hold a hearing prior to imposition of sentence, at which the defendant should have the right to be represented by counsel and to present arguments as to sentencing alternatives.

• Whenever the court feels it necessary—and always where long-term incarceration is a possible disposition—a full presentence report on the offender should be in the hands of the judge before the sentencing hearing.

• Sentencing courts should be required to make specific findings and state specific reasons for the imposition of sentence.

A root cause of the disparity in sentencing in the United States is inconsistency in penal codes. The American Bar Association in a study of sentencing alternatives noted that in one State a person convicted of first-degree murder must serve 10 years before he becomes eligible for parole, while one convicted of second-degree murder may be forced to serve 15 years.[8]

Many States now are undertaking massive revisions of their criminal codes that should eliminate some sentencing discrepancies.

In revising their criminal codes, the Commission recommends that States adopt a sentencing structure based on a 5-year maximum sentence unless the offender is in a special category of "persistent," "professional," or "dangerous" offenders. At present sentences are harsher in the United States than in any other Western country. This stems partly from the high maximum sentences authorized by law. To insure that the dangerous offender is removed from society, legislatures have in effect increased the possible maximum sentence for all offenders. This dragnet approach has resulted in imposition of high maximum sentences on persons who may not need them. Like disparities in sentences, this approach seriously handicaps correctional programs.

[7] American Bar Association Project on Minimum Standards for Criminal Justice, *Appellate Review of Sentences* (1968), p. 13.

[8] American Bar Association Project on Minimum Standards for Criminal Justice, *Sentencing Alternatives and Procedures* (1968), p. 49.

The impact of unduly long sentences on corrections is shown by studies of recidivism among offenders who have served differing lengths of sentences. A California study found that shorter incarceration was associated with no significant increase in recidivism; in some cases, it was accompanied by a decrease.[9] Among Federal parolees, a researcher found that parole violation rates increased with the length of time served. For persons serving 6 months or less before parole, the violation rate was 9 percent; among those serving 5 years or longer, the rate was 64.5 percent.[10]

**The Commission recommends a maximum sentence of 5 years for most offenders, with no minimum sentence imposed by statute. The Commission recommends a maximum sentence not to exceed 25 years for a convicted offender who is:**

1. **A persistent offender;**
2. **A professional criminal; or**
3. **A dangerous offender.**

A persistent offender is one who has been convicted of a third felony, two of them within the past 5 years. A professional criminal is one convicted of a felony committed as part of a continuing illegal business in which he was in a management position or an executor of violence. A dangerous offender is one whose criminal conduct shows: a pattern of repetitive behavior that poses a serious threat to the safety of others; persistent aggressive behavior without regard to consequences; or a particularly heinous offense involving infliction or threat of serious bodily injury or death.

The Commission decided not to speak on the question of using the death penalty to deter or punish murderers, because of the unresolved constitutional and legal questions raised by recent court decisions. Resolution of this question, it believes, should be left to referendums, State legislatures, or the courts.

The American Bar Association, noting the *Gideon* study described at the beginning of this chapter and the significantly shorter average sentences imposed by Western European judges, comments that the prison sentences now authorized, and sometimes required, in this country "are significantly higher than are needed in the vast majority of cases in order to adequately protect the interests of the public." Ex-

[9] California Assembly, Committee on Criminal Procedure, *Deterrent Effects of Criminal Sanctions* (1968).

[10] Administrative Office of the U.S. Courts, *Persons under Supervision of the Federal Probation System* (1968).

cept for a very few particularly serious offenses and under special circumstances similar to those recommended by the Commission for extended terms, the ABA standard states, "the maximum authorized prison term ought to be 5 years and only rarely 10."[11]

# Narrowing the Base of Corrections

The Commission believes that the public would be better served and correctional and other resources put to more effective use if many persons who now come under correctional responsibility were diverted out of the criminal justice process. More persons accused of illegal acts should be directed away from processing through the formal criminal justice system prior to adjudication by means of organized diversion programs.

Some conduct that may now result in correctional supervision or incarceration—drunkenness, vagrancy, or acts illegal only for children, for example—should be excluded from juvenile justice and criminal law, and not be brought before the courts and thus not channeled to corrections. (A more detailed discussion of the issue will be found in this report in the chapters on Criminal Code Reform and Revision and on Courts.) Other conduct, such as drug abuse or prostitution, may remain illegal, but, because corrections is not equipped to deal with it effectively, it should be handled through other resources. In short, to improve correctional services, it is imperative that corrections be given responsibility only for persons who need correctional services.

Corrections can do a better job, the Commission believes, if it does not have to handle persons with whom it is unequipped to deal. Among these are the drunks who in many jurisdictions go in and out of jail, forming the most conspicuous example of the revolving door syndrome, with perhaps two million arrests a year. Like the inebriates, drug addicts need treatment rather than the correctional mill. Similarly, corrections is unequipped to handle the mentally disturbed who are often incarcerated.

Some States have decriminalized public drunkenness and vagrancy, and the Commission recommends that all States do so. If States follow other Commission suggestions that there be no incarceration for certain acts that do not endanger

---

[11] *Sentencing Alternatives and Procedures*, p. 21.

public safety, corrections can put its resources to more productive use.

Indeed, for many persons accused of criminal acts, official system processing is counterproductive. To meet the needs of these persons, planned programs must be developed as alternatives to processing into the justice system. The argument for diversion programs that occur prior to court adjudication is that they give society the opportunity to reallocate existing resources to programs that promise greater success than formal criminal sanctions.

It should be noted that the criminal justice system has never processed all persons accused of criminal acts. Criminal justice personnel have used this discretion to halt prosecution for many reasons. For example, some statutes may not be enforced because the community is not really concerned about the behavior in question. In other cases, the nature of the offense, the circumstances of its commission, the attitude of the victim, and the character and social status of the accused may cause the accused to be diverted from the criminal justice system. In still other instances, some cases are not processed because the volume of cases is so large that less serious offenders must be diverted to allow law enforcement, courts, and corrections to concentrate on the more serious cases.

These processes by which some cases are not prosecuted have sometimes operated in ways that were discriminatory. They have also been used without regard to the most effective allocation of resources. The Commission therefore endorses adoption of criteria by which equitable and logical choices can be made to exclude individuals who do not need the official attention of the system or one of its parts.

Many persons, especially the young, who are arrested for minor first offenses are not likely to repeat them, particularly if they have resources available through community agencies such as counseling, medical or mental health services, employment, and job training. Legislative or administrative action that excluded many children and youth from the justice system would force development of whatever private or community alternatives were needed. It would reduce workloads of correctional staff and offer greater opportunity for constructive work with offenders remaining within the system.

In sum, the Commission recommends that each jurisdiction plan for diversion from the justice system of persons who are not dangerous to others, if prosecution may cause undue harm or merely exacerbate the social problem that led to the illegal act; services to meet their needs are available in the community; arrest has already served as a desired deterrent; and the needs and interests of the victims and of society are better served by diversion than by official processing. The question of diversion and the courts is discussed in Chapter 6 of this report.

# Emphasis on Community-Based Programs

The Commission believes that the most hopeful move toward effective corrections is to continue and strengthen the trend away from confining people in institutions and toward supervising them in the community. At least two-thirds of those under correctional control are already in some community-based program—probation, parole, work release, study release, or some other form of conditional release. The thrust of the Commission's *Report on Corrections* is that probation, which is now the largest community-based program, will become the standard sentence in criminal cases, with confinement retained chiefly for those offenders who cannot safely be supervised in the community.

## Failure of State Institutions

There are compelling reasons to continue the move away from institutions. First, State institutions consume more than three-fourths of all expenditures for corrections while dealing with less than one-third of all offenders.[12] Second, as a whole they do not deal with those offenders effectively. There is no evidence that prisons reduce the amount of crime. On the contrary, there is evidence that they contribute to criminal activity after the inmate is released.

[12] These proportions were shown by the most recent nationwide survey of offenders and correctional expenditures, made in 1965 by the National Council on Crime and Delinquency and shown in the President's Commission on Law Enforcement and Administration of Justice, *Task Force Report: Corrections* (1967), p. 1. The *1970 National Jail Census* published by the Law Enforcement Assistance Administration in 1971 and the *National Prisoner Statistics,* issued by the Bureau of Prisons (Bulletin 47, 1972) show that there has been a decline in the number of inmates of Federal and State prisons and local jails since the 1965 survey. Hence it seems likely that the proportion of offenders who are under supervision in the community may be near three-fourths.

Prisons tend to dehumanize people—turning them from individuals into mere numbers. Their weaknesses are made worse, and their capacity for responsibility and self-government is eroded by regimentation. Add to these facts the physical and mental conditions resulting from overcrowding and from the various ways in which institutions ignore the rights of offenders, and the riots of the past decade are hardly to be wondered at. Safety for society may be achieved for a limited time if offenders are kept out of circulation, but no real public protection is provided if confinement serves mainly to prepare men for more, and more skilled, criminality.

Confinement can be even less effective for children and youth. Some 19th century "reform schools" still exist with a full heritage of brutality.[13] Some newer institutions, also in rural settings, provide excellent education, recreation, and counseling but require expensive and extensive plants capable of providing for the total needs of children over prolonged periods.

The Commission believes that, if a residential facility for confinement of juveniles is necessary, it should be in or close to a city. It should not duplicate services that are available in the community, such as schools and clinical services, but should obtain these services for its residents by purchase or contract. In this way a child in a residential program will learn by testing himself in the community where he must live.

The Commission believes that some institutions will be necessary for the incarceration of adults who cannot be supervised in the community without endangering public safety, but there are more than enough facilities at hand for this purpose. The Commission recognizes, too, that some States will require time to develop alternatives to incarceration for juveniles.

**States should refrain from building any more State institutions for juveniles; States should phase out present institutions over a 5-year period.**

**They should also refrain from building more State institutions for adults for the next 10 years except when total system planning shows that the need for them is imperative.**

[13] See Howard James, *Children in Trouble* (McKay, 1970) and the chapter on juvenile intake and detention in the Commission's *Report on Corrections.*

437

Institutions that must remain in use should be modified in order to minimize the harmful effects of the physical environment on inmates. The facilities and functions of each institution should be reexamined at least every 5 years in connection with long-range planning for the State's entire correctional system.

The Commission believes that States should follow the example of Massachusetts, which has closed down all statewide institutions for juveniles. Several youth institutions in California have already been closed, and it is now proposed that the rest should be phased out.

All institutions or sections of institutions that do not meet health and safety standards should be closed down until such standards are met, as many courts have required. New facilities should be located close to cities from which most inmates come, so that family ties can be maintained. Such locations also make it easier to hire qualified staff and to purchase local services by contract.

Adult institutions should revamp their programs so that, among other things, the job training they offer trains for real jobs, using skilled supervision and modern machinery. Within about 5 years, prison industries should pay wages at rates prevailing in the area around the institution. In this event, it would be possible to obligate the inmate to repay the State for a reasonable share of its costs in maintaining him.

## Salvaging the Jail

The conditions in local jails often are far worse than those in State prisons. Local jails are old—the national jail census made for the Law Enforcement Assistance Administration (LEAA) in 1970 showed that one out of every four cells was more than 50 years old and some were more than 100 years old. Many do not meet rudimentary requirements of sanitation—50 jails had no flush toilets and investigations in many institutions have revealed filthy cells, bedding, and food. Some jails surveyed, notably in the District of Columbia, had nearly half again as many inmates as they were designed to hold. Only half of the jails had any medical facilities.[14]

Nine out of 10 jails surveyed had no recreational or educational programs. According to inmates, one of the grimmest

[14] Law Enforcement Assistance Administration, *1970 National Jail Census* (1971), pp. 1-5.

aspects of serving time in such places is having little or nothing to do, day after day.

Although conditions in some jails are better than those just described, the Commission believes that little improvement is likely over the country as a whole until jails are run by correctional authorities rather than local law enforcement agencies, whose personnel are largely untrained for custodial or correctional functions.

**Jails should be part of the unified State correctional system called for later in this chapter. The Commission also urged States to develop probation for misdemeanants as an alternative to jail sentences.**

As part of the correctional system, jails could provide services and programs many inmates need—education (in cooperation with local schools), vocational training, job placement, recreation, and various forms of conditional release.

Many inmates, including juveniles, are being held in local jails for long periods before coming to trial. The 1970 jail census showed that 83,000 persons (half of all the adult prisoners and two-thirds of all the juveniles) were being held prior to trial. In some institutions, the proportion was much higher—in the District of Columbia in 1971, 80 percent were being held prior to trial, some of them for as long as 36 months. These persons, all legally innocent, are held with convicted offenders.

Most of the detainees are in jail because they are too poor to make bail, and family and friends cannot help. The commission believes that a person's financial resources should not determine whether he is detained prior to trial. The commission commends such alternatives as issuance of citations instead of arrest; release on recognizance; and cash deposit of 10 percent of the bond with the court, a system that eliminates the bail bondsman. All of these programs have been tried in various jurisdictions in the United States, with low rates of failure to appear in court. Expediting criminal trials by requiring that a person be brought to trial not more than 30 days after a misdemeanor arrest (as recommended in Chapter 6) would also cut down on the amount of pretrial detention.

## Improving Community-Based Programs

Not all the arguments for basing corrections in the community are negative ones such as the ineffectiveness and high cost of institutions. Community-based programs have important positive value in themselves.

The wide variety of correctional programs that are available—or could be made available—in communities allows a court to select one that is suited to the needs of an individual offender. A youth, for example, may be sentenced to probation under varying conditions, such as the requirement that he make restitution to the victim or work at a public service job. Or he may be sentenced to partial confinement in a residential facility (sometimes called a halfway house) under supervision during hours when he is not working or at school. An adult may be required to live in a similar facility, working during the day and returning to the halfway house at night.

Another advantage of community-based programs is that they can make use of resources that are provided to citizens in general—health, education, counseling, and employment services. This is an economical use of resources and one that keeps the offender in the community itself or helps him to return to it after incarceration.

Perhaps the major contribution of community-based programs is that they keep the offender in the community where he must ultimately live, rather than in an isolated institution where all decisions are made for him and he becomes less and less able to cope with life on the outside. Participation of volunteers will assist in keeping the offender part of the community.

The Commission makes several suggestions designed to improve and extend community-based programs:

• Both probation and parole officers should act as resource brokers to secure services for offenders in their charge, rather than acting solely as control agents.

• The casework approach, which has dominated probation, should shift to teamwork and differential assignments.

• Probation should be extended to misdemeanants.

• Both probation and parole must follow practices that offer due process to offenders threatened with revocation of their status.

• Both probation and parole need more trained workers, particularly those who come from the ethnic and racial groups which contribute heavily to the offender population.

• Correctional authorities should develop detailed procedures to assure that probationers and parolees are adequately supervised.

The Commission emphasizes that programs and services

must take precedence over buildings. Communities that rush into construction to house new programs may be repeating the mistakes this country made over the past 200 years, when well-meant experiments like the penitentiary eventually produced monstrosities like Attica, San Quentin, and Parchman.

# Unified Correctional Programs and Total System Planning

American correction systems range in size and shape from huge State departments to autonomous one-man probation offices. Some States combine corrections with other governmental functions—law enforcement, health, or social welfare, for example. Some programs are managed in a highly professional manner, others by methods that are outmoded and ineffective.

LEAA recently reported that there are about 5,300 correctional agencies in the United States. Only one out of every six of these agencies is operated at the State level. The rest are run by counties, cities, villages, or townships, independently or in an often confusing variety of combinations.

Seeking at various times and for varying purposes to provide something more effective than prisons, State legislatures and their counterparts in counties and cities created reformatories, probation, parole, "industrial schools," and community programs for delinquent children. Agencies within the same jurisdiction often operate under contradictory assumptions, practices, and goals. With such a nonsystem, it is difficult to allocate tax dollars rationally, almost impossible to hold any one agency or agency head accountable for the results.

The Commission believes that all States should follow the example of the five States—Alaska, Connecticut, Delaware, Rhode Island, and Vermont—that now exercise control over all non-Federal correctional activities within their boundaries.

**By 1978, each State should enact legislation to unify within the executive branch all non-Federal correctional functions and programs for adults and juveniles, including service for persons awaiting trial; probation supervision; institutional confinement; community-based programs, whether prior to or during institutional confinement; and parole and other aftercare programs.**

The board of parole may be administratively part of the overall correctional agency, but it should be autonomous in

441

its decisionmaking. It also should be separate from parole field services.

An integrated, State-controlled correctional system would make it possible to streamline activities and reduce waste and overlap, thus making the most effective use of tax dollars and professional talent. Uniform staff development programs, interdepartmental career opportunities, and civil service would help provide high standards of performance. Integration of correctional planning would also minimize disparities among programs that now impede the flow and quality of services to offenders. Systemwide research and evaluation would increase feedback on how programs are working and make the system accountable to the public.

The Commission emphasizes its conviction that an integrated State correctional system is not in conflict with the concept of community-based corrections. The fact that a State agency makes statewide plans does not imply remote control of programs in the community. Rather it makes possible logical and systematic planning that can be responsive to changing problems and priorities. It implies maximum use of local personnel and fiscal resources to guarantee that programs will be developed to meet diverse local needs and local conditions.

Statewide planning indeed should be a stimulus to planning on the local level. At both levels, corrections needs to be seen as part of the total criminal justice system. Changes in one part of the system will require changes elsewhere. If public drunkenness is decriminalized, a detoxification center will be needed to replace the drunk tank in the local jail. Adoption of release on recognizance programs and probation for misdemeanants will reduce jail populations and allow resources to be allocated to programs for sentenced offenders. Within the corrections subsystem, sound planning will make it possible to supply services and programs on a regional basis in sparsely populated areas and, conversely, to provide a network of services in highly urbanized areas.

# Manpower Development

People are the most important resource in the fight against crime. In corrections they are the resource that is scarcest and most poorly used.

Corrections needs to use modern management techniques to analyze its manpower needs, recruit and train personnel to fill those needs, and retain staff who perform well and show interest in the job. Achieving these ends is hampered by lack of interest or information on the part of managers and by outmoded restraints and prejudices in hiring and promotions.

**The Commission believes that active efforts must be made to recruit from minority groups, which are usually overrepresented among offenders and underrepresented among the staff.**

At Attica in upstate New York before the 1971 riot, 54 percent of the inmates were black and 9 percent Puerto Rican, but only one black and one Puerto Rican were on the staff. More blacks and Puerto Ricans, have since been hired, but the differences in the racial makeup between inmates and staff still are great.[15]

Some correctional administrators, like those in New York, have recognized the urgency of having an institution staff that can achieve rapport with offenders, who tend to be young, to be black, Puerto Rican, Chicano, or Indian (depending on the area), and to come from ghettos or rural slums. Much more effort must be made to interest people from these groups in careers in corrections.

Community-based correctional programs also have needs and potentials for the use of minority people. In probation, for example, the minority staff member may know the problems of the offender more intimately than do his white colleagues and often can more easily locate potential sources of help. These probabilities are increased among the staff hired to serve in paraprofessional capacities in the neighborhoods from which probationers come.

Special training programs, more intensive and comprehensive than standard programs, can be devised to replace educational and experience requirements. But it must be emphasized that training in intergroup relations is essential for all recruits to corrections, with refresher courses given as standard elements of staff development programs.

**The Commission also recommends that corrections make use of other underutilized human resources, particularly women and ex-offenders.**

Because women have been discriminated against in hiring and promotion throughout the corrections field, particularly in male institutions, they have been effectively eliminated from management positions except in the few institutions for females. There appears to be no good reason why women should not be hired for any type of position in corrections.

[15] *Attica*, Official Report of the New York State Special Commission on Attica (Bantam Books, 1972), pp. 24, 28.

Ex-offenders have experience in corrections and often have rapport with offenders that gives them special value as correctional employees. They have been through the system and understand its effects on the individual. California, Illinois, New York, and Washington have pioneered in the use of ex-offenders in correctional work. There is obvious need for careful selection and training of ex-offenders. Their use in correctional programs may be high-risk, but it is also potentially high-gain.

Finally, there is a need to change current policies to secure and retain qualified personnel.

**Correctional personnel should be paid salaries competitive with those of other criminal justice personnel who work in positions calling for comparable training and performance. Outmoded requirements of residence and physique should be eliminated. Lateral entry should also be made possible, to facilitate hiring men and women of special ability from outside a given system.**

Employees with years of experience are reluctant to enter a new system if they must leave behind the pension benefits of the old. The Commission suggests a pension system that would permit benefits to accompany the employee from one agency to another, within or between States.

# Increased Involvement of the Public

The degree to which the public understands, accepts, and participates in correctional programs will determine to a large extent not only how soon, but how successfully, corrections can operate in the community and how well institutions can prepare the inmate for return to it.

Public participation is widespread in both institutional programs and community-based programs. The National Information Center on Volunteers in Courts, operating in Boulder, Colo., estimates that citizen volunteers outnumber professionals by four or five to one. According to the Center, about 70 percent of correctional agencies which deal with felons have some sort of volunteer program to aid them. Volunteer work with the misdemeanant is even more widespread.

Some volunteers supplement professional activities, as in teaching, while others play roles unique to volunteers in friendship situations, such as big brothers to delinquent youngsters. Other citizens serve as fundraisers or organizers of needed services, goods, and facilities.

In recent years institution doors have been opened to volunteer groups, including Alcoholics Anonymous and other self-help groups, ethnic organizations, and churches. Such programs have the double effect of involving citizens in the correctional system and providing services that inmates need.

Intensive efforts should be made to recruit volunteers from minority groups, the poor, inner city residents, ex-offenders who can serve as success models, and professionals who can bring special expertise to correctional programs.

Training should be provided to volunteers to instill understanding of lifestyles common among offenders and to acquaint them with the objectives and problems of corrections. A paid coordinator of volunteers should be hired in each program using volunteer help.

Although corrections has succeeded in bringing citizen participants into many institutions, it has often met resistance when it has tried to set up residential facilities in communities. Opinion surveys have shown that people who register general approval of halfway houses, drug treatment centers, and similar facilities, are often alarmed at the thought of such a facility in their own neighborhood, fearing it would jeopardize public safety or depreciate property values.

The Commission recommends that institutions plan for programs that bridge the gap between institutions and community residents. Institutions should actively develop maximum interaction between the community and the institution, involving citizens in planning and activities.

Work-release programs should involve advice from employer and labor groups. Offenders should be able to participate in community educational programs, and, conversely, community members with special interest in educational or other programs at the institution should be able to participate in them. The institution should cultivate active participation of civic groups and encourage the groups to invite offenders to become members.

For such activity to become widespread, there will have to be a general change in the attitude of corrections itself. The correctional system is one of the few public services today that is isolated from the public it serves. Public apathy toward improving the system is due in part to the tendency of corrections to keep the public out—literally by walls, figuratively by failure to explain its objectives. If corrections is to receive the public support it needs, it will have to take the initiative in securing it. This cannot be achieved by keeping the public ignorant about the state of corrections and thus pre-

445

venting it from developing a sense of responsibility for the correctional process.

# Setting the Program in Motion

The program of action outlined in this chapter will require a major national commitment on many fronts. Measures to be taken are interrelated; the effectiveness of each depends on accomplishments of the others.

## Adequate Financing

Corrections is in difficulty today partly because not enough money has been provided to support even existing programs adequately. Nothing is left for investment in change.

Anyone familiar with State and local corrections knows that it is at the end of the line when legislators and county commissioners are parceling out available tax funds. States and localities combined now are spending about $1.5 billion a year on corrections, an amount that just maintains the system at its present grossly deficient level of operation. The Federal Government contributes, through LEAA, about $200 million a year.

The Commission believes that a large increase in funding—possibly double the amounts now appropriated—is essential if corrections is to become a more effective part of the criminal justice system. All levels of government—particularly the Federal level—should increase their contributions substantially.

## Needed Legislation

State and Federal penal and correctional codes are striking examples of the problems created by passing laws to meet specific situations without considering other laws already in force. For the most part, these codes have been enacted piecemeal over generations and follow no consistent pattern or philosophy. Indeed, the lack of a basic philosophy of the purpose of corrections is as crippling to operation of the system as are contradictions between statutes. The Commission calls attention to the 1972 action of the Illinois legislature in passing a unified code of corrections and urges all States to do so.

Reform of penal and correctional codes will require time. If it is to be done in the 5-year period suggested by the Commission, the entire code of a State should be redrafted and considered legislatively as a package.

As each jurisdiction has its own history and traditions regarding the legislative process, success in reforming a penal and correctional code will depend on careful planning from the start and the involvement of progressively larger groups of legislators, administrators, judges, and other citizens as the drafting progresses.

## Manpower

This Commission has emphasized the importance of qualified manpower throughout the criminal justice system. Nowhere is the lack of educated and trained personnel more conspicuous than in corrections.

A major problem is to attract capable people to corrections in the first place. They can be persuaded to enter the field only if the image of regimentation and failure is changed to one of potential success in changing offenders and reducing crime. Changing the image will depend in large measure upon the present personnel in corrections.

Availability of education to prepare students for careers in corrections is also essential. Federal funds are available for scholarships. States must take responsibility for insuring that criminal justice curriculums with correction-oriented components are available throughout the State and that efforts are made to recruit graduates into State and local programs.

## National Institute of Corrections

A national academy of corrections has been proposed for many years. At the National Conference on Corrections held in Williamsburg, Va., in December 1971, the Attorney General directed LEAA and the Bureau of Prisons to work with the States in developing such an academy, to be called the National Institute of Corrections.

Among other proposed functions, the Institute would serve as a clearinghouse for information on crime and corrections; provide consultant services; fund training programs; and coordinate and fund correctional research. At present none of these functions is being satisfactorily fulfilled on a national basis.

A national institute with the authority and funds for this wide range of activities could serve as a powerful force for coordinating and implementing a national effort to reform corrections. The Commission urges immediate action to make it a reality.

## Accreditation of Corrections Agencies

All accreditation system for corrections would be used to recognize and maintain standards of service, programs, and institutions, and eventually to bring about higher levels of quality.

One function of the accreditation system would be to hold the correctional administrator accountable for results. In the past, custodial institutions have been required only to keep offenders until ordered to release them. Probation and parole agencies have been required to list offenders in their charge and report violations. In short, unless riots, escapes, and scandals occurred, the correctional administrator had satisfied requirements.

But if accountability is to be a basic principle of correctional management, as the Commission recommends, the manager must have tools by which to measure. It is a waste of public funds to impose penal terms without either knowing the goals to be achieved or having some method to measure accomplishments.

The Commission urges the implementation of an accreditation plan for corrections which would help measure accomplishment of individual institutions and generally elevate standards of performance in correctional programs.

# Conclusion

A national commitment to change is essential if there is to be any significant reform of corrections, for this is a formidable task. High recidivism rates, riot and unrest in prisons, revelations of brutality and degradation in jails, increasing litigation against correctional officials, and indignant public reactions attest to the need for change in corrections.

The chairman of the U.S. Board of Parole said in an address to the American Correctional Association in the summer of 1972:

> To put it bluntly, the field of corrections is experiencing a crisis in public confidence, and the crisis shows no sign of abating. Unlike times past, we can't expect to handle the problem by letting it wear itself out.

Corrections must commence reform now. But corrections cannot accomplish the needed reform in its traditional isolation. It must act vigorously to enlist the support of legislators, local officials, law enforcement personnel, community agencies, and various other public and private groups.

Reform in corrections will also require changes in public values and attitudes. The public must recognize that crime and delinquency are related to the kind of society in which offenders live. Reduction of crime may therefore depend on basic social change.

# Excerpts from the Task Force Report on Corrections

## 1: Corrections and the Criminal Justice System

... It is clear that a dramatic realignment of correctional methods is called for. It is essential to abate use of institutions. Meanwhile much can be done to eliminate the worst effects of the institutions—its crippling idleness, anonymous brutality, and destructive impact. Insofar as the institution has to be relied on, it must be small enough, so located, and so operated that it can relate to the problems offenders pose for themselves and the community....

Behind these clear imperatives lies the achievable principle of a much greater selectivity and sophistication in the use of crime control and correctional methods. These great powers should be reserved for controlling persons who seriously threaten others. They should not be applied to the nuisances, the troublesome, and the rejected who now clutter our prisons and reformatories and fill our jails and youth detention facilities.

The criminal justice system should become the agency of last resort for social problems. The institution should be the last resort for correctional problems....

### Jails and Pretrial Detention

... Detention before trial should be used only in extreme circumstances and then only under careful judicial control. The function of detention prior to trial is not correctional. However, as long as pretrial detention is used at all, it should be carried out in the recommended community correctional centers because of the resources that will be available there. Thus, by implication, corrections is assuming responsibility for the pretrial detainee, even though this is not properly its function as defined here.

## Varying Purposes of Corrections

... In the new view, crime and delinquency are symptoms of failure and disorganization in the community as well as in the offender himself. He has had too little contact with the positive forces that develop law-abiding conduct—among them good schools, gainful employment, adequate housing, and rewarding leisure-time activities. So a fundamental objective of corrections must be to secure for the offender contacts, experiences, and opportunities that provide a means and a stimulus for pursuing a lawful style of living in the community. Thus, both the offender and the community become the focus of correctional activity. With this thrust, reintegration of the offender into the community comes to the fore as a major purpose of corrections.

Corrections clearly has many purposes. It is important to recognize that correctional purposes can differ for various types of offenders. In sentencing the convicted murderer we usually are serving punitive and deterrent rather than rehabilitative purposes. Precisely the contrary is true with respect to the deprived, ill-educated, vocationally incompetent youth who is adjudged delinquent; with him, rehabilitative and reintegrative purposes predominate. ...

## Standards and Goals in Corrections

... Standards and goals must be realistic and achievable, but that certainly does not mean that they need to be modest. The American culture has not only a bursting energy but also a remarkable capacity for adapting to change. What was unthinkable yesterday may be accepted as common practice today. In the criminal justice system, such changes have been observable in recent years with respect to the treatment of narcotics addiction and in the law's attitude toward a range of victimless crimes. They have been seen in the remarkable sweep of the movement toward procedural due process in all judicial and quasi-judicial hearings within the criminal justice system. When the courts abandoned the "hands-off" doctrine that led them to avoid inquiry into prison conditions, this was another aspect of change. ...

## Corrections and the Police

... If many of the standards proposed in this report are adopted, the police will perhaps take an even dimmer view of correctional adequacy. If local jails and other misdemeanant institutions are brought within the correctional system and removed from police jurisdiction, corrections will bear the responsibility for a substantially larger number of problems that would otherwise fall to the police. Likewise, as additional techniques are implemented that divert more apparently salvageable offenders out of the criminal justice system at an early state, those offenders who remain within the system will be the most dangerous and the poorest risks. Obviously, a higher percentage of these offenders are likely to fail in their readjustment to society.

Police decisions to concentrate on particular types of offenses will directly affect correctional programming. A large number of arrests for offenses that do not involve a significant danger to the community may result in misallocation and improper distribution of scarce correctional resources. The correctional system may be ill-prepared to cope with a larger than normal influx of certain types of offenders. . . .

It should also be noted that the police can make affirmative contributions to the success of community-based programs. The police officer knows his community; he knows where resources useful for the offender are available; he knows the pitfalls that may tempt the offender. The police officer is himself a valuable community resource that should be available for correctional programs. This of course requires the police to take a view of their function as one of preventing future crime as well as enforcing the law and maintaining public order. . . .

## Corrections and the Courts

. . . Sentencing decisions by the courts affect the discretion of correctional administrators in applying correctional programs. Sentencing courts generally have accepted the concept of the indeterminate sentence, which grants correctional administrators broad discretion in individualizing programs for particular offenders.

There is growing recognition that disparity in sentencing limits corrections' ability to develop sound attitudes in offenders. The man who is serving a 10-year sentence for the same act for which a fellow prisoner is serving 3 years is not likely to be receptive to correctional programs. He is in fact unlikely to respect any of society's institutions. Some courts have attempted to solve the problem of disparity in sentencing through the use of sentencing councils and other devices. Appellate review of sentencing would further diminish the possibility of disparity.

The appropriateness of the sentence imposed by the court will determine in large measure the effectiveness of the correctional program. This report recognizes that prison confine-

452

ment is an inappropriate sanction for the vast majority of criminal offenders. Use of probation and other community-based programs will continue to grow. This essential ingredient in the integration of courts and corrections into a compatible system of criminal justice is the free flow of information regarding sentencing and its effect on individual offenders. . . .

## Overemphasis on Custody

The pervasive overemphasis on custody that remains in corrections creates more problems than it solves. Our institutions are so large that their operational needs take precedence over the needs of the people they hold. The very scale of these institutions dehumanizes, denies privacy, encourages violence, and defies decent control. A moratorium should be placed on the construction of any large correctional institution. We already have too many prisons. If there is any need at all for more institutions, it is for small, community-related facilities in or near the communities they serve.

There is also urgent need for reducing the population of jails and juvenile detention facilities. By using group homes, foster care arrangements, day residence facilities, and similar community-based resources, it should be possible to eliminate entirely the need for institutions to hold young persons prior to court disposition of their cases. Likewise, by other methods discussed in this report, it will be practicable to greatly reduce the use of jails for the adult accused. By placing limitations on detention time and by freely allowing community resources, agencies, and individuals to percolate the walls of the jail, it will be possible to minimize the social isolation of those who must be jailed.

Nevertheless, it must be recognized that at our present level of knowledge (certainly of adult offenders) we lack the ability to empty prisons and jails entirely. There are confirmed and dangerous offenders who require protracted confinement because we lack alternative and more effective methods of controlling or modifying their behavior. At least for the period of incarceration, they are capable of no injury to the community.

Even so, far too many offenders are classified as dangerous. We have not developed a means of dealing with them except in the closed institution. Too often we have perceived them as the stereotype of "prisoner" and applied to all offenders the institutional conditions essential only for relatively few. Hence, this report stresses the need for development of

453

a broader range of alternatives to the institution, and for the input of greater resources of manpower, money, and materials to that end.

Community-based programs are not merely a substitute for the institution. Often they will divert offenders from entering the institution. But they also have important functions as part of the correctional process. They facilitate a continuum of services from the institution through graduated release procedures—such as furloughs and work release—to community-based programs. . . .

## Ambivalence of the Community

If asked, a clear majority of the community would probably support halfway houses for those offenders who are not a serious criminal threat but still require some residential control. But repeated experience has shown that a proposal to establish such a facility in the neighborhood is likely to rouse profound opposition. The criminal offender, adult or juvenile, is accorded a low level of community tolerance when he no longer is an abstract idea but a real person. Planning must be done, and goals and standards drafted, in recognition of this fact. . . .

# A: Setting for Corrections

## 2: Rights of Offenders

EVOLVING JUDICIAL REGARD FOR OFFENDERS' RIGHTS

Until recently, an offender as a matter of law was deemed to have forfeited virtually all rights upon conviction and to have retained only such rights as were expressly granted to him by statute or correctional authority. The belief was common that virtually anything could be done with an offender in the name of "correction," or in some instances "punishment," short of extreme physical abuse. He was protected only by the restraint and responsibility of correctional administrators and their staff. Whatever comforts, services, or privileges the offender received were a matter of grace—in the law's view a privilege to be granted or withheld by the state. Inhumane conditions and practices were permitted to develop and continue in many systems.

The courts refused for the most part to intervene. Judges felt that correctional administration was a technical matter to be left to experts rather than to courts, which were deemed ill-equipped to make appropriate evaluations. And, to the extent that courts believed the offenders' complaints involved privileges rather than rights, there was no special necessity to confront correctional practices, even when they infringed on basic notions of human rights and dignity protected for other groups by constitutional doctrine. . . .

Eventually the questionable effectiveness of correctional systems as rehabilitative instruments, combined with harsh and cruel conditions in institutions, could no longer be ignored by courts. They began to redefine the legal framework of corrections and place restrictions on previously unfettered discretion of correctional administrators. Strangely, correctional administrators, charged with rehabilitating and caring for offenders, persistently fought the recognition of offenders' rights throughout the judicial process. This stance, combined with the general inability of correctional administrators to demonstrate that correctional programs correct, shook public and judicial confidence in corrections.

. . . Administrative convenience is no longer to be accepted as sufficient justification for deprivation of rights. Additionally, correctional administrators are subjected to due process standards which require that agencies and programs be administered with clearly enunciated policies and established, fair procedures for the resolution of grievances.

A concomitant doctrine now emerging is that of the "least restrictive alternative" or "least drastic means." This tenet simply holds that, once the corrections administrator has demonstrated that some restriction on an offender's rights is necessary, he must select the least restrictive alternative to satisfy the state's interests. . . .

## IMPLEMENTATION OF OFFENDERS' RIGHTS

It should be recognized, however, that the Constitution requires only minimal standards. The prohibition against cruel and unusual punishment has not to date required affirmative treatment programs. If courts view their role as limited to constitutional requirements, litigation will merely turn filthy and degrading institutions into clean but unproductive institutions. Courts, however, have a broader role. A criminal sentence is a court order and like any court order should be subject to continuing judicial supervision. Courts should specify the purpose for which an offender is given a particular sentence and should exercise control to insure that the treatment of the offender is consistent with that purpose. A sentence for purposes of rehabilitation is hardly advanced by practices which degrade and humiliate the offender.

On the other hand, litigation alone cannot solve the problems of corrections or of offenders' rights. The process of case-by-case adjudication of offenders' grievances inevitably results in uncertainties and less-than-comprehensive rulemaking. Courts decide the issue before them. They are ill-equipped to enter broad mandates for change. Similarly the sanctions available to courts in enforcing their decrees are limited. While some courts have been forced to appoint masters to oversee the operation of a prison, full implementation of constitutional and correctional practices which aid rather than degrade offenders requires the commitment of funds and public support. Courts alone cannot implement offenders' rights. . . .

Corrections, at the same time, is provided with an opportunity for meaningful progress. Most prisons are degrading, not because corrections wants them to be but because resources for improvement have not been available. Judicial decrees requiring change should make available additional resources. In the last analysis, the Constitution may require either an acceptable correctional system or none at all. . . .

### Standard 2.1: Access to Courts

**Each correctional agency should immediately develop and implement policies and procedures to fulfill the right of persons under correctional supervision to have access to courts to present any issue cognizable therein, including (1) challenging the legality of their conviction or confinement; (2) seeking redress for illegal conditions or treatment while incarcerated or under correctional control; (3) pursuing remedies in connection with civil legal problems; and (4) asserting against correctional or other governmental authority any other rights protected by constitutional or statutory provision or common law. . . .**

**3. Where complaints are filed against conditions of correctional control or against the administrative actions or treatment by correctional or other governmental authorities, offenders may be required first to seek recourse under established administrative procedures and appeals and to exhaust their administrative remedies. Administrative remedies should be operative within 30 days and not in a way that would unduly delay or hamper their use by aggrieved offenders. Where no reasonable administrative means is available for presenting and resolving disputes or where past practice demon-**

strates the futility of such means, the doctrine of exhaustion should not apply. . . .

## Standard 2.2: Access to Legal Services

Each correctional agency should immediately develop and implement policies and procedures to fulfill the right of offenders to have access to legal assistance, through counsel or counsel substitute, with problems or proceedings relating to their custody, control, management, or legal affairs while under correctional authority. Correctional authorities should facilitate access to such assistance and assist offenders affirmatively in pursuing their legal right. Governmental authority should furnish adequate attorney representation and, where appropriate, lay representation to meet the needs of offenders without the financial resources to retain such assistance privately. . . .

Recognizing the large and probably unmanageable burden on existing attorney resources, the standard validates supplemental use of lay assistance (law students, trained correctional staff, "jailhouse lawyers," or other paraprofessionals) even in matters requiring formal attorney representation. In this regard, a recent judicial observation in a California case dealing with right to counsel in parole revocation is instructive. The ruling, *In re Tucker*, stated:

> Formal hearings, with counsel hired or provided, for the more than 4,000 parole suspensions annually would alone require an undertaking of heroic proportions. But that is only the beginning. For if there is a right to counsel at parole revocation or suspension proceedings, no reason in law or logic can be advanced why a prisoner, appearing before the Adult Authority as an applicant for parole and seeking to have his indeterminate sentence made determinate, should not also have legal representation. The conclusion is inescapable that my dissenting brethren are in effect insisting upon counsel for a potential of 32,000 appearances annually: 28,000 parole applicants and 4,000 parole revokees. This monumental requirement would stagger the imagination.

This standard rejects that view. If the criminal justice system must provide legal counsel in every instance where a man's liberty may be jeopardized, its duty should not end

457

there. The system must and can find ways to meet the cost involved. In other situations where liberty is not directly at stake, those serving as counsel substitutes would be required to receive reasonable training and continuing supervision by attorneys. The opportunity this presents for broadening of perspectives on the part of correctional staff and a new legitimacy and vocational path for the trained "jailhouse lawyer" may prove to be valuable byproducts. In addition, full cooperation with correctional authorities by public defender programs, civil legal aid systems, law schools, bar groups, and federally supported legal service offices for the poor will be necessary to put the standard into practice. . . .

**Standard 2.3: Guarantee offenders' access to legal materials.**

**Standard 2.4: Protection Against Personal Abuse**

Each correctional agency should establish immediately policies and procedures to fulfill the right of offenders to be free from personal abuse by correctional staff or other offenders. The following should be prohibited:

1. Corporal punishment.

2. The use of physical force by correctional staff except as necessary for self-defense, protection of another person from imminent physical attack, or prevention of riot or escape.

3. Solitary or segregated confinement as a disciplinary or punitive measure except as a last resort and then not extending beyond 10 days' duration.

4. Any deprivation of clothing, bed and bedding, light, ventilation, heat, exercise, balanced diet or, hygienic necessities.

5. Any act or lack of care, whether by willful act or neglect, that injures or significantly impairs the health of any offender.

6. Infliction of mental distress, degradation, or humiliation.

Correctional authorities should:

1. Evaluate their staff periodically to identify persons who may constitute a threat to offenders and where such individuals are identified, reassign or discharge them.

2. Develop institution classification procedures that will identify violence-prone offenders and where such offenders are identified, insure greater supervision.

3. Implement supervision procedures and other techniques that will provide a reasonable measure of safety for offenders from the attacks of other offenders. Technological devices

458

such as closed circuit television should not be exclusively relied upon for such purposes.

Correctional agencies should compensate offenders for injuries suffered because of the intentional or negligent acts or omissions of correctional staff.

... In this area particularly, standards should be more prohibitive than judicial interpretation of the eighth amendment, because they give credence to the new philosophy of corrections as a reintegrative force, rather than a punitive one. This standard enumerates a variety of punitive activities which, at least on an individual basis, may fall short of the eighth amendment ban but which should be included in the legal protections available to the offender. ...

Adoption of the standard would go far toward curtailment of excessive use of the most widespread, controversial, and inhumane of current penal practices—extended solitary confinement. One recent model act—NCCD's 1972 Model Act for the Protection of Rights of Prisoners—has refused to recognize any disciplinary use whatsoever of solitary confinement. Courts as yet have failed to classify solitary confinement as "cruel and unusual punishment," except when conjoined with other inhumane conditions, although several decisions have viewed extended periods of isolation with disapproval and some court orders have fixed maximum periods for such punishment. The standard recognizes, in setting its relatively modest maximum, that most cases require much shorter use of punitive segregation as a disciplinary measure and enjoins correctional authorities to minimize use of the technique.

The Commission recognizes that the field of corrections cannot yet be persuaded to give up the practice of solitary confinement as a disciplinary measure. But the Commission wishes to record its view that the practice is inhumane and in the long run brutalizes those who impose it as it brutalizes those upon whom it is imposed. ...

**Standard 2.5: Guarantee healthful surroundings for inmates.**

**Standard 2.6: Guarantee adequate medical care for inmates.**

... Medical care is of course a basic human necessity. It also contributes to the success of any correctional program. Physical disabilities or abnormalities may contribute to an individual's socially deviant behavior or restrict his employment. In these cases, medical or dental treatment is an intergral part of the overall rehabilitation program. Most incarcerated offenders are from lower socioeconomic classes, which have a worse health status generally than more affluent persons. Thus, there is a greater need for medical and dental services than in the population at large. Since "care" is implicitly or explicitly part of correctional agencies' enabling legislation, medical services at least comparable to those available to the general population should be provided. The standard should not be "what the individual was accustomed to." Finally, unlike persons in the free community, those who are institutionalized cannot seek out needed care. By denying normal access to such services, the state assumes the burden of assuring access to quality medical care for those it so restricts. . . .

**Standard 2.7: Regulate institutional search and seizure.**

**Standard 2.8: Assure nondiscriminatory treatment of offenders.**

**Standard 2.9: Rehabilitation**
Each correctional agency should immediately develop and implement policies, procedures, and practices to fulfill the right of offenders to rehabilitation programs. A rehabilitative purpose is or ought to be implicit in every sentence of an offender unless ordered otherwise by the sentencing court. A correctional authority should have the affirmative and enforceable duty to provide programs appropriate to the purpose for which a person was sentenced. Where such programs are absent, the correctional authority should (1) establish or provide access to such programs or (2) inform the sentencing court of its inability to comply with the purpose for which sentence was imposed. . . .
2. Each correctional agency providing parole, probation, or other community supervision, should supplement its rehabilitative services by referring offenders to social services and activities available to citizens generally. The correctional authority should, in planning its total range of rehabilitative programs, establish a presumption in favor of community-based programs to the maximum extent possible. . . .

An enforceable right to "treatment" or rehabilitative services has not yet been established in the courts in any significant measure. Although much discussed in recent years, it remains the most elusive and ephemeral of the offender rights being asserted. This is so despite the firm commitment of the corrections profession for more than a century to a rehabilitation rather than a punishment goal ("Declaration of Principles of the American Prison Association," Cincinnati, Ohio—1870) and an expression of rehabilitative intent in most State correctional codes and virtually all juvenile court and corrections statutes. Perhaps the lack of an affirmative, legally enforceable responsibility to provide services accounts for the extreme inadequacy of rehabilitative resources that has plagued American corrections for decades. The resources found wanting include educational, vocational, psychiatric, and casework services.

... The standard provides that offenders have the right to programs appropriate to the purpose for which they were sentenced. Where a court sentences a person for rehabilitation, rehabilitation programs should be available. Thus in the first instance the duty is placed on correctional agencies to respond to the sentencing order. If because of lack of resources or other reason the correctional agency cannot provide appropriate programs, it should then be required to report this fact to the sentencing court. ...

The standard recognizes that not every program can be available for every offender. The test to be applied should be whether the offender has access to some programs which are "appropriately related" to the purpose for which he was sentenced. ...

The standard requires that courts and sentencing judges be regularly advised of the true extent of rehabilitative services and programs available within their adult and juvenile correctional systems. This requirement is needed for sentencing officials to make proper choices among the sentencing alternatives available to them and to avoid mistaken ideas of what can be provided to sentenced offenders. This important corollary to the right to rehabilitative services has long been neglected in interaction between courts and correctional systems.

Endorsement of the right to treatment does not carry with it the right of correctional authorities to require or coerce offenders into participating in rehabilitative programs. Considerations of individual privacy, integrity, dignity, and personality suggest that coerced programs should not be permitted. In addition, a forced program of any nature is unlikely to produce constructive results. This principle, as applied to juveniles, must be qualified under the parens patriae concept, but nonetheless it would appear to have considerable validity here also.

## Standard 2.10: Retention and Restoration of Rights

Each State should enact legislation immediately to assure that no person is deprived of any license, permit, employment, office, post of trust or confidence, or political or judicial rights based solely on an accusation of criminal behavior. Also, in the implementation of Standard 16.17, Collateral Consequences of a Criminal Conviction, legislation depriving convicted persons of civil rights should be repealed. This legislation should provide further that a convicted and incarcerated person should have restored to him on release all rights not otherwise retained.

The appropriate correctional authority should:

1. With the permission of an accused person, explain to employers, families, and others the limited meaning of an arrest as it relates to the above rights.

2. Work for the repeal of all laws and regulations depriving accused or convicted persons of civil rights.

3. Provide services to accused or convicted persons to help them retain or exercise their civil rights or to obtain restoration of their rights or any other limiting civil disability that may occur.

## Standard 2.11: Establish rules of inmate conduct.

## Standard 2.12: Disciplinary Procedures

Each correctional agency immediately should adopt, consistent with Standard 16.2, disciplinary procedures for each type of residential facility it operates and for the persons residing therein.

Minor violations of rules of conduct are those punishable by no more than a reprimand, or loss of commissary, entertainment, or recreation privileges for not more than 24 hours. . . .

Major violations of rules of conduct are those punishable by sanctions more stringent than those for minor violations, including but not limited to, loss of good time, transfer to segregation or solitary confinement, transfer to a higher level of institutional custody or any other change in status which may tend to affect adversely an offender's time of release or discharge.

Rules governing major violations should provide for the following prehearing procedures:

1. Someone other than the reporting officer should conduct a complete investigation into the facts of the alleged

462

misconduct to determine if there is probable cause to believe the offender committed a violation. If probable cause exists, a hearing date should be set.

2. The offender should receive a copy of any disciplinary report or charges of the alleged violation and notice of the time and place of the hearing.

3. The offender, if he desires, should receive assistance in preparing for the hearing from a member of the correctional staff, another inmate, or other authorized person (including legal counsel if available).

4. No sanction for the alleged violation should be imposed until after the hearing except that the offender may be segregated from the rest of the population if the head of the institution finds that he constitutes a threat to other inmates, staff members, or himself.

Rules governing major violations should provide for a hearing on the alleged violation which should be conducted as follows:

1. The hearing should be held as quickly as possible, generally not more than 72 hours after the charges are made.

2. The hearing should be before an impartial officer or board.

3. The offender should be allowed to present evidence or witnesses on his behalf.

4. The offender may be allowed to confront and cross-examine the witnesses against him.

5. The offender should be allowed to select someone, including legal counsel, to assist him at the hearing.

6. The hearing officer or board should be required to find substantial evidence of guilt before imposing a sanction.

7. The hearing officer or board should be required to render its decision in writing setting forth its findings as to controverted facts, its conclusion, and the sanction imposed. If the decision finds that the offender did not commit the violation, all reference to the charge should be removed from the offender's file.

Rules governing major violations should provide for internal review of the hearing officer's or board's decision. Such review should be automatic. The reviewing authority should be authorized to accept the decision, order further proceedings, or reduce the sanction imposed.

**Standard 2.13: Adopt procedures for change of inmate status.**

**Standard 2.14: Establish offenders' grievance procedures.**

## Standard 2.15: Free Expression and Association

Each correctional agency should immediately develop policies and procedures to assure that individual offenders are able to exercise their constitutional rights of free expression and association to the same extent and subject to the same limitations as the public at large. Regulations limiting an offender's right of expression and association should be justified by a compelling state interest requiring such limitation. Where such justification exists, the agency should adopt regulations which effectuate the state interest with as little interference with an offender's rights as possible.

Rights of expression and association are involved in the following contexts:

1. Exercise of free speech.
2. Exercise of religious beliefs and practices. (See Standard 2.16.)
3. Sending or receipt of mail. (See Standard 2.17.)
4. Visitations. (See Standard 2.17.)
5. Access to the public through the media. (See Standard 2.17.)
6. Engaging in peaceful assemblies.
7. Belonging to and participating in organizations.
8. Preserving identity through distinguishing clothing, hairstyles, and other characteristics related to physical appearance. . . .

Ordinarily, the following factors would not constitute sufficient justification for an interference with an offender's rights unless present in a situation which constituted a clear threat to personal or institutional security.

1. Protection of the correctional agency or its staff from criticism, whether or not justified.
2. Protection of other offenders from unpopular ideas.
3. Protection of offenders from views correctional officials deem not conducive to rehabilitation or other correctional treatment.
4. Administrative inconvenience.
5. Administrative cost except where unreasonable and disproportionate to that expended on other offenders for similiar purposes.

Correctional authorities should encourage and facilitate the exercise of the right of expression and association by providing appropriate opportunities and facilities.

. . . Correctional administrators' fear of unjustified criticisms, real or imagined, does not alone represent a sufficient justification for abridgment of the offender's rights. A public dialogue, with its inevitable inaccuracies and misperceptions, is as useful to the correctional process as it is to the political process. Much of the current interest in corrections reform among the general public has been developed because of the complaints of offenders, generally transmitted through court proceedings. It is clear that many such complaints are frivolous or not supported in fact. But many are true. A democratic system requires a free flow of ideas—many of which will turn out to be false. Corrections has much to gain and little to lose by allowing and encouraging public discussion of correctional practices. . . .

Several studies of prisons have indicated that their most degrading feature is their dehumanizing influence on prisoners. The institution for purposes increasingly difficult to justify, withdraws from confined offenders all semblances of their separate identity. Offenders wear similar clothing. Each has his hair cut the same way. Each is given a number rather than retaining his name. The effect of this approach is becoming increasingly clear. Offenders lose whatever self-respect they have; their adjustment to free society upon release is made more difficult if not impossible. Prohibiting offenders from maintaining their identities defeats the purposes of corrections.

Correctional authorities undoubtedly have a compelling interest in being able to identify committed offenders. In some instances the ability of offenders to effectuate extreme alterations in appearance within a short period may constitute a justification for reasonable regulations. The recommendation thus contemplates that while offenders should be allowed to maintain individuality through clothing, hair styles, and other appearance-related characteristics, the correctional authorities should be authorized to promote reasonable regulations to maintain ease of identification. However, this justification should be subject to the same restraint that the least drastic regulation be adopted. . . .

**Standard 2.16: Guarantee offenders' freedom of religious beliefs and practices.**

**Standard 2.17: Access to the Public**

Each correctional agency should develop and implement immediately policies and procedures to fulfill the right of offenders to communicate with the public. Correctional regulations limiting such communication should be consistent with Standard 2.15. Questions of right of access to the public arise primarily in the context of regulations affecting mail, personal visitation, and the communications media.

MAIL. Offenders should have the right to communicate or correspond with persons or organizations and to send and receive letters, packages, books, periodicals, and any other material that can be lawfully mailed. The following additional guidelines should apply:

1. Correctional authorities should not limit the volume of mail to or from a person under supervision.

2. Correctional authorities should have the right to inspect incoming and outgoing mail, but neither incoming nor outgoing mail should be read or censored. Cash, checks, or money orders should be removed from incoming mail and credited to offenders' accounts. If contraband is discovered in either incoming or outgoing mail, it may be removed. Only illegal items and items which threaten the security of the institution should be considered contraband.

3. Offenders should receive a reasonable postage allowance to maintain community ties.

VISITATION. Offenders should have the right to communicate in person with individuals of their own choosing. The following additional guidelines should apply:

1. Correctional authorities should not limit the number of visitors an offender may receive or the length of such visits except in accordance with regular institutional schedules and requirements.

2. Correctional authorities should facilitate and promote visitation of offenders by the following acts:

a. Providing transportation for visitors from terminal points of public transportation. In some instances, the correctional agency may wish to pay the entire transportation costs of family members where the offender and the family are indigent.

b. Providing appropriate rooms for visitation that allow ease and informality of communication in a natural environment as free from institutional or custodial attributes as possible.

c. Making provisions for family visits in private surroundings conducive to maintaining and strengthening family ties.

**3. The correctional agency may supervise the visiting area in an unobtrusive manner but should not eavesdrop on conversations or otherwise interfere with the participants' privacy....**

Correctional authorities should not merely tolerate visiting but should encourage it. This extends to providing or paying for transportation when the cost of traveling to the facility would be a limiting factor. Such a provision is plainly needed to equalize the situation of rich and poor inmates. Expenses of this type can be minimized by incarcerating offenders in their own community or through expanded use of furlough programs.

The standard recommends provisions for family visits in surroundings conducive to the maintenance and strengthening of family ties. The setting should provide privacy and a noninstitutional atmosphere. In institutions where such facilities are not available, furloughs should be granted custodially qualified offenders in order to maintain family relationships. It is recognized that the so-called conjugal visit is controversial, partly because the concept seems to focus entirely on sexual activity.

The furlough system is far superior to the institutional arrangement. However, the recommendations of this report contemplate that, as institutional confinement ceases to be a common criminal sanction, prisons will increasingly house more dangerous offenders for whom furlough programs will not be appropriate. Provision of settings where an entire family can visit in private surroundings could add much to an offender's receptivity to correctional programs and strengthen his family relationships.

### Standard 2.18: Remedies for Violation of an Offender's Rights

**Each correctional agency immediately should adopt policies and procedures, and where applicable should seek legislation, to insure proper redress where an offender's rights as enumerated in this chapter are abridged....**

... In addition, each correctional agency should assure wide-scale understanding of the rights of offenders. Inservice training programs for correctional staff should concentrate on the nature, as well as the justification, of the rights of offenders. The most effective assurance of respect for such rights in the long run is recognition by correctional personnel that protection of these rights not only is required by the Constitution but also is good correctional practice. . . .

Chapter 5 of this report recommends that sentencing courts exercise continuous jurisdiction over sentenced offenders to insure that the sentence imposed by the court is carried out. It may be necessary in assuring compliance with the rights of an offender that the court exercise similar supervisory powers over correctional officials. In exercising this power, courts should be authorized to appoint and pay a special master who would be responsible to the court. The master could engage in such inspection and supervision activities as is deemed appropriate to insure that offenders are properly treated.

## 3: Diversion from the Criminal Justice Process

The Argument for Diversion

The significance of diversion is evidenced primarily by the role it plays in keeping the criminal justice system in operation. For various reasons, people refuse to report offenses; police refuse to make arrests; prosecutors refuse to prosecute; and courts refuse to convict. Yet if all law violations were processed officially as the arrest-conviction-imprisonment model calls for, the system obviously would collapse from its voluminous caseloads and from community opposition. Cost of resources needed to handle violations officially would be prohibitive financially and socially.

To illustrate, consider some national data for the year 1971. In that year, approximately 5,995,000 major felonies—murder, aggravated assault, rape, robbery, burglary, grand larceny, and auto theft—were reported to the police. These reports resulted in 1,707,600 arrests, with juvenile courts assuming jurisdiction over about 628,000 cases. Among the remaining cases, 82 percent were processed in criminal court. Sixty percent of the cases processed resulted in conviction as originally charged, and 11 percent for a lesser charge.

On the basis of these figures it can be estimated that nearly 30 percent of all reported offenses result in arrest, and almost one-third of all arrests in criminal convictions. Not included among criminal convictions are cases handled by juvenile courts. The figures also fail to account for multiple reports against single offenders, and they are compromised by the notoriously inadequate records kept by most agencies. Nevertheless, they convey some impression concerning the extent to which the arrest-conviction-imprisonment model is circumvented in practice. . . .

## Inadequacy of the Current System

California juvenile court practices offer an excellent example of the injustice experienced by many children and youth coming into the justice system for behavior that would not be an offense if engaged in by adults. Recent figures show that arrests for major offenses equivalent to adult felony offenses accounted for only 17 percent of all juvenile arrests. Arrests for offenses generally comparable at the adult level with misdemeanors accounted for 20 percent. The remaining 63 percent was made up of arrests of youths who were "in need of supervision." In many of the cases the juveniles referred to as being in need of supervision were treated in exactly the same way as, or worse than, those referred for felony and misdemeanor offenses.

A study of the fates of serious delinquents (youths adjudicated on the equivalent of serious criminal charges) and youths in need of supervision (juveniles charged with acts that would not be criminal if committed by adults) in 19 major cities revealed the following results:

1. Youths in need of supervision are more likely to be detained in detention facilities than serious delinquents (54 percent vs. 31 percent);

2. Once detained, youths in need of supervision are twice as likely as serious delinquents to be detained for more than 30 days (51 percent vs. 25 percent);

3. Youths in need of supervision are more likely to receive harsher dispositions in juvenile court and to be sent to confinement placement than serious delinquents (25 percent vs. 23 percent), with the average length of stay being much longer for the nondelinquent group. . . .

More than three-fourths of the felonies processed in criminal courts are committed by repeaters. Recidivism rates ordinarily are highest among offenders discharged from prison at the expiration of their sentences, lower among parolees, and lowest among probationers. It therefore seems clear that prisons are failing to achieve their correctional objectives. In spite of the vocal support given rehabilitation and reintegration of the offender into community life, the fact remains that many prisoners, adult and juvenile, live under conditions more debilitating than rehabilitating—conditions that encourage patterns of immorality, dependency, manipulation, irresponsibility, and destructiveness.

In recognition of this, much effort has recently been directed toward improvement of institutional programs. Among the programs developed in the last few decades are psychiatric therapy, group counseling, casework, role playing, and academic and vocational training. Prisoners, if sufficiently motivated, can gain proficiency in an occupation. But they may be unable to find related employment when released. Or they may not have learned how to get along with other people or how to perform the various nonoccupational tasks necessary for success in the community.

Programs may alleviate some pains of imprisonment and foster better institutional adjustment. Life in the free community, however, is an entirely different matter. Prison virtues such as dependency, subordination, and compliance are not always rewarded in the world outside. Thus a good prisoner does not necessarily make a good parolee or a good citizen.

The result is that prisoners who receive special "treatment" in the institution apparently have about the same recidivism rates as those who do not. Even where treatment is institutionally successful, its effects seem to dissipate once the offender returns to the community.

Our society reflects a phenomenon that sociologist Erving Goffman has identified as "ritual maintenance," which he describes as a universal feeling that when some sort of antisocial or disapproved act occurs something must happen. What happens need not necessarily be punitive, nor must it necessarily be therapeutic. The point is that there are alternatives to both punishment and treatment and a wide range between these two extremes if a willingness exists to consider them. The alternatives run a gamut from reprimand, release, fines, and informal supervision to forms of custody and restriction on freedom. Some imply treatment, but many do not. Most imply a willingness to consider noncriminal program dispositions—forms of help that are often best offered by non-justice system agencies, groups and individuals.

## A Positive Argument for Diversion

The positive argument for diversion is that it gives society the opportunity to consider the possibility of reallocating existing resources to programs that promise greater success in bringing about correctional reform and social restoration of offenders. Given the choice between expanding the capacities of police, courts, and institutions to the point where they could accommodate the present and projected rates of criminal activity and the opportunity to establish diversion programs with public funds, the economics of the matter clearly favor a social policy decision for diversion. For example, the Project Crossroads diversion program in the District of Columbia had a per capita program cost of approximately $6.00 per day. The per capita cost of institutionalization in D.C. correctional facilities was averaging close to $17.00 a day at the time. Furthermore, the recidivism rate among Crossroads participants was 22 percent, as opposed to 46 percent among a control group which did not receive project services. . . .

## IMPLEMENTATION OF DIVERSION

### Community-Based Diversion Programs

*Comprehensive Youth Service Delivery System*
. . . It is the aim of such projects to coordinate all service programs to youth in the target area—Federal, State, county, city, private—and determine from model experimentation which agencies should eventually operate these services—private or public sector, local or State government, etc. The underlying hypothesis of the program is that crime and delinquency are due not so much to a lack of resources as to a failure on the part of the system to adequately focus on the needs of youth at appropriate times and places in ways that make existing services effective. The projects propose to provide new resources to the police and courts, on a 24-hour, 7-day-a-week basis, that will enable these agencies to divert children and youth.

*Community Responsibility Programs*
Community responsibility programs are increasing throughout the United States. Frequently located in predominantly low-income minority communities (particularly in California, Illinois, New York, and Puerto Rico), these projects are designed to assist youth involved in delinquent activities. The main focus of the programs is community involvement and community responsibility for their own children and youth. A panel of community members, both youth and adult, act as judges listening to cases of youthful offenders who have been referred by various agencies, most frequently by law enforcement agencies. Minors who have committed violations of the law appear before the citizen panel which determines the minor's responsibility. If it is determined that an alleged act did

471

in fact occur which in some way injured the community, the youth may be required to carry out some useful community work under supervision. He is also asked to undergo a program of counseling with volunteers, paraprofessionals, or even established agency personnel on an informal basis. . . .

## The Youth Service Bureau

Of all the recommendations made by the President's Crime Commission in 1967, none was regarded with more hope for diverting children and youth from the juvenile justice system than the Youth Service Bureau. Yet, in 1972, a national study was able to identify only 150 bureaus spread throughout the United States and supported by only $25,000,000 of Federal funds. The Youth Service Bureau does not appear to be the Nation's most popularly supported diversion effort. . . .

## Police-Based Diversion Models

Police-based diversion programs may be administered internally or through use of referral relationships with other community agencies. Neither arrangement, however, has met with much use in the past. On a national basis, less than 2 percent of arrested juveniles are referred to other community agencies by police departments, and probably even fewer are served through police-run diversion programs. . . .

## Family Crisis Intervention Projects

There are indications that the police, by identifying conflict situations at an early stage of development, can prevent the escalation of violence. A conspicuous example is the Family Crisis Intervention Project in New York City. Officers from a high-risk precinct are trained to work in teams to intervene in family disturbance calls attempting to resolve the conflict on the scene. If unsuccessful, they refer the antagonists to a community agency. The New York program has been successful in many other cities including Oakland, Denver, and Chicago.

In the New York experience, not one homicide occurred in 926 families handled by intervention teams. Nor was a single officer injured, even though the teams were exposed to an unusually large number of dangerous incidents. Families having had experience with the teams referred other families to the project, and many troubled individuals sought out team members for advice. It is believed that police-community relations were improved as a result and that a number of incidents were averted that otherwise might have led to arrests.

*The 601 Diversion Project*

The County of Santa Clara, California, proposed a project for funding to the State planning agency that would divert 77 percent of those children arrested and previously referred to the probation department. Referred to as the 601 Diversion Project, 12 law enforcement agencies in the county receive a reward commensurate with the degree of reduction in referrals of children "in need of supervision" to alternative community-based programs. The funds received by the law enforcement agencies are used to purchase services for the children referred from other private and public agencies or resources. The probation department administers the program, and all 12 law enforcement agencies voluntarily participate in its design and implementation.

The program identifies a kind of police behavior—diversion of children in need of supervision from the juvenile justice system—and rewards those engaging in the approved behavior. Further, the proposal identifies levels for performance; i.e., 77 percent reduction from past practice of law enforcement agencies. The program specifies objectives, outlines activities, and requires evaluation for reimbursement. It proposes a planned diversion to identified programs. It is highly visible as well as measurable. . . .

## Court-Based Diversion Models

The opportunity to divert does not cease even after an arrest has been made. Many arrested offenders are diverted at a later stage in the judicial process. Whether or not these various discretions constitute diversion is another question. In some cases, the district attorney, the court, the public defender, and others have specific programs aimed at diverting people out of the criminal justice system. They have a specific target population and specific programs to which offenders can be diverted. To the extent that these activities are formally designed to divert a defined offender population, they are diversion programs, as the term is used in this chapter. . . .

## Civil Commitment

Criminal justice concepts are being revised because of the increasing tendency of courts and the public to hold authorities responsible for the consequences of their decisions. This is perhaps best evidenced in the rapid expansion of civil commitment and other procedures based on a medical model that holds that some types of deviance, instead of indicating criminal intent, are symptoms of illness.

Civil commitment can be described as a procedure, theoretically noncriminal and employed without stigmatization, for diverting selected types of deviants from the criminal justice system. Such diversions can occur either before or after trial. The offenders—juveniles, drug abusers, sex offenders, and the mentally ill or retarded, for example—are hospitalized for treatment instead of being imprisoned. Community protection is promised by removal of the "sick" person and by therapies aimed at restoration of health or normalcy before the patient is returned to free society.

Yet there are some doubts about the wisdom of civil commitments. Such commitments are ordinarily viewed by the patient as involuntary, and his rights may be violated even though no criminal charges are made against him. Moreover, there is much concern that the treatment given may not be any different or any more effective than that received in many correctional facilities. Although these charges present some problems, the Commission endorses the use of civil commitment under certain conditions. A discussion of this concept may be found in the Commission's Report on Police and in the chapter dealing with drug abuse in its Report on Community Crime Prevention.

*Pretrial Intervention Programs*

... Pretrial intervention projects basically operate in two ways. In a number of the projects, no formal charges are lodged. Instead, after an individual has been arrested, he is screened on a number of criteria to determine whether he is eligible for participation in a formal diversion program. Such screening criteria vary, depending on the scope and range of the particular project. For example, a project may be willing to accept only juvenile first offenders or offenders who have not committed offenses in certain categories. If an individual meets the particular criteria, the project staff explains the program to the individual. If he is interested in participating, the staff will ask the court to defer formal charging. If the individual successfully completes the program, which usually involves regular participation in certain activities and acceptance of assistance, the staff will ask the prosecutor to dispense entirely with the case. For those individuals who do not wish to participate or who indicate a desire to participate but then withdraw or are terminated unfavorably, charging will proceed as otherwise would have occurred.

In the other model, formal charges are lodged but individuals are screened for eligibility in a particular intervention project. If they and the court agree, further criminal proceedings are suspended pending the outcome of the individual's participation. In these programs, successful completion of the program results in a request that charges be dropped. Unsuccessful participation results in regular proceedings on the charges.

## SPECIAL PROBLEM AREAS

### Public Drunkenness

*Detoxification Centers in St. Louis and the District of Columbia*

St. Louis opened the first police-sponsored detoxification center in 1966 for the diversion of drunkenness offenders....

Persons arrested on a drunkenness charge in St. Louis now have a choice between treatment at the center and criminal prosecution. For those who choose to undergo treatment, criminal charges are suspended pending completion of the 7-day program. At the center, patients are given food and medical care, with optional counseling and referral services.

The District of Columbia received Federal funds for a similar detoxification program shortly after the creation of the St. Louis center. In Washington, a 1- to 3-day program is available to "walk-ins" and is mandatory for intoxicated persons picked up by the police.

... Before the detoxification centers opened, public inebriates in the District of Columbia generally spent 30 days in jail. Critics of the centers feel that a 30-day sentence at least gave an offender the opportunity to "dry out" and a place to sleep. Now the large turnover and volume of cases make rehabilitation difficult, if not impossible....

The courts and jails have benefited from the detoxification programs, now that all public drunkenness offenders in D.C. and those who prefer treatment to arrest in St. Louis are routed through the centers. No police time is saved, however, as police are still responsible for keeping inebriates off the streets. Police dissatisfaction with the new procedure causes many inebriates to be ignored.

In addition to the lack of police support, both programs suffer from a lack of money. Overcrowding is a chronic problem in both centers, in effect reducing them to corrals for herds of unfortunates. A minimum of services is provided and individual programming is nonexistent....

With the virtual decriminalization of public drunkenness in St. Louis and Washington, the next logical step is to remove it completely from the realm of the criminal justice process, entrusting care and cure to social service agencies that can better address long-range projects for housing and employment. Prison does not rehabilitate drunkenness offenders and neither does forced, short-term treatment. To rehabilitate problem drinkers, an alternate lifestyle must be offered, and the problem drinker must bring with him a desire to change his habits.

Until the distribution of public monies makes feasible a transfer of responsibility, drunkenness offenses will continue to drain law enforcement resources. Diversion of such cases into therapy may, in the long run, prove to be the most practical means of dealing with this problem.

## Drug Abuse

Narcotics offenses have become more and more prevalent in recent years, burdening the criminal justice system with cases that might better be treated medically. Drug offenders today come from middle-class suburban as well as urban core areas and thus create public interest in preventive and rehabilitative programs. Diversion into therapeutic programs offers drug offenders an alternative to criminal prosecution. It completely avoids legislative and judicial entanglements, imprisonment, and the controversy over legalization of the possession of some drugs, especially marijuana. Dealing with the social and medical aspects of drug abuse is a positive approach with potential benefits both for society and for the individual.

In establishing a plan for diversion, several questions must be resolved: when diversion is appropriate; whether treatment should be voluntary or imposed; whether there should be a specified length of treatment; and whether it should be available to anyone, including non-offenders. For the success of any diversion scheme for narcotics offenders, eligibility requirements must be clearly defined. The population to be served must be a cohesive group with similar problems and treatment goals. The nature of the pending charge is also crucial: hard-core addicts should be treated separately from first offenders charged with possession. The goal of any diversion plan is to reorient the offender in society and to spare the criminal justice system the time and expense of prosecuting cases that are medical, rather than criminal, in nature.

### Illinois Drug Abuse Program

The Illinois Dangerous Drug Abuse Act in 1967 provided a diversionary procedure for narcotics offenders, especially heroin addicts, and in 1968, the Illinois Drug Abuse Program (IDAP) was established. Financed entirely by the State Department of Mental Health, the program provides for group therapy, methadone maintenance, and medical and social services in halfway houses and therapeutic communities. After 1968, Federal funds made available through the Narcotic Addict Rehabilitation Act were channeled to the program through the National Institute of Mental Health (NIMH). IDAP's budget increased from $185,000 in 1968 to $2.4 million in 1971, with the State gradually assuming more financial responsibility. By 1972, the budget increased to $4.5 million with NIMH funds accounting for only 14 percent. . . .

The structure and function of every agency involved are defined by State law. The court determines eligibility for offenders according to statutory requirements. Not eligible are offenders charged with violent crimes, drug-related criminal conspiracy, sale of specified drugs or sale of drugs to young persons, or possession of more than a certain quantity of specified drugs. Two or more previous convictions for violent crimes or a pending felony charge disqualify a person from treatment, as do two previous enrollments in a drug program within any consecutive 2-year period. . . .

The maximum referral period is 2 years for preadjudication cases. Under the statute, treatment can be successfully completed at any time during that period. If an offender leaves the program or if IDAP dismisses him, pending criminal charges are brought to court. If a person faithfully participates in the program for 2 years but cannot be certified cured by staff, the court exercises discretion in dropping the charges or resuming prosecution. The maximum term of treatment for persons assigned to the program as probationers is 5 years or the length of probation, whichever is less. . . .

### Narcotics Treatment Administration

The District of Columbia's Narcotics Treatment Administration (NTA) differs from the models described above in its primary goal: to treat all the addicts in the community, regardless of their previous offenses and program failures. The only prerequisite for enrollment is a desire to break the drug habit, and failure in treatment does not result in expulsion. . . .

Each day NTA representatives screen all defendants entering Superior Court to identify heroin users. The court approves the administration of narcotics tests, and eligible offenders are released to NTA's Criminal Justice Intake Service on bail. Thorough examinations are performed, and a counselor refers each patient to the treatment facility nearest his home that can best serve his needs. NTA operates separate units for those not yet 18 years old. . . .

From May, 1970, to November, 1971, NTA studied the progress of 450 adult and 150 youth patients, selected at random. Most of the adult patients were enrolled in methadone maintenance; most of the youths were in a methadone detoxification program. After 18 months, 46 percent of the adults were still in treatment; 19 percent were meeting all program goals of abstinence from illegal drug use, no arrests, and employment or training. Twenty-seven percent of those still in treatment failed to meet one or more treatment goals, usually employment. Twenty-eight percent of the sample had been arrested within the study period.

In the youth sample, 18 percent remained in the program for 18 months, with only 1 percent satisfying all treatment goals. Twelve percent of those in treatment failed to meet one or more program goals. Ninety-two percent were arrested within the study period. No followup data concerning dropouts are available.

Results of the study seem discouraging, but in a city with an estimated 20,000 addicts, success will not be immediate. NTA has extended its original city-wide treatment deadline of 3 years to 5 years and blames its failures on inadequate planning and management. Since 1971, efforts have been made to broaden and restructure existing services, with expansion of referral services and recruitment of a highly professional staff as priorities. . . .

**Standard 3.1: Implement Formal Diversion Programs.**

## 4: Pretrial Release and Detention

CORRECTIONS' INTEREST IN PRETRIAL DETENTION
. . . Three goals for pretrial reform can be isolated.

1. Detention and other restrictions on liberty should be minimized to an extent consistent with the public interest. As noted throughout this report, incarceration as a criminal sanction is widely overused. While confinement is necessary for the small percentage of offenders who are dangerous, it has all too often been considered the standard response to crime. In the pretrial process the detention of persons awaiting trial is far too frequent and in practice is generally based

not on any real or imagined public interest requirement but on the financial resources of the accused.

2. The treatment of persons awaiting trial should be consistent with the presumption of innocence. But persons awaiting trial in most jurisdictions are considered to be in the same class as persons already convicted and sentenced. They are housed together in the same degrading and inhumane facilities, they are deprived of the basic amenities of life, and they are treated as though their guilt had already been established. This is self-fulfilling prophecy, as the deprivations make preparation for trial more difficult and enhance the risk of conviction and harsher punishment.

3. The time prior to trial should be a constructive period in the life of the accused rather than one of idleness. Many persons awaiting trial require or could utilize assistance that only the state can provide. Many suffer from difficulties relating to alcohol, drugs, or physical or mental problems or defects. Frequently their confinement results from inability to cope with financial, employment, social, or family responsibilities. Yet few persons awaiting trial are accorded access to assistance. If detained, they are housed in local jails that typically have few resources, and there appears to be a feeling that programs for persons not yet convicted are neither authorized, desirable, nor deserving of high priority.

## PROBLEMS IN PRETRIAL DETENTION

The current picture of detention before trial is a mass of contradictions. In terms of the number of persons affected per year, pretrial custody accounts for more incarceration in the United States than does imprisonment after sentencing. In many jurisdictions, the rate of pretrial detention is rising at the same time that postconviction imprisonment is dropping. . . .

The Commission has not taken a direct position on whether preventive detention (i.e., the detaining of persons found to be "dangerous") should be implemented. This chapter is based primarily on the traditional concept of pretrial programs—assuring the presence of the accused for trial. The Commission is not unaware of the controversy over the constitutionality, advisability, or necessity of preventive detention. It is recognized that in theory preventive detention seems to run counter to many of the major principles recommended in this report. Standards and criteria for determinations of dangerousness are difficult formulations at best. The result possibly could be more detention instead of less. On the

479

other hand, we know that the present system of money bail is essentially a preventive detention system, with judges setting bond inordinately high to insure detention prior to trial. This form of hypocrisy runs counter to the need for the criminal justice system to breed respect rather than hostility for law.

The Commission feels, however, that it may be premature to recommend a system of pretrial preventive detention. In most jurisdictions, implementation of this chapter's recommendations will bring about major change in the pretrial process. Defects in the present system may be eliminated. Development of voluntary treatment programs, supervised release, and partial confinement alternatives may diminish the need for preventive detention. The experience in the District of Columbia, which now has preventive detention, is inconclusive. Its legality remains in question. . . .

Today, the status of the person presumed innocent is generally worse than that of a sentenced person confined in the same facility and far worse than that of a person confined in a felony institution after conviction for a serious offense. Thus a judicial decision requiring only that persons awaiting trial should be accorded treatment and opportunity equal to that of convicted felons would cause major changes in the construction and operation of jails. Court decisions demanding a higher standard for persons presumed innocent than for convicted persons would make obsolete existing facilities and programs, as well as many presently planned for future construction and implementation.

A few illustrations will suggest the scope of the problem faced by each administrator and jurisdiction now building, planning, or contemplating a new pretrial jail.

Take, for instance, the matter of classification. Most jails have been built to a single security system (often maximum), which assumes for administrative convenience that all detainees pose the same risk of escape or institutional misconduct. Sentenced offenders in the same institution, or in the same jurisdiction's other correctional institutions, are usually classified on a variable security basis, from minimum up. Some classification systems offer wide variations in institutional freedom, individual and group accommodations, recreational and work opportunities, etc. In this light, a pretrial institution that uniformly imposes greater security classifications and constraints on accused persons than on minimum-security sentenced offenders in the same jurisdiction may be unconstitutional.

Similarly, sentenced offenders are generally classified by

degrees of dangerousness, age, vulnerability to assault, illness, and ability to reform. Persons awaiting trial are generally classified in one class, under the rationale that they are all presumed innocent and no information base is available for distinguishing one detainee from another. The result is that young persons are detained with alcoholics, petty offenders with drug addicts, innocent persons with hardened criminals.

Another area in which many pretrial detainees in cities are worse off than convicted offenders is indoor confinement. The high cost of inner-city land, the economies of skyscraper jails, and interests of security are among the reasons why many pretrial jails offer little or no opportunity for outdoor recreation. Pretrial detainees thus are denied ingredients of personal health and individual freedom found in many postconviction prisons in the United States. These deprivations, even though cemented in the choice of a jail site and the architect's plan, may be unconstitutional.

Finally, the criminal justice system discriminates against the pretrial detainee in the length of time he serves. In most States, the sentenced felon automatically earns "good time" credit when he avoids disciplinary action, and he may obtain additional credit against his sentence by exceptional performance. More important, by participation in work and treatment programs, he may be able to secure an early release from the parole authority or even a pardon from the executive.

The person awaiting trial has no such ameliorating options. The period of detention is determined by the pace of judicial proceedings or the ability of his family and friends to raise sufficient money bail. He seldom has an opportunity to have the detention decision reviewed; indeed in most instances no affirmative decision to detain was made. There is no parole board to act as an administrative check on the judicial officer's determination of the amount of bail, the length of detention required, or the case for delay in the trial. Programs to improve his position for return to the community or for leniency in sentencing generally are not available. His ties to the community become strained or totally severed.

... Persons with short prior criminal records (or none at all) who are accused of property crimes and clearly lack economic opportunity, often are sentenced, if convicted, to probation, work release, a halfway house, or other community-based programs that address the need for job training, job finding, or stable employment. Yet these helpful dispositions all too frequently are preceded by pretrial jailing. The

481

promise or delivery of assistance is not considered until the tradition-bound system has run its course and the person pleads guilty or is convicted. . . .

**Standard 4.1: Develop a comprehensive pretrial process improvement plan.**

**Standard 4.2: Construction Policy for Pretrial Detention Facilities**

Each criminal justice jurisdiction, State or local as appropriate, should immediately adopt a policy that no new physical facility for detaining persons awaiting trial should be constructed and no funds should be appropriated or made available for such construction until:

1. A comprehensive plan is developed in accordance with Standard 4.1.

2. Alternative means of handling persons awaiting trial as recommended in Standards 43. and 44. are implemented, adequately funded, and properly evaluated.

3. The constitutional requirement for a pretrial detention facility are fully examined and planned for.

4. The possibilities of regionalizations of pretrial detention facilities are pursued.

**Standard 4.3: Formulate procedures for use of summons, citation, and arrest warrants.**

. . . When a police officer fails to issue a citation and makes a physical arrest, he should be required to indicate in writing his reasons for doing so. This report should allow his superior officers to reexamine the case, once the accused is brought to the police station. Superior officers with more time to deliberate and to verify information should be authorized to issue a citation at the police station and release the accused. This allows an internal administrative review and insures the release of those persons who are unable, in the short time available, to convince the officer on the street that their ties to the community indicate little risk of flight. . . .

**Standard 4.4: Alternatives to Pretrial Detention**

Each criminal justice jurisdiction, State or local as appropriate, should immediately seek enabling legislation and develop, authorize, and encourage the use of a variety of alternatives to the detention of persons awaiting trial. The use of these alternatives should be governed by the following:

1. Judicial officers on the basis of information available to them should select from the list of the following alternatives the first one that will reasonably assure the appearance of the accused for trial or, if no single condition gives that assurance, a combination of the following:

   a. Release on recognizance without further conditions.

   b. Release on the execution of an unsecured appearance bond in an amount specified.

   c. Release into the care of a qualified person or organization reasonably capable of assisting the accused to appear at trial.

   d. Release to the supervision of a probation officer or some other public official.

   e. Release with imposition of restrictions on activities, associations, movements, and residence reasonably related to securing the appearance of the accused.

   f. Release on the basis of financial security to be provided by the accused.

   g. Imposition of any other restrictions other than detention reasonably related to securing the appearance of the accused.

   h. Detention, with release during certain hours for specified purposes.

   i. Detention of the accused.

2. Judicial officers in selecting the form of pretrial release should consider the nature and circumstances of the offense charged, the weight of the evidence against the accused, his ties to the community, his record of convictions, if any, and his record of appearance at court proceedings or of flight to avoid prosecution.

3. No person should be allowed to act as surety for compensation.

4. Willful failure to appear before any court or judicial officer as required should be made a criminal offense.

Standard 4.5: Develop procedures for pretrial release and detention.

Standard 4.6: Legislate authority over pretrial detainees.

Standard 4.7: Develop pretrial procedures governing allegedly incompetent defendants.

**Standard 4.8: Protect the rights of pretrial detainees.**

... Persons awaiting trial should not be considered in a class with those serving a sentence. Proper classification would contemplate that persons detained awaiting trial should be treated more like those persons released on bail or other form of pretrial release. Obviously, the fact of confinement will force some dissimilarities, but only those differences that confinement inherently requires should be allowed. And where it is asserted that confinement does require modification of such rights, the burden of justifying it should be on the detention agency. To be justified, the least restrictive means needed to accomplish the state interest should be imposed.

**Standard 4.9: Programs for Pretrial Detainees**

**Each State, criminal justice jurisdiction, and agency responsible for the detention of persons awaiting trial immediately should develop and implement programs for these persons as follows:**

**1. Persons awaiting trial in detention should not be required to participate in any program of work, treatment, or rehabilitation. The following programs and services should be available on a voluntary basis for persons awaiting trial:**

**a. Educational, vocational, and recreational programs.**

**b. Treatment programs for problems associated with alcoholism, drug addiction, and mental or physical disease or defects.**

**c. Counseling programs for problems arising from marital, employment, financial, or social responsibilities.**

**2. Participation in voluntary programs should be on a confidential basis, and the fact of participation or statements made during such participation should not be used at trial. Information on participation and progress in such programs should be available to the sentencing judge following conviction for the purpose of determining sentence.**

**Standard 4.10: Develop procedures to expedite trials.**

# 5: Sentencing

CURRENT STATUS OF SENTENCING

In view of the crucial and complex nature of sentencing decisions, the current state of that process in this country is nothing less than appalling. In the vast majority of jurisdictions, the decision as to where and how a man may spend years of his life is made by one man, whose discretion is virtually unchecked or unguided by criteria, procedural requirements, or further review.

A sentence can be meted out without any information before the judge except the offender's name and the crime of which he is guilty. Oftentimes, the information base for sentencing decisions consists largely of hearsay and unreliable testimony. Some evidence used may have been seized in violation of constitutionally or statutorily prescribed standards. Resources for obtaining reliable additional information may not be available.

Furthermore, the reliability and accuracy of the available information often goes unchallenged. The judge is not required to indicate either the information he is considering or the reasons for the sentence imposed. The evidence need not be shown or described to the defendant or his counsel. It is subject neither to cross-examination or rebuttal. In too many jurisdictions, so long as a sentence is within the maximum allowable under the law, it is not directly reviewable by another court or other agency even if it is based on misinformation, bias, prejudice, or ignorance.

The law governing selection of the appropriate sentencing alternative is chaotic. In some States, mandatory sentences allow the court no discretion. In others, the judge has full discretion as to the nature and extent of the sentence to be imposed. He may choose from numerous options, ranging from suspended sentence to incarceration for life without probation or parole. With little guidance from the legislature or little training in sentencing techniques, the judge must select the proper sentence on the basis of his personal view of the purposes of the criminal law and the effect of a particular sentence on a particular offender.

The legislative branch bears a large responsibility for the lack of a coherent sentencing policy in most jurisdictions. Statutes provided little guidance in terms of what the sentencing courts are expected to accomplish through the imposition of a criminal sentence. Few procedural safeguards have been legislatively imposed to assure accurate and useful information for sentencing. Moreover, legislatures all too often have enacted a proliferation of various maximum and minimum sentences unrelated to the gravity of the offense. Inconsistency in legislatively authorized sentences makes judicial consistency impossible. . . .

**Standard 5.1: Establish judicial sentencing of defendants.**

**Standard 5.2: Establish sentencing practices for nondangerous offenders.**

... The Commission accepts the concept of indeterminacy, notwithstanding the validity of many criticisms of current practice. The major reason for this position is that the alternative—a pure determinate sentence that could not be altered—would leave little room for correctional administrators or parole boards to release the offender when it appears to them that he is capable of returning to society. As a result, offenders would serve longer sentences than necessary—a situation to be avoided wherever possible.

This acceptance of the indeterminate sentence should be considered with reference to the recommendations that would eliminate abuses inherent in broad discretion without unduly restricting the benefits of individualized sentencing techniques. Thus standards that authorize appellate review of sentences to minimize disparities, suggest more widescale and effective use of statutory criteria for decisionmaking, grant offenders greater participation in decisions that affect their sentences, and generally reduce authorized maximums would tend to alleviate many difficulties presently experienced with indeterminacy while retaining the flexibility to individualize sentences...

**Standard 5.3: Establish sentencing practices for serious offenders.**

**Standard 5.4: Establish sentencing procedures governing probation.**

**Standard 5.5: Establish criteria for fines.**

**Standard 5.6: Adopt policies governing multiple sentences.**

It is recognized that authorization of consecutive sentences provides another means for extending the recommended 5-year maximum. Like the American Bar Association which similarly wrestled with the problem, the Commission concludes that "the offender who has rendered himself subject to multiple sentences may pose the same type of unusual risk to the safety of the public [as the dangerous offender]." Consecutive sentences should, however, be limited to preclude a maximum sentence of more than double the maximum for the most serious offense. Under the recommendations of Standard 5.2, this would preclude consecutive sentences resulting in a maximum of more than 10 years. Extended terms up to 25 years could, of course, be imposed under the recom-

486

mendations of Standard 5.3 and as much as 50 years for this type of offender under the present standard.

**Standard 5.7: Disallow mitigation of sentence based on guilty plea.**

**Standard 5.8: Allow credit against sentence for time served.**

**Standard 5.9: Continuing Jurisdiction of Sentencing Court**

Legislatures by 1975 should authorize sentencing courts to exercise continuing jurisdiction over sentenced offenders to insure that the correctional program is consistent with the purpose for which the sentence was imposed. Courts should retain jurisdiction also to determine whether an offender is subjected to conditions, requirements, or authority that are unconstitutional, undesirable, or not rationally related to the purpose of the sentence, when an offender raises these issues.

Sentencing courts should be authorized to reduce a sentence or modify its terms whenever the court finds, after appropriate proceedings in open court, that new factors discovered since the initial sentencing hearing dictate such modification or reduction or that the purpose of the original sentence is not being fulfilled.

Procedures should be established allowing the offender or the correctional agency to initiate proceedings to request the court to exercise the jurisdiction recommended in this standard.

. . . If the court is properly to exercise continuing jurisdiction over the sentenced offender, it must be authorized to modify or shorten a sentence. The Commission is aware of the possibility of abuse of this power. As the American Bar Association recognized, a court could impose a long sentence for publicity purposes one day and then quietly reduce it the next. Thus provisions granting the authority to reduce or modify a sentence should be carefully drafted to require either (1) a showing of new factors that affect the original sentence, or (2) conditions that are unrelated to or inconsistent with the purpose of the original sentence. These findings should be made in open court and on the initiation of either the offender or the correctional agency. Other standards requiring that the court indicate in writing at the time of sentencing the purpose of its sentence would assist the court in further proceedings.

**Standard 5.10: Judicial Visits to Institutions**

Court systems should adopt immediately, and correctional agencies should cooperate fully in the implementation of, a policy and practice to acquaint judges with the correctional facilities and programs to which they sentence offenders, so that the judges may obtain firsthand knowledge of the consequences of their sentencing decisions. It is recommended that:

1. During the first year of his tenure, a judge should visit all correctional facilities within his jurisdiction or to which he regularly sentences offenders.

2. Thereafter, he should make annual, unannounced visits to all such correctional facilities and should converse with both correctional staff and committed offenders.

3. No judge should be excluded from visiting and inspecting any part of any facility at any time or from talking in private to any person inside the facility, whether offender or staff.

**Standard 5.11: Conduct sentencing councils, institutes, and reviews.**

**Standard 5.12: Conduct statewide sentencing institutes.**

**Standard 5.13: Sentencing Councils**

Judges in courts with more than one judge immediately should adopt a policy of meeting regularly in sentencing councils to discuss individuals awaiting sentence, in order to assist the trial judge in arriving at an appropriate sentence. Sentencing councils should operate as follows:

1. The sentencing judge should retain the ultimate responsibility for selection of sentence, with the other members of the council acting in an advisory capacity.

2. Prior to the meeting of the council, all members should be provided with presentence reports and other documentary information about the defendant.

3. The council should meet after the sentencing hearing conducted by the sentencing judge but prior to the imposition of sentence.

4. Each member of the council should develop prior to the meeting a recommended sentence for each case with the factors he considers critical.

5. The council should discuss in detail those cases about which there is a substantial diversity of opinion among council members.

6. The council through its discussions should develop sentencing criteria.

**7.** The council should keep records of its agreements and disagreements and the effect of other judges' recommendations on the sentencing judge's final decision.

## Standard 5.14: Requirements for Presentence Report and Content Specification

Sentencing courts immediately should develop standards for determining when a presentence report should be required and the kind and quantity of information needed to insure more equitable and correctionally appropriate dispositions. The guidelines should reflect the following:

**1.** A presentence report should be presented to the court in every case where there is a potential sentencing disposition involving incarceration and in all cases involving felonies or minors.

**2.** Gradations of presentence reports should be developed between a full report and a short-form report for screening offenders to determine whether more information is desirable or for use when a full report is unnecessary.

**3.** A full presentence report should be prepared where the court determines it to be necessary, and without exception in every case where incarceration for more than 5 years is a possible disposition. A short-form report should be prepared for all other cases.

... Some State statutes specifically require presentence reports for certain classes of convicted defendants, such as felons, but most do not. In the latter jurisdictions, the percentage of courts and of judges within those courts using such reports varies greatly. Federal courts appear to be the most consistent users, with presentence reports being prepared in almost 90 percent of the cases.

The importance of the presentence report to informed decision making in sentencing led the drafters of the Model Penal Code to require such reports in most instances. The American Bar Association disagreed, however, pointing out that there were some instances in which it would provide no useful information beyond that already available to the court. ...

## Standard 5.15: Restrict preadjudication disclosure of presentence reports.

## Standard 5.16: Disclosure of Presentence Report

Sentencing courts immediately should adopt a procedure to inform the defendant of the basis for his sentence and afford him the opportunity to challenge it.

1. The presentence report and all similar documents should be available to defense counsel and the prosecution.

2. The presentence report should be made available to both parties within a reasonable time, fixed by the court, prior to the date set for the sentencing hearing. After receipt of the report, the defense counsel may request:

    a. A presentence conference, to be held within the time remaining before the sentencing hearing.

    b. A continuance of one week, to allow him further time to review the report and prepare for its rebuttal. Either request may be made orally, with notice to the prosecutor. The request for a continuance should be granted only:

        (1) If defense counsel can demonstrate surprise at information in the report; and

        (2) If the defendant presently is incarcerated, he consents to the request.

This standard, consistent with the view that the sentencing procedure should be a major step toward reintegrating the offender into the society, adopts the position of requiring full disclosure, without exceptions as to confidentiality. Several reasons prompt this decision.

First, if the offender is to be convinced that his reintegration into society is desirable, he must be convinced that the society has treated him fairly. If he is sentenced on information he has not seen or had any chance to deal with and rebut, he cannot believe that he has been treated with impartiality and justice.

Second, the argument that sources may "dry up" is unconvincing. Two thoughts compel this conclusion: (1) those jurisdictions which have required disclosure have not experienced this phenomenon: and (2) more importantly, if this same evidence were given as testimony at trial, there would be no protection or confidentiality. Concepts of fair trial require that all such information be brought forward in open court and subjected to cross-examination and scrutiny. There is no reason to require less in the sentencing procedure, where the offender's liberty is at stake.

A third fear of those opposing disclosure is that certain information may be damaging to the envisioned relationship between offender and probation officer. Two observations seem appropriate here:

1. If complete candor is required for such a relationship, avoidance of disclosure surely begins the relationship on the wrong foot.

2. The less drastic alternative, recommended in the chapter on probation, is to separate the function of presentence report preparation and the supervision and treatment role of the probation officer.

### Standard 5.17: Sentencing Hearing—Rights of Defendant

Sentencing courts should adopt immediately the practice of holding a hearing prior to imposition of sentence and should develop guidelines for such hearing reflecting the following:

1. At the hearing the defendant should have these rights:

    a. To be represented by counsel or appointed counsel.

    b. To present evidence on his own behalf.

    c. To subpena witnesses.

    d. To call or cross-examine the person who prepared the presentence report and any persons whose information, contained in the presentence report, may be highly damaging to the defendant.

    e. To present arguments as to sentencing alternatives.

2. Guidelines should be provided as to the evidence that may be considered by the sentencing court for purposes of determining sentences, as follows:

    a. The exclusionary rules of evidence applicable to criminal trial should not be applied to the sentencing hearing, and all evidence should be received subject to the exclusion of irrelevant, immaterial, or unduly repetitious evidence. However, sentencing decisions should be based on competent and reliable evidence. Where a person providing evidence of factual information is reasonably available, he should be required to testify orally in order to allow cross-examination rather than being allowed to submit his testimony in writing.

    b. Evidence obtained in violation of the defendant's constitutional rights should not be considered or heard in the sentence hearing and should not be referred to in the presentence report.

    c. If the court finds, after considering the presentence

report and whatever information is presented at the sentence hearing, that there is a need for further study and observation of the defendant before he is sentenced, it may take necessary steps to obtain that information. This includes hiring of local physicians, psychiatrists, or other professionals; committing the defendant for no more than 30 days to a local or regional diagnostic center; and ordering a more complete investigation of the defendant's background, social history, etc.

**Standard 5.18: Develop procedural guidelines for sentencing hearings.**

**Standard 5.19: Impose sentence according to sentencing hearing evidence.**

## 6: Classification of Offenders

Theoretically, classification is a process for determining the needs and requirements of those for whom correction has been ordered and for assigning them to programs according to their needs and the existing resources. Classification is conceptualized as a system or process by which a correctional agency, unit, or component determines differential care and handling of offenders. To date, however, there has been considerable confusion about classification systems in corrections.

One of the basic problems experienced by corrections in adopting the concept of classification as a useful correctional tool is that too often the purpose which a classification system might serve has not been specified.

Most correctional classification schemes in use today are referred to as classification systems for treatment purposes, but even a cursory analysis of these schemes and the ways in which they are used reveals that they would more properly be called classification systems for management purposes. This judgment does not imply that classification for management purposes is undesirable. In fact, that may be the only useful system today, given the current state of knowledge about crime and offenders. It is important, however, that corrections begin to acknowledge the bases and purposes of classification systems that are in use. . . .

The fact that there is so little knowledge about causes of criminal behavior and how to eliminate it means that systems of forced treatment based on that small amount of knowledge will necessarily be extremely subject to abuse. Furthermore, since the overriding goal of institutions remains that of maintaining order and control, it is not surprising that in large measure classification schemes are based on this objective and are used to the extent that they coincide with it.

For the offender, on the other hand, the main goal is release. Thus his secondary objective becomes that of trying to figure out what he is supposed to do to obtain release and then do it, or appear to do it. Most get bogged down on the first part; that is, trying to figure out what they are supposed to do. Given the fact that the offender is classified and assigned on the basis of subjective judgments by the treatment staff and that their judgments tend to shift as it is administratively convenient to do so, the individual can feel no confidence that whatever course of behavior he may try to follow will in any way help him to reach his goal. Furthermore, he is likely to be judged less on his behavior than on his "attitude," his demeanor, his degree of "contrition," his "desire to change," or some other subjective factor. . . .

## Difficulties in Application

One of the difficulties with classification is that, even after agency goals have been clearly established and commitment has been made to a specific classification program, there continues to be a wide range of latitude for response to overall decisions by agency personnel. Because of this latitude the classification process frequently breaks down.

Correctional staff by necessity are concerned with making judgments as to appropriate levels of custody, needs for education or vocational training, suitability for counseling, and readiness for parole. In making these judgments, the staff plan the offender's education or training program on the basis of academic achievement scores, vocational preference inventories, and other devices that really provide little information on how to change an offender into a nonoffender. Security classification decisions are made on the basis of escape records coupled with an appraisal of the seriousness of the commitment offense, even though this information never has been proved a reliable indicator of the inmate's custody requirements or potential for future violence.

Amenability to a counseling program is determined by the availability of the program, the offender's willingness to participate, and the counselor's willingness to make his services available. In practice, it has been demonstrated that certain forms of counseling are of little value to some inmates and actually detrimental to others. . . .

An ideal correctional system would match offender types successfully with program types. Society must be protected against incorrigible offenders, but it should not aggravate the problem by locking up those who would do better in the community. A need to isolate offender types works both ways. An effective classification process would identify offenders who must be kept out of community programs, as well as those who should be kept in them. It would acknowledge that a screening process is sufficient for the decisions needed for most offenders and that classification as theoretically conceived is needed only for a comparative few. . . .

## Classification for Risk

It is stated elsewhere in this report and in many other documents on corrections that perhaps the greatest contribution to corrections today would be development of a scheme or system that would effectively differentiate among offenders as to their risk of recidivism or their potential dangerousness to others. It is argued that such a scheme, applied at the time of sentencing, would greatly increase sentencing effectiveness, cost-effectiveness of correctional programs, and safety of the community.

Although this theory is basically sound, it presents a number of problems. Not the least of these is that sentencing decisions are not made solely on the basis of risk or a desire to protect others. Society also expects the courts to maintain individual liberties, satisfy a common notion of justice in the sense of equal and consistent treatment, maintain an image as "fair" institutions, maintain the declarative and condemnatory functions of the criminal law, seek a deterrent effect, and operate in ways that are reasonably cost-effective. Many of these goals are by no means fully consistent with the goals of protecting society and reducing recidivism. The dilemma created by these conflicting goals of the criminal sanctioning system has been well described in a recent article by Martin A. Levin.

> . . . from what we know about the type of offenders who are most likely to fall into the recidivating group, one clearly could derive the following policy to reduce recidivism: *Incarcerate for the longest terms the youngest offenders, especially if they are black or have a narcotics history.* But such a policy, however effective it might be in reducing recidivism, is obviously unacceptable if the court is to remain in our eyes a fair and non-

discriminatory institution which exercises a due regard for equality and individual liberties. Conversely, the same findings of social science with regard to reducing recidivism would dictate that judges *incarcerate for the shortest terms possible under the law whites over 40 who have committed murder or sex crimes!* These groups have extremely low recidivism rates, and such a policy would also save the state money in incarceration costs. But there is little doubt that most people would consider such a policy wrong—both because it discriminates against the young and the black and because it does not sufficiently express society's disapproval of such grave crimes as murder or rape.

Thus, society is faced with a number of crucial social policy determinations. Given the facts stated above, a common response is to declare that the public policy must be to continue to incarcerate large numbers of offenders for purposes of punishment, retribution, deterrence, or condemnation, even though they do not present a high risk to the safety of others. . . .

### Reception-Diagnostic Centers
While the reception center concept was progressive for its time, it has become obsolete. The system is administratively convenient and efficient in that a limited staff can provide services for a large number of offenders. However, this very administrative efficiency is largely accountable for its obsolescence.

Traditionally, the reception and diagnostic center has provided summary reports including information on social background, criminal history, initial adjustment to custody, medical examination, psychological assessment, vocational skills, educational level, religious background and attitudes, recreational interests and abilities, and psychiatric evaluation. Today, it is not necessary that any of these components of the diagnostic report be completed in a diagnostic or reception center. A number of the items usually are produced by probation and parole officers in the community. Although medical examinations and psychological and psychiatric evaluations require professional services, these services also are available in the local community through both contract and public agency programs.

The reception center, because of the ceaseless repetition in the nature of its work, becomes even more institutionalized than other forms of the classification process. Schedules are adhered to rigidly, and offenders are kept too long in the centers waiting for the diagnostic skills or services of a limited number of persons. The process itself is uniformly extensive and thorough for most offenders, and more information is produced than can be used effectively for classification purposes, considering the current lack of correctional knowledge and resources.

The futility of much of this work is evident in the separation of the study and diagnostic process from operational units. Independent institutions usually do not rely on information developed at the diagnostic center and may repeat clinical evaluations and studies. . . .

. . . The basis of the intake worker's judgment may or may not be clear in his own mind. In any case, institution and personal bias are involved, because the worker rarely is apprised of the result of his recommendations. Even if he is, only an experienced worker is capable of rendering such judgments in a manner beneficial to the correctional system. Only when explicit criteria form the basis of recommendations is the system's management able to check assumptions, analyze relationships, and pass along pertinent data to inexperienced workers.

The central diagnostic facility is also in conflict with current theory over the importance of developing and programming correctional efforts at the community level. Many theorists in the field argue that a valid classification system, universally applied throughout the whole of corrections, would be more useful.

### Community Classification Teams

Another organizational arrangement for classification that is now emerging suggests that with development of a realistic classification system used throughout a correctional system, the classification function can involve a much wider range of personnel and resources than previously supposed. For instance, a classification team consisting of parole and probation officers might collect the social history, while local practitioners could provide necessary medical and psychiatric examinations. State and local institution personnel, in cooperation with the other members of the community classification team, in turn would review the appropriate correctional programs available to meet the offender's needs.

The community-based classification team concept is superior to current practice. It has already begun to emerge within the correctional system and may be generally realized within the next 5 years. Indeed, to the extent that community correctional programs become the pattern, offenders should not have to be removed to a State diagnostic center or institution for review and study. The classification process itself can be adapted to the needs of offenders, most of whom, for the purposes of community-based programs, require little more than screening for risk and matching to resources. . . .

Much more extensive research is needed to develop an effective and theoretically sound classification system for the small proportion of offenders who require more than basic screening and assessment. Corrections will have to depend on the behavioral sciences to produce a more consistent theoretical basis, and corrections itself will have to engage in research and experimentation to devise programs and resources that will be related directly to causation theory. Only with the successful outcome of such efforts will it be possible to develop a classification system that will dispel the present mythological character of correctional "treatment."

**Standard 6.1: Develop a comprehensive classification system.**

**Standard 6.2: Establish classification policies for correctional institutions.**

**Standard 6.3: Establish community classification teams.**

# B: Correctional Programs

## 7: Corrections and the Community

Dissatisfaction with incarceration as a means of correction has grown to a point where some States have almost completely abolished incarceration for some classes of offenders. In other States, experimental programs have been successful enough that once-overcrowded prisons and reformatories now are unused. Clearly, the future lies with community-based corrections.

The institution model for corrections has not been successful in curbing potential crime. But at least it exists, with its physical plant and identified processes of reception, classification, assignment, custody, work, academic and vocational training, religion, and recreation.

The substitute models are talked about and are occasionally used. But community-based corrections is not well organized, planned, or programmed. This task is the challenge of the future. Required is a complicated interplay among judicial and correctional personnel, those from related public and private agencies, citizen volunteers, and civic groups. This interplay of the correctional system with other parts of the public sector and greater involvement of the private sector, including civic participation in dimensions not foreseen in the correctional world just a few years ago, requires leadership in the entire criminal justice field to collaborate in the exploitation of all possibilities for successfully changing repression to reintegration. Policymakers must understand the essential elements of a sound community-based correctional system as well as they now understand the orderly management of the prison.

## SIGNIFICANCE OF COMMUNITY-BASED CORRECTIONS

In this chapter, the significance of community-based corrections will be assessed from three aspects: humanitarian, restorative, and managerial. The criteria of success in each differ markedly.

The humanitarian aspect of community-based corrections is obvious. To subject anyone to custodial coercion is to place him in physical jeopardy, to narrow drastically his access to sources of personal satisfaction, and to reduce his self-esteem. That all these unfavorable consequences are the outcome of his own criminal actions does not change their reality. To the extent that the offender can be relieved of the burden of custody, a humanitarian objective is realized. The proposition that no one should be subjected to custodial control unnecessarily is a humanitarian assertion. The key question is the definition of necessity, which must be settled by the criterion of public protection.

The restorative aspect concerns measures expected to achieve for the offender a position in the community in which he does not violate the laws. These measures may be directed at change, control, or reintegration. The failure of offenders to achieve these goals can be measured by recidivism, and their success is defined by reaching specific objectives set by correctional decisionmakers.

The managerial goals are of special importance because of the sharp contrast between the per capita costs of custody and any kind of community program. Any shift from custodial control will save money. But the criterion of correctional success is not fiscal. A major object of correctional programs

498

is to protect the public. Therefore, any saving of public funds must not be accompanied by a loss of public protection. When offenders can be shifted from custodial control of community-based programming without loss of public protection, the managerial criteria require that such a shift be made. Otherwise public funds will have been spent without satisfying a public objective.

It is necessary here to note that public protection is not always the sole objective of correctional programming. Some kinds of offenders, especially the most notorious, often could perfectly well be released without jeopardizing public safety. But their release will not be countenanced because public demands for retribution have not been satisfied. Offenders in custody should be there predominantly because public protection seems to require it. Decisionmakers must disentangle these objectives to assure that use of community-based correctional programs is not denied for irrelevant reasons. . . .

## RATIONALE FOR CORRECTIONS IN THE COMMUNITY

But community-based corrections cannot be limited to the services of an employment office. A man who has committed a crime and been caught and convicted has suffered a blow to his self-esteem that may be masked by bravado or indifference. He has good reason to believe that conventional persons will reject him, and he therefore seeks out the unconventional. In the prison he has no choice; he must associate with the unconventional. In the community, probation and parole resources should make accessible a whole range of social support services as needed.

The difficulty of the task is obvious. Far more is required than the one-to-one contact between probation or parole officer and the offender. The offender's predicament stems from the combination of personal deficits and social malfunctions that produced a criminal event and a social status. Most personal deficits characterizing offenders are also commonly found in nonoffenders. The social malfunctions of unemployment, discrimination, economic inequity, and congested urban living affect most citizens. The offender, like other citizens, must find a way to live with his deficits and with the disorder around him. If corrections is to mitigate alienation, it must mobilize the community services that can make such an outcome possible.

To a much larger extent than has been realized, social support services must be given outside the official correctional apparatus and inside the community. Schools must accept and help reintegrate the delinquent instead of exiling him to reform schools. Unions and employers must open doors to adult offenders instead of restricting their employment to the most menial and insecure labor. . . .

But even if we allow that some crime is deterred by the criminal justice system, the deterrent potentiality of the prison is grossly exaggerated. The argument should be framed properly in terms of the statistical chances of getting caught. In the case of most crimes other than homicide, the chances are much less than even. In most communities a criminal can reasonably assume that, even with repeated law violations, his chances of getting caught are relatively slight. The prospect of incarceration or other punishment is distant.

### ROLE OF THE COMMUNITY IN CORRECTIONS

. . . Circumstances of the past decade have had dramatic impact on corrections. The poverty programs of the 1960's, which failed to win the war on poverty but made strong impressions on the Nation, are of particular import for corrections. The ideology underlying those programs suggested that persons of minority origin and low socioeconomic status systematically are denied access to higher status in American society. They thus are persistently overrepresented among those who experience mental and physical illness, educational failure, unemployment, and crime and delinquency.

. . . If the social milieu to a substantial degree causes criminal behavior, the social milieu itself must be attacked and changed. This rationale suggests that the correctional system must involve itself in social reform to control and prevent crime. Further, it requires an understanding that, if behavior is related to events and circumstances in the offender's milieu, changing his behavior in isolation from that world will not solve the problem. Evidence of behavioral change in the isolation of the total institution is meaningless. It is behavior at home, on the job, and on the streets that matters.

The shift in correctional thought that underlies the change to community-based correctional programming also can be understood by considering empirical evidence as to the effectiveness of current programs in controlling crime and the promise of new patterns. Corrections is a large, uncoordinated set of subsystems, with large gaps in service, irrational resource allocation, inadequate information, and a range of treatment modes that lacks a consistent and workable rationale. The confusion about individual vs. social causation underlies some of the lack of coherence. Contemporary corrections has not integrated its theoretical base and its practice. Despite the shift in social science theory, notions of intervening in community circumstances have not been applied widely. Rather, the emphasis has been on changing the individual—on a "treatment" philosophy that largely ignores the enormous potential of the community as the place for reduction of criminal behavior.

## RESPONSIBILITY OF CORRECTIONAL SYSTEMS FOR COMMUNITY PARTICIPATION

### Corrections' Information and Change Agent Role

Correctional agencies must provide a continuous flow of information to the public concerning issues and alternatives involved in implementing correctional programs, so that citizens may participate intelligently in the major decisions involved. For example, a major difficulty in instituting various types of community-based treatment centers is communities' refusal to have centers located in their territory. Such resistance will not be overcome immediately, but involvement of many citizens can be expected to bring success eventually.

Similarly, experience has shown that simply being able to prove that new techniques can be efficient in reducing crime or costs of crime control does not guarantee their acceptance. Bail reform measures, for example, have been carefully evaluated and have demonstrated beyond question that costs of jail incarceration can be reduced without increasing the risk to society. In addition to such cost effectiveness, bail reform substantially reduces the inequities of a jailing system that systematically discriminates against the poor. Still, release on recognizance projects have been instituted in only a fraction of the Nation's courts.

The information program should go beyond the usual press releases and occasional public hearings. Corrections must assume an educational role, a change agent role, for it is clear that drastic changes are required to bring the community-based correctional process into being.

The change agent role also involves working with private agencies that too often have offered services in a way that favors other groups in the general population over inmates or former inmates. By selectively serving individual clients who are not as problem-ridden or difficult to deal with, these agencies have burdened governmental agencies with a disproportionate number of offenders. It is reasonable and appropriate to seek a redistribution of caseloads, so that the private sector assumes a greater share of responsibility for those with the major social disabilities of conviction and imprisonment.

## IMPLEMENTATION OF COMMUNITY-BASED CORRECTIONS

### Work Release

Work-release programs began to be used extensively in the 1950's. The practice permits selected inmates to work for pay outside the institution, returning each night. Prisoner employment is not new; the work gang for hire is a well-known feature in penal history. The work-release concept differs markedly, however, in allowing regular civilian employments, under specified circumstances, for selected low-risk inmates. Initially used mainly with misdemeanants, work release now is used widely with felons and youthful offenders. Other versions, similar in intent, provide for weekend sentences, furloughs, and release for vocational training or educational programs. All help to reestablish links to the community for the incarcerated.

In a few instances, commercial manufacturing operations have been introduced into prisons. Honeywell, Inc., has loaned a computer to a Massachusetts prison for use by inmates to do programming and data processing for various departments of State government, an up-to-date version of "state use." Union involvement in such efforts is crucial; it will add a much needed dimension to employment programs and represent a further potential resource for correctional programs. . . .

**Standard 7.1: Develop a range of community-based alternatives to institutionalization.**

**Standard 7.2: Insure correctional cooperation with community agencies.**

**Standard 7.3: Seek public involvement in corrections.**

**Standard 7.4: Inmate Involvement in Community Programs**

Correctional agencies should begin immediately to develop arrangements and procedures for offenders sentenced to correctional institutions to assume increasing individual responsibility and community contact. A variety of levels of individual choice, supervision, and community contact should be specified in these arrangements, with explicit statements as to how the transitions between levels are to be accomplished.

Progress from one level to another should be based on specified behavioral criteria rather than on sentence, time served, or subjective judgments regarding attitudes. . . .

# 8: Juvenile Intake and Detention

## SIZE OF THE PROBLEM

In 1971, persons under the age of 18 accounted for 25.8 percent of all arrests. They accounted for 50.8 percent of all arrests for crimes against property and 22.8 percent of arrest for violent crimes against persons. In specific offense categories, more youths under 18 than adults were arrested for burglary, larceny, auto theft, arson, and vandalism.

Moreover, youth crime appears to be increasing faster than total crime. The National Commission on the Causes and Prevention of Violence found that from 1964 to 1967, arrest rates for the four major violent crimes (murder, forcible rape, robbery, and aggravated assault) increased by 15.4 percent for all urban whites over 10 years of age and by 20.6 percent for such whites in the 10 through 17 age bracket. For all urban blacks over 10, the arrest rate for these crimes increased by 23.0 percent as against 48.5 percent for all urban blacks aged 10 through 17.

These statistics are hard to interpret. Recording techniques are not uniform, and police practices differ. Crime statistics are known to be economically and racially skewed because middle- and upper-class juvenile delinquency tends to be handled on an informal basis and not recorded in official statistics. Furthermore, recent population changes indicating an increase in the number of persons aged 10 to 24, which are the most crime-prone ages, may well be reflected in the overall increase in juvenile crime. In other words, there may be more delinquency because there are more young people. . . .

## THE JUVENILE JUSTICE PROCESS

There is evidence that the police handling of juvenile offenders is more a function of informal police-community relations, the nature of the community, and its geographical location than observance of abstract principles of law enforcement. For example, it has been found that the proportion of juveniles arrested who are referred to court depends on the type of community and the relationship of police and the public there. Rural communities where there is apt to be a high degree of personal relationship between citizens and police, tend to have significantly fewer court referrals of arrested juveniles than do communities with a high degree of impersonality in contacts between police and public. In each case, police reflect their perception of community attitudes toward delinquency, exercising maximum discretion in homogeneous rural areas and less in urban areas where the population is heterogeneous and therefore perceptions of the citizenry are likewise varied. . . .

The detention decision should not be made by law enforcement officers, whose professional backgrounds and missions may differ considerably from those of court or social service personnel. Since the ultimate responsibility for detention of children rests with the court, it will need to assume full responsibility over juvenile detention and admission control on a 24-hour basis. The objective is to separate the "detecting and catching" function from the "detaining, adjudicating, and correcting" function. . . .

Between 1970 and 1971, the number of delinquency cases reaching the courts increased by 7 percent, compared with a 3 percent increase in cases handled informally. This may mean that more serious cases are being brought before the courts, that increased concern with due process as a result of the *Gault* decision, 387 U.S. 1 (1967), may contribute to a concomitant emphasis on formality, or that recent emphasis on diversion techniques and community-based programs affects mostly those cases that never reach the courts. The question remains as to why so many youngsters are brought before the court when informal community alternatives have been recognized as more desirable for most juveniles. . . .

INTAKE SERVICES

. . . In all but the smallest jurisdictions, intake services should be provided by specialized staff who are assigned only to intake functions. Other staff members should be assigned to prepare social study reports, to represent the child in court, and to be responsible for supervision.

Intake personnel should have the following responsibilities:

1. They should make a determination of whether the matter in question falls within the delinquency jurisdiction of the court.

2. If the matter is not within the delinquency jurisdiction of the court, the juvenile should be released to his parents. In some cases, intake staff may assist the youngster and his parents by making a voluntary referral to another section of the court (that handles dependency, neglect, etc.) or a service

program such as a family or mental health service, a public welfare agency, or a youth service bureau.

3. If the matter appears to be within the delinquency jurisdiction of the court, intake staff should make an assessment of what action is appropriate, in the following order of priority:

    a. Dismissal of the complaint as too minor or otherwise so circumstanced as to warrant dismissal.

    b. Referral to a nonjudicial agency for services.

    c. Utilization of any of the other formal or informal dispositions available to the court other than a delinquency petition. Among them might be participation in a formally organized diversion program, a consent decree, or informal probation.

    d. A decision that a formal court hearing is required and subsequent filing of a delinquency petition. As a general rule, formal proceedings appear appropriate where:

    Accusations are in dispute, and, if borne out, court-ordered disposition and treatment appear desirable.

    Detention or removal from the home is indicated.

    The nature or gravity of the offense warrants official judicial attention.

    The juvenile or the parents request formal adjudication.

4. Screening of children for whom a delinquency petition is filed to place as many in their parental homes, a shelter, or nonsecure residential care as is consistent with the safety of others.

5. If no other alternative can be achieved for a child for whom a delinquency petition is filed, placement of the individual in detention pending a detention hearing.

6. Preparation of a report for the court to be used at the detention hearing, presenting the reasons why detention was deemed necessary. . . .

Despite the obvious inequity of the situation, most jurisdictions do not differentiate legally between delinquent and nondelinquent children. While the Standard Juvenile Court Act long has called for separation of the nondelinquent child from those who have violated the law, by requiring that the former not be placed in institutions primarily designed for the treatment of delinquents, continued indiscriminate grouping constitutes a national disgrace. Even if great care were taken to provide separate legal categories by statute, it is doubtful that such differentiated labeling as PINS or MINS would be any less stigmatizing or injurious than being adjudicated delinquent because, in most States, they are detained and institutionalized together. . . .

In the initial intake interview, when an intake officer decides whether or not to refer to the court for formal petition, the parents and the child should be allowed to answer questions without their statements being used as evidence in any formal adjudication that may result. This recommendation dovetails with those of the Model Rules for Juvenile Courts, extending them to intake services and the entire preadjudication disposition process. Only in this manner can the dispositional decision be made with adequate information. Thus, the juvenile can take advantage of the informal disposition possibilities, if offered, and yet not lose his right to remain silent if formal adjudication results. . . .

In all situations, the child and parents should be apprised of his options and the possible consequences of each. One option is formal disposition—the filing of a delinquency petition or equivalent court proceeding. The moment this option is chosen, counsel should be provided. If the alleged offense is such that informal disposition is possible, it is not likely that a formal hearing will be chosen.

Assuming the juvenile chooses the informal proceedings, he should be informed that he can, at any time, terminate such a disposition and request formal adjudication. The restraints placed on his freedom as a result of such disposition should be minimal, since no adjudication has actually occurred. Obviously, such dispositions can be used only where both parents and child are willing to cooperate. . . .

OVERVIEW OF CURRENT DETENTION PROBLEMS

In 1969, a nationwide survey identified 288 detention homes throughout the country, which admitted approximately 488,800 per year. While the latter number may not be precise, it nevertheless represents a considerable increase over the 317,860 reported for 1965. The estimated average daily population of 13,567 in 1969 also was slightly higher than the 1965 estimate of 13,000. The nearly half-million children believed to have been admitted to detention homes in 1969 represent approximately two-thirds of all juveniles taken into custody in that year. Since nine out of ten of the juvenile court jurisdictions in this country detain too few children to warrant construction of detention homes, it is estimated that at least 50,000 and possibly more than 100,000 children of juvenile court age are held in jails and police lockups each year. According to the 1970 National Jail Census, 7,800 juveniles were confined on March 15, the census date, in 4,037 jails. Of the juveniles detained, 66 percent had not been adjudicated.

Nineteen States have statutes permitting detention of juveniles in jail, provided they are segregated from the adult population. At the other end of the spectrum, Connecticut, Delaware, Rhode Island, and Puerto Rico do not keep juveniles in jails. Nine States have statutory or administrative prohibitions against keeping juveniles in jails, but these prohibitions often are violated.

About half of the 288 juvenile detention facilities reported in the 1969 survey were constructed specifically for that purpose. The rest were converted from other types of facilities. Detention homes usually are located in urban areas and are frequently of poor quality.

According to the 1969 survey, detention homes have an average capacity of 61. Administrators reportedly were more concerned about custody than any other goal. A comparative analysis of the homes' capacities and their average daily population indicates that larger homes tend to be overcrowded, while smaller ones are not. ...

... The decision to detain prior to adjudication of delinquency should be based on the following criteria:

• Detention should be considered as a last resort where no other reasonable alternative is available.

• Detention should be used only where the juvenile has no parent, guardian, custodian, or other person able to provide supervision and care for him and to assure his presence at subsequent judicial hearings.

• Detention decisions should be made only by the court or intake personnel, not police officers.

• Juveniles should not be detained in jails, lockups, or other facilities used for adults.

Thus in the predetention screening process, the following priorities should be favored over detention:

• Release of as many children as possible to their parents or guardians.

• Release to a third party with the consent of the parent or guardian and the child.

• Diversion into temporary nonresidential programs or placement into physically unrestricted residential care of all children who need shelter but not secure custody.

Most correctional administrators agree that there are too many maximum security facilities for juveniles and adults alike on State and local levels. Many urge a halt to the building of massive concrete and steel institutions. The existing institutions in too many instances are monuments to the mistakes of the past and to an "edifice complex," the propensity for trying to solve social problems by building an enclosure to keep them out of sight and mind.

It is particularly important for jurisdictions to think twice before building or enlarging juvenile detention centers because of an unfortunate but verified tendency, where new detention space is constructed, to detain more children and to keep them confined longer. Another tendency in detention center planning and construction, hitherto accepted without question, is the assumption that security can be obtained only through hardware. Whenever security is achieved primarily by physical means, the options for individualized treatment and flexibility decrease proportionately.

**Standard 8.1: Authorize police to divert juveniles.**

**Standard 8.2: Establish a juvenile court intake unit.**

**Standard 8.3: Apply total system planning concepts to juvenile detention centers.**

**Standard 8.4: Evaluate juvenile intake and detention personnel policies.**

# 9: Local Adult Institutions

## MAJOR CHARACTERISTICS OF THE JAIL

A jail census conducted in 1970 by the U.S. Bureau of the Census under an agreement with the Law Enforcement Assistance Administration found 4,037 jails meeting the definition of "any facility operated by a unit of local government for the detention or correction of adults suspected or convicted of a crime and which has authority to detain longer than 48 hours." These institutions ranged from New York City's festering "Tombs" to the infrequently utilized small municipal lockup.

With more than 4,000 jails, implementing recommendations and standards delineated in this chapter will require localities to make precise specification of their needs and resources. The prescriptive content of this chapter will consist of elements that may be combined into a suitable solution for any given situation. There is no single answer to the problems of jails.

Local control, multiple functions, and a transient, heterogeneous population have shaped the major organizational characteristics of jails. Typically, they are under the jurisdiction of the county government. In most instances, the local area has neither the necessary tax base from which to finance a jail adequately nor sufficient size to justify even the most rudimentary correctional programs. Local control inevitably has meant involvement with local politics. Jails are left in a paradoxical situation: localities cling tenaciously to them but are unwilling or unable to meet even minimal standards. "The problem of American jails, put most concisely, is the problem of local control."

Beyond their formally acknowledged tasks of correction and detention, jails have been adapted to perform a variety of "social welfare" tasks and provide easy answers to law enforcement problems. For example, Stuart Queen, a jail critic of 50 years ago, noted the "floater custom" in California counties by which transients were arrested, brought to the jail, and from there "ordered to disappear." Similarly, Sutherland and Cressey observed the "Golden Rule disposition" of misdemeanant arrest in which the individual is held with no intention of bringing him to trial but only until his condition changes (as with drunkenness, disorderliness, etc.) Such uses, as well as detention of suspects and witnesses, are understandable responses to difficulties encountered by law enforcement personnel. They are, however, short-term expedients that rarely solve anything.

Because of their multiple uses, jails house a population more diverse than any other correctional institutions. The 1970 jail census found that, of 160,863 persons held on the census date, 27,460 had not been arraigned, 8,688 were awaiting some postconviction legal action, 69,096 were serving sentences (10,496 for more than a year), and 7,800 were juveniles. Thus accused felons and misdemeanants and juveniles are all found in American jails, often unsegregated from each other. . . .

## JAIL CONDITIONS TODAY

### Physical Facilities

The most striking inadequacy of jails is their abominable physical condition. The National Jail Census found that 25 percent of the cells in use in 1970 were built before 1920. And the chronological age of the facility is aggravated by the manner in which it is used. Jails that hold few persons tend to be neglected, and those that are overcrowded repeatedly push their equipment and fixtures beyond the breaking point. Given the fact that most jails are either overutilized, and hence overcrowded, or are using only a portion of their capacity, it is not surprising that most of the physical facilities are in crisis condition.

The National Jail Census found 5 percent of jails included in their survey overcrowded, with the propensity to be overcrowded increasing with design capacity. On the other hand, on four census dates, a survey found 35 percent to 45 percent of Idaho's jails unoccupied. Neither the situation of the overcrowded urban jail nor that of the underutilized rural facility will be ameliorated merely by constructing new buildings. The means of delivering detention and correctional services must be reexamined. Otherwise, the new will merely repeat and perpetuate mistakes of the old.

In nearly all jails, the available space is divided into inflexible cells or cage-like day rooms. Rows of cells compose self-contained cellblocks that face a large cage or "bullpen." The arrangement is designed "so that a relatively small number of staff can insure the secure confinement of a comparatively large number of inmates." Items are passed into the bullpens through slotted doors, largely preventing contact between staff and inmates. . . .

### Administration by "Custodial Convenience"

The fundamental principle underlying the relationship between jailers and inmates is that of "custodial convenience," in which "everyone who can, takes the easy way out and makes only the minimal effort." Because of insufficient staffing and funding and the lack of effective screening for incoming inmates, the population is separated into several large groups and placed in specific cell blocks. Each division represents an attempt to replace continuous, or even frequent, staff supervision with a maximum security setting. With such an arrangement, jailers effectively abandon their control and concentrate solely on any untoward occurrences.

Thus the inmates are left to work out their own internal order. For this reason, "control over inmate behavior usually can be achieved by other inmates more immediately, directly, and completely in jails than in other types of confinement institutions, such as penitentiaries or State hospitals." In past eras, kangaroo courts flourished in many jails and still do in some.

While most such "judicial" trappings have gone the way of many traditions, the basic features remain in force. Jail inmates face many uncertainties arising from a threatening environment and an ambiguous relationship to the machinery of the criminal justice system. Under these conditions, individuals experienced in crime and accustomed to life in State penitentiaries assume positions of leadership and control.

The "custodial convenience" philosophy is marked by an almost fanatic concern with security, but one practice totally contradictory to security is found in many jails. To operate and maintain the jail, selected inmates are granted the rank of trusty. They have free access throughout the jail and frequently to the outside as well. All too often, the result is a jail run by its inmates. In most instances, trusties, or at least their "barn boss" or foreman, are well schooled in prison life, and jailers must offer them privileges in return for cooperation.

"Custodial convenience" also dictates a solution for the multitude of social and medical problems entering the jail. Here too, inmates are left to solve their mutual problems, with the elderly, sick, intoxicated, suicide-prone, and addicted all thrown together. The assumption is that they somehow will arrange to take care of each other. . . .

SHORTCOMINGS OF STATE SUPERVISION

In addressing the needs presented by current jail conditions, the trend toward seeking change through State-set standards and inspections of local jails is open to question. *The Passing of the County Jail*, published 50 years ago, was no isolated utopian exercise but the product of an era of jail reform, written by an experienced and tough-minded practitioner. The book assessed the growing State involvement in local correctional efforts that had occurred in the preceding two decades. State boards of charities and corrections had been established in several States and charged with inspection of jails. Results of inspection surveys were published in California and Illinois. In Alabama, a State prison inspector was granted broad powers by statute to oversee jail activities, including the right to set standards. By and large, however, these measures did not meet expectations. . . .

For individuals seeking reform of local adult corrections, precautions must be taken not to set off in the wrong direction. Hans Mattick has articulated well what must be avoided.

At least two kinds of investment should be *postponed* in any statewide jail reform program based on a phased-stage implementation of State standards: the building of new jails and the hiring of more personnel. Investment in new jails, or the major refurbishing of old ones, would merely cement-in the old problems under somewhat more decent conditions. . . . Increasing the number of personnel in existing jails would only have the effect of giving more persons a vested interest in maintaining the status quo and contribute to greater resistance to future change. By and large, new buildings and more staff should come only after the potential effects of criminal law reform and diversion alternatives have been fully considered. Such collateral reforms, combined with an increasing tendency toward regionalization of jails, would require fewer jails and fewer, but better qualified and trained, jail personnel.

This position may be difficult for some to accept because at first blush the answer to poor jails seems to be to build better ones; the response to inadequate personnel, to hire more. It must be remembered, however, that this is not the first generation to confront the plight of American jails. Concerned individuals have been speaking out for at least a hundred years. But, for the most part, the situation has not improved. New jails have been built, but they now present the same problems as those they were built to replace. History shows clearly that only a different attack on the problem holds real promise. The new approach must involve all components of the criminal justice system. . . .

FUNCTIONS OF COMMUNITY CORRECTIONAL CENTERS

**Court Intake Services**
Where at all possible, court intake personnel should be located in a community correctional center. Such an arrangement will facilitate communication between court and corrections staff by virtue of proximity and functional relationships that must be developed to attain an integrated local adult corrections system. . . .

**Standard 9.1: Undertake total system planning for community corrections.**

**Standard 9.2: State Operation and Control of Local Institutions**

All local detention and correctional functions, both pre- and postconviction, should be incorporated within the appropriate State system by 1982.

1. Community-based resources should be developed initially through subsidy contract programs, subject to State standards, which reimburse the local unit of government for accepting State commitments.

2. Coordinated planning for community-based correctional services should be implemented immediately on a State and regional basis. This planning should take place under jurisdiction of the State correctional system. . . .

**Standard 9.3: Formulate State standards for local facilities.**

**Standard 9.4: Adult Intake Services**

Each judicial jurisdiction should immediately take action, including the pursuit of enabling legislation where necessary, to establish centrally coordinated and directed adult intake services to:

1. Perform investigative services for pretrial intake screening. Such services should be conducted within 3 days and provide data for decisions regarding appropriateness of summons release, relase on recognizance, community bail, conditional pretrial release, or other forms of pretrial release. Persons should not be placed in detention solely for the purpose of facilitating such services.

2. Emphasize diversion of alleged offenders from the criminal justice system and referral to alternative community-based programs (halfway houses, drug treatment programs, and other residential and nonresidential adult programs). The principal task is identifying the need and matching community services to it.

3. Offer initial and ongoing assessment, evaluation, and classification services to other agencies as requested.

4. Provide assessment, evaluation, and classification services that assist program planning for sentenced offenders.

5. Arrange secure residential detention for pretrial detainees at an existing community or regional correctional center or jail, or at a separate facility for pretrial detainees where feasible. Most alleged offenders awaiting trial should be diverted to release programs, and the remaining population should be only those who represent a serious threat to the safety of others.

The following principles should be followed in establishing, planning, and operating intake services for adults:

1. Intake services should be administratively part of the judiciary.

2. Ideally, intake services should operate in conjunction with a community correctional facility.

3. Initiation of intake services should in no way imply that the client or recipient of its services is guilty. Protection of the rights of the accused must be maintained at every phase of the process.

4. Confidentiality should be maintained at all times.

5. Social inventory and offender classification should be a significant component of intake services.

6. Specialized services should be purchased in the community on a contractual basis.

7. The following persons should be available to intake service programs, either as staff members or by contract:

    a. Psychiatrists.
    b. Clinical psychologists.
    c. Social workers.
    d. Interviewers.
    e. Education specialists.

**Standard 9.5:** Upgrade pretrial admission services and processes.

**Standard 9.6:** Upgrade the qualifications of local correctional personnel.

**Standard 9.7:** Internal Policies

Every jurisdiction operating locally based correctional institutions and programs for adults should immediately adopt these internal policies:

1. A system of classification should be used to provide the basis for residential assignment and program planning for individuals. Segregation of diverse categories of incarcerated persons, as well as identification of special supervision and treatment requirements, should be observed.

    a. The mentally ill should not be housed in a detention facility.

    b. Since local correctional facilities are not equipped to treat addicts, they should be diverted to narcotic treatment centers. When drug users are admitted to the facility because of criminal charges not related to their drug use, immediate medical attention and treatment should be administered by a physician.

514

c. Since local correctional facilities are not proper locations for treatment of alcoholics, all such offenders should be diverted to detoxification centers and given a medical examination. Alcoholics with delirium tremens should be transferred immediately to a hospital for proper treatment.

d. Prisoners who suffer from various disabilities should have separate housing and close supervision to prevent mistreatment by other inmates. Any potential suicide risk should be under careful supervision. Epileptics, diabetics, and persons with other special problems should be treated as recommended by the staff physician.

e. Beyond segregating these groups, serious and multiple offenders should be kept separate from those whose charge or conviction is for a first or minor offense. In particular, persons charged with noncriminal offenses (for example, traffic cases) should not be detained before trial. The State government should insist on the separation of pretrial and posttrial inmates, except where it can be demonstrated conclusively that separation is not possible and every alternative is being used to reduce pretrial detention. . . .

## Standard 9.8: Local Correctional Facility Programing

Every jurisdiction operating locally based correctional facilities and programs for adults should immediately adopt the following programming practices:

1. A decisionmaking body should be established to follow and direct the inmate's progress through the local correctional system, either as a part of or in conjunction with the community classification team concept set forth in Standard 6.3. Members should include a parole and probation supervisor, the administrator of the correctional facility or his immediate subordinates, professionals whose services are purchased by the institution, representatives of community organizations running programs in the institution or with its resident, and inmates. This body should serve as a central information-gathering point. It should discuss with an individual inmate all major decisions pertaining to him. . . .

## Standard 9.9: Develop release programs for convicted adults.

## Standard 9.10: Evaluate the physical environment of jails.

515

# 10: Probation

GOVERNMENTAL FRAMEWORK OF PROBATION

... California and Washington have developed probation subsidy programs in which counties are reimbursed in proportion to the number of individuals that remain in the community rather than being sent to State institutions. The subsidy program in California was developed as a result of a study that indicated that some individuals eligible for commitment to State correctional institutions could safely be retained on probation and that with good probation supervision, they could make a satisfactory adjustment. It was estimated that at least 25 percent of the new admissions to State correctional institutions could remain in the community with good probation supervision.

The California Probation Subsidy Program was instituted in 1966 by the State's youth authority. The youth authority was authorized to pay up to $4,000 to each county for every adult and juvenile offender not committed to a State correctional institution. The counties were required to demonstrate a commitment to improved probation services, including employment of additional probation workers and reduction of caseloads. In addition, each county had to demonstrate innovative approaches to probation, such as intensive care probation units for dealing with hard-core adult and juvenile offenders.

California estimates that, even with expanded probation services, the cost of probation runs little more than one-tenth of the cost of incarceration, approximately $600 per person annually for probation, compared to $5,000 annually for institutionalization. In all, the program has resulted in substantial savings to taxpayers. In the six years between 1966 and 1972, California canceled planned construction, closed existing institutions, and abandoned new institutions that had been constructed. Almost $186 million was saved in these ways, while probation subsidy expenditures came to about $60 million. Furthermore, although there has been a general decrease in commitments to State institutions throughout the United States, the decrease is sharper in those counties in California that participate in the subsidy program. The decrease in those counties almost doubles that of California counties not participating in the subsidy program.

The State of Washington has had a similar experience with the probation subsidy program begun in January, 1970. Its purpose was to reduce the number of commitments to institutions from county juvenile courts. In the 2 years the program has been in operation, there has been a marked reduction in the number of children and youth sent to State institutions. To illustrate, in 1971, the State received 55 percent fewer commitments than expected. . . .

## SERVICES TO PROBATIONERS

### The Current Service System

Many problems have prevented development of a system for providing probationers with needed resources. For one thing, the goal of service delivery to probationers has not been delineated clearly and given the priority required. Services to probationers have not been separated from services to the court. Generally, both services are provided by the same staff members, who place more emphasis on services to the court than to probationers.

Because the goal for service delivery to probationers has not been defined clearly, service needs have not been identified on a systematic and sustained basis. Priorities based on need, resources, and constraints have not been set. Measurable objectives and ways of achieving them for various target groups have not been specified. Moreover, monitoring and evaluation of services have been almost nonexistent.

Another problem is the lack of differentiation between services that should be provided by probation and those that should be delivered by such agencies as mental health, employment, housing, education, and private welfare agencies. Because of community attitudes toward offenders, social agencies other than probation are likely to be unenthusiastic about providing services to the legally identified offender. Probation offices usually lack sufficient influence and funds to procure services from other resources and therefore try to expand their own role and services. This leads to two results, both undesirable: identical services are duplicated by probation and one or more other public service agencies, and probation suffers from stretching already tight resources. . . .

### Overemphasis on Casework

One result of the influence of social work on probation has been an overemphasis on casework. Development of child guidance clinics in the 1920's and 1930's influenced particularly the juvenile courts and their probation staff.

The terms "diagnosis" and "treatment" began to appear in social work literature and not long after in corrections literature. Those terms come from the medical field and imply ill-

517

ness. A further implication is that a good probation practitioner will understand the cause and be able to remedy it, just as the medical practitioner does. Essentially, the medical approach overlooked any connection between crime and such factors as poverty, unemployment, poor housing, poor health, and lack of education.

A review of the literature of the 1930's, 1940's, and 1950's indicates that the casework method because equated with social work, and in turn, casework for probation became equated with a therapeutic relationship with a probationer. A study manual published by the National Probation and Parole Association in 1942 reflects this equation in the table of contents. The titles of three of the chapters are: "Social Casework," "Case Study and Diagnosis," and "Casework as a Means of Treatment."

The literature discussed the development of social work skills in interviewing, creating therapeutic relationships with clients, counseling, providing insight, and modifying behavior. When practitioners began to view themselves as therapists, one consequence was the practice of having offenders come to the office rather than workers going into the homes and the communities.

Although the literature refers to probation officers working with employers, schools, families, and others in the probationer's life, the chief concern is the relationship between probation officer and probationer. Indeed, if probation staff members see casework as their model, it may well be asked how much contact and what kind of contact they should have with persons other than probationers. . . .

. . . The San Francisco Project described in a subsequent section challenged the assumption of a caseload standard. Four levels of workloads were established: (1) ideal (50 cases) (2) intensive (25, i.e., half the ideal); (3) normal (100, twice the ideal); and (4) minimum supervision (with a ceiling of 250 cases). Persons in minimum supervision caseloads were required only to submit a monthly written report; no contacts occurred except when requested by the probationer. It was found that offenders in minimum caseloads performed as well as those under normal supervision. The minimum and ideal caseloads had almost identical violation rates. In the intensive caseloads, the violation rate did not decline, but technical violations increased.

The study indicated that the number of contacts between probationer and staff appeared to have little relationship to success or failure on probation. The conclusion was that the concept of a caseload is meaningless without some type of classification and matching of offender type, service to be offered, and staff. . . .

For the most part, the probation system has tended to view offenders as a homogeneous group. The assumption has been that all require the same kind of service; namely, treatment on a one-to-one basis. Confusion exists about the form of treatment to be used and what it is supposed to accomplish. Discussion with most probation staff members reveals their difficulty in explaining what they do to "treat" a probationer and why. They speak of a relationship with each probationer as an end in itself and the sole means of providing services to individuals. Probation staff members also perceive the periodic contact they must make to account for the probationer's presence in the community as helping, treating, or rehabilitating the probationer.

Probationers are a heterogeneous group. The needs of juveniles differ from those of adults; girls and women have different needs than boys and men. There may be some common needs but one means, casework, will not meet them all. For example, casework is not a satisfactory technique for the probationer who has a drug problem. The problem of a probationer may not be interpersonal but one that should be met through specific help such as a job, employment training, or education. Reducing caseloads alone to improve supervision does not necessarily result in better probation services. Research in the past decade provides evidence that other approaches are needed. . . .

## Future Directions for Service Delivery

. . . Direct probation services should be defined clearly and differentiated from services that should be met by other social institutions. Generally the kinds of services to be provided to probationers directly through the probation system should:

• Relate to the reasons the offender was brought into the probation system.

• Help him adjust to his status as a probationer.

• Provide information and facilitate referrals to needed community resources.

• Help create conditions permitting readjustment and reintegration into the community as an independent individual through full utilization of all available resources.

In addition, probation must account to the court for the presence and actions of the probationer.

Other needs of probationers related to employment, training, housing, health, etc. are the responsibility of other social institutions and should be provided by them. Therefore, most services needed by probationers should be located outside the system itself. These services should be available to probationers just as they are to all citizens, but some social institutions have created artificial barriers that deny ready access by persons identified as offenders.

Employment is an example. Some probation agencies have created positions of job developers and employment finders. Probation systems should not attempt to duplicate services already created by law and supposedly available to all persons. The responsibility of the system and its staff should be to enable the probationer to cut through the barriers and receive assistance from social institutions that may be all too ready to exclude him. . . .

In examining the various functions within the probation service delivery system it becomes apparent that there is a range of jobs requiring different kinds of knowledge and skills. Paraprofessionals and those in other "new career" occupations can provide services complementary to those of the probation officer. The potential for assigning a group of probationers to a team of probation officers, paraprofessionals, and other new careerists, headed by a team leader who does not function in the traditional social work supervisory role, is worth testing. . . .

The responsibility for being the sole treatment agent that has traditionally been assigned to the probation officer no longer meets the needs of the criminal justice system, the probation system, or the offender. While some probation officers still will have to carry out counseling duties, most probation officers can meet the goals of the probation services system more effectively in the role of community resource manager. This means that the probation officer will have primary responsibility for meshing a probationer's identified needs with a range of available services and for supervising the delivery of those services. . . .

## MANPOWER FOR PROBATION

### New Careers in Probation

Probation and other subsystems of corrections will need many more personnel than are likely to come to them from colleges and universities. And there are other good reasons why persons with less than college education should be employed for work in probation.

520

Allied human services which have faced similar needs for more workers have come to realize that many tasks traditionally assigned to professionals can perfectly well be handled by people with less than a college education, even some who have not graduated from high school. Moreover, these people often have a better understanding of the client's problems than professionals do. Hence progressive agencies, particularly those in education and health, have made concerted efforts to recruit people with less than a professional education and to set up career lines by which these paraprofessionals may advance.

Probation has lagged behind in this movement. But the shift from a caseload model to one based on offender classification should encourage the introduction of new career lines into the probation system. This would follow the Joint Commission recommendation that agencies set up career ladders that will give persons with less than a college education a chance to advance to the journeyman level (probation officer) through combined work-study programs.

It has been amply demonstrated that paraprofessionals can be used in probation. The National Institute of Mental Health funded a program for the Federal Probation Office in Chicago, to employ paraprofessionals in both full-time and part-time capacities. The results were so promising that Congress has appropriated funds to include paraprofessionals as a regular part of the staff in fiscal 1973.

A recent study identified four groups of tasks that can be carried out by staff other than probation officers. The tasks are related to:

• Direct service—for example, explain to the individual and family the purpose of probation.

• Escort—such as accompanying probationer to an agency.

• Data gathering—collecting information, such as school progress reports, from outside sources and disseminate it to probation staff.

• Agency and personnel development—such as taking part in staff meetings for training and research activities.

Other tasks could be assigned; for example, accounting for the presence of the probationer in the community. . . .

**Standard 10.1: Place probation under executive branch jurisdiction.**

**Standard 10.2: Establish a probation service delivery system.**

**Standard 10.3: Misdemeanant Probation**

Each State should develop additional probation manpower and resources to assure that the courts may use probation for persons convicted of misdemeanors in all cases for which this disposition may be appropriate. All standards of this report that apply to probation are intended to cover both misdemeanant and felony probation. Other than the possible length of probation terms, there should be no distinction between misdemeanant and felony probation as to organization, manpower, or services.

**Standard 10.4: Develop a State probation manpower unit.**

**Standard 10.5: Probation in Release on Recognizance Programs**

Each probation office serving a community or metropolitan area of more than 100,000 persons that does not already have an effective release on recognizance program should immediately develop, in cooperation with the court, additional staff and procedures to investigate arrested adult defendants for possible release on recognizance (ROR) while awaiting trial, to avoid unnecessary use of detention in jail.

1. The staff used in the ROR investigations should not be probation officers but persons trained in interviewing, investigation techniques, and report preparation.

2. The staff should collect information relating to defendant's residence, past and present; employment status; financial condition; prior record if any; and family, relatives, or others, particularly those living in the immediate area who may assist him in attending court at the proper time.

3. Where appropriate, staff making the investigation should recommend to the court any conditions that should be imposed on the defendant if released on recognizance.

4. The probation agency should provide pretrial intervention services to persons released on recognizance.

# 11: Major Institutions

HISTORICAL PERSPECTIVE

Institutionalization as the primary means of enforcing the customs, mores, or laws of a people is a relatively modern practice. In earlier times, restitution, exile, and a variety of methods of corporal and capital punishment, many of them unspeakably barbarous, were used. Confinement was used for detention only.

The colonists who came to North America brought with

them the harsh penal codes and practices of their homelands. It was in Pennsylvania, founded by William Penn, that initial attempts were made to find alternatives to the brutality of British penal practice. Penn knew well the nature of confinement because he had spent six months in Newgate Prison, London, for his religious convictions.

In the Great Law of Pennsylvania, enacted in 1682, Penn made provisions to eliminate to a large extent the stocks, pillories, branding iron, and gallows. The Great Law directed: "... that every county within the province of Pennsylvania and territories thereunto belonging shall ... build or cause to be built in the most convenient place in each respective county a sufficient house for restraint, labor, and punishment of all such persons as shall be thereunto commited by laws."

In time William Penn's jails, like those in other parts of the New World up to and including the present, became places where the untried, the mentally ill, the promiscuous, the debtor, and myriad petty offenders were confined indiscriminately.

In 1787, when the Constitutional Convention was meeting in Philadelphia and men were thinking of institutions based on the concept of the dignity of man, the Philadelphia Society for Alleviating the Miseries of Public Prisons was organized. The society believed that the sole end of punishment is to prevent crime and that punishment should not destroy the offender. The society, many of whose members were influential citizens, worked hard to create a new penology in Pennsylvania, a penology which to a large degree eliminated capital and corporal punishment as the principal sanctions for major crimes. The penitentiary was invented as a substitute for these punishments.

In the first three decades of the 19th century, citizens of New York, Pennsylvania, New Jersey, Massachusetts, and Connecticut were busy planning and building monumental penitentiaries. These were not cheap installations built from the crumbs of the public treasury. In fact, the Eastern State Penitentiary in Philadelphia was the most expensive public building constructed in the New World to that time. States were extremely proud of these physical plants. Moreover, they saw in them an almost utopian ideal. They were to become stabilizers of society. They were to become laboratories committed to the improvement of all mankind.

When these new penitentiaries, were being planned and constructed, practitioners and theorists held three factors to be the primary contributors to criminal behavior. The first was environment. Report after report on offenders pointed out the harmful effects of family, home, and other aspects of environment on the offender's behavior. The second factor usually cited was the offender's lack of aptitude and work skills. This quality led to indolence and a life of crime. The third cause was seen as the felon's ignorance of right and wrong because he had not been taught the Scriptures.

The social planners of the first quarter of the 19th century designed prison architecture and programs to create an experience for the offender in which (1) there would be no injurious influences, (2) the offender would learn the value of labor and work skills, and (3) he would have the opportunity to learn about the Scriptures and accept from them the principles of right and wrong that would then guide his life.

Various States pursued this triad of purposes in one of two basic methods. The Pennsylvania system was based on solitary confinement, accompanied by bench labor within one's cell. There the offender was denied all contact with the outside world except that provided by the Scriptures, religious tracts, and visits from specially selected, exemplary citizens. The prison was designed painstakingly to make this kind of solitary experience possible. The walls between cells were thick, and the cells themselves were large, each equipped with plumbing and running water. In the cell were a work bench and tools. In addition, each cell had its own small walled area for solitary exercise. The institution was designed magnificently for its three purposes: elimination of external influences; provision of work; and opportunity for penitence, introspection, and acquisition of religious knowledge.

New York's Auburn system pursued the same three goals by a different method. Like the Pennsylvania system, it isolated the offender from the world outside and permitted him virtually no external contact. However, it provided small cells in which the convicts were confined only on the Sabbath and during nonworking hours. During working hours inmates labored in factory-like shops. The contaminating effect of the congregate work situation was elminated by a rule of silence. Inmates were prohibited from communicating in any way with other inmates or the jailers.

The relative merits of these two systems were debated vigorously for half a century. The Auburn system ultimately prevailed in the United States, because it was less expensive and because it lent itself more easily to production methods of the industrial revolution.

But both systems were disappointments almost from the

beginning. The awful solitude of the Pennsylvania system drove men to insanity. The rule of silence of the Auburn system became increasingly unenforceable despite regular use of the lash and a variety of other harsh and brutal punishments.

Imprisonment as an instrument of reform was an early failure. This invention did, however, have some notable advantages. It rendered obsolete a myriad of sanguinary punishments, and its ability to separate and hold offenders gave the public a sense of security. It also was thought to deter people from crime by fear of imprisonment.

Imprisonment had many disadvantages, too. Principal among them was the phenomenon that so many of its "graduates" came back. The prison experience often further atrophied the offender's capacity to live successfully in the free world. The prison nevertheless has persisted, partly because a civilized nation could neither turn back to the barbarism of an earlier time nor find a satisfactory alternative. For nearly two centuries, American penologists have been seeking a way out of this dilemma.

TYPES OF INSTITUTIONS

## Maximum Security Prisons

For the first century after invention of the penitentiary most prisons were built to be internally and externally secure. The early zealots who had dreamed of institutions that not only would reform the offender but also would cleanse society itself were replaced by a disillusioned and pragmatic leadership that saw confinement as a valid end in itself. Moreover, the new felons were seen as outsiders—Irishmen, Germans, Italians, and Negroes. They did not talk or act like "Americans." The prison became a dumping ground where foreigners and blacks who were not adjusting could be held outside the mainstream of society's concern. The new prisons, built in the most remote areas of the State, became asylums, not only for the hardened criminal but also for the inept and unskilled "un-American." Although the rhetoric of reformation persisted, the be-all and end-all of the prison was to hold.

From 1830 to 1900 most prisons built in the United States reflected that ultimate value—security. Their principal features were high walls, rigid internal security, cage-like cells, sweat shops, a bare minimum of recreation space, and practically nothing else. They kept the prisoners in and the public out, and that was all that was expected or attempted. . . .

## Medium Security Correctional Centers

... Much of the major correctional construction in the last 50 years has been medium security. In fact, 51 of the existing 110 medium security correctional institutions were built after 1950. Today, over 57,000 offenders, 30 percent of all State inmates, are housed in such facilities.

Today medium security institutions probably embody most of the ideals and characteristics of the early attempts to reform offenders. It is in these facilities that the most intensive correctional or rehabilitation efforts are conducted. Here inmates are exposed to a variety of programs intended to help them become useful members of society. But the predominant consideration still is security. ...

## Minimum Security Correctional Centers

... Most, but not all, minimum security facilities have been created to serve the economic needs of society and only incidentally the correctional needs of the offenders. Cotton is picked, lumber is cut, livestock is raised, roads are built, forest fires are fought, and parks and State buildings are maintained. These are all legitimate tasks for prisoners, especially while our system still (1) receives large numbers of offenders who are a minimal threat to themselves and to the general public, and (2) holds men long after they are ready for freedom. Moreover, open facilities do serve therapeutic purposes by removing men from the stifling prison environment, separating the young and unsophisticated from the predators and substituting controls based upon trust rather than bars. All these aspects are laudable.

However, these remote facilities have important deficiencies. They seldom provide educational or service resources other than work. Moreover, the predominantly rural labor bears no relationship to the work skills required for urban life. Separation of the prisoner from his real world is almost as complete as it would have been in the penitentiary.

One remarkable minimum security correctional center was opened in 1972 at Vienna, Ill., as a branch of the Illinois State Penitentiary. Although a large facility, it approaches the quality of the non-penal institution. Buildings resembling garden apartments are built around a "town square" complete with churches, schools, shops, and library. Paths lead off to "neighborhoods" where "homes" provide private rooms in small clusters. Extensive provision has been made for both indoor and outdoor recreation. Academic, commercial, and vocational education facilities equal or surpass those of many technical high schools.

This correctional center has been designed for 800 adult felons. Unfortunately, most of them will come from the State's major population centers many miles away. Today this open institution is enjoying the euphoria that often accompanies distinctive newness. One may speculate about the future, however, when community correctional programs siphon from the State's prison system many of its more stable and less dangerous offenders. Fortunately, this facility will not be rendered obsolete by such a development. The non-prisonlike design permits it to be adapted for a variety of educational, mental health, or other human service functions. . . .

## Youth Correction Centers

The reformatory movement started about a century ago. With the advent of penitentiary, imprisonment had replaced corporal punishment. The reformatory concept was designed to replace punishment through incarceration with rehabilitation. This new movement was aimed at the young offender, aged 16 to 30. Its keystone was education and vocational training to make the offender more capable of living in the outside world. New concepts—parole and indeterminate sentences—were introduced. An inmate who progressed could reduce the length of his sentence. Hope was a new treatment dynamic.

The physical plant in the early reformatory era was highly secure. One explanation given is that the first one, at Elmira, N.Y., was designed as a maximum security prison and then converted into a reformatory. Other States that adopted the reformatory concept also copied the physical plant. Huge masonry walls, multi-tiered cell blocks, mass movements, "big house" mess halls, and dimly lit shops were all part of the model. Several of these places are still in operation. Later, in the 1920's, youth institutions adopted the telephone-pole construction design developed for adults; housing and service units crisscross an elongated inner corridor. More recently campus-type plants, fenced and unfenced, have been constructed. Some of these resemble the new colleges.

Most recently built reformatories, now called youth "correction" or "training" centers, are built to provide only medium or minimum security. (However, the newest—Western Correctional Center, Morganton, N.C.—is a very secure 17-story facility.) These centers usually emphasize academic and vocational education and recreation. Some supplement these with counseling and therapy, including operant conditioning and behavior modification. The buildings themselves are central to the program in providing incentives. At the Morganton center, for example, as a youth's behavior modifies he is moved from the 17th floor to the more desirable 16th, or from an open ward to a single room, etc.

Youth institutions include at least two types of minimum security facilities, work camps and training centers, which present a series of dilemmas. In work camps, outdoor labors burn up youthful energies. But these camps are limited severely in their capacity to provide other important needs of youthful offenders. Moreover, they are located in rural America, which is usually white, while youthful offenders frequently are not. The other type of minimum security youth center has complete training facilities, fine buildings, attractively landscaped surroundings, and extensive programs. These, too, usually are remote from population centers. Though they probably represent our most enlightened form of imprisonment, quite possibly they soon will be obsolete. . . .

These open centers serve three important functions:

1. They bring the individual every day face to face with his impulse to escape life's frustrations by running away.

2. They remove youths temporarily from community pressures that have overwhelmed them.

3. They provide sophisticated program opportunities usually not available otherwise.

In the near future it is to be hoped, these three purposes will be assumed by small and infinitely less expensive community correctional programs.

### Institutions for Juveniles

Almost all human services in America have followed a similar course of development. When faced with a social problem we seek institutional solutions first. The problems presented by children have been no exception. Early in our national development we had to face the phenomenon of child dependency, and we built orphanages. Children would not stay put, and we established the "Home for Little Wanderers." When children stole we put them in jails, filthy places where the sight of them incensed pioneer prison reformers. They turned to a model already common in Europe where congregate facilities, often under the auspices of religious groups, cared for both dependent and delinquent children.

The first such facility in America was established in New York in 1825. Reflecting its purpose, it was called the "House of Refuge." Others followed, coinciding almost exactly with the first penitentiaries. The pioneering juvenile institutions were just about as oppressive and forbidding, emphasizing security and austerity. By today's standards they were basically punitive. In time they tended more toward benign custodial care along with providing the essentials of housing and food. They became characterized by large populations, with consequent regimentation, and by oversized buildings.

In the latter decades of the 19th century, attempts to minimize the massive institutional characteristics led to the adoption of the "cottage concept." Housing was provided in smaller buildings. "House parents" aimed at simulating home-like atmospheres. This model has remained and today continues as a common, perhaps the predominant, type of institution for juvenile delinquents. . . .

At the risk of oversimplification this section describes two predominant but conflicting philosophies about the care of delinquent children. This is done because they suggest profoundly different directions and consequently different facility requirements for the future.

One has its roots in the earliest precepts of both the penitentiary and reformatory system. It holds that the primary cause of delinquent behavior is the child's environment, and the secondary cause is his inability to cope with that environment. The response is to provide institutions in the most remote areas, where the child is protected from adverse environmental influences and exposed to a wholesome lifestyle predicated on traditional middle-class values. Compensatory education, often better than that available in the community, equips the child with tools necessary to face the world again, some day. This kind of correctional treatment requires expensive and extensive plants capable of providing for the total needs of children over prolonged periods.

The second philosophy similarly assumes that the child's problems are related to the environment, but it differs from the first model by holding that the youngster must learn to deal with those problems where they are—in the community. Institutions, if required at all, should be in or close to the city. They should not duplicate anything—school, recreation, entertainment, clinical services—that is available in the community. The child's entire experience should be one of testing himself in the very setting where he will one day live. The process demands that each child constantly examine the reality of his adjustment with his peers.

The first model clings to the traditional solution. Yet institutions that serve society's misfits have never experienced notable success. One by one, institutions have been abandoned by most of the other human services and replaced by community programs. The second model, still largely untested, moves corrections toward more adventurous and hopeful days. . . .

. . . Opened in 1967, the Reception and Medical Center at Lake Butler serves the State of Florida. The plant is campus style with several widely separated buildings occupying 52 acres enclosed with a double cyclone fence with towers. There is a great deal of movement as inmates circulate between the classification building, gymnasium, dining room, clinic, canteen, craft shops, visiting area, and dormitories.

Housing is of two varieties. Three-quarters of the men are assigned to medium security units scattered around the campus. One maximum security building accommodates the rest.

Men not specifically occupied by the demands of the classification process are encouraged to take part in a variety of recreational and self-betterment activities conducted all over the campus. An open-air visiting patio supplements the indoor visiting facility that ordinarily is used only in inclement weather. Relationship between staff and inmates appears casual. Movement is not regimented. Morale appears high, and escapes are rare.

The contrast between this reception center and one in an adjacent State is vivid. In the Medical and Diagnostic Center at Montgomery, Ala., the inmate spends the entire reception period in confinement except when he is being tested or interviewed. Closed circuit television replaces contact with correctional personnel—a contact especially needed during reception. In that center escapes and escape attempts are almost as common as suicide efforts. . . .

THE FUTURE OF INSTITUTIONS

**For Adults**

From the standpoint of rehabilitation and reintegration, the major adult institutions operated by the States represent the least promising component of corrections. This report takes the position that more offenders should be diverted from such adult institutions, that much of their present populations should be transferred to community-based programs, and that the construction of new major institutions should be postponed until such diversion and transfers have been achieved and the need for additional institutions is clearly established.

However, the need for some type of institution for adults cannot be denied. There will always be a hard core of intractable, possibly unsalvageable offenders who must be managed in secure facilities, of which there are already more than

530

enough to meet the needs of the foreseeable future. These institutions have and will have a difficult task indeed. Nevertheless, the nature of imprisonment does not have to be as destructive in the future as it has been.

With growth of community-based corrections, emphasis on institutional programs should decline. However, the public has not yet fully supported the emerging community-oriented philosophy. An outdated philosophy continues to dominate the adult institution, thus perpetuating a number of contradictory assumptions and beliefs concerning institutional effectiveness.

One assumption is that the committed offender needs to change to become a functioning member of the larger law-abiding society. But it seems doubtful that such a change really can take place in the institution as it now exists.

Another assumption is that the correctional system wants to change. Even though research results have demonstrated the need for new approaches, traditional approaches have created inbred and self-perpetuating systems. Reintegration as an objective has become entangled with the desire for institutional order, security, and personal prestige. As long as the system exists chiefly to serve its own needs, any impending change represents a threat.

Correctional personnel who are assigned responsibility for the "treatment" of the committed offender traditionally have taken the attitude that they know what is best for him and are best qualified to prescribe solutions to his problem. Descriptions of offender problems compiled by personnel also have been traditional—lack of vocational skills, educational deficiencies, bad attitudes, ...

## For Juveniles and Youths

Use of State institutions for juveniles and youths should be discouraged. The emerging trend in treatment of young offenders is diversion from the criminal justice system. When diversion is not possible, the focus should be on community programs.

This emphasis reverses assumptions as to how youthful offenders should be treated. Previously there was a heavy emphasis on the use of institutional settings. Now it is believed that young offenders should be sent to an institution only when it can be demonstrated clearly that retaining them in the community would be a threat to the safety of others.

The nature of social institutions is such, however, that there is considerable delay between a change in philosophy and a change in practice. Despite major redirection of man-

531

power and money toward both diversion and community programs, progress is slow. Use of major State institutions for juvenile delinquents is declining, but it seems likely that these facilities will continue to be used for some offenders for some time. Therefore, standards for their improvement and operation are required.

. . . It is important to distinguish some basic reasons why institutional programs continuously have failed to reduce the commission of crime by those released.

Lack of clarity as to goals and objectives has had marked influence on institutional programs. Programs in youth institutions have reflected a variety of objectives, many of which are conflicting. Both society and the other components of the criminal justice system have contributed to this confusion.

A judge may order a juvenile committed as an example to others or because there are no effective alternatives. The police officer, whose function is to provide community protection, may demand incarceration for the temporary protection it provides for the public. . . .

While it is true that society's charges to the correctional institution have not always been clear or consistent, corrections cannot continue to try to be all things to all publics. Nor can the institution continue to deny responsibility for articulation of goals or objectives. The historical tendency of corrections to view itself as the passive arm of other state agents has resulted in almost total preoccupation with maintaining order and avoiding scandal. . . .

The institution should be operated as a resource to meet specific needs without removing responsibility for the offender from the community. Direct involvement of family, school, work, and other social institutions and organizations can have a marked positive impact on decreasing the flow of delinquents into corrections and on the correctional process.

Community responsibility for offenders implies more than institutional tours or occasional parties. It implies participation in programs with institutional residents both inside the institution and in the community. Education, recreational, religious, civic, counseling, and vocational programs, regardless of where they are held, should have both institutional and community participants. Public acceptance of community-based programs is necessary, especially when they operate next door. . . .

As diversionary and community programs expand, major institutions for juvenile and youthful offenders face an increasingly difficult task. These programs remove from the institution the most stable individuals who previously had a moderating influence on others' behavior.

The most hardened or habitual offender will represent an increasing proportion of those committed to institutions where adequate services can be provided by a professional staff, trained paraprofessionals and volunteers. All staff and participants must be prepared to serve a "helping" role.

More committed offenders than ever before have drug abuse problems. The ability to cope with this phenomenon in an environment isolated from the community has not been demonstrated. The aid of community residents must be enlisted in innovating, experimenting, and finding workable solutions.

Few treatment opportunities have been offered for the intractable offender. Common practice is to move such individuals from the general population and house them in segregation or adjustment centers. The concept of an ongoing treatment program for this group is recent but will become increasingly important as institutional populations changes. The understanding and tolerance of the community will be crucial in working with these individuals. . . .

## THE CORRECTIONAL DILEMMA

A major obstacle to the operation of an effective correctional program is that today's practitioners are forced to use the means of an older time. Dissatisfaction with correctional programs is related to the permanence of yesterday's institutions—both physical and ideological. We are saddled with the physical remains of last century's prisons and with an ideological legacy that equates criminal offenses with either moral or psychological illness. This legacy leads inexorably to two conclusions: (1) the sick person must be given "treatment" and (2) "treatment" should be in an institution removed from the community.

It is time to question this ideological inheritance. If New York has 31 times as many armed robberies as London, if Philadelphia has 44 times as many criminal homicides as Vienna, if Chicago has more burglaries than all of Japan, if Los Angeles has more drug addiction than all of Western Europe, then we must concentrate on the social and economic ills of New York, Philadelphia, Chicago, Los Angeles, and America.

This has not been our approach. We concentrate on "correcting" and "treating" the offender. This is a poor version of the "medical" model. What is needed is a good version of the "public health" model, an attempt to treat causes rather than symptoms.

If the war against crime is to be won, it will be won ultimately by correcting the conditions in our society that produce such an inordinate amount of criminal activity. These conditions include high unemployment, irrelevant education, racism, poor housing, family disintegration, and government corruption. These, among others, form the freshets that make the streams that form the rivers that flood our criminal justice system and ultimately its correctional institutions. . . .

### Standard 11.1: Planning New Correctional Institutions

Each correctional agency administering State institutions for juvenile or adult offenders should adopt immediately a policy of not building new major institutions for juveniles under any circumstances, and not building new institutions for adults unless an analysis of the total criminal justice and adult corrections systems produces a clear finding that no alternative is possible.

### Standard 11.2: Modification of Existing Institutions

Each correctional agency administering State institutions for juvenile or adult offenders should undertake immediately a 5-year program of reexamining existing institutions to minimize their use, and, for those who must be incarcerated, modifying the institutions to minimize the deleterious effects of excessive regimentation and harmful physical environments imposed by physical plants. . . .

4. All major institutions for juveniles should be phased out over the 5-year period.

### Standard 11.3: Social Environment of Institutions

Each correctional agency operating juvenile or adult institutions, and each institution, should undertake immediately to reexamine and revise its policies, procedures, and practices to bring about an institutional social setting that will stimulate offenders to change their behavior and to participate on their own initiative in programs intended to assist them in reintegrating into the community.

1. The institution's organizational structure should permit open communication and provide for maximum input in the decision-making process.

  a. Inmate advisory committees should be developed.

**b.** A policy of participative management should be adopted.

**c.** An ombudsman independent of institutional administration should receive and process inmate and staff complaints.

**d.** Inmate newspapers and magazines should be supported.

2. The correctional agency and the institution should make explicit their correctional goals and program thrust.

**a.** Staff recruitment and training should emphasize attitudes that support these goals.

**b.** Performance standards should be developed for programs and staff to measure program effectiveness.

**c.** An intensive public relations campaign should make extensive use of media to inform the public of the agency's goals.

**d.** The institution administration should be continuously concerned with relevance and change.

3. The institution should adopt policies and practices that will preserve the individual identity of the inmate and normalize institutional settings.

**a.** Each offender should be involved in program decisions affecting him.

**b.** Offenders should be identified by name and social security number rather than prison number.

**c.** Rules governing hair length and the wearing of mustaches and beards should be liberalized to reflect respect for individuality and cultural and subcultural trends.

**d.** Where possible, uniforms should be eliminated and replaced with civilian dress, with reasonable opportunity for individual choice of colors, styles, etc.

**e.** Institutional visitation should be held in an environment conducive to healthy relationships between offenders and their families and friends.

**f.** Home furlough should be allowed to custodially qualified offenders to maintain emotional involvement with families.

**g.** Telephone privileges, including reasonable provisions for long-distance calls, should be extended to all inmates.

**h.** No limitation should be imposed upon the amount of mail offenders may send or receive.

4. Each institution should make provision for the unique problems faced by minority offenders and take these problems into consideration in practices and procedures. . . .

**5.** The institution should actively develop the maximum possible interaction between community and institution, including involvement of community members in planning and in intramural and extramural activities. . . .

**6.** The institution should apply only the minimum amount of security measures, both physical and procedural, that are necessary for the protection of the public, the staff, and inmates, and its disciplinary measures should emphasize rewards for good behavior rather than the threat of punishment for misbehavior.

A major consideration in institutions is the factor of time and its effects on a committed offender. The longer an offender is exposed to the negative institutional environment, the less likely he is to adjust positively to the outside world when released. Institutional regimentation produces a loss of individual identity and opportunity for individual decisionmaking and choice. Administrators presuppose that the offender is unable to make worthwhile and beneficial decisions for himself. Initiative and the will to change also are negated. Therefore, the offender loses hope, and his world generally revolves around a day-to-day existence based on surviving in the institution and obtaining release.

Since self-concept, the way an individual perceives himself, is an essential element in human behavior, it must be considered in the operation of any correctional system. . . .

**Standard 11.4: Individualize institutional programs.**

**Standard 11.5: Special Offender Types**

Each correctional agency operating major institutions, and each institution, should reexamine immediately its policies, procedures, and programs for the handling of special problem offenders—the addict, the recalcitrant offender, the emotionally disturbed, and those associated with organized crime—and implement substantially the following:

**1.** The commitment of addicts to correctional institutions should be discouraged, and correctional administrators should actively press for the development of alternative methods of dealing with addicts, preferably community-based alternatives. Recognizing, however, that some addicts will commit crimes sufficiently serious to warrant a formal sentence and commitment, each institution must experiment with and work toward the development of institutional programs that can be related eventually to community programs following parole or release and that have more promise in dealing effectively with addiction.

a. Specially trained and qualified staff should be assigned to design and supervise drug offender programs, staff orientation, involvement of offenders in working out their own programs, and coordination of institutional and community drug programs. . . .

d. A variety of approaches should provide flexibility to meet the varying needs of different offenders. These should include individual counseling, family counseling, and group approaches.

e. Programs should emphasize "alternatives" to drugs. These should include opportunities to affiliate with cultural and subcultural groups, social action alliances, and similar groups that provide meaningful group identification and new social roles which decrease the desire to rely on drugs. Methadone and other drug maintenance programs are not appropriate in institutions.

f. The major emphasis in institutional programs for drug users should be the eventual involvement of the users in community drug treatment programs upon their parole or release.

g. Because of the inherent limitations and past failure of institutions to deal effectively with drug addiction, research and experimentation should be an indispensable element of institutional drug treatment programs. Priorities include:

(1) Development of techniques for the evaluation of correctional therapeutic communities.

(2) Development of methods for surveying inmates to determine the extent of drug abuse and treatment needs.

(3) Evaluation of program effectiveness with different offender types.

2. Each institution should make special provisions other than mere segregation for inmates who are serious behavior problems and an immediate danger to others.

c. Recalcitrant offenders who are too dangerous to be kept in the general institutional population should be housed in a unit of not more than 26 individual rooms providing safety and comfort.

(1) Good surveillance and perimeter security should be provided to permit staff time and efforts to be concentrated on the offenders' problems.

(2) No individual should remain in the unit longer than is absolutely necessary for the safety of others.

(3) Wherever possible the inmate of the special unit should participate in regular recreation, school, training, visiting and other institution programs. Individual tutorial or intensive casework services should also be available.

(4) Tranquilizers and other medication should be used only under medical direction and supervision. . . .

3. Each correctional agency should provide for the psychiatric treatment of emotionally disturbed offenders. Psychotic offenders should be transferred to mental health facilities. Correctional institution treatment of the emotionally disturbed should be under the supervision and direction of psychiatrists. . . .

4. Each correctional agency and institution to which convicted offenders associated with organized crime are committed should adopt special policies governing their management during the time they are incarcerated.

a. Because of the particular nature of organized crime and the overriding probability that such offenders cannot be rehabilitated, primary recognition should be given to the incapacitative purpose of incarceration in these cases.

b. Convicted offenders associated with organized crime should not be placed in general institutional populations containing large numbers of younger, more salvageable offenders.

c. Education and vocational training would appear inappropriate for these offenders, and their "program" should involve primarily assignment to prison industries or institutional maintenance, particularly where they are unlikely to have contact with impressionable offenders.

d. They should not be considered eligible for such community-based programs as work- or study-release, furloughs or other privileges taking them into the community. . . .

*Emotionally Disturbed Offenders*

These offenders are found in most institutions for juveniles or adults but in much fewer numbers than is popularly thought. They are committed to correctional rather than mental institutions because of the diagnosis or finding that they are not sufficiently disturbed to require commitment to a mental hospital. Although these offenders are expected to receive psychiatric treatment (and this often is a factor in court's decision to commit), such facilities and resources have been nonexistent in correctional facilities until the past two decades and still are so in most institutions.

As psychiatric services for diagnostic purposes became available in some correctional systems, the response of the correctional systems was to transfer the most seriously disturbed offenders to mental institutions. This decision was motivated by the fact that a large proportion of highly disturbed offenders were prone to violent and destructive behavior and highly oriented toward escape. However, as State mental hospitals developed "open institutions," they began to discourage admission of disturbed offenders for whom more secure facilities were required. The result was that few offenders in need of psychiatric treatment were accepted or satisfactorily treated by mental hospitals. Attempts to share treatment responsibility for mentally disturbed offenders between corrections and mental health agencies have seldom been satisfactory.

These factors led many State correctional systems to develop their own diagnosis and treatment resources. Two patterns developed. The first approach was to identify a discrete living unit within a larger institution as an intensive treatment center. The second was to develop a single-purpose institution for all offenders deemed in need of special psychiatric services.

The single psychiatric facility was more efficient in terms of pooling psychiatric resources, maintaining a hospital treatment theme, and providing clear program direction. It suffered because of isolation.

Experience has shown that both the specialized treatment unit and the single-purpose psychiatric institution have disadvantages. Some basic principles must be recognized for both.

1. High-level administrative support is necessary.

2. The program must be able to handle disturbed offenders who display aggressive or assaultive behavior.

3. Specific policies and procedures must assure close contact between the psychiatric program and the larger system it serves.

Costs related to the severely disturbed offender may range from $50 to $75 per day. Unfortunately, the alternative is inadequate service or none at all. Provision of adequate services means that there is a large investment of staff time in these offenders with a consequent loss of service to other offenders. The [alternative to the] additional cost is a continual recycling of untreated, disturbed individuals in and out of the system.

... The problem of structuring the incarceration of such offenders so that they will not have communication with their outside affiliations is inherently difficult and probably impossible. This would require that they be kept in total isolation so that they could not send messages out through inmates being released, corrupt employees, or correspond or visit with family, friends, or attorneys. This would mean a denial of the constitutional rights to which they have the same entitlement as other offenders. In this respect, communication between the incarcerated criminal and his outside associates will continue to be a problem to institutions and society.

**Standard 11.6: Provide constructive programs for women offenders.**

**Standard 11.7: Develop a full range of institutional religious programs.**

**Standard 11.8: Provide recreation programs for inmates.**

**Standard 11.9: Counseling Programs**

Each institution should begin immediately to develop planned, organized, ongoing counseling programs, in conjunction with the implementation of Standard 11.3, Social Environment of Institutions, which is intended to provide a social-emotional climate conducive to the motivation of behavioral change and interpersonal growth.

1. Three levels of counseling programs should be provided:

    a. Individual, for self-discovery in a one-to-one relationship.

    b. Small group, for self-discovery in an intimate group setting with open communication.

    c. Large group, for self-discovery as a member of a living unit community with responsibility for the welfare of that community. ...

**Standard 11.10: Operate Labor and industrial programs that aid in reentry.**

Work in prisons serves a variety of purposes that often are in conflict with each other. Its functions have been to punish and keep the committed offender busy, to promote discipline, to maintain the institution, to defray some operating costs of the prison, and to provide training and wages for the offender.

To accomplish any one function, it has been necessary to sacrifice one or more of the others. Unfortunately, the job training function has not had the highest priority.

Until 30 years ago American prisons were busy places. In the late 1920's and early 1930's Federal and State laws were passed to eliminate alleged unfair competition arising from the sale of prisonmade goods. From this blow the prisons have not recovered. The result has been that only a few offenders in institutions have productive work, while the others are idle or engaged in trying to look busy at routine housekeeping tasks. . . .

## 12: Parole

DEFINITION AND HISTORY

. . . Parole resembles probation in a number of respects. In both, information about an offender is gathered and presented to a decisionmaking authority with power to release him to community supervision under specific conditions. If he violates those conditions, the offender may be placed in, or returned to, a correctional institution. Parole, however, differs from probation in a significant way. Parole implies that the offender has been incarcerated in a correctional institution before he is released, while probation usually is granted by a judge in lieu of any kind of confinement.

Recent development of informal institutions (half-way houses, etc.) used by both courts and parole boards make the distinction between probation and parole increasingly difficult to sustain. To add further confusion, some jurisdictions use the term "bench parole" to refer to a form of minimally supervised probation.

Parole and probation also differ significantly in terms of who makes the decision. Parole is almost always an administrative decision; the granting of probation, a court function.

The power to determine when an offender may be released from an institution, to fix the conditions of his supervision, and to order parole revocation almost always passes from the court to an agency within the executive branch. In the case of adults this agency is usually a parole board; in the case of juveniles, an institutional official. As a condition of probation, a sentencing judge may require an offender to spend some time in an institution before he is released under community supervision, as in the "split sentence" in Federal jurisdictions. In this situation, authority to fix conditions and powers of revocation and discharge continue with the court after the offender is released from confinement. Therefore, the case almost always is classified as probation. . . .

The beginning of parole in the United States generally is identified with the Elmira Reformatory in New York, which opened in 1876. In the Elmira system, sentences were indeterminate, dependent on "marks" earned by good behavior. Release was for a six-month parole term, during which the parolee had to report regularly to the volunteer guardian or sponsor.

Elmira drew wide attention by its new approach to imprisonment, which was markedly different from the tradition of incarceration for a term fixed at the time of sentence. The designation of certain institutions for youthful felons as "reformatories," and the accompanying practice of permitting indeterminate sentences and parole, spread rapidly through the United States in the last quarter of the 19th century and the beginning of the 20th. This sentencing system, including its provisions for parole, soon was extended to prisoners of all ages. By 1922, parole laws had been passed by 45 States, and in 1945 Mississippi became the last State to develop parole legislation.

This does not imply, however, that either parole laws or practices have developed uniformly. States still vary widely in the proportion of inmates released under parole supervision. In 1968, for example, the National Prisoner Statistics of the Federal Bureau of Prisons showed that among offenders released in the States of Washington, New Hampshire, and California, more than 95 percent were released under parole supervision. During the same period, less than 10 percent of inmates released in Oklahoma were released on parole. In Nebraska the comparable figure was 20 percent. Nationwide, releases to parole supervision were approximately 60 percent of all releases.

The history of parole for juvenile offenders is different from that for adults. For juveniles, parole usually is traced to the houses of refuge for children in the latter part of the 19th century. From these settings, children were released to work for several years in private homes. Total control of the child was vested in the family to whom he was released. It was the family's responsibility to determine when he had earned his freedom.

The child protection programs developed later assumed many of these activities. Although in recent years juvenile programs have become more correctional, they have continued to be involved closely with child welfare activities. In many States, juvenile aftercare services are the responsibility of the welfare department or a similar agency containing a broad range of services. In these settings, delinquency is seen as merely a symptom of a young person's need for State services. Labels such as "delinquent," "dependent," or "neglected" are de-emphasized. The general thrust is to treat these children within the context of child welfare.

Juvenile parole authorities usually are more than willing to distinguish their services from those for adults. Juvenile officials typically use the term "aftercare" as a synonym for parole, but in many ways the difference is more than semantic. The problems presented by the young releasee are different from those of the adult offender. School attendance and vocational training programs are much more likely to be a central feature of programs for juveniles, while employment is the major concern for adult offenders. The two concerns might be cursorily equated. But no one may be legally required to work, while school attendance is compulsory for juveniles. In fact, chronic truancy is a juvenile "crime."

Juvenile and adult parole services usually are not organized similarly. The National Survey of Corrections showed that in 1965 parole boards decided on the release of juveniles in only two States, although such boards released adults almost everywhere in the country.

SENTENCING STRUCTURES

**Sentencing Consistent with Parole Objectives**

The sentencing system that seems most consistent with parole objectives has the following characteristics:

1. Sentence limits set by legislation, with the sentencing judge having discretion to fix the maximum sentence, up to legislative limits.

2. No minimum sentences, either by mandate or by judicial sentencing authority.

3. Comparatively short sentences for most offenses, with a legislative maximum not to exceed five years for most offenders.

4. Mandatory release with supervision for offenders ineligible for parole, so that they are not held in an institution until their absolute discharge date.

5. All parole conditions set by the paroling authority, but with opportunity for a sentencing judge to suggest special conditions.

6. Legislative prohibition of offenders' accumulating consec-

utive sentences if it interferes with minimum parole eligibility.

7. Legislative provisions for alternatives to reimprisonment upon parole revocation.

8. No offenses for which parole is denied by legislation.

## ORGANIZATION OF PAROLING AUTHORITIES

### The Independent Authority

In the adult field, a good deal of reform was associated with removing parole decisionmaking from institutional control to an independent authority. Undoubtedly much of the basis for this reform came from the view that paroling authorities were being swayed too easily by institutional considerations or were not being objective enough. The change was so complete that today no adult parole releasing authority is controlled directly by the operating staff of a penal institution.

Whatever its merits in fostering objectivity, the independent parole board also has been criticized on several counts. First, the claim is made that such boards tend to be insensitive to institutional programs and fail to give them the support they require. Second, independent boards are accused of basing their decisions on inappropriate considerations, such as the feelings of a local police chief. Third, their remoteness from the institutional program gives independent boards little appreciation of the dynamics in a given case; their work tends to be cursory, with the result that too often persons who should be paroled are not, and those who should not be paroled are released. Fourth, the argument is made that independent systems tend to place on parole boards persons who have little training or experience in corrections.

Lack of knowledge about corrections, combined with the distance of the parole board from institutional programs, builds unnecessary conflicts into the system. The rapid growth of partway release programs and halfway houses has increased the probability of those conflicts. In short, critics of the independent model assert that important decisions are being made concerning the correctional system, its programs, and the offenders in it by persons far removed from the system who have little appreciation of its true nature.

### The Consolidation Model

While these arguments and their rebuttals continue, an alternate system has gained considerable support in recent years, tending to cut the ground away from both major models. This system is linked with a general move toward consolidation of all types of correctional services into distinctive departments of corrections that subsume both institution and field programs. The consolidation model, emerging from the drive toward centralized administration, typically results in parole decisions being made by a central decisionmaking authority organizationally situated in an overall department of corrections but possessing independent powers. The director of corrections may serve on such a releasing authority, or he may designate a staff member to do so. In the youth field, the centralized board may have policy responsibilities for institutions as well as parole decisionmaking.

Proponents of the consolidation model argue that there is increased concern for the whole correctional system in departments where parole releasing authority is part of a centralized system. They claim that sensitivity to institutional programs seems more pronounced in consolidated systems than in completely autonomous ones. They also contend that removal of parole decisionmaking from the immediate control of specific correctional institutions tends to give greater weight to a broader set of considerations, a number of which are outside direct institutional concerns. . . .

The trend in this country clearly is in the direction of consolidation. More than 60 percent of the State parole boards responsible for release of adult offenders now function in common administrative structures with other agencies for offenders. This trend enhances integration of correctional operations. If parole boards are to function as useful and sophisticated decisionmaking units that balance a wide set of concerns, they also must achieve and maintain some degree of autonomy from the systems with which they interface. This issue involves appointment and tenure methods, as well as the tasks and functions for which parole authorities take responsibility.

### Articulation of Criteria for Decisions

Articulation of criteria for making decisions and development of basic policies is one of the chief tasks that parole decisionmakers need to undertake. While discretion is a necessary feature of parole board operations, the central issue is how to contain and control it appropriately. Few parole boards have articulated their decision criteria in much detail or in writing, even though research has shown that criteria exist. Parole board members tend to display, with slight variations, a consistent response to case situations of which they may be only marginally aware.

Articulating the basis of decision systems is crucial to improving parole decisions, because criteria must be specified before they can be validated. For example, 75 percent of 150 board members queried in 1965 by the National Probation and Parole Institute asserted that rapists generally were poor parole risks. Research data have shown such an assumption to be wrong. . . .

## Need for Appeal Procedures

Where the volume of cases warrants it, a parole board should concentrate its major attention on policy development and appeals. The bulk of case-by-case decisionmaking should be done by hearing examiners responsible to the board and familiar with its policies and knowledgeable as to correctional programs.

Hearing examiners should have statutory power to grant, deny, or revoke parole, subject to parole board rules and policies. In cases of offenders serving long sentences, those involved in cases of high public interest, or others designated by the parole board, two or more parole members personally should conduct the hearings and make decisions. Hearing examiners operating in teams of two should handle the large part of day-to-day interviewing and decisionmaking for the board. Inmates and parolees should be entitled to appeal decisions to the parole board, which could hear cases in panels or en banc. As action is taken on these cases and the system of appeals refined, the board should further articulate its policies against which unwarranted uses of discretion could be checked. . . .

PAROLE AUTHORITY PERSONNEL

## Qualifications of Board Members

Two dilemmas that are common to most appointive public offices are also seen in deciding on the best method of selecting parole board members: first, how to secure appointees with expertise and willingness to challenge the system when necessary rather than merely preserving it; second, how to select parole board members who will be responsive to public concern, as expressed through elected officials, without making politics rather than competence the basis for appointment.

Parole decisionmakers too frequently have shown the negative possibilities of both dilemmas. In many instances they have become so coopted by a correctional system that there is no independent check against abuses of public or offender interests. Too many times appointments have been governed by patronage considerations, a dangerous criterion when human freedom is at stake and the most difficult moral, legal, and scientific issues are involved.

If parole authorities are to have the competence required for their tasks, specific statutory qualifications for board members must be developed. In 24 States there are no statutory requirements for parole members responsible for the release of adult offenders. In one State generalized references to character are made. In another 21 only the broadest references to experience or training are enunciated.

According to the findings of the first National Parole Conference in 1939, board members "should be selected on the basis of their integrity and competence to deal with human and social problems, without reference to political affiliations." More recently the standards proposed by the American Correctional Association required that parole board members should "command respect and public confidence," be "appointed without reference to creed, color or political affiliation," possess "academic training which has qualified the board member for professional practice in a field such as criminology, education, psychiatry, psychology, law, social work and sociology," and "have intimate knowledge of common situations and problems confronting offenders."

No single professional group or discipline can be recommended as ideal for all parole board members. A variety of goals are to be served by parole board members, and a variety of skills are required. Knowledge of at least three basic fields should be represented on a parole board: the law, the behavioral sciences, and corrections. Furthermore, as a board assumes responsibility for policy articulation, monitoring and review, the tasks involved require persons who are able to use a wide range of decisionmaking tools, such as statistical materials, reports from professional personnel, and a variety of other technical information. In general, persons with sophisticated training and experience are required. In this context, the standards suggested by the American Correctional Association should be statutorily required for each jurisdiction.

Hearing examiners required less specialized education and training. More critical in these roles are persons with educational and experiential qualifications that allow them to understand programs, to relate to people, and to make sound and reasonable decisions. These roles should offer particular opportunities for ex-offenders and for those persons most sensitive to the implications of offenders' lifestyles. . . .

Some type of device must be employed if competent board

547

personnel are to be selected. Each State should require by law that nominees for parole board positions first be screened by a committee broadly representative of the community. Representatives of groups such as the State bar and mental health associations should be included, as well as representatives of various ethnic and socioeconomic groups. The law should require that appointments be made only from the approved list of nominees. . . .

## ORGANIZATION OF FIELD SERVICES

### Transfer of Adult Parole to Correctional Departments

One of the clearest trends in parole organization in the last few years is consolidation of formerly autonomous agencies or functionally related units into expanding departments of corrections. Some of these departments have been made part of still larger units of State government, such as human resources agencies, which embrace a wide range of programs and services. One clear indication of this trend is the number of States that have shifted administrative responsibility for parole officers from independent parole departments to centralized correctional agencies. . . .

### Linking Institutional and Field Staffs

The lack of continuity and consistency of services between institutional and field services has been a severe problem to many jurisdictions. It often is further complicated by what could be described as rural vs. urban perspective. Institutions generally are located miles from population centers. The manpower they tend to recruit is drawn largely from small town and rural areas. The result is that institutional staff may have little understanding of city and especially ghetto life. In contrast, most field workers live in or near the large population centers in which most offenders reside, and more field workers than institutional workers are from minority groups. This cultural difference contributes to feelings of mistrust, hostility, and incredulity that handicap communication between institutional and field staffs. . . .

Most important is that institution and field staff be under common administrative direction. It is not enough that they be simply linked administratively at the top; linking must be at the program level as well. This can be done in several ways. One is to provide that both institutional and field services be regionalized and placed under common administrators in each area. Obviously, in States where there are only one or two institutions, problems are compounded for the whole community-based thrust. But even here some program consolidations are possible by devices such as placing all institutional programming responsibilities under full control of the head of parole field services for the last months of the inmate's confinement. . . .

## Flexibility in Organizational Structure

A correctional policy that assumes parolees are capable of making a major contribution toward setting their own objectives and sees the parole agency's main task as helping the parolee realistically test and attain those objectives also must place a premium on developing an organizational structure that promotes flexibility. This means that managers must learn how to administer a decentralized organization that must adhere to broad policies and yet allow for a high degree of individual autonomy.

The dilemmas that arise when a manager tries this style of administration are many. Their resolution requires a sophisticated knowledge of administration and organizational techniques. One of the highest priorities for effective development of community-based services lies in providing managers with precisely this kind of skill.

Nelson and Lovell summarize the issues well:

> The correctional field must develop more collaborative, less hierarchical administrative regimes in order to implement its reintegration programs. The hierarchical format was developed to achieve the goal of production and orderly task performance. When individual changes is the prime purpose of the organization, this format is inappropriate for people cannot be *ordered* to change strongly patterned attitudes and behavior. Nor is change apt to come about through the ritual performance of a series of tasks. . . . Power must be shared rather than hoarded. Communication must be open rather than restricted. Thus the managers of reintegration programs will need the skills of cooptation, communication, and collaboration.

Resistance to reintegration-style programs can be widespread. Take for example a job function that has been interpreted traditionally as one of surveillance, head-counting, and maintenance of order. Management says the job is best accomplished by a new set of techniques—including relaxed, open and free communication, and decisionmaking involving parolees. Staff members should perceive themselves less as policemen than as counselors. It is highly likely in such a case that some staff will resist the changes.

Persons who see themselves as professionals also can be major obstacles to change. The trend toward a reintegration model and away from a rehabilitation model has been frustrating to several traditional professional groups who perceive their "expertise" as being challenged or, at worst, rejected. Meetings are held to organize opposition to "nonprofessional practices" and to changes that are "untested" and that have strayed from the "tried and true." It is not surprising that administrators sometimes capitulate. But "let's not rock the boat" or "let's wait till next year" are the cliches of timid leadership that lead to stagnant bureaucracies. It takes great skill and perseverance to change an agency. There is no substitute for intelligence, skill, and above all, courage.

## COMMUNITY SERVICES FOR PAROLEES

... Undoubtedly, the trend toward creating new ways of delivering services to meet human needs—mental health, family counseling, physical rehabilitation, employment, and financial assistance—will modify the parole officer's tasks in several important respects. Human service centers designed to deliver a wide range of programs will develop. Part of the task of parole staff will be to support such efforts and play an appropriate role in a coordinated human-services delivery system. Increasingly, the parole officer's unique responsibility will be to make certain that the offenders obtain the benefit of available resources, to counsel parolees about the conditions of their parole, and to help them meet those conditions.

### Employment

... Many States have developed systems of "reasonable assurance," under which a definite job is not required before an inmate is released, provided some means can be found to sustain him until one can be found. This generally is a far better practice than holding him until a job is promised. Parolees find it much easier to get a job if they can personally interview employers. Research consistently has shown offenders do as well, if not better, if they can find their own job.

Partial release programs in the community go a long way toward eliminating many of these problems. While the offender still is confined, he has the chance to make contacts in the community, be interviewed by employers, work directly with a parole officer, or actually begin an employment program through work release. In terms of a broad correctional strategy aimed at coping with employment problems, prerelease programs are of pivotal importance. . . .

## Standard 12.1: Organization of Paroling Authorities

Each State that has not already done so should, by 1975, establish parole decisionmaking bodies for adult and juvenile offenders that are independent of correctional institutions. These boards may be administratively part of an overall statewide correctional services agency, but they should be autonomous in their decisionmaking authority and separate from field services. The board responsible for the parole of adult offenders should have jurisdiction over both felons and misdemeanants.

1. The boards should be specifically responsible for articulating and fixing policy, for acting on appeals by correctional authorities or inmates on decisions made by hearing examiners, and for issuing and signing warrants to arrest and hold alleged parole violators.

2. The boards of larger States should have a staff of full-time hearing examiners appointed under civil service regulations. . . .

## Standard 12.2: Parole Authority Personnel

Each State should specify by statute by 1975 the qualifications and conditions of appointment of parole board members.

1. Parole boards for adult and juvenile offenders should consist of full-time members.

2. Members should possess academic training in fields such as criminology, education, psychology, psychiatry, law, social work, or sociology.

3. Members should have a high degree of skill in comprehending legal issues and statistical information and an ability to develop and promulgate policy.

4. Members should be appointed by the governor for six-year terms from a panel of nominees selected by an advisory group broadly representative of the community. Besides being representative of relevant professional organizations, the advisory group should include all important ethnic and socioeconomic groups.

## Standard 12.3: Specify procedure and requirements for granting parole.

## Standard 12.4: Revocation Hearings

551

Each parole jurisdiction immediately should develop and implement a system of revocation procedures to permit the prompt confinement of parolees exhibiting behavior that poses a serious threat to others. At the same time, it should provide careful controls, methods of fact-finding, and possible alternatives to keep as many offenders as possible in the community. Return to the institution should be used as a last resort, even when a factual basis for revocation can be demonstrated.

1. Warrants to arrest and hold alleged parole violators should be issued and signed by parole board members. Tight control should be developed over the process of issuing such warrants. They should never be issued unless there is sufficient evidence of probable serious violation. In some instances, there may be a need to detain alleged parole violators. In general, however, detention is not required and is to be discouraged. Any parolee who is detained should be granted a prompt preliminary hearing. Administrative arrest and detention should never be used simply to permit investigation of possible violations.

2. Parolees alleged to have committed a new crime but without other violations of conditions sufficient to require parole revocation should be eligible for bail or other release pending the outcome of the new charges, as determined by the court.

3. A preliminary hearing conducted by an individual not previously directly involved in the case should be held promptly on all alleged parole violations, including convictions of new crimes, in or near the community in which the violation occurred unless waived by the parolee after due notification of his rights. The purpose should be to determine whether there is probable cause or reasonable grounds to believe that the arrested parole has committed acts that would constitute a violation of parole conditions and a determination of the value question of whether the case should be carried further, even if probable cause exists. The parolee should be given notice that the hearing will take place and of what parole violations have been alleged. He should have the right to present evidence, to confront and cross-examine witnesses, and to be represented by counsel.

The person who conducts the hearing should make a summary of what transpired at the hearing and the information he used to determine whether probable cause existed to hold the parolee for the final decision of the parole board on revocation. If the evidence is insufficient to support a further

552

**hearing, or if it is otherwise determined that revocation would not be desirable, the offender should be released to the community immediately. . . .**

**Standard 12.5: Coordinate institutional and field services and functions.**

**Standard 12.6: Community Services for Parolees**

Each State should begin immediately to develop a diverse range of programs to meet the needs of parolees. These services should be drawn to the greatest extent possible from community programs available to all citizens, with parole staff providing linkage between services and the parolees needing or desiring them.

1. Stringent review procedures should be adopted, so that parolees not requiring supervision are released from supervision immediately and those requiring minimal attention are placed in minimum supervision caseloads.

2. Parole officers should be selected and trained to fulfill the role of community resource manager. . . .

**Standard 12.7: Individualize parole conditions.**

**Standard 12.8: Develop manpower and training programs.**

# C: Cross-Section of Corrections

## 13: Organization and Administration

BASIC PROBLEMS OF CORRECTIONAL ORGANIZATIONS

. . . The national summary of the LEAA reports indicates that there were 5,312 corrections facilities in the United States in 1971 (4,503 for adults and 809 for juveniles) and 2,444 probation and parole agencies. While a cursory examination of these figures may not be startling, more detailed evaluation reveals the fact that only 16 percent of the adult and juvenile correctional facilities are operated at the State level, with the remaining 84 percent, consisting predominantly of county and local jails and lockups, dividing among the 3,047 counties in the Nation and an even greater number of cities, townships, and villages.

Dividing correctional activities into the two major divisions, institutions on the one hand and probation and parole activities on the other, provides a clearer understanding of the national corrections picture. For example, LEAA statistics show that approximately 12 percent of adult correctional facilities in the Nation are provided at the State level, while the remaining 88 percent are provided by city and county governments. Juvenile correctional facilities are distributed more equally. Approximately 45 percent of them are provided at the State level, with the remaining 55 percent supported almost exclusively by county governments. With regard to probation and parole agencies, approximately 30 percent are administered by State governments, with the remaining 70 percent at the local level. As in the case of juvenile correctional facilities, the county governments perform the majority of the local functions.

## Major Issues in Organization

The summary of the Advisory Commission's major findings indicates that in the area of organizational and jurisdictional problems, the following major issues have been identified.

> All but four States have highly fragmented correctional systems, vesting various correctional responsibilities in either independent boards or noncorrectional agencies, in 41 States, an assortment of health, welfare, and youth agencies exercise certain correctional responsibilities, though their primary function is not corrections.
>
> In over 40 States, neither State nor local governments have full-scale responsibility for comprehensive correctional services. Some corrections services, particularly parole and adult and juvenile institutions, are administered by State agencies, while others, such as probation, local institutions and jails, and juvenile detention, are county or city responsibilities.
>
> More than half of the States provide no standard-setting or inspection services to local jails and local adult correctional institutions.

... Coordination is needed not only among correctional agencies, but between them and the other components of the criminal justice system. Moreover, the interrelationships between correctional agencies and other organizations concerned with human problems (e.g., mental health, social welfare, poverty reduction) are of vital importance. Linkages must be established with the private as well as the public sector. Paradoxically, intimate relationships between corrections and law enforcement may impede the ability of corrections to develop reciprocities with the health, education, and welfare complex. Thus, coordination and unification are delicate functions, requiring finesse as well as firm use of available sanctions. . . .

**Some Directions for Change**

. . . The major arena for reintegrative programs is the local community. Administrative power and sanction must be placed there if such efforts are to be strong, well articulated with local resources, and suitably responsive to local needs and problems.

The key to such a redistribution of authority and responsibility lies in the development of new methods of financing correctional services. The probation subsidy program in California is one illustration of a strong effort to strengthen county services and reduce reliance on State institutions. Experimentation with varied subventions, grants, and other forms of intergovernmental assistance will be required. A combination of assistance and regulation—carrot and stick—will be necessary to bring about the needed changes. . . .

MANAGEMENT STYLE AND ORGANIZATION CLIMATE

. . . The control function traditionally assigned to corrections may account in large measure for the prevalence of a bureaucratic organization climate. When coercion is the prime objective, it is efficiently administered by codifying prohibited behavior and making routine the application of sanctions. A more noble objective of "equality" frequently is cited for uniformly following disciplinary procedures that may, for a particular case, be inappropriate. Even a "treatment" purpose implies a limited degree of coercion, because the individual has been sent to a corrections unit to endure his "illness." If a deviation from routine is passed to the bureaucrat for decision, he self-assuredly asserts, "Rules are rules, and if we make one exception, everyone will want to do it."

A significant part of corrections' fragmentation can be explained by the pervasiveness of a bureaucratic mentality. Postrelease adjustment is considered the parole board's problem. Probation is a court function. Halfway houses are run by a community services unit.

A bureaucratic management style is particularly inappropriate for a human services organization, because it focuses on organizational processes rather than what is being processed—people. The manager's intentional aloofness from his subordinates is reflected by the sort of inmate-staff relations that view programs as done *for* the offender, not *with* him.

The organization has established certain activities to which individuals are assigned, regardless of appropriateness. . . .

**Standard 13.1: Professionalize correctional management.**

**Standard 13.2: Develop a correctional planning process.**

**Standard 13.3: Train management in offender and employee relations.**

**Standard 13.4: Prohibit, but prepare for, work stoppages and job actions.**

## 14: Manpower for Corrections

**Standard 14.1: Discontinue unwarranted personnel restrictions.**

**Standard 14.2: Recruit and employ minority group individuals.**

**Standard 14.3: Recruit and employ women.**

**Standard 14.4: Recruit and employ ex-offenders.**

**Standard 14.5: Recruit and use volunteers.**

**Standard 14.6: Revise personnel practices to retain staff.**

**Standard 14.7: Adopt a participatory management program.**

**Standard 14.8: Plan for manpower redistribution to community programs.**

**Standard 14.9: Establish a State program for justice system education.**

**Standard 14.10: Implement correctional internship and work-study programs.**

**Standard 14.11: Create staff development programs.**

## 15: Research and Development, Information, and Statistics

. . . It is especially noteworthy that treatment program tests have been conducted in a wide variety of incarcerative settings without establishing the rehabilitative value of any. The consistency of this record strongly indicates that incarcerative treatment is incompatible with rehabilitative objectives. This conclusion is tentative, but influential. It is responsible for the present wave of interest in developing community-based alternatives to incarceration. . . .

Research will bring about change in operations. The achievement of a significant internal review of operations requires all administrative functions to undergo a difficult transition. New categories of professional personnel must be introduced into correctional operations. Their criminal justice background will be minimal. They must be familiarized with their new environment before their technical expertise can be useful.

An even more difficult transition must be made by present management personnel. Positions that once called only for intuitive planning and decisionmaking must be adapted to requirements of a new style. For many executives, continued effectiveness will depend on completion of inconveniently technical retraining.

RESEARCH

. . . Introduction of empiricism for the support of theory is immensely important for the entire criminal justice system. No human institution is more tradition-oriented. The foundations of criminal control rest on unverified and conflicting assumptions and behavior motivation and change. For correctional practice, these assumptions result in decisions made with invalid justifications. For example, to justify incarceration by the expectation that those incarcerated will be rehabilitated thereby is to substitute wishful thinking for realism. To the extent that research has reduced the influence of such expectations on policymaking, both public protection and fairness to the individual have been served. Replacement of assumptions by empirically tested principles has started, but it is far from complete. . . .

Innovation

. . . Theories about change of human behavior by agents that are not supernatural are of recent origin. There is little evidence of their effectiveness in domains other than corrections. Because change is so much to be desired, much effort has been given to adapting the practice of behavior change to the peculiar circumstances of the offender. Most of these attempts have been derived from the limited range of socialization theory. This range consists of three principal groups of theories on which practice can be based.

The first group of theories is grounded on the belief that human behavior is influenced most powerfully by administra-

557

tion of rewards and punishments. This belief is so deeply embedded in the general perception of human nature that our whole system of criminal justice depends on it. Despite popular consensus on the validity of the rewards-and-punishment theory, the punitive measures applied have never achieved predictable successes. The pattern of results from incarceration, fines, and public reprimand shows that, whatever the ultimate value of the theory, we do not know how to punish in a way that consistently achieves desired results. . . .

The second group of theories has generated the most research and probably the most disappointment. These theories are based on the idea that socialization is dependent on acquisition of insight, and on the associated idea that criminal behavior originates in defective socialization. A wide range of applications in counseling and therapy depends on these propositions. So far, conclusions on the value of treatments based on this group of theories have not borne out the hopes held by the clinical professionals. It is beyond the scope of this chapter to consider the reasons in the detail they deserve. The principal factors to which failure can be attributed are the involuntary aspect of treatment, the inapplicability of the technique to the psychological conditions addressed, lack of clarity as to the kinds of insights desired, and the overwhelming adverse social conditions faced by many offenders. Despite their failures and the cogency of the argument that well-defined reasons for failure can be identified, correctional therapy proponents have made a less than sufficient effort to refine theory to accommodate the unfavorable empirical findings.

The third group of theories is the least developed. It comes under the heading of "reintegration," a concept supported by the Corrections Task Force of the President's Commission on Law Enforcement and Administration of Justice. This set of ideas is based on the theory that a change in the nature of the offender's relation to the community, rather than a change in the offender himself, is to be sought. The focus therefore is on the interaction between the offender and his surroundings. The objective is to achieve a better "reintegration" than the integration that existed before the trouble occurred. The theory holds that nonoffenders share the same psychological abnormalities as offenders, and attempts at rehabilitation by psychological change are superfluous if the only intent is to reduce recidivism. The task of the correctional apparatus therefore should be to help the offender achieve the level of integration enabling him to choose a law-abiding career regardless of his psychological state.

The difficulty with these theoretical positions is that so far they have not lent themselves to a clearly identifiable operational technique. The a priori logic of the theory is persuasive, so far as it goes, and there should be increasing interest in deriving innovations from it.

The foregoing sketch of theoretical positions by no means exhausts all possible models available to corrections, but it does include those currently influential. Their limited value for operational use in correctional settings reflects a serious constraint on practical development. Two possible explanations might account for this constraint. First, a theory of sufficient power to support the social restoration of the offender has not been discovered. It is possible that there is no theory or group of theories to support the planned change of offenders or, alternately, to provide for their reintegration without change.

The second explanation is that some attributes of the current correctional experience and setting seem to rule out the possibility of such change or reintegration. A method for resolving these problems has yet to be devised. The importance of achieving a resolution is increasingly clear.

## MAJOR CURRENT RESEARCH ISSUES

### Measurement in Correctional Research—Recidivism

... Recidivism should be measured by reconvictions. A conviction is a well-defined event in which a recorded action has been taken by the court. Further, measurement by reconvictions is established practice in corrections. It is desirable to maintain this continuity in statistical practice. This position is not meant to discourage measurement of arrests or a study of the relationship of arrest rates of ex-offenders to release rates. The significance of such studies must be assessed in light of a realistic view of the nature and validity of the data used.

Another consideration as to the nature of events to be included relates to technical violations of probation or parole. Technical violations based on administrative action alone should be excluded from a general definition of recidivism because they are not established formally as criminal acts. Rather, they are a reflection of administrative practices and may indicate parole policy more than correctional effectiveness. (See Chapter 12.) Technical violations in which a sentencing authority took action that resulted in an adverse change in an offender's legal status should be collected but maintained separately from data on reconvictions.

A second major problem in recidivism measurement relates to the degrees of seriousness to be identified and their significance. The recidivist event may vary in seriousness from a booking and dismissal of a minor offense to conviction for a major felony. Many correctional administrators will argue that success should be measured in terms of a reduction in seriousness of an offense pattern or an increase in the period of law-abiding behavior between offenses. This logic is not persuasive. If the objective of the corrections system is to change behavior, or at least establish successful control, nothing in its operation can or should be aimed at converting major offenders into lesser offenders. A program aimed at resocialization or reintegration should be directed at a positive result. An offense above a determined level of seriousness must be charged against the system as a failure because the program has not reduced the burden of crime. The problem lies in prescribing a level of seriousness that separates those criminal acts so minor or nonserious as not to merit public attention from those major or serious enough to be reported. . . .

The length of time offenders should be followed after their release from the supervision of the courts or the corrections system is the third important element in developing recidivism statistics. Measurement of recidivism should be pursued for three years after the release of the offender from all correctional supervision. This arbitrary figure is chosen because the few recidivism studies that have followed offenders more than three years have not revealed a significant difference between recidivism before and after the three-year point. Arbitrariness of the period is less important than the need to establish a standard measure with a specific time frame so that comparisons among programs and systems will have a consistent base. A figure should be set that will not undermine the ability to get feedback within a useful time frame and take corrective action. This is not meant to discourage reporting over longer periods, which provides valuable control information concerning reconvictions and their occurrence after the three-year period.

## The Measurement of Success

The definition of recidivism does not resolve all problems for which use of this variable is responsible. No matter how faithfully the definition is followed, only failure can be measured by using it. When recidivists are subtracted from the total cohort, the remainder are not necessarily to be credited to the system as successes. In rhetoric defending their programs, some administrators make statements to the effect that although 40 percent of their releases failed, 60 percent succeeded. Success is attributed to the system or the program to be defended. The argument is fallacious.

Although the failures of corrections can be differentiated on a wide range from the inevitable to the accidental, they nevertheless are failures. But it does not follow that the program succeeded with those who did not fail. There are several reasons for this paradox.

First, some offenders commit new offenses, but not in a jurisdiction that will report them to the agency that supervised or confined them. This common deficiency may be corrected when a national retrieval of criminal histories becomes an actuality, but not before.

Second, even though no new offense has been committed, the offender may have become a public dependent of some other kind. He may be a client on welfare rolls, a patient in a mental hospital, or an alcoholic on skid row. All these ex-offenders, while not technically correctional failures, can hardly be termed correctional successes.

The third, and by far the most frequent, fallacious inclusion in a success roster is the offender who endured the program without benefit but for various reasons managed to abide by the law or avoid detection in the commission of new crimes for the followup period or who did not require correctional services to begin with. It is easy to claim such individuals as successes, but unless the success can be related to the program in some demonstrable way, the claim is an inflation of fact. . . .

## Improvement of Evaluation

. . . What is needed now is an armory of alternatives to the existing structure. Evaluation research no longer should be limited to measuring treatment variables in laboratory tests. The evaluative tools should be used instead to create a model of effective intervention including consideration of the wide range of offender careers with which the correctional apparatus must cope.

## Study of Treatment

. . . In addition to these issues, and underlying each, is the question of attribution of delinquent behavior to an identifiable psychological state. Conventional psychiatric thought traces delinquency to an ill-defined state designated by such terms as "psychopathy," "behavior disorders," or "sociopathy." No satisfactory accounting for the state has been achieved, nor has guidance been given successful treatment of the condition. To an extent that must embarrass the thoughtful clinician, there is a circularity in a diagnosis that "discovers" that a subject's delinquency is symptomatic of the psychopathy that accounts for his delinquency. This state of affairs cannot contribute to effective rationale for treatment and control.

### Behavior Modification Theory and Correctional Applications

The work of Goldiamond, Cohen, and McKee among others, has led to the hope that through behavior modification techniques it will be possible to achieve the remedial socialization of some kinds of offenders. So far, the results of explorations do not produce a clearly favorable picture. One complication has been that most of these explorations were conducted in custodial situations. Use of behavior modification techniques in community-based corrections has been scant.

Most techniques of behavior modification have been generated either in the mental hospital or for educational use. Although their application to the correctional situation is not necessarily inappropriate, sufficient attention has not been given to the nature, scheduling, and limits of the reinforcement repertory available in the correctional apparatus. Thus the use of tokens for behavior reinforcement in a reformatory may or may not be a suitable application of an approach that works well in mental hospitals, where the problems of manipulation for secondary gains are not so prominent.

The explorations conducted so far furnish a basis for continued study of an ancient correctional problem: the usefulness of incentives and punishments in changing behavior patterns. Most of the offender population is now managed in community-based programs, and the proportion will increase. Therefore, future development in operant psychology should be directed toward making behavior modification techniques available (subject to experimental scrutiny) to probation and parole officers and voluntary agencies engaged in the treatment of the offender in the community. . . .

**Stardard 15.1: Maintain a State correctional information system.**

**Standard 15.2: Provide a staff for systems analysis and statistical research.**

**Standard 15.3: Design an information system to supply service needs.**

**Standard 15.4: Develop a data base with criminal justice system interface.**

**Standard 15.5: Measure recidivism and program performance.**

# 16: The Statutory Framework of Corrections

CORRECTIONAL CODES AND THE CORRECTIONAL PROCESS

### The Instruments of Correctional Power

. . . It is not surprising that, with no consistently stated goal for corrections, correctional agencies grew in a haphazard manner. In many States, each correctional institution was created separately, with separate administration. Prison confinement was the predominant response to criminal behavior. Each new reform, generally a reaction to the harsh conditions of incarceration, seemed to require a new governmental agency independent of the prison administration.

Probation developed as an arm of the sentencing court and subject to its control. Persons were not "sentenced to" probation; the sentence to confinement was suspended. The courts viewed probation as a device to keep certain deserving offenders out of the correctional system, rather than as a more appropriate and effective correctional technique.

Institutional programming will be required to respond to the failures of probation programs. Judicially imposed sentences of partial confinement, where an offender remains under community supervision during most of the week, with his leisure time spent in a residential correctional facility, will require close cooperation between probation and institutional staff. Coordination and mutual understanding between all correctional personnel will become increasingly important. Continuing court supervision of the probation system inhibits the coordination required. . . .

There may be good reasons for separating the presentence investigation function from that of supervision of probationers. Studies indicate that where one officer does both, time-consuming investigations and report writing seriously interfere with his ability to supervise probationers. A person directly responsible to the sentencing court could perform the investigations as well as assist the court in other judicial functions such as bail investigations.

In many States, parole agencies developed independently.

To moderate long prison sentences, parole boards were established and given authority to release some offenders from confinement if they agreed to supervision in the community. Parole also was viewed as getting the offender out of the correctional system rather than altering the nature of his correctional program. Parolee supervision in the community was administered in several instances by a board of parole rather than by the correctional agency. It remains under a board in 18 States.

Parole, like probation, is one of several correctional tools. Prison programs should prepare an offender for parole and other aftercare programs—for reintegration into the community. Imaginative use of parole conditions, such as a requirement that the parolee reside at a halfway house, may involve institutional personnel directly. Effective and efficient parole planning and programming require close coordination with other correctional activities.

Juvenile and adult institutions developed independently and remain autonomous in several States. Numerous factors appear to account for this division of correctional organization. The public is more often willing to support new and innovative programs for juveniles than for adults. Proponents of juvenile programs find it politically expedient to retain their autonomy. Different approaches are authorized, at least implicitly, for juveniles.

It is assumed that adults need more punitive measures, provisions for tighter custody, and fewer correctional programs. Juveniles, on the other hand, are more salvageable. The agency designated to administer adult programs is thought to be custody-oriented. Juvenile programs, based more on the welfare model, are envisioned as directed more toward rehabilitation. . . .

Corrections is a politically sensitive function of government. Good correctional legislation requires that personnel recruitment be insulated from political patronage. However, as an arm of the government, corrections should be responsive to public attitudes. Political patronage is improper to the extent that unqualified persons are appointed. Appointment by the governor with the advice and consent of the legislature is a standard means of striking a balance. Statutory qualifications for a particular office are another. . . .

Civil service systems, with their emphasis on promotion and seniority, impede attraction of qualified personnel to top or middle management positions as well as movement of personnel from one agency to another. . . .

Three basic systems are possible. In many States, top correctional officials serve at the "pleasure" of the appointing official. This system creates no job security.

In some States sensitive personnel are appointed for a specified term. This gives some security during the term and allows periodic review of the individual's competence. The security provided by the specific term appointment will depend on the causes listed for removal during the term. A standard phrase is that the official may be removed for "disability, neglect of duty, incompetence, or malfeasance in office." A hearing where cause for removal is asserted should be required. Political considerations can be minimized by providing terms that overlap that of the appointing official.

In a few jurisdictions a person may be appointed to a permanent position subject to removal for cause. Again, a procedure requiring a hearing should be provided.

The term and permanent appointment schemes strike the balance between security and competence and provide adequate protection from political patronage and influence. . . .

## Allocation and Regulation of Correctional Power: The Issue of Discretion

. . . Some decisions required to protect an offender from abuse should be legislatively determined. Enactment of a code of rights for offenders removes discretionary action in certain areas. A statutory prohibition against corporal punishment is a noteworthy example; several States have enacted such laws. However, legislatures generally have been reluctant to codify provisions specifically protecting the interests of offenders. The absence of legislative guidance in this area has been a major factor in creating the need for judicial appraisal of correctional practices. Legislative provisions assuring basic freedoms and an acceptable level of humane treatment would have mitigated the need for expensive litigation and reduced the confusion and ambiguities that inevitably result from a judicial case-by-case declaration of offenders' rights. . . .

In corrections, sentencing decisions are particularly susceptible to direction through statutory criteria. These are decisions of direct public interest and have an immediate and substantial impact on the offender. The length of time over which the State exercises control of the offender and the relative degree of liberty or confinement imposed are basic to the correctional process and are critical from the offender's viewpoint.

Two decisions are appropriate for development of detailed statutory criteria. The first is the trial court's selection of the sentencing alternative to be imposed initially on the offender. The broader the range of sentences available, the more important become criteria to protect against disparate results. In most jurisdictions, the major decision for the court is between probation and confinement. Section 7.01 of the Model Penal Code (discussed later in this chapter) provides a useful model for the development of criteria for this determination. The code first recognizes that for most offenders probation will be the most appropriate alternative, with confinement to be used only as a last resort.

The section requires withholding a sentence of confinement unless the court finds that imprisonment is necessary for protection of the public because:

(a) there is undue risk that during the period of a suspended sentence or probation the defendant will commit another crime; or

(b) the defendant is in need of correctional treatment that can be provided most effectively by his commitment to an institution; or

(c) a lesser sentence will depreciate the seriousness of the defendant's crime.

... The decision to parole is another sentencing decision susceptible to detailed statutory criteria. Section 305.9 of the Model Penal Code illustrates acceptable criteria for this decision. They are fundamentally similar to the criteria for initial sentencing.

The code lists 13 factors to be considered in determining whether a particular offender should be paroled. In addition, Section 305.10 lists particular information the parole board must consider, including such items as the presentence reports of physical or mental examinations, institutional reports, and the prisoner's parole plan.

These sections provide useful guidelines for development of statutory structure for parole decision-making. The proposed structure should minimize the possibilities for arbitrary decisions. ...

The dramatic increase of administrative agencies during the last few decades has stimulated legislative concern for protecting the public from arbitrary administrative decisions. In 1946, the concern culminated in passage of the Federal Administrative Procedure Act. Shortly thereafter, the National Conference of Commissioners on Uniform State Laws promulgated a Model State Administrative Procedure Act for regulating State administrative agencies. The Model Act has been adopted in several States and used as a guide in others. . . .

The thrust of the administrative procedure acts is to publicize agency action. A major protection against arbitrary or inappropriate decisionmaking in a free society is to require openness and full discussion. Under most acts, major policy decisions by an agency are first announced as proposed rules. Persons affected by a rule have an opportunity to present argument or comment on the rule before it is enacted. Adopted rules are placed on file and made available to the public.

Most correctional decisions not otherwise regulated by statutory criteria are susceptible to some regulation through utilization of this procedure. The flexibility of rulemaking and the ease with which rules can be changed to adjust to changing circumstances would protect against unnecessary interferences with or disruptions of correctional programming. The procedure likewise would provide a valuable means of allowing offenders and the public to participate in and influence the formulation of critical correctional policies. Ability of offenders to participate in decisions directly affecting their liberty and property would do much to relieve the hostility and resentment the present system breeds. . . .

Since it is in the public's and the agency's interest that correctional decisions have a constructive effect on the offender, both should support mechanisms to allow the offender to challenge the factual basis for such decisions. An erroneous or arbitrary decision is not constructive; it breeds resentment and disrespect for society and its institutions.

In formulating a procedure for offender-initiated review of decisions, the legislature and the correctional agency must recognize that the procedure not only must arrive at fair decisions but also must appear to do so from the offender's perspective. Review procedures can vary in formality and extent. A procedure enabling an offender to relay a complaint to a superior of the decisionmaker constitutes a review procedure.

Some institutions may wish to experiment with an ombudsman system in which an official is specifically designated to receive and respond to offender grievances. The ombudsman should be an impartial person who is not officially connected with the correctional administration. More formalized grievance procedures are envisioned where a formal complaint is filed and a hearing is held to resolve a disagreement.

Some decisions may be appealed to a mixed board of offenders and correctional staff. The devices available for internal review are varied. . . .

The nature of the procedure for review should depend on the importance of the decision to the life, liberty, or property of the offender. Minor decisions need not be subjected to judicial review as long as a simple, informal, and fair internal review procedure is available. Some disciplinary decisions such as temporary suspension of minor privileges would not require judicial intervention. Assignment to a particular cell or dinner shift normally would not raise substantial issues, although regulations announcing how cells are assigned may do so. . . .

Some institutional decisions have a direct effect on the sentence of the offender. Disciplinary proceedings that could result in loss of "good time" credits can substantially extend an offender's sentence. Procedural safeguards against arbitrary action should be required, and, in the absence of formal and impartial internal procedures, judicial review seems appropriate. . . .

PENAL CODES AND THE CORRECTIONAL PROCESS

The penal code includes the statutory provisions that designate an activity as criminal and prescribe the applicable criminal sanction. The penal code has a direct and influential effect on the corrections component of the criminal justice system. . . .

*Effect of Maximum Sentences on Corrections*

Most criminal codes, either modern or antiquated, provide varying maximum sentences for various criminal offenses. Establishment of these maximum sentences has a direct bearing on the development and success of correctional programs.

Legislatively imposed maximums establish the length of time for which an offender is subject to correctional power. From a purely correctional standpoint, it could be argued that the legislature should not impose any maximum. The sentence for every offense would be for life with correctional authorities making discretionary decisions terminating their control when an offender's rehabilitation is complete. This model is based on a pure form of individual treatment. Commission of an offense provides the rationale for unlimited treatment. The legislature would not be forced to scale the sanction by the gravity of the offense or to reflect the intensity of retributive feelings in the community. These decisions would be delegated to other agencies, either courts or correctional officials.

In fact, however, society does have a scale of values attributing greater severity to some criminal offenses than to others. This discrimination reflects retributive notions that can be reflected through differing maximum terms. Differentiating the length of the sentence on the basis of the seriousness of the offense reflects societal notions of fairness as well. Retribution aside, it would appear unjust for an individual who shoplifts a $10 watch to be deprived of his liberty for a substantially longer period than an individual who commits armed robbery.

Maximum terms reflect values in addition to correctional policy. Our system of government long has regarded governmental intervention in individuals' lives as an evil to be avoided without good cause. And the government's intention to intervene for the good of the individual rather than for punishment seldom has been found to be sufficient cause to extend the period of intervention. The maximum limit of state control over the individual, reflected in the criminal statutes, places time restraints on correctional programs not related directly to needs of the program or the offender. This would tend to force planning for correctional activities to contemplate concentrated rather than extended programs.

There is growing recognition of the fact that inequality of sentences directly undermines correctional programs. Offenders who labor under grossly excessive sentences, as compared with other offenders who committed relatively similar offenses, are not receptive to correctional programs. The justification that the sentence is "individualized" generally is not accepted by the offender. Lack of legislatively imposed maximum sentences, graduated in relation to the gravity of the offense, increases the possibility of disparity in sentencing. Legislatively imposed maximum sentences are the first step toward equality of sentencing. To this extent, maximum limits established by law—although limiting the time available for correctional programs—tend to enhance the effect of correctional programming by increasing offender morale. . . .

Long sentences impede correctional programming. An offender who faces a long sentence is not prone to accept and benefit readily from correctional programs. Moreover, valuable resources are consumed in the care and provision of services for many offenders who do not need extended correctional supervision. And finally, no study has yet indicated that, for the majority of offenders, any socially useful benefit is derived from long sentences. . . .

## Effect of Minimum Sentences on Corrections

Legislatively established minimum terms serve a different function. Since the legislature may contemplate only the offense and not the individual offender when setting the limits of criminal sanction, the promulgation of minimum sentences is unrelated to correctional programming requirements. The diversity, length, and inconsistency of present maximum sentences may account for the present tendency for State legislatures to enact minimum sentences.

The minimum sentence imposed by statute serves only to affect the offender adversely. Since the minimum term generally determines parole eligibility, it prolongs confinement unnecessarily. This overconfinement results not only in ineffective use of valuable resources that might be allocated more appropriately to other offenders but also may undermine seriously the progress of an offender.

The argument that a statutory minimum of 1 year should apply to all felonies represents the theory that a shorter period of confinement does not allow sufficient time for the development of a correctional program. Assuming that the corrections system cannot effectively operate in less than a year, the question remains as to which agency should make that decision. By imposition of a legislatively imposed 1 year minimum, all flexibility within that year is lost. When the judge makes a mistake in terms of correctional needs, the mistake cannot be rectified.

Whether the judge should be authorized to impose a 1-year minimum is a different question. The sentencing judge is in a position to determine on an individual basis if satisfaction of retributive feelings requires that a minimum be imposed. If imposed for that purpose, then judicially imposed minimums are justifiable, regardless of what effect they may have on correctional programming.

If the 1-year minimum is essential for correctional programming purposes, the wisest course would be to adopt by administrative rule a policy of not paroling individuals within the first year except in unusual situations. Thus, the minimum sentence decision based on correctional programming in those programs. This also would allow adequate flexibility for individualized justice.

## Effect of Mandatory Sentences on Corrections

There are two important factors in fashioning sentencing

provisions: the offender and the offense. The legislature, in enacting a penal code with penalty provisions, can deal only with the offense; the offenders who will be convicted under the provision over the history of its enactment will span the spectrum of guilt. Recently there has been an increase of laws which differentiate between the killing of a policeman and other homicides. The FBI Uniform Crime Reports indicate that persons who kill police officers range from husbands interrupted in the course of a family dispute to deranged persons lying in ambush. No legislature can determine in advance the nature of the offender who will be prosecuted under a particular penalty provision.

In a number of instances, however, legislatures have, because of public reaction to a particular offense, attempted to write mandatory sentences into law. These take the form either of specifying what sanction shall be applied or eliminating certain sentencing or correctional alternatives from consideration. Minimum sentences established by law operate as mandatory provisions since they generally postpone parole.

Legislators should not impose mandatory sentences. They are counterproductive to public safety, and they hinder correctional programming without any corresponding benefit. To the extent that the mandatory provision requires an individual offender to be incarcerated longer than necessary, it is wasteful of public resources. To the extent that it denies correctional programming such as probation or parole to a particular offender, it lessens the chance for his successful reintegration into the community. To the extent that mandatory sentences are in fact enforced, they have a detrimental effect on corrections.

However, mandatory sentences generally are not enforced. The Crime Commission's Task Force on Courts found "persuasive evidence of nonenforcement of these mandatory sentencing provisions by the courts and prosecutors." Prosecutors who find that an unusually harsh sentence in a particular case is unjust will, through plea negotiations, substantially circumvent the provision. Where lengthy mandatory sentences leave little incentive for the offender to plead guilty.

Mandatory sentences in fact grant greater sentencing prerogatives to prosecutors than to courts. The result increases rather than decreases disparity in sentences and subverts statutory provisions by a system designed to enforce them. The resulting disrespect for the system on the part of both the offender and the public tends to undermine our system of criminal justice.

The Idaho Supreme Court recently held legislative decreed mandatory sentences in violation of the Idaho constitution. The court noted:

> A judge is more than just a finder of fact or an executioner of the inexorable rule of law. Ideally, he is also the keeper of the conscience of the law. For this reason the courts are given discretion in sentencing, even in the most serious felony cases, and the power to grant probation. We recognize that rehabilitation, particularly of first offenders, should usually be the initial consideration in the imposition of the criminal sanction. Whether this can be better accomplished through the penal system or some other means, it can best be achieved by one fully advised of all the facts particularly concerning the defendant in each case and not by a body far removed from these considerations.

Similar decisions in other jurisdictions would not be unexpected.

## EFFECT OF COMMUNITY-BASED PROGRAMS ON CORRECTIONAL CODES

### Administrative Discretion

... Community-based programs are short-run risk-taking programs. Lengthy confinement without graduated programs of release creates greater risks. An offender, while confined, represents a lesser risk to the public safety than one living in the community. But the offender who participates in a gradual return to society through a variety of community-based programs represents a lesser risk in the long run than the offender who serves a long prison term and then is released abruptly without supervision.

There is certainly the temptation to exclude persons convicted of certain offenses from participation in these programs, as has been done in the case of probation and parole. All such temptations should be resisted. There are sufficient practical and political restraints operating against the overuse of community corrections.

• As long as resources are scarce, correctional administrators will tend to select the "best risks" for available programs.

• Any correctional administrator will tend toward the conservative use of these programs because, in the last analysis, he personally bears the responsibility for failure.

## Parole Board Functions

As correctional administrators obtain through legislation more discretion in utilizing community resources—particularly the authority to house offenders within the community—the parole board will take on different functions. It will, under these circumstances, act more as a reviewing agency to determine which offenders ought to be participating in community-based programs but are not because of correctional administrators' refusal to assign them to such programs. It would seem proper and advisable to view the parole board in this role. It would require some modification in present statutes establishing the board.

1. The concept of parole eligibility, if it restricts the jurisdiction of the board in all cases, should be restructured to allow the board to act prior to eligibility dates for purposes of approving participation in community-based programs other than parole supervision.

2. The parole board should be given authority to assign offenders to community-based programs other than those historically designated as "parole" programs. Thus, halfway houses, work release, and educational release programs should become available resources for the parole board as well as the director of corrections.

3. A procedure should be authorized allowing an offender not assigned to a community-based program to initiate a review by the parole board. This can be accomplished either by allowing an offender to initiate a hearing before the board for the specific purpose of testing the administrator's refusal to assign him to a community-based program or by requiring the board periodically to review the record and history of each offender. The latter would allow a review of not only community-based participation but also parole eligibility. . . .

## Due Process Requirement

. . . An offender should not be removed from a community-based program without good reason. This is a simple enough statement, but it contains difficult implications. The determination of whether there is "good reason" in our society contemplates certain procedural requirements: (1) the offender should know what the reason is; and (2) he should be able to present information to the decisionmaker in the event the reason is not founded on fact. Adequate provisions implementing these procedures should be required by correctional legislation.

**Use of Community Resources**

The assignment of offenders to the community also contemplates that nongovernmental community resources will be utilized as a critical component of the correctional program. Traditionally, governmental functions may be delegated, in whole or part, to a private agency or individual. Among the ramifications of this for the correctional code are the following:

1. Statutory authorization for the correctional administrator to utilize community resources, generally on a contractual basis, is essential. In some jurisdictions, the right to contract for private services may not be considered an implied power of a governmental agency and thus should be expressly provided for in the statute.

2. Statutory authorization should be conferred for transferring custody in fact if not in law to a private party or organization. It is preferable to have the offender remain in the custody of the correctional agency as a matter of law for purposes of determining sentence, punishing for escape, maintaining control, and revoking community privileges. . . .

**Standard 16.1: Comprehensive Correctional Legislation**

Each State, by 1978, should enact a comprehensive correctional code, which should include statutes governing:

1. Services for persons awaiting trial.
2. Sentencing criteria, alternatives, and procedures.
3. Probation and other programs short of institutional confinement.
4. Institutional programs.
5. Community-based programs.
6. Parole.
7. Pardon.

The code should include statutes governing the preceding programs for:

1. Felons, misdemeanants, and delinquents.
2. Adults, juveniles, and youth offenders.
3. Male and female offenders.

Each legislature should state the "public policy" governing the correctional system. The policy should include the following premises:

1. Society should subject persons accused of criminal conduct or delinquent behavior and awaiting trial to the least restraint or condition which gives reasonable assurance that the person accused will appear for trial. Confinement should

be used only where no other measure is shown to be adequate.

2. The correctional system's first function is to protect the public welfare by emphasizing efforts to assure that an offender will not return to crime after release from the correctional system.

3. The public welfare is best protected by a correctional system characterized by care, differential programming, and reintegration concepts rather than punitive measures.

4. An offender's correctional program should be the least drastic measure consistent with the offender's needs and the safety of the public. Confinement, which is the most drastic disposition for an offender and the most expensive for the public, should be the last alternative considered.

**Standard 16.2: Enact regulation of administrative procedures.**

**Standard 16.3: Code of Offenders' Rights**

Each State should immediately enact legislation that defines and implements the substantive rights of offenders. Such legislation should be governed by the following principles:

1. Offenders should be entitled to the same rights as free citizens except where the nature of confinement necessarily requires modification.

2. Where modification of the rights of offenders is required by the nature of custody, such modifications should be as limited as possible.

3. The duty of showing that custody requires modification of such rights should be upon the correctional agency. . . .

**Standard 16.4: Unifying Correctional Programs**

Each State should enact legislation by 1978 to unify all correctional facilities and programs. The board of parole may be administratively part of an overall statewide correctional services agency, but it should be autonomous in its decisionmaking authority and separate from field services. Programs for adult, juvenile, and youthful offenders that should be within the agency include:

1. Services for persons awaiting trial.

2. Probation supervision.

3. Institutional confinement.

4. Community-based programs, whether prior to or during institutional confinement.

**5.** Parole and other aftercare programs.

**6.** All programs for misdemeanants including probation, confinement, community-based programs, and parole.

The legislation also should authorize the correctional agency to perform the following functions:

**1.** Planning of diverse correctional facilities.

**2.** Development and implementation of training programs for correctional personnel.

**3.** Development and implementation of an information-gathering and research system.

**4.** Evaluation and assessment of the effectiveness of its functions.

**5.** Periodic reporting to governmental officials including the legislature and the executive branch.

**6.** Development and implementation of correctional programs including academic and vocational training and guidance, productive work, religious and recreational activity, counseling and psychotherapy services, organizational activity, and other such programs that will benefit offenders.

**7.** Contracts for the use of nondepartmental and private resources in correctional programming.

This standard should be regarded as a statement of principle applicable to most State jurisdictions. It is recognized that exceptions may exist, because of local conditions or history, where juvenile and adult corrections or pretrial and postconviction correctional services may operate effectively on a separated basis.

**Standard 16.5:** Define personnel standards by law.

**Standard 16.6:** Ratify interstate correctional agreements.

**Standard 16.7:** Define crime categories and maximum sentences.

**Standard 16.8:** Legislate criteria for court sentencing alternatives.

. . . Confinement has traditionally been the standard against which all other sentencing alternatives were developed. Other alternatives, developed separately, were seen as ameliorating the harshness of total confinement. Modern sentencing practices require that confinement be treated as the sentence to be imposed only if no other alternative will serve.

Thus, legislation should establish the priority in which the various alternatives should be considered and the criteria that should guide the court in imposing sentence. The court should also be required to state its reasons for the selection of one alternative over another as a check on the exercise of its discretion and to facilitate appellate review.

The following alternatives should be authorized:

1. Unconditional release. Consistent with the principle of utilizing the least drastic means necessary, outright release of a person convicted of a criminal offense should be considered in many cases. This disposition would be appropriate in cases in which the nature of the offense is so minor or the circumstances such that no useful purpose would be served by imposition of a more drastic sanction. For some offenders, criminal processing and trial may have a decided impact in and of themselves, particularly for first offenders.

2. Conditional release. Judges in some jurisdictions are experimenting with shaping sanctions to fit the offense and to avoid the use of incarceration. In some cases, a sentence to confinement is suspended on the condition that the offender perform certain specified acts. Persons convicted of minor crimes may be sentenced to perform some kind of community service, such as working in schools, hospitals, or charity programs. Such sanctions provide the opportunity for offenders to make some compensation to society for their offense. Use of these sanctions should be greatly expanded.

3. Fine. In some cases, a fine rather than probation or imprisonment is the appropriate penalty. It is, in practice, the major tool of law enforcement for minor misdemeanors or traffic offenses. However, the fine, as it has been employed in this country, too often creates hardships and results which the criminal justice system should not tolerate. A fine, followed by imprisonment for nonpayment, discriminates against the indigent. The United States Supreme Court, *Tate* v. *Short*, 401 U.S. 395 (1971), has held that confinement of an indigent because of his inability to pay a fine is unconstitutional.

Studies have found that a large percentage of persons in urban jails were committed for nonpayment of fines. On the other hand, properly employed, the fine is far less drastic, far less costly for the public, and perhaps more effective than imprisonment or community supervision. Legislatively imposed criteria requiring that the fine be levied in an amount that can be paid and statutory authorization for payment in installments with civil enforcement mechanisms should be provided as one sentencing alternative.

4. Release under supervision in the community. Probation is the most common form of release of offenders to the community under supervision. Statutory requirements for probation are outlined in Standard 16.11.

5. Sentence to a halfway house or other residential facility located in the community. Courts should not have to choose between total confinement and total freedom. The trend toward use of community-based programs for offenders after a period of incarceration suggests that community-oriented programs with State control over leisure time are a valuable tool that should not be preconditioned in all cases on a period of total confinement. In addition, there may be resources available in the community which could provide a group living situation and supervision without the hardware and institutional control characteristics of most jails and other correctional facilities. Thus, courts should have "halfway-in" houses available to them for sentencing dispositions decisionmakers.

6. Sentence to partial confinement with liberty to work or to participate in training or education during all but leisure time. This form of sanction has been used predominantly for misdemeanants sentenced to a jail term. In some cases, offenders return every evening to the jail and in others, they return only for the weekend. This arrangement serves to punish and deter without totally disrupting the individual's family life, employment, and other ties in the community. Jails and other institutions are now operating such programs, many without having specific statutory authorization. Thus, while formal authorization may not be required, it would be desirable for legislatures to affirmatively authorize this form of sanction.

7. Total confinement. The proposed standards contemplate a qualified version of indeterminate sentencing with judicial power to impose a maximum below that established by statute. The indeterminate sentence has been attacked as resulting in gross sentencing disparity, and vesting unbridled power in correctional administrators to make arbitrary decisions affecting the liberty of offenders. Elsewhere, this chapter dicusses the values and disadvantages of discretionary decisionmaking and suggests methods of limiting the abuse of that power. The major value of the indeterminate sentence is to allow some individualization of program related, in theory at least, to the needs of a given offender in terms of his ability to adjust to a law-abiding life style. . . .

**Standard 16.9: Restrict court delinquency jurisdiction and detention.**

**Standard 16.10: Require presentence investigations by law.**

**Standard 16.11: Formulate criteria and procedures for probation decisions.**

... The decision to grant probation should not be left open to unchecked discretion. The legislature can and should enact criteria to direct the courts toward an appropriate goal established by public policy. At the same time, the individual defendant is protected from decisions having no relationship to the goal announced.

The conditions imposed on probationers likewise should be restricted by the legislature to those that support the function of probation. The Model Penal Code Sec. 301.1 provides 11 conditions that can be applied in a specific case and a general clause authorizing other conditions "reasonably related to the rehabilitation of the defendant." If probation is to serve its proper role, conditions must be tailored to meet the needs of the individual defendant in the least drastic manner possible consistent with public safety. ...

**Standard 16.12: Legislate commitment, classification, and transfer procedures.**

**Standard 16.13: Lift unreasonable restrictions on prison labor and industry.**

**Standard 16.14: Legislate authorization for community-based correctional programs.**

**Standard 16.15: Clarify parole procedures and eligibility requirements.**

**Standard 16.16: Establish pardon power and procedure.**

**Standard 16.17: Collateral Consequences of a Criminal Conviction**

Each State should enact by 1975 legislation repealing all mandatory provisions depriving persons convicted of criminal offenses of civil rights or other attributes of citizenship. Such legislation should include:

1. Repeal of all existing provisions by which a person convicted of any criminal offense suffers civil death, corruption

of blood, loss of civil rights, or forfeiture of estate or property.

2. Repeal of all restrictions on the ability of a person convicted of a criminal offense to hold and transfer property, enter into contracts, sue and be sued, and hold offices of private trust.

3. Repeal of all mandatory provisions denying persons convicted of a criminal offense the right to engage in any occupation or obtain any license issued by government.

4. Repeal of all statutory provisions prohibiting the employment of ex-offenders by State and local governmental agencies.

Statutory provisions may be retained or enacted that:

1. Restrict or prohibit the right to hold public office during actual confinement.

2. Forfeit public office upon confinement.

3. Restrict the right to serve on juries during actual confinement.

4. Authorize a procedure for the denial of a license or governmental privilege to selected criminal offenders when there is a direct relationship between the offense committed or the characteristics of the offender and the license or privilege sought.

The legislation also should:

1. Authorize a procedure for an ex-offender to have his conviction expunged from the record.

2. Require the restoration of civil rights upon the expiration of sentence.

# D: Directions for Change

## 17: Priorities and Implementation Strategies

PRIORITIES FOR ACTION

**Equity and Justice in Corrections**

Corrections has been characterized by inhumane conditions, arbitrary decisions, discrimination, lawlessness, and brutality. That a civilized society cannot tolerate such conditions is being increasingly recognized. Recent judicial interpretations of offenders' rights reflect the belief that such practices are unlawful and counterproductive to instilling respect for the law in offenders and other citizens. . . .

**Exclusion of Sociomedical Problem Cases**

The historic tendency to saddle corrections with sociomedical and social welfare cases overloads the system and drastically handicaps any effectiveness it may have. It is beyond the competence and proper scope of corrections to deal effectively with the mentally ill, alcoholics, and drug addicts. In fact, correctional "treatment" often exacerbates the problems of these persons and contributes to the revolving-door syndrome characterizing our jails and other penal institutions.

The propensity for outlawing private behavior that is fairly common in our society simply because it is (or has been) objectionable to part of the society, has resulted in overcriminalization. Too many laws proscribe too many kinds of behavior. The effect has been to sidetrack the criminal justice system from its mission of protecting society against crime to the uneasy role of policing private morality. As a result of such laws, correctional institutions—particularly jails—are crowded with persons they are not equipped to handle. Types of behavior commonly categorized as "victimless crimes," which are defined as crimes without an effective complainant other than the authorities, are considered in the Commission's summary report.

Attempting to control such behaviors by criminal law is not only ineffective but also expensive in economic and social terms. It is a major obstacle to correctional reform—indeed, to reform of the whole system of criminal justice. Here and there corrections is making informal efforts to rid itself of problems which are unrelated to public safety. Success in these efforts would strengthen the system by permitting more effective use of resources and personnel to fight more serious crime. It would also allow society to find more effective ways to deal with troublesome behavior. . . .

## Shift of Correctional Emphasis from Institutions to Community Programs

The prison, the reformatory, and the jail have achieved only a shocking record of failure. There is overwhelming evidence that these institutions create crime rather than prevent it. Their very nature insures failure. Mass living and bureaucratic management of large numbers of human beings are counterproductive to the goals of positive behavior changes and reintegration. These isolated and closed societies are incompatible with the world outside. Normally desirable characteristics such as self-confidence, initiative, sociability, and leadership are counteracted by the experience of incarceration. Individuality is lost and the spirit of man broken through the performance of deadening routines and endless hours of idleness. . . .

It is of utmost importance to recognize that the concept of community-based corrections does not imply new institutions and facilities. This point is especially important in light of the flurry of construction plans and projects that have accompanied recent developments in community corrections. While it is recognized that existing facilities may be inadequate for the purposes outlined in this report, replacements should be made only after the planning stipulated in the following section is completed. In its truest sense, community corrections is the widest possible use of noninstitutional correctional programs designed to reeducate and redirect the attitudes and behavior of offenders in order to fully integrate or reintegrate them into the community as law-abiding members of society.

In the absence of a moratorium on traditional construction, corrections in the 1970's could repeat a two-century-old error and fail to benefit from the lessons of history. For it was a similar reform movement in 1787 in which our fledgling country, seeking to establish institutions predicated on the concept of the dignity of man, embarked on a prison construction program without precedent. The physical and ideological legacy of this movement stands recognized today as one of the major obstacles to correctional reform and a prime example of man's inhumanity to man. So we must guard against embarking on a financially ruinous construction program that merely would replace prisons, reformatories, jails, and detention homes with facilities bearing more palatable names and wearing more attractive facades but fundamentally unchanged. . . .

The time has come for fundamental changes in corrections. Improbable as it may sound because of the high cost of prison construction, it would be easier for this Nation to replace its obsolete correctional system with another generation of institutions than to embrace the concept of community corrections. The reasons are as distressing as they are simple. Hiding our social problems behind a progressive-looking facade requires only sufficient funding. Community corrections requires radically changed attitudes toward the offender and a new social commitment.

### Unified Correctional Systems and System Planning

Since State governments already support the vast majority of nonfederal correctional programming, the long-range goal of unification and consolidation of correctional responsibilities into an integrated, State-controlled correctional system is logical. This approach would facilitate the delivery of correctional services in a coordinated and mutually supportive fashion. Streamlining activities would reduce waste and overlap, thereby promoting optimum application of available resources. Development of high personnel and performance standards would be enhanced through uniform staff development, interdepartmental career opportunities, and civil service. System-wide research and evaluation would increase feedback on program effectiveness, the knowledge base of corrections, and accountability to the public. The implementation of an integrated State correctional system is essential to attain equity, maximum diversion of sociomedical problems from corrections, and utilization of a full variety of dispositional alternatives within the system. . . .

## IMPLEMENTATION STRATEGIES

### Money

. . . Anyone familiar with State and local corrections is painfully aware that pleas for more money addressed to legislators and county commissioners fall upon deaf ears. Corrections remains where it has always been, at the end of the budgetary line in the distribution of State and local tax funds. Although sporadic support for corrections has developed in isolated instances, there is little hope that this situation can be changed substantially. In fact, as matters presently stand, the States, counties, and cities are looking to the Federal Government to finance correctional improvements and postponing such improvements until Federal aid is forthcoming. . . .

Normal State and local expenditures to maintain corrections at its present grossly deficient level of operations total about $1.5 billion a year. The annual Federal funding assistance should approach about the same figure. Otherwise, corrections will not be able to accomplish the shift to community-based programs, obtain the manpower it needs, do the research and experimentation that has been so long neglected, and correct the deplorable conditions that exist generally.

Further, the States and localities find even the 25 percent matching requirement for Federal funds burdensome, owing to the low budgetary priority accorded corrections, and as a result even the Federal funds available often do not find ready takers. The matching requirement should be reduced to 10 percent or eliminated entirely. . . .

**The Federal Model**

... There is no evidence that Federal correction programs, although operated in well-managed institutions, produce any better results than than State programs. The Federal system, like those of the States, does not collect statistics on recidivism that can be considered valid. Comparisons therefore are impossible to make. However, Federal Bureau of Investigation statistics on offenders released from Federal jurisdiction suggest a heavy reinvolvement with the law.

The FBI reported in 1970 that 63 percent of the Federal prisoners released to the community in 1965 had been rearrested by the end of the fourth year after release. Of those released on probation, 56 percent were rearrested; of those released on parole, 61 percent; of those released after completing prison terms, 75 percent. Of persons under the age of 20 who were released in 1965, 74 percent had been rearrested by the end of 1969.

While these statistics report rearrests rather than reconvictions, they do suggest failure more than success. They also suggest that this failure of the Federal system is more pronounced with juvenile and youthful offenders than with adults. ...

The Federal model also has application in the area of jails. This report urges, at the least, State inspection of local jails and eventual State operation of such facilities. The Federal system has an inspection service, and contracts with some 800 local jails for the detention of Federal prisoners awaiting trial or transportation to Federal institutions. However, contrary to popular belief, the Federal system has no written standards for inspection, and many jails with which it has contracts are fully as disreputable as jails generally in the United States. ...

**Commitment of the Public**

The new correctional philosophy is based on at least two major considerations: First, society, in addition to the offender, needs changing; and second, more emphasis should be placed on the offender's social and cultural setting if we are to obtain any substantial relief from recidivism.

While individual differences and individual responsibility will remain important factors in corrections' response to criminal behavior, they will need to be considered within the setting of the community and the culture. To salvage offenders in any great numbers, therefore, will require changes in the offender himself and changes in the community that will help to bring about his reintegration. Communities must assume part of the responsibility for bringing about these changes, for the problems to be addressed were generated in the community. Once this is recognized, corrections can be removed from its isolation and made a part of the larger social system.

Even though the public is beginning to recognize that the ultimate success of corrections depends on reintegrating the offender into the community and motivating him to refrain from breaking the law, public ambivalence about reform and traditional lack of concern for the criminal offender seriously impede efforts to make corrections more effective. This situation is aggravated whenever change is resisted from within the criminal justice system. In such instances, deliberate appeals may be made to public fears in the interest of preserving traditional practices with all their injustices and futility.

If the philosophy of reintegration is to gain public favor, there must be full recognition on the part of the public that present correctional practices do not serve the long-run interest of societal protection. Legal and economic barriers and social ostracism must yield to commitment, involvement, and sharing of responsibility. Only then will the goals of crime prevention and crime reduction be realized.

# Chapter VIII
# Criminal Code Reform and Revision

Gambling, marijuana use, trafficking in pornography, prostitution, sexual acts between consenting adults in private—the mere mention of these activities may generate an emotional response in almost every American.

Some citizens may be angry, embarrassed, or frightened because these activities take place in society. Other citizens may express resentment that these activities, which they may consider to be relatively harmless, are condemned and punished at all. Still other citizens may condemn one of these activities while at the same time practicing one of the others.

Another group of crimes—drunkenness, vagrancy, and minor traffic violations—are a constant source of irritation and dismay to society in general and to the criminal justice system in particular. For example, the FBI reports that in 1971 there were an estimated 1.8 million arrests for public drunkenness.[1]

The criminal justice system is ill-equipped to deal with these offenses. These crimes place a heavy and unwelcome

[1] Federal Bureau of Investigation, *Uniform Crime Reports— 1971* (1972), p. 118.

burden on law enforcement resources throughout the Nation. And the laws regulating these offenses are open to abuse and, increasingly, to constitutional challenge.

# Major Recommendations

The Commission looked at these two categories of crimes and concluded that States should consider substantive changes in their statutes dealing with these crimes. Detailed recommendations in these areas are set out in this chapter, but in general the Commission recommends that:

• States review criminal statutes dealing with gambling, marijuana use and possession for use, pornography, prostitution, and sexual acts between consenting adults in private, to determine if current laws best serve the purposes of the State and the needs of the people; and, as a minimum, States remove incarceration as a penalty for these offenses, except when these offenses involve a willful attempt to affect others in these areas, such as pandering, public lewdness, and sale or possession for sale of marijuana.

• States decriminalize drunkenness and vagrancy and dispose of minor traffic offenses administratively rather than through criminal process in court.

• States whose codes have not been revised within the past decade initiate complete revision, including, when necessary, a revamped penalty structure.

• States create criminal law commissions to review new legislative proposals bearing criminal penalties.

There has been considerable activity in the area of criminal code reform in recent years. At least nine States and the District of Columbia have enacted the Uniform Alcoholism and Intoxication Act which abolishes drunkenness as a crime. The possession of marijuana is now a misdemeanor in most States, and two States, Illinois and Connecticut, have made consensual homosexual acts legal.[2]

# Reevaluation of Laws

The Commission believes that the criminal code should reflect a more rational attitude toward current social practices

[2] Norval Morris, "Crimes Without Victims: The law is a busybody," *The New York Times Magazine* (April 1, 1973).

587

and a more realistic appraisal of the capabilities of the criminal justice system.[8]

Gambling, marijuana use and possession for use, pornography, prostitution, and sexual acts in private often are punished by incarceration. The Commission questions whether incarceration serves as a deterrent to these types of behavior.

The existing criminal justice system was designed to deter potential offenders by the threat of punishment, to punish and rehabilitate offenders, and to protect society by incarcerating persons who pose a threat to others. The system has failed to some extent in almost every respect.

**The Commission recommends that States reevaluate their laws on gambling, marijuana use and possession for use, pornography, prostitution, and sexual acts between consenting adults in private. Such reevaluation should determine if current laws best serve the purpose of the State and the needs of the public.**

**The Commission further recommends that, as a minimum, each State remove incarceration as a penalty for these offenses, except in the case of persistent and repeated offenses by an individual, when incarceration for a limited period may be warranted.**

The recommendation insofar as it deals with removal of incarceration as a penalty does not apply to behavior in which a willful attempt is made to affect others in areas such as pandering, soliciting, public lewdness, and the sale or possession for sale of marijuana.

The Commission emphasizes that it is not necessarily recommending decriminalization of these five activities. It is up to each State to determine whether or not such behavior should be classified as criminal in nature. Some States may

---

[8] A thorough investigation and discussion of code reform is beyond the reach of this survey. A variety of studies have been undertaken by other organizations, such as the National Commission on Marihuana and Drug Abuse; the Department of Health, Education, and Welfare; the Joint Conference on Alcohol Abuse and Alcoholism; and the National Council on Crime and Delinquency.

Other studies are mentioned elsewhere in this report. It was not within the purview of this Commission to initiate detailed studies of the activities in question, but in light of its mandate to develop a national strategy to reduce crime, the Commission has weighed the arguments on each side of each issue, noting the impact of current laws on the operations of the criminal justice system.

decide, upon reevaluation of existing laws, to retain the laws or to modify or repeal them altogether.

The Commission is aware that both prostitution and gambling may be associated with organized crime, and it urges States to take appropriate safeguards when enacting legislation. There also may be some need to control pornography where children could be exposed to explicit sexual material.

The Commission, however, recommends that States that do not decriminalize these activities reexamine the effectiveness of incarceration in enforcing the laws. The Commission has made such an examination and concludes that incarceration is an ineffective method of enforcement. The Commission believes that incarceration should be abandoned and that probation, fines, commitment to community treatment programs, and other alternative forms of punishment and treatment be substituted for incarceration.

Incarceration is clearly not an infallible deterrent. For example, the threat of punishment did not end the use of liquor, and today it does not keep an estimated 15 to 20 million Americans a year from experimenting with or using marijuana, or prevent countless cases of illegal gambling. Evidence shows that incarceration itself does not deter; study after study documents that the majority of crimes are committed by persons who previously had been incarcerated.

The characterization of prisons as "schools of crime" needs little substantiation. Prisons often do not rehabilitate or change inmates, but instead may send back to society hardened, frustrated, alienated individuals who return quickly to patterns of crime and other antisocial conduct. Thus, incarceration may backfire: rather than protect society, it may perpetuate a threat to society.

Stricter sentences are not necessarily the solution. When sentences seem too severe for a particular crime, a jury may balk at a finding of guilty and may return a finding of not guilty or of guilty of a lesser offense.

The use of alternative forms of treatment is even more essential in the case of these crimes. Because these are the least serious crimes, long sentences rarely are applied and convicted offenders often are shuttled in and out of jail—with no benefit to the offender and at a high cost to the taxpayer.

Furthermore, these acts usually consist of behavior that does not pose a direct threat to others, but that often generates strong social disapproval. Therefore, as social problems these crimes are best dealt with by social institutions capable of treating the problem and of integrating the offender into society, rather than by a criminal justice system that could further alienate the offender by treating him the same as it would a violent criminal.

The approach recommended here already is practiced by many judges and courts; adoption of the recommendation merely would regularize that practice. The uniform application of penalties will eliminate discrimination against or harassment of certain classes of individuals; it also will prevent situations in which an individual is given an unusually severe penalty as an example to others, or as a demonstration to the public of seemingly efficient law enforcement.

# Decriminalization

The Commission believes that the criminal justice system would benefit from the removal of drunkenness as a crime, the repeal of vagrancy laws, and the administrative disposition of minor traffic offenses. The benefits from these changes that would accrue to the criminal justice system would be immediate and far ranging.

The following sections contain the Commission's recommendations in these three areas, plus a discussion of the rationale for the proposed changes.

## Public Drunkenness

**The Commission recommends that public drunkenness in and of itself no longer be treated as a crime. All States should give serious consideration to enacting the Uniform Alcoholism and Intoxication Act.**

In *Crimes With No Victims*, Edwin Kiester, Jr., portrays the existence of the Skid Row drunk:

He has been drinking steadily since his teens; and he lives on Skid Row, that run-down jumble of shabby taverns, insect-infested flophouses, religious missions dispensing free meals and lodging, cafeterias selling cheap soup, and employment agencies that specialize in dishwashers and busboys. John has no ties to anyone; and he has forgotten what trades he ever knew. He panhandles for pennies and wipes the windshields of cars stopped by a red light in hopes of a handout; occasionally he works in a restaurant kitchen hauling out garbage or washing dishes. Whatever he earns goes for cheap wine or rotgut liquor at the cut-rate Skid Row bars.[4]

The plight of such persons has not been improved by laws designating the alcoholic as a criminal. For the public drunk, the deterrence factor of a criminal sanction is virtually inoperative. Alcoholism is a problem for which social services, not the penal-correctional process, are indicated. Aggression that manifests itself in other criminal conduct, accompanied by drunkenness, should remain punishable.

In 1967, *The Challenge of Crime in a Free Society*, a report by the President's Commission on Law Enforcement and Administration of Justice, began its discussion of drunkenness offenses with this paragraph:

> Two million arrests in 1965—one of every three in America—were for the offense of public drunkenness. The great volume of these arrests places an extremely heavy load on the operations of the criminal justice system. It burdens police, clogs lower criminal courts, and crowds penal institutions throughout the United States.[5]

The President's Crime Commission doubted that drunkenness should continue to be treated as a crime.

In the 6 years since that report, there has been a slight decrease in the number of arrests for drunkenness; according to the Federal Bureau of Investigation's *Uniform Crime Reports*, there were approximately 1.8 million such arrests in 1971.[6]

That decrease is insignificant considering the amount of money and police and court time spent on each arrest. In 1971, the San Francisco Committee on Crime noted the inordinate amount of time spent on chronic recidivist drunks. In discussing the costs of handling drunkenness by criminal process, the Committee said:

> The futility and savagery of handling drunkenness through the criminal process is evident. The cost to the city of handling drunks in that way cannot be determined with exactness. Only approximation is pos-

[4] Edwin Kiester, Jr., *Crimes With No Victims* (Alliance for a Safer New York, 1972).
[5] President's Commission on Law Enforcement and Administration of Justice, *The Challenge of Crime in a Free Society* (1967).
[6] *Uniform Crime Reports—1971.*

sible. The Committee's staff has computed that in 1969 it cost the city a *minimum* of $893,500. The computation was that $267,196 was spent in making the arrests and processing the arrested person through sentence, and that roundly $626,300 was spent in keeping the drunks in county jail at San Bruno. And these figures do not include the costs to the city when a drunk is taken to San Francisco General Hospital from either the city prison or county jail. While our staff has concluded that it costs the city between $17 and $20 to process each drunk from arrest through sentencing, an estimate by a police officer assigned as liaison to the Drunk Court put the cost at $37 per man through the sentencing process. Thus, if anything, our estimates are low.[7]

The Committee said that "it cost the taxpayers about $2,500 to run one morning's 'crop' of drunks through the criminal process. The split-second decision of a judge to dismiss, sentence or suspend, may cost the city anywhere from $125 to $150." The Committee concluded: "If these expenditures achieved some social or public good, they should be gladly borne. But they do not."[8]

The San Francisco figures, when multiplied by the annual 1.8 million arrests for drunkenness, present an intolerable bill paid by Americans each year for the corralling and locking up of the public drunk.

A significant step to rectify this situation has been taken by the National Conference of Commissioners on Uniform State Laws. The Conference has drafted model legislation, the Uniform Alcoholism and Intoxication Treatment Act, that calls for decriminalization of alcoholism and public drunkenness and provides States with legal guidelines for dealing more rationally with public drunkenness. At least nine States and the District of Columbia have enacted this law, which was endorsed by the American Bar Association in 1972.

The uniform act calls for the development of a department in the State government to deal with alcoholism. It authorizes police officers to take a person incapacitated by alcohol into protective custody rather than arrest him. The act provides for a comprehensive program for treatment of alcoholics and

[7] The San Francisco Committee on Crime, "Basic Principles—Public Drunkenness," *A Report on Non-Victim Crime in San Francisco* (April 26, 1971).
[8] *Ibid.*

intoxicated persons—including emergency, inpatient, intermediate, outpatient, and followup treatment—and authorizes appropriate facilities for such treatment. This Commission recommends that all States consider the adoption of this act.

As noted in the preface to the uniform act, society's attitude toward alcohol abuse has changed. There is also increasing recognition that current laws discriminate against the poor and pose possible constitutional problems.

The alternative to reform in this area is more of the same of what society faces today. The Commission urges that appropriate measures be taken to relieve the police, courts, and jails of the futile job of dealing with a massive problem best handled by social services.

## Vagrancy

**The Commission recommends that each State review its laws and repeal any law that proscribes the status of living in idleness without employment and having no visible means of support, or roaming or wandering.**

One of the faults inherent in existing vagrancy statutes is that they are too vague to provide a reasonable degree of guidance to citizens, police, and courts as to what constitutes the offense. Thus, these statutes are constitutionally suspect. Their constitutional validity is even more in doubt when they touch the rights of assembly and free association. Yet in 1971, the FBI estimated there were 91,600 arrests for vagrancy.[9]

Another serious objection to vagrancy statutes is that they discriminate against the poor and may be enforced arbitrarily. The adverse results of this situation were stated well in *Task Force Report: The Courts,* a report of the President's Crime Commission. The report states:

> One of its consequences is to communicate to the people who tend to be the object of these laws the idea that law enforcement is not a regularized, authoritative procedure, but largely a matter of arbitrary behavior by the authorities. The application of these laws often tends to discriminate against the poor and subcultural groups in the population. It is unjust to structure law enforcement in such a way that poverty itself becomes a crime. And it is costly for society when the law arouses the feelings associated with

[9] *Uniform Crime Reports—1971,* p. 115.

these laws in the ghetto, a sense of persecution and helplessness before official power and hostility to police and other authority that may tend to generate the very conditions of criminality society is seeking to extirpate.[10]

Vagrancy statutes often are used as a device for taking into custody persons suspected of other offenses. In an exhaustive article on vagrancy laws, Professor Caleb Foote discussed this misuse of the law:

> One cannot escape the conclusion that the administration of vagrancy-type laws serves as an escape hatch to avoid the rigidity imposed by real or imagined defects in criminal law and procedure. To the extent that such rigidity presents a real problem and that the need for a safety valve is not merely the product of inefficiency on the part of police or prosecutors, such a problem should not be dealt with by indirection. If it is necessary to ease the prosecution's burden of proof or to legalize arrests for mere suspicion, then the grave policy and constitutional problems posed by such suggestions should be faced. If present restrictions on the laws of attempts or arrests place too onerous a burden upon the police because of the nature of modern crime, then such propositions should be discussed and resolved on their merits. . . .[11]

The Commission recognizes that police departments in many jurisdictions have relied upon the vagrancy statute as a means of controlling disruptive conduct in public. But removal of criminal penalties for vagrancy ought not to leave police wholly without constitutionally valid means of dealing with the rowdy and brawling individual.

**Therefore, the Commission recommends that each jurisdiction enact legislation that clearly defines disorderly conduct.**

The Commission commends the Model Penal Code of the American Law Institute as an example of a sound approach to a disorderly conduct statute.[12] The Model Penal Code redefines the crime to include only that behavior that is in itself

---

[10] President's Commission on Law Enforcement and Administration of Justice, *Task Force Report: The Courts* (1967).

[11] Caleb Foote, 104 *University of Pennsylvania Law Review*, 603, 649 (1956).

[12] American Law Institute, *Model Penal Code: Proposed Official Draft* (1962).

disorderly and removes from the law behavior that "tends to provoke a breach of the peace." To constitute disorderly conduct, the defined disturbances must be genuinely public.

Elimination of the vagrancy statute and redefinition of the disorderly conduct statute may appear to eliminate or decrease police ability to protect themselves and to investigate and deal with criminal behavior on the street. The Commission, however, notes the stop-and-frisk procedure that has been upheld by the Supreme Court. The Commission recommends that each State enact legislation in accordance with *Terry* v. *Ohio*, 88 S. Ct. 1968, 1884–85 (1968). The stop-and-frisk procedure and its constitutional limits are explained in Chapter 9, Handguns in American Society, of this report.

## Minor Traffic Offenses

The Commission recommends that all minor traffic offenses, except driving while intoxicated, reckless driving, and driving with a suspended or revoked license, be made infractions subject to administrative disposition. Penalties for such infractions should be limited to fines, suspension or revocation of the driver's license, or compulsory attendance at traffic school. Provision should be made for administrative disposition of such infractions by an agency other than the court of criminal jurisdiction. The right of appeal from administrative decisions should be assured.

The Commission strongly believes that adoption of this recommendation would result in an immediate beneficial impact upon the criminal justice system. This recommendation is discussed in detail in Chapter 8 of the *Report on Courts,* a report of the Commission.

The Commission does not belittle the significance of traffic offenses; because automobile accidents are responsible for thousands of deaths and injuries annually, minor traffic violations cannot be ignored. Repeated violations indicate that a driver is incompetent. Some form of sanction is necessary as a deterrent and to protect society and the individual. Records of violations are essential for determining which persons should be forbidden the use of an automobile.

The volume of minor traffic violations clogs lower courts, preventing the speedy and efficient consideration of serious offenses. The administrative procedure recommended is an example of a viable alternative to the criminal justice system for the necessary regulation of conduct that is per se harmless.

The Commission notes that the right of appeal from administrative decisions should be assured. Recommendations for the appeal procedure appear in the *Report on Courts* of the Commission.

The extent of the burden for the courts can be seen in the fact that in fiscal year 1969, 78 percent of all criminal cases in California adult misdemeanant courts were traffic cases. More recently, more than half of the new criminal cases filed in the District of Columbia Superior Court were traffic cases.[13] A study in 1970 of the lower criminal courts of metropolitan Boston showed that approximately 75 percent of the charges were either for drunkenness or petty traffic offenses. The same study showed that 63 percent of all charges brought in the Commonwealth of Massachusetts in the lower criminal courts were for petty traffic offenses.[14]

It is obvious in view of these statistics that administrative disposition of minor traffic offenses could free valuable criminal court resources and could contribute significantly to speeding up the disposition of other criminal cases.

# Criminal Code Revision

Criminal statutes may overlap one another, use words in an inconsistent fashion, and carry inconsistent punishments. For example, after a particularly notorious or offensive case, legislatures may enact penalties that are excessive in day-to-day application.

A State's criminal justice system may be a model of contemporary efficiency; but if its basic criminal law is the outmoded product of legislative or judicial processes of an earlier generation, the protection afforded the citizen through criminal law processes can be much less than it ought to be.

**States whose criminal codes have not been revised in the last decade should initiate revisions; these revisions should be complete and thorough, not partial, and the revision should include where necessary a revamped penalty structure.**

Much of the benefit of revision is likely to be lost unless revision is a continuing process, through which omissions or duplications in coverage can be remedied, defects in administration cured, and the inevitable urge to pass new statutes resisted. Legislatures sometimes have a tendency to enact

[13] District of Columbia Courts, *Annual Reports, 1971*, p. A-2.
[14] Stephen R. Bing and S. Stephen Rosenfeld, *The Quality of Justice in the Lower Criminal Courts of Metropolitan Boston* (Lawyers Committee for Civil Rights Under Law, 1970).

new statutes without determining whether existing statutes suffice, or whether administrative sanctions or other control devices are likely to afford greater protection than new criminal statutes. Legislatures do not always have time within the pressures of a legislative session to spot duplications and contradictions in proposed legislation. The establishment of law review commissions can remedy this problem.

**The Commission recommends that States create permanent criminal law review commissions to review all legislative proposals bearing criminal penalties in order to ascertain whether a need for them actually exists. These review commissions should propose draft statutes for legislative consideration whenever functional gaps in criminal law enforcement appear.**

The membership of the review commission should reflect the experience of all branches of the legal profession, corrections, law enforcement, and community leadership. Placement of the review commission within the legislative or executive branch should be made in view of each State's governmental and political needs. Freedom to issue objective opinions without excessive political pressure is important.

Those who revise criminal codes should be warned of the potential danger to the revision process posed by emotional issues such as abortion or the death penalty. Because criminal code revision efforts too frequently founder on one or two such issues that may be quite incidental to the overall revision effort, States should consider these issues in legislation that is introduced separately from legislation calling for criminal code revision. A more complete discussion of this area is contained in Chapter 13 of the Commission's *Report on the Criminal Justice System*.

# Conclusion

The reforms suggested in this chapter will benefit the criminal justice system and society in general.

The reforms will help reduce court caseloads; they will lessen the unnecessary costs of futile incarceration; and they simultaneously will address the underlying behavioral problems associated with the crimes discussed in this chapter.

The Commission therefore recommends that implementation of the recommendations presented here be carried out by State legislatures on a priority basis.

# Chapter IX

# Handguns in American Society

Americans are accumulating handguns at a rate estimated at more than 1.8 million weapons a year.[1] The national arsenal of privately owned handguns is estimated to be as high as 30 million.[2]

Nowhere in the world is the private ownership of handguns, on a per capita basis, as high as in the United States. Similarly, nowhere among the industrial nations of the world is the criminal homicide rate as high as in the United States.

In the United States, during 1971 alone, approximately 9,-000 Americans,[3] including 94 police officers,[4] were murdered with handguns. In 1971, more than 600 accidental deaths resulted from the improper use of handguns.[5]

[1] Data received from the Bureau of Alcohol, Tobacco, and Firearms, Department of the Treasury.

[2] George Newton and Franklin Zimring, *Firearms and Violence in American Life*, A Staff Report to the National Commission on the Causes and Prevention of Violence (1969), p. 6.

[3] Federal Bureau of Investigation, *Uniform Crime Reports—1971*, pp. 7, 8.

[4] *Ibid.*, p. 44.

[5] Estimates made by the National Safety Council from data contained in "Accidental Facts, 1972."

In the past few years, handguns have also had a searing effect on American political life. In 1968, Senator Robert F. Kennedy of New York was killed by a handgun. In 1972, Governor George C. Wallace of Alabama was wounded and crippled by a handgun. Early in 1973, Senator John C. Stennis of Mississippi was wounded seriously by a handgun.

Not surprisingly, the American public is concerned about gun control. The polls show that the vast majority of American citizens favor firearm control. As long as modern polling has existed, the polls have shown majority support for firearms control. Never have less than two-thirds of those polled favored gun control.[6] Most recently, in a 1972 Gallup Poll, 71 percent of all persons polled, and 61 percent of all gun owners polled, indicated they were in favor of gun control.[7]

This citizen concern has been recognized by Congress and by the President. In 1968, Congress enacted the Gun Control Act; and since taking office, President Nixon has expressed his support for legislation banning the possession of cheap handguns.

For these reasons, and because the members of the Commission are dedicated to the goal of reducing crime and violence in America, the Commission believes that it would be derelict in its duties if it did not address the vital issue of handguns in today's society.

## Prohibition on Handguns

The Commission believes that the violence, fear, suffering, and loss caused by the use of handguns must be stopped by firm and decisive action. The Commission therefore recommends that, no later than January 1, 1983, each State should take the following action:

• The private possession of handguns should be prohibited for all persons other than law enforcement and military personnel.

• Manufacture and sale of handguns should be terminated.

• Existing handguns should be acquired by States.

• Handguns held by private citizens as collector's items should be modified and rendered inoperative.

The recommendations of the Commission apply only to handguns, a term which for the purposes of this chapter refers to a firearm designed to be fired with one hand. The

[6] Hazel Erskine, "The Polls: Gun Control." *Public Opinion Quarterly* (Fall 1972), p. 455.
[7] *Ibid.*

term also includes the personal possession or control of a combination of parts from which a handgun can be assembled. The term includes both pistols (sometimes referred to as automatics) and revolvers, but does not include antique firearms.

The Commission believes that laws currently in force regarding rifles and long guns require no change. The Commission does not wish to curtail the use of rifles and long guns by hunters and other legitimate users.

Further, the Commission makes recommendations for State and local units of government only, not for the Federal Government. Congress is on record on the subject of firearms; it has passed some controls and has encouraged States and local units of government to enact their own laws and adopt their own ordinances. It remains for the State and local government to address the problems surrounding the public possession of handguns.

In an effort to prohibit possession of handguns, the Commission encourages States to examine and implement all recommendations proposed in this chapter. The recommendations are intended to be an operative package.

Some States, however, may want to implement the recommendations in stages. They are urged to do so in the order in which they are presented in this chapter. Further, some States may already have taken steps proposed in the recommendations. In keeping with these local variances, the Commission urges each State to work out a combination of steps best suited to complete control of handguns.

Toward this end, it is the recommendation of the Commission that States study their present laws regulating handguns and take measures to insure that existing laws are enforced fully and are adhered to scrupulously by their citizens. Next, the Commission recommends that the penalties attached to committing a crime with the use of a handgun be increased. Further, to safeguard the lives of police officers, States should enact stop-and-frisk laws to authorize search of persons and automobiles when the officer has reasonable suspicion to believe that he is in danger due to a suspect's possession of and access to a weapon.

As an additional step, the Commission recommends that States prohibit the manufacture, importation, or sale of all handguns other than those for use by law enforcement or military personnel. States should also establish agencies authorized to purchase handguns from private individuals for a just price, and further authorized to modify rare and valuable guns that owners wish to retain as collector's items. Finally, States should prohibit the private possession of all handguns other than those which have been designated as collector's items and rendered inoperative.

# Why Handguns Must Be Controlled by the States

To maintain an orderly society, a government must regulate certain of its citizens' acts. Rights and freedoms cannot exist without recognition that one person's rights exist only to the degree they do not infringe on those of another.

Such a balance must be maintained in the possession and use of handguns. The Commission believes that private use and possession of handguns infringes on the right of the American public to be free from violence and death caused by the use of handguns. Public welfare does not permit the civilian possession of machineguns, flame throwers, handgrenades, bombs, or sawed-off shotguns; neither can it any longer tolerate the private possession of handguns.

Removing the handgun from American society will not eliminate crime and violence, but documentation shows there is a strong correlation between the number of privately owned handguns and the corresponding use of guns in crimes of violence.

Nationally, the handgun is the principal weapon used in criminal homicide. Reported crime statistics for 1971 indicate that 51 percent of all murders and nonnegligent manslaughters were committed with the use of a handgun.[8]

Handguns are also an important instrument in other crimes of violence. Possibly a third of all robberies and one-fifth of all aggravated assaults are committed with handguns.[9]

Countries that have restrictive regulations on the private possession of handguns have considerably lower homicide rates than does the United States. For example, in Tokyo, Japan, a congested metropolis of more than 11 million people, and where it is illegal to own, possess, or manufacture handguns, there was only one handgun homicide reported in 1971.[10] In contrast, during the same time period, Los Angeles

[8] *UCR—1971*, p. 8.
[9] Newton and Zimring, *Op. cit.*, pp. 70, 73.
[10] Data received from the Metropolitan Police Department, Tokyo, Japan.

County, Calif., with a population of just over 7 million, reported 308 handgun homicides.[11]

Cultural differences account for some of this disparity but this explanation alone cannot account for the wide difference in homicide rates nor for the fact that Japanese statistics reflect a consistent yearly decrease in the number of crimes committed with firearms since the 1964 national prohibition against all firearms.[12]

In the past 10 years in the United States, 722 police officers were murdered while performing in the line of duty; 73 percent of them were murdered with handguns. During the same 10 years, nine police officers were killed by handguns in Great Britain, 26 in Japan, and in France, "not enough to make a percentage." These countries all have stringent handgun control laws.[13]

The Commission is aware that many persons keep firearms in their homes because they fear for the lives and safety of themselves and their families. It should be known, however, that many "gun" crimes are family killings—not the "stranger" crimes where protection is needed. In 1971, one-fourth of all murders were "intrafamily" in which a family member seized the weapon at hand. When a gun was seized, the fatality rate was five times higher than by an attack with any other weapon.[14]

Further, the self-protection afforded by a handgun often is illusory. Although many handguns are acquired to defend family and property from intruders, a handgun in the home is more likely to kill a member of the family than it is to provide lifesaving protection from burglars and robbers. A survey conducted in Detroit, Mich., indicated that more people are killed in household handgun accidents in 1 year than die as a result of home burglaries and robberies in 4½ years.[15]

[11] Telephone Survey of Los Angeles County, Calif., Police Departments (conducted by the Los Angeles County Sheriff's Department, 1972).

[12] Data received from the Japanese National Police Agency.

[13] National Conference of Christians and Jews, *Hot Line* (November 1972), p. 6.

[14] Newton and Zimring, *Op. cit.*, p. 44.

[15] *Ibid.*, p. 64.

# Recommendations

In the following section the Commission sets out its detailed recommendations for the control of handguns. Each recommendation is followed by explanatory notes.

## Enforcement of Current Laws

**The Commission recommends that existing Federal, State, and local laws relating to handguns be strenuously enforced. It further recommends that States undertake publicity campaigns to educate the public fully about laws regulating the private possession of handguns.**

Federal laws, if utilized, present a sound legislative base for control of handguns. The Federal Gun Control Act of 1968 (18 U.S.C. 900–928) encourages States to enact their own legislation in the area of firearms, and provides two key statutory incentives to do so.

First, Congress provides assistance for State and local gun control by prohibiting interstate gun transactions by any person in violation of local laws. In section 922(b)(2) of the Gun Control Act, Congress provided:

> (b) It shall be unlawful for any licensed importer, licensed manufacturer, licensed dealer, or licensed collector to sell or deliver—
>
> (2) any firearm or ammunition to any person in any State where the purchase or possession by such person of such firearm or ammunition would be in violation of any State law or any published ordinance applicable at the place of sale, delivery or other disposition, unless the licensee knows or has reasonable cause to believe that the purchase or possession would not be in violation of such State law or such published ordinance.

Federal law becomes a seal at the border of the State, prohibiting licensed importers, manufacturers, dealers, or collectors from selling or delivering firearms to such persons in violation of State law or local ordinance.

Second, Congress encourages States to enact their own firearms legislation. Congress said:

> No provision of this chapter shall be construed as indicating an intent on the part of the Congress to oc-

cupy the field in which such provision operates to the exclusion of the law of any State on the same subject matter, unless there is a direct and positive conflict between such provision and the law of the State so that the two cannot be reconciled or consistently stand together.

Thus, States may legislate freely in the area of gun control, and only when Federal and State law are in direct conflict will the doctrine of Federal preemption come into play.

The Gun Control Act of 1968 contains other provisions critical to an effective national policy of handgun control. These are:

• A ban on interstate transactions of firearms and ammunition, and a prohibition against any person receiving firearms and ammunition from out of State; licensed dealers would be exempt from this provision.

• The requirement that a buyer submit a sworn statement attesting to his competence and setting out the essential facts of the transaction in interstate mail order shipment and receipt of firearms.

• Prohibition against sale of rifles, shotguns, or ammunition to persons under 18, and of handguns to persons under 21.

• Establishment of licensing provisions for manufacturers, dealers, importers, and collectors.

• The requirement that several types of firearms, including short-barreled shotguns and machine guns, be registered with the Federal Government.

• Prohibition of sale of firearms to convicted felons, fugitives from justice, or persons under indictment for crimes punishable by more than 1-year imprisonment.

Many States and units of local government have statutes or ordinances that make it illegal with varying limitations to carry a handgun on or about the person or in a vehicle, and in some areas a handgun can be carried only by a person possessing either a special permit and/or registration.

The Commission firmly believes that the enforcement of these existing laws—Federal, State, and local—would substantially reduce the availability of handguns to criminals and incompetents, and effect a reduction in the level of violence in America today.

The Commission, however, does not include current laws dealing with mandatory minimum sentences within the scope of this recommendation.

The Commission believes that some of these laws are inconsistent with current knowledge about incarceration and its effect on rehabilitation. Also, juries are sometimes reluctant to convict a defendant if they must in effect impose an exceedingly long prison term. For these reasons, the Commission recommends instead prison sentences up to 25 years but with no mandatory minimum.

The public should also be educated fully about the laws in force through State publicity campaigns, through enlisting the aid of print, radio, and television media, and by making information easily available to interested citizens and citizen groups.

## Penalties for Crimes Committed with a Handgun

**The Commission urges enactment of State legislation providing for an extended prison term with a maximum term of 25 years for committing a felony while in possession of a handgun.**

Because of its ease of portability and concealment, the handgun is by far the principal weapon of criminal gun use. Although nationally handguns constitute only one-fourth of all privately owned firearms, they account for more than three-fourths of all criminal gun violence. If the public ever is to experience a feeling of relative safety and well-being, there must be positive and effective measures enacted to remove and eliminate the constant threat of the criminal use of handguns.

The Commission does not intend that legislatures mandate minimum sentences for those committing a felony while in possession of a handgun. Rather, this recommendation provides that extended prison sentences may be imposed if there are circumstances warranting their application.

This proposal allowing for increased prison sentences is consistent with the rest of the Commission's recommendations. In its *Report on Corrections,* the Commission recommends against incarceration beyond terms of 5 years except for dangerous and repeating offenders, for whom terms of up to 25 years may be appropriate. The Commission believes that individuals who perpetrate felonies while in possession of a handgun clearly fall within the defined exceptions, and should be subject to the imposition of an extended sentence.

The benefits to be derived from enactment of legislation providing extended sentences for persons possessing firearms while commiting felonies are twofold. First, the gun-wielding criminal would be removed from society for a substantial time period; and, second, many criminals, considering the risk too great, would be dissuaded from the continued use and possession of handguns.

Most Americans appear to agree with this approach. On February 16, 1969, the Gallup Poll conducted a survey using the following question:

> It has been suggested that anyone who commits a crime with a gun be given double the regular sentence. Does this sound like a good idea to you, or a poor idea?

The answers indicated that 58 percent of respondents thought that it would be a good idea.[16]

## Stop-and-Frisk Searches

**The Commission urges the enactment of State legislation providing for police discretion in stop-and-frisk searches of persons and searches of automobiles for illegal handguns.**

The fourth amendment provides that "The right of people to be secure in their persons, homes, papers, and effects, against unreasonable searches and seizures shall not be violated."

The Commission believes that police discretion to stop and frisk persons and to search automobiles for handguns is reasonable in situations where there are articulable reasons to believe that a police officer's life is in danger. In suspicious circumstances, officers, for their own safety, must have the right to search the person and portion on the vehicle accessible to the occupants for deadly weapons, especially handguns.

In *Firearms and Violence in American Life*, a staff report to the National Commission on the Causes and Prevention of Violence, the problem is stated as follows:

> Firearms are not only the most deadly instrument of attack, but also the most versatile. Firearms make attacks possible that simply would not occur without firearms. They permit attacks at greater range and from positions of better concealment than other weapons. They also permit attacks by persons physically or psychologically unable to overpower their victim through violent physical contact. It is not surpris-

[16] Erskine, *Op. cit.*, p. 468.

ing, therefore, that firearms are virtually the only weapon used in killing police officers.

The policeman, himself armed, is capable of defending against many forms of violent attack. He is trained and equipped to ward off attacks with blunt instruments, knives, or fists, and his firearm is usually sufficient to overcome his attacker, even if surprised at close range. It is, therefore, the capacity of firearms to kill instantly and from a distance that threatens the lives of police officers in the United States.[17]

Stop-and-frisk legislation should include broad police powers to search for weapons where strong articulable suspicion exists to indicate that the suspect is engaged in criminal conduct and there is suspicion that he is armed. This is consistent with the holding of the U.S. Supreme Court in *Terry* v. *Ohio*, 88 S.Ct. 1868 (1968).

Speaking for the court in the *Terry* decision, Chief Justice Earl Warren stated:

> The crux of this case, however, is not the propriety of Officer McFadden's taking steps to investigate petitioner's suspicious behavior, but rather, whether there was justification for McFadden's invasion of Terry's personal security by searching him for weapons in the course of that investigation. We are now concerned with more than the governmental interest in investigating crime; in addition, there is the more immediate interest of the police officer in taking steps to assure himself that the person with whom he is dealing is not armed with a weapon that could unexpectedly and fatally be used against him. Certainly it would be unreasonable to require that police officers take unnecessary risks in the performance of their duties. American criminals have a long tradition of armed violence, and every year in this country many law enforcement officers are killed in the line of duty, and thousands more are wounded.
>
> Virtually all of these deaths and a substantial portion of the injuries are inflicted with guns and knives.
>
> In view of these facts, we cannot blind ourselves to the need for law enforcement officers to protect themselves and other prospective victims of violence in sit-

[17] Newton and Zimring, *Op. cit.*

uations where they may lack probable cause for an arrest. When an officer is justified in believing that the individual whose suspicious behavior he is investigating at close range is armed and presently dangerous to the officer or to others, it would appear to be clearly unreasonable to deny the officer the power to take necessary measures to determine whether the person is in fact carrying a weapon and to neutralize the threat of physical harm.

Justice John M. Harlan, concurring, stated:

> If the State of Ohio were to provide that police officers could, on articulable suspicion less than probable cause, forcibly frisk and disarm persons thought to be carrying concealed weapons, I would have little doubt that action taken pursuant to such authority would be constitutionally reasonable.[18]

## Prohibiting the Manufacture of Handguns

The Commission urges the enactment of State legislation prohibiting the manufacture of handguns, their parts, and ammunition within the State, except for sale to law enforcement agencies or for military use.

Effective immediately upon the enactment of the legislation, and under penalty of fine or imprisonment or both, all manufacturers within the State should be required to cease production of handguns, their parts, and ammunition, other than those designated or destined for sale to law enforcement agencies or to the Federal or State government for use by military personnel.

Any attempt to eliminate the private possession of handguns should necessarily begin with obstruction at the primary source, the firearms manufacturer. The usefulness of handguns would be greatly lessened by the elimination of the availability of handgun ammunition.

Legislation should be effective immediately in order to preclude the possibility of stockpiling handguns and ammunition.

The Commission urges the enactment of State legislation prohibiting the importation into a State of all handguns, their parts, and ammunition.

Effective immediately upon enactment of the legislation, and under penalty of fine or imprisonment or both, imports of all handguns, their parts, and ammunition should be pro-

[18] See also *Adams* v. *Williams*, 92 S. Ct. 1921 (1972).

hibited. Importation of handguns for law enforcement and military agencies would be permitted.

This legislation, when combined with the preceding section prohibiting the manufacture of firearms, their parts, and ammunition, would eliminate all legal sources of handguns and ammunition in a State except where the gun is already in existence in the State.

Effective enforcement of statutes prohibiting the manufacture or importation into a State of firearms or ammunition would restrict the handgun problem to those already in the hands of citizens. Of all handguns, law enforcement officials consider the so-called "Saturday night special" to be the most common and most dangerous in criminal use. This is a handgun cheaply and quickly cast in metal; it has a relatively short life span and, with normal attrition, should disappear eventually from use.

## Prohibiting the Sale of Handguns

The Commission urges the enactment of State legislation prohibiting the sale of handguns, their parts, and ammunition to other than law enforcement agencies or Federal or State governments for military purposes.

The Commission believes that any legislation to eliminate the private possession of handguns should require an immediate cessation of all handgun sales. Although a ban on production and importation of handguns and their parts would eliminate the source of any new handguns, there is a vast number of used handguns available for sale to the public. This legislation would eliminate the potential use of these second-hand weapons. Perhaps more significantly, it would also preclude any tendency to stockpile handguns in anticipation of the prohibition of their possession.

## Establishing a State Gun Control Agency

The Commission urges the enactment of State legislation establishing and funding a State agency authorized to purchase all voluntarily surrendered handguns, and further authorized to register and modify handguns to be retained by private citizens as curios, museum pieces, or collector's items.

The Commission believes that the best way to obtain compliance with any prohibitive regulation is to offer a reasonable and practical alternative.

Many handguns presently in private possession represent a substantial financial investment, and the possessor would have an understandable reluctance to forfeit possession without receiving remuneration. The convenience of having easy access to a certain and proper buyer, willing to pay a fair price, would tend to discourage efforts to negotiate private sales, and at the same time would offer a positive motivation to comply with the law.

The program can be effective only if all persons, regardless of social or economic position, are aware of the existence of the program, the location of the purchasing centers, and the time constraints involved. All communication media should be encouraged to inform the public about the program to exchange handguns for monetary compensation.

Utilization of this agency should be voluntary. Purchasing centers should operate with the single determination to achieve the goal of substantially reducing the number of handguns in private possession. If, because of the absence of the threat of prosecution, a stolen handgun or one that had been used in a crime were forfeited, and thus eliminated from potential use in another crime, then certainly it would be to the benefit of society.

Some handgun owners have collections that are both rare and valuable; the Commission does not believe these handguns should be forfeited, or the collections diminished. Personnel at the purchasing centers should be authorized, upon a sworn statement that the handgun was intended for use as a curio, museum piece, or collector's item, to modify the firing mechanism to render the weapon inoperable as a firearm. Modified weapons should be fully registered and identified, with a copy of the registration constituting authorization for possession. Any future alteration to the firing mechanism enabling the handgun to be used again as a firearm would result in a forfeiture of the authorization for possession and subject the owner to prosecution for violation of any possession laws then in effect.

## Prohibiting the Private Possession of Handguns

The Commission further urges the enactment of State legislation not later than January 1, 1983, prohibiting the private possession of handguns after that date.

Effective on January 1, 1983, and under penalty of fine or imprisonment or both, possession of a handgun should be made illegal for any person other than law enforcement or military personnel, or those persons authorized to manufacture or deal in handguns for use by law enforcement or the military.

All of the arguments against prohibiting the private possession of handguns become, by comparison, subordinate to the death, tragedy, and violence that abound in the absence of such legislation.

# Conclusion

The Commission hopes that its position on handguns will be well received and widely supported by the American people. It recognizes, however, that there may be some initial opposition from citizens who have strong convictions in favor of private possession of all kinds of firearms, including handguns. The Commission respects the opinions of these persons and urges a full airing of all views, and open and thorough debate on the handgun issue in public forums, the press, and other appropriate places at the State and local levels.

It would be easy for the Commission to sidestep this issue altogether and to limit its recommendations to the popular and uncontroversial.

After lengthy discussion and careful deliberation, however, the Commission concludes that it has no choice other than to urge the enactment of the recommendations proposed in this chapter. The Commission believes that the American people are willing to make the personal sacrifices necessary to insure that the level of crime and violence in this Nation is diminished.

# Chapter X
# A National Commitment to Change

This Commission has sought to formulate a series of standards, recommendations, priorities, and goals to modernize and unify the criminal justice system, and to provide a yardstick for measuring progress. Its purpose has been the reduction of crime.

But the Commission's work is only the first step. It remains now for citizens, professionals, and policy makers to mount the major effort by implementing the standards proposed in the six volumes of the Commission's work.

A beginning of that effort was made at the National Conference on Criminal Justice, which brought together more than 1,500 State and local leaders, criminal justice practitioners, and concerned laymen, for a major meeting and discussion of the Commission's work. That conference was held in Washington, D.C., on January 23–26, 1973.

This chapter describes some of the ways in which States and local jurisdictions can continue and expand the implementation effort. It contains, among others, proposals for:
• Efforts by the Federal Government to encourage implementation of the Commission's standards and goals at the State and local levels.
• Methods by which State and local governments can exam-

ine the standards and goals concept with the aim of possible implementation.

• Contributions that professional, civic, and educational groups can make to develop support for the standards and goals.

Each jurisdiction will, of course, analyze the reports and apply goals and standards in its own way and in the context of its own needs.

This Commission does not pretend to have the authority, responsibility, or competence to mandate the method of implementation of the goals and standards. Nor is there need to enact legislation making compliance with the standards a prerequisite to receipt of Federal funds or a requirement on the States in any other form. Such Federal control is not consistent with American practices in law enforcement.

# Federal Encouragement

While Federal endorsement of these standards is not recommended, there is still much the Federal Government, particularly the Law Enforcement Assistance Administration (LEAA), can do in translating the Commission's work into action.

## Permanent Advisory Committee

The Commission believes that the effort it has begun should be carried on by a permanent group of citizens which can monitor implementation of the standards over the long term. The Commission believes that the Federal Government, through LEAA, should continue to perform a catalytic role in this regard.

**The Commission recommends that LEAA establish an Advisory Committee on Criminal Justice Standards and Goals to support the standards and goals implementation effort.**

This committee would provide continuing guidance, information exchange, background information, and evaluation to all jurisdictions. The group should consist of private citizens, government leaders, criminal justice professionals, and community crime prevention practitioners.

The Commission recommends that the Advisory Committee perform the following functions:

• Assess progress by States in implementing the standards.

• Evaluate progress by LEAA in using the standards in its review and approval process, its discretionary grant process, and its research and development programs conducted by the National Institute of Law Enforcement and Criminal Justice.

● Assess standards in terms of their soundness, applicability, success; decide on the necessity of eliminating unsound standards; add new ones; and refine those where experience has dictated the necessity to do so.

● Provide an annual evaluation and information exchange.

● Provide further implementation recommendations.

● Provide encouragement to States to adopt the standards.

The Advisory Committee could be supported by a small permanent staff of professionals and support personnel. The cost of forming and maintaining the staff should be met by LEAA and the staff should be located in LEAA headquarters.

The staff would provide continuing guidance, information exchange, and evaluation to the Advisory Committee members and to all jurisdictions. It could provide background information to aid the States in implementing standards.

## LEAA Block Grants or Revenue Sharing Payments

The Commission believes that LEAA should use the block grant award process (or the revenue sharing payment process if law enforcement revenue sharing is enacted) to monitor implementation of its standards and goals. This process involves comprehensive plans that are developed by each State with the assistance of LEAA funds. These comprehensive plans are required to be submitted to LEAA. The purpose of the planning phase is to encourage States to plan their own priorities for crime reduction.

The Commission recognizes that LEAA, under its present authority and under the proposed Law Enforcement Revenue Sharing Act of 1973, does not and will not have authority to require States to adopt the standards and goals. Under present and proposed authority, however, LEAA can review and comment on the comprehensive plans.

Accordingly, the Commission recommends that LEAA use its review of the comprehensive plans and award of grants to inquire as to how States propose to use the Commission's standards in their planning process. If a plan does not address the standards and the State asks for LEAA assistance, LEAA should guide the State in making use of the standards.

## LEAA Discretionary Grants

The Commission believes that the discretionary grant process affords LEAA a special opportunity to encourage States to consider implementation of the standards and goals. These grants are awarded by LEAA at its discretion for innovative and meritorious State and local projects that otherwise would not receive LEAA grant funds. LEAA is authorized to award 15 percent of its action funds as discretionary grants.

The Commission believes that LEAA could require discretionary grantees to explain how their programs relate to the standards and goals. Grantees could be asked to formulate updated standards as a requirement of applying for the grant. When standards do not exist in the area in question, the applicant should be required to formulate new standards.

# Action at the State and Local Levels

With over 500 standards on such diverse subjects as referral criteria for youth services bureaus, privacy and security requirements for information systems, and bilingual capabilities for police departments, State planning agencies (SPA's) and other criminal justice agencies wishing to use intelligently the Commission's reports will have to set priorities among the many standards.

## Getting the Facts

Priority-setting must begin with an assessment of a State or locality's major crime problems and the criminal justice system's response to those problems. Program funding decisions may change drastically depending on whether the crime problem given top priority is white collar crime, burglary, or various types of violent crime.

The Commission recommends, as a first step in implementing standards and goals, that each jurisdiction analyze its own unique crime problems. Such an analysis should result in the establishment of quantifiable and time-phased goals for the reduction of priority crimes, such as those adopted by this Commission. Once this has been accomplished, an assessment of the Commission's standards and recommendations should be made in terms of their individual impact on the selected priority crimes.

## Setting Minimum Statewide Standards

SPA's bear a special responsibility for the formation of minimum statewide standards. If SPA's are to be agents of reform, they must provide incentives for desirable practices and avoid subsidizing clearly undesirable ones.

In Maryland the Police Standards Committee of the SPA in 1972 held hearings throughout the state on the desired quantity and quality of police services. The standards initially established included requirements for 7-day-a-week, 24-hour-a-day services, minimum starting salaries for sworn personnel, compliance with FBI Uniform Crime Reporting procedures, and a minimum of 10 full-time sworn officers per department. Police agencies in Maryland must meet these standards to be eligible for funding assistance in the form of Safe Streets subgrants and other State grants.

While most SPA's have not set standards for the types of operating agencies that might be eligible for Safe Streets assistance, several States have taken actions similar to Maryland's in the police area or plan to do so in the immediate future. The Commission urges SPA's not to stop with police services, but to adopt standards for courts, corrections, and prevention efforts as well.

Standard-setting efforts should be limited to those human resources, physical resources, and management and operations requirements that are clearly essential to the achievement of the goals of the criminal justice system. SPA's may have to resist the temptation to be too detailed in their standard-setting efforts. The Commission does not believe all of its standards are of such importance that they should be made rigid conditions for grants. It does believe, however, that there are elements readily identifiable in certain standards that are essential to any effective criminal justice system, and these elements serve as the basis for minimum standards for funding assistance.

## Evaluating Programs

One of the most striking characteristics of present criminal justice operations is how little is known about what works and what does not work. The Commission at the outset of its effort undertook a survey of innovative criminal justice projects throughout the country. The survey utilized news clippings, articles in professional journals, and Federal grant applications which described potentially successful programs. Commission staff members queried more than 400 agencies for information.

The agency responses, although often enthusiastic, were nonetheless not particularly useful. The outcome of some projects was described in letters and not formally set forth in documents suitable for public dissemination. Many evaluation reports contained ill-defined objectives providing no specific standards by which to judge the project. Claims of success were generally couched in subjective and intuitive statements of accomplishments.

Even when quantitative measures were used, they were frequently not accompanied by analysis and by adequate explanation.

The Commission's surveys provided direct evidence that program and project evaluation is not considered important by most public officials. The Commission believes that this lack of emphasis is unfortunate. Although many of the Commission's standards are based on a solid foundation of previous knowledge, others are more experimental. As criminal justice agencies begin putting the Commission's standards into practice, serious attention must be given to evaluating how well they contribute to the goals of the criminal justice system and particular agencies.

**In implementing important standards or groups of standards, the Commission urges that evaluation plans be designed as an integral part of all projects.**

In its *Report on the Criminal Justice System,* the Commission underscores appropriate evaluation strategies in an appendix on "Program Measurement and Evaluation." It commends that section to the reader in regard to evaluation of programs in general.

## Other State Implementation Measures

As noted in Chapter 3, honest disagreement in the criminal justice system is common and sometimes severe. Reaching consensus on basic issues presented in the Commission's report will be difficult, but necessary. The Commission believes that acceptance of its work may be reached through publicity, education, and analysis programs initiated by Governors, State supreme court chief justices, and SPA's. These programs include:

• State sponsorship of workshops in the State's regions and major urban areas attended by individuals from all criminal justice components.

• Publicizing the report and encouraging and supporting conferences or workshops sponsored by private voluntary organizations.

• Encouraging and supporting conferences or workshops under the sponsorship of the several criminal justice components: the judiciary council, the corrections department or association, and police groups and associations.

• Encouraging and supporting legislative hearings, debate, and legislation, particularly on those standards requiring legislative action.

# Professional, Civic, and Educational Support

The Commission believes that substantial assistance for implementing its standards and goals can be obtained from a variety of concerned groups.

**The Commission recommends that national professional and civic groups and appropriate university interests support implementation of the standards and goals.**

It is hoped that these groups will place discussion of the standards and goals high on their agendas and that their conclusions, recommendations, and support will be transmitted to State and local decisionmakers.

The Commission believes that national and local professional and civic associations can play a particularly valuable role in stimulating implementation of standards. Through their initiative and leadership, these groups can exert considerable influence on standards implementation.

The associations and their members have contributed much to the formulation of standards, but the magnitude of the task of implementing them demands the energy to educate and encourage community leaders and criminal justice system practitioners to adopt the standards, and legislators to provide the necessary resources and authorizations where required.

Perhaps the best existing model for professional association participation is the effort of the American Bar Association (ABA) to stimulate adoption of their recent Standards for Criminal Justice. The ABA has provided speakers for a diversity of citizen and professional groups. It has provided educational materials for implementation. It has planned, programed, and participated in State judicial conferences, sessions, and workshops. It has cooperated in joint endeavors with other criminal justice groups and has pursued an active program both to enlist young lawyers and to stimulate law school participation. With both private and LEAA funds, it has assisted implementation efforts in several pilot States, and future plans call for the establishment of programs for measuring impact and evaluating the practical benefits of implementation.

The Commission suggests that all professional associations consider developing programs of a similar nature and that LEAA, within the limits of its capabilities, provide funding to the best of these programs.

Colleges and universities should play an effective role in standards and implementation. Law schools, universities, criminal justice departments, and institutes should find the standards valuable for inclusion in their curriculums, seminars, workshops, and research projects. These efforts can play a central role in training both young students and more experienced practitioners who can carry the implementation message back to their agencies. They can also contribute to improving the standards, drafting model codes, and evaluating the impact and efficacy of standards as they are implemented.

Finally, the Commission urges the National Governors' Conference, the Regional Governors' Conference, the National League of Cities, and the National Association of Counties to call on each State and unit of local government to review its criminal justice system and to compare that system with the standards developed by the National Advisory Commission with a view toward making such changes as each State or unit of local government deems appropriate and desirable.

# Cost of Crime Reduction

The Commission examined the issue of the dollar cost of implementing its standards and recommendations. It recognizes that for all States and units of local government, the cost of implementing these standards and recommendations could be substantial, at least in the short term.

Nonetheless, the Commission urges elected officials, administrators, and planners to accept the heavy responsibility of presenting the taxpaying public with the facts of the situation and winning the public support necessary to raise the funds. The Commission believes that voting and taxpaying citizens in all jurisdictions will vigorously support sound programs of crime reduction of the sort proposed in this report.

In addition, the Commission points out that some action elements in its plan will save money. Major efficiencies and savings can be effected by implementing new administrative approaches proposed by the Commission. Programs of diversion of individuals out of the criminal justice process may result in actual savings. Indeed, some standards and recommendations probably can be implemented without any cost at all.

The Commission points out, too, that its proposals were developed in large part by working practitioners. These are not "blue-sky" recommendations dreamed up in an atmosphere of utopian unreality. They are the solid and often field-tested proposals of professionals in the criminal justice system.

In the last analysis, however, the Commission believes that the cost of crime reduction must be weighed against the cost of crime itself. New techniques of measurement are beginning only now to tell the American people how much crime they actually endure, crime that takes its toll in human lives, in personal injury and suffering, in stolen money and property. This cost must reach substantial levels in all jurisdictions.

Less crime will mean fewer victims of crime and will result in genuine, demonstrable savings, both to potential victims and to the whole society.

# Postscript

On January 23, 1973, the Administrator of the Law Enforcement Assistance Administration convened the first National Conference on Criminal Justice at which 1,500 representatives of the criminal justice system and the public reviewed the Commission's work.

A major objective of the conference was to initiate State and local criminal justice reform using the Commission's standards as a vehicle for discussion.

At this writing, the initial steps toward action on the Commission's recommendations are being taken in many States. A post-conference survey by LEAA revealed that at least 35 States plan to have seminars or conferences on the Commission's reports. A number of these States have either established or are in the process of establishing State commissions and task forces to review the standards of the Commission.

Finally, the National Governors' Conference in June 1973 adopted the following policy statement:

"The National Governors' Conference commends the National Advisory Commission on Criminal Justice Standards and Goals for its efforts in developing a comprehensive and detailed series of goals, standards, and priorities for reducing crime in America.

"The National Governors' Conference endorses the goals of reducing in 10 years the rate of high-fear crime by 50 percent from its 1973 level. As used in this context, high-fear crime refers to homicide, rape, aggravated assault, and robbery committed by people who are strangers to their victims. High-fear crimes also include all burglaries.

"In order to reach this goal, the National Governors' Conference calls on every State and unit of local government in that State to evaluate immediately its criminal justice system, to compare its criminal justice system with the standards and goals developed by the National Advisory Commission, and make such changes in their criminal justice system as are deemed necessary and appropriate by that State or unit of local government."

# Commission Members

Russell W. Peterson was elected Governor of Delaware in 1968.

Prior to his election, Governor Peterson spent 26 years with the DuPont Company in Delaware, advancing through a variety of management posts in research, manufacturing, and sales. In 1963 he was named to organize and head a new division responsible for launching the DuPont Company into new fields. He also served as Chairman of the Board of the Textile Research Institute in Princeton, N.J.

Governor Peterson has taken part in numerous community and political activities. In 1961 he led the Kiwanis Club of Delaware to organize the Three-S-Citizens Campaign against crime.

For his work in environment areas, especially the passage of legislation to ban oil refineries from the Delaware coast, he was named "Conservationist of the Year" by the National Wildlife Federation in 1971 and was given the Gold Medal of the World Wildlife Fund.

Governor Peterson has made many changes in the management of State government, including the conversion of Delaware's executive branch from a commission to a cabinet form of government. He was National Chairman of the Education Commission of the States during 1971–1972. He also served as Chairman of the Crime Reduction Committee of the National Governors' Conference (1971–1972).

Governor Peterson graduated from the University of Wisconsin with B.S. and Ph.D. degrees.

### Peter J. Pitchess

Peter J. Pitchess is currently serving his fourth 4-year term as Sheriff of Los Angeles County.

Sheriff Pitchess served 12 years as a special agent with the Federal Bureau of Investigation. He was appointed Undersheriff of Los Angeles County in 1953 and was elected Sheriff following the retirement of his predecessor in 1958.

Sheriff Pitchess has participated in many civic, professional, and fraternal organizations among which are: Past President and member of the Executive Committee of the California Peace Officers' Association; California State Sheriffs' Association; Past President of Los Angeles County Peace Officers' Association.

He holds B.S. and J.D. degrees from the University of Utah.

### Richard R. Andersen

Richard R. Andersen was appointed Chief of Police of Omaha, Neb., on Nov. 1, 1967.

Chief Andersen joined the Police Division in 1951, becoming Deputy Chief in 1965. Chief Andersen has served in all phases of the police service, with a majority of his time in rank served within the Detective Bureau.

Chief Andersen attended Nebraska University, and graduated from the University of Omaha with a degree in Law Enforcement and Education. He is also a graduate of the first police management course held at the School of Business Administration at Harvard University in 1966.

### Forrest H. Anderson

Forrest H. Anderson was elected Governor of Montana in 1968. He did not seek reelection in 1972.

Governor Anderson began his political career by serving two terms as a member of the Montana State House of Representatives in 1943 and 1945. Shortly thereafter he was elected as Lewis and Clark County Attorney. He was elected to the Montana Supreme Court in 1952 and served as an Associate Justice until 1956, when he won election to the Office of Attorney General. He served as Attorney General until his nomination for the governorship in 1968.

The Governor was educated at the University of Montana at Missoula and the Columbus University Law School in Washington, D.C.

### Sylvia Bacon

Sylvia Bacon is a trial judge of the District of Columbia Superior Court, which has general jurisdiction over criminal prosecutions, civil actions, and family matters. She has served on the court since 1970.

Prior to coming to the bench, Judge Bacon was the Executive Assistant U.S. Attorney for the District of Columbia and had served in that office as a trial attorney. She also served as Associate Director of the President's Commission on Crime in the District of Columbia.

Judge Bacon has been a Bar Examiner for the District of Columbia, a member of the Board of Directors of the District of Columbia Bar Association, and a trustee of the District of Columbia Bar Association Research Foundation and of the National Home Library Foundation. She has taught Juvenile Court Practice at Georgetown University Law Center.

Judge Bacon was educated at Vassar College and at the Harvard Law School. She also obtained an LL.M. from the Georgetown University Law Center and is a graduate of the National College of the State Judiciary.

### Arthur J. Bilek

Arthur J. Bilek has been Chairman of the Illinois Law Enforcement Commission since early 1969. He is on leave-of-absence from the University of Illinois at Chicago Circle where he holds the academic rank of Professor of Criminal Justice and has served as Director and Founder of the Administration of Criminal Justice Curriculum.

Mr. Bilek was Chief of Police for the Cook County Sheriff's Department from 1962 to 1966. From 1953 to 1962, he served with the Chicago Police Department, advancing from Patrolman to Lieutenant. He also has been a Special Investigator for the Cook County State's Attorney's Police and a special agent in the U.S. Army Counter Intelligence Corps.

He is a member of the board of the Law in American Society Foundation and is a member of several professional organizations including the International Association of Chiefs of Police, the American Academy of Forensic Sciences, the American Sociological Association, and the American Society of Criminology.

He is a graduate of Loyola University in Chicago, which granted him B.S. and M.S.W. degrees.

### Frank Dyson

Frank Dyson was appointed Chief of Police of the Dallas, Tex., Police Department in 1969.

Chief Dyson began his police career in 1950 as a patrolman for the Dallas Police Department. He rose through the ranks becoming Assistant Chief in June 1969, and Chief of Police on December 15, 1969.

Chief Dyson has instructed at El Centro Junior College, and is a member of the faculty at Southwestern Police Academy.

He is a member of the Texas Police Association, the FBI National Academy Association, and the International Association of Chiefs of Police, and has served as a member of the Texas Criminal Justice Council.

Chief Dyson holds a B.S. degree from Sam Houston State University.

### Caroline E. Hughes

Caroline E. Hughes was appointed a member of the National Advisory Council on Vocational Education by President Nixon in April 1971.

Mrs. Hughes has also been a member since 1967 of the Oklahoma State Advisory Council on Vocational Education, and served as Chairman of that council in 1969. She has been an elected member of the Board of Education of the Central Oklahoma Area Vocational and Technical School District since 1967.

Mrs. Hughes is also on the Executive Board of the Governor's Link Committee which counsels the Department of Corrections in Oklahoma. She is a member of several local civic and service clubs, including the Cushing, Okla., Chamber of Commerce and the Daughters of the American Revolution. Mrs. Hughes is also active as a consultant in the field of vocational education.

Mrs. Hughes holds a B.S. degree from Oklahoma State University.

### Howard A. Jones

Howard A. Jones was appointed Chairman of the Narcotic Addiction Control Commission, State of New York, by Governor Rockefeller on July 1, 1971. He has been a member of that commission since May 1970.

Prior to joining the commission, Commissioner Jones served for 7 years as a member of the New York State Board of Parole. From 1962 to 1963 he was assistant counsel to Governor Rockefeller. From 1953 to 1960, Commissioner Jones was an Assistant District Attorney in New York County.

Commissioner Jones also has served on the New York Temporary State Commission on Revision of the Penal Law and Criminal Code, and on the Select Committee on Correctional Institutions and Programs. He is a member of several professional, charitable, and civic organizations.

He served as a World War II combat infantryman. He attended the City College of New York and New York University and holds a law degree from St. John's University Law School.

### Robert J. Kutak

Robert J. Kutak is a partner in the law firm of Kutak, Rock, Cohen, Campbell, & Peters in Omaha, Neb.

Before joining the firm, Mr. Kutak was Administrative Assistant to U.S. Senator Roman L. Hruska of Nebraska. He also served as a law clerk to Judge Richard E. Robinson of the U.S. District Court for the District of Nebraska.

Mr. Kutak was a member of the President's Task Force on Prisoner Rehabilitation in 1969–1970. He was a member of the United States delegation to the Fourth World Congress on Prevention of Crime and Treatment of Offenders in 1970. He is a member of the National Advisory Panel to the Director of the Bureau of Prisons and is Vice Chairman of the American Bar Association Commission on Correctional Facilities and Services; Mr. Kutak also serves on other committees of the American Bar Association.

Mr. Kutak holds degrees from the University of Chicago and the University of Chicago Law School.

### Richard G. Lugar

Richard G. Lugar was elected Mayor of Indianapolis, Ind., in 1967, and reelected in 1971.

Mayor Lugar entered public life in 1964 when he was elected to the Board of School Commissioners in Indianapolis; he served as Vice President of that board in 1965. From 1960 to 1967, he was Vice President and Treasurer of Thomas L. Green and Company, and has served as Secretary-Treasurer of that company from 1968 to the present. Since 1960, he also has acted as Treasurer of Lugar Stock Farms, Inc.

Mayor Lugar is Vice Chairman of the Advisory Commission on Intergovernmental Relations, and former President of the National League of Cities. He is a member of the Board of Directors of the National Association of Counties.

Mayor Lugar graduated first in his class from Denison University, and, as a Rhodes Scholar, received his B.A. and M.A. from Oxford University (Pembroke College). He has served as a Lieutenant in the U.S. Navy.

### Ellis C. MacDougall

Ellis C. MacDougall was appointed Director of the State Board of Corrections in Georgia in January 1971.

Mr. MacDougall also has served as the Commissioner of Corrections for the State of Connecticut, as Director of the South Carolina Department of Corrections, and as the Director of Prison Industries in the South Carolina Department of Corrections. He has served as Deputy Warden and Business Manager of the South Carolina Penitentiary, and in several other positions in the corrections field.

Mr. MacDougall is a member and Past President of the American Correctional Association, is the Past President of the Southern States Prison Association, and is a member of the National Council on Crime and Delinquency.

Mr. MacDougall holds a B.A. degree from Davis and Elkins College, an M.A. from New York University, and an Honorary LL.D. from Davis and Elkins College.

### Henry F. McQuade

Henry F. McQuade was appointed to the Supreme Court of the State of Idaho in December 1956, and has been reelected to that office to the present time. He was Chief Justice of that court for the years 1964–1965 and 1971–1972.

Between 1951 and 1956, Justice McQuade served as District Judge of the Fifth (now the Sixth) Judicial District of Idaho. He also has served as Prosecuting Attorney of Bannock County, and as a Justice of the Peace in Latah County. During World War II, Justice McQuade attained the rank of Captain in the United States Army.

Justice McQuade received both his B.A. and LL.B. degrees from the University of Idaho.

### Gary K. Nelson

Gary K. Nelson was appointed Attorney General of Arizona on July 1, 1968, and has been elected and reelected to that office to the present time.

Mr. Nelson has been in the Office of the Attorney General since 1964, first in the Highway Legal Division and later as Chief of the Criminal Appeals Division and Chief Trial Counsel. He has also been an associate in the firm of Kramer, Roche, Burch, Streich, and Cracchiolo, and a law clerk to Justice Fred C. Struckmeyer, Jr., of the Arizona Supreme Court.

Mr. Nelson has been the Chairman of the Arizona State Justice Planning Agency since 1969. He is also a member of the Law Enforcement Officers Advisory Council, President of the National Association of Attorneys General, and a member of the President's Consumer Advisory Council. He is Past Chairman of the Conference of Western Attorneys General.

Mr. Nelson graduated from Arizona State University with a B.S. degree, and from the University of Arizona with a J.D. degree. He served in the U.S. Army with the rank of Captain.

### Charles L. Owen

Charles L. Owen has been the Director of the Kentucky Crime Commission since it was established in July 1967. He has also served for the past 2 years as Chairman of the National Conference of State Planning Agency Directors, which administers funds under the Omnibus Crime Control and Safe Streets Act.

A graduate of Princeton University and the University of Virginia Law School, Mr. Owen served as Assistant United States Attorney for the District of Columbia before assuming his present position in Kentucky.

### Ray Pope

Ray Pope was appointed Commissioner of the Department of Public Safety in the State of Georgia on January 12, 1971. He has responsibility for administering the State's largest law enforcement agency, consisting of the Georgia State Patrol, the Georgia Bureau of Investigation, the State Crime Laboratory, and the Georgia Police Academy.

Colonel Pope began his law enforcement career in 1939. Since that time he has held several law enforcement positions, the most recent being a Program Specialist for the Law Enforcement Assistance Administration. He was also Chief of the Waycross, Ga., Police Department for 8 years.

Colonel Pope has served as Vice-Chairman of the Georgia Crime Commission and as a member of the Georgia Organized Crime Prevention Council. During his career he also has been President of the Peace Officers' Association of Georgia, President of the Georgia Association of Chiefs of Police, and Chairman of the Georgia Law Enforcement Planning Agency Supervisory Board. He is a member of the National Council on Crime and Delinquency's Law Enforcement Council.

Colonel Pope attended the University of Georgia and South Georgia College, from which he received a degree in Criminal Justice. He also has studied Police Administration at the Southern Police Institute. During World War II, Colonel Pope served 3 years with the U.S. Navy Shore Patrol.

### Reverend Elmer J. C. Prenzlow, Jr.

Elmer J.C. Prenzlow, Jr., has been Campus Chaplain of the University Lutheran Chapel of the Metropolitan Milwaukee Campus Ministry for the South Wisconsin District of the Lutheran Church, Missouri Synod, for 11 years. He is Chairman of the Humanities Department of Spencerian Business College in Milwaukee.

Reverend Prenzlow also works as a consulting psychologist in residential treatment centers for the emotionally disturbed. He has held a number of denominational offices and responsibilities in the Wisconsin Evangelical Lutheran Synod and in the Lutheran Church, Missouri Synod.

Among his professional and civic activities, Reverend Prenzlow is a member of the American Personnel and Guidance Association and a member of the American Psychological Association, and was a member of the Wisconsin Legislative Advisory Committee on the Kerner Report.

Reverend Prenzlow holds a B.A. from Northwestern College, a B.D. from the Wisconsin Evangelical Lutheran Seminary, an M.S. in psychology from the University of Wisconsin, and has done extensive postgraduate work in his field.

### Milton G. Rector

Milton G. Rector is President of the National Council on Crime and Delinquency and has been its executive officer since 1959.

Prior to assuming the directorship, Mr. Rector was Western Consultant and Assistant Director of the Council from 1946 to 1959.

Mr. Rector has been a delegate to the United Nations for the Second, Third and Fourth World Congresses on Prevention of Crime and Treatment of Offenders. He was a member of the President's Advisory Council on Juvenile Delinquency from 1960 to 1966, a consultant to the President's Commission on Law Enforcement and Administration of Justice and a member of the Advisory Committee to the National Commission on Reform of Federal Criminal Laws. He is at present a member of the New York City Coordinating Council for Criminal Justice.

Mr. Rector is on the Board of Directors of the American Correctional Association, the Osborne Association, and several other professional organizations. He is author of a syndicated newspaper column, "Of Crime and Punishment."

Mr. Rector received a B.A. degree from the University of Southern California, and did graduate work at Columbia University and at the University of California at Berkeley.

### Arlen Specter

Arlen Specter was elected District Attorney of Philadelphia, Pa., in November 1965 and has been reelected to that office to the present time. Mr. Specter also serves as a Lecturer in Law at the Temple University Law School.

Before his election, Mr. Specter was a Special Assistant Attorney General of Pennsylvania. He has also served as Assistant Counsel of the Warren Commission, and as an Assistant District Attorney of Philadelphia.

He is a member of the National Advisory Council of the Peace Corps, and was a delegate to the White House Conference on Youth in 1971. He is a member of the American Bar Association, the Pennsylvania Bar Association, and the Philadelphia Bar Association.

Mr. Specter received a B.A. from the University of Pennsylvania and an LL.B. from Yale University Law School.

### Reverend Leon H. Sullivan

Leon H. Sullivan has been pastor of the Zion Baptist Church in Philadelphia, Pa., since 1950.

In 1964, Reverend Sullivan founded the Opportunities Industrial Center, a program that sponsors job training and retraining, and which operates in more than 100 cities in the United States and in four African countries. Reverend Sullivan also founded the Zion Investment Associates in Philadelphia, and Progress Aerospace Enterprises, Inc.

Reverend Sullivan is Founder and Chairman of the Board of the National Progress Association for Economic Development which is doing economic development planning and other urban planning in 40 cities around the country.

He is a director of several organizations and companies, including the Boy Scouts of America, the United Way of America, and the General Motors Corporation.

Reverend Sullivan holds a B.A. from West Virginia State College, an M.A. from Columbia University, and several honorary degrees.

### Donald F. Taylor

Donald F. Taylor has been President of Merrill Manufacturing Corporation since 1939. He is also President of three subsidiary companies: Basic Wire Products in Ohio; Taylor Insulation Company in Wisconsin; and Bay Insulation Company in Wisconsin.

Mr. Taylor has been a Director of the Chamber of Commerce of the United States since 1966. He is also Chairman of the Crime Prevention and Control Panel of the Chamber. He is a Past Director and Past President of the Wisconsin

State Chamber of Commerce. He is also Past Director of the Wisconsin Council of Safety.

Mr. Taylor received his education at the Merrill Commercial College and at the University of Wisconsin Management Institute.

### Richard W. Velde (ex officio)

Richard W. Velde was appointed Associate Administrator of the Law Enforcement Assistance Administration by President Nixon in March 1969.

Prior to joining LEAA, Mr. Velde served as Minority Counsel of the Senate Subcommittee on Criminal Law. He also served as Minority Counsel of the Subcommittee on Juvenile Delinquency. He engaged in the private practice of law in Washington, D.C., from 1961 to 1965. From 1958 to 1960, he served as Legislative Assistant to U.S. Representative Robert H. Michel of Illinois. He served 5 years in the U.S. Air Force, attaining the rank of Captain.

Mr. Velde received a B.S. degree in political science and an M.A. in speech from Bradley University in Peoria, Ill. He attended the University of Illinois College of Law, and received his J.D. degree from George Washington University Law School. He was also a Ph.D. candidate in government and public administration.

# The
# Commission's
# Origins
# and
# Work

In early 1971, the Attorney General asked the Law Enforcement Assistance Administration (LEAA) to take the initiative in developing goals and standards for criminal justice agencies. LEAA subsequently conducted two planning conferences of criminal justice experts which recommended the creation of a national commission as the most appropriate means to carry out the Attorney General's directive.

On October 20, 1971, the Administrator of LEAA, Jerris Leonard, established the National Advisory Commission on Criminal Justice Standards and Goals.

Thomas J. Madden, General Counsel of LEAA, was detailed to work for the Commission in November 1971. In December 1971, the Commission voted unanimously to appoint him their Executive Director.

The Commission created a number of task forces, each consisting of from 10 to 20 experts and informed citizens, to carry out its research into what was workable and practicable for crime control. Within guidelines and directions set forth by the Commission, four major task forces—on Police, Courts, Corrections, and Community Crime Prevention—undertook the preparation of individual studies in their respective areas. Funding for staff and consultants for each of these four operational task forces was provided by LEAA through the State Criminal Justice Planning Agencies of California, Massachusetts, Texas, and Virginia. The mandate given each task force by the Commission and LEAA was to draft goals and standards for State and local agencies that would reduce crime and improve the quality of justice. They were charged with finding successful models for action if they existed and, if no model existed, they were charged with developing one.

In addition to the four operational task forces, the Commission and LEAA also established eight advisory task forces on: Juvenile Delinquency; Organized Crime; Drug Abuse; Community Involvement; Civil Disorders; Research and Development; Education, Training, and Manpower Development; and Information Systems. These task forces, comprised of experts and professionals, met several times to advise the Commission and the Task Forces on Police, Courts, Corrections, and Community Crime Prevention.

The advisory task forces worked without staff support, with the exception of the Information Systems Task Force. They performed recommending and reviewing functions as contrasted with drafting and research functions. The Information Systems Task Force, however, was assisted by a staff and produced a report that serves as a major section of the Commission's *Report on the Criminal Justice System*.

Commission staff was assigned by the Executive Director to administer each of the operational task force grants and to work with each task force to assure that the Commission's guidelines were followed. Commission staff reviewed material prepared by each task force, suggesting to the Commission and to the task forces modifications, additions, and deletions of material. Commission staff members attended each task force meeting and provided insight to the task force on the requirements of the Commission. In many instances Commission staff members drafted standards for the task force reports.

In October 1971 the Commission staff assumed full responsibility for completing the *Report on Community Crime Prevention* and much of the material in that report was developed under the direction of the Commission staff.

In addition the Commission staff had sole responsibility for producing for the Commission the *Report on the Criminal Justice System* and the final report of the Commission, *A National Strategy to Reduce Crime*. And the Commission staff edited and completed final preparations on each of the Commission reports prior to printing.

Under the direction of the Executive Director, a Publications Unit was formed to prepare manuscripts for the printer. The unit was established in October 1972 and was composed of professional journalists. This group processed copy submitted to it by the Commission staff and prepared it for production by the Government Printing Office. A professional design firm developed the concept of the cover art and was responsible for selection of type and layout.

The chairmen of the Commission's task forces attended Commission meetings and actively participated in its discussions. They did not participate in Commission voting. The reports of the various task forces together with the work performed by the Commission's own staff provided the Commission with its basic working material.

Under this structure, the Commission's work was decentralized and subject to a series of independent reviews. The majority of task force members were drawn from State, local, and private agencies. The bulk of the staff and consultants for the major task forces came from outside Washington, D.C. Two task forces, those on Police and Corrections, were headquartered in Los Angeles, Calif., and Austin, Tex., respectively.

The wide diversity of geographic representation on task forces and staffs contributed to the expression of a variety of viewpoints and provided access to a number of important information sources.

While the Commission did not view its task as primarily survey-and-study, several surveys were nonetheless undertaken by the Commission and task force staffs. These included, for example, a survey of several hundred criminal justice agencies concerning innovative programs, and a survey of State and trial court administrators concerning characteristics of contemporary court administration. Each of the task forces initiated contacts with professional associations and individual criminal justice agencies. The Police Task Force alone contacted hundreds of small, medium-sized, and large police departments throughout the country.

Considerable volunteer effort was contributed by staff from agencies under the direction of particular Commissioners and task force chairmen. Among the agencies headed by Commissioners or task force chairmen whose personnel were involved in the Commission's work were the Los Angeles Police and Sheriff's Departments, the Dallas Police Department, the New York State Narcotic Addiction Control Commission, the Georgia State Department of Offender Rehabilitation, the National Council on Crime and Delinquency, the District Attorney's Office of Philadelphia, Pa., the Metropolitan Police Department of Washington, D.C., and the Michigan State Police.

A number of Federal agencies provided valuable assistance

to the Commission, including the Office of Criminal Justice, the Federal Bureau of Investigation, the Bureau of Prisons, and the Community Relations Service of the Department of Justice; the National Institute of Mental Health and the Youth Development and Delinquency Prevention Administration of the Department of Health, Education, and Welfare; and the Manpower Development and Training Administration of the Department of Labor. All offices of LEAA, and particularly the National Criminal Justice Information and Statistics Service, the National Institute of Law Enforcement and Criminal Justice, and the Office of Criminal Justice Assistance, contributed papers, suggestions, information, and staff assistance.

The full Commission met eight times for 2- to 4-day periods during the course of its work. On numerous occasions, however, individual Commissioners consulted with and advised Commission staff and the task forces. During the latter half of 1972, the Commission met in a series of meetings to review and approve reports from the task forces as well as those from the Commission staff itself. Every standard in the Commission's reports was debated and voted upon by the full Commission.

In a number of cases, standards presented by task forces or Commission staff were modified or rejected. In some areas, more than one task force presented similar recommendations. The Commission allowed overlapping between reports so that each report could stand by itself.

Each standard adopted by the Commission was subject to approval by a majority vote; however, not every Commissioner agreed with every standard adopted by the Commission or with the narrative supporting each standard.

# Task Force Members

## Police Task Force Staff

**Chairman**
Edward M. Davis
Chief of Police
Los Angeles Police Department
Los Angeles, Calif.

**Vice Chairman**
Dale Carson
Sheriff, Jacksonville, Fla.

Arthur L. Alarcon
Judge, Superior Court
Los Angeles, Calif.

George A. Bowman, Jr.
County Judge, Children's Court Center
Milwaukee, Wis.

William Cahn
District Attorney of Nassau County
Mineola, N.Y.

Benjamin O. Davis, Jr.
Assistant Secretary for Safety and Consumer
    Affairs, Department of Transportation
Washington, D.C.

Don R. Derning
Chief of Police, Winnetka, Ill.

Alfred S. Ercolano
Director, College of American Pathologists
Washington, D.C.

David Hanes
Attorney, Wilmer, Cutler & Pickering
Washington, D.C.

Clarence M. Kelley
Chief, Kansas Police Department
Kansas City, Mo.

David B. Kelly
Superintendent, New Jersey State Police
West Trenton, N.J.

Charles Kingston
Professor of Criminalistics
John Jay College of Criminal Justice
New York, N.Y.

Donald Manson
Policy Analyst, Center for Policy Analysis
National League of Cities
Washington, D.C.

John R. Shryock
Chief, Kettering Police Department
Kettering, Ohio

Joseph White
Executive Director
Ohio Law Enforcement Planning Agency
Columbus, Ohio

## Courts Task Force

**Chairman**
Daniel J. Meador
Professor of Law, University of Virginia
Charlottesville, Va.

**Vice Chairman**
Stanley C. Van Ness
Public Defender
State of New Jersey

637

Trenton, N.J.

Arthur Azevedo, Jr.
California State Assembly
Office of Assemblyman Bill Bagley
Sacramento, Calif.

William O. Bittman
Attorney, Hogan and Hartson
Washington, D.C.

William L. Cahalan
Wayne County Prosecuting Attorney
Detroit, Mich.

John C. Danforth
Attorney General of Missouri
Jefferson City, Mo.

William H. Erickson
Justice, Supreme Court of Colorado
Denver, Colo.

B. J. George
Professor of Law, Wayne State University Law
   School
Detroit, Mich.

Edward B. McConnell
Administrative Director of the Courts
Trenton, N.J.

Tim Murphy
Judge, Superior Court, District of Columbia

Frank A. Orlando
Presiding Judge, Juvenile Court of Broward County
Fort Lauderdale, Fla.

G. Nicholas Pijoan
Director, Division of Criminal Justice
Denver, Colo.

Donald E. Santarelli
Associate Deputy Attorney General
Department of Justice, Washington, D.C.

William M. Slaughter
Litton Industries, Inc.
Beverly Hills, Calif.

George A. Van Hoomissen
Dean, National College of District Attorneys
University of Houston
Houston, Tex.

## Corrections Task Force

**Chairman**
Judge Joe Frazier Brown
Executive Director, Criminal Justice Council
Austin, Tex.

Fred Allenbrand
Sheriff, Johnson County
Olathe, Kans.

Norman A. Carlson
Director, U.S. Bureau of Prisons
Washington, D.C.

Hubert M. Clements
Assistant Director, South Carolina Department of
    Corrections
Columbia, S.C.

Roberta Dorn
Program Specialist
Law Enforcement Assistance Administration
Washington, D.C.

Edith Flynn
Associate Professor, University of Illinois
Urbana, Ill.

Eddie Harrison
Director, Pre-trial Intervention Project
Baltimore, Md.

Bruce Johnson
Chairman, Board of Prison Terms and Paroles
Olympia, Wash.

Martha Wheeler
President, American Correctional Association
Superintendent, Ohio Reformatory for Women
Marysville, Ohio

## Community Crime Prevention Task Force

**Chairman**
Jack Michie
Director, Division of Vocational Education
Lansing, Mich.

Martha Bachman
Hockessin, Del.

Ronald Brown
General Counsel, National Urban League
New York, N.Y.

Paul D'Amore
Vice President for Business & Finance
Marquette University
Milwaukee, Wis.

Adrian G. Duplantier
State Senator, Orleans Parish
New Orleans, La.

Carl V. Goodin
Chief of Police
Cincinnati, Ohio

Mamie Harvey
Youth Services Administration
New York, N.Y.

Richard A. Hernandez
Attorney
Los Angeles, Calif.

Gary Hill
The United States Jaycees
Lincoln, Nebr.

Eugene Kelley
Security Manager, Bendix Corporation
Newark, N.J.

Ruby Yaryan
Staff Director, Interdepartment Council to Coordinate
   All Federal Juvenile Delinquency Programs
Law Enforcement Assistance Administration
Washington, D.C.

# Advisory Task Force Members

## Civil Disorders Advisory Task Force

**Chairman**
Jerry V. Wilson
Chief, Metropolitan Police Department
Washington, D.C.

George Beck
Deputy Chief
Los Angeles Police Department
Los Angeles, Calif.

Herbert R. Cain, Jr.
Judge, Court of Common Pleas
Philadelphia, Pa.

Gerald M. Caplan
Professor, College of Law
Arizona State University
Tempe, Ariz.

Thomas Gadsden
Civil Rights Division, Department of Justice
Washington, D.C.

Edward A. Hailes
Executive Director
Opportunities Industrialization Center
Washington, D.C.

Maynard H. Jackson
Vice Mayor
Atlanta, Ga.

Wayne A. Kranig
Chief, Law Enforcement Division
California Office of Emergency Services
Sacramento, Calif.

Robert E. Levitt
Majority Floor Leader, House of Representatives
Canton, Ohio

Norval Morris
Director, Center for Studies in Criminal Justice
School of Law
University of Chicago
Chicago, Ill.

Eugene J. Quindlen
Assistant Director for Government Preparedness
Executive Office of the President
Washington, D.C.

William A. Rusher
Publisher, *National Review*
New York, N.Y.

## Community Involvement Advisory Task Force

**Chairman**
George B. Peters
President, Aurora Metal Company
Aurora, Ill.

Victor Henderson Ashe II
Knoxville, Tenn.

Sidney H. Cates III
Deputy Chief for Administration
Department of Police
New Orleans, La.

Patricia Costello
Northshore Youth Counselling Service
Milwaukee, Wis.

Sarah Jane Cunningham
Attorney, Cunningham and Clark
McCook, Nebr.

Ephram Gomberg
Executive Vice President
Citizens Crime Commission
Philadelphia, Pa.

Benjamin F. Holman
Director, Community Relations Service
Department of Justice
Washington, D.C.

Wayne Hopkins
Chamber of Commerce of the United States
Washington, D.C.

Kenneth B. Hoyt
Director
Specialty Oriented Student Research Program
University of Maryland
College Park, Md.

Steve E. Littlejohn
Harvard College
Cambridge, Mass.

Margaret Moore Post
*Indianapolis News*
Indianapolis, Ind.

Gary Robinson
Assistant Secretary
Executive Office of Human Services
Boston, Mass.

Edward J. Stack
Sheriff, Broward County
Fort Lauderdale, Fla.

William H. Wilcox
Secretary, Department of Community Affairs
Harrisburg, Pa.

## Drug Abuse Advisory Task Force

**Chairman**
Sterling Johnson
Executive Director, New York City Civil Complaint
   Review Board
New York, N.Y.

Edward Anderson
Bureau of Narcotics and Dangerous Drugs
Department of Justice
Washington, D.C.

Kenneth Biehn
Assistant District Attorney, Bucks County
Quakertown, Pa.

V. C. Chasten
Daly City, Calif.

Judianne Densen-Gerber
Executive Director, Odyssey House
New York, N.Y.

Jeffrey Donfeld
Assistant Director, Special Action Office for Drug
   Abuse Prevention
Washington, D.C.

Robert L. Dupont
Director, Narcotics Treatment Administration
Washington, D.C.

Allan Gillies
Eli Lilly and Company
Indianapolis, Ind.

Frank Lloyd
Director, Medical Services, Methodist Hospital
Indianapolis, Ind.

Bruce Martin
Project Director, Regional Institute for Corrections
Administrative Study
Boulder, Colo.

Bernard Moldow
Judge, New York City Criminal Court
New York, N.Y.

William M. Tendy
Assistant Director
New York Organized Crime Task Force
White Plains, N.Y.

W. Elwyn Turner
Director of Public Health, County of Santa Clara
San Jose, Calif.

J. Thomas Ungerleider
Assistant Professor of Psychiatry
University of California at Los Angeles
Los Angeles, Calif.

Yaras M. Wochok
Assistant District Attorney
Philadelphia, Pa.

## Education, Training, and Manpower Development Advisory Task Force

**Chairman**
Lee P. Brown
Director of the Law Enforcement Programs
Portland State University
Portland, Oreg.

Morris W. H. Collins, Jr.
Director, Institute of Government
University of Georgia
Athens Ga.

Jay Edelson
Social Science Research Analyst
U.S. Department of Labor
Washington, D.C.

Donald E. Fish
Bureau Chief, Department of Community Affairs
Police Standards Board
Tallahassee, Fla.

Ernest Friesen
Executive Director, Institute for Court Management
University of Denver Law Center
Denver, Colo.

John B. Hotis
Inspector, FBI Academy
Quantico, Va.

John Irving
Dean, Law School, Seton Hall University
Newark, N.J.

Conrad F. Joyner
College of Liberal Arts, Dept. of Government
University of Arizona
Tucson, Ariz.

Charles V. Matthews
Director, Center for the Study of Crime, Delin-
  quency and Corrections
Southern Illinois University
Carbondale, Ill.

Frederick Miller
Executive Director, Opportunities Industrialization
  Center Institute
Philadelphia, Pa.

Gordon Misner
Director, Administration of Justice Program
University of Missouri
St. Louis, Mo.

Richard A. Myren
Dean, School of Criminal Justice
State University of New York
Albany, N.Y.

James P. Quinn
Indianapolis, Ind.

Alfred F. Smode
Executive Scientists, Dunlap and Associates, Inc.
Darien, Conn.

649

# Information Systems and Statistics Advisory Task Force

**Chairman**
John R. Plants
Director, Michigan State Police
East Lansing, Mich.

C. J. Beddome
Assistant Chief, Administrative Division
Arizona Department of Public Safety
Phoenix, Ariz.

Gerald B. Fox
City Manager
Wichita Falls, Tex.

George Hall
National Institute of Law Enforcement and Criminal
   Justice, Law Enforcement Assistance
   Administration
Washington, D.C.

Scott W. Hovey, Jr.
Director, Bureau of Services
St. Louis Police Department
St. Louis, Mo.

Joan E. Jacoby
National Center for Prosecution Management
Washington, D.C.

James A. McCafferty
Assistant Chief, Division of Information Systems
Administrative Office of the U.S. Courts
Washington, D.C.

Vincent O'Leary
Professor of Criminal Justice
State University of New York
Albany, N.Y.

Larry P. Polansky
Chief Deputy Court Administrator
Court of Common Pleas
Philadelphia, Pa.

Donald R. Roderick
Inspector, Uniform Crime Reports
National Crime Information Center, FBI
Washington D.C.

## Juvenile Delinquency Advisory Task Force

**Chairman**
Wilfred W. Nuernberger
Judge, Separate Juvenile Court
Lincoln, Nebr.

Gary Abrecht
Metropolitan Police Department
Washington, D.C.

Mary Ellen Abrecht
Metropolitan Police Department
Washington, D.C.

Robert C. Arneson
Director, Law Enforcement Planning Commission
Boise, Idaho

Allen F. Breed
Director, Department of Youth Authority
State of California
Sacramento, Calif.

William S. Fort
Judge, Court of Appeals
Salem, Oreg.

Sanford Fox
Director, Center for Corrections and the Law
Boston College Law School
Boston, Mass.

Robert J. Gemignani
Commissioner, Youth Development and Delinquency
    Prevention Administration
Department of Health, Education, and Welfare
Washington, D.C.

651

Thomas N. Gilmore
Senior Research Analyst, Wharton School of Finance
  and Commerce
  University of Pennsylvania
Philadelphia, Pa.

William H. Hansen
Chief of Police
Sioux City, Iowa

Milton Luger
Director, Division for Youth
New York State Youth Commission
Albany, N.Y.

James E. Miller
Director, Juvenile Delinquency
Indiana Criminal Justice Planring Agency
Indianapolis, Ind.

Wayne R. Mucci
Special Services for Children
Bureau of Institutions and Facilities
New York, N.Y.

Paul Nejelski
Project Director, Juvenile Justice Standards Project
Institute of Judicial Administration
New York, N.Y.

Margaret K. Rosenheim
Professor, School of Social Service Administration
University of Chicago
Chicago, Ill.

Stanton L. Young
Oklahoma City, Okla.

## Organized Crime Advisory Task Force

**Chairman**
William L. Reed
Commissioner
Florida Department of Law Enforcement
Tallahassee, Fla.

Annelise Anderson
Palo Alto, Calif.

G. Robert Blakey
Chief Counsel, Subcommittee on Criminal Law and
    Procedure
U.S. Senate
Washington, D.C.

Harry Lee Hudspeth
Attorney at Law
El Paso, Tex.

Wallace H. Johnson
Special Assistant to the President, The White House
Washington, D.C.

John F. Kehoe, Jr.
Commissioner of Public Safety
Boston, Mass.

Aaron M. Kohn
Managing Director, Metropolitan Crime Commission
New Orleans, La.

William Lucas
Sheriff, Wayne County
Detroit, Mich.

John J. McCoy
Chief Deputy, Riverside Sheriff's Department
Riverside, Calif.

William J. Scott
Attorney General of Illinois
Springfield, Ill.

# Research and Development Advisory Task Force

**Chairman**
Peter J. McQuillan
Judge, New York City Criminal Court
Flushing, N.Y.

Peter B. Bensinger
Director, Department of Corrections
Springfield, Ill.

654

Paul M. Whisenand
Professor, Department of Criminology
California State College
Long Beach, Calif.

# Task Force Staff Members, Advisers, Consultants, and Contributors

## Police Task Force Staff

**Executive Director**
Vernon L. Hoy

**Assistant Director**
Taylor L. Searcy

**Research and Editorial Staff**
Ronald C. Banks
Jeremy I. Conklin
William J. Cox
Robert S. Earhart
Laurence E. Fetters
Newsom J. Gibson
Louis J. Reiter
Charles A. Sale

**Research Assistants**
David G. Brath
Michael K. Hooper
Don G. Letney
John D. Madell

Stephen R. Staffer
John Swan
Anthony R. Toomey

**Administrative**
Amy F. Aki
Lydia Anderson
Barbara Bonino
Terry Gallegos
Susan H. Hennis
Susan Sullivan

**Consultants**
George Eastman
International Association of Chiefs of Police

## Courts Task Force Staff

**Staff Director**
Harvey Friedman

**Editor and Co-Director**
George E. Dix

**Professional Staff**
Paul Garofalo
William P. Redick
Arlene T. Shadoan

**Editorial Assistants**
Walter E. Dellinger, III
Daniel L. Rotenberg
David B. Wexler

**Clerical Staff**
Florence K. Fisher
Eleanor H. Kett
Hilda M. O'Neill
Katherine L. Watson

**Research Assistants**
Mary S. Burdick
James C. Doub
Jerome James
Jerry Kahn
Neil S. Kessler
Norman Leopold
Michael Needham

William E. Persina
Barbara F. Sachs
Mary Lee Stapp
Rodney J. Streff
Randall E. Wilbert
Charles J. Willinger, Jr.

## Contributors

Carl Baar
Ernest L. Bailey, Jr.
Herbert Beaser
Martin Belsky
John M. Cannell
James Cogan
Walter W. Cohen
Gary V. Dubin
Elyce Z. Ferster
Ernest C. Friesen, Jr.
James N. Garber
Marshall Hartman
H. Paul Haynes, Sr.
William R. Higham
Laurance M. Hyde, Jr.
Joan E. Jacoby
James Lacy
Jerome F. Lieblich
Arnold M. Malech
Donald M. McIntyre
William S. McKee
Raymond T. Nimmer
Thomas B. Russell
Shelvin Singer

## Advisers

James Beck
Winslow Christian
Richard A. Hauser
Kirksey M. Nix
Michael O'Neil
Axel Kleiboemer
Monrad G. Paulsen
Peter Ruger
Mark Sendrow
Lee R. West
Charles R. Work

## Corrections Task Force Staff

**Executive Director**
Lawrence A. Carpenter

**Assistant Director**
Marilyn Kay Harris

**Staff Director**
Ernest A. Guinn, Jr.

**Technical Writer**
Francis Smith Dodds

**Administrative Assistant**
Faye Hanks

**Staff Associates**
Harvey Perlman
Billy L. Wayson

**Contributors**
William T. Adams
Melvin T. Axilbund
Lewis P. Brusca
John P. Conrad
Edith Flynn
Norval Morris
Frederic D. Moyer
William G. Nagel
Vincent O'Leary
Clarence Schrag
Richard G. Singer
Robert L. Smith
John A. Wallace

**Advisers**
Bill Anderson
William E. Baughman
Allen F. Breed
Milton Burdman
Joan Carrerra
John P. Friedman
Kenneth K. Henning
Hazel Kerper
Barbara Knudson
Robert J. Kutak
Joseph S. Lobenthal, Jr.

659

Richard E. Longfellow
Milton Luger
Ellis C. MacDougall
W. Donald Pointer
Francis J. Prevost
Sue Shirley
Daniel L. Skoler

## Community Crime Prevention Task Force Staff

**Staff Director**
Louis Rome

**Associate Staff Director**
Kenneth D. Hines

Lori Blevins
Donald Brezine
Richard Friedman
Eleanor Hellrung
Roslyn Mazer
Patricia McLaughlin
Gail Miller
Dorothy Neubauer
Judith E. Rapp
Adelaide Reid
Rachel Shugars
Judith Zeider

**In-office Consultants**
James Fleck
Bryon Mills
Joseph Phelan
Ruth Ann Rudnick

**Law Student Researchers**
David Callet
Paul R. D'Amoto
James A. Gass
Mark R. Kravitz
Karen M. Radius

**Contributors**
David Adamany
John Adams
Herbert Alexander

660

John F. Allbright
LaVerda O. Allen
Randolph Blackwell
Bruce Brennan
James A. Brennan
Leon Brill
Carl Chambers
John Duguid
Elaine Duxbury
William Falcon
John Favors
O. C. Foster
Maurice D. Geiger
Pearldean Golightly
Jerald D. Hampton
Robert Harris
L. Bert Hawkins
Wallace T. Homitz
Leon Hunt
Francis Ianni
Peter A. Jaszi
Ernest Jones
Michael Kantor
Russell Leedy
Donald Levine
Donald McCune
Harold Meiselas
Hubert Molina
Bruce Monroe
William Moore
Donald F. Muhich
Erasmus C. Ogbuobiri
Joseph Price
Charles S. Prigmore
Stephen H. Sachs
Ralph Salerno
Nicholas Scoppetta
James Shonkwiler
Neil M. Singer
Robert L. Smith
Neil Sullivan
Robert Taggart III
George Washnis
Malcolm H. Wiener
Kenneth F. Wilhoite

661

Ben Zimmerman
California Youth Authority
Manpower Administration, U.S. Department of
    Labor, for financial assistance
Narcotic and Drug Research, Inc.

## Advisers

Howard Aldrich
Robert Atkins
Howard Braun
Albert Biderman
Lee P. Brown
Patricia Caesar
Orin C. Church
Eli Cohen
Martin B. Danziger
Hollis Devines
Robert Howe
Harold R. Johnson
Aaron Kohn
H. Joseph Meyer
M. Jean Miller
Perry Norton
Lloyd Ohlin
Vincent O'Leary
Howard Rogers
Charles C. Rohrs
John Rush
Wilbur Rykert
Ruben Schofield
Dwight C. Smith, Jr.
Edwin F. Toepfer
Mathew Wright

## Information Systems and Statistics Advisory Task Force Staff

**Staff Director**
Paul K. Wormeli

**Project Coordinator**
LeRoy B. McCabe

Ronald E. Biggie
Donald F. King
Steve E. Kolodney

Robert L. Marx
Ernest A. Unwin
David R. Weinstein
Michael A. Zimmerman

**Contributor**
Paul M. Whisenand

**Advisers**
Ronald C. Allen
Lloyd A. Bastian
Wayne P. Holtzman

## Criminal Justice System Contributors and Advisers

### PLANNING FOR CRIME REDUCTION

**Contributor**
Ralph M. Gutekunst, Jr.

**Advisers**
Richard Glynn
Peter R. Gray
Nicholas Roberts
Arnold Rosenfeld
Henry S. Ruth, Jr.
Allen Schick
Jseph L. White

### CRIMINAL JUSTICE EDUCATION

**Contributors**
William T. Adams
Charles P. Smith

### CRIMINAL CODE REVISION

**Contributor**
B. J. George, Jr.

### VICTIMIZATION: APPENDIX A

**Author**
Anthony G. Turner

### ENCOURAGING CHANGES: APPENDIX B

**Author**
Paul Solomon

**Authors**
Howard H. Earle
Rosemary Hill
Richard P. Krank

# Index

665

667

671

673

677